GEERT M

Geert Mak is a Dutch journalist and historian, and the internationally acclaimed author of *In Europe*, *In America*, *Amsterdam* and *The Bridge*. He is one of the Netherlands' bestselling writers, has twice been awarded Historian of the Year and his books have been translated into more than twenty languages.

LIZ WATERS

Liz Waters translates literary fiction and non-fiction from Dutch into English. Authors whose books she has translated include Lieve Joris, Luuk van Middelaar, David Van Reybrouck, Paul Scheffer and Douwe Draaisma. She has lived in the Netherlands for many years.

ALSO BY GEERT MAK

An Island in Time: The Biography of a Village
Amsterdam: A Brief Life of the City
In Europe: Travels Through the Twentieth Century
The Bridge: A Journey Between Orient and Occident
In America: Travels with John Steinbeck

GEERT MAK

The Dream of Europe

Travels in a Troubled Continent

TRANSLATED FROM THE DUTCH BY
Liz Waters

VINTAGE

1 3 5 7 9 10 8 6 4 2

Vintage is part of the Penguin Random House group of companies whose
addresses can be found at global.penguinrandomhouse.com

Penguin
Random House
UK

First published in Vintage in 2023
First published in hardback by Harvill Secker in 2021
First published with the title *Grote verwachtingen: In Europa
1999–2019* in the Netherlands by Uitgeverij Atlas Contact in 2019

penguin.co.uk/vintage

A CIP catalogue record for this book is available from the British Library

ISBN 9781529113044

This publication has been made possible with financial
support from the Dutch Foundation for Literature.

N ederlands
letterenfonds
dutch foundation
for literature

Printed and bound in Great Britain by Clays Ltd, Elcograf S.p.A.

The authorised representative in the EEA is Penguin Random House
Ireland, Morrison Chambers, 32 Nassau Street, Dublin D02 YH68

Maps by Kartomedia

Heinrich Böll's 'Wir kommen weit her' ('We come from afar')
from *Work*, Cologne edition, volume 23, 1984–1985
© 2007, Verlag Kiepenheuer & Witsch GmbH & Co. KG,
Cologne, Germany. Used by permission. English
translation by Liz Waters.

For Emile and Ellen

We come from afar
Dear child
And have far to go
Have no fear
All are with you
Who came before you
Your mother, your father
And all those before them
Far, far back
All are with you
Have no fear
We come from afar
And have far to go
Dear child

— Heinrich Böll

Contents

Prologue

2018–2019

I

SEEN FROM THE SKY IT'S a brownish-grey landscape. It's the moon, straight after a passing downpour, or dented earth with a thousand lakes and streams, like the pools and creeks sketched in the mud when the sea retreats, twice a day, for all eternity. Rocks and lichen, and endless desolation.

We're almost there. A lone tree, radiant yellow in the beginnings of winter. A bright red house. Then out of nowhere a couple of factory buildings, a big shipyard, a cluster of shops and homes lining a square, a few cranes, a harbour. The little town. From an icy sea a trawler puts in, blue and black; they catch king crabs here, monstrous creatures coveted by Europe's top restaurants.

It's almost nightfall, the streets are empty and silent, except for the sound of the wind. The town hall is alone in showing a light, apart from the big yellow Russian consulate with its closely barred windows. The restaurant serves whale steaks, or reindeer and mushroom pasta. On the quayside the stock of a hardware shop is still out on display: three dripping aluminium ladders, one short, one long and one medium-sized. In the little supermarket two girls are deliberating. This is their one outing of the week. Will it be a milkshake or the latest soft drink?

Soon the gate at the border, a few kilometres away, will be locked again for the night. The soldier on this side will shake hands with the two on the other side. In doing so he's allowed no further than thirty centimetres onto foreign soil. It's a rigorous ritual that they mustn't botch.

Tomorrow is another day.

*

I have to begin with distance. With distance in space and distance in time –
insofar as that's possible, anyhow. There's something contradictory about
writing the history of an era when you're right in the middle of it, of a
world in which you're fully involved. History needs distance; letting time
pass is still the best way to put things in perspective. It wasn't until late in
the nineteenth century that Napoleon could be given his due place in European history. Debate continues to this day about the deeper causes of the
twentieth century's two global conflicts, the nature and consequences of
colonialism, the frozen violence of the Cold War and the collapse of the
Soviet Empire in 1989. What to say, then, of these first two decades of the
twenty-first century, with the history factory once more running at full
capacity and our orderly European world of peace and equitable prosperity
seeming about to founder?

Twenty years ago I wrote a book about Europe in the twentieth century. It
ended in 1999 and it cries out for a sequel: what has happened to the European world in these turbulent early years of the twenty-first century? I
would of course love to look over the shoulder of a clever history student
half a century from now, in 2069, as she writes a dissertation about our
own times. It will be a far from cheerful story, I fear, but undoubtedly fascinating. Both the United States and later the European Union could be
seen as great historical projects by free citizens who tried to take the course
of history into their own hands instead of merely submitting to it; projects
with their origins in the Enlightenment ideals of human rights, liberty,
equality and fraternity – international fraternity included. Where did the
dismantling of a thing so beautiful start?

 My youthful historian, fifty years distant, has a broad perspective on all
this. I don't. I envy her.

2

Here, in this northernmost outpost of Europe, everything is clear-cut: if
you don't watch out, you'll freeze to death. Spring, summer and autumn
come and go in a flash. 'It's endless winter, then bang, it's summer,' they say
here. 'And then, bang, summer is over.' The cold usually starts in October,

with snow that lies until May. In late November the polar night closes in. The northern lights blaze across the black sky and beneath them everything freezes into oblivion in twenty – sometimes thirty – degrees of frost. On 18 January, if you climb one of the hills, you can see the first of the light. It makes everyone cheerful. They celebrate it like a second Christmas and all the schoolchildren have the day off. Afterwards, life returns to the daily rhythm of the mail boat: at the harbour, on the wharves, in the shops, at the border posts, at the airport. Everyone spends the rest of the time between their own four walls. Centrum Kafé, the talkative heart of the town, closes at five in the afternoon.

Kirkenes has barely 3,500 residents, it's a pinprick on the map, yet this remote place is a geopolitical cauldron. It occupies an extremely important strategic position, right near the Russian border. It's also the most northerly ice-free port in Europe – close to the Barents Sea, with its huge gas field in the Russian part – and the gateway to Murmansk, one of Russia's main ports. Provisional estimates suggest that 13 per cent of the world's oil reserves and 40 per cent of remaining gas stocks are in the Arctic region, along with huge amounts of iron, copper, gold and other minerals. Now that the polar ice caps are melting, all kinds of activities will inevitably take place here and everyone is making preparations. The Russians in particular are investing vast sums, and military activities are increasing to match.

Kirkenes is also a crucial harbour on the future Arctic shipping route from Asia to Europe, an alternative to the Suez Canal. The mayor sees his town as tomorrow's Singapore: 'I get Chinese delegations here every week,' he says. Thomas Nilsen, editor-in-chief of the local online newspaper, once described Kirkenes as 'the centre of the periphery of Europe'. To him the town is above all a laboratory, a place to study the relationship between Russia and Europe in particular: 'Changes are encountered here by us first, far sooner than by anyone in Berlin, Washington or Moscow.'

Today I'm walking around with a cameraman. My European journey in 1999 was given a second life when Dutch broadcaster VPRO made a television series – although the book and the series were quite different projects. Now we're starting again, and this time we're travelling together from the start. There's too much urgency for us to wait.

We walk along the dockside. The trawler, the *Salacgriva*, is from Murmansk. From close up the ship is a floating factory, a dripping clutter of cables, cranes and crab pots, the men wordless under thick hoods, as weathered as their ship and their nets. In the corner of a work shed they sit waiting to put to sea, silently passing coffee around and watching the dancing girls on TV.

Then up the hill. The last war isn't far away. At one time the beautifully crafted wooden houses seen in all other Norwegian trading towns must have stood here, but in the latter days of the Second World War almost every building was wiped off the map. During a major Soviet Arctic offensive – targeting the nearby nickel mines and the strategic naval base at Kirkenes – the town was bombed more than 300 times. Between Kirkenes and Murmansk, at least 60,000 troops died. The townspeople survived for seven months in caves and mines, throughout the winter of 1944–45. Twenty children were born. By the spring of '45, just three houses were left standing in Kirkenes.

So all these neat white wooden homes and shops are new, and they make Kirkenes look a bit like an American suburb. One of the oldest structures is a bomb shelter, now a memorial to civilian courage. Nearby, high on a pedestal, stands a Russian soldier. There are always bright green wreaths and bouquets at this liberation monument, of freshly woven plastic – you can forget about real flowers in this climate. The Russians are traditionally celebrated here as liberators. When Stalin died, some people in Kirkenes were among those who wept.

Higher we go, past the wooden verandas and a couple of sports fields, until we can see the harbour down below. We sit on a bench. On the horizon is the great empty bay, without a ship to be seen until, in the far distance, we spot the daily mail boat. A man with a dog walks past and looks at his watch. 'It's late today, at least fifteen minutes.' Life is robust, the cars and houses are shiny and spacious; the living here seems good. Under a few rare trees lies the graveyard, the sun glancing brightly off the gold lettering of the headstones. Restraint is the norm here and there are no ornate monuments. Soon we'll all be equal before God. In truth, we already are.

The mayor's name is Rune Rafaelsen. He talks about his grandmother. Her first husband was killed at the sawmill, crushed in a fall. She'd only just remarried when her second husband died in a submarine attack. Rune's father was the youngest resistance fighter in Norway, sixteen when he linked up with the Norwegian army. Rune's uncle was sent to a punishment camp as a youth, where he fell in love with a captive Russian girl, unreachable beyond barbed wire. She disappeared and he never saw her again. He asked for her even on his deathbed. As for Rune, he grew up in a house bursting with people. 'There was nothing left, after the war. Everything had to be rebuilt from scratch.' That's history here.

The Cold War was occasionally touch-and-go, especially in the Arctic. For years this part of Norway was the only place where Russia directly bordered on NATO. In 1968, in response to a NATO exercise, the Soviets showed up here with an infantry division of 200 tanks and 500 armoured combat vehicles. Kirkenes nonetheless remained stubborn, its relationship with Russia special and close. The mayor says the border 'was always inhabited flexibly . . . Sami, Norwegians, Finns, Russians – they all used to mix.' Nobody was afraid of the Russians. 'If they come, they'll first take Oslo, then Bergen and Trondheim. Then they'll come to Kirkenes for a cup of coffee.' That was the attitude.

Rafaelsen has been deeply engaged with the place all his life. His office in the town hall is plain and austere, the window bars, cameras and aerials of the nearby Russian consulate always in sight. NATO is no less powerful a presence; several times a month a mysterious ship arrives at a wharf where even the mayor is forbidden to set foot. The *Marjata* looks like a fairly normal passenger vessel with some extra antennae, but in reality it's one of the world's most advanced listening stations. 'They suck everything out of our phones and laptops,' you hear people say in the Centrum Kafé. Russian submarines, for their part, fossick about near the undersea cables in the Arctic, making the Americans nervous in turn.

In Kirkenes you look down from a great height on Berlin, Brussels, London and Rotterdam, all half a world away. Yet recent history has impacted upon Kirkenes time and again: the collapse of the banks in 2008, the crisis that followed, Russia's annexation of Crimea, Europe's migrant crisis, Brexit, Trump.

The iron ore mine, once the mainstay of the local economy, went bankrupt in 2015 in the aftermath of the banking crisis, and 400 people lost their jobs. The town took that calamity in its stride. The ice-free port of Kirkenes is now the most important base for the Russian fishing fleet and three-quarters of the big shipyard's work is commissioned by Russians. Tourism is flourishing too, with some 100,000 visitors arriving in the port by cruise ship each year. 'The town has mellowed,' the mayor says.

He shows me his appointments for the coming week. The launch of an 'open screen' film festival in Murmansk – he's known the governor there since 1992. A consultation with the mayor of Nikel in Russia, a good friend for years now. The LGBTQ+ pride parade right here in Kirkenes, with a sizeable delegation from Murmansk, where such an event is of course unthinkable. He finds border regions fascinating and always chooses them for his holidays.

Yet even in Kirkenes, relations with Russia have cooled. The Putin regime has grown harsher, independent media outlets are struggling to survive, Crimea and part of Ukraine have been occupied and the West has responded with tough sanctions. They've felt all that directly, here at the border. Russian fisheries were squeezed; football matches between the two sides stopped; shops began selling French wines and cheeses hand over fist to Russians who, with the sanctions, could no longer buy them at home.

Then there was the painful case of elderly Frode Berg, a much-loved local character: chair of the church council, one of the organizers of the town's orchestra and the cross-border arts festival, and above all an active champion of warm ties with Russia. He, of all people, was arrested in Moscow in December 2017 by the FSB. For espionage. No one can fathom it. His friends in the Centrum Kafé are shaken; they can't imagine he actually was a spy. But stories start coming out. Others have occasionally been approached by the Norwegian intelligence agency. Frode is still being held.

'At a regional level it's business as usual,' says the mayor. 'But the atmosphere has changed. Until 2014 we had casual chats with the Russians about everything, including politics. Nowadays, if I say I'm worried about Russia they cut me short immediately. "I'm worried about my grandmother," they say. "She needs her medication. So don't give me your democracy stories."'

3

Kirkenes has never been fertile ground for populists. It's far too concerned with the future for that. Just four countries have traditionally focused on the Arctic region: America, Canada, Russia and Norway. 'And here everything works, always, even in the depths of winter,' Rune assures me.

Close to the North Pole, temperatures are rising three times faster than anywhere else. Here it's an average of three degrees warmer than in 1971. More and more stretches of sea are open all year. Everyone has noticed that the landscape turns green in May, rather than June, and this summer saw the first heatwave. The melting ice is altering the polar vortex, a persistent low-pressure area high in the atmosphere that influences the weather right across Europe. In the south it can turn shockingly cold almost overnight; in the north it's growing markedly warmer and wetter.

Europeans are increasingly worried about climate change, but in Kirkenes they see new opportunities. By about 2030 the Arctic seas will probably be navigable for twelve months of the year, and sailing time from Shanghai to Rotterdam by that route is around twenty days, instead of thirty or forty via the Suez Canal. There are plans for a huge container port, and the mayor dreams of a direct railway line to Helsinki.

'This is Norway's geopolitical focal point,' he says. 'Intense negotiations are going on with Russia over gas in the Barents Sea. Lavrov has been here a number of times. The Chinese are discussing a northern version of the Belt and Road Initiative, called the Polar Silk Road. In Oslo nothing's happening; here's where the action is.'

It's no exaggeration. Right now, in October 2018, America has just announced that it will leave the historic Intermediate-Range Nuclear Forces Treaty – its NATO partners weren't consulted, incidentally. Russia promptly responded with measures of its own and after thirty years of peace the old arms race might start again, now with China joining in. The Americans are sending an aircraft carrier to the Arctic Circle for the first time in three decades. Over the past few years Russia has reopened seven of its old Soviet naval bases there, and the first military icebreaker is on its way – something else that hasn't been seen for decades.

Meanwhile, the Norwegians and the Americans are building a new radar system in the fishing village of Vardø, called Globus III, to keep track of Russian nuclear submarines. In February the Russians staged a mock attack on Vardø with eleven Sukhoi Su-24 fighter aircraft, an intimidating move that quite startled the Norwegian Intelligence Service. Such incidents can easily get out of hand.

This spring, Sweden began checking and refurbishing its old fallout shelters, and issued a new publicity brochure about civil defence. 'If Sweden is attacked by another country, we will never give up,' it reads. 'All information to the effect that resistance is to cease is false.' In Norway, Trident Juncture 18 is starting, the largest NATO exercise since the Cold War, involving 50,000 troops, 10,000 vehicles, 250 aircraft and 65 ships. The main concern: can British troops come to the Norwegians' aid quickly enough if the Russians attack? After the end of the Cold War, questions like that were not asked for years. Roads and bridges in Germany and the Netherlands now need careful inspection. Are they still strong enough to take massed military transports? It's a 'realistic stress test', the American commander tells the media.

It used to be thought that Western freedom and democracy would steadily conquer the rest of the world. Now events seem to point in the opposite direction. Europe is casting about for answers, divided and weakened, while Russia seizes any opportunity to sow dissent. China is rushing to fill the gaps that are opening up everywhere – the Middle East, the Balkans, Greece – while Western Europe leaves them unexplored. Further west, an American president has come to power who engages in much the same politics of destabilization as the Russians, and who is rapidly dismantling the rules and institutions of the post-war world order. As New York Times commentator Roger Cohen notes, quoting Baloo from The Jungle Book, the old transatlantic world of the late twentieth century is 'gone, man, solid gone'.

How could this have happened to the optimistic Europe of 1999? Many years ago, when I was a know-it-all student, an elderly Dutch journalist – a former resistance fighter – wrote to me: 'Easy for you people to talk, in the light of the present day. But what were we supposed to do, in the 1930s? We were trying to find our way through the darkness with a candle, groping and stumbling, in an utterly unfamiliar house.'

Now I'm walking around like that with a candle myself.

1. The Sky's the Limit

1999

I

IT BEGAN SO MAGNIFICENTLY. LIKE the start of the twentieth century, the start of the twenty-first was one big victory party. The Cold War was over, the stock markets danced, champagne was sold by the crate, and on Friday 31 December the popular Dutch daily *De Telegraaf* shouted from every kiosk, 'The sky's the limit!' Economic growth had continued unabated, unemployment was at its lowest since records began, and for the first time in a quarter of a century the Dutch treasury had no deficit to report. 'Never before,' the newspaper went on, 'have citizens, in the West at least, had it so good.'

New Year's celebrations were more lavish than ever. In the Netherlands a record three million bottles of bubbly were sold. 'Whether at home or for a party, the key words are chic and eccentric,' said a fashion expert. 'The boa, for example, is in again – and for women, lots of bare skin.' Europe crossed the threshold of the new century in an ebullient mood, full of confidence and optimism.

Those final days of 1999 are still fresh in my mind. I was a journalist, had been for decades, and I'd spent the whole year travelling in Europe. Every day I wrote a short item for the front page of my newspaper, NRC *Handelsblad*, and afterwards the project grew into a book.

It was intended as a kind of tour of inspection: how was Europe doing, at the end of the millennium? It was also a journey in time. How had people, all over Europe, experienced the 1930s, or the 1950s and 1960s? And how had they endured all those wars, all that persecution, all those disasters? For a year I worked my way through the century, month by

wounded countries, cities bearing scars. I also saw miraculous
I listened. That, above all.

d, for example, I interviewed actress Alexandra Vasilyeva, 102
about the Russian Revolution of 1917. She was as fragile as floss,
but her eyes sparkled: 'It was so exciting! Really dangerous! Fortunately my
husband worked in films, he was a film star, and all those soldiers and ban-
dits thought that was wonderful. They didn't shoot him.'

With elderly politician Nigel Nicolson, at his country estate in Kent, I
tried something new: we made tea in the microwave. Later he read out a
letter from his father, diplomat Harold Nicolson, written in 1919: 'So I went
in. There were Wilson and Lloyd George and Clemenceau with their arm-
chairs drawn close over my map on the hearth rug. . . . It is appalling that
these ignorant and irresponsible men should be cutting [Asia Minor] to
bits as if they were dividing a cake.'

Truusje Roegholt of Amsterdam still had a slight German accent. She
told me about her childhood in Cologne and about 1933. 'Everyone was
marching in beautiful new uniforms. The impact was stunning. All those
poor people were suddenly somebody. They sang utter tosh, but they had
new shoes!'

At the Hotel Astoria in Budapest, writer György Konrád described the
Hungarian Uprising of 1956. 'That last week we lived in a beautiful illusion.
From the countryside came rumours of Russian tank movements, but that
was simply a misunderstanding. Or so we thought.'

I visited the former president of the Federal Republic of Germany, Richard von Weizsäcker, who told me about the fall of the Berlin Wall on 9
November 1989. 'The next day there was no holding me. I crossed Potsdamer Platz completely alone. I walked to the barracks housing the East
German border guards and there a lieutenant of the Volkspolizei stepped
out. He recognized me, saluted and then said calmly, "Mr President, I would
like to report that there is nothing special to report." '

In the Brussels district of Molenbeek I wandered past the empty displays
and grubby shop windows with my friend Pierre Platteau, searching for the
remains of the 'dream palaces' of his childhood: 'That magnificent Kinox
cinema, just look what's become of it, a huge fabrics shop full of bargain
bins.'

*

It ended in late December 1999 – my journey, along with the century. The Yugoslav wars were behind us and I'd managed to break out of a snowed-in Sarajevo.

By New Year's Eve, I was home. 'In the Far East the new century has already begun,' an announcer said that afternoon on television. 'The millennium bug seems to be keeping a low profile.'

That strange phenomenon was no figment of the imagination. The innermost core of all large computer systems dated back to the 1960s, when years were expressed in two digits. So at the transition from 1999 to 2000, '99' would become '00', or 1900. On 31 December 1999, at the stroke of midnight, computers all over the world might lose their bearings, in which case there would be power cuts, bank accounts would melt into air and planes would be set adrift. The new century might start in one great apocalyptic mess. Nobody knew what would happen in the cellars of banks and other complex organizations. For the first time, profound concern arose among the public about modern technology that no longer seemed manageable, that had the potential to get out of hand. Banks, ministries, embassies: crisis teams sat in wait everywhere that night. You never could tell.

In the end, disaster was averted. People went out into the streets, lit fireworks and popped corks.

I spent that momentous evening in an Amsterdam canal house, within sight of the oldest church tower, which has watched over the city for seven centuries. It was a tradition. We always waited with the same group of friends for twelve to strike, and then stood on the balcony to watch the fireworks. One friend had entrenched himself in another church tower, and at twelve he would ring the bells himself, with a few fellow bell-ringers, scattering his blessings over the city year after year. This time the explosions drowned out everything and everyone.

The economy was humming, especially the coffee shops and drug dealers on the far side of the canal. They spared no expense; tens of thousands of guilders of drug money was set alight in thousand-bang crackers, rockets and Roman candles. Before we knew it, the dealers had made all the church towers disappear into a stinking fog of gun smoke. That too was an Amsterdam tradition.

Everyone has their own memories of that night. José Martí Font, a journalist in Barcelona, told me about a big house crammed with friends. 'We were all drunk, every one of us. We tossed our glasses out of the window as the sun slowly came up. We went nuts. Everything was going to get better, the euro was coming, money would shower down on us like manna from heaven!'

Aydin Soei, the seventeen-year-old son of Iranian refugees – later you'll hear a good deal more about him, and about Font – celebrated the arrival of the new century in an empty garage, somewhere in the backstreets of Copenhagen: 'I was with classmates from the grammar school. We often used to get together there, even to sleep. I remember that evening vividly. In a sale I'd bought socks with "2000" printed on them. Everyone was wondering whether all those computers really were about to crash. We wore party clothes. I still remember the photos, the girls in evening dresses, the boys in dinner jackets. It looks fairly weird actually, children in dinner jackets. Of course I had a very different story from all the others, but they had no idea about that.'

Gábor Demszky was mayor of Budapest in those years, and a fierce opponent of Viktor Orbán: 'We were on a skiing holiday in Austria. I'd got a new girlfriend. I had two children and so did she. My ex and hers – everyone was with us, a big family event. Orbán was prime minister at the time and he was trying to get his hands on all the money and power in the cities. To his clan I was the urban-intellectual-liberal Jew. I wasn't actually Jewish, but I was a troublesome liberal. It was a political war without end. At that time I had enough money to treat everyone. I wouldn't be able to do that now.'

Umayya Abu-Hanna, a Finnish television broadcaster of Palestinian origin I'd met during my travels in Europe, toasted the new century in a beautiful eighteenth-century house in the centre of Helsinki: 'Food was suddenly in fashion; everyone in Finland wanted to be urban and international, especially in their diet. My friends kept it low-key. There was delicious French champagne, we watched a special television programme about Finnish history: the best this, the most beautiful that. We were four couples and a few children, and no one expected anything, better or worse. It all just babbled past, as if we were sitting in a canoe.'

In Novi Sad in Serbia there was little to celebrate. Another companion of mine, filmmaker Želimir Žilnik, looked back on a decade of madness. At the start of the 1990s his city was flourishing; prosperous Yugoslavia was seen as a prime candidate for EU membership. But by 1999 the splendid Danube bridges had been wrecked by shelling, old ladies were selling their fur coats at the open-air market, the price of a pack of cigarettes was rising by the hour, and the criminals who had once worked for the communist secret services were now the heroes of the nationalists. 'It was one big long orgy of plunder,' Žilnik said. 'Grab, grab, grab. That's what ethnic cleansing amounted to.'

'Every poor man is a fool, you know,' said his friend, the writer Aleksandar Tišma. 'His clothes are dirty, his hair untrimmed. So we too are fools. We're the village idiots of the world.'

In Kirkenes in Norway, the New Year celebrations were a modest family affair, as they always had been. Thomas Nilsen was alone in being all fired up: 'I was in an environmentalist group at the time, working with two Russians on a book about the nuclear hazards posed by the Russian fleet here in the Barents Sea. For years the FSB had been after us with writs and lawsuits, but on 29 December a miracle happened: we were acquitted. It was the first acquittal in an FSB case – and the last. Two days later everything changed in Russia, but we had no inkling of that then.'

In Vásárosbéc, the village in southern Hungary where I started my story in 1999 and where it had remained 1925 for ever, the dancing went on that evening until condensation ran down the walls. A drunken Roma man began throwing punches, some scuffles with a foreigner followed and eventually the drunk was thrown out of the door, into the twenty-first century. The party died down after that.

2

'Dawn of the Century' was the name of a tune played by the British as they saw out 1899, and the front cover of the score shows all the delights that awaited them: a tram, a typewriter, a telephone, a sewing machine, a camera, a threshing machine, a locomotive – even an automobile coming round the corner.

The twenty-first century was greeted with similar optimism. What could stop us now? Buildings were going up at an astonishing rate in all the world's capital cities; the glass Eiffel Towers of our own era, the new status symbols of global corporations. Trains and letterboxes had lost their familiar colours – they'd been privatized and the brand was king. The old century was quickly put out with the rubbish. I remember how, in those years, calculators and typewriters, drawing tables, card indexes and other pieces of ingenious twentieth-century technology were dumped, overtaken by all the new IT techniques.

'The twenty-first century might yet belong to Europe,' wrote historian Tony Judt at the end of his epic account of recent European history, and at that point there was every reason to think so. Around the turn of the century, the EU was the greatest trading bloc in the world, with the biggest consumer market, the biggest economy and the biggest reserves of non-military knowledge and technology. Peace and security were solidly anchored, the alliance with America unquestioned, Russia no longer a threat. After Mikhail Gorbachev's perestroika a new 'European space' was being created, and even Russian membership of NATO was on the cards.

London and Frankfurt were the world's most important financial centres, Berlin had been reborn, Warsaw was modernizing at astonishing speed and Amsterdam had begun a new growth spurt. Reykjavík was a special case. The sober Icelanders seemed to have an uncanny instinct for speculation and moneymaking. By 2007 they held fifty times as many foreign shares as they had at the start of the century. Icelandic cod fishermen owned houses in London and Copenhagen, and businessmen held birthday parties where Elton John flew in to perform.

Europe's prosperity was boosted by extreme globalization. In 1999 the internet as we know it now barely existed; Europeans made payments in German marks, French francs and Dutch guilders; and Google and Amazon were the province of small groups of enthusiasts. A largely paperless world at home and at work was still an unimaginable prospect. The mobile phone had recently come onto the mass market, and a Dutch filmmaker interviewed people on the street about it. Hardly anyone could see the point. 'No need. I've already got an answering machine.' 'Strikes me as appalling to be reachable all the time.'

Yet many companies had long ago risen above national borders. A Renault or a Volvo wasn't made in a factory in France or Sweden any longer;

instead the parts came from all over the world and only at the
they put together to make a car – something that might equally
in Germany or the Czech Republic.

The same went for food and a vast range of other products. I remember
seeing a truck full of bright yellow bananas in the grey East German town
of Görlitz, and the excitement it caused. That was shortly after the fall of the
Wall. Barely ten years later, the former East Germans could buy whatever
they liked from anywhere – wines, electronic goods or the most exotic
fruits, often at remarkably low prices. A Chinese radio cost little more than
the Christmas issue of The Economist.

The whole world benefited. Everywhere the standard of living increased,
although huge inequalities remained. Indian author Pankaj Mishra described
the emergence of a 'vast, homogenous world market, in which human
beings are programmed to maximise their self-interest and aspire to the
same things, regardless of their difference of cultural background and individual temperament'. It confirmed the prediction of philosopher Hannah
Arendt, back in 1968: all the peoples on earth were for the first time in
history living in a 'common present'.

A new age began, and those last days of the twentieth century revealed
something of it from time to time, like hatches opening up for a glimpse
of the future. At Christmas in 1999, for instance, an astonishingly fierce
storm ravaged France, Germany and Switzerland. Millions of trees were
uprooted, a quarter of French households suffered power outages and 130
people were killed. The word 'climate' slowly started to permeate our everyday vocabulary.

In those same weeks, a disabled engineer, one Wayne Westerman, put
the finishing touches to a solution he'd found for his cramped fingers. In
deepest secrecy he'd developed what was then known as 'multi-touch technology' – the basis for the smartphone. It was a device that harboured a
better world, that sent seductive messages day and night, connected and
divided people and, along with the internet, helped to define the new century, just as the fifteenth century was defined by printing with movable
type.

Then there was a letter that appeared in the Frankfurter Allgemeine Zeitung a
week before that festive New Year. Its author, a young politician called

Angela Merkel, was better known as Helmut Kohl's *Mädchen* (girl), but she was a rising talent with the courage to denounce, in a few lucid paragraphs, the 'patronage system' of her political leader, the former federal chancellor. She did so in the midst of a political storm. Kohl had lost the previous election and was caught up in a major scandal over party financing, yet many CDU party members remained loyal. Merkel had the audacity to denounce their 'juvenile' dependence on the old 'Kohl system'. The party, she wrote, must dare to take up arms against the old warhorse, relying on its own strength: 'There is no escaping the fact that we have to take the future into our own hands.'

With her brave and balanced letter, she put herself at the centre of power in a single move. It was typical of Merkel, who was never fazed by anything. She was the no-nonsense daughter of an East German clergyman who had steered his family and his congregation through difficult times and complex dilemmas. Growing up, her ultimate dream was to visit America when she turned sixteen – travel restrictions on women were dropped at that age in the German Democratic Republic. When the Wall fell, on the night of 9 November 1989, and euphoric East and West Berliners fell into each other's arms, she had simply gone to the sauna with a friend as she did every Thursday evening.

As a child of the GDR, Merkel was an outsider who did not belong to the 'generation of compliant helpers'; to the traditional, power-addicted Christian Democrat network. And she was fearless. That was her great strength. Within six years of writing that letter, she was federal chancellor. 'No one seriously disputes,' wrote the *Financial Times* in 2012, 'that Merkel is today the most powerful politician in Europe.'

Another sign of the new times was the euro. The new currency was first used in 1999, in transactions between banks. A spectacular undertaking, it swept away in an instant all the exchange rates that had made European trade so complicated. Travel and tourism were a good deal easier now, and speculators no longer stood a chance against the single, solid euro. It was a great and logical step in the direction of further European unification.

We were a little nervous. Might a quick-change routine make everything more expensive? But warnings from a handful of specialists that a single European currency without a common financial policy would inevitably produce major problems escaped almost everyone's attention. The same went for persistent negative reports about Greece, buried in the back pages of newspapers. If there was one feeling that pervaded the European project, it was triumphalism. The Wall had fallen, communism was dead and Marxism belonged to the past. The ideologists embraced the global free market and enlightened self-interest, and Europe went along with them.

3

Seventy years after the outbreak of the First World War, on 22 September 1984, German chancellor Helmut Kohl and French president François Mitterrand stood together on the once blood-drenched fields of Verdun. Music played. There were songs for fallen comrades. The rain poured down. Mitterrand and Kohl stood silently side by side, soaking wet. Then, unexpectedly, Mitterrand put out his hand. Kohl, as he himself said, was 'overwhelmed' with emotion. Hand in hand, the men stood there. An image to last for all time.

'The fathers had no notion of how thin the layer of civilization was, or what volcanic forces were working under the surface,' György Konrád would write later. He was eleven in 1944, and by then almost all the Jews in his provincial town had been taken away in cattle trucks, including his father and mother. Only the four children were left in the house and they got by somehow. It seemed you could live like that. For the price of a house, György, with all his eleven years, arranged for a travel permit to join relatives in Budapest. He said goodbye to his cousin Vera. 'Two weeks later I was strolling along the Danube, and Vera had been gassed and burned.' Of the 200 Jewish children in his village, they were the only four to survive.

It was a spring afternoon in Budapest when I spoke to him for the last time, almost three-quarters of a century later. We drank cognac. Shafts of light fell everywhere through his shadowy house. I'd already dined with my Hungarian friends Vera and Peter, an apparently successful family, with a good business, providing enjoyable work.

Vera's mother was one of Hungary's few Jewish survivors, having been forced to move on from seventeen different hiding places during the war. Her first husband was killed in the last of the raids and Peter, her second husband, had to flee for his life after taking part in the Hungarian Uprising of 1956 while serving in the army. He lived in Sweden for many years, separated from his wife and children.

Sixty-four of Peter's relatives did not survive the war. After a childhood in Israel, his mother threw in her lot with communism rather than Zionism and became an agent of the Hungarian secret services, leading a double life. 'Only now do I understand certain things,' Peter told me.

Želimir Žilnik in Novi Sad was another war child, brought up by his grandparents and three aunts. 'My mother was a professor, a member of the illegal communist party, a partisan. After she was wounded while on operations she spent time recovering up in the mountains, and there she met my father, another partisan. She died shortly after I was born, in a concentration camp, and he died in 1944 at the Bulgarian border.'

I crossed paths with Bronisław Geremek, a central figure in the European Parliament. As a skinny boy of ten, in the summer of 1942, he'd sat in a Warsaw tram trembling with fear, believing that everyone could plainly see he was a little Jewish boy who'd managed to slip out of the ghetto through a gap moments earlier. He survived to become a leading figure in the Polish dissident movement, spent a year in prison and then, among other things, served as minister of foreign affairs. This was European history encapsulated in one person. He had known, and could still describe, a Europe without laws or rights, devoid of any kind of civilization, and that childhood experience had given his life its shape and direction.

During my journey in 1999 I spent a day with German industrialist Winrich Behr. He showed me a small box in his top desk drawer: Iron Crosses awarded to four generations. 'My great-grandfather, my grandfather, my father and I have one thing in common: we all fought in a war against France and all four of us were wounded. My great-grandfather in 1870, my grandfather and my father in 1914, and I in 1940. That would once have been a great honour for a German family. But now of course it's a miserable thing.'

Behr became one of the founding fathers of the European project, along with Frenchman Jean Monnet – a member of the French government in exile during the war – and Dutchman Max Kohnstamm of the student resistance and the Amersfoort concentration camp. Or take Helmut Kohl himself, the first chancellor after German unification, who once let slip to chronicler Timothy Garton Ash, 'Do you realize that you are sitting opposite the direct successor to Adolf Hitler?' He knew better than anyone that everything must now be different. That was his historic responsibility.

To be honest, I'm writing these paragraphs mainly for the young historian of 2069 who might at some point pull this mouldering book out of a pile, curious about the world of our day. This digression is for her: never underestimate the deep furrows those European wars and massacres ploughed through our generations. Seventy years later we are still intensely caught up in all that, consciously or unconsciously, in any number of ways.

The history is well known. The power and dynamism of Europe arose out of its diversity and variability. In the highly technologically advanced China of the mid-fifteenth century, one command from the emperor in 1433 was enough to stop all Chinese voyages of discovery for good. China was a rigid entity. In the same period, Columbus, on finding that the French king lacked any appetite for his expeditions, simply went to work next door, for the king's Spanish rival. In Europe you could choose, time and again.

Our fate was the downside of that: Europe's division, fragmentation and endless wars. Austrian writer Robert Menasse once came up with an image that says it all. If you draw on the map of Europe all the political boundaries created over the course of history with a black marker pen, you are guaranteed to find yourself at the end of the exercise with an almost completely black page. If you draw in red on the same map the front lines and battlefields of all the European wars, something similar happens. All those flourishing cities, all those productive rivers and valleys, gradually disappear beneath a single great field of red.

That too is Europe, time and again.

The world was turned on its head for months after almost 3,000 people died in the attacks of 11 September 2001. Yet during the Second World War an average of around 17,000 were killed every day, almost six times as many, and that war lasted for six years, claiming close to 75 million lives. Five million Poles did not live to see the end of the war, 20 per cent of the population. The number of civilian deaths in Russia has been estimated at 14 million. During the First World War, more Frenchmen died at Verdun in three months than Americans in all of America's foreign wars to this day. Monuments in every French village testify to that. In 1913 the dance floor was full; in 1918, half empty. It happened again in May 1940, when six weeks of war saw 112,000 French dead. As far as possible, the loss was absorbed into rituals, covered with shame and often hushed up. But the subterranean after-effects were overwhelming.

Take me as an example. I came into the world in the first full year of peace, and grew up with an attic full of war. My parental home was beside a canal in Leeuwarden, in the Dutch province of Friesland. Below the roof was a wooden structure forming two small rooms and a big space where the beams creaked. Discarded army stuff lay scattered around up there – for years we played with an old transmitter and a pair of English headphones. When the wind got up, a big, half-finished cut-out of a bomber whispered between the floorboards, a huge cardboard Lancaster that my oldest brother had once thrown away in despair. Between those same floorboards we'd discovered a den with a small mattress in it, probably a wartime hiding place. My mother, her sister and two brothers had been in Japanese concentration camps, and my father had survived the building of the Death Railway in Burma. When I was five I sometimes heard evil spirits cry out when an old green Canadian army ambulance, the only ambulance Leeuwarden possessed in my memory, drove wailing through the streets. They'd been stowed inside, I thought, and were being taken away screaming. Far away.

After the war the evil was indeed whisked away, not in army lorries but in an infinite number of stories – heroic stories, stories of national pride, and a European story too, a story of peace and cooperation, of borders that would vanish like snow, of ever-increasing prosperity in a new community of values that was the new Europe. We learned that story from our parents and grandparents. We accepted it from them and carried it through life on our shoulders.

There was something strange about the generation to which I belong. We hadn't experienced the war, we were children of peace and prosperity, we were and are anything but victims, yet the war sat at the table with us every evening, in silence. Visiting the Stadtmuseum in Dresden one day, I came upon a large sheet of paper found under a piece of roof boarding in the

1990s, a shrill cry from the father of a family: 'Ein Hungerjahr, 1947 – Wir fallen bald um!' (A year of hunger, 1947 – We're about to collapse!) That was after the war, but in large parts of Europe it was still a terrible time.

Our parents and grandparents, all over Europe, had endured hunger and ruin, they'd survived bombing and concentration camps, they'd fought at Stalingrad and on the beaches of Sicily and Normandy, they'd hunted and killed, they'd hidden or fought in the resistance – but whatever they'd done, hardly anyone ever talked about it. We all needed to move on.

Only much later did I realize that a large part of my generation, from Warsaw to Berlin, Amsterdam to Madrid, had known the same strange childhood. All too often we'd grown up in wounded families, sometimes even with badly damaged parents. That indirect war, the war at the dining table, defined us, I think, more than we realized. It defined European politics too. That silent war helped to drive the European process forward, on countless occasions. The war gave European politicians the courage to jump over their own shadows.

4

For us, America was an endless source of fascination in all this, sometimes negative, mostly positive. The United States saved Europeans from themselves at least four times: when it intervened in the First and Second World Wars, when it helped the ravaged and starving Europe back onto its feet in 1948 with the Marshall Plan, and, by way of an encore, when the Europe of the 1990s proved incapable of quenching the fires of civil war in Yugoslavia without help. For older Europeans especially, America had always been a big brother who could do no wrong – despite Vietnam, and despite the undemocratic and often cruel interventions elsewhere in the world by successive US governments, in Central and South America especially. 'Europeans have not only been influenced by America, as a kind of external presence or force, but the American presence is also deeply embedded in Europeans' own self-perceptions,' wrote Norwegian specialist on Europe John Erik Fossum at the start of the twenty-first century. 'To many Europeans, Americans are not "they", but "us".'

Europeans shared with Americans, in theory at least, the values of democracy, of the rule of law, of tolerance, freedom, equality and fraternity. Those were the values they preached to the rest of the world. At the same time, they drew different conclusions. Europeans, for example, had become far more pacifist, having learned their lesson during and after the Second World War. This was not an experience born of films and heroic stories; countless Europeans knew the reality of war and persecution first-hand, and even the younger generations had yet to recover from the shock.

European power – for which read Western European power – mainly took the form of 'soft power'. Violence was replaced by aid, hope of prosperity and sometimes even talk about joining the European Economic Community, as it was then called. As a result, the disintegration of the Soviet Empire in Central and Eastern Europe – with the exception of Yugoslavia – was remarkably peaceful. The prospect of membership mitigated all religious, ethnic and national conflicts, for the time being at least. Most Europeans didn't give the matter much thought. It seemed natural enough. It wasn't, of course.

In the immediate post-war years – and this too was typically European – there was a powerful aversion to extreme social inequality. Partly for that reason, Western European welfare states gave the average citizen a security and quality of life unattainable in the rest of the world, including the United States.

Europeans were for many years at the forefront in providing humanitarian aid, defending human rights and promoting values such as tolerance and justice. When, for example, the far-right Freiheitliche Partei Österreichs (FPÖ) joined a governing coalition in Austria in the spring of 2000, there was outrage. Fourteen EU countries introduced diplomatic sanctions.

The Europeans weren't even afraid of giving up parts of their national sovereignty for the sake of the whole, inspiring the then popular American author Jeremy Rifkin to propound a bold theory in 2004: Europe would probably overtake the United States in the coming decades. The continent was ready for the future. Europeans lived longer, they were better educated, suffered less poverty and crime, and had more free time and a higher standard of living.

It was a historic experiment. The development of a European single market, a common European currency and, gradually, a supranational European government, seemed without precedent. The European project, Rifkin predicted, would increasingly function as a vast laboratory for the rest of the world. Here new forms of collaboration were being tried; here the priority was not endless growth but quality of life. 'While the American Spirit is tiring and languishing in the past,' Rifkin said, 'a new European Dream is being born.'

In the eyes of many in recent decades, Europe and the EU were on their way to becoming a new kind of world power. The process did not run smoothly. According to Tony Judt, the European Union was nothing other than 'the largely unintended product of decades of negotiations by Western European politicians seeking to uphold and advance their national and sectoral interests'.

The merging of European countries therefore happened in fits and starts, driven by a high degree of optimism. Usually a fait accompli was created at some point – a common market, for example, or a euro, or another enlargement, the hope being that specific regulations could be agreed and everything else would follow. That was the basic assumption, and for decades the strategy of making progress by catching up with the facts worked well.

In the 1980s the European leaders realized that a political deepening of European unity was necessary. Bit by bit the European project was becoming far more than simply a matter of selling Mercedes cars in Italy, Spanish tomatoes in Britain and Dutch cheeses in Austria. Around all sorts of issues, a need arose for a common foreign policy, and there were questions about European priorities and European identity. New foundations needed to be laid. Furthermore, it had often been difficult to reach agreement between the six pioneer countries, and with twelve members or more it was hard even, as one participant put it, 'to decide which restaurant to eat at that evening'.

The fall of the Wall disrupted the process. The reunification of Western and Eastern Europe now became the main priority, and the organizational and political deepening could wait. A certain triumphalism arose too: now we can surpass ourselves; we are finally creating our own future. Internally, European collaboration became ever closer, including on a personal level.

Ministers now consulted monthly, their civil servants weekly, and as time went on there was more trust, even a kind of club feeling. Self-conscious Brussels looked like a beacon of civilization and progress, based not on military power but on the persuasiveness of its own values, its own culture and above all its own success.

After the fall of the Wall there was in any case no alternative for most of the countries of what had been the Eastern Bloc. With the exception of the former Yugoslavia, they all diligently set their course according to the Western democratic model. In all the Eastern European capitals, laws were aligned, feuds resolved, stables cleaned out, hair combed and suits dry-cleaned – whatever it took to gain access to The Club.

In 1999 I met lawyers criss-crossing Europe like travelling showmen. They were rewriting constitutions, tailoring them to the EU, and they'd developed great expertise at it. One diplomat told me the negotiators sometimes averted their eyes, knowing perfectly well that many of the agreements could never be met. 'But still, the process has to continue,' they would say. 'We'll see how things turn out – in about ten years from now, I fear.'

At the end of it all lay the definitive test: each country's willingness to accept the contents of a tome of some 50,000 pages that now fills several metres of shelving in the attic of the House of European History in Brussels: the *acquis communautaire* on which this vast system of regulations, compromises, order and peace is based. Membership of the Union followed. In perpetuity, because leaving – according to the rules at the time – was impossible.

Back in 1990, European Commission president Jacques Delors said on French television, 'My objective is that before the end of the millennium Europe should have a true federation.' French president François Mitterrand, who was watching at home, shouted with anger, 'But that's ridiculous! What's he up to? No one in Europe will ever want that.' But Delors' words set the tone for the European project for years to come. Exceptionalism – we're special, better than any other country – was the scourge of American foreign policy, but the EU suffered from its own form of extreme triumphalism in those years: we have defeated the age-old curse of Europe, wars have been consigned to the past, everything will always get better and better.

That had been the message, for example, of a historic photograph taken in June 1985 in the Luxembourg border village of Schengen, showing five young politicians in a rather jocular pose on a pleasure boat. They had just signed a treaty by which Belgium, Luxembourg, France, Germany and the Netherlands agree to do away with border controls between them. It was the start of what would become one of the EU's most important successes, the largest passport-free zone in the world.

From then on, you could cross Schengen's internal borders at a hundred kilometres an hour. But how could such a thing work without firm joint control of the external borders – or indeed without explicit agreement on a common immigration policy? In that sense, Schengen was a grand gesture without content. Everything was supposed to come right of its own accord. Jean Monnet had always said politics would conform to the facts. Not so.

5

In *Ill Fares the Land*, his final, stirring call for more social democracy, Tony Judt describes how, shortly after the Second World War, almost all the major political debates in Europe and America had a strongly 'moralized' quality to them: 'Unemployment (the biggest issue in the UK, the US or Belgium); inflation (the greatest fear in central Europe, where it had ravaged private savings for decades); and agricultural prices so low (in Italy and France) that peasants were driven off the land and into extremist parties out of despair: these were not just economic issues, they were regarded by everyone from priests to secular intellectuals as tests of the ethical coherence of the community.' The consensus on these points was unusually broad, even among those involved in economic planning, and definitely among the pioneers of European unity. 'Everyone believed in the state.'

It's an intriguing paradox, Judt writes, that in those perilous post-war years capitalism was saved by a large dose of socialism. Sensible conservatives had no objection at all to close state supervision of food supplies, for instance, and they had little difficulty accepting a fairly progressive tax system. Everyone was convinced that economic growth and the other fruits of the European project would generally come to benefit those who needed them most. Hence the 'soft' capitalism characteristic of Europe, with all its regional variations – including the German Rhineland model, the Scandinavian model and the Dutch polder model.

Half a century later the opposite mentality prevailed. After the oil crisis of the 1970s, many Western countries encountered something that became known as 'stagflation', low growth combined with inflation. It opened the way for a new economic direction, provided by a series of economists and political thinkers of whom economist Milton Friedman, with his Chicago School, was the most important.

Now known as 'neoliberalism', the new approach was based on the idea that competition is the element of human nature that dominates all others. It must therefore be given free rein, in free markets. Instead of the 'artificial' state, 'natural' competition must rule the world. It was a vision based on an idealistic view of capitalism and of human nature, a presumption that individuals always make rational choices and markets always function flawlessly.

As an economic theory, neoliberalism dates back to the crisis years of the 1930s. To enable their economies to recover, governments all over the West – especially in America – intervened powerfully, and with success. Austrian philosopher and economist Friedrich Hayek, however, regarded all those state interventions as a slippery slope; the world would inevitably slide into socialism and tyranny. *The Road to Serfdom* was the eloquent title of Hayek's most important book, published in 1944. In April 1947, he collected a group of prominent economists and intellectuals around him in the Swiss mountain village of Mont Pèlerin. That meeting marked the start of what Hayek himself was happy to call 'the neoliberal movement'.

In the years that followed, his plea for 'liberal radicalism' was further developed and modified, but it was not until the 1980s that the breakthrough came, and thanks to Friedman and his acolytes it took a radical form.

In 1979 and 1981, two of neoliberalism's most enthusiastic adherents came to power, British Conservative prime minister Margaret Thatcher and American Republican president Ronald Reagan. From that moment on, neoliberalism made the running everywhere in the US and Western Europe. It boiled down to three dogmas: liberalization, deregulation and privatization. In all kinds of fields, governmental control came to an end. Postal services and the railways were privatized, schools and hospitals were commercialized, public housing became a commodity, and the bankers were given a free hand.

The fall of the Wall had immeasurable consequences for Western as well as Eastern Europe. In 1989 a major ideological adversary fell away, a permanent opponent that had always kept Western European capitalism in balance to some degree. Anyone transported from that time to the present day would no doubt be amazed by spectacular technological developments, but above all by the wholesale dismantling of the public sector. At a European level, privatization and large-scale deregulation – in the 1999 Treaty of Amsterdam for example – were a high priority. As a result, the centre of gravity of the European project steadily shifted. In economic terms, Europe moved from a social market economy (in the 1970s and 1980s) via a capitalist market economy (in the 1990s) to a neoliberal and hyper-globalized system (from the start of the new century).

At first sight, this shift seemed extraordinarily successful. In less than thirty years, from around 1980 to 2010, the standard of living for a large proportion of humanity markedly improved. The global economy grew by more than half. The decline in poverty, all over the world, was spectacular, with more people escaping extreme poverty in those thirty years than in all the preceding five centuries. In 1990, 1.9 billion people were still desperately poor, whereas in 2017 the figure was less than 700 million. In 1955, all over the world, people lived to an average age of forty-eight. In 2020 the average expectancy was 50 per cent higher, at seventy-two. Sluggish governments were forced by the stimuli of the free market to change with the times, and in that sense, neoliberalism was undoubtedly a necessary corrective. But it was taken too far.

Under the influence of a new generation of economic advisers, politicians all over Europe increasingly took their cue from the demands of the financial markets rather than the needs of their natural supporters. The spin doctor and the strategic adviser became central figures in European governments, especially under progressive political leaders. All those unpopular messages had to be sold to the voters somehow. No longer was priority given to the interests of a support base of vulnerable people. The main objective now was to stay in power.

Labour leader Tony Blair took the lead in implementing this change of direction in the UK. The left had been defeated time and again in the Thatcher years. Around the turn of the century, with New Labour, Blair managed to win three elections in a row, in 1997, 2001 and 2005. His Third Way relinquished two features of classic Labour policy: the party's link with the unions and its stress on public ownership. Many commentators cheered, believing those old structures had stood in the way of innovation for far too long. As she would later admit, Margaret Thatcher was prouder of this achievement than anything else; she had managed to hitch Labour to her triumphal chariot.

Blair's Dutch counterpart, union leader and social democrat Wim Kok, was seen as another shining example. The Netherlands, like other countries in Europe, had changed radically since the 1960s, from an industrial society with a strong public sector into an increasingly individualist society with a strong service sector. Politicians and governments had failed to move with the times, and by the 1980s the resulting problems included a state disability benefit with so many recipients that it was clearly out of control, a high national debt and extensive youth unemployment. These were phenomena that reinforced each other. Something had to be done.

'Shaking off the ideological feathers', as Kok called it, proved extraordinarily effective. It seemed possible to combine capitalism, neoliberalism, social democracy and a reliable welfare state. In 1997, American president Bill Clinton came to see the Miracle in The Hague with his own eyes. 'The third way goes global,' wrote the international press.

In the 1990s, Germany was regarded as the 'sick man of Europe', and from 1998 to 2005 Gerhard Schröder's red-green coalition set to work to put it right. The labour market was liberalized, state benefits were drastically cut and programmes were set up to help the unemployed, while at the same time wages were kept low, rapidly improving the competitiveness of German industry. The project was led by an executive at Volkswagen, Peter Hartz. In the harsh final phase, popularly known as 'Hartz IV', welfare payments were reduced to an absolute minimum and millions of pensioners found themselves close to the poverty line. Social democrat voters never forgave Schröder.

Naturally, there were protests. In America, where a similar movement was underway, an interesting political newcomer called Barack Obama was giving fiery speeches, condemning the zeitgeist and quoting what Adam Smith had said about 'this disposition to admire, and almost to worship, the rich and the powerful, and to despise, or, at least, to neglect persons of poor and mean condition'. Such voices remained the exception, however, and they were often greeted with jeers.

All over Europe, societies were reshaped to fit the market model. Henceforth every citizen would have to behave as a calculating *Homo economicus*, even in fields in which other values had traditionally prevailed. Terms such as 'the education market', 'the social care market', 'the art market' and so on came into fashion. American political scientist Wendy Brown spoke of a relentless economization of everything and everyone, from the state to the human soul, a process that in the long run wrecked every democratic debate: 'The demos disintegrates into bits of human capital; concerns with justice bow to the mandates of growth rates, credit ratings, and investment climates.'

In Britain, the railways were privatized amid great fanfare. It proved a disaster. To boost the country's global competitiveness, the special character of schools, universities and countless other long-established institutions was destroyed, and their often deeply rooted links with local communities were severed. British journalist Anthony Barnett used the phrase 'storms shatter communities'. Communities were shattered, he believes, purely to open them up to 'natural' competition, according to the dogma of the free market.

My own country changed rapidly too. From 1995 onwards, Dutch house prices quadrupled, mortgage debt tripled, education was stripped down, housing associations were privatized and the social housing sector was depleted. Public services were increasingly contracted out to private companies, even including the guarding of prisons. A similar pattern was visible in healthcare. The patient, nurse and doctor were no longer central, their places taken by cash flow and efficiency. Public values were eroded.

Philosopher Dorien Pessers called this 'crazy' neoliberalism 'aggressively antisocial'. It distrusted everything that could not be organized like a business, or whose results could not be fully quantified. The biggest victims were the arts sector, the universities, and health and social services, all of which Pessers believed gave life meaning and created bonds between people, forming society's 'humus layer'. An acquaintance of mine, working in a care home, was faced with a new manager who consistently referred to the elderly people entrusted to her care as 'the product'.

Between right and left a kind of truce developed. The cliché was that in the 1960s the left won the 'culture war', meaning the battle against racism, homophobia, sexism and other forms of personal oppression, while the right won the economic war. 'We are intensely relaxed about people getting filthy rich,' explained Labour strategist Peter Mandelson in the late 1990s, 'as long as they pay their taxes.' Centre-left governments all over Europe followed the same line of thought.

Even in fields in which theoretically there was no market mechanism, neoliberal managers attempted to mimic the market model. I heard a council official in a Dutch provincial town introduce himself as a 'member of the executive board'. Citizens had become clients – conveniently ignoring the fact that these clients had no ability to choose, except by moving house. Organizations in the public sector, and citizens themselves, continually had to 'prove' their value in numerical terms and demonstrate how well they had 'performed'. The power of the judiciary became a 'production line', as judges themselves called it. 'Self-reliance' was now the buzzword; public services were stripped to the bone and sanctions were harsh. Social security was hollowed out by flexible employment contracts, so that the power of employees dwindled.

Everything was measured and quantified, right down to the 'performance' of the youngest children at primary school. Viewing figures determined the policy of broadcasters. In health and social care the introduction of market mechanisms had the opposite of the intended effect, creating an undreamed-of bureaucracy. Dutch district nurses and carers found themselves having to register what they had done every five minutes so that their bosses could keep the finances in order. It ate up at least a third of their time, and fifteen years passed before this insane regime was more or less abolished. In universities, the humanities – languages, history, philosophy, culture – were discredited, since their 'output' could not be measured. An entire generation of talented people felt the ground slip away from under their feet. Rebel politician Pim Fortuyn – murdered in 2002 – talked of an 'orphaned society'.

The human dimension seemed forgotten.

6

On the first Saturday of 2002, my wife and I walked through our local street market. The stalls were showing dual prices for the first time: 4.40 guilders / 2 euros. Real euros. It had happened! All over Europe, revolutionary banknotes had poured out of cash machines on the night of 31 December. Italians celebrated with street parties, eager to get their hands on the new European money, the miracle currency that at a stroke would sweep away the worthless lira, eternal inflation and all those other Italian maladies. 'That night felt like stepping into a new world, a place inhabited by serious and stable people, blessed with a respectable currency,' wrote Stefano Montefiori of the *Corriere della Sera*. 'Of course, we wouldn't be millionaires any longer [the average monthly salary was 1.4 million lira at that point], but we were overjoyed to be able to swap our millions for the prestige of being Europeans.'

At our Amsterdam market, feelings were mixed. The stallholders had to find new words, now that the *kwartjes*, *dubbeltjes* and *stuivers*, to say nothing of the modern *snippen* and the old *geeltjes*, no longer existed. Someone was selling hot soup for €2.50. 'What?' we said. 'Is the man mad? More than five guilders for a lousy little cup of soup?' I noted, as a kind of experiment, how long I carried on thinking in guilders. The first year, I converted everything back; after about four years, only house prices, annual salaries and other large sums. After six years that too was over.

In the Netherlands, incidentally, we'd had just about the most beautiful money in the world, by a brilliant graphic designer. The fifty-guilder note in particular, with its orange-yellow sunflower, was exquisite, a joy to use. After 1 January 2002, they were no more. The new money was formally introduced in 1999, but now it started coming out of the wall. It looked like greyish compromise money – cowardly money too, since the designers had not even had the courage to decorate the notes with real European bridges, buildings or artworks, or with real European personalities. It would have led to too many arguments.

That was an early clue to the euro's greatest weakness. There was certainly every reason to work towards a single European currency in due course. By the early 1970s, the agreements made under the post-war Bretton Woods system were no longer tenable. The anchors of the dollar and gold fell away, and the values of the European currencies – guilders, lira, marks, crowns, francs, pesetas – fluctuated incessantly. Agreements were made about mutual support and about a specific 'bandwidth' that limited the movement of currencies, yet there were still currency storms in which Italian liras or French francs were blown in circles like dry leaves. A new anchor was needed.

The euro was sold to us, the public, for its convenience. On holiday and in transactions we no longer had to change money; all that messing about with foreign currencies was over for good. It later turned out that, behind the scenes, other motives were at play. There was a single political aim: after the fall of the Wall, Germany must not be allowed to become too powerful. Or, as Timothy Garton Ash put it, 'The European monetary union forged during and after German unification was not a German project to dominate Europe but a European project to constrain Germany.'

The birth of the euro was therefore not a particularly democratic process. Immediately after the Berlin Wall fell, there was immense pressure on Helmut Kohl. British prime minister Margaret Thatcher was opposed to German unification, thinking a reborn Germany far too dangerous. Dutch prime minister Ruud Lubbers shared her hesitation to some extent, for which Kohl never forgave him. The Bonn-Paris axis, however, as always in Europe, held sway. That meant there would have to be a single currency. If Germany refused, Mitterrand threatened, 'We will return to the world of 1913.'

Kohl's own voters were not willing to give up their hard, safe Deutschmark for all the tea in China. Yet Kohl bowed to the demands of Mitterrand and other European leaders. 'It will happen,' he said. 'The Germans accept strong leadership.' He was in need of his closest European allies, France first among them, for the acceptance of German unification, but he did impose strict conditions: no monetary union without a common economic and financial policy, a budgetary union and a political union.

The French pulled Kohl back into line immediately. There were just two strict, basic conditions for all participants. National debt must be below 60 per cent of gross national product (roughly everything a country earns in a year); and the budget deficit must be less than 3 per cent. A European central bank was set up, but its powers remained limited to maintaining price stability by setting key interest rates and controlling the European Community's money supply. As French economist Thomas Piketty later put it, 'For the first time in history, we managed to create a currency without a state and a central bank without a government.' It was certainly the first time on such a scale.

In 1992, Europe took the plunge. The Maastricht Treaty included an official decision to introduce the euro. In the words of Timothy Garton Ash: 'In the Sturm und Drang of the largest geopolitical change in Europe since 1945, a sickly child was conceived.'

For the participating economies, the introduction of the euro had all kinds of costs and benefits, but one effect leapt out immediately: the steering mechanism that having a currency of your own provides in emergency situations had been removed. Previously, if a country's debt became too great or competitive gaps too wide, it could devalue its currency. France and Italy, for example, did this regularly. A cheap franc or lira was a miracle cure that had countless side effects, but many of the resulting problems could be put right to some degree without causing the population too much trouble. The introduction of the euro made this self-interested ploy impossible. Henceforth, all a government could do in such situations was to reduce wages, cut government expenditure – especially on the welfare state – and raise taxes.

According to American economist Joseph Stiglitz, later a recipient of the Nobel Prize, this was the euro's weakness. And was a common currency really so important for a united Europe anyhow? The EU ought to concentrate on a common foreign policy, he argued, and on a common defence policy, trade policy, social safety nets and so on. The participating countries, with all their cultural and economic differences, did not have to be squeezed into a single system that lacked any flexibility. Their opportunities to implement their own economic policies and make their own democratic choices would remain, and a European 'democratic deficit' could be avoided. 'The founders of the euro were guided by a set of ideas, notions about how economies function, that were fashionable at the time but that were simply wrong,' Stiglitz later wrote.

In 1997, 330 European economists jointly issued a warning: watch out, the euro is a mistake; monetary integration without political union can never work. They were ridiculed, and Dutch finance minister Gerrit Zalm spoke of 'timid economists', but Helmut Kohl had already said in the Bundestag: 'The idea of maintaining in the long run an economic and a currency union without political union is mistaken.'

In 1998, shortly before the introduction of the euro into the banking world, André Szász, former director of De Nederlandsche Bank, the Dutch central bank, said in an interview, 'We are building on quicksand.' The experts felt like powerless onlookers. *Newsweek* correspondent Rana Foroohar said later that she felt as if she were standing on the quayside watching the *Titanic* sail away.

Discipline and triumphalism do not sit easily together. In 1997, the 60 per cent debt and 3 per cent deficit rules of the eurozone were laid down once more in a Stability and Growth Pact. Almost all the euro countries, including Germany and the Netherlands, twisted themselves into the strangest configurations in order to comply with the rules. Following immense pressure from France, both Italy and Belgium were admitted to the eurozone, even though their national debt stood at 120 per cent of GDP, twice the permitted level. When Germany and France threatened to exceed that same norm in 2003, the rules of the game changed again. The costs of all these irregularities would not, it was believed, ever come anywhere close to cancelling out the benefits of the euro.

There arose a vast circus of bookkeeping conjuring tricks, from Athens and Rome to Paris and Berlin. Eventually, Luxembourg was the only eurozone country more or less still complying with the demands of the Stability and Growth Pact. But government leaders did not want to upset their pleasant clubbishness too much, so there were no sanctions, there was no discipline, nobody was thrown out or even called to account. Nor did the leaders want to transfer any power, so there was no clear hierarchy – a thing indispensable in a crisis.

Political motives were decisive in this phase too. France did not want to adopt the euro without Italy, because then it would soon be the weakest eurozone country. And surely what was given to Italy could not be withheld from Greece? Rarely have statistics been fiddled to the extent they were to allow Greece to adopt the euro. All kinds of expenditure – pensions, defence – vanished from the books in Athens. Taxes on petrol, alcohol and tobacco were reduced, as were electricity prices, in order to push the inflation figures down. The head of the Hellenic Statistical Authority was nicknamed 'the Magician' by insiders for his proficiency at making inflation, the deficit and the debt magically disappear. In a speech in Athens, the then German foreign minister Joschka Fischer praised the Greeks for managing to do so much in so little time. The rigorous Dutch finance minister Gerrit Zalm called the Greek accomplishments 'extraordinarily impressive'.

That magical world held up miraculously even after Greece adopted the euro in 2001. From then on, Greeks could borrow as much as they liked. They had been paying 18 per cent interest; now the rate was the same as in Germany, at 5 per cent. With the help of the bankers at Goldman Sachs – in return for some $300 million in consultancy fees – successive Greek governments became adept at concealing their true creditworthiness. Even future income, amounts from European funds included, was immediately pledged, cashed and spent.

At the same time, far too little money was coming in. The tax system and the land registry (in reality, 398 land registries) remained in chaos despite all the support from Europe. The huge Greek bubble stayed in the air simply because hardly anyone in the rest of Europe bothered to look. As long as those who lent money to Greece assumed it was a country as sound as the European Union – for which read Germany – nobody cared. Most Greeks had no desire to sound the alarm either. They were doing very nicely as things stood.

On 9 May 2002, in Aachen, the prestigious Charlemagne Prize was awarded to 'the euro', as the greatest European achievement of recent years.

7

That grey compromise money that streamed out of cash machines everywhere therefore got off to a flying start. In those first few years, things proceeded exactly as hoped; the common currency bound Europe more tightly together. In 2008, Bruegel, a Brussels think tank, took stock. The introduction had gone smoothly, as had the accession of new members like Greece, Slovenia and Cyprus. Prices had remained stable, economies were growing, travel and trade were a good deal easier than before. The Europeans were content.

At a global level too, the euro was functioning well. A quarter of all foreign currency reserves were in euros. In November 2007, press agencies reported that Brazilian supermodel Gisele Bündchen no longer wanted to be paid in dollars but in euros. With her multimillion-dollar company, she was guided by the mood of the markets. The euro was even starting to displace the dollar.

But did this prosperity and this euro mean genuine peace? From an outside perspective, Pankaj Mishra recognized a 'sanitized' European history. Peace and prosperity in Europe since 1945 had, he believed, helped to 'obscure deeper disruptions and longer traumas'. In reality, the continent's history was a story of 'carnage and bedlam', rather than peaceful unification. 'The modern world put the two world wars in a separate, quarantined box, and isolated Stalinism, Fascism and Nazism within the mainstream of European history as monstrous aberrations.' Europeans did not seem to realize it, he wrote, but the post-1945 equilibrium was 'precarious and rare'.

Despite the triumphs, that equilibrium had not become any steadier since 1999. For all the joys of globalization, a price had to be paid. Inequality of income, which had reduced in the decades after the war, started to increase again rapidly after the turn of the century. On the financial markets, now practically without any rules or national limitations, fortunes could be made in the blink of an eye. The super-rich grew in numbers, and accordingly in political influence. A new class of managers, technocrats and advisers took full advantage of the 'challenges' of globalization, and above all of the financial opportunities presented by an endless series of privatizations. No longer policy-making officials, they started calling themselves CEOs and earning two to three times their former salaries.

At the same time, at the opposite end of the social ladder, a twenty-first-century proletariat emerged that hopped from one temporary job to the next, continually driven to meet numerical targets set by management. Subtly exploited and humiliated, many workers led difficult lives, sometimes in poor housing, often with health problems and perpetual debt. Their incomes, in contrast to those of the richest 10 per cent, barely increased at all in those prosperous years.

Furthermore, there were still huge differences between European countries and regions, despite support from numerous European funds. Around the turn of the century, productivity per head in Central and Eastern Europe was still no more than half that of Western Europe. The contrasts within European countries were at least as stark. Between Greater London, for example – with its booming financial centre in the City – and the old industrial regions of Scotland, Wales and the north-east of England. Or between Bavaria with its rich capital, Munich, and the former GDR, or the faded glory of the Ruhr. Or between Flanders and Wallonia. Or between southern and northern Italy.

At the start of the twenty-first century, people in the former Eastern Bloc well remembered the deprivations and dilemmas of living through a war or a major crisis, or indeed under a dictatorship. Czech president Václav Havel had spent ten years in prison, purely for what he thought and wrote. 'Only then do you truly realize what today's Europe means.'

Many people in the West, certainly among the younger generations, no longer had any idea what might happen to them if things turned out badly. 'They're dancing on the edge of a volcano,' Max Kohnstamm sometimes muttered. I had got to know him well. 'We did that too, in the 1930s. But at least we knew we were doing it.'

2. Peace

2000

I

AT KIRKENES, THE LAND BORDER with Russia – 195 kilometres long in total – consists of a double row of posts, yellow and red, spaced exactly four metres apart with the border precisely halfway between them. In 2018, the job of guarding posts 177 to 396 was in the hands of the Jarfjord Company, a Norwegian army unit of around 120 men and women. They generally carried out surveillance and policing tasks, but should the signal 'Make ready' sound from the border station they were able to mobilize within five minutes, fully prepared for combat.

Norway has fewer than 5.5 million inhabitants, roughly the same as the city of Saint Petersburg – an indication of just how outnumbered it is by Russia. That same year, 2018, Norway reintroduced the emergency pack. During the Cold War, every Norwegian was expected to keep a stock of firewood and dried herring at home. Nowadays they are each required to make sure they have water, crispbread, porridge oats, canned food, a camping stove and a battery radio. According to the latest information brochure, citizens must be willing to take part in a 'total defence' of the country.

The Norwegian army was hospitable. Yes, of course; do come and watch. In the truck that picked me up, Bach's first piano concerto was playing – what a civilized country this was! I was allowed to accompany a patrol under Commander Widerøe, with his men Fossen, Anderson, Sørløk and Aase. They had open faces. They were conscripts, yes, but thoroughly specialized. They drove heavily armoured buggies on all sides of our jeep. Our dashboard looked old and worn, the knobs and steering wheel like those of a charming vintage car. 'You're right, this jeep dates back to the 1970s. Last year we got new vehicles, but at minus thirty they gave up the ghost. These old things never fail to start. We keep them going with parts from the scrapyard. They'll have to do.'

We walked up a hill. The former observation post was now fully automated. From there we looked out over a beautiful, isolated lake, the Russian border at our feet, and in the distance another Norwegian border post, a bigger one this time. Endless watching and listening went on here.

Contact between the Russian and Norwegian border forces was still fairly relaxed. They reported incidents and unknown passers-by to each other. They used to have annual football matches, which the Russians consistently won, but here, as everywhere, relations were cooling. 'If we come upon the Russians now, we nod to each other. No more than that. Once a year, in autumn, the top brass meet up and check the border posts. Afterwards they always have dinner together. But football matches, we don't have those anymore.' That was a shame, everyone thought.

I was aware that the Norwegians knew this inhospitable terrain better than anyone and had a thousand surprises in store for any aggressor. Nevertheless, it was strange to think that these lads, with their buggies and their snow scooters and those beautiful names on their breast pockets, these pleasant young men formed the front line.

They were all young. The junior officers were in their mid-twenties, the oldest in his mid-thirties. The highest-ranking individual was a small, dapper woman with a ponytail. Captain Carina Vinterdal had the stiff bearing of a professional officer – 'We never run here, we always walk; we don't want any excitement if there's no need for excitement' – but her eyes flashed with life every time she contemplated a question. We talked for far longer than either of us had intended, about her work, about the place of women in the Norwegian army, about what motivated her. Meanwhile the parade ground was filling up. Half the company was preparing for a four-day exercise in the forest, with three freezing-cold nights. Their faces were painted black, weapons and ammunition were handed out, two ancient-looking tracked vehicles, from the 1980s, were started up. Two girlish plaits sprang out from under a helmet.

I asked Captain Vinterdal whether she'd been watching *Occupied*, a television series that begins with the disappearance of an investigative journalist in these snowy border plains before the Russian army rolls in. She nodded.

'I thought: oh my god someone's touching on a very important issue here. As a commanding officer you always ask yourself: how would I react to an invasion? How could I explain that to my children? It's on my mind all the time, because it's what we're preparing for.'

'How?'

'We're capable of putting up a good fight, but we're small. I'm not sure how to say this, but we don't have the right resources. We do have the will. It's in our history. We have a lot to lose, a beautiful country, our values . . . The older I get, the more I realize how much there is to fight for.'

'And to die for?'

'Look, a photo of my children. That's Norway to me. We're so lucky to be able to live here, and I want to keep it that way. That's why I'm in the army.'

'And those soldiers over there on the parade ground?'

'If you put that question to them, some will say yes. Others will say nothing at all.'

2

The jubilation in Western Europe at the turn of the century concealed a darker reality. In Russia and Eastern Europe I'd witnessed optimism in 1999, but also a shocking amount of poverty. In a small town in Poland I was buttonholed by a wizened old lady. '*Ach, bitte, helfen Sie eine alte deutsche Mutti.*' (Oh, please, will you help an old German mama.) In Hungary I picked up a hitch-hiker. She was despondent. Her bicycle had been stolen and now it took her an hour to walk to work every day. There was no way she could find the money for a new one.

In Russia in those days, you came upon lines of desperate women at every railway station, standing side by side trying to sell three bottles of vodka, or two cucumbers, or an old coat. There were some who spoke English, who had once been teachers or civil servants but their pensions had evaporated. I once talked for a bit with the last in the line, who had worked all her life in a clothes shop. No, she'd never thought she might one day stand here half-frozen, holding out a plastic cup. People in Western Europe were largely blind to the heart-rending scenes playing out in public all over the collapsed Soviet Empire.

Želimir Žilnik, a filmmaker, attended many Russian film festivals in those years. 'Even at prestigious receptions they served only vodka and bad salami. And people would ask, "Could you buy me a T-shirt?" "Do you have socks for me, or shoes?" On the train from Moscow to Novi Sad the conductor came past. "If you pay me one dollar you can eat with us." ' In 1992, 50 million Russians were living on or near the poverty line, a third of the population.

The Belarusian writer Svetlana Alexievich systematically noted down the experiences of her contemporaries at the time: 'Ration cards, coupons for everything: from bread to grain to socks. We'd stand in line for five or six hours at a time . . . But you're standing there with a book that you hadn't been able to buy before. You'd know that in the evening, they were going to play a previously forbidden film on TV that had been kept on the shelf for the past ten years.' But also, 'The more they shouted and wrote, "Freedom! Freedom!" the faster not only the cheese and salami but also the salt and sugar disappeared from the shelves.' And, 'Our former life has been smashed to smithereens, not a single stone was left standing.'

In Kirkenes, Russian women went from one campsite to the next to offer themselves as prostitutes. The town's mayor was invited to climb onto a tank on the other side of the border along with the Russian soldiers, and go on a duck hunt with them.

Like so many in the East, all these Russians were victims of 'shock therapy'. It was an experiment on a continental scale that Western advisers had thought up in the 1980s and 1990s, and it forced the former Eastern Bloc countries into a Western mould with a barrage of privatizations and liberalizations. The 'therapy' produced many winners and even more losers. It got countries like Poland and Hungary quickly back on their feet, but for the Russian state it ended in bankruptcy, a huge additional dose of corruption and a traumatized population.

3

The 'Washington Consensus' was the label on the standard reform package that the International Monetary Fund, the World Bank, the US Treasury Department and a handful of other financial powers loosed upon the world

The Iron Curtain, 1945–1989

from 1989 onwards. Its starting points were neoliberalism and an absolute faith in the free market. The programme was originally intended for the moribund economies of certain Latin American countries, especially Chile. When that very year the Berlin Wall came down, no time was wasted in applying it to the utterly ramshackle economies of the former Eastern Bloc.

The need seemed obvious. Bronisław Geremek, then Polish minister of foreign affairs, compared the communist system to a vast old bunker: 'You need a huge bulldozer to flatten the thing.' But in the end, he believed, everyone would be happy, with a new Scandinavian, social-democrat version of capitalism. The socialist straitjacket was torn off, state control and state ownership were ended as quickly as possible, and banks and other financial institutions were set up at great speed.

What was still happening gradually in Western Europe took place in the East virtually from one day to the next. The mass privatization of businesses began, farms were split up and sold, small retailers were pushed aside by mega-emporia Lidl and Aldi, and slogans with words like 'collective' and 'communal' were replaced by talk of 'markets' and 'competition'. The IMF and the EC – the future EU – stepped in with tens of billions of dollars, yet their help was as nothing compared to the post-war Marshall Plan, under which the United States had given support to a haemorrhaging Western Europe.

In Poland, this shock therapy was a leap into cold water. Subsidies for food, fuel and other essentials were abolished, as were price controls, and the borders were thrown open to foreign companies. Unprofitable state firms were privatized. After a short, painful period of adjustment, so the neoliberal economists claimed, a new balance would be achieved, demand and supply would match once more, and the economy would begin to grow again.

At first, there was great disappointment. The crisis was deep and seemed set to last. In 1990 and 1991, industrial production fell by almost a third and inflation was barely kept under control; and in 1992, 2.3 million Poles found themselves unemployed. At the famous Lenin Shipyard in Gdańsk, where so many had fought for this new, free Poland, close to five out of six employees lost their jobs. 'We used to have enough money, but we couldn't buy anything,' a woman told me in 1999 on the train to Gdańsk. 'Now we can buy whatever we like, except that we don't have the money. All told, we haven't made any progress. We've just been driven crazy.'

It was no different elsewhere in Eastern Europe in those first few years. In Czechoslovakia and Hungary industrial production fell by a third; in Romania and the former GDR by around a quarter. In Hungary, 80 per cent of state-owned companies were sold – the old communist rulers and Western European businesses had a field day – and wages fell by a fifth, pushing around 30 per cent of the population under the poverty line while the 'advisers' earned millions. Young people started to leave. The population of Ukrainian cities like Lviv fell by a fifth within just a few years.

In the GDR, the former state-owned companies, including huge housing corporations and 2.4 million hectares of agricultural land, were redeveloped and privatized by the Treuhandanstalt, known as Treuhand, the agency set up for that purpose. The costs of the operation were to be covered by the proceeds of privatization. When it was all over and done with, in 1994, just 1.5 million of the 4 million Treuhand jobs were left. Against expectations, the operation was loss-making, ending with a deficit of an estimated 270 billion German marks, or 135 billion euros.

In those years, with all the privatizations, the 'Wild East' represented a bonanza for smart entrepreneurs. Within ten years of the fall of the Berlin Wall, at least half of Eastern European manufacturing was in the hands of Western multinationals. Car production was 90 per cent Western-owned. For clever young men and women who knew Western languages, the jobs were there for the taking. For them, the promised economic miracle became a reality. Spending power in Warsaw, Prague and Budapest rose by some 60 to 70 per cent between 1995 and 2000, while inflation and unemployment fell. In many cities, a new middle class began to emerge, and buildings went up hand over fist.

The statistics showed that by 1999 the former Eastern Bloc had largely picked itself up and its economy had been restructured. Adherents of neoliberalism cheered, while others believed that the same or even better results could have been achieved with a more gradualist approach, avoiding a great deal of the poverty, humiliation and other human suffering.

Furthermore, the prosperity divide remained enormous. In the reborn Warsaw, Prague and Budapest, for years a teacher continued to earn between

€150 and €205 a month. Beyond the glamour of the big cities, the situation was even more alarming. There was widespread disruption in the country-side, and in Leipzig, Magdeburg and Chemnitz unemployment in 2005 still stood at almost 20 per cent.

Twenty-five years after the fall of the Wall, the World Bank reported that the transition to Western modernity had been a real success for only 10 per cent of the population of the former Eastern Bloc. For another 30 per cent, the process had been 'moderately successful'; for 40 per cent a 'moderate failure'; and for 20 per cent it was downright catastrophic, with household incomes even lower than in 1990. The latter was true for most people in five of the twelve post-Soviet states – Ukraine, Moldavia, Georgia, Kirghizia and Tajikistan – and in four of the seven states of the former Yugoslavia: Serbia, Bosnia-Herzegovina, Montenegro and Kosovo. There was talk of countries with three or four lost generations.

4

While this entire world was on the brink of collapse, a young secret agent was laboriously working his way up through the Soviet bureaucracy. He'd had a wild childhood, liked a fight, and eventually, after much determined effort, he'd been allowed to join the Soviet intelligence agency, the KGB. His work was far from spectacular and, in 1985, he was stationed in a pro-vincial outpost, the East German city of Dresden. There he started a family, fathering two children.

His job was to snoop on foreign businesspeople, to collect intelligence on military and scientific developments in the West, and later mainly to keep an eye on the Stasi, East Germany's secret service. He spent most of his time collecting and sifting through Western news cuttings, thereby gleaning information not available to the rest of the population in the East – about the campaign of lies surrounding the nuclear disaster at Cher-nobyl in 1986, for example. He became thoroughly familiar with the logic and ethics of the KGB. It would shape the rest of his life.

In November 1989, the world fell apart for this agent, Vladimir Putin. When demonstrators threatened to storm his headquarters in Dresden, he and his colleagues, in a panic, attempted to burn as many files and contact

lists as possible – with only partial success – while at the same time desperately trying to contact their KGB bosses for further instructions. 'Moscow
is silent,' was all they were told. Lieutenant Colonel Putin would later repeat
that phrase endlessly. 'I got the feeling that the country no longer existed.
That it had completely disappeared.'

After the dismantling of the GDR in 1990, he was recalled to Moscow.
The humiliation was total. The Soviet army no longer had sufficient
resources even to pull out of the region, so its withdrawal was partly
financed by Germany. Putin had not received his salary for three months,
he had nowhere to live in Moscow and barely anywhere to sleep, and his
only possession was an ancient washing machine he'd been given by his
East German neighbours as a parting gift. On the train on the way back to
Moscow, a thief stole his wife Lyudmila's coat and all the roubles and marks
they had on them.

The uprooted agent had one great piece of good fortune: he was a member of the KGB, the Soviet Union's most powerful and astute organization.
In the KGB there was an awareness at an early stage that the Soviet system
was on its last legs, and during President Gorbachev's reforms it had been
busy setting up its own businesses and trade channels, facing West. The
West offered legal certainty and security; you could invest your money
there with confidence, as the KGB was well aware. Hundreds of dummy
companies were created to invest the wealth of party leaders and secure the
future of their intelligence work.

In the turbulent years that followed the collapse of the Soviet Union,
both state power – apparatchiks, after all, knew their way around
unerringly – and the keys to finance and commerce were largely in the
hands of the KGB. Anyone in the Wild East who attempted to profit from
the shock therapy, the expropriations and privatizations, inevitably ran up
against the KGB sooner or later.

On the street, the economy was taken over in the early 1990s by gangsters and the mafia. In provincial towns, drug dealers didn't sell heroin any
longer but a home-made concoction of codeine pills and various synthetic
cleaning products. Even vodka had become too expensive for millions of
Russians and they now drank samogon (hooch), made from industrial alcohol or window-cleaning fluid. I remember my fellow passengers on the *Red
Arrow*, the night train from Saint Petersburg to Moscow, tying the handles of

the compartment door together with string before going to sleep: 'You never know.'

Power struggles were settled by gang warfare. The murder rate rose to around thirty a day. 'I quickly realized that the new world wasn't mine, it wasn't for me. It required another breed of person,' wrote eyewitness Svetlana Alexievich. 'They raised the ones from the bottom up to the top . . . All in all, it was a revolution . . . The streets were filled with these bruisers in tracksuits. Wolves! They came after everyone.'

There had always been gangsters, even in Soviet times, but they'd been more or less underground. Many items were scarce in the communist period, so there was plenty of money to be made from smuggling, and from fixing and fiddling. Gorbachev's version of Prohibition in the mid-1980s was a godsend for these *vory* (thieves), since along with a new market for their illegal alcohol it gave them a broad following. Thieves and smugglers were now welcome everywhere and even normally law-abiding citizens made grateful use of their services. They operated in broad daylight, with criminal codes of their own that survived all the twists and turns of events.

In the chaotic Russia of the 1990s, the gangsters felt right at home. You saw them everywhere at the start of that decade, the lesser among them in the form of hucksters and money-changers around every Russian hotel – sometimes even on bicycles – busily building up starting capital in dollars and D-marks before the real bonanza began. The state had virtually ceased to function, so businesspeople hired them to secure their deals, and indeed their persons. *Krysha* (roof) became a household word for someone who offers protection while extorting money from you.

The country in which these mafiosi ruled the roost now had the population statistics of a war zone. The birth rate soon halved, the death rate resembled that of Zimbabwe or Afghanistan, and between 1989 and 1999 average life expectancy for men fell by no less than five years, to fifty-nine, the level of Bangladesh. The main causes of death were tuberculosis, AIDS and, above all, vodka.

Following upon this petty criminality, the real pillaging began. The second half of the 1990s is known in Russia as the 'Time of the Seven Bankers', the years in which power lay not with politicians or the military but with seven insanely rich oligarchs. Three years after coming to power, the president of the time, Boris Yeltsin, was barely able to pay his civil servants their pensions and salaries, so to bail out the treasury he launched a loans-for-shares scheme. In exchange for cash loans, the most important oligarchs were given control of the immense state assets of communist times. Because the loans were never paid back by the state, these magnates eventually got their hands on countless industries, oilfields, mines, housing blocks and farms for a song.

Our uprooted KGB agent made a career leap of his own in these years, becoming right-hand man to his former professor Anatoly Sobchak, who had been elected mayor of Saint Petersburg. Sobchak was a brazen and brilliant lawyer who presented himself as a liberal and was therefore unable to allow a prominent KGB member to join his staff, since the KGB was part of the old regime. But he did need the KGB. The unknown and inconspicuous Vladimir Putin was an excellent choice in such circumstances.

Putin became head of the city's Committee for External Relations. This put him in charge of, among other things, foreign investments, the registration of business ventures, and flows of money to and from foreign countries. He had gained a position of enormous power, in a place where everything came together: the state, the secret services and the Russian mafia. He worked with such brutal resolve that he quickly gained the nickname 'Stasi'.

Around Sobchak's city hall there was soon the buzz of scandal. Within a year, Putin and his civil servants were being investigated. His office had approved the export of $120 million worth of wood, metals and other supplies from the few remaining state-owned companies, in exchange for a large amount of foreign food. Famished Saint Petersburg never saw any of the food. The investigation was swiftly curtailed.

The local mafia was tamed fairly quickly with a deal: keep a low profile and arrange all your business through us, and we'll leave you in peace. Later, Putin would handle the oligarchs in the same way, laying the foundations for a powerful, orderly and smoothly functioning kleptocracy.

After Sobchak lost the mayoral election in 1996, Putin moved to Moscow. What happened in the years that followed is still shrouded in mystery. Putin was given a leading role in the management of the Kremlin and within two years he was boss of the FSB, the successor to the KGB. Within another year he was premier of the Russian Federation. Where his true loyalties lay – with the Yeltsin clan or with the FSB – remained unclear.

When I travelled through Russia in 1999, developments like these were being played out in semi-darkness. The country was bankrupt, and for the second time in ten years Russians had lost all their savings. There were plenty of scandals, but only a handful of people knew exactly what was going on.

British-Russian Peter Pomerantsev, who worked in television, later described his Moscow years as exceptionally exciting. The atmosphere was reminiscent of 1920s Berlin. 'Never had so much money flowed into so small a place in so short a time. . . . The Russians were the new jet set: the richest, the most energetic, the most dangerous. . . . "Performance" was the city's buzzword, a world where gangsters become artists, gold-diggers quote Pushkin, Hell's Angels hallucinate themselves as saints.'

In my memory, the talk of the day was not corruption but the shiny women's magazine *Cosmopolitan Russia*. Launched in 1994, it immediately became a resounding success, even in the most remote parts of the country. One of the pioneers was a former journalist, Derk Sauer, and he was as astonished as anyone. A copy of *Cosmo*, he calculated, cost a day's pay; the fact that so many people could afford to buy it meant there was a great deal of silent money stashed away among the Russians. There really did seem to be a hidden middle class, and the new post-Soviet era was being celebrated with a new lifestyle.

That observation tallied with the results of a sociological mass survey among no fewer than 75,000 Russians. Despite the chaos, by and large they seemed to be better off than in the 1980s. They had rather more spacious homes, more households had washing machines, televisions and fridges, and the number of private cars had doubled. Yet they were unhappy. More than half of those questioned would have loved, if they could, to go back to the times of the old Soviet Union, before perestroika.

The cause of their discomfort, according to sociologist Lev Gudkov, could be found in another striking statistic. A large number of Russians – a sixth of the population, in fact – had been able to take a look beyond the Russian border for the first time. That confrontation with the West was far more shocking than the realization that some of their compatriots had become staggeringly rich overnight. In the words of Russian-American writer and journalist Masha Gessen, 'They had felt themselves to be not just poor individuals but people from a poor country.'

This explains, in part, the confusion regarding *Cosmopolitan*. Everyone I spoke to had an opinion about it. *Cosmopolitan* put on show a new kind of freedom, new role models, the possibility of a better life – and in the current chaos, there was a great need for that. 'Most bosses here are either ex-communists, or criminals, or corrupt,' a woman said to me. 'And they're often arseholes, too. *Cosmopolitan* shows us unattached working women – well educated and ready for postmodern society. They're the victors over the men.' Another woman remained gloomy: 'The message of *Cosmo* is yet another story that contrasts with our daily lives in every possible way. It seems we in Russia always need a dream like that, a grim confrontation between a distant world and our own struggle to survive.'

5

In late 1999, Boris Yeltsin's position became untenable. There were rumours that the president was drinking heavily; you could actually see him sway. In reality he'd been seriously ill for several years, as the Dutch doctors who treated him would later confirm. Yet he hesitated for a long time before naming a successor. There was no way around the all-powerful FSB, but at the same time the new man had to be a trustworthy member of his own clan. There was a real danger that he, and especially his daughter, might otherwise end up in prison for corruption.

Eventually, he opted for the mouse hardly anyone knew.

Gleb Pavlovsky, adviser to the Kremlin at the time, afterwards told PBS *Frontline* and my colleagues at VPRO how preparations were made for the launch of the new Russian hero, whoever it turned out to be: 'He had to be elected as president, and this was our job . . . I knew the plot. I needed an actor.' There was something else he knew too: people no longer had faith in the old elite. The new leader needed to be part of the elite, that was inescapable, but he must not be associated with it. 'For electors, it looked as if Putin was in charge of a crowd that stormed the Kremlin and as if he took the president's seat. This was the kind of revolution that electors wanted. It was a safe revolution, a revolution inside the government.'

Back in the spring of 1999, Pavlovsky and his colleagues had researched the anxieties that prevailed among Russians and how they imagined their heroes. They found a fictional hero, Max Otto von Stierlitz, who was the lead character in a popular television series about a Soviet intelligence officer stationed in Nazi Germany. Von Stierlitz was a Russian James Bond, with impeccable dress sense and manners. As an experiment, they put him on the cover of the magazine *Kommersant Vlast* as 'President in the year 2000'. Sales of that issue were far above average. 'We realized that we needed a young, strong, powerful intelligence officer.' Putin was that man.

In September 1999 a series of extraordinary terrorist attacks took place – bombings of entire housing blocks in Moscow and two cities in the south of the country. Some 300 people were killed, and because the targets were in ordinary residential neighbourhoods, they caused immense unrest among the population. Chechen rebels were blamed, but no convincing explanation for the attacks was ever produced. In the city of Ryazan, several men seen carrying sacks of explosives into a block of flats happened to get caught by ordinary police officers. They turned out to be members of the FSB. The intelligence agency claimed they were involved in a vigilance exercise. Digging further into the affair proved deadly dangerous; politicians and journalists who attempted it did not live to tell the tale. Suspicion has therefore always fallen on the FSB, and the motive was clear. The attacks would make the call for a strong leader all the louder.

Sure enough, the recently appointed premier Vladimir Putin was on Russian television practically every night that autumn: he alone could banish fear and save the country. After the atrocious bomb attacks on the apartment buildings, he hit back hard. The destruction wrought by his tanks and bombers on the Chechen capital, Grozny, was unlike anything seen in Europe since the Second World War. According to Putin, however, the Chechens had not been attacked but liberated and 'placed under Russian protection'. He claimed it was the only way to stop further disintegration of the Russian empire; his own experiences as a KGB officer in the

dismantled GDR had been traumatic. When in 2000 peace was more or less
restored – after rebel leader Akhmat Kadyrov switched sides – Doctors
Without Borders calculated that nine out of ten Chechens had lost a close
friend or relative.

Putin's approval ratings shot up, from 33 per cent in August 1999 to 80
per cent in November. Here was a true leader. 'I started out as a historian,'
Pavlovsky said. 'You can either write history or make history.'

On that memorable New Year's Eve of 1999, at noon, Boris Yeltsin unexpectedly appeared on television. Against the background of a Christmas tree
dripping with tinsel, he announced, slow and slurring, his resignation. 'I
have understood that it was necessary for me to do this. Russia must enter
the new millennium with new politicians, with new faces, with new, smart,
strong, energetic people.' He tottered to his car, waved off by his successor.
So it was that Putin automatically became acting president of the Russian
Federation.

The operation was top secret. Putin's wife, Lyudmila, who had not
watched the New Year's message, received a phone call five minutes later
from a friend. 'Lyuda, congratulations, my best wishes.' 'And my best wishes
to you,' Lyudmila answered, assuming it was a New Year's greeting. Her
friend had to explain that her husband had just become president – *ad
interim* – of the Russian Federation.

Film director Vitaly Mansky would later let slip that Yeltsin's announcement was pre-recorded and the television crew kept isolated, not even
allowed to ring home: 'There was something fishy about it.' The timing was
perfect. On that 31 December, the Russians had thrown themselves into a
party mood that would last for two weeks, since it was followed by Orthodox Christmas and Orthodox New Year. The transfer of the trappings of the
presidency, including the nuclear briefcase and the princely pension and
dacha promised to Yeltsin, all largely escaped the notice of the Russians.
'When we awoke from our stupor on 15 January we had an acting president
who didn't give a damn about elections, because de facto he'd already been
president for ages,' said Mansky.

In a carefully crafted essay in the daily *Nezavisimaya Gazeta*, the new leader
had presented his credentials the day before. The situation was alarming:
40 per cent of the nation's income was earned on the black market, the

country had become far too dependent on exports of oil and gas, and productivity was shockingly low. A change of course was essential. 'For the first time in the past two or three hundred years there is a real risk that the country will sink to the level of a second- or even third-rank state,' the acting president wrote. Reforms were urgently needed, in all sectors. Three months later, Putin would win the presidential elections in the first round of voting. 'It was like a hot knife through butter,' said Mansky.

Yet his very first decree as acting president, on that 31 December, concerned his predecessor. It ensured that 'corruption charges against the outgoing president and his relatives' would not be pursued.

Briefly, after the collapse of the Soviet Union, it had seemed as if Russia would slowly move in the direction of the West. In 1993, the border at Kirkenes was more or less opened for permanent residents of the border region. Every day, hundreds of Russians crossed the border to do their shopping in the little town. Coffee and, above all, disposable nappies were sometimes hauled away carloads at a time. There was clearly something wrong with their nappies, the people of Kirkenes concluded. The Norwegians, for their part, filled up with cheap petrol in Russia and sometimes went to dine or dance in Murmansk, some four hours' drive away. There were cultural exchanges and sports events. The residents of Kirkenes and the neighbouring Russian town of Nikel crept closer together.

But Russia did not become a full member of the European family. That turned out to be a pipe dream, especially after the shock therapy and the Russian people's harsh encounter with Western neoliberalism and capitalism. Under Putin there was instead an intermediate set-up, typical of Russia – a modern kind of tsarism combined with Western structures and enticements, with a reborn version of the KGB at its core. Gleb Pavlovsky, who left the Kremlin in 2011, would later speak of an 'ironic empire' in which nothing was what it seemed.

The new leader had the wind in his sails. During his first few years in office, oil prices rose strongly – Russia was still largely dependent on selling oil – from $20 a barrel in 2000 to $140 in 2008. Putin and his circle earned good money. According to estimates by Russian *Forbes*, they accumulated personal fortunes of between $25 million and $9 billion within a few years.

Putin had created a modern version of medieval aristocratic rule – a 'neofeudal fiefdom', according to Russia expert Hubert Smeets. You could own things, but ultimately everything you had was property in fealty, which the ruler in the Kremlin could give or take away at will. This applied to everyone, especially the rich and powerful oligarchs that Putin, after a few painful fiscal crackdowns, had managed to bring under control just as he had the Saint Petersburg mafia in the 1990s. Immediately upon taking power, he had summoned the most important Russian business leaders to his dacha and put a proposal to them. They could make a fresh start with a clean slate, and in return, they must promise absolute loyalty to Putin. They were no longer permitted any involvement in politics. As an aide to a senior banker said to Mark Galeotti, 'Everyone understood what was being offered: be quiet, be loyal, do what the Kremlin wants, or Putin's guys would screw you good.' The oligarchs had become affluent vassals.

That system permeated all layers of society. Functions, positions and formal chains of command were increasingly irrelevant within the Russian state apparatus; what mattered were personal relationships and forms of protection, which in this adhocracy might change at any moment. The Kremlin did not pay its vassals; rather it created 'opportunities'. Ordinary property rights proved similarly relative. They were always conditional upon loyalty to a higher power, right down through the social strata. In Putin's Russia, if you did business without a 'roof' you stood no chance, whether you were running a major oil company or a corner shop. You might have all the right in the world on your side, but it wouldn't matter; the tax authorities would invent a staggering assessment and demand immediate payment, frontmen would confiscate your flat or your business with the help of a corrupt judge, and if you were even slightly unlucky you'd find yourself in jail. Without a patron, you would get nowhere, and of course your dependency on that patron had to be demonstrated in all kinds of ways.

The media were dealt with no differently. On 14 April 2001, armed units raided the building of independent broadcaster NTV, maker of the satirical show *Puppets (Kukly)*. The programme was hugely popular, with millions of Russians sitting down in front of the television every week to watch it make fun of the rulers in the Kremlin. After Putin's intervention, a few billion-aires from his entourage took over the broadcaster, *Puppets* was killed off, and the recently acquired press freedom was quashed. That was merely the start. By about 2008, 90 per cent of Russian media was directly or indirectly under Putin's control. Television editors were instructed from on high on the news items of the day, reporters were contacted by the secret services if it was felt they had stepped out of line, and from time to time a journalist was murdered.

The economy grew explosively, by 7 per cent a year, and night after night television programmes orchestrated the rejoicing with a sophisticated combination of old Soviet control and Western entertainment, always with superman Putin in the main role. This president was at last the president of stability, an effective leader, the answer to the confusion and semi-darkness of the 1990s – that was the message – and anyone who opposed him was an enemy who had taken up arms against stability. Slowly, the picture of a kleptocracy emerged, covered with a thin layer of democratic rhetoric. Stability and effectiveness were the new mantras.

6

Most people in Kirkenes, meanwhile, did not concern themselves with politics, even where the new Russia was concerned. Thomas Nilsen did. He took his job as a local journalist extremely seriously, despite living in the middle of nowhere. He kept on asking questions: about the climate, about Russia, about the future of the Barents Sea. 'Norway is addicted to oil, even more so than Russia. Wouldn't we do far better to put those huge investments into green projects?'

He had a room in a multi-tenanted office block. There, with just one colleague, he compiled the *Independent Barents Observer*, the daily online newspaper for the entire polar region, in two editions, one in English and one in Russian. On the wall was a map of the North Pole with the key words of the paper's credo written on it: 'Arctic', 'Justice', 'Objectivity', 'Independence', 'Responsibility', 'Future'.

The border itself didn't worry him too much; it had been peaceful there for years. What did worry him were the so-called hybrid conflicts that even here were becoming more frequent, so that a vague twilight situation arose, somewhere between war and peace. 'All those Russian attempts to destabilize the situation, to put an end to openness in this border region and to gag the independent media, they're all part of it.'

Headlines in the *Observer* between the autumn of 2018 and spring 2019 included 'An Arctic fight is raging between Russia's two biggest oil companies', 'Finnish nuclear safety investigator suspected of conflict of interest', 'Melting glaciers at Novaya Zemlya contain radiation from nuclear bomb tests', 'Murmansk protesters marched on government office', 'Arctic oil field could be Russia's biggest discovery in 30 years', 'Pentagon warns of risk of Chinese submarines in the Arctic' and 'Now you can circumnavigate the Arctic, at a start price of €50,000'.

Nilsen and his colleagues worked for the *Independent Barents Observer* for years, receiving their pay through a Norwegian regional cooperative. In 2015, their bosses, under pressure from the Russians and the FSB, decided to curb the *Observer*'s freedom. All the journalists resigned and started a new, independent online paper. It was kept going by donations from the public and from businesses. The FSB hit back immediately by banning Nilsen from entering Russia. The consulate in Kirkenes had already given him a dressing down: 'Moscow isn't happy with the things you write.'

Soon afterwards, the independent *SeverPost* in Murmansk got into trouble as well. In Russia, a torrent of vague accusations and fines usually indicates the beginning of the end. As Nilsen put it, 'All the signs are that the Russian security services have set their sights on regional cooperation in the Arctic region. It has to be weakened, perhaps even wrecked.'

He was worried – professionally, in part. 'As a journalist you can describe a classic war quite accurately. There are troop movements, offensives, battles. Hybrid wars are far more difficult to observe.' But he was determined. 'This is our work here: to look, listen, investigate, ask questions, whatever the complications may be. It's all we can do.'

Aydin

MY EARLIEST MEMORY IS OF my father. He's shaving and I'm standing in the bathroom watching him. I'm four years old. I find him fascinating, not having seen him for a year and a half. First we'd lived in Iran, then in Uzbekistan, and eventually he went on ahead of us, alone, to Denmark. He requested family reunification, and now we were living in a small flat on the outskirts of Copenhagen.

My name is Aydin Soei. I was born in 1982 and grew up in an Iranian refugee family in Avedøre Stationsby and Gladsaxe, two suburbs of Copenhagen. My parents were active communists during the time of the shah. My father had set up a regional branch of the party in Iran and he was in the front line of demonstrations, throwing petrol bombs. He was put in prison and tortured. He was regional party leader, and after the revolution that brought Ayatollah Khomeini to power in 1979, he ordered his men to hand in their weapons. The instructions from Moscow were that the communists must accept the new regime, since they had a common enemy in the Americans, and they would all be given an amnesty. Nothing came of that.

In 1983, a year after I was born, the ayatollah's regime started to persecute 'infidel' communists. My parents were told they had precisely one day to leave the country. My father reassured his parents-in-law that there was no need to worry, they'd see their daughter again within about four months, the regime wouldn't survive for long.

We crossed the Soviet border into Azerbaijan, and from there we fled to Uzbekistan. When we arrived my parents had no idea where they were. The local communists, who had accompanied them on their journey, refused to tell them. Security reasons. Eventually my mother asked some women at the airport where she was. They said something like 'Gate B8'. 'No,' she said, 'what country?' 'You mean you don't know? Uzbekistan.'

So for three years we lived in Uzbekistan. My father left after eighteen months, deeply disappointed. He'd seen with his own eyes how Soviet society worked. At one of the first local party meetings he cautiously asked a couple of Iranian communist refugees, 'Can it really be that we've seen beggars and homeless people on the streets here?' 'No,' he was told. 'Of course not, you must have been hallucinating.'

They both witnessed the poverty of the Soviet Union in its declining years, the long queues outside the shops, the children hospitalized with malnutrition. On top of that came the shock when they realized that Soviet hospitals were decades behind those of Iran. Their dream, all their lives long, had been to transform Iran based on the Soviet model. Not any longer.

My father was unable to reconcile himself to that reality. He kept asking questions about everything and eventually he was told, 'If you think it's so wretched here, go back to Iran!' To everyone's utter amazement, he said, 'Okay.' He was a proud man. He'd rather risk his life than stay in the Soviet Union, safe but a hypocrite. So he left, lived underground in Iran for six months, then travelled to Turkey and, from there, with the help of human traffickers, to Europe. He'd actually intended to go to France, Britain or Germany, where there were large Iranian communities, since he wanted to remain politically active. But he chose Denmark. It was easy to have your family join you there. So we ended up in Copenhagen.

'Aydin, you should be proud that I chose Denmark,' he said to me time and again in those early years. 'This country, this Danish welfare state, is the closest of all countries in the world to socialism. I thought I'd find that in the Soviet Union, but I found it here. In this country it's not the fatness of your wallet that determines how far you get in life; here education is free and everything comes down to your willpower, your own efforts.'

As a child I hated school. My father used to tell me, 'It doesn't matter, we're going back to Iran anyhow.' But of course the day never came.

You know, I didn't think I was the academic type. I was a boy from a neighbourhood of workers and immigrants and I simply wanted a job. Except that I had a criminal record. Nothing serious, a bit of petty theft, but there was no chance of finding work. When I was twelve we moved house and I had to go to a different school. My very first day there I met a boy who was eager to learn. I hated him and after a few days I went up to him and hit him – that's what you did at my old school. But to my astonishment he didn't hit me back. Instead he ran away, crying. I thought that was extraordinary, but everyone looked at me as if I was the stupid one. It seemed I was now in a new world where you didn't get credit for fighting but for getting on with your homework.

There was a teacher there who made a huge effort to help me. You've little choice when that happens. I got into the grammar school, which to be honest was a strange place, far from home, and I didn't want to go there at all. I was fifteen, so I was eligible for a study grant of about €400 a month. You could get by on that if you were still living at home, so I went to the grammar school after all. I was the exception, in every respect. There were five of us immigrant children in a school with a thousand pupils. Some of the older kids were flabbergasted when they discovered that I could speak Danish. They looked at me as if I was a giraffe.

And then came 11 September 2001. In spite of everything, my parents were still communists. I hadn't had a religious upbringing at all and I wasn't interested in religion. Of course, in the weeks that followed, people talked about nothing else, and I noticed the effect the discussion about the attacks in New York was having on the pupils in the school playground. My younger brother was at an ordinary Danish school in an ordinary neighbourhood, a school with lots of white kids and a few who were black or brown. At that point he was fourteen, an age when you're looking for an identity and want to belong somewhere.

Many young people from the Middle East suddenly became ardent Muslims after 9/11. It was their identity. My brother was asked questions like, 'So are you a Muslim or not?' 'Yes, I think so,' he said. 'My parents were born Muslims, so I am too . . .' 'And you eat pork?' So he stopped eating pork. Then he started consciously seeking Islam. He went to the mosque, spoke to imams. None of that would have happened, I think, without 9/11. He didn't have many friends at school. Here was something easy and safe. Are you a Muslim? Okay, then you're one of us. At last he fitted in.

*

I struggled with that pressure too. What Hans Magnus Enzensberger says is true: foreigners become more foreign when they're poor. In my old neighbourhood the kids called themselves immigrants. The ones with dark skin were the strongest, the best at fighting, the best at football. The children of the Danish workers were all right, actually, but that's how we lived there: two groups, close together.

After 9/11 the kids stopped calling each other immigrants. Instead of looking at ethnic backgrounds, they simply called each other Muslims. Not Pakistanis, not Iranians, not Iraqis, no: we're Muslims. In a way it united them, sharing the same faith. But it also introduced stronger social control. What do you eat? What do you drink? Who do you go out with? Young people no longer went out in their own neighbourhoods. Imagine someone seeing you. Imagine not being a good Muslim.

My brother didn't get on well at school. He failed his exams, so he had no qualifications and no chance of finding work. Islam became even more important to him then. He had a lot of spare time, so he was often in the mosque, where he was recognized and acknowledged. He grew more and more conservative. At a certain point he asked my mother, 'Why are you wearing a T-shirt? Can't you cover your arms?' My mother was taken aback. 'I'm sorry? What did you say?' I was surprised too. That seeking, that conservatism and stricter adherence – he'd kept it to himself all that time.

My mother and many of her Iranian friends finally managed to pass their exams in the 1990s and get qualifications. That led to a lot of divorces. Quite a few men couldn't comprehend their lower place in the hierarchy, let alone accept it. That was certainly true of men like my father, men with no chance of participating in the European labour market because they had no official qualifications. He became very suspicious of my mother, even violent. 'Who did you meet? Who did you talk to?' You saw it happening all over Western Europe. If you're an immigrant from a country where you were a valued worker, where you had a high status purely because you were male, and you find yourself in a society that asks for qualifications of a completely different kind, then you sink very low, as a man.

My father was a carpenter, a joiner. After we moved house we had an extra room and he converted it into a workshop. He started making things with wood again and had the idea of making three perfect Iranian guitars – because in Iran that's the most prestigious thing you can make from wood. He wanted to get into the newspaper, as a way of finding work for himself.

When they were finally finished he took them to a job centre. My mother went with him, because his Danish was still poor, even though he'd taken three language courses. He showed his guitars to the social worker and said, 'I want to work with my hands, to make things from wood, you can see what I can do.' The social worker asked, 'Do you have any qualifications? Papers that show you're a carpenter?' My father pointed to his guitars and said, 'That's proof, isn't it? You can see I'm capable of it.' 'Yes, they're really beautiful,' she said. 'But you can't get work in Denmark if you don't have qualifications. You need papers to prove you can make things out of wood.'

It was a hundred per cent Kafka. My mother said to me later, 'I've never seen him so disappointed, so fragile.' He never heard anything more from the job centre.

My story is typical of my generation. In the 1980s most immigrants weren't very 'successful'. Not in the famously prosperous 1990s either, for that matter. The first generation often felt huge disillusionment, especially the men. My family history is more tragic than most, because it ended with a murder. Yes, eventually my father murdered the father of one of my classmates, another Iranian refugee, a man with whom he was close friends. Nobody has ever been able to understand it. My father started talking about the man and his gang, saying they were watching him, tapping his phone. I was twelve then. It was 1994. He slit the man's throat. He had it all planned out. He went to the Iranian Club, the place where all those losers got together, and asked his friend for a lift. In the car he pulled out his knife and forced the man to drive to an isolated place, where he cut his throat.

The psychiatrists said my father was suffering from paranoid schizophrenia. You need to have a predisposition for that, you can't hide it, but all those years his strange behaviour was interpreted by our teachers and social workers as 'Middle Eastern culture'. No one did anything. After all, it was 'culture' and you don't want to mess with that. But all along he was ill, mentally ill.

*

You need to remember that in Iran my father was a respected man, the regional leader of the communists. In Denmark he found himself right at the bottom of the heap. I think he was driven insane by a combination of things: an awareness that for much of his life he'd believed in a lie, his complete disillusionment with life in Denmark, his loss of status, his abuse of alcohol, and on top of it all a lack of support from friends and family. Three years after the murder he was sent back to Iran. His brothers immediately saw there was something very wrong. He was completely unreachable and very violent. They did everything they could to get him back on track, sent him to all kinds of doctors and got him to take various psychiatric drugs.

When I went back to Iran for the first time in 2003, I encountered a completely different man. A smiling man, playing with nieces and nephews in the garden. When I was little he never played with me, he was always impatient, dissatisfied and tense. Now, in Iran, he was doing fine again. But I thought, okay, my childhood would have been very different if we'd had a network of cousins and uncles like this in Denmark, or if all those social workers had realized that my father's behaviour had nothing to do with 'culture'. Then my schoolmate would probably still have his father with him too.

On the last day before my flight back to Denmark, my father and I were sitting side by side in the car. We hadn't been so close together for years. Suddenly he said in Danish, 'I've been a bad father. Sorry.' I thought: is he really saying this now? Because I'd never heard him say sorry to anyone. I looked at him and he went on staring straight ahead. So again I started to doubt that I'd heard him properly. But for him it was probably such a big step . . . He stared ahead and said nothing. After I got out I thought: it's too late, Dad.

He died in 2011 and six months later my son was born. I'd have liked them to meet.

3. Fear

2001

I

IT WAS LIKE THE MURDER of President John F. Kennedy on 22 November 1963, in the sense that everyone would always remember where they were when the news broke. The spectacular attacks of 11 September in New York had that effect: the entire world witnessed, in an endless live television broadcast, the proud Twin Towers of the World Trade Center crumbling and almost 3,000 people being killed. The images etched themselves into the memory of everyone who saw them.

For us, in Europe, it started that Tuesday afternoon at about three, with reports that an American Airlines plane had flown into the North Tower of the WTC. For a short time it looked like a spectacular accident, until fifteen minutes later a second hijacked plane smashed into the South Tower. Now both towers were on fire. Half an hour after that, a third plane drilled into the Pentagon. A fourth hijacked airliner came down near Pittsburgh after the passengers, who by then understood what was going on, fought back. That fourth plane was probably intended to hit the White House, or the Capitol Building.

The images we saw were tragic. Some 200 people jumped to their deaths from the Twin Towers, and near the entrance a thudding sound was heard time and again as bodies dropped onto the projecting roof. After an hour the South Tower collapsed and half an hour after it the North Tower, followed later in the day by a third WTC building. Hardly anyone who was still in the Twin Towers at that point survived.

I recall only fragments, as if that whole afternoon were shrouded in a dark fog. The pictures rolled in as we were standing in an Amsterdam bar having a drink – my stepson had just been sworn in as a lawyer. Everyone fell silent, watching in astonishment. Out on the street people stopped to look in through the window of the bar, mesmerized by the television inside.

I once heard a description of the early morning of 10 May 1940, from someone who as a young journalist had stood on the roof of an Amsterdam hotel to watch the first bombers fly over. 'I think this is the real thing, babe,' an American colleague muttered to her. Another colleague pelted past on a bicycle, on the way to his editorial office: 'Honey, the show is on!' That same atmosphere prevailed on the afternoon of 11 September 2001, and now too a friend raced past, with his young son on the back of his bicycle. 'This is war, Geert!'

The Turkish writer and Nobel Prize winner Orhan Pamuk was sitting in a small waterfront coffeehouse in Istanbul, surrounded by cart drivers and porters, while 'his' Manhattan, where he'd spent three years of his life, burned and fell. On the quayside a woman was crying. The men in the coffeehouse watched the coverage with surprise, more than anything. It had little emotional impact. 'I felt desperately alone,' Pamuk wrote afterwards. Later he ran into a neighbour: '"Sir, have you seen, they have bombed America," he said, and added fiercely, "They did the right thing." This angry old man is not religious at all. He struggles to make a living by doing minor repair jobs and gardening, and gets drunk in the evening and argues with his wife. He had not yet seen the appalling scenes on television, but had only heard that some people had done something dreadful to America.'

Umayya Abu-Hanna, who is Finnish, was picking up her Palestinian parents at Helsinki Airport that afternoon. The taxi driver had the news turned on. She translated, and her mother kept saying, 'Please, don't let it be an Arab, please, please . . .' And then, 'No, it can't be an Arab, it's far too cleverly plotted.' She kept repeating those words, again and again.

In the West the shock was enormous. With the Cold War over, was this to be the new theatre of conflict? The American president even declared war on terrorism as such. For Europe, the phenomenon was sadly far from new. Many European countries had faced terrorist organizations in the twentieth century: Spain (ETA), Italy (Red Brigades), Germany (Red Army Faction), the Netherlands (Moluccan nationalists), Britain (IRA). Between 1970 and 1990 even more deaths were caused by terrorism than in the quarter-century after 1990. All possible means had been used at some stage: firearms, knives, bombs, chemicals, cars, trains, aircraft. But this attack was truly spectacular, and the number of casualties was disconcerting. The political and social impacts were to prove very far-reaching indeed.

9/11 was the catalyst for two American wars in the Islamic world, conflicts into which several major European countries were dragged, and that further destabilized the Middle East in particular. The attack on the Twin Towers was also the start of a fundamental change to the public debate within Europe. Antitheses that had previously been seen as primarily socio-economic now acquired a strongly cultural and even racial character. The debate about immigration in particular was increasingly pushed onto religious terrain.

The plans for the attack were hatched in Afghanistan, but the participants were mostly from Saudi Arabia. Fifteen of the nineteen hijackers were Saudis, their leader from the prominent Saudi bin Laden family. There are photos of Osama bin Laden on a trip to Sweden in 1971, a friendly lad among smiling young relatives, every one of the boys and girls dressed according to the latest Western fashions. Ten years later no such photo could have been taken, since after the Iranian Revolution in 1979 the Saudi leaders once again adopted a strict interpretation of Islam, to forestall a religious revolution in their own country.

By doing this they were reverting to the orthodoxy of the eighteenth-century scholar Muhammad ibn Abd al-Wahhab, who in 1744 had entered into an alliance with the man who gave the Saud kingdom its name, Muhammad ibn Saud. The Saudi family controlled affairs of state, while the religious leaders were responsible for safeguarding the country's spiritual and moral purity. What we now call Wahhabism demanded a strict interpretation of the Koran, unconditional submission to the doctrines of the religious leaders, and a sharp dividing line between men and women. There was to be no mercy for dissidents, apostates or adherents of other religions.

The Saudis were once dirt-poor desert tribes who came together in 1932 to form the Kingdom of Saudi Arabia and six years later unexpectedly found themselves sitting on vast oil wealth. In no time at all a country run by an absolutist regime became the biggest oil producer in the world. In February 1945 American president Franklin D. Roosevelt negotiated with its leader, Abdulaziz ibn Abdul Rahman Al Saud, on board the cruiser USS *Quincy*. Roosevelt introduced the king to films and ice cream. Ibn Saud had brought his astrologer with him, plus several sheep to roast on deck. Clearly this was a country full of ambiguities – on the one hand fabulously rich and hyper-modern, on the other strictly regulated, with norms and values unchanged since the Middle Ages.

In all kinds of fields – oil, arms dealing, intelligence, finance – Saudi Arabia was tightly bound up with the interests of the United States. That created a further ambiguity, since with their lashings of Western oil money, the ruling families had every opportunity to disseminate anti-Western Wahhabism across the rest of the Islamic world. Their missionary zeal increased after the 1970s. The Saudis threw money around and countless Wahhabi mosques, schools and universities benefited, but so did militant groups like the Taliban.

The young Osama bin Laden was highly receptive to this revived funda-mentalism. During his studies at King Abdulaziz University in Jeddah, he grew into a pious and passionate leader. In the early 1980s he joined the Islamic resistance to the Russian occupying forces in Afghanistan, an insur-gency enthusiastically supported by the Americans. 'Everyone who met him in the early days respected him,' his younger brother Hassan said years later in a rare family interview, for *The Guardian*. 'At the start, we were very proud of him. . . . And then came Osama the mujahid.'

In 1988, from Afghanistan, he set up the militant group al-Qaeda, mean-ing 'the base'. He believed that the West, especially the United States, must be driven out of the Islamic world in a 'holy war'. In 1993, a first attempt was made to blow up the World Trade Center. For a while Osama lived in Sudan. His brothers tried to calm him down, without success. 'He used to fax statements to everybody,' says the head of Saudi intelligence. 'He was very critical. There were efforts by the family to dissuade him – emissaries and such – but they were unsuccessful. It was probably his feeling that he was not taken seriously by the government.'

In 1996, Osama joined forces with Mullah Mohammed Omar, leader of the Taliban, whose activities included attacks on American embassies in 1998. Osama's relatives saw him for the last time in 1999, when they visited him twice at his base close to Kandahar airport. 'He was very happy to receive us,' his mother said in that same *Guardian* interview. 'He was showing us around every day we were there. He killed an animal and we had a feast, and he invited everyone.'

At that point, Osama bin Laden was top of the list of most wanted terrorists at intelligence agencies in Riyadh, London and Washington. Yet the family seems to have had no difficulty finding him and spending several enjoyable days with him. The French secret services knew all about him too. In early 2001 they warned the Americans there were plans to fly aircraft into important American buildings, such as the WTC.

In Washington the information was pushed aside, to the fury of the French, who had been building up vast expertise on the matter ever since the 1970s. In 1994, they'd dealt with the hijacking of an Air France plane by Algerian Islamist terrorists, who planned to fly it into the Eiffel Tower. The attack failed, and when the plane was raided during a stopover in Marseille, the pilot managed to jump out of the cockpit. It was clearly a precursor to 11 September 2001, except that in 1994 it hadn't yet occurred to anyone that hijackers could themselves learn to fly.

'I was shocked, stunned,' said Osama's other brother Ahmad of 11 September. 'It was a very strange feeling. We knew from the beginning [that it was Osama], within the first 48 hours. From the youngest to the eldest, we all felt ashamed of him. We knew all of us were going to face horrible consequences.'

2

The effect of 9/11 was indeed overwhelming. American commentator Robert Kaplan spoke of the end of a twelve-year truce, the peaceful and prosperous period between 1989 and 2001. Joschka Fischer, then German minister of foreign affairs, spoke of the 'return of history': the obsession with power, the conflicts, the continual prioritizing of security over human rights, and the fear – fear above all, since the attack might just as easily have taken place in London, Amsterdam or Paris. It also meant the all-powerful United States was vulnerable, another source of concern for a dependent Europe.

The first reaction was to express solidarity. Tony Blair regarded the attack as a 'declaration of war by a new type of enemy'. All the NATO allies were in agreement and NATO's Article 5 – an attack on one is an attack on all – was immediately invoked. Even Russia joined in, opening its airspace to American transport planes. It's striking how unimportant, as yet, was the role played by the European Union. The president of the European Council, at that point the Belgian prime minister Guy Verhofstadt, had to admit a few days later that he still hadn't spoken to American president George W. Bush. The White House phone operator had no idea who this Belgian might be.

Even before then, in the late 1990s, the great strategic question for America, and indeed for Europe, was how to preserve Western hegemony in the changing world order after the Cold War. The optimism that had predominated immediately after the fall of the Wall was no more. Western predictions based on a presumed natural affinity between democracy, capitalism and the free market were beginning to look like empty promises. Globalization, with all its new prosperity, had triggered a reaction that was now turning against Western globalization itself. Treaties were undermined, failed states emerged, national and above all religious conflicts increasingly set the tone. The rapidly rising China jumped in with huge programmes of purchase and investment, while the West lost more and more of its authority. All this was brought to a head by 9/11. The mood in the West was that something had to be done, and quickly.

On 7 October 2001, the Americans and the British, with widespread support that included Afghan anti-Taliban fighters and Norwegian, Canadian, German and Australian troops, began retaliatory action in Afghanistan. The aim of Operation Enduring Freedom was, according to President Bush, to capture the leaders of al-Qaeda and destroy the terrorist organization's infrastructure.

In November, Kabul was conquered by the anti-Taliban troops of the Northern Alliance, in December a transitional Afghan government was put in place, and by January 2002 al-Qaeda seemed defeated. In the remote mountains of western Pakistan, however, Osama bin Laden held out, along with his organization and his network. Meanwhile, the Western powers, lacking a firm peace plan, were sinking into the very morass that the

Russians had struggled to extricate themselves from more than ten years before. They were now faced with the almost impossible task of bringing some measure of peace and democracy to that chaotic, violent and inhospitable country.

In time, forty-three nations would be sucked into a bloody conflict that, at its height in 2011, saw 130,000 foreign troops deployed, including tens of thousands of Europeans. The eventual death toll on the Western side was more than 3,000. The number of Afghan civilians killed ran into the tens of thousands and more than 2.5 million Afghans fled the country. Another eleven years were to pass before the Americans withdrew most of their troops. 'We were devoid of a fundamental understanding of Afghanistan – we didn't know what we were doing,' Bush's national security adviser, General Douglas Lute, later acknowledged in an internal evaluation that was leaked to the *Washington Post* in 2019. 'What are we trying to do here? We didn't have the foggiest notion of what we were undertaking.' It was a repeat, if on a smaller scale, of Vietnam.

The terrorist attacks of 9/11 were soon being used by Washington for purposes that were almost entirely unconnected. Amid the confusion, the Republicans rapidly pushed a controversial reduction in taxes for the wealthy through US Congress. Then the opportunity arose to do something that had been pressed for in certain American political circles over the previous decade, quite independently of the attacks of 9/11: invade Iraq.

In 1991, President Bush's father, George H. W. Bush, had responded with military force against Saddam Hussein's Iraq during his own presidency, after it invaded its oil-rich neighbour Kuwait. Iraqi forces were driven back or slaughtered, Saddam was restrained by a series of disarmament treaties, with accompanying inspections, but Iraq was not occupied. Saddam Hussein continued to challenge the West yet was allowed to remain in office. It later turned out that the Americans feared even greater chaos if he was deposed. In the eyes of many Americans, especially neoconservatives in the Republican Party, this decision by Bush the Elder was an error that demanded rectification. Bush the Younger took that task upon himself. In July 2001, three months before 9/11, detailed plans were prepared by the US Department of Defense for an invasion of Iraq.

There was little disagreement about Saddam Hussein, a reprehensible figure and tyrant who, with the aid of a cruel and ubiquitous security apparatus, had ruled his people with a rod of iron, deploying torture and summary execution. He was a threat to the entire region. He had invaded Kuwait and engaged in a long and devastating war against Iran, during which he used chemical weapons – as he had done before against the Kurds. The excesses of his regime had cost the lives of at least 300,000 of his own people, and the wars he fought probably claimed over a million more.

After 9/11, therefore, there was broad support in America for tough action against this 'rogue state', and for 'regime change' in Iraq. President Bush declared there could be no doubt that Iraq possessed weapons of mass destruction. Vice President Dick Cheney predicted that in response to an American intervention, the streets of Basra and Baghdad were 'sure to erupt in joy'. Defence secretary Donald Rumsfeld believed that an invasion would pay for itself, since the costs would be offset by the value of the oil, and that the entire operation would take 'five days or five weeks or five months, but it certainly isn't going to last any longer than that'.

The American press and public opinion – including most Democrats – shared this blind optimism, while the dissident voices of experts were ignored. Huge commercial interests were at play in the background. Halliburton, the multinational corporation Dick Cheney had led before becoming US vice president, managed to sign government contracts worth $7 billion in this phase, for the reconstruction of the Iraqi oil industry.

In Europe the mood was far more cautious; in fact, government leaders were plainly divided. France, Germany and Belgium were fiercely opposed to intervention, if only because it had no basis in international law and they did not want to give the UN a mandate. France and Germany even consulted Moscow. Moreover, there were well-founded fears that such a war would further inflame anti-Western sentiment in the Islamic world. Former Dutch prime minister Ruud Lubbers, who was UN High Commissioner for Refugees at the time, warned loudly of the huge number of refugees such a new war might produce, with incalculable ramifications for the whole region.

The leaders of Britain, Spain, Italy, Denmark, Portugal, Poland, the Czech Republic and Hungary, by contrast, gave the Americans their unconditional support. In the absence of a single European voice, they made their views known in an open letter to the *Wall Street Journal* in January 2003 – a highly unusual form of international diplomacy. The Dutch position was half-hearted; initially the invasion received political support, but no troops were sent. It later turned out that the Dutch intelligence agencies had serious doubts about the reality of the Iraqi threat, but the government of the time, under Jan Peter Balkenende, took from their reports only the information that fitted the stance it had already adopted. In the end, the Dutch government, as usual, followed the Americans and the British.

Tony Blair supported the 'regime change' project in Iraq wholeheartedly. Earlier humanitarian interventions in Kosovo (1999), Sierra Leone (2000) and Afghanistan (2001) had appeared effective and he wanted to continue along those same lines. After the tragedies in Kosovo and Rwanda, he and his supporters believed, genocide and extreme cruelty could no longer be tolerated. Even a foreign country's national sovereignty had its limits.

Blair recognized that the aim of removing Saddam Hussein, whatever he might have done, was not a sufficient basis for military action. Only the demonstrable possession of weapons of mass destruction would make him so dangerous that intervention by force was justified. Like the Americans, Blair was convinced that Iraq was creating new stocks of chemical and biological weapons. A report by a British parliamentary committee claimed they could be deployed against Britain within forty-five minutes.

The American position was not based on expert analysis – by the CIA or the State Department, for instance. Instead, it was devised by the Office of Special Plans, a department set up by the Pentagon after 9/11. This particular agency leaned heavily on information from the ambitious charlatan Ahmed Chalabi and a few other Saddam deserters. The dissidents had a personal interest in regime change, but what they were providing was little more than information tailored to please. They said what the hawks in the Pentagon wanted to hear: that there were close ties between Iraq and al-Qaeda (this turned out to be completely untrue) and that the Iraqis were indeed developing weapons of mass destruction. Their intelligence was leaked to the press, and as a result three-quarters of the American public came to believe Saddam Hussein had something to do with the attacks of 11 September.

Contrasting opinions, at the State Department, the CIA and other US intelligence agencies, were systematically swept aside. In the words of American arms control expert Greg Thielmann, it was as if the American government were saying, 'We know the answers; give us the intelligence to support those answers.' So a fierce battle also raged behind the scenes, between the American intelligence agencies themselves. Later, the CIA spotted a chance to interrogate one of the dissident informers from Iraq, on his own. The man denied the claims of the Pentagon most emphatically: 'No, I never said that.' No al-Qaeda. No weapons of mass destruction.

In February 2003, further confirmation that there were no such weapons came from a team of UN weapons inspectors in Iraq. Its leader, the experienced Swedish diplomat and investigator Hans Blix, was himself initially convinced that Saddam had quietly resumed his old ways. He spoke of 'gut feelings'. But after more than 700 inspections he arrived at the opposite conclusion. Nothing of the sort had been found. Fearful of a full-scale invasion, Saddam had stuck to the agreements made in the 1990s. Afterwards, Blix said, 'The UN and the world had succeeded in disarming Iraq, without knowing it.'

None of this helped. Ruud Lubbers described in his memoirs how in those weeks he provided new information to Tony Blair in a private conversation: even the IAEA, the international authority on nuclear inspections, was absolutely convinced that Iraq did not possess enriched uranium. Blair cut him short: 'But Ruud, we're not talking here about sincerity, or about the correctness of facts. This is about a political decision to eliminate that monster.'

The Pentagon had meanwhile given the CIA the task of investigating Blix and finding 'sufficient ammunition to undermine' him. The planned invasion must go ahead at all costs.

Ultimately, nothing incriminating was found against Blix. In hindsight, he believes the entire project was an effort to mislead the public. The American and British governments deliberately exaggerated the threat posed by Saddam 'in order to get the political support they would not otherwise have had'.

His findings were later confirmed by the Americans themselves. In 'liberated' Iraq, US troops found some 5,000 old chemical bombs and shells, manufactured before 1991, but even at that point there was no indication that weapons of mass destruction had been produced after that date.

American war preparations continued unabated. Instead of waiting for further inspections, the US Army poured into the region. 'Once there got to be 250,000 troops sitting in the hot desert sun,' Blix said later, 'there was a momentum built up that couldn't be halted.' In the media and on the streets, feelings were now running high. The Europeans understood, better than the Americans, that a dishonest and dangerous game was being played. For many Britons especially, the Iraq War represented a profound breach of trust between ordinary people and the political elite. After all, vital questions were never answered.

Rarely have such large demonstrations taken place all over the continent as in the early spring of 2003. In Italy, some 3 million people came out onto the streets, in Spain 1.5 million, in London alone, at least a million. In Germany, France, the Netherlands, Belgium, Hungary, Ireland and Portugal, crowds thronged the streets and squares. In Warsaw, former foreign minister Bronisław Geremek joined them. 'To be sure, the Warsaw ghetto survivor, the Nazi soldier, the British officer, the French collaborator, the Swedish businessman, and the Slovak farmer had very different wars,' wrote Timothy Garton Ash. 'Yet from all their throats rose the same passionate cry: "Never again!" '

It was the start of the first transatlantic split since Vietnam. In America, the French obstructionists were described as 'cheese-eating surrender monkeys' and French fries were renamed 'Freedom fries'. The Hummer – the civilian version of the Humvee, the US Army's utility vehicle – became hugely popular, and other models increasingly came to resemble it: the car as a travelling fortress. At the same time, dissidents were making themselves heard even in the United States. During a demonstration in Chicago, a young senator from Illinois predicted that 'even a successful war against Iraq will require a US occupation of undetermined length, at undetermined cost, with undetermined consequences'. Such an invasion would only play into al-Qaeda's hands and 'encourage the worst, rather than best, impulses of the Arab world'.

'I am not opposed to all wars,' said the as-yet-unknown Barack Obama. 'I'm opposed to dumb wars.'

All those premonitions proved correct. The military campaign began on 20 March 2003. Three weeks later Baghdad fell, the firing stopped and Saddam's statue was pulled down by a cheering crowd. A few months after that, the dictator was captured, tried and eventually hanged. On 1 May 2003, President Bush, dressed in a US Air Force uniform, gave a speech to the sailors of the aircraft carrier USS *Abraham Lincoln*, with a banner above him that read 'Mission Accomplished'. That performance was broadcast all around the world. In reality, the Americans had no idea of the sectarian demons they had set loose with their intervention.

In Iraq, the Shiites took power and fiercely discriminated against the Sunni minority that Saddam Hussein had always relied on for support. Antagonisms intensified, instability increased and lives became even more unsafe. Iraqi prisoners were tortured and humiliated by the Americans – the pictures later leaked for all to see.

The wars in Afghanistan and Iraq had been started under the flag of 'counterterrorism'. Even in that respect, both interventions were a complete failure. With the removal of Saddam, a power vacuum was created in which new terror groups flourished, all over the region. The number of terrorist incidents worldwide grew from around 500 in 1996 to 1,800 in 2003 and some 5,000 in 2006, most of them in the Middle East.

A crucial moment in the Iraq War – and at the same time, a symptom of the ignorance in which the Americans were operating – was the decision to disband the Iraqi army. This laid the foundations for the caliphate of Islamic State, the terrorist organisation that would make the running all over Europe and the Middle East a decade later. It became an even more professional and dangerous opponent than al-Qaeda, mainly because of the huge amount of experience at the disposal of all those angry, cast-off Iraqi officers.

The invasion that was supposed to pay for itself ultimately cost the Americans, according to economists including Joseph Stiglitz, a total of around $3 trillion, or $24,000 per household. Roughly 4,400 coalition troops were lost. The number of Iraqi dead is difficult to estimate. According to the prestigious medical journal *The Lancet*, more than 600,000 Iraqis were killed between March 2003 and June 2006 alone. More recent research suggests a million or more in total.

The Iraq War was partly to blame for the Syrian civil war that broke out in 2011, the worsening of religious conflict between Sunnis and Shiites, the persecution of Christians, the slaughter of Kurds and Yazidis, the rise of Islamic State, and a long series of terrorist attacks. For Russian foreign policy too, Iraq was a turning point. Ever since, NATO has been not a possible partner but a potential enemy. All trust was gone.

The invasion of Iraq in 2003 was to a certain extent comparable to the rash Russo-Japanese War of 1904–05. A century later, it was the West that fell from a pedestal, from a great height, with disastrous results.

3

For Umayya Abu-Hanna, life changed radically after that catastrophic September day in 2001. The following Sunday, a good friend's daughter was christened. Umayya's parents, who were staying with her, were invited along. The pastor welcomed the two 'Arab guests' and explained: 'Despite everything, we shall accept you here.'

Umayya was furious. 'Just think, my father comes from Nazareth, we've been Christians for two thousand years, our whole family; we have nothing to do with this attack, and then that mumbo-jumbo clergyman from Scandinavia, who's just read out biblical texts from my father's own village, says he'll accept us in spite of everything. And everybody smiled. How nice and generous that Finnish pastor was. I thought: get lost, with your smile, with your superiority!'

In the weeks that followed, the media attention was unceasing. Umayya had to debate with an old friend on television, for example. He was introduced as a 'European Jewish intellectual', she as 'the immigrant'. 'He said things like, "All Muslims are this" and "All Muslims do that", there was no end to it. I looked at him and thought: always going on about human rights and suddenly it seems they don't exist anymore. I said, "Ruben, you're generalizing, that's a racist thing to say . . ." and he said, "Are you calling me a racist?"'

For Umayya, that debate was the tipping point. 'Backstage I burst into tears. 9/11 had got between us. It made people so frightened – it was "us" against "the Muslims". She received death threats. She wrote to the Finnish president: 'I don't feel threatened by who I am but by the changes that are happening in this country.'

'Until 11 September I was "the Palestinian" in Finland,' she told me. 'That stopped. I became – although it was complete nonsense – "the Muslim".'

Meanwhile, international jihadism was starting to take root in Europe, and the still-young internet functioned as an important catalyst for the religious revolt. In 1998, a total of twelve pro-jihadi websites were spotted; by 2005 there were almost 5,000. At first, al-Qaeda used Europe mainly as a place of refuge, a place where the practical preparations took place for attacks thought up somewhere in the Afghan mountains. On 11 March 2004, the Old Continent became the scene of the action for the first time, when a simultaneous attack on four busy commuter trains was mounted during rush hour in Madrid, resulting in almost 200 dead and more than 2,000 wounded. The following year, on 7 July 2005, something similar happened during rush hour in London, involving three trains and a bus, with more than 50 dead and 700 wounded.

Both Spain and Britain were active allies of the United States and there was a clear connection with the Iraq War. But soon some radical Muslims began to see their battle as a jihad, a holy war, against the West as a whole, including Western culture, Western democracy, Western freedom and the Western Enlightenment.

On 2 November 2004, the intractable Amsterdam filmmaker Theo van Gogh, great-grandson of the brother and confidant of Vincent van Gogh, was attacked in broad daylight in the middle of a busy street by a jihadist with a gun and a knife. His throat was cut. He was said to have insulted the Prophet and Islam with a television film about the oppression of women called Submission Part I, in which texts from the Koran were written on the body of a naked and beaten woman. For traditional Muslims, that combination was shocking.

The idea and the form the film took were the product of the imagination of charismatic activist Ayaan Hirsi Ali. Reconstructions later revealed that Van Gogh had no idea he was playing with fire. He wasn't particularly keen on the film because 'there was nothing funny in it', but he made it as a favour for a friend. Hirsi Ali and the mayor of Amsterdam, Job Cohen, received credible death threats and had to go into hiding.

There was immense panic, those first few days. 'The Netherlands is on fire,' some newspapers declared. Much was written and demonstrations were held. There were also arson attacks on mosques and death threats appeared on websites, mostly aimed at dissident Muslims. My local bar had an obscene message about Allah painted on the door. For his trad-itional entry into Amsterdam later that month, Sinterklaas wore a bulletproof vest.

We, the Dutch, were pretty confused. This was the end of our relative innocence, of the safe, cosy and free little country we knew so well. That much was clear to us all. The post-war taboos around racism and discrimi-nation were swept away at a stroke, as if the sluice gates had opened.

So began a long, useful, complicated, yet often vicious public debate about religion, immigration and the role of Islam in a Christian and secular Europe. For many foreign journalists this change of mentality in an always so tolerant country was more shocking than the murder itself. 'Articles are being published here that would undoubtedly lead to a trial for libel or racism in my country,' I heard several foreign colleagues say in those weeks.

What many Americans had explicitly avoided after 9/11 – even the most rabid media never spoke in those days about 'Muslims' but always about 'terrorists' or 'jihadi fighters' – was now regarded as perfectly normal in the Netherlands. The Dutch let fly at an entire religion, including all its variants and all its devoted, half-hearted and intermittent believers. Geert Wilders, a liberal parliamentarian who had become an independent, said Islam was responsible for '99 per cent of all problems surrounding security and public order'. His poll ratings soared. Straight after Van Gogh's murder, the website of the public broadcaster even mentioned the 'Islamic appear-ance' of the perpetrator. There were new buzzwords: 'strong', 'resolute', 'ourselves' as against 'weak', 'soft', 'politically correct' and 'multicultural'. Traders in fear seized their chance.

I was reminded of Heinrich Böll, who in his masterly German family history *Billiards at Half-Past Nine* avoided all the old, loaded labels from the 1930s and replaced them with a single magical description: those who have partaken of 'the Sacrament of the Buffalo'. Well, in the Netherlands from the autumn of 2004 onwards, people partook of that sacrament with gusto here and there. And they developed a taste for it.

A year later, on 27 October 2005, fierce rioting broke out in the Paris suburb of Clichy-sous-Bois. Two boys, of Tunisian and Mauritanian extraction, were electrocuted after they hid in an electricity substation, fearing police interrogation. For three weeks, there were riots against the police. Police stations, schools and other public buildings were stormed, and almost 10,000 cars were torched.

A month earlier, *Jyllands-Posten*, Denmark's biggest newspaper, had published a series of cartoons featuring the Prophet Mohammed. Depicting the Prophet is in itself blasphemous in Islam, and the in-house cartoonist Kurt Westergaard had given him a bomb in his turban. In the privacy of Denmark the reactions were initially mild. Aydin Soei had just taken a temporary job at another Danish paper, *Dagbladet Information*. 'We saw it simply as a stunt by a right-wing newspaper. I didn't understand the text that accompanied it at all, but I thought: so be it; everybody's free to publish this kind of thing.' Later he spoke to some young Muslims in deprived neighbourhoods. They were angry. They already felt excluded, so religion was becoming increasingly important to them, just as it was to Aydin's brother. The youngest among them wanted to riot, but the older ones held them back: 'Don't. That's exactly what they want. Ignore those cartoons. Just let it all die down.' The troubled districts of Copenhagen remained quiet.

Yet this local issue in Denmark grew into an immense international crisis. On 14 October 2005, 3,000 Muslims demonstrated outside Copenhagen City Hall – not so much against the drawings of the Prophet but against the bomb in his turban. Islam really is a peaceful religion, was the point they wanted to stress. There were cries of '*Allahu Akbar*' (God is Great). Many non-Muslim Danes didn't understand – to them the slogan sounded aggressive.

The ambassadors of eleven Muslim countries requested talks with Danish prime minister Anders Fogh Rasmussen. He refused even to receive them, to hear their protest and offer some kind of explanation. So there arose, partly because of the rude and starchy attitude of the Danish government, a short circuit between two mental worlds. On one side was the Western world of individualism and absolute freedom of expression – including the 'right' to insult. On the other was the agrarian tradition in which most of humanity lived and in which community, family and above all 'honour' were central.

Some Danish imams further stoked the flames. A delegation travelled to the Middle East, manipulated prominent spiritual leaders there and showed them, along with the original cartoons, images that had never been published in Denmark but were simply plucked from the internet. Now the issue became global internet hype that set the Islamic world on fire. Riots and demonstrations followed, most of them orchestrated by the ruling regimes. Danish embassies were stormed and set alight. Danish products were boycotted and Danish flags burned. Some 200 people died and 800 were wounded. The tumult in the media was deafening.

In those months I was working on a long piece of reportage and spent weeks amid the porters, street traders and cigarette sellers on the Galata Bridge in Istanbul, the same people as in Pamuk's coffeehouse. We talked a lot, sitting on stools in their tearoom, or sheltering from the umpteenth downpour under a couple of tarpaulins. None of them, save one, had ever heard of Theo van Gogh, and when I told them about the murder they were almost all deeply shocked. 'Only God allows a person to be born,' said a street-seller of insoles. 'And only God can take a life.'

But the cartoon issue made tempers flare. I soon understood that for my companions this was not a religious matter. Most of them described themselves as secular, and went to the mosque only now and then. Yet as we talked I noticed that the traditions of Islam were part of their deepest selves. They used them to keep a grip on their difficult and often chaotic lives. In their poverty, Islam was often their only source of pride and dignity. 'Without religion I'd lose all firm ground, I'd fall apart,' said a seller of sticking plasters.

In his essay about 9/11, Orhan Pamuk paints a sombre picture of the lives of these poor Muslims, all over the Islamic world. They know they are condemned to a hard, short existence. At the same time, films and television continually confront them with what looks like a life of luxury lived by Americans and Western Europeans. Because of their perpetual lack of money, they live almost permanently in a vicious and disorderly private sphere.

'The Western world is scarcely aware of this overwhelming humiliation experienced by most of the world's population,' writes Pamuk, 'which they have to overcome without losing their common sense and without being seduced by terrorists, extreme nationalists or fundamentalists.'

I saw the bookseller, the insoles man, the tea-seller, the street photographer, the cigarette boys, my interlocutors on the bridge in Istanbul, all wrestling with that daily. For them, their response to the cartoons of the Prophet was above all about wounded pride, about damage to their ultimate bulwark against humiliation. If you're poor as a church mouse, then honour may be the last thing of value you possess.

From then on, the offices of *Jyllands-Posten* looked like a fort. Elderly cartoonist Kurt Westergaard still fears for his life. In 2010 he survived a murder attempt. 'Blood! Vengeance!' was all his assailant, a Somali man, shouted as he attacked him in his home with an axe. The cartoonist barricaded himself in the bathroom and the man was arrested within five minutes. 'When he's freed I'd like to meet him,' Westergaard told Flemish philosopher and television personality Jan Leyers. 'I don't feel any anger towards him any longer, only curiosity. I want to understand what goes on in his head. I'm too old to hate.'

4

Elsewhere in the world, thousands died annually in terrorist attacks. But in Europe, after the attacks in Madrid and London, clearly organized under the auspices of al-Qaeda, things went fairly quiet for several years and it seemed relatively safe. Furthermore, the work of the various intelligence agencies was apparently successful. According to a study by Leiden University, in Europe an average of nine out of ten attacks were prevented.

The jihadists did not have a monopoly on terrorism, of course. In 2011 Norwegian Anders Breivik single-handedly caused mass death and destruction with a bomb attack in Oslo, followed by a mass shooting at a social-democrat youth camp on the island of Utøya. In total, seventy-seven people were killed. In a lengthy manifesto, disseminated in far-right circles everywhere, Breivik described his motives: Europe must be saved from Islam and from politically correct politicians. Violence was the only solution. 'We gave peace a chance. The time for armed resistance has come.'

That attack was the first manifestation of an extremely violent new-right movement. Like Breivik, the later 'alt-right killers' – in New Zealand, the United States and Sweden – were inspired by what became known as the 'white replacement theory'. It assumes that 'Western identity' is under serious threat, that the white population of the West is being gradually replaced by black, brown and Muslim immigrants, and that this process is being encouraged by murky groups – Jews, the progressive elite – that see it as a means to world domination. In right-wing populist thinking, this theory made increasing headway from 2011 onwards.

A new phase began in 2015, influenced in part by the eruption of a civil war in Syria and increasing bitterness at the tough attitude of the Israeli government towards the Palestinians – the seventieth anniversary of the state of Israel in May 2018, for instance, was accompanied by the shooting of sixty young Palestinians who were taking part in a largely non-violent demonstration at the border with Gaza.

Terrorism was now coming from Europe itself. On 7 January 2015 two French jihadists in Paris mounted an attack on the offices of the satirical weekly *Charlie Hebdo* – and again, it was all about a couple of cartoons. Two days later, a jihadist killed four Jews in a kosher supermarket.

Young adventurers travelled to Syria to join the fighting on the side of the terrorist organization Islamic State or some other group. They returned home as battle-hardened jihadists. The internet proved the perfect radicalization machine in this sense as well. The culprits were often discovered to be confused individuals who had ridden the slipstream of international terrorism in an attempt to achieve hero status. Many terrorist acts had a clear connection with these new jihadist networks: the Paris shootings of 13 November 2015 (130 dead, 89 of them in the Bataclan theatre); attacks on the metro and airport in Brussels on 22 March 2016 (32 dead); the truck driven into a festive crowd in Nice on 14 July 2016 (86 dead, and ten days later an elderly village priest had his throat cut in front of the altar); the truck that caused death and destruction at a Berlin Christmas market on 19 December 2016 (12 dead); the Uzbek man who on 1 January 2017 entered the Reina nightclub in Istanbul, shooting as he went (39 dead); the man who on 22 March 2017 deliberately drove into pedestrians in front of the Houses of Parliament in London (5 dead); the bomb attack on 3 April 2017 on a metro train in Saint Petersburg (14 dead); the Islamic State sympathizer who used a truck as a weapon, this time in Stockholm, on 8 April 2017 (4 dead); the bomb attack on a pop concert in Manchester on 22 May 2017 (22 dead); the jihadist who drove into the public on London Bridge on 3 June and then ferociously stabbed those around him (7 dead); the delivery van that caused carnage on La Rambla in Barcelona on 17 August 2017 (13 dead); the attack on a supermarket in Trèbes in France on 23 March 2018, largely thwarted by policeman Arnaud Beltrame, who died as a result (4 dead); a stabbing and shooting attack on 29 May 2018 in Liège, Belgium (3 dead) – not to speak of dozens of smaller or failed attacks. Europol recorded a total of 142 fatalities in 2016, 68 in 2017.

As I have said, in earlier decades at least as many Europeans had died in terrorist attacks, but the impact of this global terrorism was far greater. An attack might happen anywhere, there were often many fatalities in a single event, the perpetrators were strange, their motives incomprehensible, and everyone was a target. Some police forces and security services only added to the atmosphere of threat with their excessive shows of strength. In Brussels the state of emergency lasted for months, and in Paris and other large cities heavily armed militia on the streets created a new atmosphere.

Although daily life returned to normal surprisingly quickly after each attack, there was a general sense of doom hanging over the continent in these years. Europeans did not feel safe – which was precisely the intention. The number of anti-Semitic threats and violence against Jews increased everywhere; in the case of France, by 74 per cent between 2017 and 2018.

Moreover, the terrorist attacks had been mounted under the flag of Islam, a religion that many Europeans knew nothing about. In some circles the words of Enoch Powell in 1968 about 'the River Tiber foaming with much blood' (a quote from Virgil) were repeated more than once: 'It is like watching a nation busily engaged in heaping up its own funeral pyre.'

Populist politicians eagerly took advantage of the mood. In Germany the leader of the new ultra-right AfD party, Frauke Petry, demanded the government put a stop to the 'increasing Islamization' of Germany. The party's deputy leader tweeted about 'barbaric, gang-raping hordes of Muslim men'.

In the Netherlands, Geert Wilders wanted to ban the Koran and to introduce a tax on headscarves, which he called a *kopvoddentaks* or 'head-rag tax'. The wearing of a headscarf was banned in French schools, and on French beaches the 'burkini', a special swimsuit for Muslim women, was outlawed. The Swiss voted in a referendum for a ban on the building of minarets. In Hungary, Islam became a central theme for Prime Minister Viktor Orbán, in whose view the 'flood' of Muslim immigrants was a direct threat to the safety and integrity of European civilization. (In reality, Muslims in Hungary made up just 0.15 per cent of the population.)

Discrimination cannot exist without crude generalizations. These campaigns consistently spoke of 'the' Muslims, as if there are not countless types of Islam, heavy and light, militant and mild, just as there are diverse denominations within Christianity. In Europe alone, four types were clearly visible within Muslim communities in the early twenty-first century: the closed and traditional Salafism; the more pragmatic forms of political Islam – especially that of the Muslim Brotherhood; a so-called Euro-Islam, based on the principles of the Renaissance and the Enlightenment; and in Germany a 'Secular Muslim Initiative', a movement that renounced all religion and advocated a 'folkloric relationship with Islam'.

Ignorance therefore became a fertile breeding ground for all kinds of misunderstanding. According to a revealing study by Ipsos in 2016, most French people thought that almost a third of the population was Muslim, 31 per cent. In reality the figure at that time was 7.5 per cent. The Belgians, Germans, Dutch and Italians thought it was a fifth, 20 per cent, whereas in reality it was between 5 and 6 per cent, or in the case of Italy 3.7 per cent. The British and Danes estimated a sixth of their population was Muslim, or 15 per cent. The actual percentage was somewhere between 4 and 5. In Europe as a whole there were around 26 million Muslims, some 5 per cent of the population.

Demagogues certainly had a role to play in this, but the distorted impression was also a result of the increasing visibility of Muslims. New and bigger mosques were being built and more and more Muslim women wore headscarves, while mosque attendance among young people increased markedly. In some big cities, Mohammed (in various spellings) became the most popular name for newborn boys. In Muslim circles there was even talk of 'an Islamic awakening', a worldwide increase in religious and political consciousness among Muslims that had been underway since the 1970s.

All this did not merely concern a conflict between the values of the West and of Islam, as was so often claimed. Running right through it was a clash between secularity and religion, between belief and unbelief. Religions had a central function in all previous centuries, in all societies. They provided intellectual frameworks and strong value systems. They encouraged empathy and certain forms of citizenship and charity. These were set down in laws and commandments that were endlessly violated and contravened, but which nevertheless existed.

In large parts of modern Europe, Christianity had lost that central role. According to polling in fifteen European countries by the Pew Research Center, Western Europe became one of the most secular parts of the world in the final decades of the twentieth century, so that by the early years of the twenty-first century only a fifth of Europeans regularly attended church. These developments profoundly altered European culture. In the words of Amsterdam literary critic Kees Fens, 'Western culture has lost its two-thousand-year-old perspective, a perspective that served to bind it together.'

In the eyes of many, this dismantling of the European Christian tradition was caused by the newcomers and by 'Islamization'. In reality, the process had been going on for much longer – since the 1950s in the case of the Netherlands – without any outside intervention.

4. Greatness

2004

I

A CLOSE ACQUAINTANCE OF MINE owns a furniture factory in Bosnia. We both belong to a choir, business is good, the factory is expanding and we're all off to Bosnia: sing!

We walk up a cart track, between blossoming hedges, across an undulating green landscape. The old order has been restored: the grey men smoking on the veranda, the inquisitive housewives; the houses, half-finished, full of dreams and new plans; the neatly laid-out vegetable plots for the passing seasons. It's summertime and the war ended years ago. The toddlers of those wartime days are now in the factory tending computer-operated drills, and at the national festival in the evening the girls seem transformed – they're breathtaking dancers. And yet, only Bosnian Muslims work here, even though the Republika Srpska, the Serbian part of Bosnia, is a mere five kilometres away. 'They don't apply for the jobs,' says the owner.

Regional politics in this part of the world has been largely taken over by commerce, I'm told. All the nationalistic and ideological squabbling is over; as a businessman you now have to accept a great deal of nepotism and corruption. 'We'll never be stopped for speeding, let's say. After all, we bring jobs. They're not going to tread on our toes.'

On our way here we saw incidental signs of poverty everywhere: a shy man trying to sell a handful of books, taxi drivers pushing their cars to save fuel, an elderly person rummaging in a bin. Local unemployment stands at 35 per cent; youth unemployment at 55 per cent.

But today it's party time. In the factory's big woodshed, tables have been set out. There's beer and wine, there are sausages and pork chops, there are speeches: 'An example of European integration', 'More than fifty people at work now', 'We're hoping for an even better future, with even more machines and further expansion'. 'Machines', 'Expansion', 'Europe', 'Future' – the speaker representing the employees repeats his message over and over, and the buzzwords keep on buzzing.

In a jam pot, in a corner, are all the bullets they've found while sawing wood.

Bosnia-Herzegovina is still knocking at Europe's door. The Yugoslav federation of which it used to be a part – along with Croatia, Slovenia, Vojvodina, Kosovo, Macedonia, Serbia and Montenegro – was once at the front of the queue to join the European Union. But the country tore itself to pieces in the 1990s with ethnic wars, expulsions and reciprocal pillage, and Bosnia was hardest hit.

In December 1999 I left Sarajevo in a skidding taxi. A snowstorm had paralysed the city for days. I'd stayed in a small hotel near the Ottoman district that had barely any guests save a handful of Dutch and German businessmen. The city had been under siege and artillery fire for four years, 12,000 people had been killed and rebuilding had yet to start. At breakfast we all sat enthralled by *Teletubbies*, a children's series about toddler puppets in a heavenly landscape, always sunny and green, which was all that Bosnian television had to offer at that time of the morning. After watching those scenes of tranquillity we felt able to face another day.

Sarajevo was empty and wounded. Everywhere, tough-looking men walked around in tracksuits, the universal attire of the Balkans in those years of transition. A legion of Western aid workers were taking care of the city; in swanky Land Cruisers, they drove from one consultation to the next. A few bars and restaurants were still open and everyone crowded into them. In the legendary To Be or Not to Be bar, I was brought up to date by Hrvoje Batinić, a fellow journalist who knew the city well. He'd made a lifestyle out of his eternal pessimism – 'Then if something good happens, I'm always glad.' He had his doubts about all those bustling Western European aid workers and 'do-gooders'. 'Hey, Geert, be honest, what sort of characters are you lot sending us? The top people are fine, but the rest? Third-class, at best. Adventurers who treat us as if we need to be told what a flushing toilet is.'

Now, almost twenty years later, there are luxury cars everywhere, even parked on the pavements. The place where I used to stay has been thoroughly refurbished and extended, and around the corner are another four hotels; beyond them, a sea of white graves. For tourists there's the Franz Ferdinand tour, complete with vintage cars: experience the historic assassination afresh any day of the week. The city centre is one big café terrace. A girl walks behind a large pink balloon, an elderly woman is selling small bunches of thistles, a war invalid begs, his stump serving as a prop for a noticeboard; there are flâneurs and street musicians, and the ice cream parlours are full, everything inside them pink and pale blue.

In the evenings, celebrations are held in the restaurants. The exams are over. People sing at the tables and the girls who have made the grade dance, their hair up. Then there's World Cup football, the quarter-final, Croatia versus Russia. All the bars are showing it on big screens and everyone cheers for the Croats. Okay, we were at war, but they're still family. 'Yugoslavia remains part of our lives,' says a Bosnian I know. 'All our memories are full of holidays in Croatia, the smell of the forests of Slovenia, sleepovers in Belgrade.'

Sarajevo was always a crossroads of cultures and religions, and so it remains. Islam – a large majority of the city's residents are Muslim – is modern and free here. The black-clad women you come upon everywhere in the streets are almost all tourists from the Gulf States. They like coming to Bosnia, since the country is green, cheap, and European yet Islamic. My energetic publisher organizes a literary festival here and special things happen at it every year: exchanges with festivals in Berlin and Tehran, offers from publishers in Amsterdam, Sarajevo and Riyadh, discussions between writers from New York, Budapest and Paris. I always enjoy it.

Yet if you walk around a little longer, you notice a thick cloud of despondency hanging over the city. 'Change?' one of the festival speakers sighs. 'My hair has grown grey here, waiting for change.' Another member of the panel lets slip, almost incidentally, that this afternoon it's exactly a quarter of a century since her father was shot dead by a sniper. A young woman in the audience says, 'During the war, survival was all that mattered. It's only now that the nightmares come, and they keep on coming.' The factory owner speaks up: 'We played with everybody. At Easter we Muslim children always got Easter eggs from a neighbour up the street. Now I have girls working here who say they've never spoken to a Serb.'

After the compromise that brought peace, the Dayton Agreement of 1995, two governments held power in different parts of the country: the Republika Srpska and the Federation of Bosnia and Herzegovina. Five years later a third joined them, the tiny district of Brčko. So there are three ministers of education, health, infrastructure – and everything else you can think of. In many respects the war is still going on, but at an administrative level. Every idea from one government is adroitly blocked by the others.

The water-supply infrastructure dates from Habsburg times. It's forever failing but no one feels responsible. Each population group gets its own schooling, so children are pumped full of ethnic and nationalist myths from their earliest years. Saudi Arabia and Turkey have scattered new mosques all across the country; there's one in every village and in every neighbourhood. Young people are leaving in droves. They're well educated, Croatia and Germany have jobs on offer, and even in the smaller towns, dozens of emigrants get on the bus every day. Meanwhile the place is crawling with politicians whose obvious prosperity is hard to square with their official careers and salaries. The hills around Sarajevo, once so fiercely fought over, are peppered with their mansions.

Until recently at least, the Republika Srpska strove for total independence – the prime minister even went to inquire of Montenegro how that country managed to separate itself from the Serbian Federation in 2006. The president of the Bosnian part is an enthusiastic supporter of Vladimir Putin. My fellow panellists call him 'the Muslim Viktor Orbán'. In the book stalls at the Sarajevo Memorial for Children, in between Umberto Eco, Orhan Pamuk and Elena Ferrante, the latest edition of Adolf Hitler's *Mein Kampf* is on display.

The government is still formally under the guardianship of the European Union and the United States. Ultimate authority rests with a kind of colonial governor, the EU's High Representative. At the time of writing, the job is held by an Austrian, who has the power to intervene wherever and whenever he chooses.

One particularly large building is the seat of the OSCE, the international cooperative organization charged with promoting prosperity, peace and stability. Some 300 people work there. The American embassy is almost as big, with a staff of around 500 – in a country with a population of less than 4 million. The strong presence of the EU and the US is telling. This part of Europe remains extraordinarily unstable. New outbursts of violence threaten.

At breakfast I come upon Dubravka Ugrešić, a Croat writer who has lived in exile for many years. Briefly back for the festival, she exudes a grim resignation. 'Twenty years after the Bosnian war, the former Yugoslavia looks like a dreamland, a utopia,' she says. 'There was prosperity, education, healthcare. Everything was fine.' She stresses that the country, like the Czech Republic and Slovakia, could easily have been divided peacefully. Serbia, Bosnia, Croatia – those national entities weren't so very closely bound together. So why all the wars? 'Very simple. It was called ethnic cleansing, but in reality it was one big looting spree. Anyone forced to leave would abandon their house and their possessions. It was compounded by the fact that in all those communist collectives very little private property was registered. When the communist structure fell away, a huge battle erupted over property rights: what belonged to whom? Just look around. Everywhere here you'll see individuals who got inexplicably rich in those years.'

The nationalists proficiently wrecked the Yugoslav dreamland, and to explain this and make it acceptable, history is now being powerfully censored and rewritten. The Croats, for example, once again idolize their Second World War fascist independence movement, the Ustaša. Dubravka Ugrešić tells one story after another about swastikas and other Nazi symbols, and sure enough, here and there you can see them again. 'That's consistently dismissed as incidental, but if it happens day after day it's no longer incidental.' Charges are hardly ever brought for crimes committed during the Yugoslav wars. No European country is so obstructive as Croatia in this respect. 'If someone steals, they're brought before a judge,' Ugrešić says. 'A gang ends up in prison. But if two million people go about robbing and thieving, they'll never face any consequences. That's what happened.'

A few days later I spend an evening with old friends in the Serbian city of Novi Sad. There too the buildings have been patched up, the ruined bridges replaced or repaired, everything forgotten and smoothly paved over – yet the stories are the same as in Bosnia. Serbia's ruling party is gaining a grip on practically all sectors of society again. I spend a morning talking with my old mate Želimir Žilnik. 'Under Tito it was nowhere near as bad,' he tells me. In 1969, Žilnik was thrown out of the Party, but he was still able to make all the films he wanted to make for television, some twenty documentaries at least. 'You can only dream of that now. A commission or a job, whether as liftboy or as administrator of a school or a theatre, is available to you only if you're a member of the party. That's obvious and upfront these days.' Meanwhile, Putin is an honorary citizen of Novi Sad.

As in Sarajevo, it's often unclear what people live on. In theory hardly anyone has any money, yet the bars are full. A lot is mere show. There's rarely any work. To survive you need family; that's a vital part of every story. One of my old friends provides me with some figures. Along with his mother, he lived on her pension – one hundred and seventy euros per month – plus his own war pension of eighty euros. When she died he had to manage on the eighty euros, but he continued to live in the house that belonged to his parents. Sometimes he gets a casual security job: one euro an hour, ten euros a day.

The prices aren't much different from those of Western Europe, so food alone can easily cost you seventy-five euros a week. Our friend manages on twenty. 'If you're old and you've got no money and no children, you walk to the Danube and jump,' he says. 'That's the best solution.'

I regularly find myself thinking back to the sombre and impressive War Childhood Museum in Sarajevo. All the young people who experienced the siege of the city as children were asked to donate an object that had been of crucial importance to them in that difficult time. Donations flooded in, hundreds of them. I saw a home-made football game, drawings on toilet paper, children's clothes made from rags, photos, a splotchy diary, stories of falling in love – which went on as it always had. I remember best of all a little robot figure in blue and gold plastic, the treasured possession of a small boy who sometimes had to fetch water or firewood while shells fell around him. 'Robots ought to be able to do that for people,' he dreamed in those days. 'Think how many lives it would save.'

'It was our turn,' I heard a young woman say in Sarajevo. 'We were just going through what previous generations endured.' All the same, I wanted to ask her parents and grandparents a few questions. Because look at how prosperous and promising the Yugoslav federation was at the start of the 1990s. And then look at the state that Bosnia and Serbia are in now, after the nationalist inferno. For many Bosnians and Serbs nowadays, Europe is little more than a robot like the one the boy dreamed about, a magic little machine that can remove all troubles at a stroke. But there was no way either country could join in the great enlargement of the EU on 1 May 2004, or indeed the enlargement that followed. They were and remain far from ready. How things are supposed to go from here, nobody knows.

2

In the Berlaymont building, the headquarters of the European Commission in Brussels, Italian Claudio Di Marzio is responsible for everything that flaps and dances in the wind. Ever since 1982 he has performed his task meticulously. Flags of the member states are stored on the third floor. In a side room they are regularly ironed and in the basement they are washed, at 30 degrees Celsius.

On that historic Saturday, 1 May 2004, it was Di Marzio's task to raise ten spotless new flags next to the other fifteen: those of Poland, Estonia, the Czech Republic, Hungary, Latvia, Lithuania, Slovakia, Slovenia, Cyprus and Malta.

It seemed a triumph, but in reality it was another risky operation. Ever since part of the island was occupied by the Turks in 1974, Cyprus has been an unsolved problem; and for that reason alone it was for years refused membership of the EU. As a result of successful blackmail by Greece, which threatened to veto the accession of the others, it was let in.

Malta was a pleasant tourist island, deeply divided and corrupt. It soon took to abusing its EU membership by selling Maltese passports, and therefore EU residence, to rich Russians and Saudis, for €900,000 apiece. The trade earned Malta and Maltese politicians hundreds of millions. Then, in 2017, the island's most important journalist, Daphne Caruana Galizia, was murdered in cold blood for unearthing too many mafia connections to this 'golden visa' system. The last two sentences on her blog were: 'There are crooks everywhere you look now. The situation is desperate.'

*

The enlargement of the EU

	EU until 2004
	EU enlargement in 2004 and later
	Outside the eurozone

FINLAND

Helsinki

Tallinn
ESTONIA
Stockholm

RUSSIA

Moscow

Riga LATVIA

LITHUANIA

Vilnius Minsk

BELARUS

Warsaw
POLAND

Kyiv

UKRAINE

ZECH
PUBLIC
SLOVAKIA
Bratislava
na Budapest
HUNGARY

MOLDAVIA

Chişinău

Zagreb
CROATIA
BOSNIA
HERZEGOVINA Belgrade
SERBIA
Sarajevo
MONTENEGRO
Podgorica
Tirana Skopje
MACEDONIA
ALBANIA

ROMANIA

Bucharest

BULGARIA

Sofia

Ankara TURKEY

GREECE

Athens

SYRIA IRAQ

CYPRUS

MALTA

SAUDI ARABIA

The decision to admit most of the former communist countries in one go was taken back in 1993, but it was controversial from the start. There was a real dilemma: deepening or widening? All activities aimed at making the EU more democratic and decisive would have to be put on the back burner if expansion occurred, and some people believed those activities should take priority. Others rightly asked whether the structure of the EU was robust enough to absorb so many new members. President Mitterrand wanted to offer the Eastern and Central European newcomers an Association Agreement in this initial phase, rather than full membership. First, the fifteen Western EU countries needed to get their house in order.

For other members, especially Germany and Britain, expansion was the main priority. Collapsing empires can release a deluge of chaos and violence, and that would surely hold true for a subsiding Soviet Empire. The prospect of rapid and orderly accession might prevent a repeat of a fateful history – and that is indeed what happened.

Germany in particular, which lies in the middle of Europe, had a strong desire for an overarching European order. Geopolitics was part of the picture too; the Eastern and Central European countries must not become pawns of other superpowers such as the emerging China and later, perhaps, Russia once more.

There was also powerful moral pressure. How could the West say no to the Poles who had suffered so terribly during the two World Wars and had given their all in the fight for Europe? Or to the Czechs and Slovaks, who after the 'betrayal' of Munich in 1938 found themselves on the wrong side of history? Was there no sense of solidarity with all those Europeans who had lived such austere and burdensome lives behind the Iron Curtain?

The Yugoslav wars settled the matter: nothing like that must be allowed to happen again at any cost. Strict conditions were attached to accession, in fields including the rule of law, democracy, the protection of human rights, the free market and the transparency of politics and government. As so often in this European history, the conditions were largely disregarded once it was safe to do so – by Cyprus and Malta after the first expansion, and a couple of years later by Romania and Bulgaria. It was impossible to export a car to the latter two countries without a whole package of kickbacks, but in 2007 their accession to the EU was greeted with jubilation. Triumphalism still prevailed.

*

In the new member states, expectations were high. In the 1950s and 1960s in the West, every form of modernity was given the prefix 'Europe' – Europe Square, Europe Boulevard – and around the turn of the century the same occurred in the countries of the former Eastern Bloc. Europe bars, Europe clubs and Europe restaurants appeared everywhere. In the Hungarian village of Vásárosbéc, which I visited regularly in those days, the residents were already dreaming of riches. Ten Dutch people went to live there who between them bought at least a dozen houses, attracted by the low prices in this part of Europe. The old houses were transformed one after another into pleasant holiday homes, complete with swimming pools. They might only be used for one week a year, and the new occupants didn't bother to learn how to say 'thank you' in Hungarian, but none of that mattered. It all demonstrated the kind of life that was possible.

My host's warnings – slaughtering pigs at home, smoking in the pub; in the EU all that would be banned – were laughed off. Impossible. What nonsense.

In Budapest, meanwhile, the city council was doing everything it could to meet the conditions for membership. Gábor Demszky, mayor at the time, told me later about the thousands of rules and regulations that had to be changed. Somehow, by 2004 the Hungarian capital was ready. Unlike the rest of the country, incidentally. 'That first of May was the best day of my life,' Demszky said. 'We would finally become a member of a community that was politically, culturally and economically developed. You could see that same mood in everyone, the feeling that we now belonged with the West. There was a fear of a loss of autonomy, certainly, and there were undoubtedly nationalistic feelings, but there was no open criticism. Only the fascists were opposed.'

In a beer cellar in Warsaw in 1999 I'd sat brooding one snowy evening with historian Jarosław Krawczyk, editor-in-chief of the newspaper *Mówią Wieki* (Centuries Speak). 'Expansion of Europe?' he growled. 'But we *are* Europe, just like the Hungarians, the Czechs and the Romanians. You in the West always forget what we have to offer you: the fighting spirit of the Poles, the circumspection of the Czechs, the perseverance of the Hungarian dissidents. Aren't those things that you're awfully short of? Courage, principles, experience of life?'

We talked about all the differences between the former communist countries – which he felt the West, in this mass expansion, had completely overlooked. Just take the term 'Eastern Bloc'. Such a typically Western concept, he felt. In reality there was never any 'bloc'.

'The Czech ambassador once said to me, "We had only nitwits to deal with, but you, the Poles, were ruled by highly intelligent communists." The Czechs and East Germans were shut in, but when I was twenty no one tried to stop me from hitchhiking to Italy. That was a shock, by the way. Our reality was so grey.' All the same, in 2004 he was incredibly happy, he told me later. 'I truly believed Europe should be one, with one army, one economy, one political system.'

In Poland, 1 May 2004 was celebrated in style. German historian Philipp Ther was in Słubice, a Polish border town near Frankfurt an der Oder where champagne corks and firecrackers popped all night. On the German side of the border it was strikingly quiet. In the West, beneath all the apparent joy, there were worries. Would this really go well? The EU member states, with a couple of exceptions, had always been fairly evenly matched. That ended in 2004.

Within the EU, the differences have been vast ever since, in both a democratic and an economic sense. The Bavarian minister-president Edmund Stoiber calculated in a speech how ridiculously little a tradesman in the former Eastern Bloc earned per hour: in Poland 5.50 marks, in Bulgaria 1.40 marks, compared to a German on 48 marks. That alone might have unforeseen consequences.

To prevent a mass immigration of Eastern European guest workers, the EU had given the member states permission to limit the influx for seven years. Only Sweden, Britain and Ireland, countries very much in need of skilled workers, threw their borders wide open immediately. It was an obvious invitation. The British government predicted that some 15,000 migrants would arrive from the new member states every year. In reality, in the two years after 2004, 427,000 arrived. Within ten years, the number of Poles in Britain increased tenfold. At more than 900,000 individuals, they were the largest foreign population group.

In Germany, it was all rather less official. Philipp Ther described how the local trains between Szczecin and Frankfurt an der Oder were soon packed full on Sunday evenings, mostly with middle-aged women. 'If you got talking to them they'd tell you about their work as home helps, cleaners or nurses.' Often the women lived two or three to a room, trying to earn as much money as they possibly could to send home. Mass emigration from East to West did not happen; for most, it remained a matter of coming and going. 'The open door,' as one expert said, 'turned out to be a revolving door.'

3

The apparent boundlessness of the EU after 2004 nevertheless became a problem that worried more and more Europeans. According to German foreign minister Joschka Fischer, the fall of the Berlin Wall mean that the 'back wall' of the European house had disappeared. And out of that gaping hole all kinds of things might emerge. 'Nations hitherto unheard of are awakening and want countries of their own,' wrote Czech president Václav Havel. 'Highly improbable people from God knows where are winning elections.'

How far should the Union go to accommodate them? The question kept arising. Turkey, which had fulfilled all the initial criteria in 2004, remained in the waiting room. The biggest European countries, especially France and Britain, were eager for further negotiations because of Turkey's military and strategic position as a bridge between Europe and the Middle East. Smaller countries like the Netherlands, Austria and Denmark thought less in geopolitical terms. In their view Turkey did not fit into supposedly Christian Europe 'from a cultural point of view'. Others feared its size. Wouldn't a Muslim country with more than 70 million inhabitants pull European relationships too much askew? As former German chancellor Helmut Schmidt once said, 'We cannot manage Turkish membership since it would fatally dilute the EU.'

In 2006, negotiations with Turkey were put on ice once again, officially because of the unresolved problem of Cyprus. The Turks themselves decided they'd had enough, and under the leadership of the new premier Recep Tayyip Erdoğan their country took a different path. The secularism of Kemal Atatürk, founder of modern Turkey, gave way to national Islamism. Turkey increasingly seemed to be turning away from the West.

Quite a few of the Balkan countries – Serbia, Montenegro, Albania, Macedonia, Kosovo and Bosnia – remained outside, as we have seen. (For the time being, at least. Serbia and Montenegro have a chance of accession in 2025.) In their case too – human aspects and national politics aside – it was a matter of major geopolitical interests. The region was surrounded by EU countries and formed a power vacuum on the continent of Europe that others were all too happy to exploit: Russia, which was trying to regain its lost influence through Orthodox Christianity; Turkey, which was doing the same in Bosnia through Islam; China, which simply bought influence with hard dollars; and the mafia, which turned Albania in particular into an efficient base of operations.

Yet after the accession of Croatia in 2013 there was little enthusiasm for further enlargement. The experience with Romania gave pause for thought. Ten years after Romania's accession, the European Commission reported that the situation in the country, especially regarding the rule of law and corruption, had got worse rather than better. The same went for Bulgaria – according to Transparency International, ten years after accession it was still the most corrupt EU member state. 'Please, not another six Bulgarias,' was the collective sigh.

So Bosnia and Serbia were left in suspense, and for the European citizen a kind of uncertainty, a kind of indeterminacy, continued to hang around the edges of the apparently borderless EU.

4

2004 needed to be a triumph of the reborn Europe and of the expanded Union's only real weapon: soft power. From all kinds of EU funds, including its agricultural subsidies, billions of euros poured into the new member states. In the period between 2007 and 2013, a total of €175 billion was paid out – for Poland alone €67 billion, for the Czech Republic €26.7 billion, for Hungary €25.3 billion. In those years, the operation really was comparable to America's Marshall Plan after the Second World War.

The economic success of EU enlargement was at least as impressive, although not everywhere. In 2005, the EU invested €62 billion in the new member states, a year later €91 billion. Their gross domestic product grew

by between 7 and 10 per cent annually. The buying power of the average
Pole tripled between 1989 and 2009. There was talk of a Polish *Wirtschaftswunder*, and the standard of living improved accordingly. Average life expectancy
increased markedly in the same period, by up to four or five years in Poland,
the Czech Republic, Slovakia, Hungary and Estonia.

Enlargement had negative effects too, however. Some borders were closed.
Želimir Žilnik lived in Vojvodina in Serbia, where the border with Hungary
had been more or less open for at least a century. Under the dictatorship of
Slobodan Milošević in the 1990s, half a million or more Yugoslavs escaped
that way. Žilnik was one of them, after things got too hot for him for a while.
But it had become the border with the EU. 'You now needed a visa for a
simple trip to Budapest,' he said. 'A new Berlin Wall has gone up.'

Many Hungarian families were torn apart. The large market in the border town of Subotica collapsed completely; within two weeks there was
nothing left of it. Žilnik made a film, *Europe Next Door*, about the flourishing
trade in brides in those days. 'In the Serbian border villages, parents went in
search of Hungarian brides and bridegrooms for their children. Everyone
wanted a European passport in the family, and they were willing to pay a
good price, around three to five thousand euros. These were fake marriages
but big business. And there was always a huge wedding celebration.'

More than ten years after enlargement, I went to have another look at
Vásárosbéc, on the 'right' side of the new EU border. The old lady who
shared her home with her cow had died. The house of the one-legged man
had half fallen in. The woman who lived with one pig had died of cancer –
like most Roma in Hungary, she had no health insurance, so the hospital
sent her away. Other than that, everything seemed unchanged: the court-
yards full of chickens and ducks; the peeling paint of the houses where the
Roma lived – they still sometimes fed the stove with their own doors and
window frames; the wood fires, the crowing of cocks, the blue smoke curling out of the chimneys in the early dusk.

Yet the nineteenth century, still present everywhere in 1999, had now
truly ended. The horse-drawn carts, the dirt-poor Roma travellers in their
covered wagons, the basket makers and wood carvers who went door to
door with wooden spoons and rolling pins – all the old skills, all the little
things, had gone. A couple of major retail chains had descended upon the

neighbouring village of Szigetvár, and with their low prices they wiped most of the small traders off the map – before raising their prices again. Our friends ran into their grocer in Lidl, stocking up on bananas there in desperation, since they cost far less than his wholesaler charged him. 'I can still see his shocked and embarrassed face when he recognized us.' Two years later, he was bankrupt.

Nor had the village pub survived the coming of the EU. The pissing place at the back would have to become the site of strictly separated gentlemen's and ladies' toilets, according to the new rules, and there was no way the owner could pay for all that shiny tiling. Now the men stood drinking outdoors in the evenings, on the pavement outside the grocer's shop.

European funds had paid for a house of culture, a fine-looking building with gleaming roof tiles where there were meetings twice a month and bingo almost as often. The rest of the time it was shut. The church had been beautifully restored, but no one attended it any longer.

One of the Roma had started a contracting firm. But he was the exception. Village life still consisted of some casual sweeping and raking, a lot of hanging about, and a bit of foraging by chickens and pigs. People expressed their gratitude for the election gift from Orbán: enough firewood to last two weeks; for the elderly, four. The only entertainment behind the brown and muddy doors was sex, the one source of pleasure that cost nothing – at least in the short term.

So while the big cities regained their splendour, the villages were left behind, in every sense. Just beyond Vásárosbéc, in an abandoned field, a children's playground had been built with European money. The swings hung motionless and you never heard a cry or a laugh, since there were no children to be found for miles around. In Bosnia, Serbia, Hungary, everywhere in Eastern and Central Europe, the villages emptied. Here, mass migration, as one Eastern European commentator wrote, 'is simply a rational response to the large differences in the standard of living'.

In 2010, some 1,500 Hungarians left the country. Seven years later the figure was fourteen times that, at almost 21,000. The better doctors from Vásárosbéc and the surrounding district had almost all left to work in Austria. Estonia lost a third of its young people. In 2011, more than 2 million Bulgarians were living abroad, out of a population of little more than 7 million. By 2050, according to the latest predictions, the population will have declined by 39 per cent. Serbia expects a decline of 24 per cent by 2050, Albania 26 per cent. In 2018, more Albanians were already living outside the country than in it. One young Albanian described his ideal life to a journalist for the Dutch newspaper *de Volkskrant*: 'When I'm twenty-five I want a house, a wife, a nice car, a son and a wristwatch. If I stay in Tirana I've no chance of that.'

At his films' showings in America and Western Europe, Želimir Žilnik noticed new diaspora emerging everywhere, as they had in the 1930s. 'I come upon thousands of young people in London and New York, active in the worlds of advertising, film, literature, the visual arts and science, passionate people that their own countries would have held on to in normal circumstances. All of it talent in exile.'

The effects of mass emigration were tragic for the migrants' native countries, not just economically – businesses could no longer find good employees – but socially and politically. Those who left were mostly young, well educated and reasonably progressive, and they took that youthful, forward-looking mentality with them. Societies became more traditional, conservative and anxious.

Bulgarian political scientist Ivan Krastev noticed among Eastern Europeans a 'fear of ethnic disappearance', coupled with a fear of newcomers. The changes they saw were signs that they themselves were disappearing from history. Europe is not only divided between left and right, North and South, he wrote, but between those who have personally witnessed the disintegration of a society and those who have only read about it in history books. 'The experience of the sudden and nonviolent end of something that we were confident was permanent (until it was no more) is the defining experience in the life of my generation.'

He and his contemporaries were overwhelmed by all the new opportunities, and at the same time shocked by a newly discovered sense of the fragility of everything that was political. 'When you watch on television scenes of elderly locals protesting the settlement of refugees in their depopulated villages where not a single child has been born for decades, your heart breaks for both sides – the refugees, but also the old, lonely people who have seen their worlds melt away. ... The nation, not unlike God, is one of humanity's shields against the idea of mortality.'

5

In Poland, Jarosław Krawczyk had alerted me back in 1999 to a new religious movement centred on the broadcaster Radio Maryja. 'Nationalistic, almost fascist. Poor people's hatred.' Later I drove through the endless landscape of eastern Poland, with its snowy reed beds, birch forests, small villages and the occasional brave plume of smoke from a factory chimney. This was the country he'd been talking about, the land of dirt-poor smallholders and the redundant labourers of the old communist-era farms; the country of Radio Maryja where the population found it impossible to connect with the new Poland.

I noted down some of the things I heard from Radio Maryja on a random morning: prayers, Ave Marias, phone calls from listeners, stories about poverty, illness and misfortune, a priest promising help, a diatribe. (Have you any idea how many Jews there are in the current government?) Another prayer. Everything is sinful, the world is tarnished, only Radio Maryja and the Polish nation can save us.

'Most of us still haven't got over life under communism,' said Croat journalist Slavenka Drakulić in an interview. At that point (2016) the Iron Curtain had been gone for more than a quarter of a century. 'The West is mistaken in thinking that now, democracy and capitalism having replaced communism, we all have the same values and problems. The way people look at the world and the things they believe in change very, very slowly. You can have a new system, but not new people.'

That's certainly true, and it becomes particularly obvious when you look at the practice of democracy and the rule of law. Every democratic system needs to develop in its own way, through crises, through countless compromises, through endless debate. It takes time. I still recall an elderly lady in her vegetable plot, just after the GDR ceased to exist. 'What experiences do we have of democracy? The regime of the emperor, the chaos of Weimar, Hitler, then a lack of freedom in the GDR. We need to reinvent everything from scratch.' It was the same story for the citizens of most Central and Eastern European countries. In the twentieth century, they'd stumbled from one authoritarian regime to the next. The political systems of the new EU

member states were still young, there was little experienc
things were barely in balance. 'Imagine,' said Želimir Žilni
ation we in Serbia have experienced a 180-degree char
those in power three times over. First from communis
nationalism, then from nationalism to the neoliberalism of his successors,
and now back from neoliberalism to nationalism.'

'We don't have any sense of solidarity,' said Slavenka Drakulić. 'Among us
in the East it was destroyed by communism. An individual wasn't supposed
to stick by friends and family or even sympathize with them. You were
expected to identify with the working class, full stop.'

Then there was the relationship between citizen and state. Or rather
between private and public. In all those former communist states it was
completely out of balance. Whereas in the communist years almost everything was in the hands of the state, now the opposite was the case. In a
frenzy of privatization, practically everything that was public came to be
seen as more or less private. It led to enormous confusion and all kinds of
corruption, great and small.

Polish journalist Witold Szabłowski used a wonderful analogy to describe all
this. It told of the fate of the dancing bears with which many Bulgarian
Roma in villages and holiday resorts earned the odd penny. At the instigation
of the EU, the tradition was abolished in 2008 and the keeping of bears was
illegal from then on. Their owners were bought off and an Austrian aid
organization took charge of the bears and housed them in a delightful bear
park, not far from Sofia. No whip, no nose ring, no cruel treatment at all any
longer: for the bears as for everyone else, a new age had dawned. Bit by bit
they would learn to walk about freely, to find food, to hibernate. The park,
Szabłowski wrote, became 'a freedom research project'.

The experiment came up against a major unforeseen problem. The bears
did not hunt for food. They were so used to bread, it was almost impossible
to persuade them to adopt a different diet. They had never hibernated. They
needed to be sterilized, since their offspring would never learn to live in
the wild either. And since freedom was too complicated for a retired dancing bear, he did what he'd always done to please his boss: he got up on his
hind legs and danced.

Szabłowski wrote that when he heard this story he realized that he too, ost-communist Poland, was living in a kind of research lab, taking 'a ever-ending course in what freedom is, how to make use of it, and what sort of price is paid for it. We have had to learn how free people take care of themselves, of their families, of their futures. How they eat, sleep, make love – because under socialism the state was always poking its nose into its citizens' plates, beds and private lives.'

So when life gets difficult, the dancing starts again – in Poland, Serbia, Hungary, all over Eastern and Central Europe.

All those historical experiences in Eastern Europe, so different from those of the West, kept resurfacing in the years after enlargement, here, there and everywhere. Because what did the fall of the Wall really mean? And the removal of the Iron Curtain? And the embrace of the EU and the values that went with it? There, perhaps, lay the greatest misunderstanding of all.

In the West, 1968 was a decisive year, a breakthrough for individual freedoms, women's rights and the protection of minorities. In the former Eastern Bloc, too, it was a year of rebellion, but primarily by nationalist movements standing up against the all-powerful Soviet Empire. The cultural and individualistic revolution of 1968 largely passed Eastern Europe by, hence the later clashes between East and West concerning the rights of women, and of LGBTQ+ people and other minorities.

It happened again, even more starkly, in 1989. Seen from the West, the fall of the Wall was primarily a victory for liberalism, 'the end of history'. For many Europeans in the former Eastern Bloc – especially for the Poles and Hungarians – the collapse of the Soviet Empire was above all a triumph of nationalism, a fresh start for a thousand and one national ambitions. We should not forget that until 1918 many Central European countries were either part of the Austro-Hungarian Empire or under Ottoman rule. Later they were subsumed into the Nazi Third Reich, and after the Second World War they were governed by the Soviets. So they experienced only a decade or so as truly free and sovereign nations. Poland had been endlessly divided and torn apart; in fact, after 1795 it disappeared from the map completely for more than a century, and after 1945 it was again pulled hither and thither. No wonder its nationalist sentiment is brittle and fragile, and cherished like a religion.

This explains why the newcomers insisted on introducing an exit clause into the European treaty. After the Soviet Union they did not want to find themselves caged once again. (In the end it was the British who, fifteen years later, were first to use the emergency exit.) People in the former communist countries believed that the dream of being able to operate as free and sovereign nations had finally become a reality. But this sentiment was overlooked by political and public opinion in the West.

'The West never wanted to listen to what the Poles, the Czechs and the Hungarians were trying to say,' said Jarosław Krawczyk when I visited him again in the spring of 2018. 'But now the Poles, the Czechs and the Hungarians have no say at all. Fukuyama thought history had come to an end in the 1990s, that the mission of Light had defeated the mission of Darkness. No, no, no.'

6

Christmas 2017. More than thirteen years after that major enlargement of the EU, I'm back in the Etterem, the restaurant in the crook of Keleti station in Budapest. In 1999 I spent quite some hours there. Nothing seems to have changed: the big wooden bar, the nineteenth-century chandeliers, the strong smells, the huge Christmas tree in the corner, the elderly waiters with their velvet solemnity, the enormous pillars holding up the roof of this temple to food.

Everything is now at rest. The entire history of Europe's recent decades has washed past here – first the exodus of 1989 when the Iron Curtain began to tear, followed by the victims of the Yugoslav wars, then the tens of thousands of Syrian refugees and other migrants. If anywhere is Europe's revolving door then it's this quiet restaurant, with its stuffed cabbage and meaty pasties.

When György Konrád was telling me about writing under a communist dictatorship, he said, 'The story of my printer, the man who published all that illegal literature, is at least as interesting.' I wanted to ring the man immediately to make an appointment, that very afternoon. Konrád stopped me. 'That might be a little difficult. He's now the mayor of Budapest.'

Gábor Demszky, to everyone's surprise, was elected right after the fall of

the Wall. A dissident from the age of eighteen, he organized student demonstrations in 1968, was thrown out of university and, like many others
accused of illegal activities, was forced to try all the jobs going. For years he
was a taxi driver, before travelling the country as a pollster. 'It wasn't exactly
a career, but I saw and heard a huge amount about Hungary,' he told me.
'The world of the poor villages was one that the communists understood
very well. What matters isn't the reality. What matters is what people think.'
He started printing samizdat, forbidden literature, in print runs of several
hundred. 'They're classics now.'

In the 1980s, Demszky became a leading figure in the resistance to the
communist regime. He was mayor for twenty years, re-elected four times.
In the 1990s, he said, it was mainly a matter of clearing the debris, literally
and figuratively. Next, despite endless obstructionism by the first Orbán
government, came a wave of investment in new buildings, theatres, roads,
metro lines and other infrastructure. After a series of scandals, Orbán was
removed in 2002 and Demszky's Liberal Party came to power again. He says
it made a 'huge mistake' by working throughout with the former communists, who now called themselves socialists.

The turning point came in 2006. At an internal party meeting, the
socialist leader, former prime minister Ferenc Gyurcsány, gave a fiery
speech in favour of more reform and innovation. Gyurcsány was a courageous and passionate man, but at that moment he was rather too candid. 'We
lied in the morning, at noon and at night,' he said. 'There is not much
choice. There is not, because we have fucked it up. Not a little but a lot.' The
speech leaked. It marked the end of the Socialist Party – the voters felt
misled – and the Liberals went down with them. As Demszky put it, 'That
cost us millions of votes; people saw it as a betrayal.'

Viktor Orbán, once just as much of a hippie dissident as Demszky, seized
his chance. Two major shocks – the banking crisis and later the refugee
influx – helped him back into the saddle, this time for good.

The 2008 financial crisis in particular hit many Hungarian families hard.
They'd taken on risky mortgages in euros or Swiss francs, and when the
Hungarian forint lost value they could no longer meet their obligations.
Forced sales and evictions took place all over the country. Orbán blamed the
urban elites and promised to compensate the homeowners affected. In the
2010 election, his party, Fidesz, gained a two-thirds majority in parliament.

'A revolution happened today in the polling booths,' Orbán said. In reality, only 2.7 million of the 8 million voters had turned out, and he had gained a narrow majority of 53 per cent of those who did vote. Yet on that basis he claimed he had been given a mandate by 'the Hungarian people' to turn the Hungarian constitution completely on its head – to his own and his followers' advantage, naturally. He aimed high, with a reform of the voting system, limitations on the power of the high court and a tightening of the government's grip on the media and culture. EU criticism of the new constitution was not aimed at his government, he believed, 'but against the Hungarian people'. He even went a step further: 'It is not the government the European Union has a problem with, much as they want us to believe that ... The truth is they attack Hungary.'

At the same time, he handed out gifts to keep his voters sweet – firewood, new mortgages, citizenship for all ethnic Hungarians living in neighbouring countries – and introduced a successful economic programme. Wages rose by more than 10 per cent and unemployment fell by close to two-thirds. Orbán had revealed himself to be a classic populist: anyone who attacks my government attacks my people; leader and people are one; what binds us together is an external enemy.

A couple of years later, in 2016, he spent billions of forints on a campaign of lies about immigrants. As part of its efforts to share the burden fairly, the EU had asked Hungary to take in 1,294 Syrian asylum seekers, but according to the Orbán government this 'forced placement' meant a dangerous acceptance of terrorists and a 'threat to our culture and traditions'.

The Orbán regime was of course largely financed by that same EU. For years, Hungary was the biggest net recipient of EU funds by head of population; at least half its investments in roads and other infrastructure – plus the bribes that went with them – were paid for by the European Union. Orbán was consequently able to 'buy' the support of his faithful voters, meaning the EU was subsidizing its greatest opponent and saboteur. The solid support of the conservative and Christian democrat grouping in the European Parliament, the European People's Party, enabled this to go on for years. Orbán filled the remaining holes in the budget by raiding the privatized pension funds. Hungarian employees who between them had put around €10 billion aside for their old age saw their money disappear into the state coffers.

Demszky's term as mayor had ended long before then. Three years later I sat next to him at a dinner in Amsterdam. At that point, for security reasons, it was impossible for him to return to Budapest. There had been anti-Semitic threats, and a show trial was underway against his four most prominent members of staff in which it was clear that Demszky was the real target. He was living more or less in exile. It was the first time I'd met an exile from an EU country.

Now I'm spending a day with him once more. The trial ended in acquittal for all those involved – 'Don't forget, the only power in Hungary that is still independent to some degree is the power of the courts' – and Demszky himself is less important now. He is back in Budapest, living alone in a small apartment. He takes me with him to a complex of buildings around an old courtyard. I meet the chair of the special Roma Parliament, which has its office there. In a dilapidated room, as part of an alternative night school, a small economics seminar is being held. There are twelve attendees. 'These were all top people,' Demszky whispers. László Lengyel, once a groundbreaking scientist and commentator, and winner of a Pulitzer Prize, delivers an introduction. 'This is the only place where meetings like this can still be held.'

Around the corner is a hostel for the homeless. There's a queue for breakfast; some of the residents are grimy from poverty. A woman walks around in a tartan hat, her eyes big, her face thin. 'Grotesque-looking figures, as though hauled from the lower depths of world literature,' Joseph Roth once wrote about the homeless of Berlin. 'Faces chiseled by hunger and toughness . . . eyes that look at you with a mixture of fear and confrontation. Women in brown rags, shameless and shy.' Here, almost a century later, the scene is exactly the same.

Demszky does voluntary work now and then, along with a few of his old political associates. The party still gets no more than a few per cent of the vote, but they keep their spirits up. I'm introduced to a former ambassador, a party chairman and a former minister of internal affairs. They work hard, and they're busy sharing out supplies: coffee, bread and a banana for each of those shy faces.

Demszky tells me about the press, which toes the line, the strict censorship of state radio and state television, the independent media bought up by friends of Orbán and sometimes closed down, the huge fines for disseminating news that the authorities decide is 'not balanced', and the critical journalists who have been sacked one by one. In 2015 some 30 news media outlets were regarded as pro-Orbán; the figure in 2018 is more than 500. After the application of pressure and blackmail, and mass 'donation' by the original owners, over 400 newspapers, websites, and radio and television stations are now in the hands of a huge media conglomerate tightly controlled by Orbán loyalists. It's a structure very much like the communist propaganda machine that Demszky, Konrád and indeed Orbán rebelled against.

We walk in through a door and pick our way across a warehouse with a dusty offset press, a sewing machine, an old radio, and piles of books and boxes. Through another door, and there it is, a small printing press quietly thumping away, turning out a newspaper with opposition news for distribution in the villages. Once again, samizdat is being printed here in Hungary.

Later, I walk with an old friend past the time-worn frontages on the boulevards. He tells the same story. 'Even György Konrád doesn't appear anywhere any longer, not on any of the television stations. He's clearly on a blacklist.' My friend is fairly desperate, and depressed. 'I know every street corner here,' he says. 'Yet for the past few years I've seen my city above all as decor. The decor of a cruel and noxious stage play, one from which, for our actors, there is no escape.'

5. Numbers

2004

I

THE YOUNG NIGERIAN SPEAKS. 'YES, Lord!' The others join in, rocking and singing as they pray.

'So many of us died ... Most were shelled and bombed ... We went across the Sahara ... Rapes and murders, many people, and we couldn't stay! We fled to Libya, and Libya belonged to Islamic State ... Many of us were imprisoned, died ... No food in the prison, no water ... We knelt and cried out, "What are we to do?" The mountains couldn't hide us! The people couldn't hide us! And we ran to the sea ... There were ninety passengers on the boat. Only thirty were saved, the rest died ... Oh, but today we're alive ... God, save us.'

The men stand between the beds in a dormitory on Lampedusa. Documentary filmmaker Gianfranco Rosi has recorded everything, images that haunt the conscience of Europe to this day: the mechanical solidarity of the Italian coastguards, who in white protective coveralls spot yet another craft on the sea that's crammed with refugees. Bringing their inflatables alongside, they climb aboard to empty it. First the half-dead, the unconscious and the dehydrated who have laid themselves down on the deck to die, then the hundreds of living, then the dead, dozens of them, lying every which way, suffocated in the hold. The legendary village doctor Pietro Bartolo says he sees it as his humanitarian duty to continue to help. 'But everything makes you so angry. It leaves you with a hole in yourself.' We hear the last of the calls to the coastguard: 'Please can you help us, please.' 'Please, your position, your position.' 'We are sinking, we are sinking.' 'Madam, please, calm down. Your position, please.' 'Help us.'

Between 1999 and 2019 almost twice as many people took off for the unknown as in previous decades – some 65 million worldwide in total, driven by wars, violence, drought, poverty and the hope of a bite to eat. On the bridge in Istanbul, the cigarette boys would sometimes sigh, 'My god, Europe, how we'd love to go there! There's money, you can do whatever you like, people respect one another.' Some had occasionally tried to hide in a container but failed. The police beat them black and blue: 'Why are you leaving our country? Isn't it good enough for you?'

People have always set out in search of a better life. New, since the start of the twenty-first century, were the overpopulated cities, the early impacts of climate change and the available means of communication. After the turn of the century, the effects of better healthcare in Africa were increasingly visible. Population growth became exponential, with the population of the continent passing a billion in 2010 and on course to reach 2.5 billion by 2050. Deforestation and climate change – widespread drought, floods – drove countless small farmers to the already crowded cities. According to a Gallup poll, by 2019 close to one in three African adults wanted to move to a richer country, compared to one in seven in the rest of the world.

Large 'zones of disorder' arose, and the biggest geopolitical movement of the first two decades of this century was made up of millions of people trying to leave those zones for the 'orderly world'. Furthermore, with the arrival of access to the internet, the modern, prosperous world came within reach. The introduction of the iPhone in the summer of 2007, quickly followed by cheaper smartphones, was truly revolutionary. On Facebook, WhatsApp, Twitter and other applications, potential immigrants could keep each other up to date. They could unite and organize, all practically cost-free, from any spot on the globe. Meanwhile those prepared to exploit the desire to seek a better life could effortlessly optimize their business. Human trafficking became a lucrative and popular profession.

A mass trek northwards began, in South America, Africa and the Arab world. Some spoke of a new revolution by the poor, not with demonstrations and street-fighting this time, but simply on foot.

For Europe the influx began in the 1990s, when refugees and immigrants from Albania and Tunisia crossed into Italy. In 1997 the Schengen Agreement took effect, the EU's internal borders were abolished and migration quickly became an industry. For big money, human traffickers from Tunisia or Libya transported their clients in the direction of Lampedusa, an Italian island not far off the Libyan coast. They were often 'saved' or 'detained' halfway by passing ships, or by the Italian navy, which enabled them to complete their journey. From Lampedusa they were transferred to Sicily and given notice to leave Italy within two weeks. They were then free to go. Because of Schengen, migrants could fairly easily travel onwards through Europe and make their own way in life, legally or otherwise. The vast majority did just that. Money and documents were sent on to them by family and friends. Little Lampedusa soon became Europe's entry valve. More than 400,000 refugees and migrants landed on the island in those two decades.

With so many ramshackle boats, disasters were inevitable. On 7 March 2002, a ship carrying around eighty immigrants was caught in a storm a hundred kilometres off Lampedusa and capsized. Only eleven of those on board were saved. In June 2003, two tragedies occurred within a week, one involving a ship that probably had seventy people on board – three were saved – and another carrying some 250, of whom more than 200 drowned. In October that year, the police found a boat holding fifteen emaciated survivors and thirteen dead. They had been adrift at sea for ten days without fuel, food or drinking water. Some seventy passengers, including seven children, had not survived the voyage; most of the corpses had been thrown overboard. The mayor complained there was no way his island could cope with the deluge any longer. Coffins were running short.

On 10 September 2004, a record was broken on Lampedusa. In one day, on three boats, more than 800 immigrants arrived. On one little wooden craft, twenty-five metres long, 478 people sat packed like sardines. On 3 October 2013, a similar boat capsized near the island, leaving 368 dead, mostly from Eritrea. A week later another capsized, again near Lampedusa, and more than 200 people died. A further disaster, in April 2015, close to the Libyan coast, claimed the lives of more than 700. These were merely the most costly disasters. In the part of the Mediterranean close to Lampedusa alone, between 1999 and 2018 around 15,000 men, women and children drowned.

There are no precise numbers. No one knows exactly how many people disappeared without trace in the Mediterranean or the Sahara in those years. Huge efforts were made to identify some of the dead, often based on the most minimal evidence: a soaked identity card, a toothbrush, a comb, a tattoo, a faded photo of a cheery young Eritrean woman. They were recognized by family members and DNA techniques were used to find a match. Despite all these efforts, most of the victims remain nameless.

The mass drowning of the poor off its coasts became so normal in twenty-first-century Europe that it often went unmentioned by the media. Activists tried to compile inventories based on newspaper articles, reports by aid organizations and records held by the coastguard. Starting in 1993, one of them, an organization called UNITED for Intercultural Action, has published an annual 'List of Deaths', and it is by far the most accurate survey of the casualties of mass migration to Europe. The results are shocking. In total, between 1993 and June 2018, 34,361 migrants died. They disappeared en masse in the Sahara, suffocated in shipping containers and lorries, were killed in accidents or met violent deaths, set themselves alight or jumped in front of trains – in around 600 cases there was evidence of suicide. Most people by far drowned at sea: 80 per cent, or some 27,000.

Every line of its final tally represented a tragedy.

- Chandima Endirisinghe and another seventeen migrants from Sri Lanka: suffocated in a sealed trailer in Györ, Hungary.
- Nameless, a woman from Georgia: froze to death in an attempt to cross the border between Bulgaria and Greece in the snow.
- Manuel Bravo (35): knew that his thirteen-year-old son could not be deported alone. He hanged himself at Yarl's Wood removal centre in Bedfordshire on the day before he was due to be sent back to Angola. In his suicide note he wrote, 'I kill myself because I don't have a life to live any more. I want my son Antonio to stay in the UK to continue his studies.'
- Nameless, two migrants from China: killed on their way from Hungary to Austria because they could not pay the smuggler.
- Nameless, two Turkish women, stowaways: fell out of an aeroplane wheel bay in China after hiding in the wrong plane in France.
- Nameless, twelve migrants from Africa: their corpses were found on a tourist beach on the Costa Teguise, Spain.
- Nameless, baby: drowned in the Neisse river as the mother tried to cross the Polish-German border, having bound her baby to her belly.

- Nameless, Iraqi (32), asylum seeker: set himself alight in Diever, the Netherlands, after being caught stealing.
- Nameless, fifteen migrants: drowned when their boat overturned during a rescue attempt near Fuerteventura, Spain.
- Nameless, from Morocco: died after jumping into the water when discovered by Spanish police.
- Nameless, four men from Liberia: drowned after being forced to jump from a Maltese ship near Gran Canaria.
- Christelle M. Nsimba and another nine people, from Zaire, Angola, Lebanon and Togo: died in an arson attack on a refugee hostel in Lübeck, Germany.
- Nameless, 87 migrants and refugees from Albania: drowned when their boat capsized after colliding with an Italian coastguard ship.
- Akim (24), from Togo: jumped out of the window of his house in Bremen, Germany, during a police raid.
- Nameless, stowaway: crushed to death in the back of a truck travelling to Spain.
- Nameless, twelve migrants from sub-Saharan Africa: starved to death on a boat on their way to Gran Canaria.
- John Madu (31), from Nigeria: bled to death in Liège, Belgium, after being denied medical treatment.
- Nameless, 283 migrants and refugees from India, Pakistan and Sri Lanka: drowned after the Greek captain deliberately sank their vessel off Malta.
- Nameless, child, from sub-Saharan Africa: died of hypothermia in a boat with twenty-one other migrants during an attempt to reach Tarifa, Spain.
- Yaguine Koita (14) and Fodé Tounkara (15), stowaways: frozen to death in the undercarriage of a plane flying from Conakry, Guinea, to Brussels.
- Lin Fa Ming and seventeen other migrants from China: suffocated in the sealed trailer of a truck during the crossing from Zeebrugge to Dover.
- Nameless, two men: drowned when they tried to swim to shore; bodies found in Ceuta (Spanish Morocco).

- Nameless (+/- 25), from India: probably a stowaway in a truck, died of heat exhaustion and deprivation; found two weeks after his death at the side of a road in Essex.
- Danielle Dominy (30), from Brazil: suicide by drinking antifreeze; feared being separated from her daughter by immigration officials in Cornwall.
- Nameless, twenty-four migrants, from Maghreb: drowned when the rubber boat in which they were attempting to reach the Canary Islands sprung a leak.
- Nameless, fourteen migrants: their corpses, wearing life jackets and floating in the sea, were spotted by military pilots off Lampedusa.

2

A WhatsApp exchange between a young man in Calais and his uncle in Britain. It's noon on Tuesday, 7 October 2014. 'I can see England,' the boy writes. Perhaps he could find a boat, or swim across. It's a lot further than you think, the uncle tells him. 'You must not try to swim. That wouldn't work. Hide in a lorry.' The boy replies, 'I will try today.' A few hours later he sends a message to his youngest sister and other family members in Jordan: 'I miss you.' It's the last time anyone hears a word from Mouaz al-Balkhi from Damascus, twenty-two years old.

Mouaz was a quiet, friendly boy with roguish curls. He was studying electrical engineering but the regime forced him to flee. He came from a family of dissidents. After a failed attempt to continue his studies in Turkey, he decided to go to Britain. 'They have good refugee legislation,' his sister told him. 'You'll be able to study, and your uncle lives there.'

Nine months later I stood next to Mouaz's unmarked grave, in a peaceful spot between the soughing trees of the public cemetery on the Dutch island of Texel, tucked in safely next to Ate Sijtsma and Anneke Molenaar-Van den Brink and the other islanders. 'The Lord is my shepherd. I shall not want.' A few flowers lay on the sand.

That same Tuesday afternoon, 7 October. A telephone conversation between another Syrian young man, Shadi Omar Kataf (aged twenty-eight), and his

uncle in Leuven: 'It's Shadi. I'm in Calais in France. You have to come pick
up my laptop and backpack. I don't have enough money to use the people
smugglers so I'm going to buy a wetsuit and swim to England.' The uncle
responds by saying, 'Don't be a complete idiot! You can't swim to England.
It's way too far, and there are huge waves.' The uncle says he must come to
his house, and that he can bring his things. Then the phone battery dies.

Shadi was the eldest son of a wedding singer; the name Shadi actually
means 'singer'. He'd been living in Yarmouk Camp, a district of Damascus
that once housed more than 150,000 people but was later so badly shelled
and fought over that barely 20,000 were left. It was described by the *Guardian*
as 'the worst place on earth'. In 2012 he fled to Libya along with his sister,
who soon disappeared, perhaps kidnapped.

Mouaz's unrecognizable body, dressed in a wetsuit, washed ashore on a
cold beach on Texel on 27 October 2014. Shadi's stinking, tattered wetsuit
was found on the Norwegian island of Lista on 2 January 2015. A couple of
blue swim fins were sticking out of it with two white bones inside. Anti-
theft chips sewn into the wetsuits enabled the police to trace them back to
Decathlon, a large sporting goods shop in Calais. The cash registers revealed
that two cheap wetsuits were bought on the evening of 7 October 2014, at
three minutes past eight, along with a waterproof A4-sized folder for keeping valuable documents dry. There was no further trace.

Norwegian journalist Anders Fjellberg eventually managed to reconstruct
the tragedy of the two anonymous refugees. He asked around in Calais, had
DNA samples taken from possible relatives of the two men, and finally succeeded in confirming their identities. From their families he heard the
stories of their flight.

Mouaz turned out to have travelled very quickly. On 17 August 2014 he
flew from Turkey to Algeria. He then spent two days crossing the desert in
the direction of Libya. He said little about that over the phone, except that
it was difficult and dangerous. After ten days he got himself a place on a
refugee boat bound for Italy. He was picked up by the Italian navy, taken to
the safety of the coast and from there travelled north. On 5 September he
arrived in Dunkirk.

In the two weeks that followed he tried to hide in a truck that was going to Britain. He was in regular touch with his obviously concerned family. 'Are you keeping warm? Have you got enough to eat?' He wrote that they shouldn't worry. There were rumours that it was possible to fly from Italy to England. Mouaz travelled to Italy in vain, took the train back to Dunkirk and again tried to hide in a truck, twice over. He couldn't afford to pay any more smugglers, so he was attempting to make the crossing on his own. On the morning of 7 October he set off for Calais.

Shadi had crossed to Italy on 25 August 2014, a trip that took him three days. It's unclear how he travelled from there to Calais. In late September he rang his father: life was hard, he was sleeping on the streets in France, he couldn't pay the smugglers. The family got some money together. It was transferred on 7 October 2014.

Shadi and Mouaz paid at the counter in the Decathlon shop for two flimsy wetsuits – meant only for summer – some swimming things, plus that watertight plastic folder for valuables. They paid €256 altogether, in cash.

3

The Europe of Schengen, that great European achievement of the 1990s, proved ten years later to be a source of despair, anxiety and abuse. At its root it faced the same problem as would trouble the euro. Here too, amid the optimism of the time, things had been done back to front. Instead of first putting in place a robust policy on refugees and immigration and only then removing its internal borders, the EU did precisely the opposite. Most of the internal borders of Europe were thrown open, while control of the external borders was neglected, and nothing resembling a proper common immigration policy was introduced.

The political line taken, especially in northern Europe, largely involved looking the other way. The Dublin Convention, renamed the Dublin Regulation, was still in place, most EU countries having accepted it in the 1990s. It meant that a request for asylum must be dealt with in the country where the applicant first set foot in the EU. That country remained responsible. It was an unbalanced and unfair rule that placed a heavy burden on the southern member states. Greece, Italy and Spain had long external borders that were hard to patrol, and they were being asked to deal with the entire influx of migrants.

Italy and Greece 'solved' this problem by letting most immigrants travel onwards. The Netherlands Court of Audit concluded that 90 per cent of migrants who asked for asylum in the Netherlands had entered Europe through another country, but only half were registered elsewhere. If such a registration existed, that country had to 'take back' the asylum seeker, according to the Dublin system. This turned out to be happening in only one case in six. The rich northern member states remained wilfully oblivious to all the wheeler-dealing. It was a price they were happy to pay to avoid being in the front line themselves.

In 2001, the northern states set up a new barrier. The Carrier Sanctions Directive meant that whoever had provided transport – a shipping company, an airline – was responsible for any passenger travelling without the right papers. After three charter flights full of Eritrean refugees landed unexpectedly at Schiphol Airport in 1997, the Netherlands became one of the strongest advocates of this rule. The hole must be closed right away – at the expense, yet again, of the southern member states. Countless immigrants who had enough money for a ticket were now forced to use people smugglers and flimsy little boats, with predictably catastrophic consequences.

Furthermore, the perverse situation arose that even the most threatened of refugees, guaranteed to be given asylum, first had to endure an expensive and horribly dangerous trek though the desert, then try to stay out of the clutches of dozens of Libyan robber bands, then risk their lives again in an unseaworthy rubber boat before they could be received with open arms in hospitable Europe.

It was not until 2005 that the EU agency Frontex, based in Warsaw, started to coordinate the guarding of the common external border. Frontex was largely a product of politics as theatre. Since all EU member states wanted to retain sovereignty over their own borders, the agency was allowed to operate only under the leadership of the member in question. At crucial moments – when refugee riots broke out on the Greek islands, for instance – Frontex could only stand by and watch. 'No instructions from Brussels.'

Brussels looked away. A fully fledged European border force remained taboo.

*

Meanwhile, Spain and Italy, largely in silence, were seeking answers of their own. Spain initially accepted many migrants through Ceuta and Melilla, its two enclaves in Morocco. There were dramatic scenes in which every day thousands of men stormed the fences around the two settlements. From 2005 onwards, such movements declined, the fences having become taller and more ingenious in design, and the migration route switched to the Canary Islands where, on packed fishing boats, almost 32,000 people arrived in 2006 alone.

Spain then decided on a new approach: joint border controls in combination with economic support. In Las Palmas de Gran Canaria, a coordination centre was set up that directed the search and rescue efforts at local, national and international levels, in close collaboration with Frontex and the Red Cross – along with the customs services, navies, air forces and police forces of Spain, Morocco and the countries of West Africa. The European Union funded these cross-border operations generously, paying out some €300 million by 2014. Morocco and the West African countries were rewarded for their selfless efforts with additional investment and economic aid, and the money filtered down to local holders of power.

Thus the European border moved to Africa. Frontex carried out operations in Morocco, quite often under the pretext of humanitarian aid. In *Illegality, Inc.*, a much-praised study of this border-control industry, journalist and anthropologist Ruben Andersson describes how before very long everything was held at bay. Every fishing boat, sound or not, was designated a 'virtual shipwreck' and a 'risk to life' from which those aboard needed to be 'saved' – and therefore sent back whence they came. He writes that the humanitarian ideal was thereby misappropriated to shift Europe's border away to the south. And it worked. After 2009, the Spanish patrol ships off the coast of West Africa had practically nothing to do.

Italy too moved its borders, in its case mainly into the Libya of tyrant Muammar Gaddafi. In Libya, some 2 million migrants were said to be awaiting their chance to cross the Mediterranean. Gaddafi used them mainly to put pressure on Europe: he wanted money, rehabilitation and a lifting of the economic embargo. Italian premier Silvio Berlusconi entered into a secret deal with the dictator. Ships with Italian-Libyan crews were allowed to patrol the Libyan coast to keep migrants away.

Providing help to migrants was then made a criminal offence for the first time. In the summer of 2004, three members of staff at the aid organization Cap Anamur were arrested in Sicily after saving thirty-seven dying Sudanese refugees on a drifting rubber dinghy.

Migrants could now be 'taken back' by Libya from Lampedusa as well. In October 2004, several hundred were returned without any kind of legal process. In exchange, Italy provided Libya with everything needed for effective border control: radar installations, planes, patrol boats and much more besides. It even paid €5 billion as compensation for Italy's colonial occupation of Libya. The agreements were laid down in a 'treaty of friendship' in 2009. The Sahara became Europe's new border.

Gaddafi remained fickle, however, capable of blackmailing Italy again. Europe drew a new Iron Curtain around itself.

Between the huts and rubbish of Calais, meanwhile, the men sing of their fate:

> I've been warned: don't head for London.
> I'm going anyway, I said. Let go of my collar.
> If I can't pick up the threads of my life here,
> Then I will die a lonely death.
> There's no one who cares about me or wants to care for me
> Darling, I cannot bear the loneliness,
> My whole life was full of care,
> But I never felt lonely before.

Documentary-makers Frans, Sylvia and Ruben Bromet recorded it all. They were treated to an encore:

> You come from the Netherlands and are now in Calais.
> You don't know what is happening to us.
> In that sense we resemble each other.

The men nod and smile.

6. No, Non

2005

I

I WILL NEVER FORGET THE old Luxembourg Square, the way it looked in January 1999. It was a tranquil place, where the nineteenth century and the friendly-looking station of the Leopold quarter still held sway, but behind them a tsunami of glass and aluminium was rising. The new European Parliament building was almost finished; the concrete mixers were taking their final turns. The glass wave would then roll on, everyone knew it would, and overwhelm all the things they were fond of, from the quirky baguettes and unpasteurized cheeses to the affable one-toothed woman who ran the confectionery stall at the station.

That has since happened.

On the lawn in the centre of the square, at the foot of the statue of quarrying magnate Jean Cockerill, EU interns meet up with cans of beer from the local supermarket. Those a little above them in the pecking order – young journalists and up-and-coming Eurocrats – cultivate their networks on the café terraces that now set the square abuzz. But the real work goes on in the restaurants and bars around two great European palaces: the Berlaymont building that houses the European Commission, the EU's governing body; and the Europa building occupied by the European Council of heads of state or government.

Brussels is a bubble, or more accurately an endless assortment of bubbles, all rubbing up against each other. It's still a tormented city – in fact, in that sense it has only got worse over the past twenty years. A hundred paces beyond the gleaming Brussels-South station and the sparkling new Pullman otel, you find yourself walking along dilapidated streets, past abandoned building sites, past alleyways devoted to drug dealing and haggling, past an impending knife fight. The terrorists who carried out the most devastating jihadist attacks in Paris and Brussels came from Molenbeek, still to some extent a traditional working-class neighbourhood in 1999, now a North African urban district. Knowledge of Dutch has halved over the past two decades.

Brussels is one of the richest metropolitan regions in Europe, with a big labour market for highly educated professionals. Nevertheless, rates of poverty and long-term unemployment here are shocking. It's a typical expat city; of its 1.2 million residents, 65 per cent were not born in Brussels. Over the past twenty years, 1.1 million people have left and 1.2 million have moved in, an astonishing rate of turnover. Its flexibility and relativity are visible everywhere. High finance and Europe's big grazers continue to eat away at the urban fabric, taking great bites out of the glorious past of the city year after year. Yet it continues to embrace all comers. 'Brussels fed me, deflowered me, was the primeval mother,' said my old friend Pierre Platteau as we wandered its streets in 1999, and the city, miraculously, has retained its almost physical personality.

In competition with Strasbourg and Luxembourg, Brussels has slowly managed to work its way up to the position of unofficial capital of Europe. 'Capital' would not be entirely accurate, which is part of the tragedy. The presence of the EU and various other international institutions means that Brussels has never been seen as a city. Instead, it's a 'function' – I'm quoting city historian Sophie De Schaepdrijver now – an administrative centre for 'the province', the homeland that 'the commuter needed to return to as quickly as possible when work was done'. Twenty years later, the Brussels 'province' stretches out all across Europe.

Some 50,000 civil servants work for the EU, led until recently by the brilliant German careerist Martin Selmayr as secretary-general of the European Commission. Behind the scenes he was regarded as the most powerful man in this European inner world, the Rasputin of the Berlaymont. 'What's the difference between Martin Selmayr and God?' goes the joke in Brussels. 'God doesn't think he's Martin Selmayr.'

All those civil servants bring their partners and families with them. The number of 'Bruxpats' from EU countries has been estimated at 100,000, and there are some 20,000 more from countries outside the EU. The city is home to almost 600 permanent representatives of cities, regions and countries, more than 5,000 diplomats and some 150 international law firms. Flocking to feed on them are between 20,000 and 30,000 lobbyists and about 1,500 journalists.

All these life forms now caper and gambol about on Luxembourg Square, or the Place du Luxembourg to give it its French name, often shortened to Plux. It's a beautiful spring day in 2019 and I'm sitting looking about me, along with two veterans: Bart Beirlant, who has been reporting on this world for years for Belgian newspaper *De Standaard*; and Vincent Stuer, adviser and speechwriter to members of the European Commission. Most of the suits walking by are stiff, the women's especially expensive and stylish, their jewellery and other finery an extravagant presence. The medium of communication – twenty years ago French for at least half of them – has since the enlargement of 2004 been English almost exclusively. There's a kind of reversed 'upstairs-downstairs' here: French is used only to address the canteen staff.

'Look, there's a prominent German member of parliament, with a camera crew around him, he must have news.' 'Ah, interesting, a Dutch liberal, a fairly important one. Who's he talking to?' Every species on this square can be recognized by the badges dangling from necks. 'Those three young women are interns, you can tell by the colour of their badges. That journalist there – he has the highest status; that's the colour of permanent accreditation.' The man is lugging a fat briefcase, his jacket askew, and he walks with a slight stoop as if carrying half the EU on his shoulders.

The inner world of all these European councils and institutions is fascinating, yet until recently it was a game mainly of interest to enthusiasts and insiders. The eternal problem for those who wrote about it was summed up in the word 'sexy'. Brussels politics, despite all the flirting, was simply not sexy. There were great dramas with massive ramifications, especially in times of crisis, but in contrast to national politics, the political theatre here never got off the ground. The parliamentarians and the real holders of power – the leaders of national governments – rarely looked each other in the eye. There were too many institutions and too few human faces. Only very slowly does that seem to be changing.

2

In 2017, Robert Menasse published an exuberant caricature of life around Luxembourg Square called *The Capital*. It's a novel loosely modelled on *The Man Without Qualities*, that classic parody written in the 1930s by another Viennese author, Robert Musil, about his own city's dying days as the Habsburg seat of power. Musil's imaginary nation is called Kakania, 'that state since vanished that no one understood, in many ways an exemplary state, though unappreciated'. In Kakania everything is political theatre. 'In this country one acted – sometimes to the highest degree of passion and its consequences – differently from the way one thought, or one thought differently from the way one acted.' Nobody ever gets anything done. The fundamental maxim of this 'incredibly clever state' holds good, however: 'muddling through'.

Menasse's Brussels, just short of a century later, likewise teems with incompetent dandies and power-hungry fools. There are 'Salamanders' in sleek suits and ties, not Europeans but careerists within European institutions. There are minor wars between the executive boards of AGRI, TRADE and GROW, with countless inter-service meetings and PowerPoint presentations. A promotion-craving woman is deeply disappointed to be assigned to 'Directorate C, "Communication"' of the 'EAC-C-2 department: "Cultural Programme and Measures"'. It is known as an 'alibi ministry', she says, low down in the ranking. At all those lunches and meetings a continual battle is fought for power and prestige: a microcosm, a world in a drop of water.

The Capital is hilarious, yet it was the result of a research project. Menasse had observed the European centre of power at length, he had looked until he could look no more, for a full five years, and he had talked to EU civil servants of all stripes. 'I wanted to understand how they think, how they live, how is their daily life, why they are failing and so on,' he said afterwards, describing the Union as a 'slowly happening revolutionary project'. He moulded the civil servants into caricatures in his novel, but at the same time he revealed that many of the clichés are wrong. He had found that, at the top especially, people worked hard and with conviction; they were expertly trained and extremely competent.

'I encountered one surprise after another,' Menasse wrote in *Enraged Citizens*, an earlier book, referring to the openness of the European Commission, the limited size of the Brussels bureaucracy – smaller than that of the city of Vienna – and its frugality: the offices are functional; no state bureaucracy was ever this cheap. (For the sake of comparison, of total annual government expenditure in the rich Netherlands in 2017, amounting to €264.9 billion, €3.4 billion all told went to the EU, or 1.3 per cent, or €199 per citizen. Of that, €2.4 billion was returned in the form of all kinds of subsidies.) Then there was the pleasure officials took in their work, 'as if there had been a secret agreement to debunk all of the clichés and fantasies about the Eurocrats and invert them in reality'.

'So which is it really?' I asked Menasse at a meal we shared in Vienna. 'Is it Musil's Kakania all over again? Or is it the cheerful, open capital of *Enraged Citizens*?' He said nothing for a moment, clearly troubled by the conflict of loyalty that many observers feel regarding the European project, but then said, 'I wrote *Enraged Citizens* to show how it ought to be. *The Capital* is what it actually is.'

I feel the same internal conflict. In Brussels many of my prejudices melt away. Almost everyone working here feels an emotional involvement with the European project. Vincent Stuer, for years an insider, says to me, 'You don't find many vegetarians working in butcher's shops, either.' All the same, too often I have the feeling that people working for the EU are spending their lives in an artificial reality, a computer game, a dream world that produces the illusion that everything is permanently under control and everything that doesn't fit into certain frameworks simply doesn't exist. Time and again I see European leaders defending this little Brussels world to the hilt, while the rest of Europe tells a very different story.

In that respect too, Brussels is a bubble. The entry requirements are strict and participants work till they drop. They see each other regularly, their children attend the same schools and they often spend time together at weekends.

The central bubble is around the European Commission – everyone agrees about that. 'It's where the true believers are,' says Bart Beirlant. 'If you criticize EU policy it causes them almost physical pain.' It's a bubble reminiscent of a religious sect, complete with its own scripture called the

Treaty on European Union. 'Just as a preacher or vicar can point to Matthew such-and-such verse so-and-so, they refer to Treaty article such-and-such. For them, everything revolves around the regulations.' 'We are the keepers of the Treaty,' says Vincent Stuer. 'That feeling is indeed very strong within the Commission.' 'If you call them bureaucrats they're shocked,' Beirlant tells me. 'No! They're civil servants.' Being so often right, they tend to be unusually arrogant, but, Beirlant admits, also open. Everyone is very approachable. I hear that time and again. The Commission, in defiance of all preconceptions, is strikingly transparent.

By contrast, the bubble around the European Council of government leaders is not transparent at all. It's all about power there, and endless compromises. People are more cynical, and they tend to look with some suspicion at the 'idealists' of the European Commission. The European Parliament forms its own bubble, if only because of its buildings, which are worlds of their own, with kiosks, bars, restaurants, even a hairdressing salon. You could spend your whole life in there. 'It's as if the parliamentarians offer a complete cocoon,' is how Beirlant puts it. It's therefore inevitable that relationships develop, often across party lines. Stuer compares it with institutions like the Concertgebouw Orchestra. 'When you travel together a lot, and you're working on the same things, then naturally attachments may sometimes develop.'

Since everyone is far from hearth and home, normal social control is lacking. Marietje Schaake, one of the most important of European parliamentarians between 2014 and 2019, spoke in a farewell interview about the sexism and abuse of power that remain ubiquitous: about members who wanted to meet her in a hotel room late at night, about a male colleague who reprimanded her for not wearing high heels, about the times she was thrown out of meeting rooms because she was assumed to be 'only' an assistant. A dedicated website for the European Parliament, called MeTooEP, has reports of lewd comments, but also of careers cut short, indecent assaults and even rape. The exuberant female interns and assistants attached to the Eastern European parliamentarians are known as 'the modelling agency'.

Last but not least, there's the journalistic bubble. Every morning, the vast EU machinery starts churning out points of view, about anything and everything, known as 'Lines To Take' or LTTs. They are read out at the daily twelve o'clock briefing by the various spokespersons, who must not deviate from them; and the hundreds of journalists present might just occasionally hear something interesting, but only as an aside. Nevertheless, journalists do well to make their presence felt at those briefings, with intelligent questions and astute comments, because that's the way to get noticed. They'll gradually receive more invitations to background discussions, and if they're really lucky they might, until recently that is, gain access to the pinnacle of EU journalism, lunches with Cardinal Selmayr himself, on the 13th floor of the Berlaymont building. The few permitted to call him 'Martin' know they are close to the gates of paradise.

Within that journalistic bubble there was in the past a great degree of institutional loyalty. For many years a critical attitude, the proper starting point for reporting of any kind, was regarded as slightly inappropriate in Brussels: the EU must at all costs be explained and defended. That deference to authority has gone, killed off in the wake of the chaos surrounding the euro crisis and the refugee crisis, but even now most journalists group up with compatriots, sitting at the same table, often concentrating only on briefings by their own government leaders and spokespeople. Reporting therefore inevitably remains national in its orientation, although that too is at last starting to change.

This bubble is small, like all the others, a world in which everyone continually runs into everyone else. Those who write sensible things about the EU at a theoretical level can be confident that after a while invitations will start to arrive: to keynote speeches, symposia, discussion panels and other worthy chin-tickling. But I hardly ever see on the lists of participants the names of those of my journalistic colleagues who have reported on the business of Europe systematically 'from below' – from the refugee camps, the farms and the banks.

The Brussels bubbles are not inquisitive; in fact, they often want to know nothing more than what is absolutely necessary to allow them to continue to exist as bubbles. A friend of mine who did a lot of research in Greece into the practical aspects of European immigration policy was reproached from all sides for missing too many meetings in Brussels and told that her reporting – she merely wrote of the misery she had seen with her own eyes – was 'consistently negative'.

'We work here as embedded journalists,' another friend once said to me, referring to those who, under strict conditions, are allowed to travel with the armed forces. Only in the last few years has the EU begun to show a degree of democratic maturity in that respect.

A few streets from Luxembourg Square is Schuman Square, the true power centre of the EU. On one side is the surly old Justus Lipsius building that once housed the European Council – replaced in late 2017 by the spanking new Europa building – and on the opposite side is the overwhelming Berlaymont building of the European Commission: two daunting, inward-facing – and at the same time anxious – compromise structures. This is not the place to see thrilling architecture.

The area is ringed by embassies in nearby streets and, again, a series of relatively modest cafés and restaurants where sandwiches and takeaways are fetched for the late-night workers and where everyone sees everyone else from early morning to deep in the night: the Berlaymont Café, Il Viticolo, Exki for the staff of the foreign service, The Old Hack – the Brexit pub frequented by Nigel Farage – and the Maxburg, loved by all Germans. Then there is of course the famous restaurant Chez Nardi, and La Rosticceria Fiorentina, where traditionally, over pasta, deals are cooked up – all the way to Brexit.

The few experiences I've had here confirm the conclusions reached by Menasse. I've come upon the crème de la crème of diplomacy – intelligent and highly competent men and women, impeccably educated, at home speaking four or five languages. The many small rooms add up to a pressure cooker of talent and hard work. The same goes for the European Parliament, where you can find a wealth of uncommonly capable and dedicated representatives of the people. Beneath it all, however, is a layer of mediocrity, replete with the small-mindedness of Kakania.

I recall a meeting in about 2013, before the great storms began. José Manuel Barroso, then president of the European Commission, wanted to launch a project called the New Narrative for Europe. Writers, artists and scientists were to create a 'new story', in any number of ways, and with it a new European identity, alongside major debates in the national capitals, citizens' dialogues, a book and a website, because young Europeans must 'have their say' too.

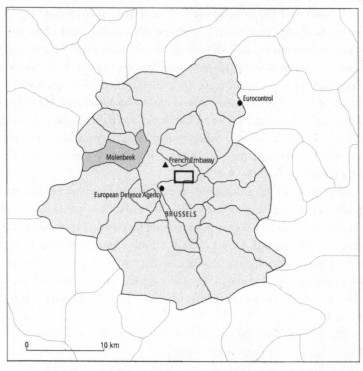

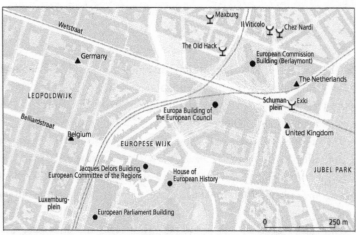

Brussels and the European 'bubble'

- ● European Parliament buildings
- ▲ Permanent representatives to the European Union (country name)
- ⅄ Pubs etc.

ndful of European 'storytellers' and 'purveyors of culture' were
to the Berlaymont for the purpose. What did we think of the idea?
The president had set aside an hour and twenty minutes. We waited a long time for him to turn up. His entourage was copious; at any moment a Byzantine potentate might make his entrance. Then we were allowed to have our say – in as far as the haziness of the concept allowed. There must have been about twenty-five of us. The French and Italian authors, as usual, piled in straight away with elaborate disquisitions; Björn Ulvaeus of pop group ABBA started talking about copyright; György Konrád said a few sensible things about the past.

Next to me sat Rosie Goldsmith of the BBC, and together we started to prick at all those European soap bubbles. We asked a few questions and got no further. It was time for the potentate and his courtiers to depart. In any case, the meeting was not intended as a forum for critical remarks; this was, we soon realized, above all a PR exercise, not just for the president and his entourage but for many of the others present. I had an image of Good Intentions being passed around the table like slices of cake. Everyone had stopped listening.

The 'Austrian Year', the 'Big Jubilee Project' and the 'New Narrative for Europe' all died the same quiet death.

chapter about Bits not fitting into Brussels life.

3

Dutch philosopher and historian Luuk van Middelaar once drew an enlightening distinction between the three Europes we were dealing with at the start of the twenty-first century: the Europe of States, the Europe of Citizens and the Europe of Offices.

The Europe of Citizens was above all a legal construct. The European citizen, after all, had yet to be created, the European Parliament was in need of further development, and the dreamed-of European coffee house, where an ongoing public debate would take place, was only slowly getting off the ground.

The Europe of States was the world of historians and diplomats, who think in terms of international relations. There was a dark past, and out of it stepped a hero: the state or the EU. Its motto was collaboration, its institution the European Council. Maltese premier Joseph Muscat once gave *Politico* a glimpse into those inner rooms. The meetings of the Council sometimes seemed so tedious and slow that European leaders laid their heads on the table and slept. Equally, on certain issues they almost came to blows. Rather remarkably, the debates were hardly ever a matter of 'right' against 'left', and even less were there 'parties' of leaders from the same political blood group. 'I wouldn't say it's always about national interest,' Muscat said. 'I've seen some genuine cases where decisions were taken in the European interest – and there were some prime ministers, some presidents who said quite clearly "this is not popular back at home", but they would do it because it's what needs to be done.'

The Europe of Offices was the domain of the administrators, civil servants and economists. Here everything was quantifiable and always moved the same way, namely in the right direction. An astonishing amount had happened since the establishment of the European Coal and Steel Community in 1952, which marked the start of European unification. Borders had been abolished, a thousand and one legal barriers removed, billions invested in the modernization of the member states, roads and railways laid, education systems made compatible, multinationals restrained and basic rights enforced – and permanent peace seemed guaranteed. For the younger generations all this seemed so natural by 2019 that no one any longer stopped to think about it, yet it was a unique political and diplomatic achievement.

Ironically it was Brexit that demonstrated how far that interweaving of nations had gone. All the fibres, threads, nerves and arteries connecting the EU with a member state, in this case Britain, were unsparingly exposed by the breach. In the autumn of 2018, *The Economist* presented a summary of all the things that would change for the British now that they were about to step out of the EU. It went on for several pages: air transport agreements, import arrangements covering gas and electricity, the right to reside in other EU countries, the financial buffer system between the banks, the delivery of pharmaceuticals, exchange programmes for young people and students, mutual recognition of qualifications, social rights, patents, access to cheap mobile phone networks, subsidies for farmers, fishing rights, legal protections for workers and other employees . . . It was endless.

Customs controls – young Brits and other young Europeans had never experienced that crippling bureaucratic rigmarole – would return, with devastating consequences. From the port of Dover alone, tens of thousands of lorries entered the UK unhindered daily in 2018, transporting € 133 billion worth of goods each year, 17 per cent of Britain's trade. Entry was quick and easy, without any customs hold-ups, and it needed to be. A typical British car like the Mini (owned by Germany's BMW, incidentally) was held together by parts most of which were made elsewhere in Europe, some four or five thousand of them. Conversely, around 60 per cent of car parts made in British factories were for export, as were eight out of ten British-made cars. To keep the Mini factory in Oxford going, parts had to be brought in via Dover according to a strict schedule, in some 200 lorries daily. One hitch and the entire production process, turning out a thousand Minis a day, would grind to a halt. And that was just one pan-European production chain out of many thousands. The often practically invisible Europe of Offices made it all run smoothly.

There was a downside, however, to the glorious project of Jean Monnet and friends. After more than half a century, the Europe of Offices had in many respects grown to become an amorphous technocracy. Everything was calculated and negotiated down to the finest details, from the composition of goat's cheese in France to the maximum length of a window cleaner's ladder in Amsterdam. The Europe of Offices had become a kind of upside-down federation. Brussels was weak at the things the centre of a normal federation is good at – fiscal policy, foreign policy, security, defence – whereas it was often all-decisive in matters that a normal federation leaves to its member states, such as ladders and goat's cheese.

It was, moreover, a bureaucracy with a tendency to keep enlarging its field of activity. After all, in the ever-expanding European project there were no clear boundaries or brakes. Jean-Claude Juncker, who spent five years as president of the European Commission, once described as one of his greatest achievements the fact that, 'taking my life in my hands', he had prevented the commission from standardizing toilet cisterns. At the same time it was a bureaucracy that at crucial moments failed to enforce its rules and agreements. The budgetary rules within the eurozone and the Dublin Regulation on immigrants, for instance, were consistently and systematically evaded.

In truth, many of those monstrous European regulations were not the product of Brussels but of the conflicting interests of member states, there being no other way of reaching a compromise. When German and French carmakers got into a fierce row about the standard colour of a headlight, yellow or white (yes, this actually happened), Brussels needed to come up with something.

The most famous case concerns the seat of the European Parliament, located in Brussels and, to keep the French happy, in Strasbourg. Twelve times a year a mammoth ritual takes place as parliamentarians, civil servants and documents are transferred from one to the other. Every month a special train is chartered for the purpose. The cost of this removals circus is more than € 10 million each time, quite apart from all the stress and discomfort for those concerned. It is passively accepted. The EU, in the words of Tony Judt, remains 'a compromise on a continental scale, designed by literally hundreds of committees'.

Be that as it may, the regulations remain a source of irritation and they undermine the authority of the EU. Citizens will not respect a person in authority who announces rules that defy common sense, over which they can no longer exert any influence. A clash between the Europe of Offices and the Europe of Citizens was inevitable.

The first major collision took place in the spring of 2005. The constitutional structure of the EU was neither strong nor clear, and nor was the Union particularly democratic. All member states agreed about that. The problem would inevitably become acute after the enlargement of the Union by no fewer than ten new member states, almost a doubling of their number. So in 2002 the Convention on the Future of Europe had been assembled, a large gathering of representatives of governments and parliaments that, after much deliberation, came up with the draft of a European constitution. The European Parliament in particular was to be given many more powers, and together with the European Council it would become the EU's legislative body, able to approve the European budget. Henceforth, members of the European Commission and the president of the European Council would be elected by the European Parliament. It would not make Europe a true federation, but these were obviously steps in that direction.

In Spain, Luxembourg, France and the Netherlands, referendums were held. In Spain and Portugal the outcome was positive, although turnout was poor, at around 40 per cent. Completely unexpectedly, however, the citizens of France and the Netherlands, the most faithful of EU members, voted against. They were not prepared to transfer yet more sovereignty to far-off Brussels. On 29 May 2005, the French rejected the new constitution by 55 per cent to 45 per cent, with a turnout of 69 per cent. Three days later the Dutch result was even clearer: 61 per cent against, 39 per cent in favour. It was the end of the whole convention and constitution project. A British referendum was cancelled, since after such results the outcome was beyond doubt. In Germany, according to the polls, something similar would have happened.

That chorus of 'no', in the core region of Europe, was a moment of truth. It was the first open mass protest against the slowly expanding Europe of Offices. The European structure's democratic deficit became bitterly palpable.

What were the immediate causes? The French, as it turned out, weren't so much against a constitution as such, it was just that they wanted a different constitution, with fewer economic freedoms for the EU. The opposition, strongly pro-European, campaigned for a 'no' vote on that basis, but its main motivation was to give the conservative government a slap in the face.

The Dutch result was predictable. Ever since separating from Belgium in 1830, the Netherlands has had a tendency to shut itself off mentally from events on the European continent, however close its relations with other European countries are in reality. Successive Dutch governments had re-inforced that tendency, impressing upon voters over many years that the EU was a necessary evil that, more than anything else, cost money. The official referendum campaign by the Balkenende government was fought under the less-than-compelling slogan 'Europe. Rather important'. The information put out consisted mainly of the proposed constitution itself, an unreadable wad of newsprint that was thrust through letterboxes all over the country. To be honest, after such a campaign it would have been a mira-cle if a majority of the Dutch had voted 'yes'.

In both countries, as polls by Eurobarometer showed, the rapid enlarge-ment of the EU had made many voters uneasy. They had the feeling they were sitting on a train that was thundering ahead long after the driver had jumped out of the cab.

*

Sure enough, the European leaders strode calmly on, in precisely the direction their voters had rejected. As Jean-Claude Juncker had said before the French referendum, in a sudden outburst of honesty, 'If it's yes, we will say, let's proceed, and if it's no, we will say, let's continue.' In great haste, under the leadership of the recently elected German chancellor Angela Merkel, the rejected constitution was transformed into a treaty. Treaties are agreed in the name of the member states, so European citizens no longer had any direct say. The notion of an unimpeded democratic continuum from the base to the summit of Europe was abandoned.

The result was the Treaty of Lisbon, signed on 13 December 2007. It welded together many of the separate components of European integration. There was to be a high representative for foreign affairs – a minister of sorts – and the Union would speak with one voice on foreign policy rather more than it had before. The European Parliament increased its influence and the European Council was given a new status, with a permanent chair, an 'EU President'.

The rejected draft constitution had been presented in the public arena of the Capitoline Hill in Rome. The presentation of the Lisbon treaty took place in the privacy of the nearby Jerónimos Monastery. That said a great deal. The Europe of Citizens grumbled. The Europe of Offices was content, since if the EU as an organization was to continue functioning, adjustments like this were unavoidable.

The 'no' of 2005 was a historic hiatus. The coming together of all those different European nations, each with its own history, with its own wounds and its own expectations, had been possible in the past only because countries were prepared to embark on a journey together. They moved step by step. Every major European treaty, from the 1950s onwards, contained the seeds of the next treaty. All those steps were in a forward direction, inevitably, because returning back down that long path might have tragic consequences.

The Treaty of Lisbon, however, contained few if any seeds of further development. The treaty as a whole gave the impression of a final destination, for the time being at least. The European Union remained in theory an intergovernmental organization, and it was the job of the representatives of the national governments to continue shaping the EU, in an endless process of negotiation. The treaty did not as yet create the conditions for a decisive European federation. The European project was left hanging between two constitutional structures, hazy, nebulous, and eternally complicated. The travellers had lost their way.

4

In 2069 my clever history student will ask: what was the mood of the ordinary European citizen at this point? Well, there were still ideals, certainly. Three years later, in 2008, a referendum took place in Ireland on the Treaty of Lisbon. Extensive research was done into the motives of voters. It turned out that 'yes' voters had voted primarily in favour of 'the idea of Europe'. Less than 20 per cent of them were able to say anything meaningful about the proposed treaty itself. As for the European Union, most Irish pro-Europeans had the 'feeling' that the EU was 'good for Ireland', but again only a few knew what sorts of things went on in Brussels. I suspect the results would not have been very different in, for example, Germany or the Benelux countries, then or now.

The European project was still reasonably popular in those years. According to Eurobarometer, in 2000 only 14 per cent of EU citizens were opposed to their country's EU membership. Yet enthusiasm was clearly waning, even then. One indication was the turnout for elections to the European Parliament, which fell from 62 per cent in 1979 to 45 per cent in 2004. The proportion of people firmly in favour of the EU fell too, from 72 per cent in 1991 to 49 per cent in 2000. Comfortable majorities had been transformed into uncomfortable minorities.

There was something unjust about this, as if all the achievements of the EU – peace, open borders, multiple forms of legal and social security, a power bloc with more than 500 million inhabitants – were as natural as getting water from a tap. Close cooperation within the EU set an example to the rest of the world: this was how to tackle crucial shared concerns, climate change foremost among them. The EU also provided a solid framework for smoothly resolving the countless frictions and conflicts between European countries, which in earlier years had produced immense tensions. The Union could hold its own in a world increasingly governed by the almost inviolable power of international corporations, the financial sector, high-tech companies and, not least, the big criminal networks.

In the years that followed, several major monopolies were brought to heel. The EU led the way in taking on the powerful tech giants that had emerged in the first decade of the century: Alphabet, Amazon, Apple, Facebook, Google and Microsoft. They were fined billions of euros for stifling competition, restricted by new digital copyrights, and confronted with advanced forms of privacy protection. Since a quarter of the turnover of five of the six giants related to activities in Europe, such measures had real effect. EU standards were often copied elsewhere in the world. The basic rules for data protection – you are in charge of all the data held on you and have the right to examine it, add to it, and decide who is allowed to use it – are largely attributable to the EU.

This steadily growing interconnectedness was itself a source of tension, however. On the one hand the EU was increasingly becoming a single economic system, a world power in the making with a dynamic financial sector and extensive exchange in all fields – not least at a human level. On the other hand, after 2005 political integration more or less stopped or was even reversed. The result was a fundamental internal contradiction, a constitutional design fault that created bigger and bigger problems as the years went on.

Not long after the 'no' of 2005, in the spring of 2007, three conferences were organized in the grand rooms of the Noordeinde Palace in The Hague, under the auspices of Queen Beatrix of the Netherlands. What exactly was Europe? Why was Europe different from the rest of the world? As for the EU, was it still a peace project? Or was it increasingly a political project, a glorified trade project?

I was one of the organizers and these were the questions that occupied our minds. We were able to invite the best thinkers in Europe, and thanks to the magic of palace and monarchy, they came. The discussions were uncommonly interesting, and at the same time those meetings, I realize now, were a telling snapshot of the time.

I sat at a table with top British diplomat Robert Cooper, for instance, who as the Council of the European Union's director-general for external and politico-military affairs was right at the centre of the Brussels bubble, a genuine old hand. He was not unduly concerned. 'All kinds of things are wrong, some organizations function terribly badly, but the Union is only fifty years old, it has developed at the speed of an express train and it urgently needs to change and go on changing.'

He was unreceptive to complaints about relinquishing national sovereignty, saying that the Union was ultimately led by the nation states. That was exactly what made it all so complicated, he argued, and above all desperately tedious. 'In earlier times, history was written on the battlefield, which is where we got our monuments and flags. Nowadays history is written at three in the morning when everyone is tired and starting to get bored and the meeting room is in a complete mess and they're yet again inching towards a worthless compromise that's sure to bring them grief when they get home, because you can't achieve a compromise without going beyond your remit.'

Polish historian Krzysztof Pomian blamed the European identity – or rather the lack of one. Europeans think in terms of difference, of a multitude of languages, cultural areas and religions. We are self-evidently Poles or Dutch people, he claimed. 'But there is nothing self-evident about being a European.'

American-German philosopher Larry Siedentop, author of several standard works about Europe, took up the point, saying that in recent years the European project, with all its adjustments large and small, had gradually been transformed. 'Ordinary people are beginning to feel, to realize, that European integration influences not just their interests but their identity.' He predicted that all across Europe a nationalist backlash would arise – and that Britain in particular would be receptive to it.

Bronisław Geremek, survivor of the Warsaw ghetto, who with his bright blue eyes dominated the table, was worried. The abrupt rejection of the constitution was not just a crisis of legitimacy, it meant the end of the natural forward movement of the European process as a peace project, the ideal to which he had devoted his life. The 'no' was in his view a symptom of a far broader crisis of confidence. How it was dealt with would, he believed, determine the future of Europe and the Union.

A year later Geremek was dead, killed in a car crash.

5

Europe's old maladies surfaced again in all their severity in the early years of the twenty-first century. Dutch writer Nelleke Noordervliet once compared the feelings of the average citizen towards Europe and its Union to the mood of the hero of Stendhal's novel *The Charterhouse of Parma*, the young Milanese idealist Fabrizio del Dongo, who crawls around in the mud after the defeat at Waterloo with no idea what is happening to him. Where is he to fight for his emperor? Where is the battlefront? That strange whistling sound above his head, what on earth is that? And should he set out with that little group of irregulars or with that other one? Our hero desperately searches the battlefield for the fulfilment of his ideals, but he no longer has anything like a comprehensive picture.

Historically, European integration, in the words of Danish political scientist Sara Hobolt, was 'a project spurred on by the elite, supported by a "charitable consensus" among European citizens'. When the most prominent figures in national political and business life decided to collaborate more closely in certain fields, the rest of the population initially went along without too much complaint. There was no need for real involvement, a few exceptions aside. Most Europeans, like Stendhal's hero of Waterloo, barely noticed what was going on. At the same time there was a strategy of fait accompli, in which each major step towards further integration meant there was no going back. This applied even to membership of the EU. As we have seen, for many years it was impossible to leave, since there was no exit clause.

In the 1990s, the consensus began to break down. European integration became a point of contention, at what was actually a very late stage. It was not just a matter of all the economic and political differences but of the image of the EU itself. As the project grew, the expectations of the member states diverged. Countries like Finland and the Netherlands saw trading advantages, Germany wanted above all to live in peace with its many neighbours, France dreamed of a great European ideal, Spain and Italy wanted to modernize, Poland saw the EU as a shield against the Russians, while Hungary, Bulgaria and Romania mainly hankered after the fleshpots of Brussels. Each nation had its own priorities and its own sensitivities.

Luuk van Middelaar, who from 2010 to 2015 worked for the president of the European Council, Herman Van Rompuy, described afterwards how difficult it had been for a speechwriter to tell a common European story and how 'this one "Europe" from Dublin to Sofia and from Madrid to Helsinki forms a continually changing projection screen for national desires and fears'.

The result of all that integration, in short, was not a union but an unfathomable network of nation states. As Robert Cooper once wrote, 'The European Union is a highly developed system for mutual interference in each other's domestic affairs, right down to beer and sausages.' That remarkable system had grown to become a huge economic power, but it was a power that could make decisions only with great difficulty and could resolve its internal contradictions only through endless debate between its members.

After his time in Brussels, Luuk van Middelaar rightly concluded that the EU had been for decades a system of 'rules politics', of norms and compromises to keep all those different powers in balance. But, he said in a speech, 'this European rule-making factory is not set up to deal with misfortune, danger, or unexpected events, in short, with crisis situations'. Such moments – and any major power will inevitably be confronted with them from time to time – require 'events politics', enabling decisions to be made quickly. In an unexpected situation, such as a euro crisis, an invasion of Crimea or a sudden influx of immigrants, what central body is to take the initiative? Who has the authority to step forward and act?

Van Middelaar described a masterclass he gave in 2015 to mid-career Brussels officials. Since the 1980s Europe had found itself in a new, demanding world, and it seemed obvious to him that the European Union needed to respond accordingly. But through Brussels spectacles, apparently, this was hard to see. At least half the participants made light of the difference between patiently tinkering around with rules and reacting rapidly to problems on Europe's external borders; between commentary in professional journals and Europe-wide screaming headlines. 'They reduced the issue to fit their own box of tricks: sharing pain, smoothing away conflicts of interest, depoliticization.'

Time and again the EU was shown to lack the necessary means of exercising power. Most things, if not everything, had to be arranged through the national governments. When the EU attempted to impose its authority by force, it often failed. Agreements and instructions – eurozone rules, Schengen, Dublin – were ignored again and again, undermining the credibility of the EU every time.

All kinds of strategies were deployed to mask this impotence. The endless postponement of responses to questions of principle, for example, or the concealment of every issue beneath vague linguistic formulations, so that even in cases of deep disagreement an apparent harmony was created. The most common trick became known as the 'politics of announcements'. It was defined by experienced EU politician Guy Verhofstadt as 'the repeated launching of major initiatives and projects without providing the necessary resources'. The common migration policy was one example, decided upon in 1999 in Tampere in Finland. Another was the Lisbon Strategy, agreed in 2000, which said that by 2010 the European economy must be 'the most advanced knowledge-based economy in the world'.

The EU regularly took refuge in political theatre. Instead of an actual state – which it was forbidden to become – it developed symbols of statehood. Hence the single currency, without a common financial policy. Hence an organization like Frontex, without the powers of an effective border force for the entire Schengen zone. The Europe of Offices, the Europe of States and the Europe of Citizens had come to seem almost incompatible.

6

The EU system thus remained fragile, internally as well as externally. An army of lobbyists were still active everywhere, on behalf of countless businesses and institutions, big and small, all over the world. Perhaps this was unavoidable, since the 'hard' power of the EU resided to a great degree in purely technical issues – trade agreements, public health regulations, environmental norms – for which the knowledge possessed by the business world and other concerned parties was indispensable. Furthermore, when the EU bowed to pressure from lobbyists, the problem often did not lie in the EU itself. There tended to be powerful players at the table who refused to allow themselves to be talked around. For lobbyists, the national governments were therefore a far more attractive target, since they could be worked on thoroughly before their leaders adopted a stance in the European Council.

So it was that after the crisis of 2008, of which more later, the banks generally speaking had a narrow escape. Effective national lobbying meant that little survived of the many proposals intended to curb their freedom. The same went for tax avoidance by multinationals, which was eventually reined in to some degree, but only after years of sabotage by a coalition of the unwilling to which the Netherlands in particular – home to Unilever, for instance – made an important contribution. And because of lobbying by Spain and the Netherlands, the controversial agricultural poison, better known as the weed-killer Roundup, remained on the market despite being described by the World Health Organization as 'probably carcinogenic'.

Nevertheless, lobbyists could sometimes operate with great success in Brussels. As a result of skilful delaying tactics, it took a full thirteen years for excessive roaming charges by telecoms providers to be tackled. The short-stay room rental network Airbnb received the full support of Brussels for years despite the fact that it was causing immense distortions to the housing market in cities including Berlin, Barcelona, Paris and Amsterdam. The CO_2 lobby was notorious; measures against climate change involved huge vested interests and a great deal of money. The combined efforts of calf fatteners and pig slaughterers drove the agricultural commission of the European Parliament to the point where terms like 'vegan sausages', 'veggie burger' and 'soya yoghurt' were declared taboo, just in case the consumer was misled into thinking they contained real meat or real milk. These are just a few examples among many.

Then there was the farming lobby. Shortly after the Second World War a vast subsidy system was set up to protect the farmers of the time against impoverishment. Everything changed in the years that followed, except for the subsidy. Seventy years later, some €60 billion – almost 30 per cent of the entire EU budget – was still being distributed to European farmers, whether they needed it or not. In a national context farmers would never have been given so much support for so long, but within the EU the outdated system simply hurtled onwards. Again, it was all down to first-rate lobbying.

*

A major lobbying scandal played out in the declining years of the diesel car. German car manufacturers especially had made huge investments in their efforts to perfect diesel technology. They gambled and lost. It soon became clear that the future lay with electric vehicles. There followed a long and ferocious rear-guard action, with a powerful Brussels lobby of European carmakers working to avoid the introduction of stricter testing methods for diesel emissions during 'normal' driving. A law firm was even engaged to raise questions about the concept 'normal'.

A Swedish researcher, Per Kågeson, had published a detailed study back in 1998 about the way in which carmakers, by manipulating the onboard computer, had been able to come out of testing looking as if theirs were the cleanest diesel cars. In normal traffic, those same diesel cars produced up to forty times as much pollution as in tests. Volkswagen was at the forefront of this widespread fraud. Between 2008 and 2015, 11 million Volkswagens worldwide were fitted with software that lowered the emission of poisonous substances to within legal limits, but only during testing.

This large-scale deception was common knowledge among engineers. Even the scientists of the European Commission had been warning about it for years; a study by its Joint Research Centre from 2013 outlined all the tricks and techniques. But the car lobby, with massive support from major car-producing countries like Italy, France and Germany, blocked all moves against it. As an EU official later said to me, 'We clearly felt that the brakes had been put on from within the Commission.'

It was not until 2015 that the scam blew up in the carmakers' faces, ultimately as the result of an American study. When everything was on the table, Bas Eickhout, Dutch member of the European Parliament for the Green Party, told the *New York Times* he was not surprised – other than by the fact that Volkswagen had invested its budget for innovation in duplicity, rather than in making actual improvements to its engines. The story demonstrated once again the rewards of lobbying.

In such situations, democratic forces struggle. One thing that came to the fore increasingly frequently from the 1990s onwards was what became known as the EU's 'democratic deficit'. Important powers had been transferred from the national parliaments to the European level, but what had become of the means of keeping them under democratic control?

Of course, national sovereignty and democracy within the EU did not simply disappear into thin air. Voters had a great deal of indirect influence on Europe via their government leaders in the European Council. 'Sovereignty is a seat at the table,' was for years Robert Cooper's response. In other words, citizens often had more of a say in the world at large through the EU than they had through their national parliaments. In addition, there were two forms of direct democracy. One was the European Citizens' Initiative, which meant that a petition from a million or more European citizens from at least seven countries could force the Commission to propose new legislation on a specific subject. Then there was the European Parliament. In the 1980s and 1990s it still functioned mainly as a kind of democratic think tank, but the Treaty of Lisbon gradually gave it more power. Laws and almost all major treaties now had to be passed by the Parliament, the EU budget needed parliamentary approval and the same went for the appointment of all the members of the Commission.

It was a parliament that slowly gained teeth. In 2013, for instance, the SWIFT agreement was blocked, since it would have given the American security services unfettered access to European citizens' financial data. In 2017, the Parliament ensured that extortionate roaming charges were abolished all across the EU. Since 2018, CO_2 emissions from cars have been subjected to far stricter norms. In 2019, a package of new European social rights was introduced, including the right to paternity leave. Unfair competition created by importing cheap labour from poorer member states was blocked by the Posting of Workers Directive, which meant that from 2020 the same minimum wage must apply as for citizens of the host country.

Through a system of *Spitzenkandidaten*, or lead candidates, the Parliament tried to assert its influence on the appointment of the president of the European Commission. The government leaders could propose a candidate, but they needed to take account of the results of the most recent elections to the European Parliament. Problems emerged right from the start. In 2014, the chosen lead candidate, Jean-Claude Juncker, was eventually given the post despite opposition from some government leaders; and in 2019 back-room politics returned when the new Commission president, Ursula von der Leyen, appeared fully formed out of thin air. Supreme authority once again lay with the national capitals. Not with the Parliament. Not with democracy.

By trial and error, every bit of European democracy needed to be secured. It remained impossible to vote out individual members of the Commission through a motion of no confidence. Furthermore, the Parliament lacked the usual weapons of inquiry and initiative. This meant there was no obvious, dynamic relationship between government and opposition, and none of the permanent political debate that shapes any normal democratic process.

During the great crises that came after 2005, practically all decision-making lay with the executive institutions – the Commission and above all the European Council. At the height of the Greek crisis, Jeroen Dijsselbloem flatly refused to attend debates on the subject in the European Parliament, since his responsibility lay with the national ministers in 'his' Eurogroup of eurozone finance ministers. During the financial crisis, the Greek crisis, the refugee crisis and Brexit, the European Parliament, despite all good intentions, stood on the sidelines wringing its hands.

Nor was the Parliament a truly representative body for the people of Europe. Women were in a small minority and, although almost 50 million Europeans have their origins in ethnic minorities, it was an almost completely white assembly – 97 per cent white, in fact. Furthermore, citizens can vote only for candidates from their own countries. 'More than 60 years of European union have, in short, signally failed to create anything that might reasonably be called a European political space,' concluded The Guardian on the eve of the European elections in 2019. 'When EU citizens go to the polls this month, they will vote under national electoral laws, for candidates representing national parties, campaigning on domestic issues.' European democracy was still no more than the sum of Europe's national democracies. There was hardly any public debate at a European level of the kind that takes place in nation states, and the formation of pan-European public opinion about matters affecting the whole of Europe – about climate, security, employment or immigration – was still only just beginning after all those years.

This was compounded by the way the Parliament was composed, which for the average voter remained hard to fathom. The European groupings consisted in practice of a jumble of factions. Anyone voting for a Christian democrat, for example, was also supporting Hungary's anti-European governing party Fidesz; a vote for the social democrats was a vote for the corrupt governing parties in Romania and Malta; while liberals found themselves in the delightful company of Andrej Babiš, known as the Czech Berlusconi. The condition of the European representative chamber in 2019 was not unlike the condition of many national parliaments at the end of the nineteenth century. Everything was in flux, but there was still a long way to go.

This lack of effective democratic foundations, this lack of legitimacy, spread across the entire European project like a moorland fire in the early decades of the twenty-first century, smouldering below ground before unexpectedly flaring up. Public support for the EU had traditionally arisen from its achievements: peace, open borders, free trade and so on. It had never been legitimized by 'input', in other words by elections and democratic debate; instead its popularity was based on its 'output'. When those accomplishments increasingly became the subject of debate, its weak legitimacy in the field of democracy came back to bite it. The 'no' of 2005, despite the fact that its motivations were diverse, therefore arose from a single concern, however hard for many to articulate, that threw its shadow across Europe like a thickening cloud: the fear that we, as simple citizens, were losing a grip on our future. Not only that, our unique national characters seemed increasingly to be evaporating in the new Europe and in the globalized society of the twenty-first century.

In the corridors during that 2007 meeting at the palace in The Hague, the 'no' result was played down by some as merely an expression of mindless populism. At times I even had the feeling I was back in the old days of the GDR, when after the popular revolt of 1953 the leaders openly wondered whether 'the people' really deserved all their wisdom and efforts.

It was not mindless at all, of course. The 'no' was an expression of the fact that, as *International Herald Tribune* commentator William Pfaff rightly reflected, 'the first obligation of any political society, whether national or multinational, is to itself, its own security, integrity, and successful functioning'. Hence the fiasco of 2005: there was virtually no room for a normal opposition, and therefore many voters were not going to pass up the chance to say 'no' for once, to shout, to scream.

7

When everything had once more been neatly ironed and folded, when the Parliament and the voters had been tossed the necessary bones, when it was all over, we, the citizens of Europe, woke to important news on the morning of 20 November 2009. The practically unknown Belgian prime minister Herman Van Rompuy and the anonymous British professional politician Catherine Ashton had been appointed as our most important helmsman and helmswoman. Van Rompuy was to be the first European 'president', Ashton the first high representative for foreign affairs. British journalist Geoffrey Wheatcroft took a small poll of his colleagues. Nobody other than the Belgians could tell him anything about the new European president, and as for the new foreign minister, even her own compatriots knew little or nothing about her.

I had followed the process leading up to these appointments closely. I knew they were coming, I was familiar with the European circus and, after all those years, nothing could surprise me. Yet on that November morning I was abruptly and quite unexpectedly seized by an intense anger. Is this what all that endless deliberating and campaigning was about, first over the draft constitution, then over the Treaty of Lisbon? Have we, stupid Euro-enthusiasts, spent years working like Trojans at our books, articles, readings, debates, conversations, campaigns – travelling and complaining and nagging – for this? For this shameful display of spinelessness, impotence and non-democracy? No more Europe for me, I thought in my fury – and I wasn't the only one. Sort it out for yourselves!

My anger had nothing to do with wounded national pride. On the contrary, since for various reasons it was a relief to hear that my own prime minister Jan Peter Balkenende, briefly one of the favourites, had not been appointed. Nor did I have anything against Van Rompuy or Ashton personally – in fact Van Rompuy was a pleasant surprise, emerging as a wise and highly competent leader. Both no doubt had what it took to maintain, as its central-heating technician and electrician, the pipes and cables of the European compromise machine, or even to make improvements. No, what shocked me, again, was the way in which they had been chosen, and the motives behind that choice. I knew exactly how it had gone in Brussels.

This was a decision by the European Council, the gathering of Europe's national leaders, and these appointments, given the relationships between the European powers, were probably the best that could have been achieved: two seemingly grey figures who showed no signs of charisma, who would definitely not give the EU the face it needed and would present no threat to existing relationships. But from the perspective of an ordinary person, this apotheosis of years of debate about the convention and the constitution was an outright insult to 508 million European citizens.

We knew all about the menu for the dinner enjoyed by the leaders of government, we knew exactly what they were served for dessert, but we knew nothing at all about the candidates and their vision for Europe. Decisions had been made, and no one could do anything about them. It was as if, at a European level, nothing had changed since the Congress of Vienna in 1815.

A European and a democrat had lived in my head for decades. They had always got along reasonably well together. But now they were quarrelling, repeatedly, and they never stopped.

Steven

MORALITY? THIS MAY SOUND HARSH, but it's a great mistake to think that banks have any morality. Aside from a few idealistic banks, it's nowhere to be found among their statutes or their principles. They comply with the laws and regulations, but still, they're institutions that exist to make money. Morality doesn't come into it.

You think that's scandalous? I can assure you that if you were to investigate the psychological profiles of the traders in the banking world you'd conclude they were people of a particular character. Are they immoral by definition? No. Do they think morality is of any relevance to their work? No. Do many other people think morality is of great importance? Yes. But they work in other sectors. They become nurses, say, or teachers. They work just as hard, for a pittance.

As for me, how could I ever forget our New Year's Eve party in 1999? Four of us organized it, four friends. It was in Amsterdam, at a girlfriend's house, in her home cinema. It was fantastic. Everything happened that could possibly happen on a night like that. Couples where one partner fell for someone else, setting off a buzz of gossip, two good friends who got into a fistfight, and meanwhile lots and lots of dancing and fun.

I was thirty-two and everything was going swimmingly. After a couple of intermediate appointments I'd joined the Belgian-Dutch Fortis Bank, the start of a fantastic career. My specialty was assets and liabilities management, which put me at the financial nerve centre. A bank has to be able to get money from somewhere or, if more than enough comes in, to have somewhere to put it. Those flows of capital – and indeed changes to interest rates and the risks that go with them – need to be kept running smoothly; there always has to be a proper balance between outflows and inflows.

The balance is managed by a relatively small outfit. It's the absolute financial heart of the bank, the 'bank within a bank'.

When I started in 1996 there was a sense of optimism fit for the *fin de siècle*. We had absolute faith in the New Economics, a feeling that we'd got beyond certain economic rules, the rules of boom and bust. After new financial legislation in the early 1980s, banking had become a different kind of business. In the past many banks had all kinds of grandiloquent goals in their statutes, such as 'encourage saving'. With the rise of the 'universal bank' most of those laudable aims were abandoned and there were no longer any moral or public-interest restraints. From then on, things could only get better.

That boundless optimism was reflected in lending. The rise of the internet meant that cash flows were far more rapid than before. Growth increased, and confidence along with it. We believed we could assess risks far more precisely than in the past, that as a result those risks were reduced, and we could therefore lend far more money than before.

It used to be regarded as responsible for a bank to lend five to ten times the amount of capital it held. That now rose to thirty or fifty times. So the 'reserve buffer' fell from 20 or 10 per cent to 3 or 2 per cent. The same optimism prevailed everywhere, a sense of certainty, a firm faith in the new method of calculation – within banks, but no less so among the regulators. It was further boosted by the dot-com bubble of the last three years of the twentieth century. There was a brief dip in the spring of 2000 when the bubble burst, but nobody was particularly worried. That was regarded as an isolated phenomenon, a slight overestimation of the strength of state-of-the-art technology, nothing more.

Oddly enough, the attack on the Twin Towers in New York only reinforced our self-confidence. I was in Mexico with my wife on 11 September 2001 and people came up to us who thought we were Americans. 'You must go and look,' they said. On the corner was a McDonald's with a television screen. All we saw was a skyscraper putting out smoke; we didn't speak much Spanish and we assumed we were looking at a movie. We couldn't understand it. After about ten minutes I thought: what a boring film, there's hardly anything happening. Only very slowly did it dawn on us: this is real!

Of course, I tried to get through straight away. I had colleagues who knew people in the towers, so in that sense it affected me closely. But the system held out. The central bankers consulted almost instantly and that worked fine. I think 9/11 only served to strengthen our faith in the robustness and quality of our financial system. Something had happened that was utterly unthinkable, with enormous potential consequences, yet everything carried on just fine, because people rang each other and did the right things.

It was and remains a special world. Those with the wherewithal to survive in it were unbelievably capable people, every one of them, but they were able to stand their ground only because they were prepared to compromise. Even with themselves. Because to hold your own in a bank you needed to have a certain way of thinking.

The huge rewards were actually a golden cage. I often heard my former colleagues at the top of the banking world say, 'The day I can leave here, I'm gone.' They were nice people, they really were, but they were completely tied to their income, habituated to it, and to their status within the bank. That life gave them their identity.

Take the people in the dealing room. All due respect, but most of them had no more than an average education. In twenty years in the job they'd learned how you could manage certain positions, but they were doing it in a world in which insane amounts of money were changing hands. So they had relatively high salaries, too. But if you were unexpectedly forced to leave that golden cage, in a round of job cuts for example, the best you could hope for was to become something like a bus driver – and even for that you first had to get your HGV licence. They went from eighty thousand a year to twenty-five. Only then did they realize what their skills were worth in ordinary life.

In those years we laughed and cried a good deal at all the slogans and motivational diagrams served up to us by management about the value of our work. At Fortis they thought up thirteen 'Fortiomas' – thirteen rules to live by. They included 'Set an example' and 'Show courage'. There came a point when you'd see them on display at every important meeting, on big billboards. There was something absurd about injunctions like that, but there they were, and people believed in them.

It's almost impossible to think autonomously in a system like that, to maintain a sense of perspective, to resist being pulled in. Those who did would generally quit, somewhere between the ages of thirty and forty. Anyone who remained as a 'senior' was therefore, in a sense, part of a value system.

In 2007 there were a few slight hiccups. It was the time of the great wave of takeovers and yes, we were still hugely optimistic. My bank was trying to buy ABN Amro, one of the biggest of the Dutch banks. It was a matter of coming up with around €80 billion, the kind of money that's almost unimaginable now. The financing came through after some calls to a couple of American banks, which then arranged for backers and stood surety for them.

So all that was possible, but some concerns began to arise. De Nederlandsche Bank, the Dutch central bank, doesn't ring the assets and liabilities manager of a bank every week if there's nothing wrong. I was starting to get frequent calls from them. We'd borrowed a vast amount of money because of the takeover, and the parties that lent to us from then on were willing to do so for shorter and shorter periods.

If you borrow €80 billion for six months, that gives you a bit of time, but if you have to pay off a sum like that after a month, then you need to find a way to get the same amount back out of the market on a monthly basis. You get it from pension funds, American banks, Norwegian bond funds, PIMCO (that's the biggest), Saudi Arabia . . . There are around 150 major lenders worldwide. And that market, we noticed, was less and less willing to lend to us. In 2008 you could see the durations reducing and the prices increasing. The financiers felt that things might not be going all that well with the banks and wanted to limit their risk.

When the period for which a bank can be sure of borrowing money reduces, it's referred to as a 'liquidity risk'. We had discussions about it internally, and in retrospect they were incredibly friendly. We on the risk side would say, 'Is this still realistic?' And on the other side they'd say, 'We've always pulled it off before. We've rung all the parties, we've got a good reputation, no problem at all.' Our colleagues in Belgium especially, who worked flat out to get financing time and again, remained firm believers. 'It'll be fine, we know these people, we talk to them every day, they're still giving us money . . .'

It's like the interesting story of the frog in a pan of hot water. The people who were speaking to our financiers in person every day kept the faith. We, who were watching from the outside, thought: yes, but as time goes on this is getting to be pretty unpleasant. The term is getting so short, and the amount of money we need to find every month is getting bigger. You know that if ever the day comes when you can't get your hands on the cash it's all over.

From the spring of 2008 onwards I came home more and more often with stories. 'Let me tell you what happened, this is really incredible.' My wife sat here at the kitchen table listening in astonishment. But I still found it impossible to imagine that the bank would actually collapse or that there really would be a liquidity shortfall.

All supervisory boards at banks have a subcommittee that oversees the bookkeeping and the financial risks. The chair of the supervisory board usually chairs it, since it's such an important committee. It's laid down in law that staff with certain important risk-assessment functions must have formal access to it, without needing to consult their own managers. So in certain circumstances, messengers with less-than-welcome messages can get through to the supervisory board. It's an important aspect of the governance of banks.

At one of those meetings I was allowed to give a brief report. It was a shocking experience. I told my story, said that the capital position of Fortis Bank in the Netherlands was weak and that it was profoundly dependent on the funding position of its mother bank, the Belgian Fortis Bank, which was having increasing difficulty getting hold of all those billions. When I mentioned the fact that in Belgium we had a serious risk, I was told the information wasn't relevant to the situation at Fortis Bank in the Netherlands, and I ought not to have said anything about what was going on at Fortis Bank in Belgium.

The next day I spent an hour talking about all this with my own chairman of the board. I was of course in the Dutch arm of the bank, whereas the power lay in Brussels. Belgium and the Netherlands have a particular relationship at the best of times, so if a Dutch person criticizes something that may not be going too well, it's not appreciated.

*

You know, the entire financial world ultimately depends on confidence. As long as there's confidence, everything holds up. As soon as it falls away the entire structure collapses, taking other financial structures with it, like dominos. Chaos ensues. In 2008 we came very close to that.

The funny thing is, we measure everything, we have all kinds of base figures and endless interim calculations, but we know nothing at all about concepts like 'confidence'. You may have gut feelings, but that's not concrete. Only when it goes wrong do you say, 'Yes, I had a feeling about that.'

I've given it a lot of thought, with hindsight. How could things have got to that point? In light of what we know now it was too crazy for words! There were concerns, but only a tiny clique realized that there might be massive consequences. In any case, we didn't have the means to do anything about it. On the other side, within the bank, there were any number of people who were entirely focused on making a lot of money, who had tremendous authority internally and thought it would all be fine.

That summer I took another trip to Brussels to sound a critical note. In vain.

On 15 September 2008 Lehman Brothers, one of the biggest of the American investment banks, was forced to ask for bankruptcy protection. Billions in losses came to light; it was the start of the great banking crisis of 2008. Even then, in those first few days, our initial reaction was still fairly technical: what might this mean for us? There was no great sense of shock. Others may have realized straight away how closely interlinked the financial world was, but we didn't. Many people in banking thought it was mainly an American affair. That didn't last long. When confidence melts away and that feeling seeps out to the public at large, there's no stopping it. That's where a run on the bank starts. Savings are withdrawn. You can survive for another two days, but no longer. Within two weeks we reached that position ourselves.

That weekend my boss on the management board rang me and asked me to come to the office immediately. 'Should I put on a suit?' I asked. 'No, just get over here.' Everything was kept within a very small circle, of course. No one could be allowed to find out how bad it was or the panic would be total. How many of us were there? Let's see. Three on the management board who really got it, three or four of us in assets and liabilities, another couple of staff who could actually carry out transactions, so maybe fifteen people altogether. Beyond that, the supervisory board was in constant touch with De Nederlandsche Bank, The Hague and Brussels. It had now become a matter for national governments.

We worked all weekend to salvage what we could. There was a large corner room, the treasury room, full of screens. I moved in there. It was close to the floor where trading took place. On Monday morning a man walked in. It turned out to be his office. 'Sorry, but we need this room,' I told him. 'All kinds of things are going on, I need to stay here.' He was affronted, rang the boss, looked at his phone in astonishment, then at me, and trailed out. I couldn't tell him what was happening. I can still see him walking away, in disbelief.

There are all kinds of procedures in place for emergency situations like this, and they work as a cascade: we go from green to orange, then to red, then to black. Except that as soon as a bank lets it be known that it's going from green to orange, it's instantly in the black phase. Once you've stuck up a finger in the financial world to say how serious your situation is, no one will ever lend you a euro again. So you have to tack back and forth continually between openness and secrecy. Confidence is all.

On Monday, 29 September 2008, it was announced that to defuse the crisis, Belgium, the Netherlands and Luxembourg would take over half of the Fortis Bank. Together they paid more than €11 billion. But on that same day we watched customers withdraw several billion more, and that went on for two or three days in a row. We were watching savings flow out by the hour. So you see, confidence is all you've got. When that disappears, when savings start moving, you've had it.

I was a player in a far bigger game. That didn't sink in until later, but that weekend I did dwell on all kinds of horrors. 'I'm frightened that the whole system is going to topple,' I said to my wife. After the American debacle of Lehman Brothers, Fortis was the first big European bank to be hit, and if it couldn't meet its obligations, more big banks on the continent would tumble and the misery would be unfathomable. If you couldn't get money out of the wall tomorrow, if shops couldn't purchase supplies, then you were going to smash each other's brains in like primitive peasants. At one point

I looked through the window of our office, saw all the people walking outside and thought: you've no idea what's hanging over your heads.

Crazy things happened that week. The mortgage bank was more or less a separate bank within Fortis. The director was a man I respected, competent and honest. We rang him in the evening at eleven o'clock and told him to come to De Nederlandsche Bank immediately to sign the documents. All his mortgage clients had put their homes up as collateral, which was transferable, and because we were desperate for money, we needed a signature so that all that collateral, all those houses in which our clients lived, could be used as additional security for emergency credit.

The director arrived in the middle of the night. It was a matter of around €30 billion and he said, 'I'm not just going to sign, it's all the collateral we have, I want to take a good look at this.' But the documents were needed by the morning, otherwise the bank couldn't open. He sat there, everyone was tired, so after a while he was told, 'Now go ahead and sign.' 'I'm still reading,' he said. We were actually contemplating the possibility that if he didn't sign, we could hold a special shareholders' meeting and appoint a new director. Those are the kinds of contingencies you come up with. In the end, at four in the morning, he signed. Then you go home and realize: well, that man is rung at eleven in the evening and needs to sign for €30 billion so he hesitates, conscious of his responsibility. But we didn't have any time left for responsibility. Bizarre.

I began with the issue of morality. Perhaps I ought to have put it rather better: it's not a matter of individual morality. I watched the people in my field, even under huge pressure, set to work with a great sense of responsibility, even those who've been pretty fiercely vilified since as rapacious. But the system has no morality, and it's the people who, together, keep that system going. It entails both risks and opportunities to do the right thing, but to use those opportunities you need not just strict rules but confidence as well.

The following weekend, Fortis, including the remaining share of ABN Amro, was nationalized. The Dutch part was bought by the Dutch government for almost €17 billion, the rest by Belgium, Luxembourg and the French bank BNP Paribas. With all those guarantees and all those billions, confidence was restored. The bank survived. We'd made it through.

7. Brothers

2008

I

I WITNESSED A STRANGE, APOCALYPTIC scene during the final moments of 2007. We had joined our traditional New Year's Eve gathering once more, in that spacious house on an Amsterdam canal. Firecrackers clattered on the pavement outside, we kissed cheeks, the Chinese residents and the drug dealers started their pyrotechnic displays, the church tower disappeared as ever in a greasy fog of gunpowder smoke, and all at once there were swans, an immense throng of swans squeezing along the canal. Where they'd come from, nobody knew. They swam in a silent dash, in tight formation, the youngest protected in the middle, the strongest on the outside, in one long surge of disciplined panic.

People stopped their conversations to watch from the windows and the canalside. There was something haunting about it. After a few minutes it was over, and we resumed our talking, whizz-banging and laughing.

2008 was to be the year of the great economic crisis, a pivot point in this European history. Saving private banks with taxpayers' money damaged faith in financial and political elites immensely. The reaction of European governments to the economic crisis that then set in – austerity – reinforced the negative mood. The euro, and with it the European project, was soon in dire straits. Millions of families were impoverished, in southern Europe especially. In Greece, Spain and Italy an entire generation of young people was more or less written off. The process of ongoing European democratization that had started thirty years before in Spain, Portugal and Greece began to falter and stagnate.

Had it not been for dramatic intervention by governments and central banks all over the world, the crisis could easily have led to even worse disruption than the Depression of the 1930s. The decline in prosperity following the 2008 crash has been estimated at 6 to 9 per cent of the gross domestic product of the eurozone. Neoliberalism – one of the causes of the crisis – received a boost; the destruction of the public sector gained momentum across the board, from culture, healthcare and education to housing, law enforcement and defence. Populist parties and movements made a breakthrough, all over the West. The years of certainty were over, fear of outsiders increased, a past that had never existed became the future, and everywhere pied pipers played their tunes.

Where did it start? As I ploughed through the analyses and statistics I realized that I'd more or less witnessed it myself when, in the first decade of the century, I travelled regularly in the United States. At breakfast in all those local diners and Burger Kings I heard the same stories again and again: that until the 1980s you could keep a family on one worker's wages, that from the 1990s onwards you needed a partner's income as well – usually the wife's – and that from the turn of the century American families had to borrow more and more to keep themselves going. By about 2010 many of those insecure households would no longer be able to keep themselves afloat.

Now we were seeing the same story on a larger scale – in America above all, but elsewhere in the West too. After the collapse of the dot-com bubble in early 2000, the American economy never properly got itself going again. Middle-class salaries fell behind and the resulting discontent was bought off, temporarily, by making cheap and easy credit available to anyone and everyone.

In that same period, in the spirit of neoliberalism, almost all restraints on banking were cast aside. In America, the Glass-Steagall Act of 1933 had protected savers for more than half a century by drawing a firm distinction between supposedly safe retail banks and risky investment banks. In 1999 Bill Clinton repealed the Act, under great pressure from Wall Street, thereby opening the way to limitless speculation with other people's money. In recent years the amount of capital held by banks had fallen sharply, so the buffers maintained to cushion setbacks were a mere fraction of what had previously been required. The banks, European banks included, were given far more scope and were at the same time weakened internally as a result.

The effect was breathtaking. From 2002 onwards there was an apparent economic revival in the developed world. This new economic growth, however, was driven by the same struggling people I'd met in all those diners. On uncommonly tempting terms, they had borrowed money they would probably never be able to pay back. Between 2002 and 2011 the total debt burden hanging over the world economy more than doubled, from an estimated $80 trillion – that's $80,000 billion – to almost $200 trillion. The major banks were willing to take on so much risk because in practice they were no longer regarded as ordinary private enterprises but as indispensable outposts of their national governments. The thinking was that they were simply too big to fail. In a crisis, they were sure to be saved by the states in which they resided.

At many banks, caution was thrown to the winds. Paul Moore, in those years head of risk management at HBOS, one of the largest of the British banks, described the professional climate as almost psychopathic: lacking in empathy, reckless, manipulative and extremely narcissistic. He told my colleagues at VPRO Television about some of the nicknames given to top bankers: 'The chief executive of one merchant bank, for example, was called Whacker. The chief executive of Lehman Brothers, his nickname was the Gorilla. The chief executive of Credit Suisse was ALF, which stood for Arrogant Little F*****, you know, the F-word. The chief executive of Morgan Stanley: Mack the Knife. So I'm afraid that we have got into the habit of promoting ruthless, dishonest, narcissistic people to the top of societally important organizations.'

An investigation into American hedge fund Hayman Capital revealed that by about 2007 the debts of the European banks were out of all proportion to the tax income of national governments, which in an emergency were going to be saddled with all that risk. The guarantee given by Ireland, for example, was more than twenty-five times the annual Irish tax income. In the case of Spain and France it was more than ten times. In Britain, the 'big four' banks between them held assets to the value of almost four times the country's gross domestic product. The equivalent ratio in the Netherlands was almost six times.

In America, most of this borrowed money poured into the housing market. People on low incomes were able to buy their own homes, and their houses were rising in value, so they could borrow even more, to buy a car or a sofa. The mortgages of these NINJA house buyers – No Income, No Job or Assets – were ingeniously concealed within larger bundles and then traded. Despite the fact that many homeowners would never be able to pay their debts, all those dubious mortgages were given triple-A status by the credit rating agencies.

In Europe too, subprime mortgages were extraordinarily popular, and in the early years it was possible to earn a lot of money from them. Deutsche Bank in particular – in the 1990s still a sleepy financier of the car industry – managed to palm off synthetic collateralized debt obligations on a vast scale to wealthy clients and fellow bankers. Within ten years, Deutsche Bank had become a world player. It later negotiated a settlement of $7.2 billion with the American authorities for mass deception, because towards the end especially, it knowingly rammed poisonous mortgage bundles down the throats of investors in order to get that last little bit of profit out of them.

In Germany, money poured in by another route as well. As a result of the Hartz reforms introduced by Gerhard Schröder from 2003 onwards, which included wage restraint, exports grew strongly. Hardly any of that new stream of capital reached German employees, however. Because of the reforms, Germans were increasingly being channelled into flexible, low-paid work. The German banks preferred to put their easy money into loans to countries on the periphery of the eurozone, where far more profit could be made. The Portuguese, Greeks, Irish and Spanish were delighted, and German exports further increased. Everyone was living on credit, but that was a problem for another day.

The financial world was jubilant. Bonuses and premiums were at unprecedented levels, and cocaine use in the banking sector was, as one Amsterdam researcher put it, 'almost functional': 'It reduces stress, relieves tension; you're in command of your work again for a while.' In the financial district of south Amsterdam, so much coke was snorted that it was clearly measurable in waste water from the sewage system.

Money was all-decisive. Paul Moore suspected that his former colleagues actually believed they deserved the fortunes they were making, year after year: 'They had lost all perspective on things.' In reality, he believed, banking is infinitely simpler than the work of a nurse or a midwife. 'In the mid-1970s a trader didn't earn much more than a car salesman.' Thirty years later, he might be getting millions annually.

In 2004, Moore decided to warn his own board of directors that its strategy for sales growth was creating huge risks. 'There was a pause. This was
an arrow right at the heart of the strategy. And after the pause the chairman
said, "Good, finally we've got ourselves a head of risk who will tell us what
we need to hear. Thank you, Paul."' Shortly after that he was sacked.

Paul Moore was convinced that the most important bankers, certainly at
the very top, knew perfectly well the risks they were taking. So why didn't
they act? 'Because they were making a fortune out of it.'

Amid all this financial euphoria, Iceland was a special case. It had 300,000
inhabitants, no more than a large European provincial city, and everyone
knew everyone else. Icelanders treated each other with caution, as people
do in any small community. The man you argue with today might cross
your path tomorrow as a new colleague, or as your daughter's boyfriend.

The rugged landscape had always imposed a solitary frugality. Traditionally, everyone lived from the fisheries, and in 1900 the average Icelander
was twice as poor as the average European – who was not at all well off in
those days. In the 1970s all that began to change. The government introduced fishing quotas, which fishermen traded for considerable sums. Young
people were increasingly well educated, and the slick shuffling of money
and credit assumed a central role in the country of elves and trolls.

From 2003 onwards, the three biggest Icelandic banks spread their wings
wider. Using the power of advertising combined with favourable interest
rates, they began to attract savings from the rest of Europe. Glitnir expanded
at an astonishing pace. Landsbanki lured British and Dutch savers with
interest rates that were twice the norm. Kaupthing Bank worked on the
Germans. The banks' success was partly attributable to the image of Iceland
as restrained, respectable, Scandinavian. The name of Landsbanki's foreign
savings arm spoke volumes: Icesave.

The Germans invested more than €20 billion in the Icelandic banks, the
British €30 billion, the Dutch more than a billion and a half, the Swedes
€400 million. In the space of just over three years, the assets of the Icelandic banks grew from a few billion to more than €140 billion. The Icelanders
themselves often borrowed money from abroad, in euros, which considerably reduced the interest rate they were charged.

An expert at the IMF explained to American financial journalist Michael

Lewis that Iceland was no longer a country, 'it's a hedge fund'. An entire nation, and one that lacked any experience with big money, had looked at Wall Street and thought: we can do that too. Furthermore, Lewis wrote, they seemed to succeed. While the total value of the American stock market doubled between 2003 and 2007, Icelandic shares reached nine times GDP. Between 2000 and 2008, house prices in Reykjavík climbed by almost 300 per cent. The average Icelandic family became three times richer over the same period, and all that new money had been generated by the young and brilliant Icelandic investment bankers.

'They were the new rock stars,' film director and activist Benedikt Erlingsson said afterwards to a television crew. 'When top banker Jón Ásgeir Jóhannesson walked into a bar in Reykjavík, excited whispering would start up.' At the high point of the Icelandic boom, Jón Ásgeir and his wife owned a boutique hotel in Reykjavík, a fifty-metre yacht, and a luxury apartment on Gramercy Park in New York that included a bulletproof panic room. Older Icelandic bankers muttered to each other about the 'Hitler Youth', meaning the new generation of go-getters, educated at American business schools, who put their business morality into practice with an iron fist.

Later, Erlingsson still spoke of this period with astonishment, as if Iceland had briefly been flung back into the darkness of the Middle Ages, where there was no limit to the excesses. 'We found ourselves dealing with a group of people with a totally different morality from the rest of the population.' Of course, neoliberalism had influenced Iceland, but this group went a step further, he believed. 'They deliberately abandoned all the rules and structures; they didn't care one iota about public well-being or the long term. We noticed a group of people living among us that operated without any conscience at all, that would stop at nothing. All those bad and ugly things that had always been thought and said about the "upper class" turned out to be true.'

He'd seen Tina Turner flown over for one of their parties, which cost a fortune. 'But when Turner started singing, the young bankers began talking noisily among themselves. To show how rich they were. They didn't even need to look at the global star for whom they'd paid millions. That was the epitome of cool.'

*

All kinds of wild explanations were doing the rounds to account for Iceland's success. The Icelanders were said to have a natural instinct for banking. Quickness of wit and a willingness to take risks had been bred into them by centuries of fishing. 'Our heritage and training, our culture and home market, have provided a valuable advantage,' the president explained to foreign journalists and investors.

The financial world outside Iceland saw things rather differently. 'It was simply a group of young kids,' said the man from the IMF. In this egalitarian society, with so little worldly experience, they came in, smartly suited, 'and started doing business'. Enterprises were financed without the youthful bankers knowing anything at all about them – which didn't prevent the lenders from issuing all kinds of instructions about how to run, for instance, an airline company. In 2006, Michael Lewis talked with the top man at a British hedge fund who was so astonished that the Icelanders were financing so many notoriously shaky companies that he set up an investigation. The Icelandic miracle turned out in reality to be one big network of friends who traded shares mainly with each other, pumping up their prices further and further. Benedikt Erlingsson compared it to the owners of a gold mine who went into the mine, painted bits of rock yellow and said to everyone outside, 'These are nuggets of gold.' The chunks of rock were then given a whole lot of paperwork and sold on between the same people time and again at a profit. It was a classic bubble, comparable to the internet hype of the 1990s or Dutch 'tulip fever' in the seventeenth century.

After a thorough investigation, economist Robert Aliber of the University of Chicago arrived at the same down-to-earth conclusion. 'I give you nine months,' he said in May 2008 to an audience of students, bankers and journalists in Reykjavík. 'Your banks are dead.' The Icelandic bankers tried to prevent publication of his speech. The Central Bank of Iceland refused to talk to him. All those who knew something was wrong had an interest in keeping quiet.

2

The first fissures and fractures became visible in the spring of 2007. Within the financial world something like it had been expected for a long time, but at that point attention was focused on the position of the dollar. Under President George W. Bush, the Americans had built up massive debts with their wars in Iraq and Afghanistan and their simultaneous tax cuts. The deficit was largely financed by the Chinese. If China were to lose confidence in the American debt position, the bubble was bound to burst. Except that then, along with the US economy, Chinese exports would grind to a halt. That joint risk kept the two countries in a mutual stranglehold for years. It seemed clear it would end in a crash.

But something else happened instead. Rather than the American government, the housing market emerged as the problem. American house prices eventually stopped rising and even started to fall slightly. Forced sales followed – ultimately, there would be almost 9 million of them – and slowly, out of those apparently safe, triple-A mortgage-backed securities, a huge amount of junk came to light. From February 2007 onwards, a few American banks started to cut their losses and write off billions. In Europe, the German bank IKB hit a rough patch. Those were the warning signs.

On the morning of Thursday, 9 August 2007, the then president of the European Central Bank (ECB), Jean-Claude Trichet, was rung at his holiday home by his chief of market operations: the international money market had come to a standstill. Banks were no longer lending to each other. Total panic ensued. 'From one moment to the next there were no dollars to be had,' Trichet remembered later. The market was brought back to life when the ECB allowed the banks to borrow unlimited sums in euros – €95 billion that very day. Eventually, more than €300 billion was pumped into the financial system. '[We showed] with a maximum of vigour,' said Trichet, 'that we remained the boss of our own money market.'

The general public had little inkling of this unprecedented emergency. The same did not go for Trichet and others in the inner world of finance. 'Central bankers were aware of the threat of a global catastrophe,' he said. They tried to get the message across to the American and European governments. For them, with hindsight, the great crisis began on that summer's day in 2007. 'It was the first sign that the financial system was extremely fragile and that in the period that followed we would have to deal with many more dramatic events.'

A month or so later, on Friday, 14 September 2007, came the first run on a bank. Panicky savers formed long queues outside branches of the British savings bank Northern Rock. Nothing like it had happened since 1929. Then in early 2008, the American government was forced to rescue the bank Bear Stearns. Every single American bank, with the exception of Goldman Sachs, made a loss that year, and American share prices and house prices plummeted. In the first week of September even the immense mortgage lenders Fannie Mae and Freddie Mac needed rescuing, with huge injections of money by the US government.

For the public at large, the crisis began on Monday, 15 September 2008. We saw television pictures of distraught bank employees leaving the headquarters of Lehman Brothers on Seventh Avenue with their personal possessions in cardboard boxes. Fired. Lehman Brothers was the fourth-largest investment bank in America, and it was bankrupt. The shock was all the greater because this bank, despite its vast size, had not been saved. International finance had never doubted that the biggest banks, too big to fail, would be supported by their governments if it came to it. Clearly that was not the case. The new uncertainty gave fresh impetus to the general disquiet.

Less than two weeks after the fall of Lehman Brothers, Europe was in a full-blown crisis of its own. Some 40 per cent of American financial 'malware' turned out to have been sold to European banks. Their position was weakened with immediate effect. Belgian giant Fortis was now in danger of collapse, taking the Dutch banks with it. Fortis, in collaboration with the Spanish bank Santander and the Royal Bank of Scotland, had recently acquired one of the largest banks in the Netherlands, ABN Amro. In retrospect it was an astonishingly reckless transaction, such a huge takeover in such uncertain times.

Dutch finance minister Wouter Bos had been looking after his children that Friday; now he had to rush to save a bank. In Brussels, he engaged in round after round of talks with the Dutch prime minister and the president of the European Central Bank, trying to catch a bit of sleep on a rolled-up carpet in the pauses in between. In two hectic weekends the bank was saved. The Dutch government bought back the Dutch part of ABN Amro. The price would be paid by the taxpayer – €16.8 billion in the case of the Netherlands, around three times the cost of the controversial new Amsterdam metro line.

The chairman of the executive committee at Fortis Belgium, Maurice

Robert Josse Marie Ghislain, Count Lippens, was forced to resign. 'Maurice Lippens's brain retired two years ago already' was the headline in the weekly *Humo* magazine. After an investigation by the Belgian authorities that took ten years, a prosecution for providing misleading financial information and deploying false documentation ran aground in 2018, partly because many offences were by then beyond the statute of limitations. Lippens personally lost some €40 million in the affair, yet the Lippens family could still, as the Flemish say, 'walk on its own land from Knokke to Brussels'. It remains one of the richest families in Belgium.

In the weeks that followed, financial support was needed for other Dutch banks and insurance companies, including Aegon, NIBC and SNS. To pull the largest Dutch bank, ING, back from the brink, a rescue operation had to be set in train involving more than €32 billion in support and guarantees. Nationalization was seriously contemplated.

Yet the crisis of 2008 was very different from that of 1929. Then, it had taken three months for American problems to infect the rest of the world. In 2008 it took no more than half a day. Still, extreme globalization presented one big advantage. The central banks worked closely together this time to tackle the crisis, consulting continually, pumping huge quantities of dollars and euros into the system to keep it going. 'We were in the worst crisis ever since World War Two,' Trichet said afterwards. 'And it could have been the worst crisis since World War One, had we not taken appropriate decisions, which were swift and bold.'

The role of America's Federal Reserve System was crucial. Behind the scenes, the Fed propped up central banks all over the world, including those of Britain, Switzerland, Norway, Sweden, Denmark, Australia, Japan and, lest we forget, the European Central Bank. Historian Adam Tooze has calculated that it took more than $10 trillion, or $10,000 billion. The ECB alone was given more than $8 billion. As Tooze puts it, the Fed's response to this crisis gave an 'entirely new dimension' to the dollar as a global currency.

'We've had around a year in which everything was possible,' Wouter Bos said afterwards. 'At the very highest level, at G20 meetings, supervision turned out to be feasible after all, and all the major countries participated. We have never been so close to a world government as in that period.'

*

All over Europe that autumn, the same pattern was repeated. In contrast to the Americans, European governments and central banks intervened everywhere. They had no choice, since many European banks did indeed prove too big to be allowed to fail. Furthermore, the social role of the banking sector was far greater in Europe; more than 70 per cent of all civic activities were in one way or another financed by the banks. In America the figure was less than 30 per cent.

A week after Fortis, on 8 October, the Royal Bank of Scotland and HBOS – Paul Moore's bank – threatened to fail within hours. Together they formed one of the biggest banking conglomerates in the world. As with Fortis, the government – in this case the British – did everything it could to prevent the collapse of the bank, and with it the economy of the United Kingdom and the rest of the world, by investing £20 billion.

It was the same story elsewhere. In Denmark, Roskilde Bank was taken over by the Danish national bank. In Switzerland, the huge UBS investment bank needed €60 billion in government support to keep its head above water – plus silent help from the Americans. The French government bailed out its banks with €360 billion in guarantees and new capital. The German government did the same, having already saved the country's largest mortgage lender, Hypo Real Estate, with an injection of almost €90 billion.

In Italy, Spain and Portugal, and in the case of ten banks in Central and Eastern Europe, governments rescued whatever they could. In 2007 there were forty-five regional savings banks in Spain. After the crisis, just two were left. In Russia, the oligarchs found themselves in difficulties and the state intervened. Putin seized the opportunity to consolidate his power further.

The Icelandic pyramid collapsed on 6 October 2008. The value of the three biggest banks was reset to zero in early October and the Icelandic króna went into freefall. The flashy bankers weren't heroes any longer; some of them seized their chance to stuff a couple of holdalls with dollars, euros and yen and slip quietly away. Even at the very last moment they'd been trying to pull in new money from Europe. More than €2 million was spent on one last television commercial for Icesave. No expense spared, it showed images of pure nature and a completely transparent bank building, while a serious voice intoned lines such as 'What is, for humanity, the ideal savings account?' The advert was never released. The bank was bankrupt.

Far from the hubbub of Reykjavík, at the foot of an extinct volcano on the peninsula of Snæfellsnes, Guðrún Arnórsdottir and Bjarni Sigurbjörnsson were running a farm. A handful of red roofs in a white infinity, some sixty cows, a hundred sheep – it was a tough life, partly because the profit margins on milk and lamb were steadily declining. They told my television colleagues about the trials and tribulations of those years. They hadn't participated in the great gamble. 'We weren't programmed that way.' Everyone was telling them to build a new barn, to step up the pace of their lives. 'We were a bit too old-fashioned for that,' they said with hindsight. 'Which was our salvation.' They had succumbed to one temptation: in 2007 they bought a small tractor, 'our dream', with borrowed money. 'Yes, it was crazy, all our earnings were in Icelandic króna, but the bank insisted we take out a foreign loan. In the end we took half the money in foreign currency.'

Many Icelanders got into deep trouble that way. They had to pay off their loans in a foreign currency after the króna lost four-fifths of its value. In 2007, Iceland had an enviable national debt amounting to just 28 per cent of the country's gross national product. Two years later it was 130 per cent, most of it owed to Germany, Britain and the Netherlands, which between them had lent Iceland more than €6 billion, mainly to bail out their own savers. In the Netherlands, the province of North Holland and several local authorities were among the losers. Seduced by the high interest rate, they had invested their reserves in Icesave and were now in trouble to the tune of almost €100 million.

Guðrún and Bjarni felt the impact too. Their half-foreign loan became increasingly expensive. It kept them awake at night. For years they had to economize. 'Yes, we paid far too much. But we still have that tractor. We're rather fond of it.'

Ireland was a case apart. When I travelled around the country in 1999 it had only just shaken off centuries of poverty. According to the statistics it was, at that point, already one of the richest countries in Europe, with unemployment at less than 4 per cent. Everyone was talking about the 'Celtic Tiger'. At the same time, the old frugality was still very much in evidence. I took a room in the countryside, where people still weren't earning very much. 'But you can always go hunting, and the river is full of trout,' said my host. 'Now it's time to cut sods of turf again and fetch them in.'

Wealth increased explosively in the years that followed, mainly because the Irish banks, like the banks in America, financed huge spending on real estate without sufficient security or collateral. Shortly before the crisis, the Irish banks lent 40 per cent more capital to a handful of property developers than they'd lent to the entire Irish population in 1999. When that bubble burst, there was a real danger the three biggest Irish banks would fall: the seemingly distinguished Bank of Ireland (1783), the Allied Irish Banks (1966) and the Anglo Irish Bank (1964).

These were banks that had traditionally enjoyed immense confidence among the Irish people. In reality, the dynamic Anglo Irish Bank in particular had been taking enormous risks for years; according to insiders it was 'probably the world's worst bank'. Michael Lewis compared this behaviour to the Icelandic gamble: 'Even in an era when capitalists went out of their way to destroy capitalism, the Irish bankers had set some kind of record for destruction.'

On 29 September 2008, all three banks collapsed. Ireland would have to introduce massive cuts to public spending, but the Irish government hesitated – and with good reason. Wouldn't it be better simply to allow these banks to go under? The next morning, however, Ireland capitulated: the country would guarantee for two years not just the savings but all the other liabilities of the Irish banks, including bonds. Michael Lewis spoke to an analyst for Merrill Lynch, an investment and wealth management division of Bank of America, who had been planning to cut his losses and sell his Irish bonds for 50 per cent of their value. But when he woke on 30 September he found to his amazement that they were worth 100 per cent again. An unexpected gift from the Irish government.

That financial show of strength stopped the run on the banks. But was it necessary? Later it turned out that the Irish government had given a comprehensive guarantee only as a result of extreme pressure from the European Central Bank. Confidence in the European banking system as a whole needed to be maintained. Not just savers but holders of bonds and shares must be spared.

The Anglo Irish Bank could not be called a 'systemic bank' by any stretch of the imagination. It was not tightly interwoven with the Irish business world, it had no savers, no cash machines and only six branches. It was an undertaking that took money from foreign investors and speculators and

lent it to Irish property developers. That was all. Its bankruptcy would not
have had the severe social impact of the fall of a systemic bank. Yet this bank
too, with its debt position of €34 billion, was nationalized.

Ultimately, Irish taxpayers had to pay off all these debts. Their finance
minister, with his promise of 30 September, had saddled his country with
guarantees and liabilities worth a total of €440 billion – in a country of
fewer than 5 million people. The national debt rocketed to more than € 100
billion, money that largely flowed back to the foreign bankers who had
miscalculated but still saw their full stake returned: Goldman Sachs, the
German and French banks, and German investment funds.

Ireland, riding high in Europe just a year earlier, was now more or less
bankrupt. It found itself in IMF aid programmes and subject to all the con-
straints of the eurozone. There were extremely severe rounds of cuts,
government expenditure was reduced by a fifth, the economy shrank by
more than 10 per cent, unemployment rose from 4.2 to 14.6 per cent, the
number of people drawing welfare benefits climbed to more than 400,000,
and average disposable income fell by a sixth. In 2012, a quarter of Irish
households could no longer afford one or more of their necessary expenditures: heating, rent, basic clothing and so forth. In the end the Irish banks
gambled away more than € 100 billion – or the entire country's tax take over
a period of four years.

3

In the early months of the 2008 crisis, a sense of quiet pride still prevailed
within the European Union. The common currency and the social safety
nets of most European member states ensured, in this difficult patch, that
Europe was more stable economically than anywhere else. 'Suddenly, Europe looks pretty smart', read one headline in the *International Herald Tribune* in
the autumn of 2008. There was talk of a Europe that had always seemed
soft, slow and divided, but had now proven that it could react with unity,
efficiency and speed. In his history of European politics, Luuk van Middelaar described it as an 'instructive experience ... arrogant global "flash
capitalism" cannot do without the order provided by states'.

This feeling was reinforced by the inventive statesmanship of the French president of the time, Nicolas Sarkozy, who developed the French presidency of the Council of the EU into an example for the future. This was how a charismatic leader could lead Europe. He regularly made toes curl, he trampled on European relationships at will and much of his policy was pure showmanship, but – essential in a leader – he evoked in the average European a sense of urgency and dynamism. My goodness, it seems to be working after all, I thought in that first month – this strange edifice made out of a handful of ideals and thousands of compromises that we call the European Union.

The celebrations were short-lived. In early October, at the annual meeting of the IMF, American and European finance ministers agreed – after harsh reproaches aimed at the Americans for letting Lehman Brothers go bankrupt – that no more 'systematically important financial institutions' would be allowed to fail. At a European level, agreements were made about coordinated rescue operations and a European stimulus policy.

A French plan to have the European Union regulate the financial system, with joint European bank guarantees, was blocked by the Germans. 'Chacun sa merde' remained Angela Merkel's motto: 'to each his own shit'. Instead, banks like Fortis were saved and split up along national lines. The banking sector operated across borders, and facing it were several separate national governments. That was how things would stay. The European Union was greatly fragmented as a result in the years that followed. There were regular meetings and improvisations, but a central European financial regulatory authority never got off the ground.

From 2009 onwards the banking crisis led seamlessly into a European debt crisis. What had brought little Ireland to the edge of the abyss took place all over Europe on a massive scale. With the rescue of the banks, a huge financial problem in the private sector was transferred to the public sector, with all the inevitable consequences.

In 2007 the average national debt in the European Union was 57.5 per cent of gross national product, well within the norm of 60 per cent. Two years later, in 2009, the figure had reached 72.5 per cent, and it continued to rise. Financially speaking, the Netherlands had long been a particularly prudent country. For years it had done all it could to get its state finances in order and keep them that way. Lending billions to the banks wiped out all those efforts at a stroke: in a single year, 2008, Dutch national debt rose from 45 to 58 per cent. It went on to reach a peak of 75 per cent in 2013. By 2019, incidentally, it had fallen again to around 50 per cent of GDP, 10 per cent below the eurozone norm.

Because of the banking crisis, public debt in Greece, Ireland, Italy, Portugal and Spain reached alarming levels. Their economies went into deep recession, tax income fell accordingly, and they survived the situation financially only with external help of all kinds: from the European Commission, from the IMF or from the European Central Bank, and sometimes from all three together, the 'troika'. The conditions under which help was given were strict, mainly involving cuts to public spending. Little came of the recommendation at the G20 summit of November 2008 to 'invest our way out of the crisis'.

America has a phenomenon known as 'state mobilization'. In emergencies, the government, normally reticent, can fire on all cylinders to keep the country on course. That had occasionally happened in the past – the New Deal during the crisis of the 1930s; the general mobilization in the Second World War – and it happened again during the crisis of 2008. US president Barack Obama, who had only recently taken office, supported the financial sector and boosted the real economy with cheap loans. The stimulus package of 2009 pumped no less than $831 billion into the American economy.

State mobilization was impossible for the EU, so there was no massive stimulus policy. The European Commission initially got no further than the invention of 'project bonds' (to help attract additional private sector financing for infrastructure projects) to the value of €200 million – one four-thousandth of the American investment. The 'free market' would simply have to do its job.

From one moment to the next, politicians and policymakers ceased to worry about poverty and unemployment and spoke only of financial shortfalls. 'Austerity' was the guiding principle of those years. Not until 2015 was an investment fund of any size launched, at 300 to 500 billion euros: the Juncker Plan, set up to support some 700,000 small businesses.

The indirect effect of the financial crisis, however, was far bigger and far longer-lasting. Any banking crisis almost inevitably leads to an economic recession, and the social damage that results ultimately amounts to many times the cost of saving the banks. Which is why the responsibility of the bankers is so great, and why the consequences of their recklessness cut so deep. This proved true yet again. To take the Netherlands as an example, the crisis of 2008 turned the predicted 1.5 per cent growth rate into a contraction of 3.5 per cent. So at least 5 per cent less money came in than expected, and that went on year after year, an annual setback of many tens of billions. The budget deficit shot up. Something similar happened, to a greater or lesser degree, in other European countries. Governments were forced to respond.

Yet warnings from economists came thick and fast. It was said that the financing and austerity dogma had no basis in carefully considered economic analysis. In fact it went directly against the established principles of economics and the great lesson from the 1930s: don't cut spending during a recession, invest instead. In any case, were government finances the eurozone's biggest problem, as many government leaders and commentators suggested? In some countries the situation was certainly worrying, but the eurozone as a whole was doing fine. Of all the major economic powers in the world, Europe had the lowest deficit by a long chalk.

Moreover, in Europe, with the exception of Greece, there were no structural deficits. Where such deficits exist, a government does indeed need to take a close look at its expenditure, but in the rest of Europe the deficits were attributable to – admittedly high – one-off expenditures: bank rescue operations. Practically all economists agreed that those costs could have been spread over a longer period. Then the pain would not have been anything like as great.

An impressive array of economists, as well as respected conservative institutions like The Economist and the IMF, involved themselves in the debate, saying the cuts must stop. Indian economist and philosopher Amartya Sen – winner of the 1998 Nobel Prize in Economics – stressed that 'very few professionally trained economists were persuaded by the direction in which those in charge of European finances decided to take Europe'. Another Nobel Prize winner, American economist Paul Krugman, talked of 'deficit fetishism'. A third Nobel Prize winner, Joseph Stiglitz, proposed pumping far more money into the economy – which is what happened, but mainly to save the banks, not to stimulate economic recovery; that was merely a by-product. As Sen put it, 'The European debacle demonstrated, in effect, that you do not need economists to generate a holy mess: the financial sector can generate its own gory calamity with the greatest of elegance and ease.'

The warnings led nowhere. They were stones tossed into a bucket of mud. After the shock of the banking crisis, the Netherlands found itself in an all-consuming frenzy of tight-fistedness. It seemed like a return to the rigid policies of Calvinist prime minister Colijn in the 1930s, except that Colijn did at least invest in large infrastructure projects like the creation of 1,600 square kilometres of new land by draining the IJsselmeer polders. His twenty-first-century successors, in these new times, were a good deal more frugal.

Politicians told stories about 'household finances' and the need to 'balance the books', conveniently forgetting that the rules of households and those of a national economy are utterly different. It looked very much as though something else was going on, as though cuts in the prosperous Netherlands were motivated by politics, not economics. The liberal government of the day, with the collaboration of the social democrats, energetically implemented a stern neoliberal programme. One wave of cuts after another was announced: €18 billion in 2010, €12 billion in 2012, followed by another €16 billion, and a further €6 billion in 2013.

The public sector was expertly fleeced, all the way from defence, housing and education to culture. The Dutch minister of state for culture even took pride in the fact that he rarely if ever attended a play or a concert, claiming such things were purely 'for the elite'. The massacre he carried out had nothing to do with financial problems, let alone with cultural policy.

Coen Teulings, director of the CPB Netherlands Bureau for Economic Policy Analysis at the time, recalled the head of the IMF delegation saying to him, with great concern, 'Coen, we must talk.' But the few commentators and economists who emerged as dissident voices – including some who were anything but minor figures, such as former IMF boss Johan Witteveen – were dismissed as village idiots.

The results were exactly as predicted: high unemployment, low tax revenue, an economy hovering on the edge of deflation, irreparable damage to the public sector – to say nothing of the sour atmosphere of austerity and a steadily declining faith in politics. America regained its 2008 level within two years, whereas in Europe the recession lasted a full six years and some countries were still not back on their feet after ten. 'The eurozone, through wilful policy choices, drove tens of millions of its citizens into the depths of a 1930s style recession,' wrote Adam Tooze, the first to venture to put together a history of the crisis – and it is an impressive one – adding: 'It was one of the worst self-inflicted disasters on record.'

The figures are unambiguous. The first stimulus measures in 2008, intended to save the banks, also helped the rest of the economy. From early 2010 to the end of 2011 the eurozone grew again, by 2 per cent. From early 2012, however, austerity policies began to bite and there followed a second recession, lasting until mid-2013, which had far more serious consequences. After that the European economy was sickly for years, with growth figures below 1 per cent.

The pain could be relieved somewhat in states with good social security systems, such as Germany, Austria, the Netherlands and the Scandinavian countries. Germany recovered remarkably quickly; its economy began growing again in 2010. The Netherlands lost, roughly speaking, a full year of economic output. Poland escaped the crisis. It had seen no real-estate bubble, government debt was not excessive, and because of the recession elsewhere in Europe, 2 million Polish emigrants returned home with their savings. To a certain extent, the same was true of the other post-communist countries. In addition, Eastern Europeans had built up plenty of experience in recent decades at getting themselves through a crisis, with or without the help of a government.

Elsewhere, this 'failed experiment on the people of Europe' – the expression is from statistician David Stuckler and his colleagues – ended in total catastrophe. In Spain and Greece, hundreds of thousands of people lost their homes. Youth unemployment rose above 40 per cent, matching that of the Palestinian territories. In Ireland, the Baltic states and Italy, 30 per cent of young people were jobless, as many as in Tunisia and Syria. In Estonia, unemployment quintupled; in Latvia and Lithuania it tripled. In Britain, according to the Office for National Statistics, more than half a million public sector jobs were lost between June 2010 and September 2012.

In Spain the percentage of jobless reached historic levels. In 2013, 6 million Spaniards still had no work, or around 25 per cent of people of working age. The situation in Greece was little better. Meanwhile in Italy, cuts to pensions hit home hardest, since among the poor, whole families might live on a single pension. A third of Italians were unable to make ends meet on their own income, according to a 2014 survey. UNICEF and the Council of Europe (the continent's leading human rights organization) discovered that child labour had begun to emerge again.

In Barcelona in those years, I saw supermarkets everywhere collecting for food banks, and more and more people were living on the streets. The countryside was plagued by minor theft: chickens, rabbits, a bunch of onions, a few tools. As one of the victims told the *New York Times*, 'You don't steal eight rabbits to sell them. You steal eight rabbits for food.'

In the autumn of 2011 I spoke to a Spanish author. None of her friends and acquaintances dared to have children. The statistics confirm this. According to demographers at the Wittgenstein Centre in Vienna, a fifth of Spanish, Greek and Italian women born in the 1970s would probably never have children. Birth rates were at their lowest since the Second World War.

Whatever your level of education, however well qualified you were, it made no difference – there was no work. Young talent emigrated en masse, a brain drain that only made the dislocation even greater. Latvia lost almost 10 per cent of its population between 2009 and 2011. Romania lost 2.4 million residents, 1.5 million of them in 2011 alone.

José Martí Font, the journalist from Barcelona who in 1999 celebrated the arrival of the new century with such ebullience, lost his job too. 'I continued to get a bit of money from my paper, *El País*, but beyond that I had to sort things out for myself. My brother went bankrupt. He had a button factory, with five employees. He ended up with no money, and nothing to do, in our family home outside the city. He literally smoked himself to death there.'

The loss of work, income and status led to a rise in mental health issues everywhere, especially among older people. The EU suicide rate had been falling until 2007, but it increased again from 2008 onwards. Almost 8,000 suicides were probably attributable to the crisis. British research comes to a similar conclusion, with around a thousand additional suicides in the United Kingdom alone. In the Netherlands the figure rose after 2008 from 9 to 11 per 100,000 of the population.

Just how badly the politics of austerity hurt the very weakest in society is clear from the statistics for pensioners. Their pensions were frozen or reduced, all kinds of subsidies were abolished, and social care and medical facilities were subjected to swingeing cuts. Mortality rates for those aged between seventy-five and ninety-five speak volumes, rising starkly from 2011 onwards. In 2015, both Italy and Britain saw their highest mortality for half a century.

In the countries of southern Europe especially, old social rifts and divides re-emerged. Between workers with long-term employment contracts and those without, for example. Or between young people who could fall back on the old patronage networks of family and friends – the young people who filled the bars and café terraces even in the most difficult years – and those who had no such social cushioning.

The figures published by Eurostat were telling. All across Europe, the percentage of people aged between twenty-five and thirty who were living with their parents – generally out of necessity – rose by almost half after the crisis, to 42 per cent. The same statistic revealed a gap between North and South: in Denmark, only 4 per cent of this age group had yet to move out, whereas in Italy the figure was a full 67 per cent. A political time bomb.

'But in this crisis you saw the strength of family ties,' said José Martí Font in Barcelona. 'For Spain the past twenty years have meant a gradual rise in prosperity and then, abruptly, from 2010 onwards, a steep fall. And we have survived it. The country hasn't fallen apart. Hardly anyone died of starvation. Friends joined forces, children went to live with their parents, whole families might live on one grandmother's pension. The blows were absorbed. We turned out to be far tougher and more flexible than we ever imagined.'

4

The banking crisis and the euro crisis that followed dominated European politics for years. The political and financial chaos in Greece, as we shall see later, brought everything to a head, but the direct political repercussions were profound too. In Hungary, Gábor Demszky, mayor of Budapest, lost his job. 'I didn't stand for election in 2010. It was clear that we wouldn't be able to do anything anymore, that the city would be paralysed.' His main opponent, Viktor Orbán, capitalized on the chaos and uncertainty surrounding the crisis, seizing back power and holding on to it.

In Poland in 2010, a majority of voters swung behind the traditionalist-nationalist Law and Justice party (PiS). In that same year, the British Conservative Party came back into office after thirteen years. Under the leadership of Jeremy Corbyn, Labour returned to its radical-left principles. In the Netherlands, Geert Wilders's right-wing populist Party for Freedom had the wind in its sails, gaining twenty-four seats, up from a previous nine.

In Spain, Ireland, Italy, Portugal and Greece, similarly profound power shifts took place. In Ireland the centre-right governing party Fianna Fáil suffered the biggest defeat in its history. In Spain, both the socialists and the conservatives ceded a large part of their traditional power base to two new parties, with the left-wing protest movement Podemos and the centre party Ciudadanos eventually managing to gain the support of a third of voters between them. The possibility of secession by Catalonia poisoned the debate, with support for independence reaching unprecedented heights, largely consisting of protest votes against the spending cuts. In Greece, a similar dissatisfaction became visible. The social democratic Pasok, the most powerful party over the past forty years, was defeated in 2012 by radical-left newcomer Syriza. In Italy, the omnipotent media politician Silvio Berlusconi – partly as a result of pressure from the EU – made way for technocrat Matteo Renzi in 2014.

In northern Europe, protest parties arose in response to the financial help given to southern EU member states. In Finland, the far-right True Finns came from nowhere to take almost 20 per cent of the votes with their slogan 'Do NOT bail out Portugal'. In Germany the new-right AfD, Alternative für Deutschland, was set up in 2013. As its then leader Frauke Petry later explained in an interview, 'Alternative' was a direct response to Merkel's claim that her European policy was *alternativlos*, 'without alternative'.

In Portugal, something anomalous happened. There too the socialists initially lost power, but they won it back in 2015. Under the leadership of finance minister Mário Centeno, the country took a completely different course, defying the austerity demands of the rest of Europe by stimulating the economy in all kinds of ways, including investment and increases to salaries and pensions, while limiting government expenditure at the same time. Within a few years the country was back on its feet. The stimulus programme was not even particularly big, but it set a completely different tone. There was energy and optimism again, and above all self-confidence. Even in Brussels circles, a furtive recognition arose that Portugal might have chosen a better way out; in late 2017 Centeno was appointed president of the Eurogroup, as the successor to Jeroen Dijsselbloem.

The crisis had far-reaching effects outside the EU as well. Ukraine began to falter, needing tens of billions to avoid bankruptcy. In America a shady property developer called Donald Trump was hit hard. In the hope that real estate prices would go on rising, he had borrowed far too much money from Deutsche Bank, his only remaining financier after a series of bankruptcies. As Adam Tooze points out, having a stab at the presidency became very interesting for him, since if he won he would be able to escape many of his problems, even a possible criminal prosecution.

Meanwhile, China seized its chance. The weakened European countries were forced to sell off land, ports, airports and other infrastructure, and so it came about that the strategic port of Athens came under majority Chinese ownership. The same happened with land and facilities in Iceland, of crucial importance for the new Arctic route, and with Energias de Portugal, that country's most important electricity provider. The Chinese could not understand European policy: first create a currency, and then do far too little to ensure it survives into the future.

In the long term this was perhaps the most important effect of the crisis. The euro missed out on a chance to take over from the dollar as the global reserve currency. After 2008 that opportunity was lost. For China, the long term meant something rather longer.

So what had become of the ordinary European citizen amid all this political and financial turmoil? Aydin Soei saw it happening all around him, in that neat and proper Denmark. The state had intervened to save the big banks but it let the little local banks in the provinces fail. There had been a few prosecutions of top bankers, but they were all acquitted, whereas small provincial savers lost everything. 'In the provinces the crisis meant all the work disappeared; the middle classes were gone.' He watched motorcycle gangs, with their tight subculture, offering forgotten young people a new identity, both in the urban ghettos and in the neglected countryside. 'People who already felt that politicians in the big cities were not there for them were confirmed in that view more than ever. And there was a grain of truth in it.'

The spending cuts were regarded by the troika and the national governments as largely technical operations, all about interest rates on government bonds and positions on the financial markets. Confidence in the financial sector must be preserved at all costs. The confidence of the European populations in their national governments and in the European project was sacrificed to that cause, with inevitable social and political consequences.

Citizens began to rebel everywhere, first of all in Iceland. Straight after the collapse of the banks, thousands of angry Icelanders took to the streets, and eventually more than a quarter of the population was participating in the weekly demonstrations. After five months, this Icelandic 'pot and pan revolution' led to the fall of the government and to lawsuits against those primarily responsible. Italy also responded quickly. In the autumn of 2008 and the spring of 2009, a movement swept through secondary schools and universities under the heading 'We're not paying for the crisis!' Later there were more huge demonstrations, although they failed to grow into a lasting movement.

In Portugal in 2010, a long series of demonstrations began, the biggest since the country became a democracy in 1974-75. In 2012 there were more than 500. On average, a group took to the streets every fifteen hours. Their slogans spoke for themselves: 'You'll never own a house in your fucking life.' 'Till debt us do part.' 'The future has been erased.' 'To hell with the troika, we want our lives back.'

Meanwhile, in October 2010, a pamphlet had appeared under the title *Indignez-Vous!* (or *Time for Outrage!*). It was written by ninety-three-year-old French diplomat and former resistance fighter Stéphane Hessel. In one final protest he called on today's young people to come together to defend basic European values by speaking out against the growth of inequality between rich and poor, the way immigrants were being treated and the degradation of the environment – just as he and his comrades had done during the Second World War. 'The basic motive of the Resistance was indignation. We, veterans of the French Resistance and the combat forces that freed our country, call on you, our younger generations, to revive and carry forward the heritage and ideals of the Resistance. Here is our message: It's time to take over! It's time to get angry!'

The pamphlet was passed around by young people and more than a million and a half copies were printed in Europe. On 15 May 2011, some 20,000 demonstrators occupied the central square in Madrid, the Puerta del Sol, and built a tent city there. Adopting the term used by Hessel, they called themselves the indignados (the indignant). The flames spread to France and Greece. In France the indignés demonstrated in more than twenty cities in late May, and there were protests in thirty-five Greek cities. Syntagma Square in Athens was occupied, just as the square in Madrid had been, and on 5 June a huge demonstration took place, attended by as many as 200,000 to 300,000 people. Across Spain two weeks later, on 19 June, a total of some 3 million marched in the largest demonstration in modern Spanish history.

In opinion polls, a third of Greeks and a quarter of Spaniards said they had taken part in a march against austerity. Yet the European protest movements waned in the summer of 2011. In part they were transformed into political parties such as Podemos and Syriza.

In New York in September 2011, under the slogan 'Occupy Wall Street', a new wave of protests began. One sign of the extent of the anger, especially among young people, was the speed with which the Occupy movement spread. Barely three weeks later, on 9 October, demonstrations were held in more than 950 cities, all across Europe and far beyond. In America, 'occupy' was named 'word of the year for 2011'. The movement raised awareness, bringing the social impact of the banking crisis to public attention once more. At a local level, occasional concrete results were achieved, especially in the field of debt relief, but Occupy too ran into the sand, partly because of its loose organization and the vagueness and multiplicity of its aims.

Why were people in general not far angrier? At the peak of the crisis, Mervyn King, governor of the Bank of England, expressed his surprise, saying 'The people whose jobs were destroyed were in no way responsible for the excesses of the financial sector and the crisis that followed.'

He was right. The moderate nature of the protests was striking. With a few exceptions, there was nothing that could be described as a 'popular revolt'. The rage went underground, where it was transformed into despair and resignation, a smouldering desire for democracy that flared up only when a suitable opportunity arose: a candidate who finally 'spoke plain language', a referendum that might just teach 'the elite' a lesson, a party that promised to smash the 'establishment', an internet that, crackling with thousands of slogans and lies, raged on like an unstoppable inferno.

5

What has been said of the American presidential system applies equally to the European Union: a crisis doesn't change you, it reveals who and what you truly are. Many banks had gambled purely in pursuit of private profit, yet they were saved with public money. Never had the neoliberal bankers and politicians been interested in the public sector, but now an immense problem from 'their' private sector had been completely taken over by the public sector. The crisis was thereby transformed into a problem between nations, instead of a problem between banks.

It wasn't just the misconduct of the banks that astonished everyone, it was 'the overpowering sense of amorality' that it laid bare, wrote thriller author Tana French, herself a victim of the Irish crisis. As a writer of psychological crime novels she recognized the pattern of behaviour: for these people, as for many criminals, there was no longer any connection between action and consequences; they had lost all sense of responsibility.

The banking crisis was a crisis of morality. The impunity and even rewards enjoyed by the bankers, the genuflection to the demands of the financial markets, the division between winners and losers, the desolation and despair with which so many ordinary Europeans paid the price for wrongdoing in the financial sector – it all gave the average European, however briefly, a glimpse of the values that dominated the boardrooms of the free West.

Thomas Piketty ventured a small calculation. Although not perfect, it gave an idea. Between September and December 2008, the European Central Bank and the American Federal Reserve between them pumped almost €2 trillion in new money into the financial system. That money was 'lent' to the banks at an interest rate of around 1 per cent. The banks then lent it to companies, private individuals and governments for 5 per cent or more. So for the banks, 4 per cent was pure profit, amounting to some €80 billion, or four-fifths of the total profits of those banks in 2009.

This cheap 'loan' was no folly on the part of the ECB and the Fed. It was a way to prevent the banks falling like dominos, which would have caused far greater misery still. But then, Piketty writes, the governments should have imposed strict regulation on the banks, otherwise citizens might quite rightly think that the whole episode was an economic absurdity. 'Bank profits and bonuses rebound, job openings and wages remain weak, and now we have to tighten our belts to pay back the public debt, which was itself created to clean up after the financial follies of the bankers.'

There was little sign of any such regulation, in Europe at least. The directors of the Royal Bank of Scotland handed out more than a billion in bonuses again in 2010. Its hundred top executives each received an average of a million that year. ABN Amro boss Rijkman Groenink, despite the huge mess he had created, pocketed €30 million. Dick Fuld, CEO of Lehman Brothers, where it all started, left with $71 million in bonuses and premiums.

For the countries of the eurozone, after the banking crisis and the debt crisis came Act Three: the euro crisis. Yet after 2013 and 2014, Ireland and Portugal were able to stand on their own two feet again. In fact, in 2017 Ireland grew more than any other country in the eurozone and unemployment fell back to 6 per cent. Spain too served as an example to European policymakers. Partly as a result of radical reforms to the labour market in 2012 – making it far easier to dismiss employees and therefore less onerous to take them on – its unemployment rate halved by 2018, and the Spanish economy grew faster than those of Germany and France. On the street the Spanish saw things rather differently. The pay and quality of jobs had degenerated rapidly, many middle-class households had been forced to make huge sacrifices, and the likelihood that they would lose out even more in future was considerably greater than their chances of ever fully recovering.

I'm reminded of the mother of a Spanish acquaintance of mine, a dignified lady who had lost her secure job because of the crisis. In 2018 she found herself working in the kitchen of a tourist restaurant, for five euros an hour, ten hours a day, six days a week. Officially this meant she was earning the minimum wage, but she was working 50 per cent longer for it than the norm and no one checked. She'd become blind in one eye and could barely stand because of arthrosis in her legs, but she couldn't quit because there was no other work, let alone state benefits. She was one of the hundreds of thousands who after the crisis of 2008 found themselves in a new kind of slavery.

In the summer of 2017 I took a boat trip to Iceland. In Bergen in Norway, where we stopped off, many Norwegians caught the boat to go shopping in Newcastle, England. Oslo was too far away for them. On the Shetland Islands, our local guide explained that many of the residents would love to be part of Norway again. The bare, windswept islands were annexed by Scotland in 1472, and after half a millennium the islanders still found that hard to accept.

Next stop, Iceland. Reykjavík was indeed the astonishing, lonely, lichen-covered provincial town I was expecting. A third of Icelanders were still struggling to make ends meet, but in Reykjavík the cranes were at work everywhere again, the café terraces were packed and brand-new SUVs traversed the few streets of the city centre. The economy had grown by 4 per cent in the previous year – mainly from the mackerel and the tourists. That spectacular influx of tourists, incidentally, had everything to do with the fact that Iceland was not part of the eurozone and therefore had been able to manoeuvre at will. The government had significantly reduced the value of the króna.

I needed to arrange something at the Landsbanki. The former owner of the bank, Björgólfur Guðmundsson, a flamboyant billionaire who had always walked the streets of Reykjavík in extravagant suits, sporting a bow tie and greeting everyone amiably, seemed to have vanished without trace, but in the stately wood-panelled concourse of the head office, the Icelanders waited their turn in a quiet, orderly manner. Money poured out of the cash machines. Everything was just fine once again.

'We, the Icelanders, had forgotten how we got rich,' said Guðrún and Bjarni at the kitchen table in their lonely farmhouse. 'Our wealth came from fishing and farming, not from shares or from boutiques in shopping centres.' They gave me an example: knitting. Icelanders had always knitted their own socks, hats and sweaters. That stopped. People bought imported clothing. They forgot how to knit.

'You know what the positive thing about the crisis was?' said Guðrún. 'People bought wool again, bought handicraft magazines again, started to knit again. It wasn't so bad for us, in the end, to get one hard slap in the face.'

Close to the beautiful theatre café stood an elegant statue of a man with a briefcase. A seemingly respectable, hard-working man. Except that his head was a stone, he had no face at all, there was nothing from the chest up but a chunk of rock.

6

Was everything resolved, as far as the banks were concerned, after the crisis? Banks that get into trouble don't always have to be rescued with public money, as became clear when a fifth eurozone country found itself in deep water: Cyprus. Between 2003 and 2010 its banking sector more than doubled in size. Relatively high interest rates were paid on savings and the little island increasingly acted as a port of refuge for tainted money. In early 2013, the two biggest banks were in danger of failing. The magazine *Der Spiegel* rightly wondered whether European taxpayers would now have to come to the rescue of 'Russian oligarchs, businessmen and mafiosi who have invested their illegal money'. For the first time, the Eurogroup, under the leadership of its recently appointed president, Jeroen Dijsselbloem, decided to follow a different path: taxpayers were not asked to save a bank; instead, the wealthy savers and financiers were made to pay. After all, they had been profiting from high interest rates for years. In some circles Dijsselbloem was jeered, but it was a fundamental about-turn. There did indeed turn out to be alternatives.

On a second front too, Dijsselbloem achieved a breakthrough. With the formation of a European banking union in 2014, he put an end for the time being to the stranglehold that governments and systemic banks had on each other. The new standard was the 'bail in', supervision of the hundred largest banks now lay with the European Central Bank, and there was a European banking fund, financed by the banks themselves, with which to rescue banks in difficulty or, if that proved impossible, to wind up bankrupt banks in an orderly manner. At last the European governments had got some kind of grip on the almost untouchable international financial sector.

But beyond that? In the revelatory 2018 documentary *De Achtste Dag*, about the Fortis crisis, British central banker Mervyn King expresses astonishment at the lack of discussion afterwards: 'After the Great Depression in the

1930s there was really deep questioning about whether a capitalist economy was the right way to run our affairs. After the 2008 crisis what was so noticeable was how little intellectual turmoil there was, how little political interest there was in asking seriously the question: are we really running our economy in the right way?'

Meanwhile Nout Wellink, former president of De Nederlandsche Bank, the Dutch central bank, pointed out that the instruments for steering an economy – interest rates, investments – were all set to maximum. 'There is a danger that, if circumstances once again propel us into a major existential crisis, governments will not, or will no longer, have their instruments available to a sufficient degree.' As Jean-Claude Trichet said, 'It is very naive to think that we are, at the moment we're speaking, in a world which is potentially much more stable than was the case before the crisis. I have, on the contrary, the sentiment that some indicators are telling us that we are in a universe which is as vulnerable and perhaps even more vulnerable than before the crisis.'

In practice, little had changed. 'Anyone who fell asleep in 2006 and woke up to look at the financial markets today would have no idea there had ever been a crisis,' wrote *The Economist* in the summer of 2018. The banks had been put under stronger supervision, they were obliged to retain more of their own capital – the 'capital ratio' – and the largest banks had been subjected to stress tests. As a result of effective lobbying, however, nothing at all had been done to split each bank into a savings arm and a risk-taking arm, as so many people had recommended. Capital ratios remained dangerously low, at between 4 and 8 per cent. Nor had limits been placed on the ever-increasing size of the mega-banks. Between 2008 and 2018, the global debt mountain had doubled.

In any case, all the new regulations had been created for the banking sector of ten years before. Any number of new risks had arisen that escaped the greater regulatory stringency almost completely. 'Banking services are now being split up,' said Steven Seijmonsbergen, former assets and liabilities manager at Fortis, from whom we heard earlier. 'Everything is being cut up into tiny pieces, spread over separate companies, all over the world. So control of the sequence of financing that we still call "banking" has become far more complicated in recent years.'

And the scandals kept coming. Deutsche Bank, Danske Bank in Denmark

and the Dutch bank ING were involved in huge money-laundering esca-
pades, and quite a few banks indulged for years in rate-fixing, with the
Dutch Rabobank fined €774 million. The British and American authorities
alone imposed fines amounting to around €10 billion between 2014 and
2019.

In the autumn of 2018, Danske Bank occupied the main role in Europe's
biggest money-laundering scandal, in which €200 billion of Russian money
was channelled to America and Europe via a branch in Estonia. Deutsche
Bank had collaborated, concealing 20 billion through its American subsidiary. Earlier still, between 2010 and 2014, Deutsche Bank had been involved
in a huge Russian money-laundering operation nicknamed the 'Global
Laundromat', with links to the Kremlin, the former KGB and the FSB. Since
2012 Deutsche Bank has reached settlements with the courts at a cost of
more than $11 billion for manipulating the interbank Libor interest rate, for
money laundering, for manipulating gold and silver prices, and for fraud
involving mortgages in the US. The value of shares in the bank fell by 90 per
cent between 2008 and 2019.

In 2018, the journalists' collective Follow the Money revealed that,
between 2001 and 2016, European governments had been cheated out of at
least €55 billion by investors. Using sophisticated fiscal tricks, they managed to get the dividend tax they had paid returned to them twice over, or
to recoup dividend tax that they had never paid in the first place. Pulling
the strings were, yet again, the notorious Deutsche Bank, UBS, BNP Paribas, Barclays, JP Morgan, Merrill Lynch, Banco Santander, Morgan Stanley
and a subsidiary of ABN Amro. All these banks had been rescued in 2008
by the governments they had now ruthlessly plundered. 'This wasn't Bonnie and Clyde robbing the banks,' a financial specialist said later. 'No, this
time the banks robbed Bonnie and Clyde.'

Paul Moore, the former risk manager at HBOS, was one of those rare
figures from the banking world who decided to break his non-disclosure
agreement. He became a whistleblower. He said that the crisis of 2008 was
a unique opportunity to discipline the financial sector and bring a degree
of order to 'the terrible mess we're in': 'With profit, power and fame as the
only criteria you have a system in which the destruction of the planet is
built in.'

That opportunity was wasted, but Moore had not given up hope.

Ultimately, everything was and is the work of people, and above all of the social systems in which they operate. The problem really is in our heads. The banking world should at last draw lessons from that.

As Moore put it: 'They're the sort of people who, when they're children, pull the wings off flies. Because there's something missing. It's actually a mental health issue, so I actually have compassion for them. But don't put them in boardrooms, for god's sake. Because if you put them in the boardrooms, forget the regulation. Nobody'll stop them.'

Anna

THE NEW MILLENNIUM? I SPENT New Year's Eve in Hungary with friends, all Hungarian Jews. Each in our own way, we were all outsiders, but we formed a nice, special little group. I actually felt pretty comfortable in Poland in those days – everywhere really.

In the 1980s and 1990s I was intensely involved with Solidarność, the big dissident movement. Four of us, all women, put together the *Gazeta Wyborcza* at my kitchen table, the first free newspaper in the Eastern Bloc. Adam Michnik had dreamed it up; he always pursued ideas further than the rest of us. Solidarność was a huge success, although there were no real winners then, not among the nationalists, not in the Church and not among the democrats either. Geert, you sat at my kitchen table then too, in 1999. But after our common enemy disappeared, the movement quickly collapsed.

Still, I felt at home in Poland. In those years it was all about Europe, and about hope. We were full of that. And now, twenty years later, I'm an outsider again. In my own country. Because of the things I believe in, and yes, also because I'm Jewish. Perhaps that most of all.

I never used to think about my Jewish roots. I wasn't even aware I was Jewish. My mother didn't do family, and as a child I regarded that as perfectly natural. My mother was fairly independent and headstrong and I thought that must have something to do with it. She had a perfectly respectable Polish maiden name – at least, she did from 1942 onwards, after a Polish man who was in love with her arranged Aryan papers for her, including a fake baptism certificate. Her old name, Lea Horowicz, disappeared for good and was never spoken of again.

Out of gratitude she married that Polish man, then after the war she left him and married the man who became my father. Not Jewish, another Pole. She never wanted to talk about it, about the long-lost Lea Horowicz and the marriage she entered into during the war just to be safe. My grandmother and the rest of the family had to stay in the ghetto. They probably died in Treblinka. My mother didn't want to burden us with all that misery. She believed it shouldn't be passed on to the next generation.

I didn't hear the story until I was thirty-three, from a man I happened to meet at our dacha outside Warsaw. He turned out to be a first cousin of mine, the son of my mother's sister, who was murdered in 1937 in Stalin's Great Purge. He told me everything he knew about my family. I was delighted and rang all my friends: 'I'm Jewish!' But nobody was particularly impressed. I turned out to have a problem, too: was I Polish or Jewish? I kept having to prove I was Polish above all else, circumspect and polite. I actually had to be more Polish than the average Pole.

In 1999 I felt increasingly concerned about it, and the following year I started my project in Jedwabne, a little town in the east of Poland, where on 10 July 1941 hundreds of Jews were dragged out of their homes, locked into their wooden synagogue and burned alive while a jeering crowd looked on. Their own neighbours and fellow townsfolk did that. Poles. There wasn't a single German anywhere near at that point.

Jan Gross, a Polish-American historian, drew attention to the mass murder in Jedwabne in 2000 with his book Neighbors. 'Half of the population of a small Eastern European town murdered the other half,' Gross wrote. When I read that I immediately wanted to write a report about it, about the little town where the truth had come to light after sixty years of silence, how people reacted and what their feelings were now.

My editor-in-chief, Adam Michnik, was dead set against it, to my amazement. 'Don't go there, don't do it!' I was deeply shocked. It was the first time that someone at 'my' newspaper had forbidden me to do anything. I sensed it was because I was Jewish. I think behind that fact lay the vague idea that I actually wanted the perpetrators of the murders to be Polish, not German. Completely ridiculous of course, but apparently not for some of the people at my paper. It was all very painful. Suddenly my Jewishness came into play. It was actually getting between me and my newspaper.

I decided to take unpaid leave. If I couldn't write the report for my paper, then it would have to take the form of a book.

That's how *The Crime and the Silence* came about, a book about a town, about keeping quiet and about the truth. I investigated everything about Jedwabne, everything I could possibly find out about the people and the town – before, during and after the war. To be honest, it became an obsession. I did all I could to bring the place back to life. I've forgotten the names of many of my classmates, but I know everybody who used to live in Jedwabne. I even reconstructed a complete map of the town. And yes – the Jews were killed by their neighbours.

I went there regularly, I spoke to the last eyewitnesses and survivors and noticed that the people of Jedwabne hated the Jews, the Jews of those days, the Jews who were killed. I wasn't the first, Gross had already written about it, and again there was that total denial that you couldn't get past. Nothing seemed to have changed. It was unbelievable, this everyday anti-Semitism that I'd known nothing about.

All the same, there were real Polish heroes. Even in Jedwabne I came upon a handful of impressive people who had hidden Jews and saved their lives. My own mother's life was saved by a Pole. You might say that a permanent battle went on, underground, between Poles, between those who chose to betray Jews and take their houses and other property – because often it was as trivial as that – and those who went on protecting them.

I worked on it for four years and the book was published in 2004. I was worried. At the launch, two of my friends, big strong men, acted as bodyguards of a kind, but that turned out to be unnecessary. The responses were far more favourable than I could ever have expected. In that period there was tremendous openness here. Poland had become a member of the European Union and the country was trying to make something of its own history.

All the same, after my book about Jedwabne came out I seriously asked myself whether it was a good idea to stay in Poland, as a Jewish woman. I actually thought it wasn't, and I made plans to emigrate to the United States. But my daughters refused to contemplate going. 'No, no, this is the best place to be! Go if you like, but we're staying in Poland.' They were enjoying school, they were fourteen and sixteen then, and it was of course unthinkable to leave without them. So I stayed. But I no longer felt completely at ease here. No, not even with my old comrades in Solidarność. You know, in the Solidarność period many people were courageous and showed solidarity, but they might still have a deeply rooted distrust of Jews. It was ingrained in them, in Polish identity. Far more so than in other countries. Not in an aggressive form, but as an innate abhorrence.

Its origins lie, I think, in the fact that the Jewish community here traditionally had a strong identity. The Poles had quite a negative self-image in the nineteenth century. The country didn't even exist the way it does now. Nationalism and identity needed to compensate for that: we're Catholics, not Jews. There was a belief that Poland was different from all other European countries, that it was 'made' by Poles, by Catholic Poles. No one else really belonged. Something similar is true of Hungary, also a relatively small country with, in those days, a large Jewish community.

I was once invited to a conference about anti-Semitism, as a guest. Its title was 'The black hole of Polish identity'. I heard stories there about young people who had developed a psychotic hatred of Jews and how difficult it was to do anything about that.

I don't think it's got worse over the past ten years, it's just that under this new government it's more acceptable to speak in public about it, to go on television and tell anti-Semitic jokes or parade anti-Semitic attitudes. For example, I heard two television commentators talking about how to refer to the concentration camps. You're not allowed to call them Polish camps. Lots of Jews, they said, helped the Germans to fill up those camps, so you'd do better to call them Jewish concentration camps. They laughed a little as they said it, as if it was a good joke.

Or take one of the leading figures in a new trend here in Poland, a popular writer, very active on the internet. Without batting an eyelid she claimed that, during the war, the Jews built the ghettos so that they could lead pleasant, protected lives of their own in them, separate from the impoverished Poles outside. Seriously. And that connects with the feeling of victimhood among many Poles, victimhood that the rest of the world simply refuses to acknowledge. Poles think that during the Second World War they suffered more than the Jews. Right-wing websites compete with each other in putting out anti-Semitic texts expressing hatred of Jews – ridicule, contempt, it's all entirely 'patriotically correct' again.

You ask me about the moments in this century that have been decisive for Europe? Poland largely 'missed' them. For me personally, 9/11 was a huge shock. New York was my second home. When I visited the city again two months after the attacks, that caustic smell was still hanging in the streets. By nature I'm an optimistic person, having grown up in a communist state in which you learn that things can only get better. 9/11 was the moment when I thought: no, things won't get better, there really is something wrong.

For most people in Poland it was different. There were hardly any Muslims living here, so Poland was still mainly concerned with its own history. The same goes for the banking crisis of 2008. We had a lot of small businesses that were mainly supported by family money, not by the banks. In those years it was a different society, the fear hadn't got into it yet.

No, Poland's 9/11 was Smolensk, 10 April 2010. The air crash at Smolensk, in which the president and almost a hundred prominent Poles were killed, wasn't just a political disaster, it was a tragedy laden with symbolism. All those politicians were on their way to the commemoration of Katyn, so the disaster was directly connected with that other great Polish trauma, the murder of thousands of Polish officers by the Red Army in April and May 1940 in the forest of Katyn. Smolensk reopened an old wound. It affected the country to its very core.

Smolensk was the moment when Poland became truly divided. Of course, there had always been differences of opinion about all kinds of things, but now there was a deep split. On one side were all those people who believed it was a malicious plot; on the other those who thought it was a tragic accident. It was a definitive divergence of opinion.

The right-wing regime that we have in Poland now didn't arrive out of the blue. In the two decades before and after the turn of the century we went through a liberal phase, with a free press, with Solidarność, with a Jewish newspaper – anything was possible. Now I'd call that period an interlude. It was a phase that had nothing to do with Polish history or Polish identity. Whereas now, well, now we have the real Poland again, the way it's always been, Poland as it is. I know a lot of people who have become pure nationalists again now, old friends from Solidarność – unbelievable. Maybe I ought to have known, because the liberal tradition was always weak in Poland. Solidarność was a movement with three undercurrents: the workers (the trades unions), the nationalists and the democrats. That all went disastrously wrong. Our newspaper is still in existence, but the government is trying to destroy it financially by boycotting us and scaring away advertisers. So we're in a bind. In reality we're preaching to the converted. Most of the workers movement has become nationalistic, and the same goes for some of the democrats – democracy is hard to handle, it seems – and the young people. They are now the pillars of the right.

It's not nationalism arising from a kind of nostalgia for the nineteenth century, such as you sometimes see in Western Europe. No, these movements are focused on the future. In Hungary you have Orbánism; nothing seems to touch that man nowadays, he can't do anything wrong in the eyes of his people. In Poland it's different. Of course, here too we have cliques who pass the good jobs around between them, but we don't have oligarchs, we don't have widespread corruption. Here the nationalism is real. There's a new zeal in our thinking. We don't have a culture of shame any longer, we have a culture of pride. We're proud to be Polish and we're proud of our history.

Poland is old, but at the same time it's a very young nation. It's still trying to discover itself, including its anti-Semitism. A law was recently introduced that makes it a criminal offence to tell 'untrue stories about the Holocaust'. If my book about Jedwabne was published now, then in theory it could get me three years in prison – in theory, because after the new law was passed by parliament, it was put away in a drawer in response to pressure from other countries. It was all a show staged for the Polish public, not actually meant to be used. They didn't want a whole lot of court cases and endless trouble with Europe. But the law did serve to create a collective story, by force if necessary, and at the same time to push out of sight all the stories that contradict it.

I never worried too much about myself, even if many of my friends did. What concerns me most is that young historians at the start of their careers will think twice before stepping onto this terrain. Are you going to dig around in Polish-Jewish issues if that alone is enough to lose you your job, your research grant and your chances of promotion?

*

So I escaped a prison sentence, thanks to pressure from the EU. Not every-one was pleased by that. Poland has always been afraid of Russia, but its dislike is more and more being turned against Europe, against the EU. Poles think Europe interferes too much in Polish affairs, that it wants to take over Poland and dictate to it. 'We didn't fight the communists to be ruled by others.' That's the feeling now.

As for me, I think we gained a great deal by joining the EU. We've been given a huge amount, so perhaps it's time to give something back. But apparently it's a question of different values. Poland is and remains Cath-olic. Europe isn't. Our prime minister declared that we must 'Christianize' Europe. Oh, oh, oh, nothing new under the sun.

Twenty years ago we had problems too – workers struggled to preserve their livelihoods and it was hard to honour the ideals of Solidarność – but I had hope. That's gone.

You know, after 1999 I focused on Jedwabne, I wrote books, did research, concentrated on the Holocaust and lived part of the time outside Poland. For my old friends at the newspaper and in Solidarność it's far worse. All their lives they've concerned themselves entirely with change in this coun-try. They've been in prison, they've been through god knows what. For them it's tragic – giving everything, and then realizing that you're being portrayed as an enemy, as a traitor to the nation. It makes me bitter. Just think, Adam Michnik, one of the most courageous of dissidents, is now regarded as one of Poland's biggest reprobates: editor-in-chief of the *Gazeta*, one of the leaders of Solidarność, and Jewish.

The current regime acts as if the Poles always fought flat out against communist domination. All kinds of nationalists, all kinds of people we never saw in those days, now claim to have been in the forefront of the resistance. We know it isn't true, that there were a handful of us, no more, but this is the new history of Poland. A fairy tale. At the expense of the people who truly loved freedom.

8. Truth

2010

I

SEAGULLS WHIRL OVER GDAŃSK, BRILLIANT white in the sun. It's spring, and in this bright light the city has colour again. The early April morning is quiet. I hear only my own footsteps, the sparrows in the trees and the brooms of waiters sweeping the pavements where the tourists gather. A fine mist still hangs in the streets of the old city centre – the sea is nearby, always. The frontages here rival those of Amsterdam, the squares have the charm of Antwerp, the pastel colours in which many of the houses are painted have something Italian about them: pale green, pink, yellow ochre, mysterious brown. This place is connected, in the very fibre of its being, to Flanders, Holland, northern Germany, Italy, Europe.

A merchant from 1609 has covered his front wall with the stone heads of Cato, Horace, Virgil and Scipio: *Tue recht und scheue niemand*. (Do right and fear no one.) Every house is a person, with an endless history. It's no accident that the collapse of communism began in this city, since all the weaknesses of the system came together here: religion, nationalism, rebellious workers and the bullheadedness of an old German mercantile city.

In the ancient gatehouse, a few black-and-white photos from 1945 are on display, showing the city as a blackened set of rotting teeth, with just a few teetering houses left. Out of the rubble its historic centre was rebuilt in all its glory in the years after the Second World War. The Poles are impeccable restorers, the city was constructed anew, history replicated with great skill, more beautiful than ever. It strikes me that I've been walking through a delightful decor all morning, a Potemkin past. But what does it matter?

The city has been given roots again, and pride, and what could be more important for a citizen than that?

I've been here before, in 1999, and my memories too are in black and white: the forest of churches and cranes; the hotel suite I stayed in; the old Lenin Shipyard where Solidarność was born, which was then still working at full capacity; the church packed with elderly peasant women, praying for Mary and for Poland; the wet snow.

Now everything is in colour: the old city centre, the flats in the workers' districts. The European fairy has been here with cans of paint and building materials. All that's left of the original Lenin Shipyard is the porter's lodge, a small structure that now has European Heritage status. An enormous monument has gone up next to it, with crosses and anchors, and beyond that is the European Solidarity Centre, very big and glassy. Aside from five security guards and a huge photo of a gathering of gentlemen, I come upon no one at all.

The new Museum of the Second World War is impossible to miss. It's close to the harbour and the former post office, at the very spot where the Second World War began, on 1 September 1939, with an endless series of salvos fired at the harbour from the German battleship SMS *Schleswig-Holstein*. The building itself is a gigantic shell strike, apparently drilling its way into the earth, and the exhibition is indeed mostly below ground level.

This is the biggest war museum in Europe and its effect is devastating. The paving of a former street – the district around it almost completely swept away – forms the axis of the exhibition, with rooms to the left and right, often showing entire side streets, that each tell their own story. You walk along a meticulous replica of a shopping street from the 1930s, full of cheerful innocence, no one yet knowing what awaits their pleasant villages and towns. In one hall a Stuka dives towards you, and in the narrow streets you almost literally lose yourself in suffering great and small, at one point coming upon a complete goods wagon like those that took people to the concentration camps. A fragment from the diary of someone who witnessed the pogroms in the villages reads, 'We are dealing with an untamed, shameless, callous, blind brutality. Anything is possible, absolutely anything.' You walk across the battlefields, past the air raid shelters, and at last you find yourself in a courtyard, surrounded by ordinary houses ruined by shelling, with a Red Army tank in the background.

This is an honest museum. Jedwabne is given due attention. In a glass case are the keys to gates, doors, houses and drawers, found in large numbers next to the exhumed bodies, as if the victims hoped they were merely going on a journey, that the film would soon be rewound and normal life could resume.

It's also a European museum. During the Second World War, 5 million Poles died, yet almost as much attention is paid here to the fate of other Europeans. You can see the Schüsselmaschine E, better known as the Enigma machine, a triumphant prize of the Poles, who made an incalculable contribution to the liberation of Europe just by breaking the German codes. But there's also an impressive side room entirely devoted to the siege of Leningrad and the fate of its millions of Russian victims. The exhibition transcends national suffering, and that above all makes it great and exceptional.

Right at the end the achievement is oddly marred. When the museum first opened, the tour ended with a film that included shots of the Nuremburg trial, then moved on through Martin Luther King, Nelson Mandela and Solidarność to the European refugee crisis. It was a cosmopolitan film, posing questions such as: what have we left behind, and what remains with us?

In its place I'm shown a crude propaganda film. 'With Enigma we saved millions of lives,' I note down. 'We were the first to warn of the Holocaust.' 'But despite everything we did, we were betrayed.' 'Amid the violence of the war, we continued to resist.' 'The Iron Curtain falls. The war is over. We win. Invincible!' Music. The heroes-and-villains story is back, after an intervention by the new regime. This too is Poland – the Poland of today.

The war museum in Gdańsk has become a battleground between two histories, and actually between two kinds of fatherland, one that appeals to myths and stories telling of heroism, and one that is secure enough to look truth in the face, including its darker sides. It's not a problem specific to Poland. In countries like the Netherlands, Belgium, France and Britain, similar squabbles arise when it comes to addressing colonial history. But here the debate goes right to the heart of politics.

The plans for the museum date back to 2004, to the liberal Poland that had just joined the EU and felt a powerful need to rediscover its history, in openness and freedom. It was determined not to make the leading story yet another summary of heroic deeds; instead the stress would lie on the fate of European citizens, those who had suffered most in the war, and on the global dimension of the conflict. The intention, in the words of the museum's initiator and first director Paweł Machcewicz, was 'to give a place in the historical memory of Europe and the rest of the world to the experiences of Poles and the people of Eastern and Central Europe'.

With the coming to power of a new conservative government in 2015, that ended. Machcewicz had been a friend of the previous president; now he was a traitor. 'You're a dead man,' he was told. According to the new regime, the museum was 'unpatriotic'. The fact that other countries and the suffering of citizens all over the world were part of the exhibition signified a dangerous undermining – or 'Europeanization' – of all that was special about Polish history and identity.

Great efforts were made to prevent the opening of the museum. The police raided Machcewicz's house, he was accused – and later absolved – of corruption. Nevertheless, he pulled out all the stops and managed to get the museum ready to open on 23 March 2017. A legal device was used to have it formally closed down two weeks later and then immediately reopened under the leadership of a new director, a government figurehead. The museum would be thoroughly rebuilt, was the plan, in adherence to new cultural guidelines.

The film, with its slogans and catchphrases, is the first visible result of the new direction to be taken, but a year on there is still no sign of a major about-turn. Even the controversial glass case about Jedwabne remains untouched. Clearly all that fuss was for appearances' sake; in reality, the censors are in no hurry. Machcewicz has meanwhile left for Berlin and no longer sets foot in Gdańsk.

In front of the museum is a building site and in the distance a demolition crane clatters away. The last of the houses in an old workers' district are being pulled down, the last of the chimneys, attics, children's rooms, the yellow tiles of a bathroom, the wrenchingly evocative wallpaper in a kitchen where so much happened and so much was discussed: ordinary history relentlessly swept aside.

Poland is modernizing rapidly. A lightning-fast express service, with all the latest creature comforts, has replaced the creaking train from Gdańsk to Warsaw. The road system looks brand new – almost two-thirds of the cost

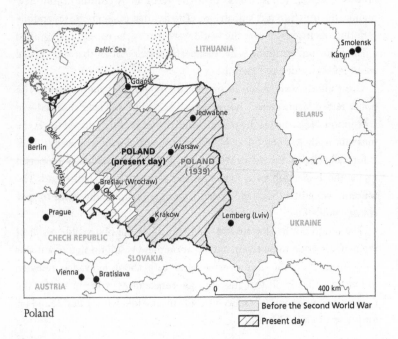

Poland

Before the Second World War

Present day

has been covered by the EU. In Warsaw, the older parts of the city, after renovation, have regained some of their Parisian allure. Close to the station and the old Stalinist culture palace, a busy and dynamic business district has arisen over the past twenty years – often referred to as 'boomtown Warsaw', a cross between Rotterdam and Berlin. Here the office blocks of Deloitte and ING dominate, along with the sparkling shopping centre Złote Tarasy, or 'Golden Terraces', and the Żagiel tower block where you can pay € 15,000 per square metre. Between 1992 and 2012, 250,000 new homes were built in Warsaw, practically all of them by the private sector, quite often in the form of gated communities.

In the autumn of 1999, with the help of a photo book, I spent a whole day searching for rare remains of the Jewish ghetto. Here and there I found a detail: a doorway, a step, a stone seat near the courtroom, a fragment of a wall, tram rails. Now, almost twenty years later, I try to find a few of those places again, but it's almost impossible. This city is still full of history, but glass and Deloitte are winning, and the past has increasingly gone underground.

The economy has been growing for more than a quarter of a century, non-stop. Gross domestic product has tripled since 1990. Doing business has become far easier; in the space of ten years Poland rose up the World Bank rankings from 72nd to 24th place. In many respects Poland has out-stripped the countries of southern Europe over the past twenty years. The statistics suggest that a well-educated young Pole who speaks one or two foreign languages has a better chance on the jobs market than a Spaniard or an Italian.

True, the Poles are still enamoured of their coal, which they produce and burn in prodigious quantities. Of the fifty European cities with the worst air pollution, thirty-six are in Poland. But unlike Hungary, for example, it has not become a kleptocracy under the banner of God and Fatherland. OLAF, the European Union's anti-corruption office, discovered in 2018 that a company belonging to Orbán's son-in-law had got hold of more than €43 million of EU money. The Hungarian leader had a ridiculous stadium built close to his native village, with a dedicated railway line. Such things are unthinkable in Poland. Even the most vehement critics of the Polish regime confirmed to me that there is no systemic corruption in Poland comparable to that found in Hungary.

*

Yet in 2015, everything had to change. The right-wing nationalist party Prawo i Sprawiedliwość (Law and Justice), PiS for short, won the presidential elections and went on to gain an absolute majority in parliament. Set up in 2001 by identical twins Lech and Jarosław Kaczyński, the party aimed to restore a 'truly' Catholic Poland. It opposed both communism and the free market, declared war on the liberals, urged women to know their place (at the kitchen sink), encouraged municipalities to declare themselves LGBTQ+-free zones and wanted nothing to do with Muslims, foreigners and immigrants. The liberal *Gazeta Wyborcza* was Satan. In 2004, an angry crowd turned up at its editorial offices with a priest, to drive out the devil with prayer. In the countryside especially, the true Poland was felt to be under threat, and the blame was placed on the EU.

It was not just nostalgic nationalism that drove voters. On the contrary. Like the Hungarians, many Poles were impatient. Some 2 million Polish citizens had lived in the West and knew the kind of life that was possible. Research into their motives shows that many PiS voters did not feel neglected, or disappointed with their lives; they just wanted more, and they wanted it now.

What happened under the leadership of PiS was therefore not simply a conservative revolution, it was a generational change. The PiS presidential candidate, Andrzej Duda, was a dynamic and good-looking figure, the election campaign was a mixture of promises and intimidation, and its success was astonishing. Polish commentator Jacob Mikanowski describes Polish political culture as having two main factions that took turns at monopolizing the conversation: the 'rebels' and the 'nation-builders'. For a full two centuries, from the eighteenth-century revolt against Russia to Solidarność at the end of the twentieth century, a heroic rebelliousness in the face of a powerful oppressor had formed the moral core of Polish politics. In rebellion lies the heart of the nation, Mikanowski concludes, but responsibility lies with the nation-builders.

The parties that predominated until 2015, the United Left and Civic Platform, were typical nation-builders. But twenty-five years after the fall of communism, Mikanowski writes, the cycle of the nation-builders came to an end. The PiS party, for all its conservatism, represented a twenty-first-century rebellion. 'Poland is more prosperous than ever. It has a convincing football team and it makes outstanding video games. It is, in short, at last a more or less normal European country. And that might actually be the problem.'

Historian Jarosław Krawczyk sees things rather differently. 'The PiS and Jarosław Kaczyński created impossibility,' he told me when I saw him in Warsaw. 'They promised things a normal government could never bring about. But for Kaczyński everything was possible. He believed it was purely a question of will. Do we want to conquer China? Perfectly possible. Conquer the moon? Okay!'

I asked him whether they were disappointed. 'Yes, we were, because we cherished a surreal belief that in no time at all we would become a rich country, even an empire. But all their election stories – that Poland was a mess, a country on its knees, about to be caught off guard – were complete nonsense. Nobody wanted to conquer Poland, it was a safe and relatively prosperous place. In no sense at all was it in crisis.'

Kaczyński openly claimed that the museum in Gdańsk was doing the bidding of the Germans. 'I was on the advisory board of that museum,' said Krawczyk. 'I saw the mood change from month to month. You know, half my family was wiped out by the Germans. They hanged my grandfather. But when I hear Kaczyński talk about Germany it's never about that. Everything now has to revolve around the "heroes" and the "good" war that created our "heroic character". For them that was the main thing. They were insane.'

2

'Smolensk' was a key word in my conversations in Poland, time and again. 'Without that air crash, the Kaczyńskis and their PiS would probably have gone into decline,' said Krawczyk. 'But what happened happened.'

Smolensk. On the morning of 10 April 2010, a Tupolev belonging to the Polish government was on its way, with a large delegation, to Katyn in Russia for the commemoration of the massacre. Power in Poland was at that point shared, with the government led by prime minister Donald Tusk of Civic Platform, and the presidency in the hands of PiS leader Lech Kaczyński.

After the discovery of the thousands of victims, Katyn was a point of fierce contention for decades: who had executed all those Polish officers, the Germans or the Soviets? For years the communist regime insisted the

Germans were to blame, until the lie eventually became untenable. At that point even the word 'Katyn' became taboo. In 1990, the Soviet Union finally accepted responsibility for the tragedy.

Three days before the crash, on 7 April, Tusk and Putin had both attended the official seventieth anniversary commemorations. It was a historic moment in relations between Poland and Russia. Which explains why the leaders of PiS were absolutely determined to be present at further commemorations on 10 April.

So on that Saturday morning a second Polish delegation, made up of close to a hundred prominent politicians and high-ranking military officers – including President Kaczyński and his wife – got into a Tupolev. Thick fog blanketed the airport in Smolensk. Two earlier flights had been diverted, visibility was deteriorating by the minute and the pilot was urgently advised to divert to Minsk. The airport really ought to have been closed by that point, but air traffic control didn't dare take that decision, since with all those highly placed guests it might have caused a diplomatic incident.

In the cockpit meanwhile – the voices were all captured by the black box flight recorder – a tense situation had arisen. The crew understood that a landing at the rudimentary airport in Smolensk in these circumstances would be very difficult, but on the other hand they feared the anger of their VIP passengers if they decided to land somewhere else instead. The chief of protocol can be heard saying, 'The president hasn't yet decided what to do.' 'He'll go crazy,' says the navigator, probably referring to the Polish president and the prospect of giving him the message that they would need to divert for safety reasons. Something similar had happened two years earlier and the person in charge found himself in deep trouble as a result.

The captain therefore asked for permission to make one attempt to land. He had to communicate with the control tower himself, since he was the only member of the crew who spoke Russian. The cockpit voice recorder reveals how the plane cautiously descended through the thick fog and how the crew, not realizing they were flying in a valley, gave their altitude – 'A hundred metres' – when in reality it was a mere fifteen metres. The automatic system continually warned them, 'Pull up, pull up. Terrain ahead,' and then, in their very last moments, swearing, the crew saw the first treetops appear before them through the fog. The Tupolev started touching the trees and within five seconds it hit the ground and broke into pieces. Everyone inside was killed instantly.

'It was inconceivable and yet it happened,' said Jarosław Krawczyk. 'I heard about it as I was drinking coffee that morning. Friends rang me. Everyone was in shock. It was almost impossible to comprehend. All the political parties were hit hard, because there were representatives of all sides in that plane. The entire political debate was silenced then and there. We were all one.'

It was a while before Krawczyk realized this might have incalculable consequences. 'The majority of Poles believed it was an accident. But for people in the PiS, in all their paranoia, the disaster immediately became a central theme in the political battle.' A huge crowd of mourners laid flowers outside the presidential palace, a vast demonstration was held, and at the end of that week Kaczyński and his wife were buried like monarchs in Wawel Cathedral in Kraków, where the Poles traditionally bury their sovereign rulers and national heroes.

Jarosław Kaczyński, twin brother to the deceased president, visited his sick mother that evening and told her lies: her son was away travelling, to Peru and Argentina, and a volcanic eruption in Iceland had delayed his return. He even showed her faked newspaper articles with reports of the journey. Only after Lech Kaczyński had been buried and his mother recovered did he tell her the truth. 'There were moments that I wanted to believe those stories myself,' Jarosław said in a rare interview about the accident. 'That Lech was alive.'

Jarosław was single and childless and lived alone with his cat. At the time of the crash his brother was working on his presidential re-election campaign, and Jarosław took over his role immediately. He lost the election but became the central figure in the background of PiS, a shadowy but crucial player in Polish politics. The disaster and the martyrdom of his twin brother remained the central theme of all subsequent campaigns. There were monthly commemorations, the names of the victims were read out repeatedly, and soon they came to be referred to as *polegni*, a Polish term reserved for heroes of the nation who have fallen in wars or rebellions.

A similar conflict over the truth arose concerning Smolensk as had arisen over Katyn many years before. According to two independent investigations, the cause was undoubtedly human error. Mistakes were made by air traffic control at the airport, but the main faults were those of the pilot and the navigator, who were probably put under pressure by the Polish head of protocol, by the commander of the air force and perhaps by the president himself. It was simply a miserable accident in which Lech Kaczyński may himself have played a decisive part.

That sober conclusion was of course painful, especially for Lech's twin brother. Jarosław Kaczyński therefore seized the initiative by launching one wild theory after another: that the fog around the airport was created artificially to make the runway invisible, or that a special kind of bomb had exploded, leaving no trace. He ordered investigations in which, in search of evidence of the mysterious bomb, victims' bodies were exhumed. No new evidence was found, yet in essence his endless accusations lingered on: it was a deliberate act, the Russians were the culprits, and the treacherous Tusk government had not even taken the trouble to investigate properly. His campaign had the desired effect. In 2012 almost everyone still believed Smolensk was an accident; five years later a third of Poles were convinced it had been a monstrous plot, organized from Moscow.

The conspiracy theories surrounding Smolensk became the PiS party's most important ideology. It was for or against, good versus evil, in Polish politics. For Bulgarian political thinker Ivan Krastev, 'Smolensk' became illustrative of the way in which a broadly shared conspiracy theory – true or not – can play the part reserved in earlier times for religion, or for ethnic origin: 'The "assassination hypothesis" helped consolidate a certain "we": we who do not trust the government's lies, we who know how the world really works, we who blame liberal elites for betraying the promise of the 1989 revolution.'

In 2015 that 'we', with two landslide election victories, got its hands on power in Poland.

3

In some respects, the spring of 2010 was a turning point in European history, just as 1956 had been with Khrushchev's 'de-Stalinization', the Suez Crisis and the Hungarian Uprising.

A month after Smolensk, on 6 May, Labour lost the general election in Britain, an event that heralded many years of Tory government, a growing impasse in British politics and a chaotic Brexit. During that same weekend there was a run on the banks in Athens and the crisis in the eurozone reached its climax, with the euro dragged back from the edge of the abyss at the last possible moment. Viktor Orbán had won the Hungarian elections that April, a victory that marked the start of a long campaign against the EU and European democratic norms and values, a campaign in which boundaries were pushed back again and again. Negotiations between Orbán and the other European leaders soon took on a destructive character. In the words of Timothy Garton Ash after yet another confrontation, 'Brussels has been playing chess against a kickboxer. The kickboxer wins.'

Populist governments, certainly in Eastern Europe, have three features in common. Firstly, they regard democracy as above all a *people's* democracy: the majority is all-powerful. This means that, secondly, over time they try to gain control of the entire state apparatus. Thirdly, they rely on what is known as 'mass clientelism' – giving large groups of citizens favours, money and other benefits in return for political support.

All this made Orbán an exemplary populist, and the representatives of Poland's PiS likewise believed that they alone were the voice of the people. The opposition was no longer listened to. The Polish diplomatic corps and the upper ranks of the army were thoroughly 'cleansed'; judicial and constitutional checks and balances were dismissed as 'legal obstructiveness'; members of the constitutional court and the judiciary were rapidly replaced by PiS supporters, and confidence in the judiciary fell accordingly. A poll by Eurostat in the spring of 2019 indicated that half of Poles regarded the independence of their own judges as 'poor to very poor'. (The same applied, incidentally, to three-quarters of Hungarians, two-thirds of Slovaks and half of Spaniards and Italians.)

Interference by the Polish government caused a breach in European legal unity. An Irish judge refused to extradite a Polish drug dealer to Poland 'because of fundamental shortcomings in the Polish legal system'. The European Court of Justice eventually supported extradition, but clearly basic mutual trust had gone, on this terrain as on others.

Like every sensible populist party, the new rulers of Poland bought the sympathy of the average voter immediately on coming into office. The pension age was reduced again and, from a second child onwards, families were given a child benefit payment of 500 złotys (some 115 euros) per month per child.

Meanwhile, the Polish state apparatus was expertly hijacked. The Civil Development Forum in Warsaw has calculated that within three years of PiS coming to power in 2015, more than 11,000 civil servants were sacked based on lustration laws that determined whether a person had behaved well or badly under communist rule. The party, ultimately, was allowed to decide whether an ex-communist was a 'contrite patriot' – PiS was full of such types – or a hardened 'enemy of the state'.

There was even a risk that Bronisław Geremek, shortly before his death and despite his impressive record of service, might become a victim of a precursor to this campaign. He warned even then of a special 'ministry of truth' and a 'memory police', in the face of which citizens would be powerless: 'A state that we treated as a common good is being treated as a trophy to be seized by the rulers.'

One of the Polish government's favourite scapegoats was the EU. Or rather Brussels, because 88 per cent of Poles supported the EU – as did 67 per cent of Hungarians, incidentally – according to 2017 polling. 'Tell me honestly,' I heard Kaczyński say to his voters. 'What has Europe actually done for us?' It was the only story Poles wanted to hear, all they were allowed to hear, and whether it was true didn't matter. Europe had spent some €100 billion on new Polish infrastructure alone, and a lot more besides that, but European solidarity did not fit into the Polish story of eternal victimhood and of national courage betrayed.

4

For centuries, a wide band of anti-Semitism stretched across Eastern and Central Europe from the Baltic states, through Poland and Hungary, into Romania. To this day, according to data published in The Economist, 23 per cent of Lithuanians are unwilling to accept Jews as fellow citizens. In Romania the figure is 22 per cent, in Poland 18 per cent. In many Ukrainian towns, where before the war more than half the population was Jewish, not a single monument to their memory can be found. In Poland, a fierce campaign against the Jewish 'fifth column' was fought as recently as 1968 and at least 13,000 Jews were forced to flee the country. In Kraków – where of nearly 70,000 Jewish residents only a few survived the war – I saw supposedly comical souvenirs on sale everywhere in the form of Jewish figures with hats, shawls and Hasidic curls.

Historically, anti-Semitism rose and fell according to the political line taken, and with every increase or decrease in nationalist sentiment. Many Poles wanted nothing to do with it, especially in the big cities. The Second Polish Republic (from 1918 to 1945, from 1939 in exile) made it a point of honour to represent all citizens, including the Jews.

From 2015 onwards, however, the brown-shirt mentality cropped up again all over the place. On Poland's Independence Day, 11 November, nationalists marched through the streets in their tens of thousands, a larger crowd with each passing year, shouting slogans like 'We want God' and 'Poland for the Poles'. Between 2015 and 2017 the number of reported hate crimes rose by 40 per cent. Meanwhile, the recently established Council Against Racial Discrimination and Xenophobia was abolished.

That mentality was especially evident in right-wing propaganda targeting George Soros, the Hungarian-American financier who in the past had contributed huge amounts of money and personal energy to the democratic reconstruction of Eastern Europe. It was a deliberately orchestrated campaign of hate thought up in 2013 by two American spin doctors and deployed first of all, with great success, in Hungary. After his initial victories, Orbán needed a classic enemy, a mythical monster with a secret agenda, limitless sources of finance and tentacles everywhere. Soros fitted the bill perfectly, so he was held responsible for every setback – the euro crisis, the sudden influx of migrants, or whatever it might be. The accusations were utterly unfounded, but that was irrelevant. The campaign soon proved contagious, and elsewhere in Eastern Europe politicians began to condemn Soros, especially in Poland.

'We are fighting an enemy that is different from us,' Orbán said of the type of person he associated with Soros. 'Not open, but hiding; not straightforward but crafty; not honest but base; not national but international; does not believe in working but speculates with money; does not have its own homeland but feels it owns the whole world.' The terminology was all too familiar, a code that was understood near and far, a dog whistle that made anti-Semites everywhere prick up their ears, those in Poland included. In a small poll by the University of Warsaw in 2017, with a sample of 1,000, 43 per cent of Poles endorsed the view that Jews were after 'world domination', while a quarter believed that in the past Jews used to 'kidnap Christian children'.

Anna Bikont, the woman who investigated the Jedwabne murders, spoke of a 'tide of hatred towards the Jews' with which, to her amazement, she was inundated during her research in the remote area around Jedwabne. Her diary – included as part of her book – makes repeated mention of abuse and insults, especially after it became known that she was Jewish herself. She'd heard of a Polish priest who wanted to make a model of the Holy Sepulchre with the caption 'Jews murdered Our Dear Lord and the prophets, and persecuted us too. Poles, save Poland.'

I need to stress here once again that the picture is mixed. Tens of thousands of Poles, risking their lives, did all they could to hide and protect Jews during the war. The Israeli remembrance centre Yad Vashem has a list of the Righteous Among the Nations, people who helped persecuted Jews, and it includes more than 6,400 Polish names. Anna Bikont also found survivors of Jedwabne who were saved by people from the village. One farm boy had hidden a Jewish classmate, and after the war he said to her, 'Now my sweetheart, you're free; go where you will.' She had no desire to leave. They remained inseparable for the rest of their lives.

But after the publication of her book, Bikont again received letters saying things like, 'What's keeping you here in Poland? May hell swallow you up for your disloyalty and mendacity.' Or, 'Mrs Bikont, you Jewess possessed with insane anti-Polishness, we'll run into each other very soon now.'

In this Eastern European competition for heroism and victimhood – because that's what it was often about – history was all too readily rewritten to suit the new holders of power. Monuments and memories of the war framed the great national story, and by doing so created a new identity for 'our people' and 'our leaders'. That reshaping of the truth could be taken to extremes, as happened in various parts of the former Soviet Empire.

In Ukraine in 2015, for instance, any denial of the 'heroic character' of the nationalist paramilitary groups that belonged to Stepan Bandera's

Organization of Ukrainian Nationalists (OUN) during the Second World War was made a criminal offence. Any mention of the fact that the country's declaration of independence in Lviv on 30 June 1941 was 'celebrated' with a series of pogroms against the local Jews was forbidden, and the same went for acknowledging the enthusiastic participation of OUN militias in the mass murder of as many as 100,000 Polish Jews in order to create an 'ethnically pure' Ukraine. Even the epic *Stalingrad* by renowned war historian Antony Beevor became a banned book, simply because it mentioned the murder of ninety Jewish children by a unit of the OUN.

Earlier, in 2007, the nationalist Roman Shukhevych, leader of the notorious Nazi Nachtigall Battalion that in 1941 advocated the liquidation of all 'Polish, pro-Moscow and Jewish activists', posthumously had the title 'Hero of Ukraine' conferred on him. In Babyn Yar, a wooded area in Kyiv where in 1941 more than 30,000 Jews were murdered and thrown into a ravine, an exhibition was held in 2017 in honour of Ivan Rohach, an ultranationalist who in that same year, 1941, described the Jews as 'the greatest enemy of the people' – although no mention was made of that.

In Poland, the Holocaust was converted into, in the words of one commentator, 'a theatre of collective heroism'. On the recommendation of the Polish parliament, the year 2018 became the 'Year of Irena Sendler'. This particular heroine was said to have smuggled 2,500 Jewish children out of the ghetto, for which she was cruelly persecuted after the war by the communists. Anna Bikont dredged up her past. Sendler was indeed a courageous woman, but according to reports the most she actually did was to support somewhere between 100 and 300 children with money and clothing. She never personally smuggled anyone out of the ghetto. The Jews themselves did that. She was never prosecuted by the communist secret police, simply because she was herself an active and high-ranking communist. Thus new heroes were constructed, pieces of their life story added or taken away like Lego bricks.

In Hungary too, attempts were made to put a fresh shine on the history of the nation. In 2014 Viktor Orbán had a pompous monument built in Budapest to commemorate the German occupation seventy years earlier. It depicts the angel Gabriel in a kind of Roman temple, being attacked by a big aggressive eagle. The message is clearly that innocent Hungary was caught off guard by satanic Germany. In reality, German troops occupied

Hungary in March 1944 because the regime of the time, after all those years as a faithful Nazi ally, could no longer hold its own against the advancing Red Army. The Hungarian fascist organization the Arrow Cross Party was notorious. In three anti-Semitic laws, Jews were downgraded to second-class citizens in 1938. In 1941, 'innocent' Hungary handed some 16,000 'illegal' Jews over to the Nazis. They were then executed in Ukraine in the presence of Hungarian officers.

This 'shameful monument to the falsification of history', as it was described to me, provoked a response. Professor of art history András Rényi organized a successful protest on the opposite side of the street in the form of a 'living memorial' made of flowers, candles, suitcases and other personal objects, which were lined up along the pavement in memory of Hungarian victims of the Holocaust. A group of citizens took turns guarding it against neo-Nazis – that too was necessary in 2015.

Sometimes I'm reminded of my walks through Novi Sad, in 1999, in the company of film director Želimir Žilnik. 'Far too much is being promised, and far too much expected of the EU,' he used to mutter in those days. 'And then . . . You have no idea who we have waiting in the wings, ready to jump onstage!' He was right. In Eastern Europe new figures did indeed pop up with movements that didn't fit into any Western plan. The stories these leaders acted out in their theatre were completely foreign to those of us who grew up in the West.

Western blindness was partly to blame. In Western Europe, after all, people had little time for the importance many Eastern Europeans attached to concepts such as sovereignty and national identity, and the political priorities that resulted. The twentieth century as a whole was often seen quite differently in the East. For most Eastern Europeans, 1945 did not have the same significance as in the West, since it had meant, above all, the replacement of one dictatorship with another. Instead, 1989 was the pivotal year, and they regarded events in those crucial months as their national liberation from a foreign oppressor.

After generations of dictatorship, there was hardly any experience with the phenomenon of democracy, in its Western form at least. A free press was unknown, and entire generations had grown up with a deep distrust of all forms of journalistic expression. I remember the confusion just after the

Wall fell. When an East German newspaper reported that five people had been killed in a train accident – stating the unvarnished facts for the first time – everyone was shocked. It must mean at least fifty dead, they thought; in communist times, news items always needed to be decoded. Faith in facts was therefore weak, and older people in particular preferred religious or consoling stories that united people, whether or not they were true.

In the West we had spent decades chewing over questions such as: What can be achieved by means of a liberal democracy and what cannot? What is the relationship between democracy and the rule of law? What is the role of minorities and of opposition parties? In the East there was hardly any time or space for that after 1989. Results were expected immediately, here and now, and when miracles failed to happen great bitterness arose.

Poland, Hungary and some of the other former Eastern Bloc countries became known as 'left-behind nations'. The nation state, a concept that developed all over the Western world in the nineteenth century, came to fruition in the East only at the end of the twentieth century, after the collapse of the Soviet Empire. That time lag expressed itself less in reflection – what good things have we done as a nation and what have we done wrong? – than in pride.

After the world wars, the Holocaust and the end of rule over its colonies, the West acquired a certain hesitancy in its dealings with the past. In Eastern Europe, people had a completely different perspective. There, patriotism, honour, *Volk* and Christianity were not 'dirty words' at all. Leaders like Orbán and Kaczyński wanted nothing to do with the West's 'pedagogy of shame'.

Every nation is a product of history, an 'imagined community' of countless memories and stories, an entwined fate of shared experiences, generation after generation, a solidarity across time. More even than the cultural rift between North and South, friction between Eastern and Western Europe increasingly revolved around the question: what is, in fact, our shared European 'imagined community'? It was a divide that as the years went by became harder and harder to bridge.

In the summer of 2014, Orbán proudly proclaimed that, like Turkey and Russia, Hungary must break with the 'dogmas and ideologies of the West' and strive to become an 'illiberal democracy'. It was a term coined almost twenty years earlier, in 1997, by American political commentator Fareed

Zakaria, who intended it to refer to a democracy in which the majority was
all-powerful, in which there was little if any place left for the protection of
minorities, or for the checks and balances of a liberal state under the rule
of law. In using it, Orbán introduced a new political phenomenon onto the
map of Europe – a mixture of nostalgia and modernity, of the local and the
global, of old and new politics that transcended the traditional split between
right and left. In his own words, 'Thirty years ago we thought Europe was
our future. Today we believe we are Europe's future.'

So, from 2010 onwards, the old European consensus about democracy
and the rule of law was increasingly breached. Gradually, Europe began to
see the start of an anti-liberal world order.

When Jarosław Krawczyk and I, long ago, on that snowy winter's evening
in 1999, sat in melancholy conversation, his new girlfriend called by, cheerful and smiling. She was working for the Soros Foundation. She was a
symbol of the new era that was approaching, and with her appearance
everything at the table became radiant, banishing the gloom. 'We're all
Soros's whores,' said Jarosław. 'Yes, that's what they think at Radio Maryja.
To them the only true Europe is the Church, and Poland. Soros lays another
Europe over the top, a Europe of liberals and intellectuals.' The battle was
already fully underway, but it seemed logical that freedom would win. 'I'm
getting a divorce for her sake,' said Jarosław, and I could imagine why.

When I meet him almost twenty years later, everything has changed. 'In
those days I truly believed that Europe would become one, with one army,
one shared politics, one economy. And now? It's nothing. The social face
everyone was talking about then? I don't see it.'

As a Pole, he feels stuck. 'Here it's Polish, Polish, Polish. The EU is experienced as an organization that provides money, but we don't want to
recognize its basic principles. So then the question inevitably arises: which
Europe do we actually want? Just the market and the butter? Or something
more? That's the great question of Eastern Europe, and the answer is clear:
the former.'

He adds, almost to himself, 'I feel and live like a European, and my own
country is part of Europe. But it refuses to be European.'

Kostas and Efi

KOSTAS: IN OUR SHOP WE'VE seen everything and everyone. I've lived here since I was six, when the city was half the size it is now and all the districts of Athens were villages, each with its own look, its own character, its own atmosphere. This part here, Kypseli, was a fashionable area, very green, home to artists, rich families and affluent elderly ladies. Even then there were immigrants, but they came from Greece, from all those villages up in the hills, just like we did. They came here to work. Because, however poor everyone was, there was always a lot of work in Athens – in construction, in the shops, in tourist restaurants. My father could get a job anywhere.

Life was simple then. We boys played here in the square and on the street. There weren't many cars yet. Hide-and-seek, football, we had bicycles, the square was full every evening with playing children. All around it, sitting on the benches, were the parents. Those tower blocks over there hadn't been built yet. Instead there was a sort of little wood with farmland beyond. At home we lived as if we were still in the village, very traditionally – until I was about sixteen, at least, when rock 'n' roll erupted.

I started a kiosk on our local square, and in 1996 it became a shop, on the corner with Iakinthou. That was a street with lots of old-fashioned trades in those days, like furniture makers, even small factories. There were specialist shops that sold just one kind of item, watches perhaps, or cold drinks. Around the turn of the century things started to change. Megastores popped up everywhere and swallowed everything. But our street went on doing well.

Our business wasn't a real shop at first, it was more like an outsized kiosk, selling mainly newspapers and cigarettes. Later the law changed and we were allowed to sell whatever we liked, bread, groceries and a whole lot more, so it became a proper little supermarket. Then in 1999 Efi and I managed to buy this flat, in the first block to be built here. Many more quickly followed. The banks started handing out big loans for the purchase of expensive apartments like this, to anyone who wanted to buy.

EFI: New Year's Eve 1999? I certainly do remember it, yes. I don't regard round numbers like 2000 as particularly symbolic, but Kostas and I had just got married and it was our first New Year's celebration in our new home. We were saying goodbye to the century in which my grandmother had her children, then my mother. A new century was coming in which I would have our children. We stood there together on the balcony, with that view out across the city, surrounded by fireworks. How optimistic we felt!

KOSTAS: We were just in time to buy our apartment with drachmas. All those other new flats were finished after the euro came in, and they were far more expensive, costing more than twice as much. At first everyone was confused by the euro. Older people especially. They couldn't deal with it at all. Why had everything become so much more expensive overnight? A hundred-drachma bottle of wine cost three euros, a thousand drachma. Yes, we shopkeepers did good business. There was more money going around in our neighbourhood; wages rose more quickly. Even the Albanians working in construction here found themselves with money to spend. How pleased they were! They came into our shop more and more often. We watched it all happening and thought: where on earth is all this money coming from?

EFI: When I look back, I think what a madhouse it was, from the introduction of the euro until 2010. Even the people back in my village dreamed and fantasized wildly. All of a sudden they wanted the nicest houses and the best cars; they thought the good times would never end. They went on holiday, and a long way away too. They weren't wealthy, either; no, they were ordinary people like us. We kept saying to each other: does it really add up?

KOSTAS: Friends and acquaintances would call in to buy the financial newspapers, for the share prices and for news from the stock exchange. They'd stand there and hold forth: 'I'll invest ten thousand and it'll become a hundred thousand . . .' Well, I don't understand things like that at all, so I just let them talk. Yes, in hindsight, out of all those people maybe five had some success, the rest only lost money. The government of the day goaded them on, continually telling them how brilliantly the economy was doing, that anything was possible now. Share prices rose to unimaginable heights.

EFI: The women who came into the shop said they too sometimes had a little bet on the stock exchange, but they mainly talked about the fashionable clothes and handbags they were buying: Gucci, Armani, Prada. One expensive shop after another opened up. We saw it all around us. Our shopping street, our neighbourhood – everything was flourishing, our customers had plenty of spare cash.

You'll think this is crazy, but there was something I didn't like about that strange prosperity. I sometimes told Kostas it frightened me. It wasn't normal. Even my own mother, in that farming village, thought she could buy anything she liked now, and she filled up her house with all kinds of ridiculous rubbish. Something's getting totally out of hand here, I thought, even in my home village. The villagers had started going to nightclubs. Imagine that! It was decadent.

KOSTAS: You ask where the money came from? The farmers got subsidies from the EU. Of course, they were supposed to invest in their businesses, but many farmers – not all of them you understand – preferred to spend the money on a Mercedes or a BMW. Take my brother. He was forty-five and he was given a retirement pension. At forty-five! Those were things that were simply impossible. You could surely see then that something was badly wrong. Where was Europe all those years? Where were the checks and balances? It wasn't our style. Efi and I didn't go on foreign holidays, we didn't buy a house that we couldn't afford, but anyone who refused to join the festivities was labelled an anarchist, or a romantic.

EFI: We first noticed that something really had gone haywire from the turnover of our shop. There came a time when it started falling again. Newspaper sales dropped, and we were making less profit on our cigarettes. In our personal lives we didn't notice much difference. On television we saw all those Lehman Brothers bankers out on the street, and we were told a whole lot of banks were in trouble, but we thought: that's there, not here, it's a long way away. Even a year later when our own finance minister Giorgos Papakonstantinou said openly that Greek finances were a mess, we still didn't take it seriously. You see, we were used to politicians who made all kinds of claims all the time. We weren't really surprised or shocked. They said so many things . . .

KOSTAS: It was only in 2010, when the pensions were cut, that it started to dawn on us what was going on. People bought less and opted for cheaper products. They clearly had less money. Our turnover declined by 20 to 30 per cent. We were very worried. Many shops in the neighbourhood went bust, even the old fishmonger's, and the shoe shops were struggling to keep going long enough for the owners to reach retirement age. The restaurants cut their prices, so that local people, at least, would keep coming. We had only a small shop, and at that point we expanded to take on an empty neighbouring property. That allowed us to stock a wider variety of products. With hindsight it was a huge risk, but it's what got us through the crisis.

EFI: In the shop we noticed that at first our customers were surprised, more than anything. It was only later that they got angry. Then you began to hear a lot of despair, because it was the elderly who were the worst hit, with the cuts to pensions. They might need medicines that they were now unable to afford. Some were helped by their families, sometimes they moved in with their children, and sometimes they bought stuff from us on credit. We had a book where we wrote it all down, very old-fashioned. No, we weren't afraid customers would disappear without paying, but we did fear that some of those grannies and granddads might die. We didn't lose any sleep over it. Almost everyone paid in the end; we remained a neighbourhood shop, and that means you trust one another.

KOSTAS: That's how we survived those years. Syriza came along and we hoped things really would change, because there was so much corruption. But they didn't have a proper plan either. Their minister of finance, Varoufakis, was popular mainly for his flamboyant style. If you were eighteen, you liked him. He was a rock star who pretended he could change the world.

EFI: I thought he was irritating more than anything else. He was so sure of himself, but he was responsible for our whole country and he hardly seemed to take that seriously. When the negotiations with the EU started I felt really uneasy. Yes, I voted in the referendum. I voted 'no'. I didn't actually want to leave the EU, I couldn't see any advantages in leaving, but it was a safe way to register a protest vote – or so I thought.

KOSTAS: I didn't vote. I didn't believe in it. It wouldn't change anything. The world is complicated and it was out of our hands by that point.

Schäuble and the others were going to decide about Greece now. In the shop everyone was talking about it, left-wingers, right-wingers, but few of the customers talked any sense. As for me, I thought: perhaps this is simply how capitalism works. The people are the people and 80 per cent of them have no idea what's going on.

In Kypseli, on the corner with Iakinthou, we just carried on with our lives. Most people who had money bought houses in the suburbs and left. Newcomers from the villages took their place and bought the rather more expensive apartments, while Albanians and Eastern Europeans came to live in the cheap rental apartments. That's how we live here now. Are there still any Greeks on the square in the evenings? Not many.

EFI: We met on that square. Remember, Kostas? My parents moved here in 1991. Quiet or not, for me, a girl from such a tiny village, this really was the big city. The kiosk was like a beacon; it had a phone, you could ring everyone from there. That's how I came upon Kostas, when I was just starting out as a city girl, simply by making phone calls. We got talking, I went there more and more often, I fell in love, my goodness I did. No, I didn't say anything. He felt it. That was enough.

That's how it started, and that's how it is still.

9. Solidarity

2012

I

'GREECE IS THE ONLY EXAMPLE known of a country living in complete bankruptcy since the day of its birth,' wrote French journalist Edmond About in his travel account *La Grèce contemporaine*, published in English as *Greece and the Greeks of the Present Day*. 'The tax-payers do what the farmers did – they do not pay . . . . The officials, ill paid, without a certainty as to the future, sure of being dismissed on the first change of ministry, do not, as with us, take care of the interests of the State. . . . All Greeks know and love one another a little; they do not know anything of that abstract being, called the State, and they do not at all love it.'

He wrote those lines in 1854. More than a century and a half later, Greece was still a special case.

The Greek crisis had little to do with the international financial meltdown. There were no big banks in danger of failing that needed to be rescued by the Greek state. The Greek crisis was at the start thoroughly Greek, a home-brewed affair, and the Greeks themselves and their successive governments bore full responsibility for it. When the bubble burst in 2009 it wasn't just the Greek government that was deep in debt but around half of Greek adults personally. They'd been living on credit for years. What happened subsequently is a different story, but that's how it began.

Athenian thriller writer Petros Markaris describes the Greek drama as a mass escape from the 'culture of poverty' in which the Greeks had lived for centuries. It was reminiscent of Iceland, except that the pivot point came later, in the 1980s, when the country joined the European Economic

Community. Money poured in – wealth of a kind Greece had never experienced before – and after the country became part of the eurozone, Greeks were able to borrow cheaply and easily. As Markaris writes, they could at last leave their 'culture of poverty' behind, with all the thrift and creativity that went with it, but they proved incapable of developing a 'culture of wealth': 'Consumption became the driving force in society.'

Great imbalances had existed for centuries between the northern European countries – especially Germany, the Netherlands and Scandinavia – and the southern periphery. The northern Europeans were right up with the times at the end of the twentieth century, whereas Greece had plainly fallen behind in the rapid process of European modernization. All kinds of subsidies were granted in an effort to help it catch up. The Greek economy was largely dependent on small and medium-sized businesses, and a whole series of reforms was needed to give those businesses a place in the vast economy of Europe. Greece's poorly functioning government was equally in need of reform.

Instead of setting in train a sorely needed process of change, successive Greek governments – three cheers for party politics! – chose to take the route of least resistance. Under the cover of a few fine-sounding socially conscious slogans, they all liberally shared out money, jobs and privileges among their own supporters. The result was a clientele of faithful voters that kept establishment parties in the saddle for decades, purely out of self-interest. In the space of barely thirty years, the Greek governmental apparatus tripled in size. Between 1998 and 2008 Greek wages rose by 80 per cent, almost three times as quickly as in the rest of Europe, and civil servants were kept sweet with a pay rise of 117 per cent. The Greek public sector, Markaris writes, became a 'hazy state of affairs', in which 'you could put people to work at random tasks, the only aim being to attract votes'. So public service expanded on a help-yourself basis, paid for out of public funds. 'State and citizen compete to see who can spend most.'

Pensions were a case apart. As the years went on, there were so many giveaways – a lowering of the pension age, cuts to pension contributions, pension increases – that year after year it was impossible for the Greek government to cover the costs. Meanwhile it expertly staved off any reform of the system, which in Greece would have been political suicide since there was barely any other form of welfare. In 2010 that approach hit a brick wall. The Greek government could no longer finance its deficits.

Moreover, Greek attitudes towards taxation were essentially unchanged since 1854. In 2010 the country was still owed almost €40 billion by its citizens. Payment was hardly ever enforced, and the large Greek shipping companies didn't actually have to pay any tax at all. According to unofficial estimates, as much as €60 billion of Greece's money was stashed in Switzerland alone. A remarkable number of Greek mansions were built there, while Greek yachts could be seen moored all along the French Riviera.

What everyone had overlooked was the toilsome drudgery of the silent minority of tradespeople and small entrepreneurs, whom Markaris describes as 'the one driving force remaining within Greece'.

There was no lack of extravagant governmental expenditure. The Olympic Games in Athens in 2004 are rumoured to have cost €11 billion. Later you'd come upon signs of that exuberant period all over the city: beautiful museums, a fabulous highway from the airport, excellent sports facilities. The Greeks were spending some €6 billion a year on defence, way above the European average, because of tense relations with Turkey, but also to dissuade the army from contemplating an attempt at a coup. Greek tank battalions had 1,600 tanks, four times as many as Germany's. Between 2003 and 2007, the country was the world's fourth-largest weapons importer. A good deal of slush money was involved. For one German submarine contract, the defence minister of the time and his staff received more than €60 million in kickbacks. As recently as 2006 the Greek government was planning to reserve €27 billion over the coming decade for arms purchases. Germany with its Eurofighters and Leopard tanks, France with its Mirages and Russia with its Tor missile system all stood ready to do business.

By a statistical sleight of hand, this pattern of extreme defence expenditure was expertly concealed, both from Greece's taxpayers and from its partners in Europe. In September 2009, the then Greek government, under Kostas Karamanlis, claimed that the country's budget deficit was 3.4 per cent. Later, when the facade collapsed completely, it turned out to be more than 15 per cent – five times higher than permitted in the eurozone.

In the small world of Brussels, Greece had always been regarded as a problem case. Shocking stories had been circulating internally for years, and in 2005 the country was even placed under fiscal monitoring for a while. After the banking crisis, further warnings came from the EU and the IMF, but the Greek economy was regarded as too small and too marginal to cause very much damage. Then a new government, under the leadership of George Papandreou, decided to lay all its cards on the table and admit that the country's financial problems were in danger of getting completely out of hand. That disclosure, on 19 October 2009, had previously unimaginable consequences.

On at least three occasions over the next few years, the eurozone teetered on the edge of the abyss: in the spring of 2010, in the autumn of 2011 and in the summer of 2012. The drama – for that is what it was – looks in retrospect like a hurdle race. So perhaps it is best described in terms of seven hurdles, the first coming on that 19 October 2009: the revelation of the truth.

Recently appointed finance minister Giorgos Papakonstantinou later described to financial journalist Michael Lewis how he spent the early weeks of October 2009 trying to discover the true state of the government finances. It wasn't easy. On taking office he found that all the hard disks in the computers in his ministry had disappeared without trace. Skeletons fell out of the cupboard daily.

A pension debt that was rising by a billion every year had somehow been kept off the books. Everyone claimed the debt didn't exist, yet every month the government faithfully paid the pensions. The hole in pension provision for the self-employed was not €300 million, as everyone had assumed, but €1.1 billion. And so it went on. 'At the end of each day I'd say, "Okay, guys, is this everything now?"' Papakonstantinou said later. 'And they'd all say "Yes." But the next morning a hand would go up at the back of the room. "Actually, Your Excellency, there's another problem too, somewhere between a hundred and two hundred million."' Greece's planned deficit was €7 billion. Eventually the annual hole in the budget proved to be five times as big, at more than €35 billion.

On the evening of that Monday, 19 October 2009, in Luxembourg, during his first meeting with the Eurogroup, newcomer Papakonstantinou was immediately invited to speak. He told the group frankly about what he had discovered, saying his predecessors had fiddled the figures, and he revealed the actual budget deficit, which at that point was 12.7 per cent. Everyone listened open-mouthed and a deep silence fell. Then Dutch finance minister Wouter Bos let fly at him, saying, 'Giorgos, we know it's not your fault, but shouldn't someone be jailed for this?'

The figures became public. Eurostat, the EU's statistical office, sounded the alarm. A team of specialists flew to Athens to hold the Greek statistics up to the light. The Greeks had indeed, it turned out, compiled false reports deliberately, and on a large scale. European public opinion was profoundly shocked: after the banks, are we now going to have to bail out those spend-thrift Greeks with our tax money? Politicians, in northern European countries especially, assured their voters – in defiance of reality – that every euro lent to Greece would be repaid. The markets tumbled.

Up to that point, lenders had regarded the eurozone more or less as one big safe haven, underwritten by a reliable Germany. Now the mood changed. Distinctions were made between 'strong' and 'weak' eurozone countries when it came to interest rates and access to credit. Greece was blacklisted; practically all its lenders pulled back and from one moment to the next the country was suddenly unable to borrow a penny, other than at extremely high interest rates. All confidence had evaporated.

'When the euro crisis hit, no one knew what to do,' Luuk van Middelaar wrote later. As right hand to Herman Van Rompuy, he had been in the eye of the storm. 'Given the chorus of commentators who claimed with hind-sight to have predicted everything, it can do no harm to remember that. No one had contemplated a crisis spreading from one eurozone country to another, the risk that drove the subsequent financial turmoil.'

The Greek crisis was indeed contagious. Ireland, Italy, Spain and Portugal came under immense pressure because of rapidly rising interest rates. The banking crisis of 2008 had already darkened their economic outlook con-siderably. Between them, the problem countries still had more than €3 trillion in outstanding national debt, so with a rise in interest rates of even 2 or 3 per cent, they each had to cough up additional billions. It pushed their economies further into the mire. A 'doom loop' was created, and as time went on it was no longer a matter of saving each country separately but of attempting to ensure the survival of the eurozone as a whole.

Early in 2010, the IMF concluded that Greece would never be able to pay its debts and was therefore theoretically bankrupt. Yet it took another year and a half, until November 2011, for European governments more or less to acknowledge the fact. If Greek debt had been substantially relieved in that first phase and, by deploying European emergency funds, firebreaks had been created around the other endangered countries (as the American government strongly urged) – in other words, if the eurozone had shown it could act quickly, collectively and decisively – then the crisis might quite possibly have been nipped in the bud. 'If Greece had been not a country but a northern European bank, then the problem would have been solved long ago,' one commentator wrote dejectedly. He was more right than he knew. There was no sign now of the generosity with which the banks had been rescued only a year earlier.

In the autumn of 2009, the governing coalition in Germany had changed. The Social Democratic Party (SPD) left government and a new minister of finance took office, the conservative Wolfgang Schäuble. Schäuble had been paralysed from the waist down in an attack in 1990, but with enormous willpower he had continued his political career. He was a legalist who regarded legislation and the rule of law as central; rules must be obeyed, the necessary discipline shown. His role proved decisive.

Thursday, 11 February 2010, was the crucial date for the second hurdle. On that day, it became clear where the line taken by the new German government would lead. It declared itself prepared to use all available emergency measures to save the euro and recognized that the stability of the eurozone was a 'shared responsibility'. But specific support for Greece was ruled out. So now there was a veto.

This came as no surprise. In the Maastricht Treaty and the Treaty of Lisbon, rescue operations of this kind were explicitly ruled out. The euro was not intended for bailouts of other member states; each country had to solve its own problems. The northern member states in particular had insisted on this. Even an appeal to the IMF was rejected. Schäuble felt it would be a 'humiliation' for the eurozone, while Nicolas Sarkozy said the IMF wasn't intended for Europe: 'It's for Africa. It's for Burkina Faso!'

Among German taxpayers, a mood of 'enough is enough' prevailed. They felt they'd been bled dry to pay for German unification, in the west of the country especially. They'd also been through the mill of Hartz IV and had to rescue their own financial sector in 2008. They refused to take any more. The Greeks and their banks would have to sort things out for themselves this time. Most Germans failed to realize that their own German banks were as up to their necks in Greek problems as anyone. Along with the French banks, they had lent no less than €477 billion to Greece, Ireland, Portugal and Spain.

Behind the scenes, therefore, huge financial and political interests were at play. Angela Merkel knew all too well that her voters would never agree to another bailout of the German banks, having rescued them during the crisis of 2008 with more than €400 billion of taxpayers' money. As one EU official said, 'When it comes to financial assistance, Germany is now slamming on the brakes. On legal, constitutional and principled grounds.'

Both the Greeks and the financial markets reacted with shock. There would be no convincing financial safety net for the faltering economies in the form of emergency funds. Greece deteriorated rapidly, investors did all they could to rid themselves of Greek government bonds, interest rates rocketed, and the crisis was in danger of spreading to Spain, Italy and possibly Ireland.

Behind all this lay a fundamental conflict between Germany – supported by the Netherlands and Finland – and the southern eurozone. The countries of the South, accustomed to regular waves of inflation, demanded that the European Central Bank start functioning like a normal central bank. In emergencies, central banks create new money in all kinds of ways, the currency devalues, the prices of products fall, exports increase and the economy rebounds. Some inflation results, but the pressure is taken off and debts evaporate to a degree.

In Berlin, by contrast, even the word 'inflation' was traumatizing, after the hyperinflation of the 1920s. In the northern EU member states there was a desire to make use of the situation, to force eternally ailing southern Europe to modernize. Greece had a chaotic bureaucracy on top of everything else, and a deeply troubled relationship between its citizens and the state. As Jeroen Dijsselbloem said afterwards, 'The euro wasn't the problem, it was the weak and calcified institutions, it was the totally obsolete economy, it was Greece itself. Even without the euro, Greece would have got into huge difficulties.'

This crisis, however, was also about norms, values and life stories. Dijsselbloem, as a social democrat, felt that solidarity always entailed obligations. 'So the opposition between rules and solidarity is a false dichotomy.'

The solid Protestant norms with which Wolfgang Schäuble, by his own account, grew up were typical: don't steal, don't burden the future with today's problems. He told the *Frankfurter Allgemeine Zeitung* how his mother, a Swabian housewife, had once found herself without enough coins for the parking meter. She had no choice but to park without paying. The next day she drove to the meter and fed it the twenty pfennig she owed. 'We laughed about that at the time. But today I'm no longer laughing. The principle is right: don't steal, don't cheat, don't pull a fast one.'

In the German and Dutch tradition, therefore, the economy was closely bound up with morality. A state economy was seen as ultimately a matter of family housekeeping. Growth was the reward for diligence, discipline and good behaviour. Debt was to be avoided as far as possible. Both languages – and they alone in the world – have the same word for 'debt' as for 'guilt': *schuld*. It had to be recompensed, and could not be written off. Dijsselbloem once labelled interest 'sin money'.

Chasing after economic growth by getting deeper and deeper into debt was naturally taboo in this so-called ordoliberalism. Rarely, however, did anyone ask about the responsibility of the northern lenders – the German and French banks especially – whose excessive loans had done as much as anything else had to stoke the conflagration. Rarely too was it stressed that practically all the support for Greece had come from those same banks. And hardly ever was it pointed out that the northern member states themselves had benefited from the crisis. Their economies, after all, were doing just fine – better than those of the rest of the eurozone. In earlier times this would have caused their guilders and D-marks to rise in value, increasing the prices of their products and thereby putting a brake on exports. Now the euro remained relatively cheap, their exports went on growing as a result, and their trade surpluses had been above the eurozone norm of 6 per cent for years. Meanwhile, interest on German government debt fell by 3 per cent, partly because of the mass flight of capital from Greece and the other countries of southern Europe, benefiting Germany to the tune of several tens of billions a year.

Greece was endlessly admonished by Dutch ministers of finance. Rightly so, since far too little tax was being raised. But the Netherlands itself – in those years one of the biggest tax havens in the world, along with Bermuda and Ireland – was making the channelling away of Greece's black money possible in all kinds of ways. (To the Cayman Islands, for example, safely removed from tax-raising of any kind.) The profits of the twenty largest companies in Portugal, a poor country also forced to make deep cuts to government expenditure, were likewise tempted away to the Netherlands, with the result that those businesses contributed hardly anything to the Portuguese exchequer. In short, it was like the preaching of a Calvinist minister who chastises his congregation on Sunday and has his way with his housemaid on Monday.

All the old prejudices about the difference between rich and poor and between North and South strode back onto the European stage. The euro crisis was in essence a clash of mentalities, a fundamental rift between the societies of northern and southern Europe. It was that, more than anything, that made attitudes so uncompromising.

2

For the European Central Bank a major dilemma emerged. If the ECB had been a normal central bank, like the Bank of England or the Fed, then the wildfire could have been extinguished fairly easily. The Greeks hadn't borrowed in foreign currency but in their own euros; it was just that as members of the eurozone they'd transferred to the ECB the right to print money and to buy government bonds – the things every country does in such circumstances. Had the usual measures been put in place, the ECB and Greece could have calmed the markets, for the time being at least.

Jean-Claude Trichet, president of the ECB at the time, was opposed to any such moves, since they would mean that, by a circuitous route, northern European taxpayers would be paying for Greek debts. The Bundesbank in particular, Germany's central bank, would never accept such an outcome. Furthermore, Angela Merkel feared the wrath of her voters. On 9 May 2010 elections were due in the important state of North Rhine-Westphalia, and they were make or break for her CDU party.

In the spring of 2010, therefore, the European situation was in deadlock, with growing risks for the rest of the world economy. The Americans now started to become deeply concerned, since their banks and pension funds had parked hundreds of billions of dollars in the French and German banks. A downturn in Europe would hit American savers and investors hard. President Obama began to involve himself personally in the euro crisis, urging the IMF to intervene. This time Merkel listened. An emergency regime was set up in which the IMF, the ECB and the EU were to act in concert: the troika was born.

In the meantime, the Papandreou government had done all it could to get back in the good graces of the financial markets. With tax rises, drastic cuts – especially to pensions and welfare payments – and a long series of redundancies for government employees, he tried to get the deficit down to an acceptable level. For hundreds of thousands of Greeks the impact was devastating. Aside from pensions, the country had hardly any social safety net. Entire families found themselves living on the pensions of parents or grandparents, which were being substantially reduced. Mortgages and electricity bills could no longer be paid, so homes were lost and children moved in with their parents or vice versa. The homeless started to fill the squares of Athens, while soup kitchens grew busier by the day.

Investors, however, barely reacted to this drastic policy change. With a huge effort, Papandreou managed to squeeze one final loan of €6 billion out of the markets. There was no hope of more. On 23 April 2010, he made a public appeal to Europe: without financial help from outside, Greece would go under. Two months earlier, on 11 February, the EU had recognized that there was 'a shared responsibility'. Now a third hurdle had to be overcome: material support was needed, and fast.

In macroeconomics there is something called Dornbusch's Law, named after economist Rüdiger Dornbusch: 'If a situation is unsustainable, it can go on for far longer than you would ever think possible, but when the crisis does come, it escalates much more quickly than you could ever have imagined.' So it proved. On 23 April the crisis became dangerously acute, and contagious. For certain other eurozone countries, interest rates now soared – especially for Ireland, Spain and Portugal. Flows of capital between banks stopped, since they no longer dared lend to each other. The bottom fell out of the global financial system.

Amid great tension, an agreement within the troika was made concerning Greece on 2 May 2010. The conditions were stricter than ever: draconian cuts in all sectors of public life, and the sale of all kinds of state-owned property. There was an expectation that the Greek economy would at last be forced to modernize and restructure. In return, Greece would be given loans up to a value of €110 billion. In Athens the plans sparked riots, a couple of Molotov cocktails set a branch of Marfin Bank alight and three of the staff died in the flames, including a young woman who was four months pregnant.

Wall Street grew restless as well. On Thursday 6 May, when the stock exchange opened in New York, panic struck: the euro began to plummet, American shares fell – $1 trillion in value was wiped off the stock market – and investors fled the eurozone. Olli Rehn, then European commissioner for the monetary union, said afterwards, 'We saw before our eyes a financial meltdown of Europe.'

The next day, the European Council met in all haste. During an unruly working dinner, Jean-Claude Trichet warned that this wasn't just a European problem any longer by any means, let alone a Greek problem. 'It's global. It's a situation that is deteriorating with extreme rapidity and intensity.' According to one of those present, Nicolas Sarkozy was white as a sheet: 'I've never seen him so pale.' He shouted angrily that Trichet must intervene immediately. How could the ECB as a central bank stand idly by while the financing of the entire eurozone was in danger? Trichet remained unmoved: 'You governments are responsible; this is for you to solve.' Germany, Finland and the Netherlands also dug in their heels, terrified that a 'transfer union' would emerge, in which money would continually flow from the 'strong' member states to the 'weak'.

That weekend it was a close-run thing. But this was about far more than Greece alone. A huge safety net had to be put in place for the entire eurozone, a massive firewall to deter further speculation, and the deal had to be done before the Asian markets opened early on Monday morning. The G7 sprang into action. Obama rang all the government leaders. The Europeans proposed a fund of more than €60 billion. It was laughed off the stage by the Americans: 'Make it at least ten times that.'

On the Sunday afternoon, the European leaders once again rushed to Brussels for emergency consultation. Wolfgang Schäuble was in bed, too ill to come. Angela Merkel was in Moscow for the commemoration of the end of the Second World War. She was flown back as swiftly as possible. Eventually the Germans gave their consent. After all, this was no longer a matter of supporting one country, Greece, it was about rescuing the entire eurozone. In the historic words of Angela Merkel shortly afterwards in the Bundestag, 'If the euro fails, Europe fails.'

A temporary fund was set up, the European Financial Stability Facility (EFSF), with €60 billion from the European Commission, €440 billion from eurozone member states and €250 billion from the IMF. On that basis, Trichet felt able to go further: the ECB would support the rescue project by buying government bonds. This too broke a German taboo, since in reality it meant printing money.

At the very last moment, at two in the morning, just as the Asian markets were opening, Olli Rehn was able to announce a deal. 'We shall defend the euro, whatever it takes,' he said. It was by far the biggest commitment ever made by the IMF, and it characterized the seriousness of the situation, but with a big bazooka of €750 billion all speculation against the euro was curtailed. The markets calmed. So on Sunday, 9 May 2010, the third hurdle had been overcome, with a fund worth billions and a money-printing operation.

The arithmeticians of the EU and the IMF predicted that after a few years of pain and austerity, the Greek economy would emerge reborn. In reality, as we have seen, those billions served mainly to buttress the German and French banks. There was rightly talk of a round trip via the Acropolis. The ESMT business school in Berlin calculated that of the first two rescue packages, 95 per cent was spent on interest and debt repayments to the IMF and to foreign financiers. By March 2012, of the total Greek debt to German banks of €119.2 billion, only €795 million remained. Debts to French banks were settled even more quickly, and by December 2012 they were off the books.

The price paid by the Greeks was high, especially by the young and the most vulnerable groups. Professional Athenian flâneur Chrístos Chryssópoulos noted a new sound in the streets: the metallic rattle of the supermarket trolleys in which rag-pickers collected cans, wood, scrap metal, cables and other finds of some paltry value. Everywhere he saw people who had lost their homes, sometimes whole families, sleeping on the pavements and in parks, settling in there for good. 'The city has been turned inside out,' he wrote.

There was something else that was new in the streets of Athens: the shaved heads, cudgels, black leather jackets and swastikas. In the 2012 general election, the neo-Nazis had won 7 per cent of the vote; in the European elections two years later they won almost 10 per cent. Golden Dawn was on the rise.

The fourth European hurdle, on the sunny Monday afternoon of 18 October 2010, was taken not in a meeting room in Brussels but on the promenade of the beach resort of Deauville in Normandy. It looked like an ordinary photo opportunity, a cheerful stroll along the shoreline for Nicolas Sarkozy and Angela Merkel, under the eye of the cameras. But it wasn't. As they walked and talked, without any consultation with other member states, the pair made several firm deals. The EFSF would be given a permanent and legal basis, but the taxpayer would not be asked to cover any shortfalls. From now on, the banks and the other creditors must pay, and heftily too.

It was a purely political decision. Both leaders were all too aware that their voters would no longer accept the system of bailouts. Nevertheless, the Finns, the Dutch, the Swedes, the ECB, the IMF and the rest of the financial world were enraged by this two-person coup. 'You're going to destroy the euro,' Trichet exclaimed. It was seen as a second Lehman moment, since from now on the banks would be willing to lend money to 'weak' countries only at huge risk premiums, and the uncertainty would break out all over again. The *Financial Times* spoke of a 'Merkel crash'.

A month later, Ireland went belly up. The guarantee of 30 September 2008 to the savers and investors of the Irish banks had cost Irish taxpayers some €85 billion, and the deficit had climbed rapidly. There was increasing concern about Spain, Portugal and Italy too, and the interest rates they had to pay on their government bonds became impossibly high. If the eurozone can't handle the problems of little Greece, was the reasoning – at less than 2 per cent of the European economy – then what happens if Spain comes to grief or, worst of all, Italy? Was the firewall strong enough? If Italy got into difficulties, it was calculated, then there would be a need for not €200 billion or €400 billion but a trillion or two.

The Italian premier, former media magnate Silvio Berlusconi, denied there was a problem: 'Italy is rich, the planes are full, the restaurants are full.' On 15 February 2011 he was indicted for having sex with the underage 'Ruby the Heartbreaker', but he refused to resign. Angela Merkel tried in vain to convince him of the seriousness of the situation.

In Washington, unease grew. The IMF believed a reset was needed, a clear declaration by European leaders that the crisis that had flared up once more would stop and confidence would be restored. Dominique Strauss-Kahn, managing director of the IMF, was due to fly to Europe on 14 May to achieve that task, and he needed to convince Merkel above all. But the drama took a bizarre turn with a second sex scandal. A few minutes before take-off from New York he was removed from the plane by police and arrested. He was accused of sexual assault, of having forced a chambermaid in his hotel to perform lewd acts – it had been, in his own words, an 'inappropriate relationship'. The prosecution was eventually dropped, but Strauss-Kahn, who turned out to have acquired something of a reputation in this regard, was forced to step down. In the middle of a huge crisis, the IMF had to find a new boss.

On 21 July 2011, the European leaders declared that they had found a definitive solution. There was talk of fresh support for Greece: a loan of more than €100 billion, recapitalization of the banks and a European Marshall Plan. The Slovak premier Iveta Radičová acted with particular courage. Her country was poorer than Greece, she knew she was risking her re-election, but she declared herself willing to contribute to help save the euro. Greece's private creditors also had to take their losses now, amounting to as much as 75 per cent. Foreign banks and investors had largely been bought off with the first loan, however, so the price would be paid above all by the Greeks themselves, especially by their pension funds. In the end, this part of Greece's national debt was mostly written off or postponed indefinitely.

But in the end the crucial measure was not forthcoming: the creation of firebreaks, plus a convincing European safety net for faltering economies.

Meanwhile, the doom loop was having its effect. Economic forecasts for countries like Italy and Spain continued to worsen, and the interest they were having to pay on their government loans – interest is, after all, compensation for the risk taken by an investor – rose to even greater heights as a result, which undermined their economies yet further. In addition, the banks, after the crisis of 2008, needed to bring their reserves up to the mark before June 2012 (by which time European banks were required to increase their Tier 1 capital ratios to 9 per cent), so like misers they were sitting on their money in the autumn of 2011 instead of lending out capital to stimulate the European economy.

Greece saw little benefit from all that hard-won support. It had been a series of gestures more than anything, intended to restore some degree of confidence in the financial markets. Among Greeks, poverty rapidly grew. The narrow street on the corner of which Efi and Kostas had their shop, Iakinthou, was busy and lively in 2009, with a fishmonger's, a wine shop, a business that specialized in supplies for christening parties, a shop selling orthopaedic aids, a supplier of building materials, a second supermarket, a sports shop and two shoe shops almost opposite each other, run by two women who were also friends. Now the street went downhill rapidly. The old fishmonger's and the wine shop had to close; the second little supermarket – run by a mother and daughter – succumbed to the many new tax demands; the festive shop for christenings was suddenly empty, its big windows bare; and even the two friends with their shoe shops found it impossible to carry on.

By early 2012, a third of Greek households were living at or below the poverty line. According to the National Centre for Social Research, the number of prostitutes (both male and female) rose rapidly, eventually by some 150 per cent. Their prices fell accordingly, to less than ten euros per 'contact'. But worst of all, Greeks confirmed to me later, was the loss of dignity. Greek premier Papandreou announced he would put this latest deal to a referendum. Greeks must decide for themselves whether they wanted to continue along this path.

On 3 and 4 November 2011, during the G20 summit in Cannes, the euro crisis reached an unprecedented climax. The European leaders played hardball. Obama, without being asked, took the lead – 'trying to help save Europe from itself', as the Americans put it. The US president, supported by Sarkozy, proposed the American central bank, the Fed, as a model, saying that with a similar approach Europe would have got on top of the crisis long ago, and that a far bigger protective mechanism was needed, 'a big bazooka'. But the German Bundesbank in particular refused to contemplate such a thing. The discussion became heated. Merkel had tears in her eyes when she left the room; slowly but surely she was becoming completely isolated.

Concepts like national democracy and sovereignty fell away. Behind the scenes, Papandreou was hauled over the coals. He was given to understand that the Greek referendum must be about whether voters wanted to be in or out of the eurozone. He withdrew the referendum proposal and flew back to Athens humiliated. It was also made clear to Berlusconi that his position was untenable. 'The Italian economy isn't the problem,' Sarkozy snapped at him. 'The Italian problem, that's you. Those high interest rates, that's because of you. If you want to do your country a service, resign!' The Greek interest rate shot up to an astonishing 33 per cent, while Italy's rose to 7.45 per cent.

Within a week, both Papandreou and Berlusconi were replaced by EU-backed technocrats. Cannes was the fifth crucial hurdle – and according to some participants it was then that the eurozone really did hang by a thread.

'Is it possible to be both terrified and bored?' wondered economist Paul Krugman during those crisis months. Yes, it was possible. The story surrounding the euro crisis became increasingly dull, and at the same time everyone who understood it broke out in a sweat. Never before had I heard of journalists being kept awake at night by the economic analyses they'd made during the day. I did now. I was regularly told such tales in those autumn weeks of 2011, and I was tormented by the whole thing myself. Twenty-first-century societies had grown extremely fragile, and the repercussions of a collapse of the euro were unthinkable: vanished savings, blocked welfare benefits, cash machines without money, shops and businesses no longer supplied, a completely snarled-up economy.

The British chancellor of the exchequer, George Osborne, would later reveal to the BBC that in London in those weeks there were detailed plans to fly large quantities of cash to the Greek islands should the euro collapse – pallet-loads of sterling banknotes to get British tourists home in one piece. European Commission president José Manuel Barroso, asked for his reaction, said, 'Of course, we knew that. We did the same.' He emphatically denied at the time that there was a plan B, since that would only have increased the panic. 'And it was true. Plan B didn't exist. We had a plan Z.'

Until Cannes there had never been any serious talk of a Grexit, but at this point many European governments decided they'd had enough. They couldn't ask their parliaments to rescue the Greeks again, but the refusal of further support and an open Greek bankruptcy would mean Greece having to leave the eurozone. In the deepest secrecy, therefore, from early 2012 onwards a scenario was developed for a possible Greek exit. The country would be thrown back on its own resources, unable any longer to shift responsibility for its finances onto 'Europe' or the troika, but Greece would be free of its debts at a stroke. Bankruptcy might be liberating and bring clarity, while the isolation of Greece would prevent further contagion of the eurozone.

Conversations about this top-secret plan Z went on until August 2012, when Germany put a stop to its further development. The consequences were too immense and unpredictable, not just for Greece but for the rest of Europe. It was calculated that the European banks and governments would have to write off €342 billion in debt, and several large banks would need saving again. A new currency for Greece would have to be created in secret − at about half the value of the euro − while Greek banks would be unable to borrow money and would fail en masse. Two million Greeks would find themselves well below the poverty line, basic amenities would fall away and unprecedented numbers of migrants would set off for northern Europe. The chaos might drag in other weak member states. Adam Tooze, the great chronicler of these twenty-first-century crises, wrote that 'the rest of the world would regard Grexit as a failure not just of Greece, but also on the part of the larger European states'. Europe's pretensions as a world power would be null and void.

Meanwhile, a new president of the ECB had been appointed − Mario Draghi. Unlike Trichet, he was prepared to stretch the boundaries of his mandate as far as he could. From December 2011 onwards he started a silent support operation, and over that winter he pumped a trillion euros into the refinancing of European banks.

Yet the eurozone began to deteriorate again. There was brief talk of

Chinese capital as a possible solution, as if the Chinese would want to put money into an emergency fund in which the Europeans themselves had no faith. Even a layperson could see that it was all hot air, and the investors realized that immediately. France was sinking, losing its triple-A credit rating on 13 January 2012. Even the virtuous Germany could no longer get a bond loan fully signed up. For international investors, Europe was a contaminated zone.

The Greeks meanwhile were demonstrating not just on the streets and at the polls – on 6 May the reigning Pasok went down in a crushing defeat, with newcomer Syriza in alliance with the communists getting twice as many votes – but through their bank accounts. They were withdrawing their money and the ECB kept having to intervene. To mask the extent of the run on the banks, transport aircraft were hired to fly banknotes to Athens from all the eurozone countries, to a value of almost €30 billion in total.

On that same day, 6 May, France broke with the politics of Sarkozy and Merkel. Sarkozy lost the presidential election and French voters expressed a clear preference for the anti-austerity, pro-stimulus programme of the socialist François Hollande.

Three days later, on 9 May, Spain's BFA-Bankia started to collapse and another banking crisis was in prospect. Interest on government loans soared to 7 per cent and the Spanish government deficit spiralled. The situation was reminiscent of the Irish crisis, since in Spain too the overinflated housing market was the root cause, except that in Spain it was ten times as great. 'Zombie banks' emerged, overburdened with loans that could never be repaid. They might have a promising building project on their books valued at millions of euros, for example. Two journalist friends of mine went to film the sober reality, and I can still see the images they brought back: a rusty abandoned building site, a few unfinished concrete structures, dilapidated and without any appreciable value. It was the same everywhere.

Spain's credit rating fell to Baa3, barely above junk status. The Spanish foreign minister predicted that the country's financial demise was only days away; but, as he put it to Berlin, 'If the Titanic sinks, it takes everyone with it, even those travelling in first class.' The country was given emergency credit of a hundred billion euros, but more was required. There was a desperate need to break out of the dynamic of the doom loop, the vicious circle of failing banks and weak government finances.

Under huge pressure from the United States – 'Do you really want to be responsible for wrecking the world economy?' – Germany along with Finland and the Netherlands finally came around after fifteen hours of consultation. At the European Council meeting of Thursday, 28 June 2012, a dual breakthrough was achieved, ending the stalemate between North and South in Europe. The three northern countries now seemed prepared to support problem banks directly by means of a permanent European emergency fund – something that had been unthinkable just two years earlier – on condition that a central European banking regulator was introduced. It was the start of a banking union.

Nevertheless, the sum raked together for the bailout fund – €500 billion as against debts of €3 trillion at the problem banks – was still far too little to convince the markets. In fact, it would probably be interpreted as a motion of no confidence by the northern European countries in the southern countries. Setting up too modest a fund would be counterproductive and only deepen the crisis.

So the concession won from Merkel by Mario Draghi in a nocturnal head-to-head was far more important: at last the European Central Bank was given the scope it needed to act decisively. When the summit was over, Draghi cheerfully stepped into the office of exhausted Council president Van Rompuy and said, 'Herman, do you realize what you all did last night? This is the game-changer we need.'

So that was the sixth hurdle, the eternal blockade. On Friday, 29 June 2012, at 4.20 in the morning, it was finally overcome.

It was a historic moment, but still the markets were not calmed. In Spain a silent run on the banks had started and the ECB had to come to the aid of the Spanish banks to the tune of almost €400 billion. Close to a month later, on Thursday 26 July, Draghi gave a speech to a select group of financiers and investors at the Royal Lancaster hotel in London. The mood was grim. Draghi later told a friend that his audience was furious with him. Without conferring with anyone, he had decided to hone his speech on the spot. The markets needed to understand that the eurozone, under the pressure of the crisis, had now changed fundamentally. He said that an incredible amount of political capital had been invested in the euro, and the member states would not let it be taken from them. At that point, improvising, he added the historic words: 'Within our mandate, the ECB is ready to do whatever it takes to preserve the euro. And believe me, it will be enough.'

So, almost in passing, on 26 July 2012 the seventh hurdle was overcome: the markets. What Draghi said was almost word for word what the European leaders had said at the summit of 29 June, but their bailout fund of €500 billion had not been the least bit convincing. The markets listened to Draghi and the ECB. They calmed immediately. Interest rates fell and no one talked about the eurozone fragmenting any longer. It was over.

3

As a result of huge political and diplomatic efforts, the euro and the eurozone were dragged back from the brink. On 10 December 2012 in Oslo, Martin Schulz, Herman Van Rompuy and José Manuel Barroso accepted the Nobel Peace Prize on behalf of the EU. Europe had changed. But for whom?

Many important decisions were taken in a situation of chaos and crisis, when, as they say in Brussels, 'under pressure everything becomes fluid'. Jeroen Dijsselbloem, who was appointed Dutch finance minister in late 2012, was incredulous when he first joined the Eurogroup. Meetings often lasted until three or four in the morning, he said later, and ministers disappeared into rooms to consult with each other. 'Everyone was scrambling. There were continual adjournments.'

'We didn't have so much as a second to think about improvements to the system as a whole,' I heard later from a senior civil servant in the Eurogroup. 'We were running around an ancient steam engine, unable to repair one safety valve before the next one failed; we were in simple survival mode.'

Yet in hindsight, a relatively consistent line can be detected in that series of decisions. First of all, there was a clear historical development. To address the crisis, permanent funds and institutions were established, substance was given to the euro and a common fiscal policy began to emerge. It wasn't only rules that mattered; political decisions became increasingly important too. 'Whatever it takes' didn't come out of the world of rules. It was pure politics.

Second, beneath the guise of neutrality, the priorities in decision-making became clearly visible. For the first few years after the crash especially, they unmistakably lay with the protection of the banks and the financial sector, often at the expense of the taxpayer. In 2010 Ireland made a bold effort to take a different approach, but it stood not a cat in hell's chance at the ECB. Even in 2013, during the Cyprus banking crisis, when Jeroen Dijsselbloem finally confronted the Russian magnates and other speculators with the price of their gambling, his decision to do so was met with a storm of criticism.

Again and again, those choices were at the expense of the national democracies: the total bank guarantee that had to be provided to the international money markets in 2008 and in 2010 by Irish taxpayers; the way in which Spain and Italy were put under pressure by the ECB and the EU, and Germany by America and France; the Greek referendum that in 2011 was more or less forbidden; and the way the Greek and Italian prime ministers were replaced within months of each other by two former bankers, Loukas Papadimos and Mario Monti, who, without any form of democratic legitimacy, forced through massive austerity programmes. European citizens, in short, increasingly had the feeling they were part of a financial experiment over which they no longer had any control. In the words of former British diplomat Ian Kearns, the misleading idea that no alternatives were available, that voters had no choice, 'perhaps did more damage to the ideal of European integration than any other development in recent decades'.

Meanwhile, behind the scenes at the European theatre, national interests all too often predominated. In the powerful protection given to the German and French banks, for instance. Or in the peculiar demand by the troika that the definition of 'fresh milk' must be stretched from five to eleven days, making the import of foreign milk possible – a gift to the Dutch dairy industry at the expense of small Greek farmers. Or in the obligation of Greek shops to open on Sundays, forced upon them purely and simply because it suited the interests of the large European retail chains. Or in excessive Greek defence expenditure, from which Germany in particular profited. Note that, amid all the demands for cuts, Greek military spending was miraculously spared.

The problem lay deeper, however. By adroitly shifting the burden of debt onto taxpayers during the banking crisis, a difficulty in the private sector became a public matter – and not only that, it was squeezed into all kinds of national straitjackets. Intentionally or not, an issue for the EU about the future structure of the eurozone was transformed into a fierce confrontation between European nations. The old ghosts, pushed aside with so much effort after 1945, came roaring back.

One striking thing, finally, was the almost ideological rigidity of the participants, especially Germany, Austria, Finland and the Netherlands. It was continually suggested that the euro, despite all its design faults, was a given, and that there was no alternative to the policy of austerity. Political choices were sold, in the spirit of neoliberalism, as technical solutions, inevitable and inescapable.

In reality there is a great deal more to be said on the matter. The euro was and remains an extremely problematic currency, because it forces nineteen very different economic cultures into a single monetary set-up. So within the eurozone there was a lack of much-needed monetary flexibility, which in turn blocked the chances of recovery. Iceland and later Denmark, moreover, showed that banks could be put in order or simply allowed to go bankrupt with far less social damage than would be caused by rescuing them – and, yes, at the expense of the creditors.

When it came to Greece there was another problem too. It was the member of the eurozone that had sabotaged all the rules and forfeited all confidence, but was a rigid regime of austerity really the right way to make such a country toe the line? Was it not rather more a case of a punishment expedition than of a carefully considered policy?

As I have said, warnings came thick and fast regarding both the euro and the policy of austerity, from all corners of the economic world. As early as the summer of 2012, the IMF admitted that it had seriously underestimated the negative impact of spending cuts. Prognoses from the IMF – and the same went for those of the EU – had been wildly inaccurate in many cases. In practice, the economic harm done by austerity was at least half as great again as had been expected, far greater than any possible economic benefits.

In June 2013 there was nothing to be seen of the predicted Greek

recovery. On the contrary, the economy had shrunk by 25 per cent. As Adam
Tooze concluded bitterly, 'Bad economics and faulty empirical assumptions
had led the IMF to advocate a policy that destroyed the economic prospects
for a generation of young people in Southern Europe.' With, once again, all
the inevitable political consequences.

4

'Words are such feeble things,' wrote George Orwell in the crisis year 1936,
reporting from the dirt-poor British mining towns. 'What is the use of a
brief phrase like "roof leaks" or "four beds for eight people"? It is the kind
of thing your eye slides over, registering nothing. And yet what a wealth of
misery it can cover!'

Numbers do exactly the same. Take for example the memoirs of Jeroen
Dijsselbloem about his time as president of the Eurogroup. For my young
historian of 2069 it's a great source. Dijsselbloem writes clearly and expres-
sively, making us privy to what happened in those inner rooms of the EU
during the euro crisis. But one thing becomes strikingly obvious: all the
thinking in those circles was purely from a financial point of view. Everyone was locked into the same system. Not for a moment was there talk of
broader social concerns. Not for a moment does anyone seem to have asked
themselves whether the 'cure' of sometimes-draconian spending cuts
might be far worse than the disease. Unemployment and poverty were
merely percentages that, indeed, 'your eye slides over': not broken families,
not anxiety, illness and humiliation.

Based on the raw data, things did go better with Greece from 2013
onwards. The economy seemed to grow again – both the IMF and the
European Commission were actually expecting a growth spurt of some 3
per cent. The number of unemployed began to decline and the deficit, after
all those cuts, fell to 3.7 per cent. With the privatization of state-owned
companies – aimed at bringing in an estimated €85 billion – the 'efficiency' of the economy was successfully boosted. The Greek government
was able to borrow money on the capital markets again, first €5 billion and
later perhaps as much as €20 billion. By 2014 the troika wanted to begin
thinking, cautiously, about an end to the support programmes for Greece.

That was in Brussels. In Athens the reality looked very different. In the street where Efi and Kostas had their business, two out every three shops were gathering dust, empty and forgotten. The minimum wage had gone down by between a quarter and a third, while pensions – on which whole families might have to get by – had roughly halved. Unemployment had risen to almost 30 per cent; for young people, closer to 60 per cent. Greece, according to the IMF, found itself in one of the deepest recessions in economic history. It was to last for six years.

To quote from a Greek website called 'Diary of the Unemployed' in April 2013: 'There's a small advert in the newspaper. "Office requires part-time staff member aged up to 25, working hours from ten till four, salary 150 euros per month, telephone . . ." I've been unemployed for three years and my hand goes automatically to the phone to ring the number. . . . Unfortunately the job was quickly and efficiently given within two minutes to someone who agreed to a salary of 110 euros. What a triumph. Here are the promised new jobs. Here lies the future.'

For years, little or nothing came of the economic growth predicted by the EU, the reward for all those spending cuts. Privatization all too often amounted to a fire sale, and between 2011 and 2015 it produced a mere €3.2 billion. Only a quarter of those meagre earnings found their way to the Greek treasury; the rest went to the creditors. At the same time, from 2015 onwards hundreds of thousands of refugees crossed from Turkey to Greek islands like Chios, Lesbos and Samos. Greece had become the centre of both major European crises – the financial crisis and the migrant crisis.

On Omonia Square and Victoria Square in Athens, migrants and the homeless lay sleeping side by side, day and night. Despite their own worries, many Greeks assisted the migrants as best they could, but there was no money to accommodate them properly. Between the islands where they arrived and the rest of Europe stood, as a local journalist put it, 'a wall of indifference'.

5

In January 2015 the epilogue to the Greek tragedy began, and it became a drama in its own right. For the rest of the eurozone the financial risks were small this time, but emotions loomed larger than ever. All of Europe was now watching the domestic politics of little Greece day by day, and at many kitchen tables – including ours – the discussion was heated. Fundamental questions had arisen. How far does European solidarity stretch? How much weight is given to national democracy these days? To what degree is it right to use economic coercion? And what would a 'good' Europe look like now?

Luuk van Middelaar saw at first hand that European political leaders were dumbfounded by the new performance in which they found themselves. They had only just come to realize that such discussions mattered nowadays, not just to their own voters but to a far larger arena, to 'an entirely new European public sphere, created precisely by and through those events'.

The new drama began on 25 January 2015. On that day, Greek voters settled scores with the old establishment of both left and right. The left-wing radical Syriza movement gained 149 seats, which gave it a firm grip on Greek politics. Under the leadership of Prime Minister Alexis Tsipras, a completely new government was appointed. The cabinet was dominated by former communists as well as newcomers from the academic and intellectual world, full of fresh plans and ideas but often without much experience of normal working environments, or the wheeling and dealing that is an inevitable part of them.

A typical exponent of this bloodless revolution was the self-assured Yanis Varoufakis, the new finance minister. He had grown up in a prosperous left-wing family, studied maths and economics in England, lectured at the universities of Cambridge, Sydney and Texas, and was a specialist in game and decision theory. Along with prominent Labour Party member Stuart Holland and American economist James Galbraith, he published *A Modest Proposal for Resolving the Eurozone Crisis*, in which he was fiercely critical of the policy of austerity and advocated the opposite: a strong policy of investment, a European New Deal. He enjoyed support from progressive academic circles in America, where 'Bailoutistan', as Varoufakis called Greece, was regarded as an interesting experiment.

Immediately on taking office, Tsipras and Varoufakis brought things to a head. They would raise the minimum wage, thousands of civil servants would be given back their jobs, and planned privatizations would be cancelled. Debt restructuring would be done differently too. After all, financial support was mainly going to the creditors, while the Greek economy had nothing to gain by it and was not growing. An investment programme was therefore needed, taxes must be reduced to boost growth, and corruption and privileges must be tackled head on.

Syriza believed that part of the national debt would simply have to be written off. There was no other way. Greece was now in a nineteenth-century debtors' prison like those described by Charles Dickens, a captivity that permanently blocked any opportunity to earn anything, and therefore any way to pay off the sums owed. As Varoufakis put it, 'Even if God and all the angels were to invade the soul of every Greek tax evader, turning us into a nation of parsimonious Presbyterian Scots, our incomes were too low and our debts too high to reverse the bankruptcy.'

This might have developed into a groundbreaking confrontation right across Europe, a necessary corrective to the rigid dogmatism of the northern member states. Many economists and commentators, outside Europe especially, broadly shared the vision of Syriza and Varoufakis. As President Obama said in an interview with Fareed Zakaria of CNN, 'You cannot keep on squeezing countries that are in the midst of depression. At some point there has to be a growth strategy in order for them to pay off their debts to eliminate some of their deficits.'

The IMF itself, in February 2017, recognized that the Greek national debt – estimated in late 2015 at 179 per cent of gross national product – was 'unsustainable' even in the most favourable of circumstances. Remission was inevitable, it said. Syriza rightly identified the main problem about the whole euro debate: its pseudo-objectivity, the denial that there was any possible alternative, whereas in reality, major political choices were being made.

The problem with Varoufakis, however, was that, along with many positive qualities, he had a unique talent for driving even his most sympathetic discussion partners to distraction in no time. Since in such delicate negotiations personal relationships matter, with him as finance minister Greece soon had one more problem on top of all the rest. The image that emerges from the lively memoirs published by Jeroen Dijsselbloem, by Varoufakis himself and by other central players, as well as from a number of different reconstructions of events – in particular the BBC documentary *Inside Europe:*

Ten Years of Turmoil – is of a disastrous collision between two ingrained attitudes: conservative austerity dogma and progressive academic arrogance.

Varoufakis was a minister for just five months, but in the words of his opposite number Dijsselbloem, 'he left behind him an indelible impression and untold damage'. The very first meeting between the two was disastrous. Varoufakis claimed that Greece was bankrupt, that the new Greek government would not pay back to the ECB the agreed instalments that summer, but that there was an urgent need for a bridging loan, with no conditions attached. Dijsselbloem pointed out that this was not an available option, that the rules were anchored in treaties and that voters in other countries would not accept such a wholesale cancellation of debt – for that was what it came down to. During the press conference that followed, Varoufakis explained: 'We do not aim to work with a tripartite committee whose objective is to implement a programme which we consider to have an anti-European spirit.' Dijsselbloem, caught off guard, was astonished. As they left, after an uneasy handshake, he whispered to Varoufakis, 'You just killed the troika. And without the troika, you are on your own.'

On a tour of European capitals later that week, Varoufakis followed the same pattern. He quickly forfeited the sympathy of the Italian government by suggesting – contrary to the facts – that Italy was bankrupt too. He treated his largest financial backer – in the person of Wolfgang Schäuble – with contempt, by lecturing Schäuble at length on Germany's Nazi past, and everywhere he went he repeated his anti-establishment slogan: 'Let's stop extending and pretending.' It worked brilliantly in the more progressive circles at home, since it amounted to saying that Greece was bankrupt and could no longer meet its obligations. Varoufakis was terrifically popular in Greece in those first few weeks.

Other sectors of European society, however, were listening closely. Here was a Greek finance minister who was using a slogan to declare the bankruptcy of his own country. The Greeks quietly began emptying their bank accounts, shares in Athens fell by tens of percentage points, the Greek banks lost access to the ECB's normal payment channels and interest on Greek government bonds rose rapidly.

Greece, meanwhile, urgently needed a fresh injection of money, and for that purpose the Eurogroup met in haste on 11 February. But to everyone's surprise and irritation, Varoufakis merely gave his colleagues a good talking to, apparently unaware that he was there as a representative of the country that, with its lies and deception, had caused the euro crisis in the first place. In a long lecture, he explained to his fellow ministers that they were complete idiots. 'I'm sure he was right,' Schäuble said afterwards to the BBC. 'But say that to people trying to help you, and they won't be impressed.' The French finance minister, Michel Sapin, recalled the reaction of his colleagues: 'Yanis, you want us to help pay for your pensions, when they're higher than ours?' The meeting lasted seven hours and led nowhere, not even to a press release.

A series of subsequent meetings about emergency aid for Greece proved equally fruitless. There was a point when Varoufakis started endlessly talking to Tsipras on the phone during a meeting. All the other euro ministers could only sit and wait. After an hour, Schäuble angrily wheeled himself away in his wheelchair and the other ministers followed. Varoufakis carried on talking until Dijsselbloem tapped him on the shoulder. 'Yanis, you can put the phone down. The ministers have left. There's no deal.'

Problematic too was the fact that the Greek negotiators made constant reference to their 'democratic' decisions. The academics around Syriza seemed impervious to the fact that the other eighteen eurozone countries had voters too, with wishes of their own. Lithuanian minister Rimantas Šadžius pointed out during one consultation that the minimum wage in his country was 300 euros a month, and that his government had wanted to raise it by 25 euros, but that his country was being asked to contribute to a loan to Greece so that the minimum monthly wage there, according to plans made by Syriza, could be raised from 500 to 700 euros. Did Varoufakis actually have a true picture of European reality?

All this churlish behaviour, in the words of Schäuble, made 'the final remnant of confidence in the Greeks melt away'. It meant the Greek economy was dealt another heavy blow. I recall from those weeks an interview with a Greek fellow journalist. Halfway through our conversation, he burst into tears.

The damage done by Varoufakis's brief term in office was later estimated by Klaus Regling, CEO of the European emergency fund the EFSF, at €100 billion or more. Dijsselbloem later described him as 'the most expensive finance minister in history', writing: 'I had rarely seen so much arrogance and vanity in one place, along with a willingness to take huge risks at his country's expense.'

In the streets of Athens, the staff of the troika had meanwhile been subjected to physical threats. While the Portuguese and the Irish were searching for solutions of their own – the Irish Times wrote, 'It is the incompetence of the governments we ourselves elected that has so deeply compromised our capacity to make our own decisions' – many Greeks refused any form of ownership of their problems, placing the blame on 'the old politicians' and 'other countries'. Meanwhile, practically all Greeks, each in their own way, had an interest in maintaining the status quo. Businesses had no wish to lose lucrative government contracts, the unions were happy to let abuses in state companies continue to multiply, the middle classes and professionals cherished the countless holes in tax legislation, and millions of families were dependent on the bankrupt pensions system. The representative of the IMF labelled Greece the 'most unhelpful client' in all the seventy years of the institution's history.

The few people within the fiscal system who wanted to tackle Greece's poor record on tax collection were given a hard time. Renowned statistician Andreas Georgiou, former head of the Hellenic Statistical Authority, was even taken to court. He had been the first to publish reliable figures, in 2010, and from then on he was bombarded with accusations, including a prosecution for treason, which carried a life sentence. So instead of cracking down on the falsification of data, the government allowed those investigating and revealing the true problems to be attacked. Giorgos Papakonstantinou, the minister who, when the music stopped on 19 October 2009, 'turned on the lights and told everyone the party was over', became persona non grata in his own country. 'Walking the streets became a dangerous sport,' he wrote in his memoirs.

The Syriza experiment, largely because of Varoufakis's attitude, was in the end totally counterproductive. Berlin was confirmed in its tough stance of demanding spending cuts, and more and more member states joined it, even countries that had initially been sympathetic to the notion of a new approach. At the suggestion of Slovenia, the secret plan Z was contemplated once again, more seriously now than ever. If Greece did not want to stick to any agreement, then it could not possibly remain a member of the euro-zone. This was no longer about a clash between different economic approaches, it was about the protection of the system of rules as a whole, the system that in Europe had quelled evil spirits and prevented wars for decades.

Varoufakis and his American sympathizers had meanwhile thought up an alternative of their own, an experiment with a digital payment system that would create a parallel currency. It was in conflict with all the rules of the eurozone and would also have led to a Grexit, and it wasn't even par-ticularly practical. The Greek internet was still under development; it was as slow as a freight train and a significant proportion of the rural population didn't even have a connection. The lifestyle in a village on Samos was rather different from that of the Bay Area.

In the months that followed, the crisis escalated. On 5 June 2015, the Greeks failed to pay back €300 million to the IMF. Only Zambia had ever dared to do such a thing before. Varoufakis denied there was a problem, and in meetings the other ministers could no longer conceal their astonishment: 'amateurish', 'gambler' and 'unbelievable, unbelievable' were some of the responses heard at the table.

On 18 June, Varoufakis once again subjected the Eurogroup to a long lec-ture, proposing among other things the establishment of an independent budgetary authority to keep an eye on all European budgets. His colleagues fell silent. Did Varoufakis really not know that every euro country had been obliged to have such an institution for years already? Tsipras meanwhile had demanded hundreds of billions from Germany as 'compensation' for the German occupation of 1940–45. Tactful it wasn't, but his supporters thought it magnificent.

Meanwhile, the Greeks were continuing to empty their bank accounts. By mid-April the ECB had shipped more than €75 billion to the Greek banks and the sums were continuing to rise. On a single day, 22 June 2015, no less than €1.2 billion was withdrawn from Greek cash machines.

In the streets of Greece, malnutrition became increasingly visible. Child mortality rose. Because of all the cuts, anyone who lost their job was entitled to unemployment benefits for merely a few months. After that they lost their right to free medical care as well. That left at least a million Greeks with no access at all to doctors and hospitals – quite apart from the fact that, because of the crisis, dozens of hospitals and clinics had been forced to close their doors. Clinics staffed by volunteers tried to provide some comfort. 'One of the biggest problems we face is that patients come to us only when the pain becomes unbearable,' said a doctor. 'And by then it's sometimes too late.' A quarter of the people they saw were in a bad way, but further tests were hard to arrange, since the budget of the average hospital had fallen by 40 per cent. The psychiatric clinics were packed. According to a report by the Council of Europe's commissioner for human rights, the number of suicides in Greece rose by 40 per cent between 2010 and 2015. Many of those who ended their own lives were retired people who could see no other way out.

On Friday, 26 June 2015, the Greek delegation failed to arrive at the negotiating table. In the afternoon, Prime Minister Tsipras unexpectedly announced a referendum on the 'new deal' that had been reached with the eurozone. A loud 'no' from the Greeks, which Tsipras was calling for, would strengthen their negotiating position, he claimed. In reality it was all a sham. There was no deal; the talks, especially about reforms to the pension system, were still very much underway. The Greeks had not agreed to anything and neither had many eurozone member states.

His fellow negotiators were taken completely by surprise. Donald Tusk, the new president of the European Council, was furious. 'Do you realize that other prime ministers can organize their own referendums?' he asked Tsipras. 'On one question: Do you want to pay the Greek bill? Can you imagine, Alexis, what the answer will be then?'

The conclusion of all the other eighteen members of the Eurogroup was now clear. There were no grounds for further negotiation. The ECB ceased to support the Greek banks, money in cash machines began to dry up, welfare payments stopped and the banks did not open that Monday morning. The 'Europeans' were blamed. On 5 July, 61 per cent of Greeks voted 'no'.

For the European leaders, plan Z now became a matter of urgency. Wolfgang Schäuble wrote a memo to five of his colleagues in which he proposed excluding Greece from the Eurogroup for five years, while giving its population all kinds of economic and humanitarian aid: 'We can't go on like this.' 'Are you all from another planet?' Dalia Grybauskaitė, president of

Lithuania, snapped at the Greek leaders. 'It's a crime against your own people.'

Even Prime Minister Tsipras realized he had swum into a trap. Varoufakis found him on the evening of the referendum in anything but a celebratory mood. 'We've made a hash of it,' said the premier, sitting hunched in his chair. He'd just been on the phone to his last ally in the EU, the president of France. François Hollande had, by his own account, given Tsipras a stern warning: 'You've won but Greece has lost. There have always been people who believed there was no place for Greece in the EU, and at the next EU summit they may actually throw you out.' With that, Hollande asked Tsipras point-blank whether he wanted to stay in the eurozone. 'Yes,' said Tsipras. 'I do.'

After that conversation the Greek prime minister performed a U-turn. Plan Z was hanging above his head like the sword of Damocles and, along with the French, the Syriza government came up with an emergency plan with largely the same proposals as the Greeks had voted 'no' to less than a week earlier. In fact they were more stringent, since after all its poker bluffing, the position of the Greek government had deteriorated. By then, Yanis Varoufakis had resigned.

In Berlin, however, all confidence in the Greeks had evaporated. Germany now demanded the sale of Greek state assets to create an independently managed trust fund worth €50 billion – there was even talk of the sale of the Acropolis and of entire islands – as well as a reduction in state pensions. Schäuble repeated his threat of a timeout – in other words, suspension for five years – if the Greeks refused to back down. Tsipras and the French protested fiercely that the costs were impossible for ordinary Greeks to bear. Many of the almost 3 million retired Greeks had already lost nearly half their pensions since 2010, and this foreign 'contingency fund' made their humiliation complete.

During the weekend of 10–12 July 2015, the eurozone creaked at the seams for the umpteenth time. The atmosphere was exceptionally grim. The young French minister of economic affairs, Emmanuel Macron, spoke of an almost religious European civil war, with on one side Germany and the Netherlands, plus Scandinavia and Eastern Europe, and on the other side France, Italy, Spain and the other countries of southern Europe. When Tsipras spoke to the European Parliament that Friday, he was greeted with approving whistles from the left and the extreme right, and with shouts and jeers from the centre.

After that, behind the scenes, his furious fellow government leaders laid into him for hours – some called it 'mental waterboarding'. Why had he not stuck to a single agreement? On the morning of Monday 13 July, after seventeen hours of laborious negotiations, Merkel, Tusk and Hollande reached a compromise with Tsipras. Schäuble's timeout was withdrawn; the contingency fund was set up, but part of the proceeds would be used for investments in Greece itself.

In Athens, the extreme wing of Syriza met to discuss a coup. There were plans to breathe new life into the Greek drachma. But the parliament gave its consent and, in the general election in September, Tsipras won a big majority – although four years later, in 2019, he was dethroned. Greece remained a eurozone country.

Reactions were mixed. 'This is a coup!' wrote Paul Krugman in the New York Times. 'This Eurogroup list of demands is madness . . . . This goes beyond harsh into pure vindictiveness, complete destruction of national sovereignty, and no hope of relief.' In Germany, philosopher Jürgen Habermas declared that his country had emerged as Europe's disciplinarian. Angela Merkel had set out to punish Greece. 'I fear that the German government, including its social democratic faction, have gambled away in one night all the political capital that a better Germany had accumulated in half a century.'

There was also great discontent on the right. What had Germany actually achieved in that crucial weekend? Why had Merkel buckled by giving the ceaselessly obstreperous Greece yet another chance? Habermas might complain about German discipline and hegemony, but Germany was not omnipotent – in fact far from it. The AfD ended up profiting. Merkel's 'capitulation' in the Greek crisis came to be regarded in right-wing nationalist circles as a prelude to the 'betrayal' that would follow later that year, during the next major European crisis.

6

When it was all over, Yanis Varoufakis wrote an engaging account of his 'clash with the EU establishment' and then set out on an endless promotional tour. After resigning, Jeroen Dijsselbloem built a chicken coop, and later also wrote a book. Mario Draghi simply began printing money and used it to put out the euro fire. At the height of the crisis, the European Central Bank was buying bonds worth 80 billion euros every month. Not until the summer of 2018 was the end of this cheap money announced. By then the ECB had bonds on its balance sheet worth some €2.5 trillion. That's €2,500,000,000,000.

In Greece, the recovery was nevertheless hard-going. In total, after eight years and three aid programmes, it had been lent €273 billion. The Greek problem was frozen for the time being, since until 2033 the country would not have to pay back any of the loan, nor even a single euro in interest. The government debt remained, however, at €357 billion, or 180 per cent of gross domestic product, three times higher than permitted under EU stability rules. In that sense, Varoufakis and Tsipras were completely right: growth in the squeezed economy was far too low for the huge debt ever to be paid off. In the view of the IMF too, in its annual report on 2017, Greek debt was still unacceptable; the old debts would come back to hit the country like a boomerang when all the postponements were over, in 2033. It described that future prospect as 'explosive'.

According to economist Daniel Gros, director of the European think tank CEPS, just one lesson could be drawn from the Greek drama: coercion from on high doesn't work. 'We have seen that you can impose whatever reform you like on a country, but that it is then unlikely it will actually be implemented. A country can reform only if it feels itself to be the owner of both the problem and the solution.'

Yet on 20 August 2018, all the aid programmes for Greece finished – formally, at least. The troika was dismantled, paternalism came to an end and the Greeks squeezed themselves into a financial straitjacket. Until 2022 their budget surplus was capped at 3.5 per cent, and until 2060 (!) the maximum would be 2.2 per cent – a level that even countries like Singapore and Switzerland had never managed to achieve for more than a few years in a row. Commentators described these prognoses as 'extreme wishful thinking', and that was putting it mildly.

Surviving a major crisis together can strengthen mutual ties. The opposite outcome, however, is equally likely. For decades, the phenomenon of 'trust' had oiled the wheels of Europe. The euro crisis had immense consequences in that respect, especially for the trust of the public in each of the member states. Both the policy pursued and the lack of vigour shown in pursuing it had seriously undermined support for the European project in the financially strong countries of the North as well as the weaker South.

Figures from Eurobarometer confirm this picture. At the start of the crisis, in 2007, 57 per cent of Europeans 'tended to trust' the EU. By 2014 that figure had fallen to 31 per cent. Later it increased somewhat – to 42 per cent in 2018 – but the old confidence did not return. Trust in national politicians and governments in Europe was far lower still, incidentally. In 2018, it stood at only 34 per cent.

In the Berlaymont building in Brussels, the aftertaste was bitter. 'We shouldn't have made such a fuss about saving the euro,' said a senior official afterwards. 'We set fire to the house and then save the furniture? For the first time it turns out that keeping Europe together has cost a very great deal.'

The Greeks had been put through the wringer. A 2018 progress report from the OECD clearly sets out the facts. After ten years of so-called reconstruction, Greece's gross domestic product had declined by a quarter and investment had fallen by 60 per cent. The level of investment was not recovering, partly because of the lack of finance. The number of households living at or below the poverty line had risen from 12 per cent in 2008 to 26 per cent in 2018. Unemployment had fallen somewhat in recent years, but still almost one in five Greeks was jobless. Productivity was still paltry and many Greeks had jobs far below their educational level. In its welfare provision, Greece was way behind all other OECD countries.

Since 2010, more than 700,000 Greeks had left the country. These included 18,000 doctors, and most of the others were well educated too, and young. The birth rate had declined dramatically, so the country was ageing, with demographers predicting a decrease in the population of at least a quarter by 2050. Fewer and fewer young people would have to pay the pensions of more and more elderly people.

In the spring of 2019, the shelves in the shop owned by Efi and Kostas were once again full of washing powder, tinned vegetables, biscuits, chewing gum, tissues, crisps, sweets, coffee, toy cars, beach balls, wine, newspapers, soft drinks, stuffed Donald Ducks and a thousand other items. As in earlier times, jobs were being handed out, by Syriza now. There was growth in public service employment again. But Iakinthou, the shopping street round the corner, was still quiet. Most of the shop windows were empty, the fridge display at the old fishmonger's was covered in a thick layer of dust, and behind the shop doors, letters and old newspapers lay yellowing on the mat. Only in the former sports shop was a bit of life in evidence. There, for as long as it lasted, was a nail salon.

Athens slowly picked itself up. In 2014, an estimated 40 per cent of the shops in the city centre were empty; in 2019 the figure was around 25 per cent. The illegal 'grey' economy was booming and more than a quarter of all transactions were once again happening out of sight of the tax authorities – in the rest of Europe, the average proportion was a sixth. Meanwhile, it seems there was enough money again for the rental of two hypermodern frigates in the FREMM class from the French, in response to increasing tensions with Turkey.

I walked through Exarchia, a neighbourhood full of stealthy, anarchistic plantings. In the spring sunshine, greenery was popping out of every crack and corner. The street music and the murals were of a high quality, after all those years of deprivation. Collectivist projects were flourishing. I sat for a while on a bench in a lovingly laid-out play area. There were little tables and chairs, and all kinds of toys, for every child. From the walls of the neighbouring buildings the murals burst out at me: a cat playing the cello; a city beneath which, deep in the earth, people germinated into magnificent flowers, and below them the words 'You tried to bury me in all kinds of ways. But you forgot that I was a seed.'

In front of the parliament building stood a small group of people with pamphlets, a few holding Greek flags – propaganda for an American Greek who claimed to have a fortune of €600 billion that he could use, if he had his way, to pay off all debts in one go. They believed firmly in this redeemer. 'It would be fantastic, wouldn't it? We're so poor,' said a man with no more than two or three teeth in his head.

Victoria Square was still teeming with Afghans and other immigrants who had run aground in the city. Many were living nearby, ten to a room.

The benches on the square were full, newcomers were greeted with joy and there wasn't a Greek to be seen. Here and there men were waiting for something, transport or whatever it might be. Among them were young teenage boys who were regularly picked up and taken to the far side of the square for a while, to the park. Everyone has to eat.

10. Old Ghosts

2014

I

IN LATE NOVEMBER 2013, I flew over a frozen Moscow for the first time in years, over the Russian farmland, over the snow-covered gardens and rooftops around Sheremetyevo Airport. Dusk was coming down in the early afternoon and it was a short visit. I needed to be in Moscow to introduce a film about Amsterdam and to show my face at a book fair. Vladimir Putin had been elected president again. In 2008, his milder and more congenial right-hand man Dmitry Medvedev had taken over as fill-in president for four years, and then, in 2012, after a turbulent election and fierce street protests, Putin returned to power.

When I had last walked through it, in 1999, the centre of Moscow was one mammoth Lego set, full of cranes, diggers, and Ladas with big moustaches of snow and ice. The whole place was swarming with construction workers. At the gates of the Kremlin a huge underground shopping mall was being built, and in the GUM department store on Red Square the gilt glittered as if nothing had changed since the last tsar. Everyone had two or three jobs and was dashing across the city from a bit of contractual employment here to a bit of casual work there. One trendy café after another was opening up, and at lightning speed the city was preparing itself for new, unprecedented times. After so much inflation, money had assumed an insubstantial character. It no longer counted. The atmosphere made me think of something Erich Maria Remarque wrote about the Berlin of 1922: 'It is the great sellout of thrift, honest effort, and respectability.'

The McDonald's on Pushkin Square was the place to be in those days: schoolgirls, businesspeople, old ladies – a whole new middle class was unfolding its wings. Now the hot spot was Jean-Jacques, a restaurant close to Red Square where the entire blogging opposition got together; as in Paris during the French Revolution, in the Moscow of 2013 restaurants were the centres of resistance. It was packed full. The bloggers were Moscow's new rock stars, and all the pretty girls flocked around them.

In the 1980s and 1990s the protests were bolstered by real singers and musicians. 'So there we sat, young, angry and passionate, in the heart of the Empire of Lies, and somehow or other we had to survive,' wrote pop journalist Artemy Troitsky of that time. Boris Grebenshchikov was regarded as the Bob Dylan of the disintegrating Soviet Union. He sang lyrics like:

> Sons of the days of silence
> Look at other people's films
> Play other people's roles
> Knock on other people's doors.
> Please, won't you give a sip of water
> To the sons of the days of silence?

Meanwhile entire stadiums went into raptures over rocker Mikhail Borzykin of Televizor: 'A fish rots from the head down, all of them are lying, a fish rots from the head down.'

When I went to visit a couple of singers in the late 1990s, little was left of that lively rock culture. 'Half took to drink,' said Borzykin, 'and the other half went into business and within two years they'd forgotten what music was.' He eventually emigrated to Sweden, while Grebenshchikov, as his former colleagues put it, was 'destroyed by popularity'. Artemy Troitsky left with his third wife for Tallinn, the new refuge for Russian writers and artists who could no longer stick it out under Putin. 'The fear is back,' he said in a rare interview. 'The people are passive, apathetic, cynical.'

To introduce the film I went onstage in a café-cum-cinema practically identical to the fashionable venue in Amsterdam where I'd eaten the evening before. The audience was similar too: the same clothing, the same youthfulness, the same look. Almost everyone had plenty of money to spend, that was obvious. A young journalist wanted to talk about modern cities. The financial crisis – at its height at the time – didn't concern him in the least.

'Nobody here is interested in Europe. We'll go through something like that every ten or twenty years.' He believed Russia was doing better than ever before. A middle class was clearly emerging, with more to spend with each passing year, and you could say or write whatever you liked as long as you didn't provoke the system too much – talking about homosexuality, for example, was still off limits.

Postmodern Moscow had become far too expensive, that was true. 'All those Russians who go shopping in Europe – it's down to the fact that Europe has become extremely cheap for us. Moscow is expensive, Russia is expensive. And that's mainly because of the corruption. You have to add around 20 per cent to the price of everything, a corruption tax let's call it. With public works it can get up to 100 or 200 or 500 per cent. Of course, one day that will hit the buffers.'

On Red Square, workmen were demolishing a giant Louis Vuitton suitcase. It had been there for only a few days and had caused a minor uproar on the internet. Red Square is and must remain exclusively a place for public ceremonies. A huge advert like that was sacrilege. Sure enough, the authorities caved in and agreed it was a step too far. Nearby, in the GUM department store, the Christmas decorations were unaffordable. First prize was a suitcase with three unusual Christmas tree decorations: a bag, a large coin and a wallet. All three had one word printed on them: money.

A Russian guide described the mood of Moscow in 2013: rich, yes, better than it used to be, but everyone distrusted everyone else and on the streets no one smiled any longer. I decided to try a brief spot check. Without exception, every one of the young people I spoke to in the days I spent there was eager to leave. All that was holding them back was penury, children or an elderly mother.

This fits neatly with the figures. While Medvedev was keeping Putin's seat warm for him, few Russians emigrated, an average of 35,000 a year. As soon as Putin got his hands on power again the number of emigrants soared, from some 30,000 in 2011 to ten times that – more than 300,000 – in 2014.

One evening I 'hitchhiked' – for a small fee, the way it works here – to a theatre café where friends were due to perform chansons and some songs by Brecht. I was picked up by a young couple with portraits of Putin on the lock screens of their mobiles. The girl spoke some English. She wanted to become an opera singer. They were warmth personified. No more than forty people attended the event; it was all very intimate and the concert was unforgettable. Brecht in Russian. One of the singers, a tall, bald man, had stood singing on the barricades in demonstrations against Putin. He was a famous instigator of protests. Now he was singing songs by Kurt Weill and they were painfully topical. Again that sardonic, cruelly sweet accompaniment to a dance on the edge of a volcano.

The past has a long reach. Old ghosts are not easily placated. That's certainly true of the collapse of the Soviet Union in 1991 and the emptiness it left behind – on a personal level as much as anything. In 1991 the Russians suffered a threefold loss: their political system disintegrated, their empire vanished as their European vassal states went their own way, and the Soviet fatherland ceased to exist. 'There were few committed Communists left by 1991,' British journalist and Russia expert Shaun Walker wrote later, 'but that did not make the collapse any less traumatic. Russians felt they had not lost an empire or an ideology, but the very essence of their identity. If they were no longer Soviet citizens, then who were they?'

A liberation for some was all too often a source of shame and humiliation for others. Putin called the break-up of the Soviet Union 'the greatest geopolitical tragedy of the twentieth century'. Despite warnings from many experts – in the *New York Times* the elderly George Kennan, architect of America's Cold War 'containment' policy, castigated NATO enlargement as 'the most fateful error of American policy in the entire post-Cold War era' – the West has never shown much understanding for Russia's sense of loss. It turned out from documents released later that in 1990, during negotiations between NATO and Soviet Russia after the fall of the Wall, Baker and several others had suggested that NATO would resist the temptation to expand any further to the east: 'Not one inch eastward.' US president George H. W. Bush was not of the same mind, however, and nor was British prime minister John Major. Party leader Mikhail Gorbachev, his hands full with a thousand other problems, neglected to have that vague promise set down in a treaty. In fact, his ultimate aim was to secure NATO membership for Russia.

And so, promise or no promise, NATO calmly rolled into the formerly Soviet world. In 1999, Poland, Hungary and the Czech Republic all too eagerly joined, followed in 2004 by Bulgaria, Romania, Slovakia and the

The expansion of NATO

Baltic states. Russia was thereby reduced, in the words of Barack Obama, to nothing more than a 'regional power'. The statistics reinforce this impression. By 2013 Russia was an ageing country with a gross national product of barely $1.5 trillion – not much more than the Benelux countries and less than a tenth of the figure for China, America or the EU.

Putin never forgave the American president those words. I wouldn't be surprised if my student in 2069 ultimately places the treatment of an exhausted and beaten Russia from the 1990s onwards in the same category as the humiliation of Germany in the years after 1918.

In less than a decade, Russia was transformed from a potentially useful ally of NATO into an outright opponent once again. But for a long time, its hostility was not targeted at the EU. Good relations with Germany and several other EU countries were of vital importance to the Russian economy, and anyhow, Russia saw itself as a bridge between a more or less united Europe and Asia. That changed when the EU and Ukraine, by far the most important of the former Russian vassal states, sought closer relations.

Ukraine was a typical transit zone, half Western, half deeply rooted in Russian history. Since the seventeenth and eighteenth centuries it had belonged partly to Russia and partly to the Habsburg Empire, and in the Treaty of Versailles of 1919 it was divided up between the Soviet Union and Poland.

Although Ukraine became independent in 1991, questions and debates about the country's identity remained unresolved. Was it European, or part of the Russian mir (world)? In 1994 Ukraine – officially the third biggest nuclear power in the world – had given up its nuclear arsenal in exchange for security guarantees from Russia, the United States and the United Kingdom – but according to Putin, the country ought not even to exist. 'You are surely aware, George, that Ukraine is not a state at all?' he said to President Bush Jr at the NATO summit in 2008, according to the daily *Kommersant*. 'What is Ukraine? Part of its territory is Eastern Europe. Another part, a large part, was given away by us.' In short, as one commentator wrote, Ukraine was a country with a big red neon sign flashing over it: 'Caution. Fragile. Handle with care.'

All these tensions came to the surface when, in 2004, the corrupt presidential candidate Viktor Yanukovych looked likely to come to power by means of intimidation and rigged elections. The 'Western' opposition candidate, Viktor Yushchenko, was poisoned with a high dose of dioxin. He miraculously survived, but his face was badly disfigured. Tensions erupted and fierce street protests forced a fresh election. The Orange Revolution brought Yushchenko to the presidency in spite of everything, but the enthusiasm of the Orange revolutionaries soon melted away. Yushchenko focused mainly on his pro-Western voters, breathed new life into nationalism and did little about Ukraine's biggest problem, its corrosive corruption. Europe stood by and waited.

Meanwhile the young and enthusiastic Georgian president Mikheil Saakashvili was pioneering a 'Georgian model' for the post-Soviet states – a clear answer to the corrupt Putin system, involving a mixture of liberalism and pro-Western nationalism. Financed and galvanized by the CIA and the Bush-Cheney government in America, he pulled away from the Russian sphere of influence, turned his face towards NATO and raised EU flags on all government buildings. In August 2008 he overplayed his hand by allowing himself to be tempted into invading the rebel Georgian province of South Ossetia. Russia intervened in support of the rebels and swept the Georgian troops out of their own province in the space of five days. A year earlier, in April 2007, Estonia had been paralysed for weeks by a cyberattack, the first ever, probably mounted from Russia. Now Georgia was hit. The websites of the president and the press bureaus were hacked, and the internet was all but shut down.

The EU wasted no time in reacting. Nicolas Sarkozy, at that point president of the Council of the EU, immediately flew to Moscow and then the Georgian capital, Tbilisi, where, supported by all the other EU governments, he arranged a ceasefire. It was one of the first occasions on which the EU acted as an independent geopolitical power in a matter of war and peace, without the Americans, and indeed contrary to American intentions. Earlier, during a NATO summit in Bucharest, Germany and France had blocked a possible entry of Georgia and Ukraine into the NATO waiting room, and now Russian intervention meant that a frozen conflict had developed concerning Georgia – an insurmountable obstacle to Georgia's NATO membership. Yet Bush, who towards the end of his presidency wanted at any price to put down a 'marker', managed to have included in the closing statement the sentence 'We agreed today that these countries will become members of NATO.' It was an empty promise, but one with major consequences.

During the struggle for Georgia, Putin was merely prime minister. Yet the five-day war was for him a high point. Russian state television continually showed pictures of the Russian army's relentless advance. This was the new Russia, once again capable of mounting a patriotic war: a Russia victorious. Valery Gergiev, in those years conductor of the London Symphony Orchestra, was flown to Tskhinvali, the capital of South Ossetia, to conduct Shostakovich's Leningrad Symphony on its half-ruined main square, a victory concert that was of course broadcast on all the national television channels. Ben Judah, one of the few Western journalists present, stood on a tank to listen, next to an exhausted Russian soldier, who whispered, 'I feel the way my grandfather must have felt.' Putin's popularity rose in the polls to 83 per cent.

2

But what kind of country was this 'new' and 'patriotic' Russia? In the twenty-first century, under the leadership of Vladimir Putin, the Russians, so it seemed, were marching towards a glorious future. At least, most of them kidded themselves they were. In reality, behind a nostalgic facade lay a state in which crime syndicates and former KGB officers called the shots, where justice was available only to those able to buy it, and where everything that went wrong – which was a lot – could be blamed on 'foreign powers'. It was the price paid for the fact that Russia, in contrast to Germany after the Second World War, had never been through a phase of reflection and reorientation after Stalin's atrocities. The Germans call such a phase *Vergangenheitsbewältigung*, which roughly translated means 'working through the past'.

Economically the country remained weak, highly dependent on oil and other raw materials – not exactly the route to sustainability. It was doing little to modernize itself and was becoming even more deeply corrupt. In the words of Ukrainian-born British journalist Peter Pomerantsev, 'Russians have more words for "bribe" than Eskimos do for "snow".'

A common form of company takeover in Russia was 'raiding'. A competitor would pay off a firm's security people, then the owner would be arrested, and while he was in jail his company would be renamed and sold on, with the help of a corrupt judge. It happened even to major conglomerates. In 2003, for instance, the Kremlin had the owner of the huge oil company Yukos, Mikhail Khodorkovsky, arrested. It then transferred ownership of the business to friends of Putin. Khodorkovsky spent more than eight years in prison in Siberia. In 2008, Sergei Magnitsky, a lawyer who investigated raiding of this sort, was arrested and tortured, before dying in prison. He had chanced upon a mechanism of enrichment known to insiders as 'the Kremlin's black till'. Political parties could receive donations only via the Kremlin, which took a 20 per cent cut.

In February 2008, during the election of Medvedev, a full-on protest movement arose for the first time. Former vice premier Boris Nemtsov and Vladimir Milov, once a junior energy minister, published a pamphlet in which they revealed the business interests of Putin and his friends in detail for the first time. Putin's 'economic miracle' was, they wrote, a mirage. In reality it consisted mainly of a rise in the price of oil. At the same time, all structural problems were covered up, including corruption.

In just eight years, from the moment Putin first took power, Russia had fallen in the annual ranking of least corrupt countries from 82nd to 143rd place. In the spring of 2008, three friends of Putin appeared for the first time on the Forbes list of billionaires, and at that point Putin's own wealth was estimated by some, including the CIA, at around $40 billion. Others went a good deal further, citing figures approaching $200 billion, but that was pure speculation.

There was general agreement that Putin was more interested in power than in wealth. When Mark Galeotti, an expert on international crime, once asked a Russian insider how much money Putin had, the response was a burst of laughter: 'Putin doesn't go looking for money – money goes looking for him . . . He probably doesn't even know where his own money is stashed or how much he has.'

But was Putin really the strongman behind all this, the brilliant chess player who gradually bent the world to his will, as many in the West believed? That was highly questionable. He spoke less and less to diplomats and other experts, so that practically all the information reaching the great leader came in the leather folders he received every morning with briefings from his three most important security services: the FSB on domestic matters, the FSO – Putin's personal security detail – on everything concerning the Russian elite, and the SVR, in charge of overseas agents, on international issues. By means of the contents of those three leather folders alone, the three services had a firm grip on their leader.

Furthermore, Putin was anything but a chess player. He liked judo, and Galeotti describes him as a typical judo player, a fighter who doesn't know exactly what he's going to do but who circles, continually weighing up his opponent's strengths and weaknesses, striking only when he sees an opening. Putin knew that the West, if it acted in unison, was far more powerful than Russia, with twenty times the productive capacity, six times the population and more than three times the military strength. 'But he's waiting for us to make a mistake and give him what looks like a good chance to strike,' writes Galeotti. 'He wants us to be divided, demoralised and distracted to the point where either we are willing to do a deal with him or, more likely, not in a fit state to challenge him.'

In his revealing portrait of the early Putin, documentary maker Vitaly Mansky filmed the low-key party thrown for his first election victory, in March 2000. The partygoers who had helped him to that victory sat around a large table, with Putin, in a comfy sweater, snugly in their midst. It was a small but highly competent team of planners and media experts, and everyone was cheerful and relaxed, rather like the editorial team of a major newspaper that had just won some kind of press award. They were probably hoping that this relatively untried bureaucrat would share their liberal opinions. After Yeltsin, surely, things could only get better.

Within a dozen or so years, they had all either joined the opposition, like Boris Nemtsov, or were dead. Lyudmila, Putin's wife, had divorced him. Mansky was in exile. Only Dmitry Medvedev was still part of the leader's circle. Since the constitution allowed Putin no more than two consecutive four-year terms as president, Medvedev had succeeded him in 2008. But as prime minister, Putin remained a dominant presence, and in the autumn of 2011 he announced he would be running for president again.

Medvedev did indeed turn out to be merely a figurehead. It was all simply a trick to get Putin's presidency around the limitations imposed by the constitution. In 2012, the presidential term of office was extended to six years, so if Putin was elected again he would be able to remain president until 2024, by which time he would have held that office for twenty years in total; Stalin alone had been in power longer.

Putin's coup was far-reaching, but he and those close to him anticipated few problems. In Putin's 'new' Russia, elections had the same function as in the Soviet Union. They were rituals, expressions of support for the regime, like parades. This time, however, the scheme did not go well. After the announcement of a forthcoming straight swap, Putin's popularity reached its lowest ebb since he first took office.

The crisis of 2008 had hit Russia hard. Oil prices plummeted, more than $1 trillion was wiped off the Moscow stock exchange within a few months, the rouble lost value and the economy shrank by 8 per cent, while wages and pensions fell and were sometimes not paid out for months. It marked an abrupt end to the economic boom, and Russia once again found itself in a serious recession. Putin's popularity took a hard knock.

Boris Nemtsov and those associated with him took advantage of the situation, and in 2008 they started a new dissident movement called Solidarity, after the great Polish example. At first it was tough-going, but the movement took off when Putin announced in late 2011 that he was going to play musical chairs with Medvedev and wanted to be president again. When he turned up at a mixed martial arts match in Moscow he was greeted with whistles and jeers. Footage of the occasion became a hit on YouTube.

Dissatisfaction spread like wildfire on the internet and Putin's political party, United Russia, was dismissed as a poor imitation of the Soviet Union's Communist Party, and even more corrupt. To maintain the appearance of a democratic election, the Kremlin hastily set up its own 'opposition party', A Fair and Just Russia. Meanwhile, also on the internet, a citizens' initiative had emerged called Golos (meaning 'vote' or 'voice'), which monitored the election all over the country and carefully kept track of all the violations it discovered. Even relatively government-friendly media used its data.

The citizens of Putin's Russia had seen almost everything in their time, and there had always been abuse and manipulation, but in the parliamentary elections of 4 December 2011 exceptionally cynical ballot-rigging took place, on a scale previously unknown. With the help of the internet and the activities of Golos, even ordinary Russians now saw fraud taking place in front of their eyes. They watched the director of polling station number 2501 in Moscow, for instance, sitting at his desk calmly filling in a whole pile of ballot papers. The indignation became even greater when it turned out that, even with all the tampering, United Russia had got less than half the votes, yet on that basis it had won a majority in the Duma by acquiring the 'lost' votes for smaller parties that failed to reach the electoral threshold.

That spelled trouble for the presidential elections three months later. On the evening after the parliamentary elections of 4 December, Solidarity held a protest meeting. Normally it could have expected a few hundred dissidents, but this time several thousand demonstrators stood waving flags and home-made banners reading 'Putin: thief'. The organizer, opposition leader and blogger Alexei Navalny, declared that he was going to 'gnaw through the throats of these villains'. Immediately afterwards, he and Boris Nemtsov were arrested, along with dozens of others. The next Saturday, alerted via Facebook, tens of thousands of demonstrators turned up at Bolotnaya Square, across the river from the Kremlin. They sang the 1980s song by dissident rocker Viktor Tsoi:

> Our hearts require changes,
> Our eyes require changes,
> Into our laugh and our tears,
> And into our pulse and veins
> Changes!
> We are waiting for changes.

The demonstrations continued, bigger than ever. Former president Mikhail Gorbachev called on Putin to step down. On 4 February 2012, in twenty degrees of frost, more than a hundred thousand demonstrators – some estimates suggest 160,000 – gathered on Bolotnaya Square and in the surrounding streets. On 21 February, five members of Pussy Riot, a women's punk band and performance art group, staged a bizarre performance in the virtually empty Christ the Saviour cathedral called 'Punk Prayer', with lines including 'Holy Mary, Mother of God, banish Putin! Banish Putin!'

During this winter of discontent, when the demonstrations were at their height, it briefly seemed Putin might get less than half the votes. That would have forced a humiliating second round. But in February he rose in the polls again. A few cautious concessions were made, along with promises about tackling electoral fraud, and the Kremlin's propaganda machine systematically presented Putin in his former glorious role as the steadfast leader of a country besieged by enemies both domestic and foreign. In the elections on 4 March he gained 63 per cent of the vote. There was undoubtedly some fraud, but even his critics had to admit that he enjoyed the support of a large majority of Russians.

Demonstrations were part of the election ritual from then on. The dissidents showed they were there and were duly arrested; the remainder of society saw the power of the regime, felt reassured and bowed to authority. But the fundamental clash between Putin's restored Russia and modern life outside its borders was suppressed, not resolved.

On 6 May 2012, the evening before the transfer of power, one final protest meeting was held on Bolotnaya Square. The place was packed, and there was pushing and shoving. The police began bludgeoning and arresting demonstrators; the crowd bombarded the police with lumps of asphalt; Alexei Navalny was seized, swearing and yelling, and Boris Nemtsov shouted from an empty sewer pipe, 'Russia shall be free,' before he too disappeared into a patrol van. Even the Jean-Jacques restaurant, the opposition's informal headquarters, was emptied by force. These were the biggest riots in Moscow for twenty years. By the end of the day, at least 400 people had been arrested. In the words of one of the opposition, 'I think this is to show who is boss. A new czar has come.'

The next day, Vladimir Putin drove with his escort through a silent and deserted city, on his way to his third inauguration.

A year and a half later I sat with my publisher, Oleg Zimarin, in a Belarusian restaurant in Moscow. Oleg is a passionate and witty man who published the collected works of Mikhail Gorbachev, so I was in good company. 'Any trouble with pressure from the authorities?' I asked. 'Unfortunately not. We sell far too few books to be a danger to them. We can do as we like.' Oleg talked with enthusiasm about the publishing business in the old Soviet days. 'It wasn't easy, sometimes it was hard to manoeuvre, but we had far more influence. If we managed to get a good book past the censors, then people really did buy it and read it. Masses of them. That time, unfortunately, has gone.'

A man and a woman were meanwhile singing Belarusian songs without the slightest hint of a smile, the waitresses wore 'national' costume miniskirts, the food – potato pancakes with lots of onions and meat – was as foul as ever, and the heat was unbearable. We talked long and happily about the delights and maladies of the internet, the decline in reading all over the world and the poor education of the young in particular – all without exception problems to which the Putin regime was making its own unique contributions.

The flexibility my publisher spoke of was telling; the new repression was no longer ideological but practical. It was now all about Putin staying in power. You could write whatever you liked, since you were dangerous only if you stood out from the crowd by selling books in large numbers. In fact, this new twenty-first-century repression was stimulating, dynamic and creative. Nashestvie (meaning 'Invasion'), Russia's biggest rock festival, where you needed to appear if you were ever to make your breakthrough, has been sponsored by the Russian army since 2013. Between performances by exotic punk groups, soldiers parade and tanks roll past. Culture and history have come to be seen as powerful binding agents, helping to support the regime.

Želimir Žilnik, who attends Russian film festivals every year, had noticed a number of films that looked very much like those of Soviet times, with astounding spectacles based on major historical events. There was Viking, for example, about the founder of Russia, the medieval prince Vladimir the Great, a film with thousands of horses and extras, and a budget of more than $20 million. At the same time there was plenty of room for shocking and provocative films like Shopping Tour, about a family in Saint Petersburg that decides to go shopping in a mall in Helsinki, gets lured into a shop, finds blood spattered all over the walls and discovers that the Finns have a special festival day on which they eat Russians. The family runs to the police, but they too eat Russians. 'The film proved insanely popular in Finland in particular,' Želimir told me. 'The money poured in.'

Peter Pomerantsev, who as a television producer had worked for the Russian channel TNT for four years, describes in his book Nothing is True and Everything is Possible how from the very start the Putin regime had one guiding principle: Russian television must never again be boring, as it was in Soviet times. TNT introduced a Russian sitcom and a Russian talk show in the style of Jerry Springer. Satire came out from underground, since – up to a point at least – in the new Russia you could laugh at even the Kremlin and the Duma. It gave people breathing space.

'This is a new type of Kremlin propaganda,' Pomerantsev writes, 'less about arguing against the West with a counter-model as in the Cold War, more about slipping into its language to play and taunt it from inside.' Control must be combined with Western-style entertainment, Russian television news must have exactly the same slick format as a CNN broadcast and propaganda must be hidden inside shows fizzing with activity. The president was central, of course, filling all the macho roles imaginable: soldier, businessman, negotiator, half-naked angler and huntsman, superman, even mafia boss if need be. It all made reality thoroughly malleable. 'The news is the incense with which we bless what Putin does, making him into a president,' the people at TNT told each other.

The 2014 Winter Olympics in Sochi, on the coast of the Black Sea, was the high point of that period. The costs climbed to some $50 billion, more than all the twenty-one previous Winter Olympics put together. Half that money, according to calculations by Boris Nemtsov, was spent on bribes. The opening ceremony, 'Dreams of Russia', was a dazzling show in which Putin presented his refurbished Russia to the world as a country that cherished its rich and impressive past – in a highly varnished form, of course. Russian athletes won the largest number of gold medals, with the help of an intensive doping programme in which the FSB played a central role. Indeed, nothing was as it seemed.

So began a new game with the truth. The Russians were used to it, since in the Soviet era facts were continually being manipulated, but even Western propagandists – think of the second Iraq War – now knew how to play. The Putin regime chose to use twenty-first-century social media, 'objective' and 'Western' styles of programming, and a stable of 'convincing' reporters and commentators. The products of this mendacity factory were far more effective than before, and its impact gradually became noticeable in the West too. In broad circles, in both the East and the West, a new, postmodern norm emerged: 'post-truth'.

'The truth has become irrelevant,' said Pomerantsev in an interview. 'It's now all about the tactical goal.' The more the Kremlin felt threatened – by the popular revolts of 2011–12, by the West, by Ukrainian independence – the more urgent the need to sow panic and fear. Every form of common sense was eliminated, the craziest theories were given air time, foreign hatemongers were flown in. Night after night Russia had to be entertained and numbed. 'It's not lying any longer, it's more than that: facts no longer matter.'

3

The war in Ukraine in 2014 was the culmination, thus far, of this game of deception. It was also the biggest and most dangerous East–West conflict since the end of the Cold War. Peace between the great powers could no longer be taken for granted.

This was a conflict that, starting with a spontaneous popular revolt, took everyone by surprise, and it brought both the Kremlin and the West up against the limits of their triumphalism. Ukraine no longer bowed to its powerful neighbour, but Europe's expectation that the country could simply throw itself into the arms of the EU proved an illusion. The sequence of events was revealing. The EU proved as yet unequal politically, let alone militarily, to such unexpected international developments. There was a major divergence of interest even between Europe, which was addicted to Russian gas, and the United States. More than ever, 'alternative facts' shaped the public debate on the confrontation. The conflict itself was fundamental in nature: was international politics about 'subjects' or about 'citizens'? In other words: which takes priority, the legal order derived from empires and spheres of influence of a previous century, or the freedom of choice of 45 million citizens of an independent country who want to set off down a new path?

After its Orange Revolution in 2004, Ukraine found itself in the same vicious circle as before. A handful of reformers took on the corrupt system, the ruling powers successfully fought off their attacks, and the Kremlin meanwhile did all it could to preserve its sphere of influence.

In 2010, the pro-Russian Viktor Yanukovych won a legitimate presidential election, and from that moment on corruption boomed as it never had before, even in Ukraine. More than ten years earlier, in 1999, the country still had a part-liberal, part-black-market economy. It was corrupt, but the system of kickbacks and favours was still tolerably balanced. I heard from businesspeople that you paid some 20 or at most 30 per cent extra for transactions, and the profits were shared out reasonably fairly. Under Yanukovych, however, everything was channelled towards the top and prices

Ukraine

Since 2014 in the hands of separatists
or occupied by Russia
Former border of
the Danube monarchy

were sometimes driven up by 90 per cent, which made doing any kind of business almost impossible.

Yanukovych was helped into the saddle by Paul Manafort, a notorious American political conman who advised several oligarchs. Later, he briefly led Donald Trump's election campaign and was then jailed in America for his criminal practices. It says a lot about the sums available in these circles that, according to later court cases, within a period of five years Manafort earned some $60 million from his activities in Ukraine.

Yanukovych was initially regarded by Putin as a trouble-free vassal. Straight after he became president, Ukraine extended the right of the Russian navy to use the harbours of Crimea until 2042, thereby ruling out for the time being any possible Ukrainian overtures to NATO. The Kremlin did all it could to bind Ukraine to it economically by means of the Eurasian Customs Union, set up by Russia in 2010 along with Belarus and Kazakhstan as a kind of alternative to the EU. Under Russian leadership, it would bring together states that were unable or unwilling to become EU members, plus states that might, in the future, decide to leave the disintegrating EU. This Eurasian Union became the basis of Russian foreign policy from 2013 onwards, and Ukraine was the cornerstone of the new power bloc. The EU continued to beckon, however, with an attractive Association Agreement.

The choice between Moscow and Brussels was exceptionally difficult, even for a figure like Yanukovych. The majority of the population leaned towards the West but Ukraine remained divided, along the classic fault lines of course but in mentality too, as people were faced with a choice between modernity and the tried and tested. For Yanukovych and his clique, there were important private interests to take into account, since through the EU they could far more easily safeguard their investments. Rinat Akhmetov, for example, a coal and steel magnate from Donetsk who was worth some $15–18 billion, was able to register his holdings in Amsterdam. Yanukovych himself had long ago secured his investments at an address on the respectable Alexander Square in The Hague.

On 13 September 2013, Ukraine informed the EU that the Association Agreement could be signed in November at the EU summit in Vilnius. Brussels regarded the treaty as above all a technical matter. Vincent Stuer, who was speechwriter to Commission president José Manuel Barroso at the time, wrote, 'They sat in the Berlaymont Building simply ticking off regulations. It seems nobody said, "What would Putin think of this?" '

There was still a refusal to acknowledge, in this world of rules and agreements, that major geostrategic and political interests were at play. Yet 'the standardization of jam pot lids', as a friend put it to me, had totally different implications for Moscow than for the EU. Those jam pot lids, and infinitely more besides, were in Russia's view the umpteenth example of the West's urge to expand, which had to be checked by any and all available means. For the Kremlin, the place of Ukraine in the Europe of the future was an essential aspect of power relations in the twenty-first century and it acted accordingly. It placed Kyiv under extreme pressure, threatening to close the border and increase gas prices. In August 2013, as a taster, practically all goods traffic between Russia and Ukraine was halted.

To the astonishment of many Ukrainians as well as the EU, on 21 November 2013 Ukraine reported that the country was backing out of signing the Association Agreement. A week later, at the summit in Vilnius, Yanukovych proposed dual membership of the EU and the Eurasian Union, but European government leaders refused to yield: the rules would not permit it. The EU's mindset presumed increasing economic integration, while at the same time it regarded dividing up the world into spheres of influence as a thing of the past. So Ukraine, as Luuk van Middelaar wrote later, was 'stuck between two incompatible discourses, two irreconcilable narratives'. The magnetic attraction of the EU released forces that Brussels and the government leaders totally failed to foresee, which they then stood looking at in amazement. 'Strategic insouciance went hand in hand with geopolitical inaction.'

Yanukovych was motivated mainly by self-interest and opportunism, but pure necessity was a factor too. His country's banking sector had suffered serious damage during the crisis of 2008 and billions were needed to stave off bankruptcy. The EU was offering just €610 million if Ukraine signed the Association Agreement. It was nowhere near enough. Taking into account the anticipated punitive sanctions by Russia, the European deal, if only in financial terms, was impossible for Ukraine. Putin was offering to make a loan of €15 billion available, along with a very attractive agreement on gas – including, as a nice little bonus for Yanukovych and his associates, a substantial private share in the profits from gas sales.

So the country was pulled back into the Russian sphere of influence, partly because of the legalistic attitude and short-sightedness of the European negotiators. It took a war and the loss of Crimea for the EU finally to start behaving as a geopolitical power by declaring a preparedness to give Ukraine meaningful support and by putting a revised Association Agreement on the table.

4

How does a popular revolt begin? 'Men harangued the crowd at street corners with frenzied eloquence; others set all the bells ringing in the churches; lead was melted down, cartridges rolled; on the boulevards the trees, public urinals, benches, railings and gas-lamps were all pulled down or overturned.' Gustave Flaubert's description in *Sentimental Education* of the Paris revolution of 1848, during which the king was dethroned, is a classic. 'Wine-shops were open, and every now and then somebody would go in to smoke a pipe or drink a glass of beer, before returning to the fight. A stray dog started howling. This raised a laugh.'

In Kyiv in 2013, alarm bells no longer sounded from the church towers but instead on the internet, the street corner had been replaced by Facebook and the 'frenzied eloquence' was that of an investigative journalist, but otherwise nothing had changed. As soon as journalist Mustafa Nayyem heard on 21 November that the EU deal with Ukraine had fallen through after all, he wrote an angry call to arms on his Facebook page: 'Likes don't count', there must be a demonstration right now, people must take themselves out onto the street, to Maidan Nezalezhnosti – Independence Square – in Kyiv. And they did. At first a few hundred, but every evening there were more of them. It began as mainly a student protest; even the Ukrainian opposition didn't quite know how to handle it. But when the security police set upon the students with their cudgels there were soon tens of thousands of people on the Maidan. Small groups started camping out, the demonstration spread to other cities – in the centre of Lviv, students pitched tents with EU flags flying over them – veterans came to help the 'Euro-Maidanners', and in no time at all a popular movement emerged. It continued to grow.

On the internet, 'demonstration kits' were advertised: 'Contains everything necessary for anyone who, in this cold time of year, is planning to go out onto the street for a while for the sake of their convictions.' The kits included a thermos flask, an insulated bag, an umbrella, a roll mat, a raincoat, a sleeping bag, a wireless phone charger, a flag, a camping stove, enough food for three days, and a memo listing certain articles of the law that might come in handy for any confrontation with the police.

In the town hall, where there was still a little warmth to be had, people slept in shifts. Around the square great barricades of snow were thrown up, reinforced with thick planks. 'At night, it felt like a medieval army encampment on the eve of battle,' wrote reporter Shaun Walker. 'Flags fluttering in the icy breeze above the barricades, crackling bonfires, and bubbling cauldrons of borscht.'

After three weeks, on 10 December, the Berkut, the riot police, made a second attempt to clear the square. People poured in from all over the city. Stories tell of demonstrators who 'shaved and put on clean clothes in case they died that night'.

Every afternoon the citizens of Kyiv carried firewood, food, money and endless supplies of coats, sweaters and other warm clothing to the square. A grandmother arrived with the equivalent of fifty dollars, half her pension – 'For your victory, children!' The Maidan had meanwhile been transformed almost overnight into a well-appointed tent city, complete with first-aid posts, soup kitchens, a fixed contact point for legal advice and a Christmas tree.

It was populated by workers, veterans of the Afghan War, businesspeople, housewives, students, priests in army fatigues, girls with flowers in their hair, an elderly shepherd, a man in a Superman costume, and thousands more, young and old. Oleksiy Radynski, a Ukrainian television reporter, came upon a retired mineworker from the Donbass region who had become an activist after the 2010 presidential election. At the polling station he had seen the names of countless long-deceased colleagues on the electoral roll: 'dead souls'. He was deeply shocked. 'This was voting from hell, the underworld!' – and he meant it literally. By giving dead souls the right to vote, powers from the other side had been summoned and they'd influenced

Ukrainian politics ever since. It was up to the people to drive this diabolical energy back into the underworld.

Giving was central. There was talk of a 'spontaneous welfare state'. 'You walked through the Maidan and were presented with food, clothing, a place to sleep and medical care,' said a Polish activist. Hubert Smeets wrote in the Dutch daily paper NRC *Handelsblad*, 'Just try staying sober in Kyiv in early 2014. Only someone who ingests a double portion of "analyse and reflect" three times a day might possibly avoid being turned hot or cold by Maidan.' Sergiy Gusovsky, one of the demonstrators, called it a 'fledgling utopia', a city 'as primitive as it is holy': 'I would love to believe that the Maidan of today is an embryo out of which the new Ukraine will grow. This is a city that gives its citizens not just energy and strength but a special faith in the victory of justice and honour.' That, he wrote, could become the ideological basis for the new Ukraine.

Russian and Ukrainian were spoken interchangeably, as they were all over Kyiv. The language issue was irrelevant. In response to a survey, slightly more than half the people on the Maidan said they spoke Ukrainian, a sixth spoke mainly Russian, while a quarter spoke both languages. But not everything was idyllic. Under the surface there was soon a distinction between the modern, liberal and strongly Western-oriented demonstrators and those driven by a revived Ukrainian nationalism. As the weeks went on, Shaun Walker experienced more and more uncomfortable moments. 'One night, a well-drilled group of young men marched by, sticks in hands. They looked ready to inflict violence.' On 1 January, despite protests, the trad-itional torch-lit parade was held on the Maidan in honour of the nationalist fascist Stepan Bandera.

The Russian troll factory, meanwhile, attached its own meaning to the revolt. These weren't just Ukrainian nationalist fascists; there were signs of an 'impending homodictatorship'. A spectre was haunting the Maidan, 'the spectre of homosexuality'. 'It's a well-known fact,' said one Russian televi-sion commentator, 'that the first and most fanatical instigators in Ukraine are local sexual perverts.'

There was one condition placed on the help offered to Ukraine by Putin in December: the Maidan had to be cleared as soon as possible. The Kremlin sent reinforcements to Kyiv in the form of a handful of FSB agents and instructors from the interior ministry, specialists in quashing protests.

On 16 January, Yanukovych promulgated a series of 'dictatorship laws' in which he gave a legal gloss to the use of violence. From then on, demonstrators could be treated as criminals by the regime and, if it came to that, killed. The peaceful phase of the protest seemed to be over.

At meetings, banners were seen reading 'No songs and dances any longer'. Right Sector, the violent extreme-right faction at the Maidan protest, began to stir. The first big riots started, with television pictures that spoke for themselves, showing burnt-out cars and buses amid great clouds of tear gas. 'A godforsaken country, with smoke rising from it,' noted Ukrainian writer Andrey Kurkov in his diary. 'Under that smoke, we are sharing power. Crooks and revolutionaries. In the future, the revolutionaries might become crooks. I doubt that the crooks will ever join with the revolutionaries.'

The first deaths occurred six days later, on 22 January, when two demonstrators were shot. Sympathizers promptly poured in from all over the country; Yanukovych now had blood on his hands, so in their view it was impossible to let him remain in office. This was an attack on Ukrainian political society, orchestrated by the old imperial power. The pro-Europe Maidan revolt was gradually transformed into a patriotic movement. Timothy Snyder, chronicler of Eastern Europe, wrote, 'Ukrainians who began by defending a European future found themselves, once the propaganda and the violence began, fighting for a sense that there could be a past, a present and a future.'

On 24 January, Andrey Kurkov walked across the Maidan once more. A Pole was giving a speech in Polish, but even so at least a thousand people were standing listening, at 10 degrees below zero. Kurkov described an iron pipe sticking up through a hole specially cut in the canvas of a large army tent, with smoke curling out of it. Inside, firewood was burning in a cast-iron stove.

6 February. 'Yesterday, a first wedding was celebrated in the Maidan! A story worthy of a romance novel: injured during a protest march, young Yulia, from Rovno, went to the infirmary. Bohdan, a volunteer from the Zhytomyr region, bandaged her hand. . . . At the end of the ceremony, Yulia and Bohdan went to the barricades together.'

19 February. 'In Kyiv, they are counting the dead, the wounded and the disappeared. . . . All night, there was fighting and gunshots . . . . The hospitals are overflowing right now. But many of the wounded are in hiding, from

their friends as well as from strangers. They are afraid of going to hospital because the police have often abducted injured protesters from there to take them to the station, without offering them any medical care . . . . The Maidanistas are asking for glass bottles (to make Molotov cocktails), waterproof capes (to protect them from water cannons), and anything that will burn . . . . Then they trapped the Party of Regions deputy, Dmitriy Svyatash, who has for the past two years been refusing to repay a 100 million dollar loan from the Paribas bank. Terrified, he begged the Maidanistas not to kill him. They didn't. They sprayed him with tear gas and let him go.'

The day before, 18 February 2014, the 'holy city' of Maidan had erupted in violence. Snipers appeared on rooftops in the area, the 'self-defence units' of the Maidan movement were increasingly well armed, and on that fateful Tuesday a firefight started that lasted for several days. In total around 100 people were killed and at least 700 wounded, most on the side of the demonstrators although there were victims among the riot police too. Who started this street battle remains unclear. It may have been an independent initiative by the riot police or a provocation by the FSB, but it's impossible to rule out a reckless act by a handful of demonstrators.

That killing spree marked the end of the Yanukovych regime. Even Russia and the parliamentarians who still backed him now withdrew their support. On the night of Thursday 20 February he accepted a deal worked out by a negotiating team from Germany, France, Poland and Russia. After putting in place a broad coalition, a new constitution and fresh presidential elections, Yanukovych would step down at the end of the year. (Before anything could be signed, incidentally, the Russian ambassador left for Moscow, giving Putin a free hand.) Representatives of the Maidan movement refused any compromise with this super-thief, however, and the foreign delegation left empty-handed. Yanukovych's own counter-insurgency troops began to desert him and that Friday evening he fled to Kharkiv. There, according to persistent rumours, he attended a congress where he was urged to declare his own Ukrainian state. He refused to go that far, the congress was broken up halfway and Yanukovych fled further, into Russia. Putin meanwhile spoke of a 'fascist coup' and a 'junta'.

Had the Ukrainian nationalists and fascists indeed taken over the Maidan movement in those last days of February? To judge from reports by the motley collection of journalists on the spot, the Right Sector and other fascistoid groups were certainly present on the square. They did not call the tune, however. The Right Sector eventually managed to mobilize only about 300 people, and in the presidential elections of 25 May 2014 their leader Dmytro Yarosh got no more than 0.7 per cent of the vote. It is indisputable, nonetheless, that the later Ukraine government, in response to the Russian takeover of Crimea and the revolt in the Donbass region, pursued an increasingly nationalist course.

Was this 'junta' able to seize power purely because of the trouble stirred up by the Europeans and above all the Americans, as some claimed? That too would be to underestimate the strength of a spontaneous popular movement. Naturally, as in all situations of this sort, any number of intelligence agencies, including the CIA, enjoyed fishing in troubled waters. Behind the scenes, moreover, the IMF played a central role.

One month before power changed hands, Victoria Nuland, Barack Obama's special envoy, was already busy putting together a new Ukrainian government. A far from professional conversation by mobile phone was tapped by the Russians and ended up on YouTube. You can hear Nuland going through a series of names, and adding a heartfelt 'Fuck the EU' when a possible role for Europe is mentioned. After the change of government, when journalist Hubert Smeets attended a meeting with the Ukrainian National Security and Defence Council to talk about intelligence and other Western aid, he didn't even need to bring up the subject. 'American English rolled out of the stairwell to meet us. The building was bursting with Americans, with or without Ukrainian forebears.'

Many European ministers and parliamentarians were naturally influenced by all that passion and all those European flags. They liked to call by, and one pro-European speech after another rippled across the Maidan: 'No, we won't let you down.' There were warnings – the Germans in particular were more cautious – but on 10 February 2014 in Brussels, a promise of membership was bandied about. The EU's foreign ministers, in their Foreign Affairs Council, declared that the Association Agreement was 'not the final goal', a far from realistic promise that was nevertheless repeated countless times by European politicians in front of cheering crowds on the Maidan.

All this verbal support was, in retrospect, mainly theatrics, an expression of misplaced European triumphalism. For the West, Ukraine was of less than essential importance. When it came down to it, not a finger would be lifted in its defence – quite apart from the fact that the military capacity to defend it was lacking, in Europe at least. In the phase of initial fraternization between NATO and the Warsaw Pact, immediately after the fall of the Wall, a great deal of heavy military equipment had been destroyed, including at least 50,000 tanks, artillery pieces and helicopters. By 2008 Europe was left with armed forces a mere 30 per cent of which, according to a scathing report by the European Council on Foreign Relations, were in a fit state to operate outside their national territories. 'What the other 70 per cent do with their days is a mystery,' the report went on to say.

'The West is not a suicide squad' had once been the headline in NRC Handelsblad above a piece about the Hungarian Uprising of 1956. It sparked a legendary argument among the editorial team. It was the same with Ukraine in 2014. Even accession to the European Union was an illusion for the time being, if only because of Ukraine's extreme corruption. A European effort to make Ukraine into a neutral buffer state, like Finland, would have been far more realistic in the circumstances. The encouragement of the American hawks and the European idealists may have been emotional, warm and principled, but from a military and economic point of view it was quixotic, given the actual capacities of the West. The stubborn and brave fighters of the Maidan movement were kept warm with hot air.

At the same time, statements and promises from the West were further stoking unease and paranoia in Russia – a reality to which the Americans paid even less attention than most. Putin lives in 'a different reality', Angela Merkel told President Obama in a telephone conversation. She meant that Putin experienced the crisis very differently and had a completely different perspective on Ukraine and on international politics. She didn't agree with his vision, but she understood him nonetheless. The American hawks, led by assistant secretary of state Victoria Nuland and Republican warhorse John McCain, remained, in this respect, oblivious.

There was bound to be a Russian reaction, and it was Crimea that suffered most. For the Kremlin, the Crimean Peninsula – because of its naval bases and its access to 'warm water' – was of great strategic value. There were deep historical ties as well, and Sevastopol was one of the heroic cities of the Second World War. No Russian president could permit himself to lose his grip on Crimea. Even Mikhail Gorbachev said later that he would have responded in the same way as his later successor.

Putin acted with great speed. The decision-making now took place within a very small circle; not even foreign minister Sergey Lavrov, a legend among diplomats, was invited to the meeting where the decision was made to annex Crimea. Putin and his intelligence services resolved to act. Other considerations and interests no longer counted for anything.

The Russian army had learned a great deal over the preceding few years. An excellently prepared and trained force of some 10,000 troops – in uniform but without insignia, which led to them being dubbed 'little green men' – overwhelmed most of the peninsula within a few days. The Olympic Games in Sochi, which had started two weeks earlier, were used as cover; the ships and troops supposedly needed there for security reasons were simply sent on to Crimea when the Games ended. They were referred to as 'self-defence units', deployed against the 'advancing fascists' of the Maidan movement. At the same time, the Russian troll factory began a cyber campaign peopled by fictional characters with shocking stories about the 'fascist' cruelties in Crimea and equally fictional interviews with Russians who had fled.

Kyiv was still in chaos as a result of the transfer of power, so the Ukrainian authorities in Crimea offered little resistance. There was immense confusion. One telling fact: the Ukrainian defence minister had two passports, one Ukrainian and one Russian. Andrey Kurkov wrote in his diary that the captain of the Ukrainian corvette *Ternopil*, in the harbour at Sevastopol, responded to the Russian demand for capitulation with the words 'Russians don't capitulate'. In response, the Russian admiral explained that he too was an ethnic Russian, as were at least half his crew. For the time being, the admiral left empty-handed.

Kurkov wrote that 'events are progressing very quickly in Crimea, and very slowly in Europe. As if the news were arriving not by internet but by messengers on horseback.' On Monday 24 February the invasion gathered pace; on Thursday 27 February a provisional government was established, with a local gangster as prime minister; and on Friday 28 February the Russian parliament decided to annex Crimea, making it part of the Russian Federation. By 21 March, less than a month after the start of the military campaign in Crimea, the Russian flag was flying over almost all its military installations.

The annexation was finalized with a pseudo-referendum in which people were given two options, both of which involved a split from Ukraine. This was an outright land grab, breaching all the rules of international law. With the annexation of Crimea – and later the surreptitious invasion of eastern Ukraine – Putin was violating one of the most important post-war security agreements, known as the Budapest Memorandum of 1994, under which Ukraine gave up all its nuclear weapons in return for 'security assurances' from Russia, Britain and the United States, guaranteeing its borders in perpetuity.

The West responded with sanctions. A new period of isolation dawned. Russia was suspended as a member of the G8 group of world leaders, but the Russians cared little about that. Everywhere there was proud talk of a 'clever' Russian invasion of Crimea, while at the same time, officially, it was emphatically denied. In Moscow a sad joke circulated about a quarrelling couple. Wife to husband: 'Our son has died in action, in Crimea.' Husband to wife: 'We never had a son.'

The propaganda machine meanwhile performed intriguing pirouettes. Within a few weeks Ukraine, the country of Russia's close cousins, was recast as a hostile nation, ruled by 'fascists'. On 20 March 2014, Russian television showed a new, extended weather map: the rain, storms and anti-cyclones above Crimea, the Donbass and Kharkiv were henceforth its own. The annexation was complete.

5

Does history show a pattern? Can lines be discovered in it, and plans, and strategies? Or does history repeat itself? None of the above, wrote Julian Barnes in *A History of the World in 10½ Chapters*: 'History just burps, and we taste again that raw-onion sandwich it swallowed centuries ago.'

The belches did indeed come with a vengeance, mixed with every conceivable kind of propaganda, after the annexation of Crimea. Ukrainians saw the Russians as having the terrible famine of the 1930s on their conscience – the Holodomor, the enforced collectivization of agriculture during which between 2 million and 4.5 million Ukrainians starved to death. Russian propaganda, for its part, kept knowingly referring to the role of Ukrainian Nazis during the Second World War – the Banderivtsi who cleared out the Polish resistance and did the dirty work in the death camps. Russian television showed repeatedly, day after day, images of the destructive February riots around the Maidan, intoning 'The Ukrainian fascists are seizing their chance once again.'

On 8 May 2014, Shaun Walker was invited to join a village meal in Ilyicha, an hour's drive from Donetsk. He found himself sitting beside seventy-eight-year-old Nadezhda, grey and thin, barely able to walk and almost completely blind. When the war started she must have been five. Walker gave her a little help with the food, since her hands were trembling, and suddenly she said, 'Yura, is that you? Yura, dear, have you come back?' Walker said sorry, no, he wasn't Yura, he was a British journalist. 'Yura! But it is you! You were away for so long. And now you're back. Will there be another war?' The music grew louder, tears poured down Nadezhda's cheeks, but when Walker stood up to leave she grabbed him by the arm. 'Will there be another war?' 'No, I don't think so,' Walker replied. 'Are you sure?' she said. 'I am scared. On television it's war, war, war. Everyone is talking about war, and I am scared there will be another one. Let God stop it, please, nothing is worse than war.' She was shaking, trying her hardest to work out who he was. Walker reassured her, telling her everything would be fine, for want of anything better to say.

The next day it became clear that yes, there was going to be a war.

The village of Ilyicha is in the Donbass, the easternmost part of Ukraine. The region was a melting pot like all the old mining and industrial areas in Europe, populated by the descendants of the hundreds of thousands of workers drawn there in the past, in this case mainly from the vicinity of Moscow and from the Baltic states. According to the most recent census, which dates from 2001, 60 per cent of inhabitants of the Donbass at the time regarded themselves as Ukrainian, 40 per cent as Russian. As far as languages go, the proportions were reversed, with 75 per cent speaking Russian and 25 per cent Ukrainian.

Work in the mines was extremely tough. In the past the workers had always been placed on a pedestal, as the ultimate Soviet heroes. Their fall in status and income after the collapse of the Soviet Union was deep, and the social dislocation in eastern and southern Ukraine was even greater than elsewhere. Their meagre salaries and pensions were eaten away week after week by hyperinflation. Hunger and terror prevailed, the mafia flourished – all those mines and industries were up for grabs – and businesspeople negotiated with machine guns close at hand.

In 2014 the landscape was scattered with the carcasses of a huge industrial region that, as if in the aftermath of a natural disaster, had abruptly come to a standstill: ruins of factories with not a single window left whole, rusted mine shafts, huge spoil heaps that were half overgrown, and amid it all the former workers, still dazed, poor as church mice. Everywhere in the Donbass, Shaun Walker saw posters calling on women to sell their hair if it was more than thirty centimetres long. Even that simple source of dignity, one's own hair, was for sale.

The people of the Donbass, as opinion polls showed, were far more focused on Russia than other Ukrainians, yet in 2014 the vast majority wanted to remain part of Ukraine. At that point, only a small proportion of the population supported the struggle for independence. In the impoverished towns and villages, however, soldiers could be found everywhere who were all too eager to take up arms to split from Kyiv and return to the glorious bosom of Mother Russia.

The Maidan revolt was therefore experienced very differently in the Donbass compared to in the rest of Ukraine. In Kharkiv, thirty kilometres from the Russian border, separatism was inflamed by Russia. A Kremlin fixer, Vladislav Surkov, set up a chain of sports clubs where paratroopers and other servicemen were trained for what was to come. In Donetsk, the region's second city, Walker saw continual clashes between pro-Kyiv demonstrators and thousands of pro-Russia demonstrators. He saw above all a conflict between those who had successfully survived the chaos of the past few years and embraced modernity, and people who felt they'd been left behind – mirroring the uprising that Europe and America would eventually face in their own populations, with a rebellion by forgotten groups to whom no one had paid any attention.

The pro-Russia protests did not remain limited to the east, however. In other parts of Ukraine too, people rose up against the 'Western coup' on the Maidan, in demonstrations that sometimes ended in armed skirmishes.

A major fire in Odesa on 2 May 2014 was a watershed. Several hundred pro-Russia demonstrators had sought refuge in the union building, pro-Ukraine demonstrators threw petrol bombs through the windows – even after the building had already caught fire – and forty-two of those inside died in the resulting conflagration. Russian propaganda labelled the tragedy a 'fascist bloodbath' and Russia's supporters in Donetsk and Kharkiv saw their worst fears confirmed: this has happened, and therefore the 'fascists' of the Maidan movement will invade the Donbass.

From that moment on, clashes between local militias became increasingly fierce. In Kharkiv and Odesa the separatists ultimately made no headway. In the Donbass, the fighting escalated to become a civil war. I say 'militias', but often they were heavily armed criminal gangs, especially on the rebel side. Even Moscow sometimes had great difficulty keeping a grip on these 'allies'. The airport in Donetsk was shot to pieces – that particular battle went on for almost a year. The Ukrainian army, having recovered from the humiliation of Crimea, fought back hard, deploying tanks, helicopters and heavy artillery, and from mid-May 2014 onwards an all-out war raged in eastern Ukraine, in which Russia increasingly became involved.

In that same May of 2014, I was in New York for the annual PEN festival, attending a debate between Adam Michnik, the great strategist behind the Polish anti-communist resistance, and his Hungarian counterpart, György Konrád. The two embraced like old comrades-in-arms, yet ten minutes later they were sitting side by side like polite fighting cocks. That's right: Ukraine.

Both men reasoned from their own historical experience. Michnik, to loud applause from the American audience, advocated a hard-line approach: show solidarity with the young people of the Maidan movement, draw strict and clear boundaries; this is about the foundations of our world order and our Western values, and any compromise stinks of betrayal.

Konrád was more cautious. He pointed to powerful feelings of humiliation in Russia, to the military balance of power on the ground, to the extremely limited options for both NATO and the EU. Great expectations – and this is what Konrád's story came down to – had been aroused. If they could not be fulfilled there would be huge disappointment. And then everyone would be even worse off. That had been his experience in 1956 and the situation looked similar now.

It was a quarrel I would come upon countless times in those months, even between good friends and colleagues. Russia had always been a major colonial power, although with land rather than ocean between the mother-land and the colonies. The collapse of such an empire meant, as it always did, pain, violence and humiliation for the former rulers. There was a need for caution, but where did caution stop and passivity begin? Had Russia's former colonies not in theory as much right to go their own way as coun-tries elsewhere in the world? In that light, did the cautious attitude of quite a few European politicians not look like a repeat of the 'treachery' of Munich in 1938? Or was this situation more like the building of the Berlin Wall in 1961, when a self-assured Kennedy decided against intervention? It was not a sign of weakness. He knew that rescuing the people of East Berlin was completely beyond his capabilities. He was aware of his limits. This was very different from treachery.

There in New York, both men had a point, but they were speaking from completely different worlds. Michnik spoke from a *Gesinnungsethik*, an 'ethic of conviction', based on the classic ideology of the free West, and from the heart, as an old revolutionary. Konrád spoke from a *Verantwortungsethik*, an 'ethic of responsibility', and from the sober reality of geopolitical relations, bleak but realistic. 'I have lived with Russians all my life,' he said afterwards. 'I know them.'

Once again, everything turned on the biggest geopolitical issue of these decades: should smaller states really be allowed to decide their own fate? Should the Panamanians therefore be able to opt for China, if it suits them?

That afternoon another difference became clear too, and it was at least as important. Michnik was showered with applause, which had everything to do with the fact that his vision fitted seamlessly into the American story about freedom, democracy and heroism. There was barely any applause for Konrád, with his sober and cautious approach, but he represented a vision that prevailed in Europe, even though, there too, opinion was very much divided. While 68 per cent of Americans advocated the expansion of NATO to include Ukraine, 67 per cent of Germans were opposed. In Hungary, Bulgaria, Slovenia and Greece there was much understanding for the Rus-sian viewpoint, while Poland and the three Baltic states, supported by Britain, argued for a hard line.

The cautious European attitude was in part a matter of practicality. In

New York it was easy for the Americans to talk. In Europe, Russia was right next door. Europe's trade with Russia was more than ten times America's, the French had pulled in more than a billion euros' worth of Russian defence orders – in 2014 they were working on two new Mistral-class amphibious assault ships – and London had become the financial centre for the Russian oligarchs. Then there was Europe's dependency on Russian gas. The Netherlands still had its own, if rapidly depleting, supplies, but Britain was dependent on Russia for a quarter of its gas, France for half, and Germany, Spain and Italy for as much as three-quarters.

6

Putin, meanwhile, was in a bind. His dreamed-of 'reconquest' of a large part of Ukraine quickly came to seem limited to the Donbass. In contrast to the strategically important Crimea, this left-behind industrial region was of little use to him. The Donbass would bring him only trouble and expense, and new Western sanctions time and again. Furthermore, the conflict had boosted nationalist sentiments in the rest of Ukraine. Polls showed that, during the occupation of the Maidan in 2013, at least half of Ukrainians had remained on the sidelines. Two years later, some three-quarters saw themselves as Ukrainians pure and simple. Just one in ten still felt a bond with Russia to some degree. Even in an eastern Ukrainian city like Kharkiv, only 20 per cent of people wanted to return to Russian rule, while some 40 per cent opted for Europe.

The Russian president seemed trapped inside his own rhetoric. After telling so many stories about this 'New Great War for the Fatherland' he had no way back, even though in early May he called for the referendum on independence for eastern Ukraine not to be rushed. Russian weapons kept pouring in, and from 11 June onwards Russian tanks rolled over the border.

Among the reinforcements was a Buk anti-aircraft system, type 9K37, belonging to the weaponry of the 53rd Brigade from Kursk. As part of a large convoy, it crossed the border in late June, and on 17 July the Buk missile launcher was set up in a field close to the provincial road between the tiny settlement of Balka and the town of Snizhne. Heavy fighting was going on there at the time, and every fifteen minutes or so a commercial aircraft would pass overhead, at a considerable altitude. The war zone was directly under the busy flight path between Europe and Asia, and over recent days there had been warnings from various quarters about the possibility of military 'accidents'.

What occurred on the afternoon of 17 July was exactly that. When they fired their Buk missile, which had been delivered without its radar system, the pro-Russian anti-aircraft crew thought they were targeting an Antonov An-26, a Ukrainian supply plane. In reality it was a Boeing 777, Malaysia Airlines Flight MH 17, on its way from Amsterdam to Kuala Lumpur with 298 passengers and crew on board – including 193 Dutch people, mostly families going on holiday.

Shortly before the fatal moment, the Ukrainian intelligence service, by its own account, was listening to a conversation between a 'spotter' and one of the commanders of the pro-Russian separatists. 'A bird is flying in your direction.' 'A drone or a big one?' 'Impossible to tell through the clouds; it's flying very high.' So the spotter had no idea what kind of plane it was. 'Understood.' Two minutes later, a short distance away, suitcases, bags, books, children's toys and body parts started to rain down on the gardens and sunflower fields. Soon afterwards, the separatists issued a press release. 'An An-26 has just been shot down near Torez, somewhere beyond the Progress coal mine. The bird came down behind the spoil heap. There are no civilian casualties.'

The Kremlin immediately denied any involvement in the tragedy. Local witnesses, however, had seen the Russian Buk missile launcher with four missiles aboard drive past the previous day. The missiles were filmed and photographed – a day later there were only three – and parts of the tail and warhead of a Buk missile were found at the site where the plane came down. Fragments of the hull of the aircraft showed signs of an impact consistent with being hit by a Buk. In short, it was soon clear what had happened, and it was confirmed by meticulous research – especially that of the independent investigating collective Bellingcat and the official Joint Investigation Team (JIT) of the five countries affected.

A fierce propaganda battle broke out immediately. Within forty minutes of the disaster, the Russian troll factory in Saint Petersburg – the so-called Internet Research Agency – was working flat out. Data from Twitter indicates that within two days, at least 65,000 tweets about the event were fabricated. With the help of the Russian defence ministry and the Russian media, conspiracy theories came in quick succession. 'There are radar images that show it was a Ukrainian missile.' 'A fighter plane shot down flight MH17.' 'President Putin was flying in the area; he was the real target.' 'There was a bomb in the cockpit.' 'It was a Buk, but a Ukrainian Buk.' At one point the trolls even came up with the absurd story that the victims were already long dead and had been thrown out of a plane at that spot to discredit Russia. Like every conspiracy theory, they were eagerly picked up and passed on.

In the West, meanwhile, there was talk of an 'act of terror' and an 'act of war'. It was soon clear from practically all the investigations and reconstructions – including that of the JIT – that there had been unimaginable nonchalance and stupidity, and therefore a large degree of guilt. Those manning the missile launcher were almost certainly Russian and well trained, and given the height and speed of MH17 they should have known it couldn't possibly be a military aircraft. 'Putin's missile' was the headline in The Sun, and it was typical of the mood. Without Putin's endless trouble-making and without his weapons deliveries, none of this would have happened. His denial of all responsibility and the absurd theories he propagated made everything even worse.

After that tragedy the debate between the hardliners and the Putin-Verstehers, as they had become known, fell silent. With remarkable unanimity, EU leaders imposed unprecedentedly harsh sanctions. Following America, Europe now also decided to block the export to Russia of technology for oil and gas exploration and of military equipment. (The two French assault ships were eventually sold to Egypt.) The financial sanctions were particularly drastic. There was a ban on the provision of credit to large Russian banks and businesses, including Rosneft, Transneft, Gazprom, Novatek, Kalashnikov, Gazprombank and the Bank of Moscow. American banks were banned from extending credit to the banks most closely associated with Putin and his entourage, which effectively froze hundreds of millions of dollars. Major NATO exercises took place in Poland and the Baltic states.

Moscow retaliated with a ban on the import of certain agricultural products from Europe. Many wealthy Russians found themselves searching for a safe place to stash their assets. In 2014 alone, capital flight from Russia amounted to some $150 billion. Investment fell, the value of the rouble plummeted once again, oil prices dropped – according to Putin because of a plot by the US and Saudi Arabia – budget deficits rose, and spending cuts became the order of the day. The sanctions led to a new economic crisis at least as profound as those of 1998 and 2008. Relations with the West had not been so tense since the end of the Cold War.

Over the months that followed, the Ukraine war grew into a major armed conflict. On 5 September 2014, after mediation by the EU, America and Russia, a ceasefire was agreed in Minsk, but in January 2015 the war flared up again. Pro-Russia rebels captured Donetsk Airport and fierce fighting resumed in the rest of the Donbass region. The Ukrainian government, hard-pressed by Russian armed violence, asked the West to come to its aid with high-tech weapons systems. The Americans were in favour. Surely you couldn't abandon the freedom-loving Ukrainians? Such advanced weaponry, however, could not be deployed without Western 'advisers', and consequently America and Russia, the world's largest nuclear powers, would find themselves in an almost direct confrontation on the EU's doorstep. The situation was deadly dangerous.

In early February 2015, Angela Merkel, in a desperate tour de force, set out to forestall that disastrous scenario. She took a frenetic trip around the world, within a week calling at Kyiv and Moscow, then Munich followed by Washington, then Minsk and finally Brussels. The American hawks, with their cheap heroism, accused her of appeasement and put Obama under intense pressure. Merkel believed that a better-equipped Ukrainian army would not deter Putin in the least, saying 'I cannot imagine any situation in which improved equipment for the Ukrainian army leads to President Putin being so impressed that he believes he will lose militarily. And that is the reality of the day. You have to look reality in the eye.' On Wednesday 11 February, after an all-night meeting between Merkel, Hollande, Putin and the new Ukrainian president Petro Poroshenko, and after powerful pressure by Putin on the rebel leaders, a new ceasefire was finally agreed. Heavy weapons were pulled back on both sides of the front line, there would be local elections with more autonomy for regions like the Donbass, while Ukrainian control of the border between Russia and eastern Ukraine would be restored.

Despite peace having been achieved on paper, fighting continued to break out. When eighteen months later, on 1 September 2016, the umpteenth truce came into effect, BBC correspondent Tom Burridge wrote, 'It is the first time there has been a true halt to fighting in 11 months.' Yet at the end of that year, on 24 December, another ceasefire was needed, the tenth. In the new year the fighting resumed in full force. By March 2017 at least 10,000 people had been killed since the start of the war, a quarter of them civilians.

On 27 June 2017, Russia opened a new front: Ukraine was faced with a large-scale cyberattack. This was the third of its kind, after comparable attacks on Estonia and Georgia. Computers all over the country had been infected with a vicious virus that brought life almost to a standstill. Banks ceased to function, hospitals could no longer access their patients' notes, airports, railways and power stations could not operate, and in the television studios the screens went blank. This time the rest of Europe was badly affected as well. Two Rotterdam shipping terminals, for instance, were out of action for weeks. Ultimately, 10 per cent of Ukrainian systems were found to be affected. This was virtual precision bombing, with some companies losing 60 to 80 per cent of their computer infrastructure. It took the Ukrainians weeks to get everything more or less working again.

Meanwhile Russia, at lightning speed, had built a huge bridge from the Russian mainland to Crimea. Although Crimea was still firmly linked with Ukraine – which continued to supply its water and electricity – the bridge quickly became a symbol of Russian sovereignty in the peninsula. Contrary to all existing agreements, the Sea of Azov and the Kerch Strait were blithely declared to be part of Russian territorial waters. As a result, in late 2018 clashes broke out between Ukrainian fishermen, the Ukrainian navy and the Russian coastguard. By the time a short-lived ceasefire was achieved, the conflict had cost around 13,000 people their lives.

7

'In essence the war was the collision of three hubristic projects,' wrote correspondent Ben Judah about the Georgian war of 2008. Georgian hubris, in thinking it could crush Russia's mini-client state of South Ossetia without consequences. American and EU hubris, in thinking they could take a core ex-Soviet state into their sphere of influence without consequences. Russian hubris, in thinking it still had a veto on the foreign policy choices of its former vassal states and colonies.

Precisely the same was true of the Ukraine war six years later. Again there was hubris on the part of the Americans – as if their Sixth Fleet could steam through the Bosporus and save Crimea from the Russians. There was hubris on the part of the Europeans – as if their 'technical' Association Agreement would not have huge political repercussions. There was hubris on the part of Ukraine – as if, after so many years of dislocation and corruption, full EU membership was just around the corner. And again, above all, there was hubris on the part of Russia.

Putin had allied himself unconditionally with the old ghosts he had aroused in eastern Ukraine. But what had he ultimately achieved by this? Almost nothing had come of his proposed alternative to the EU, the Eurasian Union. Of his plans for 'Novorussia', a Russian-speaking confederation that would split from Ukraine, all that remained were two semi-criminal enclaves that were totally dependent on Russian money and a Russian military presence. Ukraine itself had slipped out of his hands.

In the old Soviet Union, major decisions were often taken within the tight circle of the Politburo, but even so, various sectors and interests were represented and internal debates were common. Putin, by contrast, had steadily narrowed his circle and was barely listening to diplomats, economists or other specialists. The sober, pragmatic Putin of the early years had disappeared completely by 2012. All politics had become personal and secrecy was paramount – internal secrecy included. Even after the 'little green men' had been active in Crimea for several days, foreign minister Sergey Lavrov and his advisers still didn't know exactly what was going on.

According to Putin's biographer Steven Lee Myers, decision-making in the Kremlin concerning Ukraine quickly became a huge mess. The president decided everything himself, off the cuff, and even his most faithful advisers floundered. Kremlin commentator Fyodor Lukyanov wrote: 'It seems the whole logic here is almost entirely the product of one particular mind.' Paul Quinn-Judge, an adviser at International Crisis Group, remarked, 'If one looks back at the four years of Putin's Ukrainian adventure, they make him seem more a sorcerer's apprentice than a tactician.'

Shortly before it all began, in late 2013, over 40 per cent of middle-class Russians said, when asked, that their lives were good. After three years of sanctions the figure had fallen to 22 per cent. More than 20 million Russians, a sixth of the population, were by then living below the poverty line, and more than a third were having difficulty getting enough food and clothing. Relations with the West had reached rock bottom and Russia found itself in profound isolation, which put a brake on all further modernization.

On the evening of 27 February 2015, Boris Nemtsov was shot dead on Bolshoy Moskvoretsky Bridge, in one of the best-protected parts of the city, right outside the walls of the Kremlin. Nemtsov was at that point the most important opposition leader, yet in his own way he was a member of the Russian elite. He had been a governor and vice premier, he had helped Putin in the early years, and he was among those who had brought about the big deal with the oligarchs. The attack was spectacular and highly professional. Eventually, five Chechen men were tried and convicted, but in reality the murder was probably the work of the FSB or other security services, part of a complicated power struggle with the Chechen leader Ramzan Kadyrov.

The murder was also a provocation. Putin probably knew nothing about it beforehand, and those close to him say he was surprised and shocked. So things of this sort could happen independently of him – even an attack so close to home? That too was telling.

In Ukraine, in the aftermath of the Maidan rebellion, businessman and confectionery manufacturer Petro Poroshenko had come to power. His new slogan was 'Army, language and faith'. In 2013, the country had still been multilingual; even the leaders of the Maidan movement spoke Russian at home and Ukrainian on the podium. Five years later, Russian could be spoken in only a quarter of Ukrainian television transmission time. In cinemas, nine out of ten films had to be in Ukrainian, and in shops the staff were allowed to speak Russian only if a customer specifically requested it.

The Poroshenko regime, which would never have come to power without the Maidan uprising, was no less corrupt than its predecessors. The confectionery king was heavily defeated in the presidential elections of

2019. 'I know 100 per cent that the current guy is a disaster,' one voter told *The Guardian*. 'So of course I'll go for the 10 per cent chance we could really change things.' She, like the vast majority of her fellow citizens, now opted for Volodymyr Zelenskiy, an untarnished figure, an actor lacking any experience in politics who had played the likeable president in an entertaining television series: the dream candidate, in every sense. To everyone's surprise, three years later, partly because of his talents as an actor, he revealed himself to be a second Churchill, an exceptionally courageous war leader.

Umayya

AT THE AGE OF FIFTY I found myself in Amsterdam. I had a young daughter, I was living on a modern housing estate, and here, in Amsterdam, I was semi-literate. The other mothers at my child's school saw me as a backward, older immigrant who didn't speak a word of Dutch. I had to join in with the picnics and excursions and pancake-eating, otherwise my daughter and I wouldn't integrate. It was a nightmare. A close friend said, 'In the mornings all those mothers come to the school and they see the good mother, the bad mother, the stepmothers and Umayya.' They simply didn't know how to pigeonhole me.

In Finland I was a different person, as you know. I was a journalist and a member of the Helsinki city council, and when we met, in the spring of 1999, I'd just stopped being the presenter of *Ajankohtainen Kakkonen*, the big weekly news programme on the Finnish television channel YLE. Finnish television wanted to try me out as the first 'non-native' broadcaster. The effect was incredible. I'd never had a problem as a journalist, but as soon as they saw my face on the screen all hell broke loose: threats, a letter bomb, I even had to move house. I was quickly replaced by a blonde Finnish woman, and after that no one ever mentioned it again. That was the first time I had the feeling I was the canary in the coal mine.

We're Protestants, we're Palestinians of Christian origin. The Palestinian population has always been about 15 per cent Christian. I grew up in Haifa. Then from one day to the next I became a resident of Finland, having fallen in love with a Finn. That's how things go sometimes. It took a bit of getting used to. Helsinki can be grey for months, with lots of rain and sleet. You have to learn to walk all over again in that snow, straddle-legged, leaning forwards. Those first few winters I felt like Jonah in the belly of the whale.

You and I spoke twenty years ago in the basement of the Stockmann department store. Their slogan in those days was 'You can dress inconspicuously because you know you've got more important things to do.' Where else in the world could you sell clothes with a slogan like that? That's how Finland was in those days. I'd been living there for years by then. I was active on any number of fronts. I studied, wrote, but there was always the suggestion: you'll never get a normal job, you're an Arab, your Finnish will never be good enough. Television and radio were just about possible, but written journalism wasn't for the likes of me. Ever.

I switched to the university, where I taught audio-visual journalism. It was an escape from that constraining atmosphere, the students treated me normally, they were the new generation of Finns. You know, in Finland I was a sort of icon, for years. I was 'Miss Diversity', a model for the nation to put on show. I was in demand, I spoke fluent Finnish, I did a good job as a member of commissions and delegations. I flew to the United States with the Finnish prime minister of the time, and we visited the UN and lunched at the World Bank. A delegation of that sort could make an impression by having me along: aha, so those Finns are people of the world, they're really with it. I was their mascot.

I got a new job. The Finnish National Gallery had an opening for a 'diversity adviser'. I started off by ringing other museums, all over the world: 'What do you do about diversity?' I soon found out that the question hadn't arisen from the community at all; nobody was the least bit bothered about diversity. No, it was an issue created by the international museum world itself, purely because it was politically correct. The Finns talked to the Americans about it, and to others, it was a fashion thing. And I was invited to be an icon again. I gave talks in Vienna and Stockholm, with three-course dinners in museum cafés, conversations with the kind of elderly ladies who can always be found in museum cafés. Wonderful. But totally detached from the real world, that's for sure.

In that period I decided to adopt a little girl. From South Africa. It took a long time. The social worker from the Helsinki local council couldn't imagine how a non-Finn could bring up a child to be Finnish. 'You're an Arab,' she said. 'How are you going to celebrate Easter? How will you make your child into a Finn?' Those are the kind of conversations we had.

At last she arrived, my little daughter. Well. I thought I knew what racism was. But what happened with her . . .

Finns aren't much used to this sort of stuff, and I knew they weren't. But there came a point when I no longer felt like justifying myself to 5 million people on the tram, on the street or at friends' houses, and explaining what it means to be black.

I tried for three years, and I had the feeling that in Helsinki, with my adorable little girl, I was living in a human zoo. We were exhibits. I withdrew, it broke me. I thought: my god, I've adopted a child from a different continent, I ought to be giving her safety and security, but I can't even walk from my home to the shops with her without feeling fearful. It was as if everyone might spit on us.

On Christmas Day 2009, on my daughter's birthday, I took a decision. I had to leave. Where to? Boston? Too far. London? Too expensive. My brother has lived in Amsterdam for years, a kind and friendly city, but strange too – you can't understand anyone. Nevertheless he persuaded me. A year later, I left. It was sad and scary; hardly any of my friends had commented on my decision. I fled.

For days I trailed around Amsterdam with my little girl looking for a house, and eventually I bought something with no idea what the neighbourhood was like, I just knew it had a good school. My new roost was on an island in the harbour, I believe it had once been an abattoir, and now we called it home. My daughter had a lot of trouble adjusting; she was proud, but she couldn't yet understand Dutch. The children told her she was dumb, so she walked behind me whispering, 'Mie mouder is dum . . . Is that how you say it?'

As for me, I cried a lot. I was totally confused. Thirty years of my life were in Helsinki, the best part of my life, and mentally I was still living there. The Finnish media were intrigued. I'd fled their country. Why? Two years after I left, on New Year's Eve 2012, I gave an interview for the first time. The next day old friends started calling me: 'What have you done?' The conversation was a real bombshell.

See, the Finns always say, 'It's like getting the winning lottery ticket, being born in Finland and living here.' They say, 'Finland's the best country to be educated in.' They say, 'For single mothers too, Finland, with all its facilities, is the best country.' And then they see that someone who enjoyed all those privileges has fled, saying, 'Ultimately I'm not welcome here after all. I can't step out of my door with my child, so you can keep your lottery ticket.' The country was dumbstruck.

Others appeared, with similar stories, which nobody had wanted to believe. The floodgates opened. From the other side too, come to that. Once again I was inundated with sick emails, sometimes death threats. People in forests – and that goes for a lot of Finns – don't like other people. They walk outside, see a bear and think: right, I'll shoot you, I don't know you, I don't like you. It's an extreme feeling of xenophobia. And they're not even ashamed of it.

I gradually started to lose clients. It was 2016, and here in Amsterdam I was being supported entirely by my Palestinian parents. I was in a real panic. But thank god, I was incredibly lucky. There was a debating centre that saw something in me. I was given a job there, I could get to work on things that I'm good at. Now I'm in a place where I feel at home, it's great.

I love Amsterdam. It's beautiful and friendly, it's a city of the future, full of inventiveness and endless fun. Oh yes, I know that in many ways things aren't so very different here than in Finland. I'm among white people everywhere, everything is white. At school my daughter's classmates ask why I'm not a lunchtime supervisor, because all the lunchtime supervisors are Arabs. Or they're cleaners. So, although people are sweet and pleasant, the door to power is well hidden from non-whites.

Yes, I'm the canary in the coal mine. Slowly I really am starting to think of myself that way. It seems it's my fate.

Intermezzo

EUROPE IS A MAGNIFICENT CONTINENT, and its praises aren't sung often enough. Just look, for instance, at how the light on a March day falls across the hills of Thüringen. Or across the warehouses at the port of Gdańsk. Or across the rugged valleys of Lozère, the winding alleys of Lisbon, the pastel shades of old Budapest and the market stalls on the Campo de' Fiori in Rome. Or across the green expanse of my own Friesland, with its church towers that, when the bells are rung, seem to talk to each other.

Just listen to how beautiful Europe sounds, the splashing of the fountains in Zürich, the waves on the rocks of Wales, the sedate voice of Big Ben, a busker in Barcelona, the carillons of Amsterdam. No, no artillery today, not for quite a while now, and no cries for bread.

To my young historian in 2669 I'd say that, despite everything, we average Europeans in 2019 were happy compared to previous generations. Europe was better-off and more peaceful than ever. The sun still shone on most of the citizens of this continent. Yet the mood had changed. Many people felt less at home, strangers in their own world.

Why? Let me limit myself to my home environment, two places on this beautiful continent – the good city of Amsterdam and the headstrong province of Friesland in the north of the Netherlands, where you're almost in Scandinavia already. What has happened there, in these twenty glorious years of globalization and the free market?

About Amsterdam I can be brief: it became a tourist destination. From the turn of the century onwards, the city, like so many in Europe, was faced with a jump in scale, with growing pains as it acquired new dimensions, a new dynamism, a new magnitude of life. Such periods, when great changes take place in the technological, economic and social realms, are inspiring but often difficult and painful, since the forms and structures of a reinvented city and a new era are still lacking. The city had made similar leaps before: around 1660, when tens of thousands of immigrants transformed it into the New York of the seventeenth century; and again later, around 1880, when under the motto 'Electricity, industry and steam' – words that can still be read on the front wall of Centraal Station – the city rapidly expanded and modernized. In 2000 the third jump in scale began, this time under the motto 'Globalization, digitalization and individualization'. No one was eager to carve those words in stone, but they capture the spirit of the time.

From the 1960s onwards, Amsterdam had been through some tough years – extreme dilapidation, a prolonged youth revolt, drugs, high levels of street crime – but in the 1990s the city regained its balance, its centre was beautifully restored, and the mood was cheerful and optimistic. In 1998 British author Ian McEwan described the city as restful, open and tolerant, with delightful brick houses, 'modest Van Gogh bridges' and 'unstuffy-looking Dutch on their bikes with their level-headed children sitting behind. Even the shopkeepers looked like professors, the street sweepers like jazz musicians.'

Twenty years later that city no longer existed. Amsterdam was growing at three times its previous rate and the number of casual visitors had exploded. Between 2011 and 2016 the turnover of the cafés, bars, hotels, restaurants and brothels doubled; in 2018 alone the number of tourists increased by 10 per cent. None of this showed any sign of slowing.

In the spring of 2019 Bertelsmann Stiftung reported that the Netherlands was among the eight countries that had profited most from the EU and the European single market. Of the twenty top European regions, three were in the Netherlands: Utrecht, Brabant and Amsterdam's own province of North Holland. The Netherlands, like Germany, had benefited enormously from the euro. The common currency had removed the final obstacles to its flourishing export trade, and everything was working like a dream.

That economic success could be felt all over the city. Amsterdam was experiencing a new Golden Age. Unemployment continued to fall and the city was a magnet. Everyone with plans and talent wanted to be there. The universities grew into international hotspots and thousands of foreign students and academics created a new ethos, partly because of exchange programmes, the mutual recognition of diplomas, and the EU's open borders. The city's blossoming was reflected in its appearance. Practically all the old canalside houses had been renovated and restored, squares and streets skilfully reconfigured. Amsterdam had never been in such good shape as it was in these years.

Yet the city wasn't happy.

In 1999, I could take delight in a simple cycle ride along the canals. How beautiful our city was, in all seasons. How pleasant and attractive – the whole world had started to discover the fact and was buzzing around it. Now, after twenty years, you saw her ravaged face, especially in the old, relatively small city centre: the pushing, jostling and grumbling, the local shops giving way to tourist frippery, street life crowded out by the room-hire company Airbnb, policing wrecked by austerity, escalating house prices, and families leaving as soon as children came along – primary schools had 10 per cent fewer registrations in 2018 than in the year before.

Around the inner city lay the old middle-class districts, now with many migrants. Around them a new shell was growing, made up of gleaming residential areas, business centres and entertainment districts. That divide became starker by the year. Feelings sometimes ran high between the various population groups, drug crime was exploding, and an outburst of violence seemed a real prospect. Contract killings – extremely uncommon in the Amsterdam of 1999 – took place regularly. In 2018, there were nineteen.

Many of the workers who had always kept everything going – police officers, nurses, teachers – could no longer afford to live in this expensive city. Between 2014 and 2019, 40 per cent of parents left Amsterdam after the birth of their first child. It seemed many neighbourhoods were no longer suitable places for bringing up children. Every month my local paper – for almost forty years I'd lived in or near the Wallen neighbourhood – published a piece by an active citizen who was calling it a day and leaving the inner city for a distant province.

I steered casually through the Amsterdam of 2019 on my bicycle. Hen and stag parties lurched across the 'modest Van Gogh bridges': girls wearing bunny ears, men carrying enormous fake penises. The open curtains in the evenings – a much remarked-upon Amsterdam custom – had started to close. The 'professors' at the counter had left by the back door, shop rents had tripled or quadrupled, sometimes far more even than that. In the legendary bookshop where a young Joop den Uyl – a future prime minister – wooed his wife with a poem by Slauerhoff, rucksacks were now on sale instead, costing an arm and a leg: 'Travel Gear for the Urban Explorer'. The monthly rent my faithful baker had to cough up rose from 400 guilders in 1999 to 2,000 euros twenty years later.

In the inner city I saw internationalization of a kind that no longer produced variety but rather its opposite. The predictability and monotony increased with each passing year. All surprises seemed planned. Like Barcelona and so many other popular destinations, it had turned into an internationally interchangeable city of ice cream parlours, tourist shops and Nutella outlets.

Partly as the result of a services directive issued by Brussels, the creed of the free market had monopolized the conversation for years. Investors and venture capitalists were given a free hand in renting out homes. They could ask as much as they liked. The quality shops in my neighbourhood were helpless when faced with the big retail chains and monied speculators, and were mercilessly driven out of their old streets.

There used to be a fabulous shop with the tastiest Dutch cheeses in the city. The range was overwhelming and it was always full of customers. The owners were bought out for several times their annual turnover and now there was a mysterious cheese shop that sold just one type of tourist cheese, dyed deep yellow to make it look 'mature', in daft segments four times as expensive as in the supermarket. Another retailer sold nothing but bath ducks. Some businesses were doing remarkably well, but some shops were manifestly empty. We couldn't fathom it. 'You can hear the money-laundering machines humming away in the cellars,' neighbours said. All the illegal drug money that our 'tolerant' narco-state generated every year – according to one estimate roughly the equivalent of the turnover of Philips, some €20 billion – had to resurface somewhere, didn't it?

That spring of 2019 I'd been to a show at which the city's latest statistics were proudly presented. Everything had got better and better over the past twenty years, outstripping even the rest of the country, despite the fact that almost a third of Amsterdammers felt their jobs were insecure. Under the heading 'Migration' large coloured discs were displayed: Amsterdammers of Dutch origin were now in the minority and the city was populated by the most disparate array imaginable. The Turks and Moroccans of earlier migratory flows had been supplanted in part by 'expats', highly educated immigrants from all over the Western world. Their stay had something fleeting about it, they came and went, and at the same time the traditional Amsterdam middle class seemed to be disappearing.

One series of maps showing voting habits in Amsterdam and the surrounding area was particularly telling. In the 1990s, Amsterdam had a strong tendency to vote for parties of protest, of opposition to the system. Twenty years later the pattern had completely reversed and it was the periphery of the city that opted for dissent, often by voting for the extreme right. The city itself now favoured the established order and celebrated the fun and festivities of the expats, the propertied and the highly educated. Further out lived those who felt forgotten and excluded. My city was not unique in this; it was a phenomenon visible around all the big European conurbations.

In the early decades of this century, Amsterdam was full of self-confidence, and rightly so. It remained an uncommonly beautiful, convivial and interesting city. Several of its strongest characteristics enabled it to respond brilliantly to times of great change: openness, tolerance and a sense of citizenship, accompanied by an astonishingly methodical approach, as ever.

The city's charismatic mayor, the late Eberhard van der Laan, once put it saliently: 'We have a huge problem: Amsterdam is the most beautiful city in the world.' In 2016, he wrote that Amsterdam was one of the winners of globalization, but he also pointed to the risks created by its many drastic changes. That was the great sadness; the city's cement was starting to crumble, and its mystery, its ability to surprise and its solidarity were disappearing. My old Amsterdam was slowly dissolving, and around its jubilant heart rings of bitterness grew.

2

I live on two ice floes, which is a piece of great good fortune. With my other leg I stand in my village, a scrap of higher ground in the flat Mondrian country of Friesland, 330 souls around a medieval church. This northern-most part of the Netherlands has Scandinavian features. The melodious Frisian language still spoken in all the villages will get you a long way in Denmark or Norway, and the reverse is also true.

In 2019, over recent years everything here had stayed more or less the same. The bell, cast in 1354, was still rung every day at twelve, and at nine in the morning too if someone had died, or at eleven to mark a birth. The village had gained a handful of newly built homes, bright structures with lots of glass, sound roofs and fenced front gardens. There was a new clergy-man who, along with his wife, had begun an unusual experiment by setting up a modern monastic community close to the village. With verve, deter-mination and enthusiasm they brought life back to the old church. Behind closed doors, meanwhile, the usual joys and sorrows played themselves out: deaths, new happiness, deceptions large and small, a man who terrorized his neighbours, a village boy killed in an accident.

The community was still central to the lives of many villagers. At funer-als, several times a year, they dutifully walked around the church behind the coffin. Afterwards there would be coffee in the pub with the traditional *krakeling*, a type of biscuit that symbolizes the continuity of life. Village par-ties were still popular. The children who in the 1990s danced in the reception room above the bar were now the organizers, the life and soul of the gatherings. All this went on as it always had. The first question asked about every new family was: have they got children for our village school?

In this part of the world most people were not rich, and the official sta-tistics about education, work and income were no cause for celebration, yet there was a remarkable amount of happiness and satisfaction. According to the provincial statistical office, 92 per cent of people declared themselves happy and 89 per cent were content with their lives. Almost all the villagers worked hard, from early morning until late in the evening, whether for money or as volunteers. They spoke with pride of how the village had joined forces to renovate the former community centre, so that a family of Syrian refugees could live there. Carpentry, paintwork: the volunteers worked night after night to get the rooms ready in time. The newspapers wrote about it and other villages came to look. 'How did you do that, can you advise us?'

It turned out to be a Muslim family with no fewer than eight children. The youngest were a welcome contribution to the village school. They ran around with the rest of the kids and were soon speaking a fair smattering of Frisian and Dutch, with English thrown in. All the Syrian children had a self-assured stance in life and knew, young though they were, what they wanted to be: policeman, doctor, software engineer, architect. They were resolute by nature, quickly learned fluent Dutch, and helped to redecorate the school. The father had once been a teacher; they had owned land, olive trees and two houses. For him, everything had fallen apart.

In our village pub too, little had changed over the past twenty years. A new barman had come, with new volunteers and fresh enthusiasm, but the Persian carpets, the bar, the red beams and the old clock were the same as ever. On Tuesday evenings rehearsals were held by the drama society, on Wednesday nights it was still draughts, on Friday nights billiards, once a month women's night, and once a year the village party and a big theatrical performance in the notary's garden.

The main role in the plays was often taken by my neighbour, a schoolteacher in a neighbouring village. For thirty-five years he'd taught and raised children here. He was an excellent actor and an even better teacher – the two often go together – but he'd taken early retirement. His little school had been swallowed up by a large governing body, staffed by slick managers that neither he nor the parents had any grip on.

'They come into the classroom and don't even glance at the children,' he'd grumbled over recent years. 'They just stare at their notebooks, at the results of the written tests. We don't teach the children anything any longer, we just drill them.' The managers and head teachers met every month at a nice restaurant. Meanwhile, the school grew filthy as a result of the austerity mania. In his last few years of teaching, my neighbour took to buying all the toilet rolls himself.

The biggest changes happened mainly in outlying areas. The village certainly wasn't anxious. People had never been fearful of globalization here; even in the sixteenth century, Frisian farmers bought entire herds of cattle from Denmark to fatten them up and then sell them on for slaughter in Leiden and Amsterdam. Now I knew farmers who got their calves from Romania, raised them on powdered milk from New Zealand and then sent them to market in France. Only their dung remained.

I recall conversations in the pub about a large boatbuilding yard in a small town some miles away, where the biggest and most luxurious yachts in the world were made. Quite a few acquaintances and relatives worked there and they came home with the most unbelievable tales. They'd mostly been working for an American millionaire, as 300 people did eventually, on what was to be the most expensive yacht in the world, with onyx walls and gold taps and doorknobs, worth 330 million guilders, the *Trump Princess* II. But the American abruptly turned off the tap; he was about to divorce and that would cost a fortune as well. To avoid the boatyard confronting him with contracts and penalty clauses, the millionaire simply bought the entire business. It was far cheaper for him than all those fines; and in any case, the price had plummeted after his huge order was cancelled. The boatyard was eventually sold on and kept going, after much tribulation and many sleepless nights. So even my fellow villagers had plenty to say about the bizarre ways of hyper-capitalism.

One evening I got talking with a farmer who lived in a nearby village. He had a modern dairy farm with two milking robots and he ran it along with his son, who was at university in Ottawa. I looked surprised. 'Yes, my son does the paperwork,' he said. 'He keeps track of everything by internet. Last night he rang our farmhand, who had just set off home on his bike. "You need to go back, there's something wrong with Aaltje VIII. She's got a problem with her left front teat." He could see it from the milk production figures on his laptop, there in Ottawa. Yes, we're right up to date.'

At the same time, businesses continued to close. In spring 2019 our former neighbour stopped farming and we watched all the cattle being driven away. His family found it hard to take. Who didn't, in fact? They'd lived and worked there for generations, the place had been farmed since 1600. A complete history was driven away in a couple of cattle trucks.

In 1999 more than half of traditional Frisian farms were still going concerns. The number fell quickly, since an elderly farmer was frequently unable to find anyone to take over the business. Furthermore, in their optimism many dairy farmers had invested too much, urged on by the banks. Great floods of milk were produced – plus three litres of slurry for every litre of milk – and when milk prices collapsed, quite a few dairies found themselves in a hopeless mess. From 2018 onwards they were forced to buy phosphate rights for all the muck they produced. Manure production had to be drastically cut, as the Netherlands kept breaking through the European phosphate ceiling. Of all the dozen or more working farms close to our village, only three were left by 2019.

Here and there in the province we could now see the first ruins – an unusual sight in the Netherlands – of the once so proud head-neck-body farmhouses, their red roofs partially collapsed, great sorrowful mounds of brickwork. They'd become too expensive to maintain and could not have survived even if all the rich pensioners from all the big cities had come and adopted those great cathedrals of the farming world. Meanwhile, contact with friends and relations who had left for America or New Zealand was more intensive than ever, business contact included. At kitchen tables the word 'emigration' became common again.

One thing struck me in particular about the village plays put on in recent years. The baddie of the story, the character with power who was nevertheless consistently ridiculed, was no longer a city gentleman or a capitalist but a manager, a pathetic figure who trimmed his sails to the wind, who thought only in numbers and clichés and cared only about his own position, with no idea of what the work actually involved. Here too it was a plague they were encountering more and more.

The schoolmaster, my friend and neighbour, worked in the 'education market'. He had always been a traditional village teacher, utterly driven and highly experienced, respected by the whole community, a staunch social democrat. After school hours he would often call on his pupils, to inspect a new aviary, or to stand beside the grave of Afke's dead rabbit – all the things that are so important to children. His bosses had no idea what he was up to and didn't want to know. One night there had been a ferocious storm and the children were full of it. My neighbour used that morning to explain to his class what lightning was, and electricity. It was one lesson they'd never forget. That afternoon he was reprimanded by his 'supervisor' for failing to stick to the timetable imposed from above.

He told me about his run-ins with the steadily advancing world of numbers and managers, the way reality was being moulded into a uniform shape. He said some families were displaying a striking characteristic: they no longer had conversations. 'Sit down!' 'Soon!' 'Go upstairs!' 'That's the way!' 'I'm off then.' They were entirely normal families, but that was their style and always had been. My neighbour had one such boy in his class. Not at all stupid, yet it was hard for him to keep up. He turned out to have an astonishingly limited vocabulary. As a small child he'd never had the opportunity to pick up new words, and whatever was tried, it turned out to be hard to catch up later. He therefore performed hopelessly in the centrally organized primary-school assessment test. The official number-crunchers concluded he'd never amount to anything. A few years later the boy had a reputation as an excellent carpenter, an accomplished craftsman. 'If they'd asked him in the test about dovetail joints, adhesives and types of roof construction, he'd have got ten out of ten,' my neighbour said.

All those little schools were judged based on the standard national test. What the world of numbers left out of account, however, was the fact that in village schools the classes were often too small for a meaningful assessment. If the oldest class of eight or ten pupils happened to include the notary's child, plus one of the clergyman's, then it might do brilliantly. If it happened to have more than its fair share of children with learning difficulties, the result would be a good deal less impressive, which meant the school had a serious problem. Those same children – often diligent and reliable workers – might grow into fantastic citizens, but not according to the norms of The Hague or Brussels.

Sometimes the lines of communication were short. At a dinner I found myself next to a government minister, another social democrat. I explained to him this particular village problem. He listened attentively and advised me to send a letter to the relevant secretary of state, using our teacher's village school as an example. In my innocence I did so, the education machinery spat out a carefully nuanced response, and after that I let the matter rest. Until I ran into my neighbour again. 'Well,' he said. 'That letter certainly had an impact.' I looked at him, slightly surprised. 'Yes, two weeks later I was called in by the governing body. Severe reprimand. I must never speak to outsiders about such things again.' A file had been opened on him, he was told. It kept him awake at night.

The governing body had meanwhile appointed a new head-cum-manager for the school. She didn't speak a word of the Frisian language – a bit of a drawback in a village school where it was the main medium of communication. She attended the twice-monthly meetings in the pleasant restaurant and she consistently put the wrong ending on the past participle of every verb.

3

'I have to take part in a meeting at a hotel,' wrote György Konrád in 2005. He was to help choose Europe's cultural capital, a city in a predetermined region that would then be the centre of interest for a year. At least, that was the hope.

It was a serious game, in which money and fame were shared out. 'How do you make a city fashionable?' Konrád wrote. 'A designer is hired for a lot of money. The master comes for a year and tracks down the local obsessives and their hangouts. He's a dreamy imposter who understands advertising and knows what will sell.'

One member of the jury, 'a lazy member', was Konrád himself. 'The seven of us in a bus, writers, artists, academics' visited everyone up to and including the local poet. Konrád looked at stunts by the 'circus artists . . . who promised everything and embellished everything'. 'The city's bigwigs, the vintners and sausage-sellers, wanted this important role at any price. If industry was no longer going to bring prosperity, perhaps culture might.'

When Konrád looked in the bathroom mirror in the mornings, he saw a conman. 'How do you know? What do you know about anything? Aren't you ashamed?'

That was how Pécs in Hungary came to be awarded the honorary title of European Capital of Culture for a year. In 2018 it was the turn of my own bit of Europe, the Frisian capital Leeuwarden, and the 'serious game' was exactly as Konrád described. A newspaper was pushed through the letterbox announcing 'Leeuwarden and Fryslân, the centre of Europe'. And: 'Music, dance, theatre, exhibitions, architecture, comedy: you know right away that Leeuwarden qualifies for the title of most important city of culture in the whole of Europe for a year.' What was going on? Had our provincial capital, where the only college that taught music and drama had recently closed because of cuts and poor management, been touched with a magic wand?

The Capital of Culture phenomenon was thought up by Greek actress and singer Melina Mercouri, minister of culture in the reborn Greek democracy. In 1985, Athens became the first European Capital of Culture, followed by big names including Florence, Amsterdam, Paris, Glasgow,

Madrid and Copenhagen. Later, attention more often turned to less well-known cities and regions: Sibiu, Maribor, Košice. Officially the decision was taken by the European Council; in reality, the jury's advice was decisive.

The chosen capitals were required to embody the richness and variety of a shared European culture, to promote dialogue between representatives of various distinctive cultures, to initiate lasting cultural collaboration with other European cities by staging events, to involve broad layers of the population in the project ... There was no end to it. The local community (mienskip in Frisian) had made the crucial difference, as I understood it from the newspaper: 'The unique involvement of Frisians with their local surroundings, with families, neighbourhoods, clubs, associations or choirs, made a big impression right across Europe.'

The reality, I soon realized, was rather more trivial. The core of the European jury, of which Konrád had once been a member, turned out in practice to be a travelling ensemble that was informed and fêted everywhere by rival candidate cities and over the years had clearly developed certain preferences and sensitivities. It was preceded by a troupe of international experts and copywriters who provided candidate cities with advice, for a huge fee, and knew exactly what the jury wanted to see and hear. Leeuwarden had reached deep into its pockets, hiring the two best advisers, meticulously preparing and rehearsing its presentations, and producing a 'bid book' perfectly tailored to the jury. Wholly in accordance with the laws of Menasse's The Capital, it was made virtually impossible for Friesland to fail to win the honorary title.

Actually, there were a good many intrinsic arguments for the choice. The province of Friesland was indeed a small but interesting European region, an important centre of early-medieval North Sea culture. For centuries this had been rich farming country, with excellent connections and close trading links – Brussels might be a long way off, but Stavanger and London were only a few days' sailing from the Frisian coast. Traces of all this could still be found everywhere, in discoveries of hoards of jewels and coins, for instance, and in the language. Frisian often had more in common with English than with Dutch: lyts = little, bern = bairn, tsiis = cheese, swiet = sweet, it = it; I heard dozens of examples all around me every day.

In any number of fields – in music, drama, literature, technology, you name it – the phenomenon of the 'eccentric individualist' flourished here. People did their own thing, refusing to be distracted by the whims of fashion. It was an extraordinarily infectious kind of pride, and from time to time it produced great talents. My little village had a drama society and its own rock group, not to mention its big annual open-air theatre production for which everyone laboured mightily, and it was not alone. The word *mienskip* in the propaganda was no empty slogan. Despite all our reservations, 2018 looked promising.

The illusion didn't last. As in Pécs, here too the vintners and sausage-makers took over as soon as the title was conferred. Reports appeared in the local press. A board had been appointed made up of five mostly local cultural big shots, headed by a former television journalist. 'We will leave a legacy throughout Europe,' they promised. The top man called himself not 'director' or 'intendant' but 'CEO'. All five had annual salaries to match. A few hours after the local media uncovered the sums on their website, the information was removed. The world is small here, the press and the board members were closely interrelated, and such reports were too painful for all those thousands of volunteers who had been run off their feet day and night – for free, gratis and for nothing.

At first there was little sign of *mienskip*. The Frisian encounter with Europe was mainly top-down. A cyclone effect soon developed, such that most of the money made available for culture was inevitably sucked into the magic year 2018. Anyone wanting to organize a Bach contest or a theatre festival in 2016 or 2017 could forget it; power now lay with the CEO and his team. A plan was launched to build a fountain in each of the province's eleven towns, designed by eleven world-famous artists. In most places local artists were hardly involved at all – in contravention of the guidelines for Capitals of Culture. So, European culture descended from the ivory towers onto places like Dokkum, Hindeloopen and Workum. A lady from the Randstad directed the project. We watched kitsch, poetry and theme park emerge, all replete with good intentions and supplied with edifying explanations, but one small thing had been overlooked: no one had asked for any of it.

The result was an interesting social experiment, which I followed with particular interest. How does a community deal with an alien element, imposed from above? Some of the designers of fountains seemed to have a distinct preference for a kind of inflated realism: faces, symbols and traditional forms, but hugely magnified, the street art of an earlier age. Friction and dismay – tastes inevitably differ – often had to be resolved by a switch of location. The elegant fountain for Franeker was shoved up against the wall of a church, in IJlst a cheerful Chinese flower fountain was pushed away into the car park, and in Harlingen a spouting whale was moved so far out towards the sea that it was barely visible.

In Workum, two kitschy water-spewing lions were supposed to be sited near the mouth of the harbour. The plan met with universal protest: the townscape would be blighted and water sports hampered by the spouted water. A less prominent place was proposed, but local residents there began to object, refusing to look at such ugliness for the rest of their lives, art or no. Of course, in the end the two monstrous lions arrived there anyway. What sort of say are ordinary people in a working-class district likely to get?

Dokkum was thoroughly upset. It was to be given an ice fountain, surrounded by trees, as a reminder of the Elfstedentocht skating race and Saint Boniface, who was killed there. It was a remarkable and impressive project, but a large part of the local parking area would have to be sacrificed to it. Furthermore, its annual upkeep, financed by Dokkum itself, would severely deplete the small culture budget.

Both local tradespeople and the town's cultural enthusiasts rebelled. Yet there was no way to stave it off. The two most critical members of the local advice commission, including a respected architect, were shown the door and a special 'process manager' was hired for several tens of thousands of euros to massage the unwanted gift past all snags and objections. Eventually the European prestige project stood alone on a nice empty square, steaming – in anything resembling fine weather there was no ice to be seen. Next to it stood the subsidy text that had pulled the thing over the line. 'To achieve the maximum shadow, the sculpture uses a systematic arrangement of leaves around a center point – the result of more than 100 million years of evolution in the plant world.' Understandably, there was no money left after that for a small contribution to a local brass band.

'Leeuwarden 2018' was meanwhile acquiring more and more of the characteristics of a sect. Hardly any important public initiatives about Europe were developed, and instead large projects were simply bought in. Cooperation with neighbouring provinces and regions was minimal, the artists engaged were snapped at like schoolchildren, and the place was abuzz with horror stories. The board was in charge, with its corporate culture, and meanwhile the board members fought like rats in a sack. The village theatre could have made something of that.

Everyone was waiting for the Redeemer, a Fleming who was an old hand at all this. He turned up six months late, and a few months before the festivities began he dropped the whole thing. An American retail magnate who wanted to 'do something with culture' had offered him an even more generous fee. He told the local media, who meekly concurred, that everything was now on track and he had fulfilled his task. In reality, as everyone was aware, the final months before the launch of such a project are crucial. Furthermore, in this case, despite five years of the CEO regime, an awful lot was not on track at all. To organize the opening, a costly Amsterdam events agency had to be hurriedly brought in.

The CEOs did have one piece of immense good fortune: Friesland is populated by Frisians. The concept of mienskip had by this point been cheapened to the level of management-speak, but it turned out to be real enough. An army of volunteers took the project in hand, a sensible mayor assumed leadership, and with tremendous energy and dedication, an impressive series of local projects was finally set in train. The Frisians are good at this kind of thing. Entire villages were transformed into the decor for music and drama, thousands of volunteers came forward – an estimated 10 per cent of the population – and I watched entrancing performances. Leeuwarden was given a thorough facelift, another thing of lasting value. The summer of 2018 became, day after day, an impressive pyrotechnic display of culture and community spirit. So there was a happy ending after all.

No, Leeuwarden did not become 'the most important city of culture in the whole of Europe'. Foreign visitors made up no more than 6 per cent of the total, while 60 per cent came from Friesland itself. Europe, the feverish Europe of 2018, had little if any part to play. In hindsight, it was a great celebration of all that is exceptional about Friesland: its mutual warmth, its shared language and history, the home the Frisians have made together. There was nothing wrong with that, but the need for exceptionality was now so great that the 'European' part seemed rather tacked on.

The human tendency to stay close to hearth and home is strong. In 2019,

60 per cent of Britons were still living no more than thirty kilometres away from where they grew up, while 70 per cent of French people have always been resident in the region where they were born. The average Dutch person has parents no more than twenty kilometres away, and half of Dutch grandchildren live no further than fourteen kilometres from their grandparents.

Place et espace (place and space) were once an important theme for French philosopher Michel de Certeau. 'Space' stands for dynamism, for possibilities, for fresh air and freedom, but also for the risks and disorder that inevitably accompany the taking of untrodden paths. Europe was and is the perfect example of such a space, with its efforts to facilitate the free movement of goods, capital, people and services, with its removal of borders, its creation of new opportunities, its making of previously unimagined connections and the risks and unrest that go with them. All of that is Europe.

'Place' is the spot where we feel at home, where tradition and conventions offer predictability, order and safety, where old and new stories bind people together, where a shared history makes faith in a shared future possible. When I lived outside 'our' village for a couple of years, I discovered that for myself. What an operation the move turned out to be! In 'our' village we knew who was working on a tractor far off on the land, and which girl he was courting. We knew the history and all the stories. We knew the dead in the graveyard and their children and grandchildren. So many threads pulled us, held us tight, and we became aware of them only after we left.

We came back.

What we felt was the force, the power and also the importance of phenomena like 'place' and 'home'. Everyone knows feelings of this sort, even if the word has a different charge in each language, from the cosy 'home' and the proud *lieu* to the loaded *Heimat*. In Friesland the Frisian language is a familiar, binding element, which explains why it's so fiercely defended.

'Be from here,' writes my Flemish namesake and fellow author Geert van Istendael. 'Recipes for chili sauce and couscous salad are nowhere to be found in the 1972 edition of the Farmers Union cookery book *Ons Kookboek*, but they're included in the 2013 edition. So acknowledge identity in all its solidity, but also in all its changes and layers.' Neo-liberal globalization is steadily eroding that feeling – as is the accompanying ideology, which makes everything quantifiable and forgets about humanity.

Within the European project too, the balance between 'space' and 'place' had been upset, with 'space' increasingly devouring 'place'. The semi-illegal raw milk cheeses at the market in Dieppe, the smoky café without a toilet in the Hungarian village of Vásárosbéc, the chocolate sold in Bruges, the work of local companies for the local community – because Europe-wide tendering was now compulsory everywhere – and even the seeds in our vegetable plot: everything unique was at risk of succumbing to a hailstorm of well-intended Brussels regulations.

My neighbours and fellow villagers were highly sensitive to this. They understood perfectly well the need, in the twenty-first century, to develop a common climate and energy policy, and they knew that a small country on its own could not take a strong stand on the world stage. But many of those countless detailed interventions were seen, rightly, as an insult, as signifying a lack of respect for their feelings about 'home' and 'place'. If anything undermined public support for the European Union, along with its lack of democracy, it was this.

The liberals and the social democrats had never paid sufficient attention to such feelings, seeing them as right-wing and provincial, no matter how human and legitimate they might also be. They left such matters to others and, in the political space thereby created, populist rabble-rousers seized their chance. '*On est chez nous!*' became a battle cry for Marine Le Pen: 'This is our home.'

An idealization of what typifies 'us', a romanticizing of the past and of the 'pure' native peoples, a national and European renaissance, a boundless aversion to the political and cultural 'elite', the scent-markings of *Blut und Boden*: where had we seen all this before? The pied pipers were successful, and the Sacrament of the Buffalo, to quote Heinrich Böll, was being avidly taken once more.

In this atmosphere of uncertainty, ferocious conflicts arose over 'our traditions' and 'our heroes', which 'they' must not be allowed to take from 'us' – arguments that were sometimes as absurd as they were vicious. From 2011 onwards a real cultural battle began in the Netherlands concerning Saint Nicholas or Sinterklaas. From the sixteenth century onwards, this precursor to Santa Claus handed out sweets and gifts to children on the eve of his birthday on 6 December. It was the main Dutch family celebration of the year, more important even than Christmas. The Sint was traditionally accompanied by one or more bogeymen by the name of 'Black Pete'. In the late Middle Ages they were devils, blackened by tar from hell. In the mid-nineteenth century, Black Pete underwent a radical transformation and began to dress up as a black house servant. In the late twentieth century, large groups of citizens were increasingly offended by this. The much-loved fantasy figure was in their eyes an expression of racism and a residue of slavery. Demonstrations were staged, there were minor scuffles, innovations were tried and Petes were seen in all colours of the rainbow. Traditions do, after all, change with the times.

But supporters of the tradition would have none of it. 'We aren't racists. Leave our children's festivals alone!' Hatred of the protesters echoed across the internet: 'Black man's whore!' 'Up against the wall with them and good riddance!' When the children's ombudswoman declared that Black Pete did contribute to bullying, discrimination and exclusion, she received dozens of death threats, not to mention much shouting and cursing. One anti-Pete demonstrator, for his part, wanted to put a price on the head of Sinterklaas: 'Twice as much if it's during the national procession so that all the children see it, even if they get covered in his brains and splinters of bone.'

The shamelessness of the internet was new. No one was embarrassed by anonymous declarations put out for the world to read. The overturning of norms was new as well. Those who protested were pilloried. Now it wasn't racism that was taboo but anti-racism.

Friesland had a culture war of its own. Pro-Pete activists were taken to court for blocking the highway to stop a couple of buses bringing anti-Pete activists. In court they wore, in the style of local heroes, clogs and Frisian flags. The Randstad dismissed the demonstrators as racists, although I had the feeling that in this case it was about something else: the eternal clash between city and countryside.

By chance I got to know their leader, a single mother who ran her family business with verve, on a terrain covered in cherry pickers and forklift trucks. Her village was a tightly knit entity. With poor soil and a tradition of hard graft, it was populated by construction workers who built houses for each other. 'So they decided to get together and block the road,' she told me afterwards. 'All demolition men and builders, but no punches were thrown. Oh all right, one man showed his bare bum.'

She wanted nothing to do with extremists, it was all about having an undisturbed children's party. 'I'm not an activist, I hardly know that language, I normally talk about boom cylinders and last-minute safety measures.' Racism? 'Listen, my best friend is a refugee from Bosnia. A good friend from the Gambia stays here almost every year and he's as black as can be but he's one of us. Another friend of mine lives in Groningen and she's got a dark-skinned son. She's happy he doesn't have to go to school in a rural area because she's afraid he'd be bullied – if something like that happens you go straight over and say something. But you're not going to solve it by banning Black Pete.'

She immediately became a hero of the far right, even though she didn't want anything to do with them. 'Still, take someone from my family, a postman who was chucked out of work. He's sitting at home in his chair and along comes Geert Wilders, who links all that to the immigration problem. So now he says, "Those foreigners want to change Black Pete." You have to listen to someone like that. What's behind it? Why that fear of change? Right, Brexit happened because of feelings like that. And Donald Trump. I'm for freedom. You mustn't force people to change.'

Two weeks later the leader, along with her fellow demonstrators, was sentenced to 240 hours of community service for 'hampering freedom of expression'. She was cheered as a local 'Jenny of Arc'. She gloried in it.

Eventually the mood changed even in our free and peaceful village. The Syrian family began to struggle. It started, as far as I could make out afterwards, with pestering by a couple of village children: banging on doors and windows; ringing the bell and running away. 'Go back to your own country!' The Syrian children were no softies. They hit back. Some parents then came to sort things out. One angry father even stood in their hall with his two big dogs, raging. The tension hung in the air after that.

Ultimately only a handful of villagers were involved, fired up by a voluble troublemaker. But what was striking was the bitterness that seemed to take hold of some people, even in this warm-hearted village, as soon as it became a matter of 'outsiders' and 'strangers'. Every children's quarrel – an angry word, a bit of pushing and shoving – was blown up by that little group into a riot and endless insinuations.

One evening in April 2019, not long after a spectacular election win by the far right, a second man tried to get into the house, with a knife this time. The man was drunk and what had sparked his anger was another argument between schoolkids. One of the Syrian children managed to slam the front door in his face just in time, although the man smashed a big hole in the window with his knife. Another child, having learned from earlier situations, filmed the entire incident on his phone. They showed me the pictures: the ranting man, the big knife he pulled, the tumult, the women screaming, the kids yelping like puppies. For a week the family didn't venture out and the children no longer dared to attend the village school.

My wife and I had only just got back from a refugee camp on Samos, but the family we encountered in our own village was suffering a whole other level of fear. The youngest son, about eight years old, showed us a lump and a deep scratch on his forehead. In a panic 'when that angry man came' he'd run into a doorknob. The oldest son said, 'I'll never be able to get that moment out of my head. No matter how long I live.'

The parents and children – who had already been through a lot in Syria and during their escape – were now stiff with terror, partly because the culprit was allowed to go about as normal. 'If I, as a foreigner, had stormed at a Dutch family with a knife like that they'd have arrested me straight away,' said the oldest son – and he was embarrassingly right.

The village was deeply shocked, especially when the regional press got wind of it. 'That's not who we are.' 'My heart weeps.' At the same time, many people felt sorry for the perpetrator, a man who had endured many misfortunes in life. The self-correcting system of the village community came into play, impressively in some respects. Conciliatory conversations took place, the local council did its very best, many villagers leaned over backwards to make things right, the family felt embraced and supported.

Yet one Monday morning in the middle of the school holidays a removals van appeared in the street. Two hours later, the Syrian family was gone.

4

In a short story called 'Do You Love Me?', Australian author Peter Carey describes an imaginary country in which things – buildings, entire landscapes – inexplicably fade and eventually disappear, 'like the image on

an improperly fixed photograph'. The story's title holds the key to the secret.
The cartographers have taken power in this magical world and everything
they draw on their maps and rub out again is reflected in reality. Structures,
regions, even people are declared unloved, and they all slowly dematerial-
ize and finally vanish. 'We had no use for these areas,' says the narrator,
'these deserts, swamps, and coastlines which is why, of course, they disappeared. . . . If they had any use at all it was as symbols for our poets, writers
and film makers.'

In 2011 I walked with a handful of friends through just such an erased
world. It was a delightful Sunday afternoon in April, with all the fresh foli-
age emerging, and we strolled in the sun across the meadows in a classic bit
of Friesland, from one village church tower to the next. Suddenly something struck us and we said as much to each other: it was deathly silent.
Spring in Friesland had always been spectacularly beautiful, its praises sung
endlessly. The meadows would burst with colour in dazzling contrasts: the
white of the daisies, the yellow of the dandelions, the red of the clover and
sorrel, the brownish grey of the flowering grass, quite apart from all those
little jewels of flowers in between. Above it all tumbled the black-tailed
godwits, the lapwings, the oystercatchers, the geese and other hell-raisers,
and the noise on a spring day was enough to waken the dead, especially
when you walked across the meadows. Around the turn of the century it
still woke me early in the morning. Twenty years later there was only
silence, a 'Silent Spring' as described by Rachel Carson in 1962.

Data from birdwatchers confirms the impression. Godwit and oyster-
catcher numbers are down by more than half, while the ever-jubilant
skylark has almost died out; in the 1970s there were almost a million of
them in the Netherlands, in 2019 only 35,000.

Pesticides have played a part – there are fewer and fewer insects – but
the decline is probably mainly a result of all that pumping and draining the
Dutch are so mad about, with their artificial rivers that flow one way in
winter and the other in summer, with changing water levels that turn
Mother Nature's seasons on their heads: wet in summer, dry in winter and
spring. No farmland bird could hold out over the long term on that rock-
hard clay.

Whole stretches of the centuries-old Frisian landscape have become agrarian industrial terrain. The *National Geographic* once called the Netherlands a 'global agricultural powerhouse'. In a country already densely populated by people, there were 4 million cows, 13 million pigs and 100 million chickens. After Brazil, it was the world's biggest net exporter of agricultural produce.

We could see the consequences right in front of our eyes. Despite the difficulties faced by farmers, over the past twenty years huge unsightly farm buildings popped up everywhere like dandelions – monstrosities wholly out of keeping with their surroundings. The astonishing variety of grasses and flowers was replaced by immense expanses with one uniform species of rye grass, like green asphalt. Gone were all the ditches, all the undulations, all history, leaving a landscape as efficient as a billiard table. No bird could find peace on land that was continually fed and mown, where the last of the nests with baby birds were shredded by the cyclone mowers.

Improbable amounts of milk were produced by super-cows, and here in Friesland the farmers were at the top of the agritech game. It was what the free market and the world wanted. In 2019, Royal FrieslandCampina was one of the six biggest dairy processors on earth, and 80 per cent of the food produced by the 13,000 or more farms with which it worked went for export.

'We feed the world, so be grateful,' some farmers said. In practice, the old milk factory in a nearby town had been taken over by a German company called Hochwald, which processed the milk from 150 local farmers into cream and sweet drinks with chemical flavours – Bonny banana milk, 55 per cent sugar – for the Arab world. A local journalist, Jantien de Boer, published a calculation. For the production of this tooth-rotting children's drink alone, 7,500 hectares of Frisian land had been turned into a slurry-injected desert; and for the sugar beet needed to sweeten it, other farmers used thousands more hectares. She quoted a farmer's son from the area: 'It's enough to make you weep. Agricultural subsidies have helped to turn thousands of hectares of land into a green desert.' Unloved.

In her much-read pamphlet, de Boer laid out all the problems, and her term *landschapspijn* ('landscape pain') entered the Dutch language. In 2000, there were still almost 5,000 small farms in Friesland, with a little over half a million cows. Twenty years later the number of farms had dropped by a third, but there were 50,000 more cows. 'Fewer farmers now have more cattle.' In the words of one of those larger farmers, 'To hold your own on the world market you need scale.'

At the same time, the soil was pumped full of excrement – because it had to go somewhere, phosphate rules or not. The real catastrophe was visible only beneath the sod. Jantien spoke to a soil researcher who, night after night, lay on his belly on a kind of cart, counting worms. He broke down completely when he attempted a recount on a stretch of land where he had previously, before slurry was injected, found a lot of worms. 'The soil had been torn to pieces. There was hardly a living creature in it. I lay on my cart sobbing in the field.'

When she published her cry for help in 2017, Jantien organized a bus trip to show people some examples of landscape pain. I went along. I heard stories about farmers who were furious with her, but also about the increasing number who knew all too well that things could not go on like this. Young dairy farmers in particular realized that if they wanted to be farming thirty years from now, something fundamental would have to change. They sowed wild flowers on the edges of their fields for the insects, tried to reverse the decline in farmland birds, and searched high and low for better ways of farming. In places you did indeed see the return of flowering meadows. There was hope.

What I remember above all was a walk across what, from the perspective of nature conservation, was an exemplary farm. The grass was long and varied, and not mown until mid-June; the level of the groundwater was kept high; the birds were spared and pampered in all kinds of ways. In this bare landscape the farm was an oasis for the black-tailed godwit, with plenty of nests and broods. Yet of the almost 400 young godwits, only four had survived that year. 'We put cameras beside the nests,' the farmer said. 'We watched them starve in front of our eyes.' The first wave of insects the young birds relied on never came. Was it the insecticides? Or was mass insect death one of the many effects of climate change?

5

Not many climate change deniers lived in rural Friesland in 2019. In the city you can perhaps still permit yourself head-in-the-sand politics, but in the countryside the confrontation with the weather and nature and all the ways in which they are changing is too direct. The local benchmark is the Elfstedentocht, the skating race that passes through the province's eleven towns. As soon as temperatures fall below zero they start talking about it in the pub, but the men who once took part – they used to stuff newspaper under their shirts and sweaters – are getting very elderly.

It has to freeze hard for at least two weeks before the 200-kilometre marathon can go ahead. My childhood memories are full of such moments, a combination of biting cold and boundless excitement. In 1950 the likelihood of a really cold spell was one in four each year, according to the Dutch meteorological office. In 2019 it was one in sixteen and by 2050 it's expected to be one in two hundred. According to something known as the 'Hellmann number' – the sum of all the daily temperatures below zero – a winter that scores more than 100 is regarded as cold. Between 1901 and 1980, seven winters scored above 200, but the last winter to get above 100 was in 1997, which was also the last time the Elfstedentocht was held. In 2014, the Hellmann number for the Netherlands fell below zero for the first time since records began, with not a single day having had an average temperature below freezing.

During my European journey in 1999 the climate problem was already visible. In southern England, winters with snow had become rare; in northern France the snow line was moving northwards year by year; and in Eastern Europe everyone was talking about the unprecedentedly hot summer. On Christmas Day that year, a storm raged across France and Central Europe. I came upon worried farmers everywhere.

Four years later, in 2003, Europe was tormented by the hottest summer in 500 years. In France, an estimated 15,000 people died of the heat, most of them elderly. Paris brought in refrigerated trucks as temporary mortuaries, its crematoria and graveyards unable to keep up with the surge in deaths. The newspapers printed full pages of the names of all the Parisians killed by the heatwave. The 'White Plan' for emergencies was implemented. Intended to deal with a major terrorist attack, it was now set in motion to tackle a climate catastrophe.

For a long time it was thought that the Industrial Revolution, which began around 1780, marked the start of these developments. Later most scientists identified a far more recent time, around 1950, as the starting point. What happened in my village on a small scale, with horses replaced en masse in the 1950s by tractors and other machinery, with farms expanding massively in size and activity, and with free time and luxurious lifestyles making their entrance, took place all over the world. Climate scientists speak of a 'Great Acceleration' in human activity of all kinds after the Second World War. Wherever you look, from consumption and industrial growth to car ownership and the use of raw materials, the graphs show a steep incline after 1950. The Great Acceleration brought more agreeable times, with a far better standard of living. Child mortality fell spectacularly and the world population quickly grew. But three-quarters of the total quantity of CO_2 produced by the human race was pumped into the atmosphere after 1950, while the absorption of CO_2 fell dramatically. Millions of hectares of woodland were felled and burned at such a rate that deforestation alone caused a significant proportion of total CO_2 emissions.

I have the most recent graph from NASA in front of me, giving the CO_2 content of the atmosphere, a meticulous analysis of the ice layers in the polar regions over a period of 400,000 years. It is shocking. Until 1950 the line goes up and down within a limited bandwidth, before abruptly shooting upwards to a height never before seen in all of history (modern humans appeared on earth around 200,000 years ago). Within a single generation, the concentration of greenhouse gases has risen to levels not seen in the 4,000 centuries that came before. Even all those hard-working farmers in my part of the world contribute, unintentionally. The livestock sector – methane! – produces 12 to 15 per cent of all Dutch emissions of greenhouse gases. For the sake of comparison, the much-criticized air traffic produces just 2 to 3 per cent.

The gloomy predictions of scientists in the 1970s, '80s and '90s have started to become reality in recent decades, and the results have proven worse than expected. Animal species, especially birds and insects, are disappearing at a great rate, while numbers of mammals, reptiles and fish have fallen by almost 30 per cent. European summers, compared to the summers of the mid-twentieth century, are hot to extremely hot. In 1960, Rome experienced eight days above 32 degrees, in 2019 there were thirty. Athens had ten in 1960, twenty-six in 2019. Barcelona had two in 1960, and in 2019 nine.

All over southern Europe, schools regularly have to shut because of the heat. In the bone-dry summer of 2018, the Rhine became hard to navigate. In the winter that followed, Greece endured three hurricanes, with force 10 winds in the streets of Athens. Water shortages and forest fires are increasingly problematic. In Britain, France and Central Europe, torrential downpours cause flooding. The glaciers are melting and in northern Italy, soldiers of the Alpini, the First World War mountain infantry, are emerging one by one out of the ice.

It is all bad news. It turns our entire worldview on its head. It's so dramatic that many of my contemporaries have difficulty believing the reports. But it is a reality, and it's happening in front of our eyes.

The tendency to ignore or even deny remains strong nevertheless, a temptation that increases for each individual according to the extent to which accepting reality has a greater impact on their daily lives.

Huge vested interests are involved. Up against the worldwide movement of tens of thousands of concerned scientists is an equally powerful lobby of representatives of polluting industries, including most oil companies. Research by the London think tank InfluenceMap shows that, between 2015 and 2018, oil giants ExxonMobil, Shell, Chevron, BP and Total spent almost $200 million between them on publicity campaigns to give their companies a green image, while almost exactly the same amount was spent on political lobbying to block, delay or disrupt measures intended to protect the climate. It was reminiscent of the aggressive campaigns by the tobacco industry in the 1960s and 1970s. Here too, the truth was to be suppressed at any price.

In 2019, ExxonMobil became the first company forced to defend itself in front of the European Parliament for deliberately misleading the public on climate change. Internal documents show that even in the 1970s the company was employing some of the world's best climate researchers, who enabled it to make accurate estimates about the warming of the earth and its disastrous repercussions as early as 1978. So ExxonMobil was aware even then, for example, that the ice sheets at the North Pole would shrink dramatically, although it regarded that mainly as an interesting investment opportunity. The company's bosses knew from their own research that the alarming conclusions drawn by climate researchers were correct, yet it ran a powerful campaign for decades in which it claimed the very opposite and continually sowed doubt about the integrity of climate scientists.

*

The biggest problem is that the climate issue is complex and global, and the world has no experience to draw upon, no instruments or institutions. The effects will be seen over many decades, which means that most of the damage caused by climate change will be felt by later generations, whereas the generation that can still do something to prevent it – our own – is little troubled by it as yet. Moreover, the people who will suffer most from the damaging consequences, from floods, drought, famine and mass migration, are among the poorest and most powerless of the world's population.

Greenhouse gases are a global problem, inflicting damage all over the world, no matter where the gases are emitted, and often not until many years later, so every country and every generation taking action now will pay the costs but see few of the benefits. From a political point of view, therefore, tackling climate change is a thankless task. To press ahead with the necessary measures and projects, governments and politicians will need to renounce practically all the existing laws of politics. They need to think globally and very much long-term. They need to develop a head-strong, liberated mentality that's open to a completely different worldview and a completely different political culture. Above all, they need to convince others to do the same.

At first the solution was sought, in part at least, in the all-powerful free market. In 2005, as agreed under the Kyoto Protocol of 1997, the EU set up a trade in CO_2 emissions. Companies were given 'rights' to emissions. If they stayed below their limit they could sell their rights on, whereas if they exceeded them they had to pay. After the 2008 economic crisis the system quickly broke down. Lower productivity meant that demand for emission rights fell sharply, bringing down the price. Polluting the atmosphere became increasingly cheap. There were also countless flaws in the system, which 'carbon crooks' skilfully exploited.

The Paris Agreement, signed in Paris on 12 December 2015 and covering the years 2020 to 2050, was a big step forward, the result of pioneering work by European diplomats and a courageous change of course by President Obama. Close to 200 countries signed a binding agreement to reduce CO_2 emissions to zero within thirty years. It marked the start of a global approach to tackling the threat.

Less than two years later, in June 2017, the accord was undermined by the new president of one of the biggest polluters, the United States, who wanted at any price to protect his own high-emission industries or even to give them extra stimulus. Nevertheless, many American states, cities, companies and individuals continued to modernize. California, New Jersey and Connecticut developed climate policies of their own, while experiments with countless micro-initiatives continued everywhere.

In 2010, technology set out on an impressive sprint. Sustainable energy sources grew by tens of per cent each year, sun and wind energy fell in price more quickly than anyone had expected, the electric car made its breakthrough, and huge offshore wind parks were planned for the North Sea that would eventually be able to produce enough power for all the surrounding countries. New inventions came thick and fast: green roofs, sustainable commercial spaces, clever forms of insulation and heating, and tiny solar power stations suitable for every roof.

Climate Action 100+, a group of super-investors that include the world's biggest investment manager BlackRock and nine of the ten largest pension funds in the world, started to deploy its immense wealth – it held \$32 trillion in total – to create a more sustainable world. In late 2018, Shell became the first oil giant to announce that it would stick to the aims of the Paris Agreement, with a pledge to reduce its carbon emissions by 20 per cent by 2030 and by half by 2050. The European environment ministers, the European Parliament and the European Commission meanwhile set climate targets for 2020, 2030 and 2050. From 2021 onwards member states would be obliged to reduce their emissions of greenhouse gases in a number of ways. In March 2019, the European Parliament even demanded that emissions must be reduced by 55 per cent by 2030.

A year later, a freshly appointed European Commission came up with an ambitious 'Green Deal', which includes placing a legal obligation on member states to strive to make Europe carbon-neutral by 2050. It was allocated a total budget of €1 trillion for the coming ten years and a whole series of legislative proposals were introduced, ranging from biodiversity conservation, more sustainable agriculture and the planting of forests, to the cleaning up of the transport sector and the insulation of homes.

Quite a few member states protested, despite the urgency of the issue, saying the EU's target dates were unachievable. Anyone travelling through Poland – where coal is still the dominant fuel – realizes that there is indeed a long way to go. The same goes for Hungary, Bulgaria and Romania, and typical villages like Vásárosbéc still look blue with woodsmoke every afternoon. People don't know any better. In Brussels, it has been practically impossible to tackle systematically one of the biggest polluters, the airline industry. Although by 2018 roofs in Germany, the Netherlands and elsewhere gleamed with solar panels, in sun-drenched Spain I saw hardly any. With the help of a handful of corrupt politicians, Spain's national electricity provider, with its monopoly position, has managed to block almost all private initiatives to install them.

Meanwhile, we are faced with a whole series of ominous prognoses. The rise in average global temperatures this century is expected to be far more than the two degrees agreed upon in Paris, which means that by about 2050 the summer heat in major cities including Rome, Madrid and Athens will be unbearable. By mid-century, the oceans will be suffering mass death and a lack of oxygen. There might even be a major extinction event of the kind seen by palaeontologists in layers of the earth's crust dating back millions of years, except that in the twenty-first century the changes will take place at many times the speed.

In the distant past, such high temperatures meant no ice was left at the poles. After the twenty-first century, the vast amount of water released, along with the shifting of weight on the planet, may cause sea levels to rise rapidly by several metres. Traditional dams and dykes will be inadequate to the task. At such levels, the water will seep under the dykes and it will be far harder to flush river water out to sea. The first great inundations will therefore probably take place in river deltas like the Dutch Randstad. It's odd to cycle through Amsterdam, much of which lies below sea level, conscious of the fact that after centuries the city's days are now numbered.

In November 2017, the American scientific journal *BioScience* published a 'warning to humanity' written by more than 15,000 scientists from over 180 countries: 'Soon it will be too late to shift course away from our failing trajectory, and time is running out. We must recognize, in our day-to-day lives and in our governing institutions, that Earth with all its life is our only home.'

The UK's Institute for Public Policy Research warns that 'a new, highly complex and destabilized "domain of risk"' is developing, and that all kinds of social and economic systems might abruptly collapse as a result – a situation in some ways comparable to the near-collapse of the global financial system in 2008. The degradation of natural infrastructure, including a stable climate and fertile soils, will have a disastrous effect, the researchers write, on human health, wealth, inequality and migration, and that in turn will increase the likelihood of political tensions and conflicts.

At the opening of the UN climate conference in Poland in December 2018, the UN secretary-general, António Guterres, set out the facts once again: the twenty warmest years since records began had occurred in the past twenty-two years, with the previous four as the warmest ever; the concentration of CO_2 in the atmosphere was now at its highest for 3 million years; and after a brief period of restraint, emissions of greenhouse gases were rising steadily, a trend mainly driven by China, the United States and India. As Guterres put it, 'We are in trouble. We are in deep trouble with climate change.'

It's happening at great speed. 'The world of my childhood is long gone,' a Frisian friend of mine, a farmer's son, sighed. 'But even the world I knew in my thirties and forties has disappeared now too.' He has always been proud of his farming background, but he's becoming almost ashamed of it. That shame and that pride have the same source: the natural connection that my friend had once experienced between the land, the people and the community.

In late February 2019, everyone in our village sat outside basking in warm sunlight as if it was June. The skating rink was rarely used. At night, when there was a storm, our roof beams still creaked, but the safe and cosy feeling those wild noises used to evoke in me had been replaced by a vague sense of unease.

'Is there still a way back?' my friend wondered. Or was everything evaporating, fading like a forgotten photograph?

11. The Promised Land

2015

I

WE GALLOP OVER THE WAVES. Survival suits, headphones live, helmets on, like helicopter pilots. It's late January, night-time, on the cold Wadden Sea at wind force seven. I've joined the crew of a lifeboat, the *Annie Jacoba Visser* of the Royal Netherlands Sea Rescue Institution (KNRM), at the Lauwersoog station. 'Ed, watch out, fishing craft at two o'clock.' The searchlight flashes on then dies away. Wave after wave rises high, glittering in the light of the full moon. 'Goodness, what breakers.'

'Before we start talking, you first need to experience the sea, the way we do,' Ed Huisman had said. Now he's deftly manoeuvring through the straits and channels between the Wadden Islands; these men know all the shallows, and then don't, since they change by the week. The waves grow taller, the little lifeboat rears and stamps and seems about to turn over. 'If we hit a sandbank with these waves we have a problem,' he mutters. 'In the Mediterranean it sometimes got this rough too, except that the water was clear, and we didn't crash onto sand but on rocks. The effect is the same. The sea can be rock-hard, insanely dangerous. People don't realize that.'

Afterwards there's the ritual beer and a couple of bags of crisps are upended onto the table. They all live nearby – they have to be ready to launch within fifteen minutes. Most have been doing this for years, training every Monday. They're exceptional men, from all kinds of backgrounds, hard-working, loyal and utterly committed. 'It's our job to save people, to prevent them from drowning. Full stop.' Those people might be fishermen or owners of expensive yachts, who can sometimes be cocky. It makes no difference. Which explains why, in 2015, Ed and a colleague left for the

Greek island of Lesbos. As professional lifesavers they could no longer just watch. A year later, after two large donations, the KNRM was able to set up a lifeboat station on Chios with two boats.

Later, at his house, I see the photos: rubber dinghies in which refugees and immigrants arrive, some so weak and thin they're little more than balloons. Your heart clenches. Lifejackets with just a few wads of polystyrene inside. 'They charged fifty euros for those; you'd sink like a stone.' Washed-up clothing. A child's shoe. 'People were sometimes thrown overboard just off the coast, like cattle – out at sea no one's any the wiser.'

From 2014 onwards, on Greek islands like Chios, Kos, Lesbos and Samos, illegal immigration grew into a major industry. 'As we flew in we could actually see them from the air,' says Ed. 'There was a football field covered in old inner tubes and lifejackets, all dragged together, a great hump of red and black.' In daily life Huisman has a glass company in Dokkum. He and his colleagues were far from faint-hearted, yet they felt deeply upset afterwards by everything they'd seen.

Their place of work was a busy shipping lane, and for that reason alone the crossing in rubber boats was treacherous. 'One of those huge Hellenic Seaways ships can't see an inflatable like that, it doesn't even show up on the radar, so at night they might sail right over it.' They had to operate cautiously, and after countless well-meaning amateurs they were the first professional rescuers on the island. 'Our main task was to make sure those little boats landed safely, on sheltered parts of the coast. But you always had to keep your distance. If you got too close they'd throw three children at you just like that. A wobbly inflatable with fifty to a hundred people on it can easily capsize, and in the water desperate people grab hold of whoever is closest. They drown each other. Nothing surer. Yes, rescuing is a profession.'

But it is the children above all that haunt him. 'Approaching a jam-packed inflatable like that you'd see only the men. But they would sit on the edge and when you got close you'd often see that the middle was full of children, hypothermic or worse. How quiet those children were; it astonished me every time. In the space of two weeks we took on board three women in labour. If a newborn gets cold it's soon over. The light goes out.' He shows me a toddler's shoe that he found on the beach, a tiny thing, white and grey, with laces mouldy from the sea and treads on the sole shaped like smiling faces.

Of course, he heard people talk about refugees who 'don't belong here'. He didn't get involved in that sort of debate any longer, he understood how complicated it all was, but you surely couldn't just let thousands drown? It went against everything they stood for at the KNRM, which was to rescue people because they are people.

'I hadn't ever really been through anything tough,' he says now. 'I had a life that I'd wish for anyone, and then there I stood, at the gates of hell. I saw how great the need was, and what one person can do to another. If you're a refugee and so vulnerable, how can it be that you're robbed, beaten and raped on top of it all, and then have to risk your life in a wretched little boat? You read the reports, but that's only the newspaper. Then you see it. You see that it really does happen. All those children, forced to set out onto such a dark sea. What a start in life. I had no calluses on my soul, that was my problem.'

He shows me a couple of pictures, a group of young black men dancing in front of the wreck of a rubber dinghy, having just made it ashore, over-joyed to have finally reached Europe, the Promised Land.

2

In 1927, the eternally wandering journalist Joseph Roth wrote about the animal protection societies that every year would catch migratory birds and take them to southern Europe. What civilization, what empathy. 'Is there a comparable society for the protection of humans, one prepared to take our fellow beings, those without passports and visas, to the land of their heart's desire?'

Mass migration is inextricably bound up with Europe's fate. In the 1920s and 1930s, after the Russian Revolution and the collapse of the Ottoman Empire, hundreds of thousands of displaced men, women and children trekked across the continent. After Hitler took power they were joined by countless German and Austrian Jews. At some borders, dramatic scenes played out. National heartlessness could be appalling, but sometimes the 'society for the protection of humans' did its work. Something known as the 'Nansen passport', issued from 1922 onwards by the League of Nations, enabled almost half a million stateless Russian refugees to travel to places where their relatives lived, or where they could find jobs.

After 1945, in a devastated world, some 20 million displaced Europeans took to the road. Every inhabitant of Czechoslovakia who spoke German was deported, and before long the derelict American zone of southern Germany had more than a million refugees to deal with. A few years after that, Western European countries faced large-scale migration from their former colonies. In France alone, after the declaration of independence by Algeria in 1962, three-quarters of a million repatriated pieds noirs came into the country. Time and again the society for the protection of humans set to work. One of Europe's greatest achievements of the period is that, in the midst of the chaos and dislocation immediately after the war, it managed to find a place for almost all its migrants.

Half a century later, in 2014, the United Nations calculated that in the world as a whole, some 19.5 million people were fleeing armed conflict. That was far more than ever before, and largely attributable to the wars in Iraq and Afghanistan. Iran, Pakistan and Turkey between them had taken in more than 5 million Afghans, and now they were starting to send them on into Europe. The fall of Libyan dictator Muammar Gaddafi in 2011 added to the numbers. It turned out later that in his declining years he had flouted all earlier agreements with Italy, sending huge numbers of refugees to Lampedusa, to punish Italy for its involvement in the struggle to bring him down.

Then there was the civil war in Syria. In 2014, after three years of fighting, bombing and Islamic State terrorism, almost half the population of 22 million Syrians had been driven out of their towns and villages. Jordan, Lebanon and – once again – Turkey had taken in millions of them, but there too, little capacity was left. They increasingly needed to travel on to Europe. Many refugees never arrived. The number of drownings on the annual List of Deaths (see chapter 5) increased markedly as the war in Syria intensified, from just over 900 in 2013 to around 3,500 in 2017.

As time went on, other migrants – people in search of a better life – mingled with the exodus. For young Africans in particular, despite the expense and hazards of the journey, Europe remained exceptionally attractive. Hundreds of thousands of immigrants crossed the Bosporus or the Mediterranean, legally, semi-legally or illegally, into Europe.

Maria Makrogianni and Michalis Georgalis were clearly members of the society for the protection of humans. In their old house on the Greek island of Samos they had grown together like Philemon and Baucis, the elderly couple in Greek mythology who, despite their own poverty, respectfully welcomed two strangers driven out of the villages, who unbeknown to them were gods.

Maria and Michalis had been in love for almost thirty years, and had left earlier marriages and braved scandal in order to be together. In 2015 they were running a small taverna on Samos. One evening they saw a group of Syrian boys wandering about who had crossed from Turkey in a rubber boat. Having made it ashore they were now trying to pick some unripe tomatoes in an abandoned garden. 'Hey, those boys are hungry,' Michalis said. 'Go and cook something.'

That was how it began. One of the boys wanted to pay, but Maria and Michalis wouldn't hear of it. The visits became more and more frequent, so they started to make sandwiches and take them to the refugees' huts and tents – there were as yet no organized camps or food supplies – and some help and financial support came from abroad. Soon everyone had heard of 'Mama Maria'.

'We made hundreds of sandwiches a day,' says Maria. 'Every night we had fifty people to dinner and the boys slept all over the taverna, on little camp beds.' Why? 'Jesus taught me always to welcome strangers.' She was the daughter of refugees herself; her family had been driven out of Turkey when that country was 'cleansed' of all Greeks. 'When my mother arrived on Samos as a child refugee she was spat at and kicked, purely because she was a stranger. I don't want history to repeat itself. You have to help. That's how I was brought up. It's in my nature.'

Six Algerian boys stayed for a while and did various jobs. Ali, a fifteen-year-old Afghan, lived in the taverna for three months. 'He was like a son to us.' He went on to study medicine in Austria. 'We picked up three women with children who were sleeping on the beach. They didn't even have a blanket.'

They were obstructed by some villagers and even threatened a couple of times. Why did they carry on? 'If someone knocks on your door and says

"I'm hungry" then you don't turn them away,' says Michalis. 'Because I love them,' says Maria.

As a traveller you could see signs of the exodus all over Europe in those years. Next to the railway in Budapest, tents and huts had been cobbled together out of plastic bags by refugees. In Ostend, in the elegant Venetian Galleries along the promenade, full of children and beach toys, black migrants lay asleep all over the place, exhausted. In Calais an illegal tent city grew up in the dunes. In Paris, on wasteland near the Gare du Nord, faded rags and tarpaulins were everywhere, with the occasional wooden hut and the smoke of a few fires. In Oslo there were beggars on every street corner, right out into the suburbs. In London and Berlin you could see the places where they slept under the bridges and walkways, sometimes with elaborate structures made of sleeping bags, plastic and cardboard boxes.

They made it even to far-off Kirkenes, where normally the biggest border problem was a few reindeer on the loose. In the autumn of 2015 the border guards spotted a handful of men and women cycling from Russia towards the border, in thin clothing, straight into the icy wind. They turned out to be Syrian refugees who, probably in response to tip-offs from the Russian security service FSB, had arrived in the High North via Turkey and Moscow. They were able to enter Norway easily because of a legal loophole. Russian rules stated that crossing the border on foot was forbidden, while Norwegian law banned crossing it by car. Nothing was said about bicycles, so apparently cycling across was allowed.

It was the start of what became known as the 'Arctic Route', in practice a trip of no more than 300 metres across the snow. The news of this unprecedented opportunity passed around the world in no time, and soon hundreds of migrants were using it every day. On the Russian side a lively trade in bicycles started up. Local journalist Thomas Nilsen reported that the whole circus was devised by the FSB, including the bicycle trade. 'I was there. Two hundred dollars per bike, and bicycles might be sold two or three times. Then, just as abruptly, it stopped. It seems someone on the Russian side had said "enough".' The motive for this FSB initiative? Nilsen had no idea.

In total, more than 5,000 refugees and migrants came into Europe by that route. In little Kirkenes they were met with hospitality. 'It was winter, you know,' said Nilsen. 'You can't leave someone out in the cold in these parts.'

What was the average journey like for a refugee? I once asked a boy who lived a few doors away, Safwat, the oldest son of the Syrian family in our village. What he told me was a matter-of-fact story about a smuggling oper-ation of the kind taking place day after day at that time, everywhere: dangerous, difficult, but without any great dramas. He was twelve back then, and he travelled with an uncle and a cousin. Their city was under heavy bombardment, Islamic State was close by, the family had to leave, it would be irresponsible to delay. Both despite and because of his age, he was selected to go on ahead. Through him, the family could be reunited in Swe-den or the Netherlands.

The crossing started at a hotel close to the Turkish coast. That was the gathering point. After a few days they were given the green light. Everyone was loaded into a bus in the middle of the night and driven to the shore. The journey to Italy was supposed to take fifteen days and they were told to bring their own food. He sent a message home: 'We're leaving. If you haven't heard anything from me in fifteen days then something's wrong.'

They were taken to a ship by rubber boat. But the ship turned out to be only about thirty metres long, and more and more rubber boats kept arriv-ing that night. 'Eventually there were about two hundred of us crammed on there together, the boys and men on deck, the women and children below.'

He found the first day exciting. 'The sea, the seagulls, the dazzling water, I thought it was quite beautiful.' But then he became seasick. For days he couldn't keep anything down and he grew limp as a dishrag. 'You're sup-posed to eat sweet chocolate, that's what everyone said, but we hadn't brought any with us.' After a while the food started to run out and he lost several kilos in weight. On top of that, they all kept having to switch places on the fully laden ship. On the afterdeck conditions weren't too bad, but on the foredeck everyone was continually soaking wet. 'On other ships, just as crowded, big fights broke out and they capsized. Sometimes people were thrown overboard. Fortunately that didn't happen on ours.'

After thirteen days, the captain contacted the Italian coastguard. 'We're out of fuel, we're drifting, help us.' A few hours later a helicopter appeared. 'Now we're saved,' said the captain, who had clearly done this before, and

•

he hid among the passengers. 'The ships that came alongside were beautiful,' my Syrian neighbour told me. 'The sick were taken off by helicopter and after a few hours we were brought to land and registered.' Then everyone was allowed to travel onwards. He was supposed to go straight to Sweden with his uncle and cousin, but at the station he realized he'd lost them. The Italian police took charge of him and eventually everything came right. 'They gave us delicious pizza and a nice policeman handed me a couple of banknotes. I showed them to my uncle, thinking they were residence permits or something. He said, "That's money, lad. Those are euros!"'

3

A year later, in 2015, more than a million migrants made the journey across the Mediterranean. The majority, some 850,000, entered Europe not through Italy or Spain but instead via the Greek islands, which lie no more than a few kilometres from the Turkish coast. It had come to be regarded as the best smuggling route. For a thousand euros, you could buy a place on a flimsy rubber dinghy in the streets of Izmir or Bodrum. If you made it to Samos, Chios, Kos or Lesbos alive, then along with thousands of other migrants you could travel to the mainland in one of the rusty ferries the Greek government had chartered specially for refugees. From there, again with the help of people smugglers, you could be in Berlin or Budapest within a few days. In the Balkans, networks of smugglers were operating, mainly Bulgarians, and almost every Syrian or Afghan refugee had a list of addresses and telephone numbers.

Was there any other way? No. For a refugee, no matter how dangerous life in their home country had become, these shady dealings with smugglers represented virtually the only way to get into Europe in 2015. Even in the 'golden years' the EU had been unable to put together a consistent policy on immigration, with good border controls and places in various countries where refugees and other immigrants could apply for asylum.

According to the Dublin Regulation, the country of arrival – in reality meaning Greece, Spain or Italy – remained officially responsible for a refugee. The northern member states defended that system fiercely – against their better judgement, since they knew perfectly well that the southern member states had been ignoring it for years. The EU's border control agency, Frontex, was still in its infancy. When in 2015 hundreds of thousands of refugees arrived, European countries instinctively revived controls on their national borders. From that moment on, southern, eastern and northern Europe were at loggerheads.

On 14 April 2015, a ship on its way from Libya to Italy, crammed with refugees, capsized with an estimated 550 people on board. One hundred and fifty were saved by the Italian coastguard; the rest disappeared beneath the waves. On 16 April, on the same route, another forty refugees were lost to the sea, and on 19 April an old freighter capsized near Lampedusa carrying some 800 men, women and children. Almost all of them drowned. The sea was full of corpses, their few meagre possessions scattered around them. In a single week, some 1,200 people died crossing the Mediterranean.

For Italian premier Matteo Renzi, enough was enough. Italy no longer wanted to bear the whole burden. It must be shared out between all European countries. A week later, the twenty-eight European leaders met in Brussels. Jean-Claude Juncker said later to the BBC that it was a matter of a fundamental choice. Was the EU to be a family in which problems were shared, or an ordinary international organization like any other? Donald Tusk acknowledged his point, agreeing that the problem was a European one, concerning European values. He added that Renzi had begged the European leaders to do something that their voters weren't happy about at all. He had asked for solidarity. But what was mandatory solidarity?

Sure enough, Viktor Orbán reacted immediately: 'Such a European distribution is simply an invitation for even more immigrants.' He set about surrounding his country with a barrier of razor wire. Germany, with its past of walls and barbed-wire borders, wanted no part in that. In a private moment, Angela Merkel said to her vice chancellor, Sigmar Gabriel, 'Promise me one thing, Mr Gabriel, the two of us won't build any fences.' Eastern Europe, which regarded immigrants mainly as a threat and was allergic to being patronized by Brussels, grumbled. The other European leaders preferred to wait and see. Ukraine was virtually at war and the Greek euro crisis was approaching a climax – that was where their attention lay.

From the spring of 2015 onwards, a long procession of the displaced walked right across Europe, a scene not witnessed since 1945. The smuggling industry was thriving, in a perverse interplay with governments and with aid workers who had come from all over Europe. Rescue ships saved tens of thousands from drowning, and gradually the smugglers came to rely on them, increasingly making the rescuers an unwilling link in the smuggling chain. On the Greek islands, one battered inflatable after another came in. Rescuers helped those on board to dry land, NGOs arranged for shelter and onward transport as best they could, and the boats were written off and put out of action. Journalists, however, noticed abandoned outboard motors being dragged to the road at night, loaded onto pickups and taken back to Turkey by ferry, ready for reuse, in a never-ending cycle.

For a refugee, the trip from Damascus to Berlin, via Lebanon, Istanbul and Lesbos, took around twenty-five days on average. The Greek islands were merely a transit point, Athens became a popular stopover, and in no time Victoria Square filled with dome tents and became known as 'Afghan Square'. The new Syriza government in Greece was virtually bankrupt, while the civil service was barely functioning and regarded all those migrants as a problem that would resolve itself. 'These people arrive, and after twenty days they simply disappear again,' said the migration minister. But the influx swelled. In the autumn of 2014, there was barely a migrant to be found on the Greek islands – the policy of previous governments had been notoriously strict. In March 2015 there were 7,800; in October, 212,000.

By late August 2015 the country could no longer cope. In northern Greece the borders were opened, and in Macedonia and Serbia all controls were abandoned. Thousands of illegal immigrants who had been 'shut up' in Greece for years seized their opportunity and travelled northwards, along with record numbers of Syrians. Macedonian taxi drivers now charged €400 for the trip across the country, while their Serbian colleagues were asking €1,500 to go as far as the Hungarian border. When that August some 50,000 migrants entered Hungary, Orbán spoke of an 'invasion' and an 'Islamic threat' to Christian culture. Hardly any of the arrivals wanted to stay there, of course; they were all trying to get to Germany. Thousands camped out at Keleti station in Budapest, waiting to be registered so they could travel on to the West.

Many journalists spent time with this 'Grande Armée of emigrants'. A reporter for NRC *Handelsblad*, for instance, came upon a man from Mosul with his elderly mother in a wheelchair – the Turkish people smugglers had thrown her wheelchair away and she'd been forced to buy a new one – as well as two young Congolese men who wanted to become footballers; a young Syrian couple contemplating Sweden, Denmark or, perhaps best of all, the Netherlands ('They give you an allowance and the education is excellent'); a quick-witted youth from Damascus who was hoping eventually to study in the United States; and a family from Afghanistan, with a husband who wanted to study law in Utrecht, a wife who had been in shock ever since their rubber boat tore during the crossing and would eat nothing but aspirin, and three children who were all plagued by nightmares.

Everyone wanted to get to Germany, the Netherlands or Scandinavia. Everyone expected a hearty welcome, a quick processing of applications, and respect.

In late August 2015, with the Greek euro crisis barely behind us, the refugee crisis reached its climax. On 27 August, the Austrian police found an abandoned refrigerated lorry beside a motorway and inside it the bodies of seventy-one men, women and children, suffocated on the trip from Hungary to Austria. The next day the Austrian police stopped a similar truck and released twenty-seven stowaways just in time. On 2 September, the whole world was hushed by a single photo. It showed a three-year-old Syrian boy called Alan Kurdi, dressed in a red shirt and dark blue shorts, lying serene in death on the beach at Bodrum, washed up after his overloaded refugee boat capsized on its way to Kos, just five minutes after departure. Alan's mother and brother had also drowned.

That picture changed everything. Here was a huge moral problem for Europe. Angela Merkel warned that unless other EU countries were willing to share the burden, the foundations of the EU and the Schengen system might collapse. A week later, in his State of the Union address to the European Parliament, Jean-Claude Juncker made an impassioned plea for European solidarity: 'Europe is the baker in Kos who gives away his bread to hungry and weary souls. Europe is the students in Munich and in Passau who bring clothes for the new arrivals at the train station.' There was an immediate need to distribute 160,000 refugees across all member states, and in due course a fairer European asylum system would have to be introduced. Given the numbers, 160,000 was at that point already a drop in the

ocean, but the proposal created a precedent; from then on, refugees were
the shared responsibility of all EU member states. All these political solutions, however, were almost instantly overtaken by the facts.

In that same August, something remarkable happened in Germany. The
Federal Republic was the main destination of choice for most migrants, and
within a few years requests for asylum had increased from 30,000 a year to
200,000. In 2015, however, that number was reached halfway through the
year and the influx was still growing, mainly because of the horrific war in
Syria. Yet public opinion did not turn against the refugees. On the contrary,
a *Willkommenskultur* emerged, a 'culture of welcome'. At all the major railway
stations, hundreds of helpers gathered, with food, toys and clothing. Juncker
was referring to them in his speech. The trains were met with cheers and
applause, and after the hardships of Greece and the Balkans, Germany did
briefly seem like the promised land. Everyone sent cheerful selfies and
messages to those left behind: come too!

It was a rare and popular movement, which had everything to do with
the sense of national pride reborn in Germany since the turn of the century, a new patriotism that had shaken off ignominy and shame. Germany
was a respected nation again, its dark past confronted and assimilated. The
German flag could fly proudly everywhere now. Germany had transformed
itself from an *Übermacht* into a *Gutmacht*, a country, as Merkel put it, 'of hope
and opportunity'.

'Why we must help the Syrian refugees' was the headline even in the
reactionary tabloid *Bild* on 28 July. The internal government research publication *Ergebnisse aus der Meinungsforschung*, which collates the most important
public opinion polls, showed a shift the country had never experienced
before. In early July, 80 per cent of Germans still regarded the Greek euro
crisis as the most important issue, while only 7 per cent mentioned the
influx of refugees. By mid-August the mood had changed completely, and
by September 'refugees' had top priority for 80 per cent of people. Sigmar
Gabriel spoke of Germany's 'deep desire finally to show Europe a friendly
face again. And to free itself from the memories of that darker Germany.'

In Hungary, which had meanwhile become a transit country for all those
refugees, attitudes were completely different. The Europe that Viktor Orbán

had in mind was a Europe of autonomous Christian nation states, a vision of the future diametrically opposed to Angela Merkel's idea of Europe as a community of values, embedded in international law. He described the refugees as the 'Trojan horse of terrorism' and forced many to travel through as quickly as possible. Others, including children, were put into concentration camps surrounded by razor wire. Orbán later dismissed condemnation by the UN and human rights organizations as 'charming human rights nonsense'.

In late August, he arranged for a special refugee train to depart for Germany. It was greeted with applause at the station in Munich by hundreds of volunteers bearing milk, fruit and teddy bears. Nevertheless, Germany and Austria protested fiercely to Orbán, since according to the Dublin Regulation, the refugees ought to have stayed in Hungary. Orbán thought the German attitude hypocritical: embrace all refugees at the stations, but make every possible effort at a governmental level to keep them out. 'The problem is not a European problem,' he explained. 'The problem is a German problem.'

What could Angela Merkel do? Friday, 4 September 2015, which began as a normal working day, became for her a historic date on which she unexpectedly had to take a decision that would define her chancellorship, and indeed European politics in the years that followed.

Merkel's day began at half past eight – I'm now following the reconstruction by Robin Alexander, Berlin correspondent for the *Welt am Sonntag* – with a staff meeting in the Federal Chancellery. Everyone was still feeling cast down by the tragedy of Alan Kurdi and the seventy-one dead in a lorry, but other than that it was business as usual. The authoritarian populist Orbán and the scrupulous Merkel had been on opposite sides for years, and the Germans resolved to 'return fire in a controlled manner' by reminding Orbán of his European and international treaty obligations. The weekend was approaching, the chancellor had a tough working day ahead and the rest of her staff would shortly be leaving. The bridge from which Germany was captained would be largely deserted that historic weekend.

Later that day, Merkel flew to Munich then travelled on by car to the Bavarian village of Buch am Erlbach, where she visited a small innovative workplace. She examined an electronic nesting box and gave an encouraging speech, providing good pictures for the newspapers and television. Back in the car she heard that the situation in Budapest was worsening rapidly; Orbán was refusing to continue to act as Germany's gatekeeper and had ordered all trains bound for Western Europe to be stopped. Hungary was no longer a transit country, but the refugees were unaware of that as yet and were walking into a trap. Dramatic scenes developed around Keleti station, featuring many thousands of refugees with nowhere left to go. Merkel didn't ring Orbán; instead she flew from Munich to Cologne and then went by helicopter to Essen for a propaganda speech as part of the mayoral election. Fresh reports came from Budapest. Several thousand refugees had decided simply to walk. They were trekking with their few possessions along the Hungarian motorways towards the Austrian border. These too were scenes not witnessed since 1945. A member of the public handed Merkel a piece of card. She thought he was asking for her autograph, but it was a photograph of drowned toddler Alan Kurdi. It touched her, but there was another appearance planned, back in Cologne, a celebratory speech marking the seventieth anniversary of her party, the CDU, in North Rhine-Westphalia.

On her official iPad, Merkel was meanwhile watching footage of the refugee column, with blue EU flags at the front. Some refugees carried photos of her. The Austrian chancellor Werner Faymann tried to ring her, but by that time she was making her speech and he managed to reach her only much later. Orbán put him on the spot. Was Austria going to let the multitude in, or would he be forced to have the situation 'solved' in the coming hours by his police and armed forces? Faymann, like Merkel, found that unacceptable and proposed Austria and Germany should take half the column each. During the flight from Cologne to Berlin, Merkel consulted feverishly with her staff and her SPD coalition partners. Eventually, at eleven thirty that night, she agreed, but this was to be the single exception.

Faymann rang Orbán and offered to send buses from Austria to pick up the refugees. That wasn't necessary. Orbán turned out already to have arranged for buses to take the refugees away. Shortly after that, the Austrian border guards saw hundreds of buses appear, full of refugees from all over Hungary. Orbán could never have organized such a huge armada in such a short time. Plainly he was making use of the opportunity to empty all his refugee camps.

Later, Merkel and Faymann would defend their decision as a response to a 'humanitarian emergency'. In reality, as Robin Alexander rightly concludes, it was forced upon them 'by a carefully planned and prepared move by the Hungarian government'. Orbán had achieved his goal: Hungary was 'refugee-free'. Some 22,000 Syrians, Afghans, Iraqis and other displaced people entered Germany that weekend.

Merkel had spent half the night on the phone, and she continued her calls on the Saturday morning at home. Would fellow government leaders not take some of the refugees? This was after all a European problem. She pleaded in vain.

Orbán, meanwhile, was celebrating his grotesque ruse at the Kötcse picnic, an annual meeting of conservative politicians, columnists and artists on the shores of Lake Balaton. Merkel's humanitarian decision was wrong, he sneered in his speech. In fact, it was fatal. 'A country with no borders is no country at all', Europe must protect its ethnic and cultural composition, refugees were coming here purely because of our 'higher quality of life'. In a reference to Alan Kurdi, he declared – he was, after all, among sympathizers – 'Who killed this little boy? His parents!'

At the station in Munich, meanwhile, trains full of refugees were arriving, welcomed by doctors, police officers and around 700 volunteers. There were makeshift places to sleep, there was food and warm clothing, there were bottles of water, nappies and boxes of toys for the children, the organization was perfect, the enthusiasm overwhelming. Countless mayors, local officials and volunteers, improvising furiously, then arranged shelter for the refugees all over the country. Berlin may have come up with plenty of fine words, but only a tremendous effort by countless individuals prevented all the good intentions from culminating in drama and tragedy.

Public euphoria reached its high point that weekend. In other cities where refugees arrived there was singing and dancing, special songs of welcome, tears and shouts of jubilation, and endless comparisons to 1989. The pictures were seen all over the world. 'Mama Merkel!' shouted refugees on Chios and Lesbos. Employers cheered too, since in rapidly ageing Germany these Syrians might become the highly qualified workforce the country so desperately needed. Dieter Zetsche, CEO of Daimler, regarded the influx as a basis for 'the new German *Wirtschaftswunder*'.

Angela Merkel, according to those close to her, had tears in her eyes. 'Our country is a good country.' Henceforth, the world would see Germany as a place everyone wanted to emigrate to, a little America in the twenty-first century. Right across Germany, all through September, the country's new moral status was celebrated.

Amid all this rejoicing the German government made one fatal strategic error. Neither in the reporting nor at the border was it made clear that this was a one-off exception and that Germany neither could nor would take in any refugee who turned up. For the Germans themselves that would not have been a welcome message during those euphoric weeks. After being deprived of it for so many years, feeling good was addictive. The consequences of this oversight were far-reaching.

Via Al Jazeera and Al Arabiya, the festive pictures reached even the remotest villages and refugee camps. On the internet the most delightful fantasies circulated, such as that Angela Merkel had chartered ships to take refugees direct from Beirut to Hamburg. Donald Tusk later told the BBC that he had come upon refugees in a camp on the Syrian border who were firmly convinced they would be greeted in Europe with open arms. He said they had even apologized to him and to Angela Merkel for not having left yet; it was just that they didn't have the money to buy a ticket to that paradise immediately.

Hundreds of thousands of new immigrants were getting ready to leave for Germany, refugees or not. In the countries they needed to cross, politicians and border guards were now making little effort to stop them. Why should they create difficulties for migrants who were going to be welcomed with open arms in Germany? The influx was so great that it was impossible for German border officials to note the names of all the newcomers. The asylum system burst at the seams.

Immediately after the festive 'weekend of welcome', fourteen German states confronted Berlin with reality. They could not accommodate any more refugees. Everything was crammed full; 40,000 new migrants were on their way and there were only 850 places for them in reception centres. 'Even accommodating refugees in tents or shipping containers is almost impossible now,' wrote 200 members of local government a little while later in a furious letter to Berlin.

On the night of 12 September, a final attempt was made to close the borders by a combination of spectacle and force. To block the influx of migrants, a heavily armed police unit was mobilized, with helicopters and other impressive equipment; old border posts were rapidly reinstated; and at the Austrian border no one would any longer be let through without a passport or visa, even if they were applying for asylum. The operation was called off at the last moment. German public opinion would not accept a shoot-out at the German border, certainly not in those weeks.

Three days later, on 15 September 2015, Merkel uttered her historic proclamation – not triumphantly, almost fatalistically. 'Ich sage wieder und wieder. Wir können das schaffen, und wir schaffen das.' 'I say it again and again. We can do this, and we will.' So the German culture of welcome did not start with those words, as was often suggested later. The wir schaffen das was not a prelude but an incantation intended to conceal the panic. The true cause of the German welcome was an unexpected and exceptionally emotional settling of accounts with history, a national mass movement by which Angela Merkel, ultimately, allowed herself to be carried along. After that, the German borders were in practice open for six months.

4

In 2015 and 2016, a little over a million refugees and immigrants came to Germany. Some 8 million Germans devoted themselves to helping them, for months, sometimes day and night. As Holger Michel, an exhausted Berlin aid worker, wrote after a year, 'Someone somewhere said, "Wir schaffen das." We still don't know precisely what schaffen means, but we now know who wir is. We found each other, we joined in, we learned, motivated each other and pulled each other along. We simply did it. And we'll carry on doing it.'

That was one side of the story. But was it that simple? Philosopher Peter Sloterdijk wrote, with fury, that the German government had allowed itself to be rolled over, waiving its sovereignty. 'There is no moral obligation to self-destruct.' And who in fact were the people who had arrived? As we have seen, in 2015 there was no way for most world citizens to emigrate to Europe legally, except by acquiring refugee status. Hundreds of thousands of migrants therefore entered Europe under the heading of 'refugee' despite

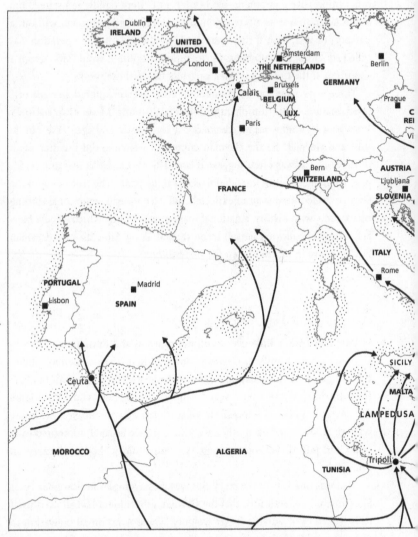

The most frequently used refugee routes from Africa and the Arab world to Europe

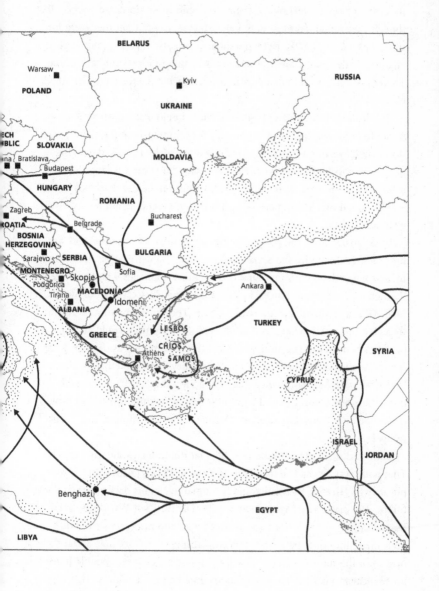

the fact that with the best will in the world they did not fit that definition. Everyone projected feelings of their own onto these uprooted people. To the left they remained most definitely refugees, to the right they were fortune seekers, to the far right potential terrorists, to many aid workers victims, to the politicians immigrants, and to employers migrant labour. There was some truth in many of these feelings, but the full truth remained elusive.

Saskia Dekkers and Pieter Nijdeken, television journalists and friends of mine, interviewed dozens of supposedly Syrian refugees at the railway stations. Their Syrian interpreter carried out spot checks. He talked to as many people as possible, to see whether they really did speak his language. The result was one in four, at the most. In the camps on the Greek islands it was at best one in two. The experiences of other observers, including my own, were comparable.

In Germany, however, people continued to refer to 'refugees' and 'asylum seekers'. In reality the Syrian and even the Afghan refugee influx was increasingly mixed with immigrants from other countries who had seized their chance to get into Europe by the same route. They came from Algeria, Mali, Ghana, Nigeria and the Ivory Coast. They often had every reason to seek a future elsewhere, and an increasing percentage could accurately be described as 'climate refugees', but a few exceptions aside they were not the victims of war or persecution. When they discovered that the promised land stretched no further than a muddy camp on Chios or Lesbos, there was great bitterness, and within the camps fighting sometimes broke out, especially between Algerian migrants and the Afghan and Syrian refugees.

Time and again the question was: how far did human solidarity stretch? That point was debated all over Europe. How in all this chaos could Europe preserve its fairness, its balance and its humanity? In his dark vision of the future, *Den danske borgerkrig 2018–2024* (The Danish Civil War 2018–2024), Kaspar Colling Nielsen has a 475-year-old man and his 350-year-old dog – both made immortal by a stem cell programme – philosophize about the origins of the future in which they live: an endless civil war, people holed up in heavily guarded neighbourhoods and houses, countries that, like Israel today, can stand their ground only by being armed to the teeth, and the ending of the European Enlightenment and European humanism. I met Nielsen at a literary festival and we discussed all these impossible dilemmas. 'If we open ourselves up we lose ourselves,' he said. 'And if we close ourselves off we lose ourselves. It's that simple.'

In October 2015, at the high point of the German culture of welcome, the opinion polls ticked downwards. More than half the population had a feeling that the refugees were not the people the media had presented to them, with those pictures mainly of women and children. A scenario leaked from the interior ministry in which another 920,000 asylum seekers were expected. The internet buzzed with conspiracy theories: this mass immigration was part of a government plan to change the ethnic composition of the German people.

According to the German Institute for Economic Research, in 2015 some 40 per cent of the population was earning less than in the late 1990s. Pensions in particular had dropped in value and one in six Germans of pensionable age had an income below the poverty line. This too generated envy and fierce debates. In Kassel, the CDU leader of the local governmental district, Walter Lübcke, explained during an angry exchange that by accepting refugees they were putting the country's values into practice, 'and anyone who doesn't hold those values can always leave the country'. The video clip was shared endlessly and earned him the eternal hatred of the far right.

The definitive reversal came at the very end of 2015, on New Year's Eve. Hundreds of mostly Arab and North African youngsters had gathered in front of the station in Cologne. The men were drunk and aggressive, and large numbers of them started to lay their hands on passing women, some of whom were robbed and more than twenty reported being raped. Police reports state that in the end more than 1,200 women reported crimes, almost 500 of which were sexual offences. Around 200 suspects were eventually arrested, most of them Moroccans and Algerians. Close to half described themselves as asylum seekers.

It was an uncommonly aggressive display, a thumbing of the nose at the Willkommenskultur. Strikingly, the German media at first made no mention of the mass sexual assaults. Nothing about them was published for several days. Journalists were clearly at a loss. This went directly against everything they had propagated over all those months with such verve. How was a Gutmacht to deal with it?

5

In that same period I visited Copenhagen. It was a different world. The Danes are said to be the happiest people on earth, not because they storm heaven but precisely because they are unassuming, content with what their own little country has to offer them. In the afternoon dusk, my taxi took me from the airport in Kastrup into town, past long rows of flats with none of the curtains drawn. Little Danish still lifes slid by: a man cutting vegetables at a kitchen counter, two children walking on their hands across a living room, shops displaying irreproachable furniture and neatly folded clothing, a brightly lit gym, blonde women on cross trainers, people dancing to inaudible music.

Rain lashed the city. I was staying with friends in the centre. They brought me up to date on the country and its politics: some kind of crisis was going on and lights were burning everywhere in Christiansborg Palace that evening, just like in the TV series *Borgen*, and everyone did indeed know everyone else. In front of the building, six royal guards marched pointlessly back and forth in soaking wet bearskin hats. The crown prince cycles past every morning on a cargo bike, I was told, taking his children to a nearby crèche. The rest of Europe might be raging and thundering; in Denmark a quiet domesticity reigned.

The Danes have a word for it – *hygge*, cosiness, a sense of comfort that they cherish. As soon as the German culture of welcome erupted, Denmark closed its borders, blocked its highways and halted all railway traffic from its neighbour. Some of the migrants wanted to travel on to Sweden, which meant Denmark would have to register all those thousands of people as refugees, and the little country could not cope with such an influx. So everything shut.

Denmark was an outsider within the EU at the best of times. It did not join the euro and it stayed out of several other EU treaties as well. That was in part the achievement of the right-wing Folkeparti, the Danish People's Party, which had an anti-immigration and anti-Islam programme dating back to the 1980s. The party adopted the populist script of Viktor Orbán and more and more voters were attracted by giveaways, such as a bonus for pensioners and the building of hospitals, and by the party's left-wing social policies. In contrast to all other movements of its kind elsewhere in Europe, however, the Folkeparti wanted nothing to do with the mirages of the far right. In the words of prominent member Søren Espersen, 'No racists, neo-Nazis, village idiots or angry bikers.' In fact, several of the party's founders were from families who had joined the resistance during the Second World War. Denmark sometimes reminded me of Poland. It too had a nineteenth-century history in which it lost much of its territory and population, it too had a historical trauma that made itself felt in a profound fear of invasion, and it had an obsession with *danskhed* (Danishness).

So despite some extreme standpoints, the Folkeparti became an acceptable supporting partner to successive Danish coalition governments, a professionally led power machine that set the tone in Danish politics for years. Ideas long regarded as extreme elsewhere in Europe became acceptable in Denmark. Twenty years later I could find hardly any sign of the friendly, tolerant Denmark of 1999. 'We Danes have always earned our daily bread in two ways,' a Danish acquaintance told me. 'Roughly speaking, as farmers or as seafarers.' Seamen were used to other cultures and had little if any problem with newcomers. For farmers, anything strange and foreign meant danger. 'The farmers have won,' he said gloomily. 'They've taken over the whole of politics, the whole of the country.'

Scandinavian like-mindedness, I heard everywhere, was a thing of the past. Norwegians and Swedes spoke of Denmark in the same breath as Orbán's Hungary. The integration of newcomers had been abandoned as a political goal. You had to become totally Danish, including the eating of pork and the shaking of hands. That or leave.

There was probably a correlation between this hard line and the terrorist threat still hanging over the country. Denmark had produced a remarkable number of fighters for Islamic State and for Syria, more than 300, and the Danish security service, the PET, had only narrowly managed to prevent a series of jihadist attacks. One of them seemed to presage what happened later in Paris with *Charlie Hebdo*. In 2009, a Pakistani terror group developed a detailed plan to storm the offices of *Jyllands-Posten* and kill all the journalists present.

Yet most Danes did not feel that to be the greatest threat. They were more concerned about their way of life, their *hygge*, and especially those ultimate symbols of solidarity, their excellent welfare state and their *arbejdsglaede* – their flexible, relaxed, friendly and at the same time decorous workplace culture. Aydin Soei's father was far from deluded when, after his flight from Iran, he claimed that as a communist he had found in Denmark the land of his dreams. As the result of a clever combination of state benefits and a flexible economy, almost everyone had a job, as well as a right to a prolonged and good education, excellent healthcare, free childcare and a lot more besides. For the almost 6 million Danes, that was a great collective achievement, but for outsiders who wanted to join, it was a rather different matter.

Aydin told me about his mother's career. She had graduated in physics in the Soviet Union, and in America her degree would have been accepted as valid. If the family had fled there, his mother would have been able to work from day one. In Denmark she was given to understand that her bachelor degree was worthless. 'My mother said she'd like to become an engineer. How should she set about it? She was told you couldn't go to a Danish university unless you had a diploma from a Danish grammar school. Okay, so how do I get into a Danish grammar school? She was told you couldn't, unless you'd been to a Danish primary school. It seemed immigrant mothers were expected to stay at home with their children, no matter what qualifications and skills they might have.'

Eventually his mother did become an engineer. She found an advertisement in the local paper for a course in mathematics and Danish, not for immigrants in particular but for people who hadn't finished school. Next she went to the grammar school and then she went back to university. Most of what she was taught there she already knew, of course, since she'd learned it all in the Soviet Union. In the end she got a good job at IBM. That little diversion cost her ten years.

Denmark, in short, has such a lavish welfare state that newcomers can easily be seen as a threat and a burden. Legislation surrounding family reunification was tightened as early as 2002. Foreigners convicted of crimes were deported more quickly than before. Refugees were deterred by the fact that their jewellery and money might be confiscated at the border.

Under earlier immigration policy, most new arrivals were sent to live in certain suburbs – that way Danish *hygge* wouldn't be too badly disrupted. So problems surrounding immigration became concentrated there: high unemployment, low levels of education and training, drugs, serious criminality. These 'ghettos', 'parallel societies' or 'black holes in the map of Denmark', as then Prime Minister Lars Rasmussen called them, have dominated the public debate ever since.

Based on a series of criteria – more than 50 per cent of residents with their origins in immigration, more than 40 per cent unemployment, three times the average crime rate – a list was compiled of twenty-two districts. Since 2018 their 60,000 residents have been subjected to a programme of forced integration. Anyone committing a crime receives twice the usual punishment, children from the age of one – rather than the normal six – have to go to nurseries to ensure they learn Danish, troublesome tenants can be evicted relatively easily, while at the same time Danes with good prospects are enticed in by all manner of means. It is a crude form of social engineering that human rights organizations, the UN among them, have fiercely protested. The Danish government stuck to its guns for years, however. It has recently agreed on some changes to the policy and is still promising that the 'ghetto' problem will be solved by 2030.

Meanwhile, under the heading of deterring refugees, yet another new plan was proposed under which failed asylum seekers would be taken to a remote island with only an occasional ferry service. 'They're unwanted here,' wrote the minister for integration, Inger Støjberg, on Facebook. 'And they must be made to feel it.'

At the airport in Kastrup all passengers leaving were, as usual, thoroughly examined and screened. Female passengers were frisked by male officials as if it was the most normal thing in the world. Why not? Well, there was another option, but that was mentioned only on a tiny notice that nobody saw. Some women were clearly so embarrassed they didn't know what to do with themselves. A young girl turned beetroot red. I spoke up, saying it went against all the international rules of etiquette. 'We're a free country, sir,' the man said.

6

So Europe drifted between those two poles, Germany and Denmark, two extreme points of view represented by neighbouring countries that are often of the same mind. Increasing migration brought to light a new European divide, this time between 'nationalist' and 'multicultural' Europe. After years of expecting salvation and prosperity from Europe above all, many Eastern Europeans were now withdrawing into their national frameworks again. They still didn't trust their national governments, but now that the 'cosmopolitan' European elite seemed to be throwing open their doors and casting their limited welfare states to the winds, they were choosing the least worst option.

For Europe as a whole, the number of immigrants was not the main issue. With more than half a billion inhabitants, the continent could in theory absorb several hundred thousand newcomers a year with ease. But all those immigrants ultimately wanted to go to a limited number of countries and cities. That created a very different situation.

Furthermore, the fears and worries of many Europeans were not so much about the refugees as about the fact that the European Union and European politicians had created the impression that they'd completely lost control of this mass migration, and therefore of their borders and their sovereignty. The *Willkommenskultur* and Merkel's decision to open the borders on 4 September 2015 put the other European leaders on the spot. President Hollande later told the BBC he'd been astonished. 'How can you do this, without checking whether they are genuine refugees?'

All over Europe the cry went up for the return of the old border controls. Now, after the euro, that other great European achievement – the Schengen Agreement that opened the borders – was under serious threat. After Denmark closed itself off, temporary border controls were introduced in several places, including between Germany and the Netherlands, between Denmark and Sweden, and between Austria, Germany, Hungary and Slovakia. Hungary extended its fences, the border with Croatia was shut, and Slovenia started building a border fence too.

The plan Juncker had described in his State of the Union address was now highly topical. Even though it concerned only a fraction of the total number of displaced people, it was a gesture with which the EU could demonstrate the beginnings, at least, of some decisiveness and solidarity. The Eastern European leaders continued to be obstructive: 'You said yourselves that the refugees were welcome. You can't now pass the problem on to us.' Italian premier Renzi pointed angrily to the billions of euros of support that Eastern Europe had been receiving all those years. 'If you refuse to send out a message of solidarity, you need to understand that this isn't just a place of "rights", "rights", "rights". Yes, there are a whole lot of rights. But there are duties too.'

It culminated in a vote. To avoid a complete break between East and West, Poland was drawn with great difficulty into the Western European camp. On 22 September 2015, the EU's interior ministers decided to transfer and accommodate a total of almost 160,000 migrants who had reached Greece or Italy. The majority of EU countries cheered; this was an important symbolic moment. Those voting against spoke of a 'terrible atmosphere'. Tusk called it the most dangerous decision possible for Europe, putting the entire Union on the line.

For some time now the debate had ceased to be about the numerical allocation – for a country like the Czech Republic it was a question of a mere seventy asylum seekers, who would move to Berlin the first chance they got, as everyone was aware. Instead it was a matter of principle. From now on, Czechs feared, by order of Brussels, their society would have to become 'multicultural'.

In no time at all Juncker's approach came up against predictable obstacles. How do you select refugees and migrants if there are no controls, no registration, no clear agreements; if no one knows exactly who are refugees and who are simply migrants; if there are no systems for sending unwanted strangers back whence they came – in short, if border controls are a mess? Although more officials were brought in later, at that point there was just one Greek functionary responsible for interviewing and registering refugees in Moria, a village on Lesbos with around 6,000 residents. He worked through a total of between one and three cases a day.

Countries differed immensely. While Germany had been preparing since early 2015 to receive some 200,000 Syrian refugees – and would ultimately take five times that number – British prime minister David Cameron refused to go beyond a commitment to accept 20,000 refugees over a period of five years. The preferences of the individuals concerned pulled things even further out of balance. The Luxembourg government, for example, had offered to take thirty refugees from Greece, but not a single one could be found who wanted to go to Luxembourg. 'It's Germany, Germany, Germany,' Juncker – himself a Luxembourger – complained, 'as if Luxembourg is the poorhouse of Europe.'

In the end, in early 2018, after endless wrangling, just 34,000 migrants were accepted by other member states – roughly 20 per cent of the total of 160,000 agreed in September 2017. The European Commission had overplayed its hand.

The obvious next move was to close off the Balkan route more securely. Germany would then be less easily blackmailed by Greece in the euro negotiations. Letting migrants through was after all an excellent lever. Politically, however, that solution was extremely risky, as Merkel's staff warned again and again. Hundreds of thousands of refugees might get stuck in Greece and a crisis of that magnitude, so soon after the euro crisis, might lead to the collapse of the Greek state and a split with the EU. Even for Washington that was an alarming scenario, since strategically placed Greece might end up in the arms of Russia.

The young Austrian foreign minister, Sebastian Kurz, paid no attention to such geopolitical considerations: the flow must be dammed no matter what. At a Balkan summit on 24 February 2016, the Balkan countries decided to close their borders and let into Macedonia only Syrians, Iraqis and Afghans from war-torn areas. Two weeks later, practically every transit route was closed off to those groups too.

At the Macedonian border, dramatic scenes unfolded almost immediately. A crowd of at least 7,000 men, women and children got stuck at the station in the small Greek border village of Idomeni in wretched conditions. Many had simply followed the railway line between Thessaloniki and Skopje on foot. In the first few days they tried to storm the recently closed border, some attempted to swim across a nearby river, there were rumours that Merkel would send trains and planes to fetch everyone, and at least two people tried to set themselves on fire. It could be freezing cold in the border area, but they all stayed there, desperately waiting amid the tents, fires and discarded railway wagons for news. An aid worker spotted something he'd never seen before: 'People got used to standing in line, just for a scrap of information.' A strange kind of normality developed around the camp, with stalls offering food and clothing, but also criminality and, increasingly, prostitution. It was May before the muddy ad hoc town was cleared away by the Greek police. The migrants – some 15,000 by that point – were transferred to other camps in Greece.

There was an alternative to this closing off of the Balkan route. Gerald Knaus was the leader of a small Berlin think tank that specialized in producing clever solutions to complex European problems. In September 2015, he launched a new policy proposal on his website entitled 'Why People Don't Need to Drown in the Aegean'. He advocated an exchange: Germany would accept 500,000 Syrian refugees straight from Turkey, and then Greece would be allowed to send back to Turkey all the refugees entering the country through the islands. In return for its cooperation, Turkey would be given financial support and long-coveted visa freedom. He initially called it 'The Merkel Plan', although he had no idea whether Merkel had ever actually read it. Later he found a greater degree of interest among the Dutch social democrats – the Netherlands held the presidency of the Council of the European Union at that point – and he rechristened his proposal 'The Samsom Plan', after the party's leader.

Merkel's hesitation was understandable. Turkey had already shown interest in such a deal, but she preferred Juncker's 'European' solution, under which refugees would be distributed across the continent. Only when that plan ran aground was she forced to turn to President Erdoğan. For Merkel it meant eating humble pie. Europe was now the requesting party; Erdoğan was a tough negotiator, and he knew that Europe was vulnerable and open to blackmail. 'We can open the doors to Greece and Bulgaria any time and we can put the refugees on buses,' senior EU representatives were told. 'If there's no deal, how will you stop the refugees? Will you kill them?'

On 6 March 2016, an agreement was finally reached in Brussels between Angela Merkel, Turkish premier Ahmet Davutoğlu and Dutch prime minister Mark Rutte, then president of the Council of the EU. In return for a series of European promises including €3 billion for refugee aid, visas, and a resumption of talks on accession, Turkey was prepared to take back all the

Syrian refugees who reached Greece by sea. For every Syrian taken to Turkey, another Syrian would be able to travel legally into Europe from Turkey. It was a deal that made the risky sea voyage to the Greek islands pointless. At least in theory.

Most of the misery, however, was farmed out so that it occurred outside Europe's field of vision. Italy and France made their own deals with Libya to block migration from there. Some 60,000 immigrants have since been held by the Libyans in degrading conditions. A report by Human Rights Watch documented 'malnutrition, lack of adequate healthcare, and disturbing accounts of violence by guards, including beatings, whippings, and use of electric shocks'.

Still, there was cautious celebration. The number of migrants fell immediately after the measures were put in place, probably mainly because of the Hungarian and Macedonian fences, although Germany and the western EU countries wanted nothing to do with those. Without the fences and without the Turkey deal, it was said, millions more migrants would have come to Europe, 'and imagine how the elections would then have gone in France, the Netherlands and Germany'. Or, in the words of a former leader of Amnesty International, 'You have to see with open eyes that, unfortunately, everything is finite. Money is finite, but also people's empathy. There are limits to that too.'

Other reactions remained critical. The fences and the Turkey deal were disgraceful from a legal point of view, because it was as if asylum rights no longer applied. They were politically objectionable, as promises were made to Turkey that the EU had no intention of keeping. They were dangerous strategically, since Erdoğan was in reality being handed the keys to Europe. And they were unachievable in practice, since all those registrations and selections meant that poor and chaotic Greece would have to set up from scratch an asylum system that did not exist even in the most developed countries. With European help, meanwhile, the Turkish border with Syria was expertly nailed shut.

Brussels was bitter too, although no one said so openly. When it was all over, the members and staff of the European Commission were left with a huge hangover, an almost physical sense of depression. 'Europe hasn't tackled the great migration crisis wrongly. Europe hasn't tackled it at all,' said Vincent Stuer, one of the Commission's former policy staff. The banking crisis and the euro crisis, however difficult, were on the terrain of the Brussels institutions, which proved able to manage them. 'But now, for the first time, there was a profound European crisis that was no longer our game. It produced a feeling of deep despair.'

7

It's now 27 March 2019, three years after the Turkey deal. I'm writing the final lines of this chapter on the island of Samos, in an 'oubliette', one of those places where the uprooted of this earth survive, in the cold and the filth, amid excrement, brawling and fires. This happens to be a European oubliette.

Today the refugee camp is shining in the sun, a giant cage of razor wire that can hold around 700 people. It's morning. The gates are wide open and the cage is surrounded by a small town of improvised huts and tents where another 3,000 migrants are camping, including 200 children and minors left to their own devices, without supervision. Thousands of sounds and smells rise from the slope. People creep into view from under the grey canvas to brush their teeth and fetch food. Only in the main camp are there a few showers and toilets, and there the migrants must gather and wait. As far as Europe is concerned, the problem has been bought off with a generous €250 million in the past two years alone. Yet, after all these years, no mobile shower cubicles or toilet units have appeared.

The number of children pottering about here is striking. At the top of the hill, amid the acrid smell of sewage, some boys have got themselves a plastic go-cart. They tear down the slope, having great fun in five languages. Five hard-working volunteers – thank heavens for the Samos Volunteers; yes, this too is Europe – play children's games in an open space in a field of mud, surrounded by a throng of singing and jumping toddlers.

> Commela, commela, commela vistas
> Chop banana, chop banana
> Mush banana, mush banana
> Eat banana, eat banana
> Mmmyum banana, mmmyum banana.

A shipping container has tarpaulins around it. 'This is our crèche.' A little further on is a closed-off space for young girls who are alone on their journey and who need the extra protection. They are mostly sixteen or seventeen, some twelve or thirteen.

There are queues everywhere – for the kitchen, the asylum service, the doctor, for anything and everything. At the asylum service is a boy of about eight with Down's syndrome. He and his brother are inseparable and they're trying to get 'a priority'. They lost their parents along the way. Everyone does their best for them. This is the forgotten side to all the stories – I come upon a great deal of kindness here, especially from the women. Together they're trying to make the best of things.

In these first three months of 2019 alone, over the winter, some 3,500 migrants have already crossed from Turkey into Greece. The smuggling routes have changed once again and Samos is now a popular destination, with rubber boats arriving every day. Men are busy putting together new frameworks of bamboo, and new huts and tents are going up all the time. It's a good trade, since a rudimentary tent costs around forty euros and for a family hut you'll pay seventy. Only a select group of refugees is allowed to travel on to the mainland. The waiting time for families currently stands at about eight months, for lone individuals at least a year and a half, although I hear that smugglers are active on that leg too, with speedboats heading for Patmos. 'And the ferry to Athens leaves from there at four in the morning. No one is watching at that hour.'

A lone Afghan woman tells her tale of woe. The winter has been terrible, the rain and the cold wind raged straight through the canvas, and the rats sometimes chased her out of her tent at night. Many people are sick, her daughter is in a bad way. A boy comes to stand nearby. He arrived here eight days ago from Kabul, expecting to be able to travel straight on to Britain.

An Afghan man who once taught English tells me he wanted to come to Europe to advance his career – 'I couldn't get a step further in Kabul' – and because of the Taliban. 'Did you expect this?' I ask. 'No, I imagined a large reception centre with a huge roof, a kind of big school. A wait of a couple of weeks and then on to Belgium. A good country, I thought, in which to start a new life.' He shows me his refugee pass: *Date of interview or examination* 25/07/2021. I take a photo of it, since I can't believe my eyes. More than two years to wait. 'Have you warned the people at home?' I ask. 'Absolutely. But I know from my friends and acquaintances that the same messages are still being sent: "It's good here. Come!" After such a difficult journey and the terrible trip across the sea, nobody wants to go back.'

Manos Logothetis has worked as a doctor for the coastguard since 2015. He sees all the refugees as soon as they get off the boat. Yesterday there were two easy boats, more than a hundred exhausted Arabs and Afghans but little trouble. Last week there were another three deaths.

'No one can say I haven't involved myself with this immense human tragedy,' he says. 'I've given it three years of my life. But still, I have to be honest.' He now calls the crossing an 'asylum baptism'. Whatever their real motives, once the migrants have survived the dangerous sea journey they are 'baptized' as 'refugees'. Europe's broad-mindedness has painful consequences. 'People forced to flee Syria with children in tow now have to go through the same miserable process as an adventurous young man from Afghanistan.' He thinks it's a great injustice.

There are things everyone knows but no one talks about, he says. For example, the embarrassing question of where the money goes. 'A lot has disappeared; there are very few checks. Thousands of blankets have been donated, they've been paid for, but they never arrive, they disappear. In a camp five thousand meals might be provided officially, three times a day. That costs a lot and it's organized by the army. But what if in reality there are only three thousand people in the camp? Millions are earmarked, all EU money, to improve the infrastructure in and around the camps. So why are the camps still in such a state after three years?' Journalists from the daily *Phileleftheros* started to investigate. In September 2018, they reported that those millions, or some of them at least, had ended up with business friends of the defence minister Panos Kammenos. At the request of the minister, the journalists were promptly arrested and prosecuted.

From African migrants Logothetis always hears three kinds of stories and they confirm the theory of asylum baptism. Either you were a relative of a tribal leader who was killed, or you were involved in a rebellion against the president, or, as a woman, you were abused and raped. 'We always accept that last story, because we don't want to risk missing real victims.'

If none of that helps, there are dozens of diseases and ailments that can get you a 'vulnerable' stamp on your refugee pass, often the only way to get off Samos. 'We run a strange medical practice here,' the doctor says. 'Normally nine out of ten of the people you see are genuinely ill. Here it's the other way round. Nine out of ten aren't actually sick. But you have to be damned careful, because at all costs you don't want to miss that one patient who really is ill.'

The senior physician at the local hospital, which I visit later, confirms this impression. All the major problems of the past few years come together here: the pressure of extra work because of the huge influx of refugees, the terrible conditions in the camp, and on top of that all the cuts because of the euro crisis. The budget has fallen sharply, the number of doctors has almost halved. Even though they now have extra help, thanks to the Syriza government, nurses are each responsible for fifty to eighty patients, and of the three ambulances only one is still in operation. The head doctor keeps his spirits up. 'It's not easy, but neither is it a disaster.'

In the hall is a long queue of African men. Many are unwell, and sure enough there is a lot of sham sickness too. 'Yes, it kills time,' says the doctor. Sometimes someone feigns a coma, sometimes a dramatic epileptic attack, and there used to be a lot of fake TB. 'Men came in hawking and coughing. Thank god we now have our own X-ray machine.' The senior physician shows me the figures for the past few months. More than 11,000 refugees have been examined and only 700 ultimately needed treatment. Less than 7 per cent.

In the corridor meanwhile, an elderly Greek man is waiting alone in a bed. And last week they brought in a shipwreck survivor who had just watched her husband and two children drown. Twenty-four-hour suicide watch in the psychiatric department – that too must be provided.

'At the centre they've no notion of the problems at the periphery,' says the coastguard doctor on Samos, who incidentally has not received his salary in two months. 'For Europe there's no crisis any longer, the numbers are small now, but for us the refugee crisis goes on. We're right in the middle of the storm.'

From Brussels and the national capitals come positive noises, but anyone who takes the trouble to go and look soon notices that little has been done to solve the problems. The redistribution of refugees across Europe was a complete fiasco, and now that the crisis is apparently over, that project has been laid to rest.

Meanwhile, Greece received 67,000 new asylum applications in 2018 alone. In the Netherlands, for the sake of comparison, there were 20,000. New agreements were made, mainly meaning that new reception centres were to be built here, but little has come of that so far. The extent to which the European asylum system has jammed up is clear from the most recent data. On average, only a tiny proportion of failed asylum seekers actually leave. In the Netherlands the figure is one in five at best, in Germany one in thirty, in Italy one in a hundred. The majority of rejected migrants simply vanish and live under the radar.

The Turkey deal? Between 2017 and 2018, according to the UN, the number of refugees landing on the Greek coast rose from 36,310 to 50,511. Sixty thousand refugees are still firmly stuck in Greece, of whom around 13,500 are in the stinking camps on the islands. A mere 2,400 refugees have been sent back, 4 per cent, whereas surely that was the main point of the policy? Turkey is still guarding its borders tightly, but for how long? Four months after the deal, on 15 July 2016, there was a failed coup in Turkey by elements of the armed forces. According to Erdoğan, the influential spiritual leader Fethullah Gülen was the main instigator, and since then suspected members of the Gülen movement have been persecuted relentlessly and ruthlessly. Stopping Gülen suspects from slipping out of the country is currently the most important motive for the Turks to guard their borders closely, but if that pressure falls away they could easily open the floodgates again. Europe remains highly susceptible to blackmail.

In Athens I sat talking for a while with Markos Karavias, director of the Greek asylum service. He'd just been to Brussels during a meeting of the European Council. 'It's very disturbing to hear in Brussels that the problem is over, simply because the numbers have gone down. It seems that as soon as an acute crisis ends, solidarity is no longer needed and everything springs back to the national level.'

The latest figures show that, in numerical terms, the flow of refugees from Syria was long ago overtaken by an influx of newcomers from other trouble spots. 'Afghanistan is now at number one, followed by Pakistan, Iraq, Turkey – yes, that's right – and Syria in fifth place. On Lesbos alone we processed 17,207 asylum applications last year, and on tiny Samos 6,743.

We've been trying to create a good asylum service since 2016, with good staff – and all in a time of insane spending cuts. We're continually having to improvise.'

No, ultimately it wasn't a matter of numbers, he said. He wanted to implement an effective and humane refugee policy, but he couldn't stress enough that to make that possible you first of all need responsible selection. In the past he'd done it himself. 'It's tough work that takes its toll, people always forget that. You might start your morning with a Georgian woman. She's honest, she wants to work here so she can care for her parents. No, sadly no asylum, that's clear. A Chinese man who can't talk, whatever we try. My colleague and I look at each other. He's probably had terrible problems at home because of his sexual orientation. What should we do? Then the door opens. A man from Sudan. He talks about how he was tortured and you hear things you really don't want to hear on an ordinary Tuesday morning. The longer you do this job, the more you realize that all those words on paper are ultimately irrelevant.'

8

It has been said often enough: in a crisis, people show their true colours and it becomes clear what a community really stands for. Or indeed what ultimately makes a community not a community at all – another possible outcome.

In 1999, immigration, in the exuberant Europe of those days, was not usually regarded as a major issue. That year Želimir Žilnik filmed the immigration police in Trieste. All refugees came together there – the Yugoslav wars had only just ended – and it was one great marshalling yard of hope and expectation. It struck him then that the Italian police were acting very humanely, even though they were inundated with hopeless asylum cases. The most senior officer took him aside. 'I've got a big problem. There are three hundred men under my command. Every week one of them falls in love.'

Twenty years later little is left of that relaxed attitude. Europe is ageing rapidly – the average European was 37.7 years old in 2003, in 2050 the figure will be 52.3 – and the continent will need more and more newcomers in the future. Germany, with 1.7 million people who applied for asylum there between 2015 and 2019, is now the country with the fifth-largest refugee population in the world. More than half of them are working and paying tax, yet since the refugee crisis, fear of immigrants has only increased. Everywhere in Europe the political consequences of *wir schaffen das* can be felt.

In Poland, the nationalists regained power in the wake of the migrant crisis. In Britain, immigration became a core theme of the Brexit debate. In Hungary, Viktor Orbán cashed in on the situation in all kinds of ways, with immigrants proving the ideal target when he needed to boost Fidesz's declining popularity. He had posters printed showing George Soros and the leaders of all the opposition parties, each holding bolt cutters, the message being: see, they'll cut our borders open again.

In France, Germany, Sweden, the Netherlands and Denmark, forms of 'welfare chauvinism' arose. Immigrants, it was feared, would gnaw at the roots of the welfare state. Marine le Pen's Front National in France reaped the benefits, as did the Dutch Party for Freedom. Sweden, once famous for its generous refugee policy, sealed itself off. The ultra-nationalist Sweden Democrats attracted more and more voters, but their main success lay in the fact that the large centre parties adopted a great many of their anti-immigration views. A similar shift took place to an even greater extent in Denmark. In December 2015 a majority of Danes voted against adopting EU rules on cross-border policing.

In Germany, the elections of 2017 marked a breakthrough for the AfD. The right-wing nationalist party took ninety-four seats in the Bundestag. Walter Lübcke, the politician who had spoken so passionately in 2015 about refugees, humanity and a society's values, received numerous threats from AfD supporters. In June 2019 he was murdered by a right-wing extremist.

The once-so-tolerant Italy, the country that had for years sustained Europe's moral authority with its rescue campaign Operation Mare Nostrum, grew bitter. The Italians felt let down by Europe. It was they who were left with all those immigrants, especially those from Africa, who couldn't go anywhere and simply wandered the country. 'The majority of Italians now feel like the victims of Europe, of the banks, of the institutions and of the state,' was how *La Repubblica* described the atmosphere in 2018. The number of racist incidents increased, and in several cities migrants were fired upon with air rifles. In Naples, a Senegalese street seller was shot at by two men on a scooter, in Rome a thirteen-year-old Roma girl was hit in the back, and in Calabria a migrant was shot dead when he tried to steal a few bits of scrap metal.

The nationalist Matteo Salvini was meanwhile converting his separatist party Lega Nord into an anti-immigration movement, thereby attracting millions of new voters – in southern Italy too this time. From May 2018 onwards it entered government, along with the anarchist Five Star Movement created by actor and comic Beppe Grillo. Both parties were supported by the Kremlin, which meant that, in Italy, Russia-friendly parties now had the upper hand.

Since then, Italy has refused access to all rescue boats. Rescuers are prosecuted as people smugglers. As we have seen, the guarding of the border in this part of the Mediterranean was handed over to Libya. The Libyan coastguard was given money and patrol ships for the purpose, and good training, with the financial and political support of the EU. The number of immigrants crossing the Mediterranean has fallen sharply since then, while the number of drownings has increased.

On 6 November 2017, the German organization Sea-Watch, which has its origins in a group of observers, took pictures of a confrontation with that supposedly well-trained Libyan coastguard whose ship, in contravention of all the regulations, sailed straight at a flimsy rubber boat. It is shocking to watch. You see more than a hundred people fighting for their lives in the water, you hear their panicked cries, you see them swallowed by the waves right in front of your eyes while the Libyan crew barely lifts a finger, not even launching a lifeboat. Forty people are estimated to have drowned in that incident.

According to figures from the UNHCR, in the first half of 2019 around 2,000 migrants made it across the Mediterranean. Close to 350 drowned.

Membership of the 'society for the protection of people' became a punishable offence in those years. My television colleagues spoke to a Danish man who was convicted of the crime of helping a Syrian family. 'I gave them coffee, cold drinks and currant buns, and let them use the toilet. Then I took them to the station. The punishment was 20,000 kroner [2,500 euros] or fourteen days in prison.' An aid worker on Lesbos spent 107 days on remand without any clear charge being brought. A Frenchman who took refugees to the border and offered them shelter was threatened with four months in jail. The captain of the rescue ship *Iuventa* was arrested in August 2017 in the harbour on Lampedusa with the rest of his crew. 'Because we have rescued people, a show trial lasting years awaits us and it's going to cost us around half a million euros.' The work of Sea-Watch has been made all but impossible.

'Mama' Maria and her husband Michalis have had a rough time of it too. The neo-Nazis of Golden Dawn came round and intimidated their customers, their takings fell, and eventually they had to close their taverna. When I visited them, Michalis struggled to make coffee for me on a camping stove and it was stone-cold in the house. They apologized. The electricity had been cut off that morning. They could no longer stay on Samos. Michalis, who had trained as a plumber, would try to find work on Crete, and Maria would move in with her daughter in Athens for a while. Their old house, full of rugs, trinkets, portraits, icons – the baggage of thirty years together – would be sold.

The grateful gods transformed Philemon and Baucis into two trees at the end of their lives, right beside each other, 'arising out of human form' with their branches entwined. 'They had just enough time to say farewell and to speak each other's name before their mouths disappeared simultaneously into the green of the boughs . . .'

That's how it should be. But these are different times.

12. Wigan

2016

I

SO THERE WE WERE, IN the spring of 2016, with that tumble-down temple from the 1950s and that half-built Tower of Babel from the 1990s.

'L'Europe est-elle mortelle?' (Is Europe mortal?) was the headline in Le Monde that April. The promise of prosperity, represented by the euro, had been 'broken', according to the paper, by the various crises and by mass unemployment. The political ambition to 'lay the foundations of an ever closer union among the peoples of Europe', as the Treaty of Rome puts it, had collided with populism. The message of peace had been negated by terrorism and by the wars in Syria and Ukraine. 'And what does it have to offer the world if it needs to entrust to the Turks the guarding of its gates and the holding back of refugees?'

Regarding immigration, nothing had actually been resolved. We'd got stiff necks from looking away. After years of turbulence, the European project had entered a vicious circle. The system was failing, so public support for the European project was on the decline, and reduced support meant that the opportunities to fix a failing system were few and far between.

We were still living with the after-effects of the crisis of 2008. In the developed world, Europe included, the incomes of roughly two-thirds of households had fallen or stagnated. In southern Europe, a third of young people were still unemployed. The public sector was damaged and weakened. Many voters no longer saw any connection between their personal lives and politics, especially at a European level. Inequality continued to grow. Hardly any bankers had ever been punished.

'How did you feel, in that spring of 2016?' my student of 2069 wants to know. Well, we were shocked. We were confused and sad. Above all we were worried, with no idea what awaited us.

The failed democratic revolutions of 1848 were once called 'the turning point at which modern history failed to turn'. The same could be said of the collapse of the banks in 2008, a crisis that showed just how wrong it was to believe that markets could regulate themselves. Neoliberalism seemed bankrupt, but, as in 1848, the opposite was true.

If you ploughed through all the statistics about the crisis years, the conclusion was inescapable: the weakest had suffered most. Election results all over Europe reflected the resulting unease. The traditional parties of government melted away and new faces appeared on the scene everywhere. Crisis of democracy? Not at all, democracy was working just fine. The results were disturbing for many people, but the system unerringly registered feelings of humiliation and injustice.

Didier Eribon, son of working-classes parents in Reims, wrote, 'My family divided the world into two camps, those who were "for the workers" and those who were "against the workers", or, in slightly different words, those who "defended the workers" and those who "did nothing for the workers". . . . Nowadays who fulfils the role played by the [Communist] "Party"? To whom can exploited and powerless people turn in order to feel that they are supported or that their point of view is expressed? . . . A source that, in the simplest terms, takes into account who they are, how they live, what they think about, what they want?'

Undine Zimmer, who grew up in the Berlin 'underclass', said, 'Poverty in Germany is not primarily a matter of hunger, disease or a lack of drinking water. It's poverty at the social level, a lack of faith in the opportunities offered by education and careers. Poverty is more than a shortage of money.'

Geert van Istendael, in Brussels, put it like this: 'Those who have never had pots of money. Those who are told day in and day out that they need to make sacrifices, that their wages are too high, that we cannot any longer cover the cost of health insurance, that tuition fees are too low – in other words, that it's they who are living beyond their means – those people feel they've been screwed. At the same time, they can see twenty-four hours a day how the rich bathe in increasingly extravagant wealth. There's no more efficient means of whipping up envy.'

Philipp Blom in Vienna wrote, 'This is nothing less than the end of the great post-war promise in the liberal countries that anyone who works hard and has a good education can build a life, climb the social ladder and participate in economic growth. The link between work and social progress has been broken and with it another central promise, namely that today's children will one day be better off than their parents.'

Erik Vlaminck quoted a working-class woman in Ghent: 'How are you supposed to cope if your water is cut off? How are you supposed to cope if you have two children and your water is cut off? How are you supposed to wash the children's clothes? I smell them, my children's unwashed clothes. And I know that other people smell those unwashed clothes too. The other children at school . . . The teacher . . .'

As far back as 1997, philosopher Richard Rorty predicted that the old industrialized democracies were heading for a tumultuous period of transition. Workers with little education and training would eventually realize that their governments were no longer even trying to prevent their wages from dropping back and their jobs from disappearing abroad. They would then become aware that white-collar workers in the suburbs – themselves frightened of falling off the social ladder – would not be prepared to pay the cost of providing others with social benefits indefinitely. 'At that point,' he wrote, 'something will crack.'

The revolution had begun, but it didn't happen the way we had always imagined. The traditional parties of power, especially after the rise of neoliberalism and the Third Way laid out by social democrats like Tony Blair, Wim Kok and Gerhard Schröder, all started to look alike. Their priorities lay with the middle class, while the classic working classes slid off to the margins of society. Everywhere a search was going on for new stories and new contexts, because the twentieth-century versions were clearly no longer of use.

In all these developments, the internet had a decisive effect. The fortress of the political and intellectual elites was demolished and everyone gained access to all available information. Everyone could communicate with everyone else, everyone could broadcast whatever they liked to the world – it was an unprecedented revolution from a historical point of view, with unimaginable social and political repercussions. We knew it was a revolution, but in those years we had little idea of its nature or extent. Twitter and Facebook, which grew at astonishing speed, turned out to be more than merely messengers, bearers of all possible feelings of discontent; they shaped those feelings and further fuelled them. The unrestrained language and aggression displayed on them generated further division and insecurity.

The new parties and movements had plenty of space in the void created by the free market creed. With the dismantling of the public sector, the phenomenon of 'politics' lost much of its appeal in many European countries. Quite a few of the newcomers in the political arena, especially the populists, did not seem to take seriously the complicated and often tedious task of governing, with its wrenching dilemmas. For at least three decades, neoliberalism had trampled on every political debate. 'Market forces' were regarded as neutral, and any political alternative seemed excluded by definition.

Margaret Thatcher was famous for saying 'There is no alternative'. Schröder quickly acquired the title 'Basta-Kanzler' (enough-chancellor). At the Labour conference in 2005, Tony Blair told delegates, 'I hear people say we have to stop and debate globalization. You might as well debate whether autumn should follow summer.' As to the question of what was right or wrong – especially in a moral sense – there was no need for further discussion. Every decision favouring the interests of the economic elite could be camouflaged behind the apparent objectivity of 'the market'. Market thinking steadily drove political considerations and democratic choices out of the public debate. The entire terrain grew quiet and barren.

This depoliticization had enormous consequences for the way in which many Europeans experienced the concept of citizenship. They no longer felt themselves to be part of a larger whole for which, each in their own way, they were partly responsible. Instead, they came to regard citizenship as above all an innate or acquired title from which they could derive rights – preferably as many as possible, even though over the years those rights became increasingly scant and paltry. 'Identity' – national, religious, cultural or otherwise – became the exclusive basis on which those rights, or alleged rights, could be obtained. For many voters, identity became increasingly important, while 'politics' and 'democracy', the traditional means of bridging divides, acquired a bad name. This 'democratic recession', spurred

on by the new media and some politicians, increasingly put Western societies under pressure. Any compromise now quickly came to be seen as a
'betrayal' of one's own group and one's own identity. Citizens had, indeed,
become 'clients'.

Those who had always been the greatest advocates of democracy –
especially liberals and progressives – were perplexed when democracy
finally gave its verdict on the state of Europe. For European social democrats, trouble arrived well before the crisis of 2008. Between 2001 and 2006
they lost power in the Netherlands, France, Germany, Portugal, Denmark,
Sweden and Finland. They had been unable to offer sufficient protection to
their core voters, the weakest groups in society.

At a congress of European social democrats in Lisbon in December 2018,
one of the speakers called out to the audience, 'Are you dead?' He should of
course have been answered with a deafening 'No!' but instead there was a
softly mumbled denial. Several delegates left the hall.

Other twentieth-century parties were no less tired and decrepit. They
carried on because they generated power and jobs, but you could no longer
expect innovation from them. In Italy, the once all-powerful Christian
democrats had been dethroned in the 1990s by the populist Berlusconi; and
in France a total newcomer, Emmanuel Macron, won the presidency in
2017, leaving all the established parties trailing far behind. The *Guardian* tried
an in-house audit. In 1998 the words 'populist' or 'populism' appeared in
around 300 of its articles. For 2016 the figure was more than 2,000. 'Populism is sexy.'

Of course, Europe had been familiar for many years with the phenomenon whereby the outsider challenges 'the elite', uses words like 'pluralism'
and 'tolerance' as terms of abuse and promises to give their 'own future'
back to a 'united people'. In the 1980s there were figures like Jean-Marie Le
Pen in France, Filip Dewinter in Belgium and Jörg Haider in Austria, who
fulminated against immigration and the supposedly corrupt establishment:
'Our own people first.' They proved more lasting than many expected, they
forged links with countless kindred spirits, and they laid the foundations
for everything that came later. It is therefore a mistake to assume that populism arose out of the decline of social democrat parties or out of the crisis
of 2008. As early as 1988 Le Pen won 14 per cent of the vote in the French
presidential elections and in 2002 he even reached the final round. The

right-wing nationalist Vlaams Blok, in 2004 renamed Vlaams Belang, was active in Flanders from 1978 onwards. And in 2002, before the social democrats lost ground, Pim Fortuyn made his breakthrough in Dutch politics.

Nevertheless, it was around the time of the European crises that the disintegration of the large centrist parties accelerated. In the European elections of 2014, the United Kingdom Independence Party (UKIP), led by rabble-rouser Nigel Farage, garnered more votes than any other British party. In January 2015 newcomer Syriza won the Greek elections overwhelmingly, and shortly afterwards Labour was wiped off the electoral map of Scotland by the Scottish National Party (SNP). In Spain, left-wing Podemos emerged; in France, Marine Le Pen's Front National grew to become the country's second party; and in Britain the Labour Party, in a political earthquake, chose the radical left-winger Jeremy Corbyn as its leader.

In 2017, the Party for Freedom led by Geert Wilders became the second-largest political force in the Netherlands. In Germany, the AfD managed within three years to reach a position that had taken comparable parties like the Front National in France or the FPÖ in Austria decades of hard work.

Populists and religious newcomers once again called the ideals of the Enlightenment into question. They rebelled against globalization, against the dismantling of the welfare state and against neoliberalism, including the freedom to migrate. The old powers weakened, and with them the traditional values and conventions of liberal democracy. In 1936, Dutch essayist Jacques de Kadt called the same phenomenon 'decency under siege'. 'In most cases people inflict their idiocy on harmless things: eastern and western religious sects, football and sport, pigeons and rabbits, etc. etc.,' he wrote. 'But let all those idiots gather together in politics without sufficient resistance of any kind and you get a dictatorship of idiocy.'

That was now repeating itself, and you could see why.

2

We were experiencing what always happens in times of unrest. An army of prophets, quacks and charlatans trekked though city and countryside, trailed by singing, praying, flagellating and dancing followers. For every opponent a pyre was built, while the leaders preached hell and damnation in colourful language. 'Troy is burning!' shouted Dutch prophet of doom Thierry Baudet in 2017, for instance, to deafening applause from his supporters. 'We find ourselves in a dizzying process of destruction.'

In reality, his country was purring with satisfaction. According to the Netherlands Institute for Social Research, the average Dutch person rated their life – housing, income, happiness, friends – at eight out of ten on several counts: 85 per cent believed their own families were living in prosperity; 68 per cent, more than in earlier years, had faith in democracy; 80 per cent were proud to be Dutch. Tolerance had not declined but rather increased. In 1994, almost half of those asked had believed that 'too many people of a different nationality are living in the Netherlands', whereas a quarter of a century later the proportion had fallen to a third. Although the prophets and preachers of hell and damnation got all the attention in the media, in practice their far-right political message won them no more than 20 to 25 per cent of the vote.

Yet the Dutch did feel insecure. 'Among those in the centre ground an end has come to optimism about the future,' wrote the Netherlands Scientific Council for Government Policy that same year. It was an insecurity that made itself felt all over Europe and to which the complacent political powers paid no attention, or far too little. After two decades of expansion, the middle class had been shrinking everywhere since 2008. The risk of slipping down the income ladder was greater than the likelihood of rising. 'Fear of falling', the title of a classic by Barbara Ehrenreich about the American middle class, was taking hold in Europe as well.

The old politics had been based to a large extent on identity. As Eribon wrote, you belonged to a particular camp, to a particular party. When that sense of self-evident belonging was lost, many voters went in search of new forms of identification. They arrived, as if by the nature of things, at outsiders who clearly demonstrated, by their behaviour, their clothing, their use of language, that they were not part of the grey order and the old elite. In the content of their messages too, these outsiders did not engage in classical opposition but in an opposition of principle, meaning opposition to the system as a whole. They showed themselves ready to defend every inch of ground gained against all comers, and with tremendous force.

The phenomenon of the apolitical politician arose all over Europe, on the left and especially on the right. 'Authenticity' became a mark of quality. In Portugal the left-wing actress Catarina Martins caused a stir; her jeans and effusive red blouses alone amounted to a statement in the grey-suited world of establishment politics. In 2015 in Spain, two such 'anti-politics' women, Ada Colau and Manuela Carmena, came from a standing start to win mayoral elections in Barcelona and Madrid. In Britain the chaotic Conservative Boris Johnson, with his knapsacks, his jokes and his flapping haircut, confounded expectations by winning the 2008 mayoral election in that Labour bastion, London. Yanis Varoufakis stole the show in Greece with his motorbike and his fashionably casual lifestyle. In 2002 Dutch populist Pim Fortuyn did something similar with his Jaguar and his butler. He managed to be both a total outsider and 'our Pim'. His later successor, radical conservative Thierry Baudet, played the intellectual, had a piano carried into the parliament building and began his maiden speech in Latin.

Clowns and cabaret artists are supposed to ridicule the powers that be. Now they were themselves the powers that be. In Ukraine the comic Volodymyr Zelenskiy came out of nowhere in 2019 to win almost three-quarters of the votes, mainly because he played such a likeable role on television: a history teacher who unexpectedly becomes president. That ought to happen in reality too, thought Ukrainian voters. No sooner said than done. In Italy the part was played by court jester Beppe Grillo. On 8 September 2007, he got 2 million people out onto the streets for a 'V-Day' demonstration against the establishment, the V standing for victory, vendetta and *vanffanculo* (kiss my ass). Grillo knew what he was doing. 'You shouldn't underestimate us,' he warned in 2010 on Dutch television programme *Tegenlicht*. 'You see us as spaghetti eaters, as pixies. But we're deadly dangerous. We invented fascism. . . . We invented banking . . . . We invented all the misdeeds of the world – and exported them.'

Sure enough, the first of the new-style populists emerged in Italy, in 1993, when media magnate Silvio Berlusconi filled the void left by the corrupt, ravaged established parties. His Forza Italia was fresh and new. He unashamedly used himself, his wealth, his football club and his sexual conquests as campaign material, and deployed in the battle for power all the television channels he controlled. He spoke the language of the street. He was 'one of us', and his unspoken promise was to make every Italian as rich as he was. For Berlusconi, the truth was entirely malleable and he staged an endless parade of obtuseness. In that sense he was already doing what Donald Trump would do almost a quarter of a century later, by recreating himself as a permanent television show. This was all a long way from normal politics and normal government, but the personal relationship he created with his voters, bypassing party politics altogether, became a bond of steel. He was elected prime minister three times over.

Italy meanwhile sank ever deeper into the morass. In the early 1990s the Italian economy was roughly the same size as the British. By 2018 it was 25 per cent smaller, while Italian GDP had fallen by 10 per cent since 2008 and some 2 million young Italians, most of them well educated, had left the country. In barely ten years the number of Italians living in poverty had grown from 1.8 to 5 million. In 2011 *The Economist* devoted a special issue to Berlusconi and the state of Italy under the heading 'The man who screwed an entire country'.

There was now room for new magicians. Beppe Grillo bridged the gap between citizen and politics in a way all his own. His Five Star Movement was a creation of the internet; decision-making was unusually flexible, fluid, anarchic. New ideas could be launched, debated and tested ceaselessly. A motley collection of floating voters, from neo-fascists to former communists, soon felt at home in this new movement. After all, they could participate in everything online, and if determined to do so they could fairly easily make their party change course. Grillo's success was initially overwhelming and in 2018 his 'first floating party in Europe' became the dominant force in Italian politics.

Grillo's right-wing counterpart Matteo Salvini was at least as good at playing the internet, in his case mainly through Facebook. In 2013 he had assumed leadership of the Lega Nord, a regional independence party that he successfully reshaped into a national anti-immigration party called the Lega. Salvini repeated the Berlusconi recipe, but with more modern ingredients. Running a permanent election campaign, with weekly shows all over the country, he created again and again a sense of unanimity between himself and his electorate. He was given all the space he needed, since in the aftermath of Berlusconi, Italy had barely any independent mass media left. Racist jokes, coarse language – everything was permitted, and if he felt it expedient, Salvini would appear onstage with neo-fascist leaders. With its vague promise to deport half a million 'illegal immigrants', his party's popularity rose rapidly in March 2018, from 4 per cent to 18 per cent of the electorate. More than half the votes in that election went to anti-establishment parties, and for a year and a half Salvini was in charge of the country, along with the Five Star Movement.

All these new figures were described as 'hyperleaders'. They were politicians whose names echoed endlessly in the cathedrals of the internet and who were incessantly mobbed by a huge 'super base' of faithful followers. With a relentless bombardment of tweets and Facebook posts, hyperleaders held the attention and demonstrated, time and again, their total independence from the musty and corrupted elite, even if in reality their ties with it were strong. They were the future, authentic and original.

In their craving for attention and spectacle, they deliberately broke long-standing taboos. Salvini, for instance, directly attacked the pope by reproaching him for encouraging and financing 'an unprecedented invasion' of immigrants. AfD leader Björn Höcke described the Holocaust memorial in Berlin as a 'memorial of shame', and the old populist Jean-Marie Le Pen called the gas chambers 'merely a detail' in the history of the Second World War, unashamedly dug up Vichy fascism, and by doing so influenced Dutchman Thierry Baudet among others. Baudet himself, once a cheerfully questing conservative, was now radicalized and took to talking about 'our boreal world' (not everyone was convinced he meant 'northern' rather than 'white') and 'the systematic dilution of the homogenous population by waves of mass immigration'. In the spring of 2019 he came from nowhere to make his Forum for Democracy (FvD) the biggest party in the Netherlands, for a short time at least.

A powerful example of such a hyperleader was Nigel Farage, one of the most dangerous demagogues in British history. Like Berlusconi and later Donald Trump, he was a paradoxical figure, a capitalist populist, a former stockbroker with a character shaped by the wild 1980s in the City of London. His language was engaging and nostalgic. He talked about a 'lost' England, about decline and injustice, about sovereignty which had been forfeited to Brussels, and about a cosmopolitan elite that had betrayed the country.

Like many other populists, he spoke of immigration as a 'dilution' of the already eroded welfare state, affecting the poorest citizens disproportionately. 'The historic right wing provides their only defence,' wrote Derk Jan

Eppink, a columnist and prominent FvD member. 'They are putting out distress signals.' Farage energetically propagated a nostalgic utopia, repeatedly harking back to an idealized past to which 'our people' must be led: the glory of the British Empire; the victories of 1918 and 1945; the proud, independent Albion.

It was the same nostalgia indulged in by populists elsewhere – in Poland, Hungary and the Netherlands. Long periods and far-reaching developments were casually passed over. The Vienna of the FPÖ shone again with the gilding of the lost empire, and at a corner of Saint Stephen's Cathedral I saw students of the Burschenschaften lounging about as if nothing had changed since the nineteenth century. Sometimes the film was turned back by a century (the Brexiteers, the Vienna of the FPÖ), sometimes a century and half (the Dutch radical conservatives), sometimes two or three centuries (the nationalists in Poland and Hungary), sometimes thirteen centuries (the Salafist Muslims).

In reality, Nigel Farage's political agenda reflected above all the priorities of the modern banking world from which he came. He wouldn't hear of increasing the minimum wage or reducing the retirement age: people must work harder for less money. 'Singapore-on-Thames' was his ideal for the future, and leaving the EU was the first step towards it. The second step must follow immediately: throwing overboard as much 'obstructive' regulation as possible, to give his buccaneers free rein.

In 1992 Farage was one of the founders of UKIP, a marginal group made up of frustrated Conservatives and the occasional ex-fascist which he reforged from 2006 onwards into an uncommonly destructive weapon. The party swiftly grew and gnawed such big holes in the Conservative electorate that the then Tory leader, David Cameron, felt forced to hold a referendum in 2016 on leaving the EU.

Three years later, in the European elections of 2019, Farage again leapt onto the political stage, this time using his Brexit Party to put pressure on the Tories to take the country out of the EU that autumn at any price. It was a one-man crusade this time. The party had no members, no programme, the candidates were chosen by Farage himself and, as it was for the Five Star Movement, the internet was the most important discussion platform. This was a typical party of objection; the lemmings, opposing everything and everyone, ran forward with just one goal, to throw themselves into the abyss, a 'no-deal Brexit', an England for Jack the Lads.

3

In the summer of 2015, during the start of the presidential campaigns, American reporters pointed to a phenomenon never previously seen in the United States. One of the Republican candidates was staging unprecedented performances, insulting immigrants by calling them criminals, rapists and drug dealers, flouting all the civilized rules of etiquette, flirting with racism, calling his rivals idiots, pulling off all the window dressing – 'They hate each other, but they can't say it. They hate each other . . . . I am so tired of this politically correct crap' – and thereby managing to attract audiences of thousands every evening. 'Today, everybody's politically correct. Our country's going to hell with being politically correct. Going to hell.'

He lacked even the most basic respect for facts, institutions and democratic principles. To him, political opponents were enemies, a compromise was not a dignified agreement but a capitulation. He allowed the journalists present to be jeered, indeed he even encouraged the audience to boo them. He castigated the lobbies and interest groups that all the other candidates depended on, the system that had inserted itself between the voters and the politicians. 'The whole thing is rigged, but I can beat it.' He felt no less angry than his audiences. He too was an underdog, and it was good to release that pent-up rage. He unfailingly managed to touch on that sense of being misunderstood. 'They call them "the elite". These people. I look at them, I say, "That's elite?" . . . We're smarter than they are, and they say they're elite? We're the elite. You're the elite. We're the elite.' The audience cheered, screamed, clapped till it could clap no more.

Donald Trump was soon a phenomenon in his own right, a political ringmaster such as America had rarely seen. Nobody thought much of his chances at first. He had no experience, the only world he knew well was that of the real estate market on Long Island – a rather exotic milieu even from a business point of view – and, later, that of television shows. His coarse language, his pathological narcissism and his many extramarital affairs would surely be enough to deter most Republican voters. But what was happening on TV every night was certainly extraordinary.

The famous political reporter Thomas Frank, author of *What's the Matter with Kansas?*, followed it all closely: 'I saw the man ramble and boast and threaten and even seem to gloat when protesters were ejected from the arenas in which he spoke.' It was repulsive. But he noticed something surprising. 'In each of the speeches I watched, Trump spent a good part of his time talking about an entirely legitimate issue, one that could even be called left wing.'

Trump talked about the industrial lobbies, about the military-industrial complex, about the ideology of the free market and the loss of millions of jobs to Mexico and China that went with it, as a result of which countless American families had found themselves in serious trouble. Like Farage, he rode high on the bitterness of the average citizen, who felt their personal life was increasingly in the grip of uncontrollable and impersonal forces. As Frank put it, 'A map of his support may coordinate with racist Google searches, but it coordinates even better with deindustrialization and despair, with the zones of economic misery that 30 years of Washington's free-market consensus have brought the rest of America.'

Trump was a phenomenon that in America, and to some degree in Europe too, turned the public debate upside down. Nothing else seemed to occupy so much space.

4

What could be more British than this small, dark-red tin of peppermints? 'Ellen Santus made her first batch of Uncle Joe's Mint Balls in 1898,' I read on the label. 'They were produced in the kitchen of her small terraced house in Wigan.' Her recipe has since been passed down from one generation to the next and is still 'a closely guarded family secret'. To this day, we're assured, Uncle Joe's Mint Balls are 'manufactured in the traditional way over open gas fires using only three ingredients and are a delicious reminder of how sweets used to taste'. England as it should be: the colours, the language, the flavours and traditions, the pubs, the pasties, the rituals, the village squares, the big old trees, the gently rolling landscape, the grey farmhouses, the stone walls between the fields, unchanged for generations. That's how England must be, full of memories, and that's how it must stay.

Wigan, close to Manchester, is an old industrial town – cotton, coal mines – like so many in Europe. I was given the Premium English Mints by a proud resident, and anyone walking to King Street walks into that same dreamed-of past: the Clarence Hotel, the Royal Court Theatre, the Grimes Arcade, the County Playhouse cinema, the once great Hippodrome Theatre – all of it nailed shut. Further on, beside the River Douglas, lie the huge red-brick factories the town used to live off, except that now all the dirt and sweat has been scrubbed off the walls. Trencherfield Mill, a vast cotton mill from 1907, is now the Academy of Live and Recorded Arts. The imposing Gibson's Warehouse, a Victorian cotton depot, is a restaurant, and another warehouse has been converted into a museum called The Way We Were.

George Orwell described Wigan Pier in 1937 as a 'lunar landscape' of slag heaps, with factory chimneys sending out smoke day and night – he counted thirty-three of them. He recalled a winter evening, insanely cold, when the ice on the River Douglas was brown with iron oxide, 'the lock gates wore beards of ice' and the bargemen had wrapped themselves up to their eyes in sacks. 'It seemed a world from which vegetation had been banished; nothing existed except smoke, shale, ice, mud, ashes and foul water . . . . And the stench! If at rare moments you stop smelling sulphur it is because you have begun smelling gas.'

Now you can almost swim in the Douglas. Everything here is clean, impressive, beautifully restored and deathly quiet. This was the toiling heart of a bygone world. It no longer beats.

When he wrote those words, George Orwell was living in a lodging house run by the Brooker family, a stinking place where tripe was cooked and sold, and full chamber pots were left under the breakfast table. He moved out after a few weeks, unable to stand it any longer: the dirt, the vile food and above all 'the feeling of stagnant meaningless decay' that surrounded the couple. He brought the family and the town of Wigan worldwide fame with The Road to Wigan Pier, a probing piece of social reportage about the lives of British mineworkers during the crisis years.

The people of Wigan were not at all pleased. American travel writer Bill Bryson was astonished when he visited Wigan. He expected, as people generally do, a dirt-poor shambles, and instead came upon a neatly tended town centre. My impression is the same as his. All those I speak to are pleasant, robust, hard-working people, certainly not victims. The Wigan Observer – 'Trusted News Since 1853' – fills today's edition with a wealth of lively advertisements, as well as reports on a successful dog show, a drunken man who sank his teeth into a police officer, and Elizabeth Cash who on her hundredth birthday received a card from the queen. The newspaper approves of tough measures; a 'Wigan child porn pervert', who has been given only a community service order by the court, is identified by name, along with the street he lives in. That'll teach him!

'Orwell did enormous damage to our town,' says local historian Tom Walsh, who, along with councillor Chris Ready, gives me a tour of the place. 'He came here with a political agenda; the miners' lot must be described vividly and animatedly. There was little money, that's true, but we had our dignity, and the vast majority lived in clean and well-maintained houses, even in those days. Women like my mother scrubbed their homes every day, that was their pride, and woe betide you if you walked across the wet floor. I was born nine years after Orwell wrote his reportage, but I heard all the stories from my father and mother. No, the real Wigan is a million miles from Orwell's Wigan.'

One of the things Orwell wrote little about was the close-knit community that existed everywhere. On New Year's Eve the entire neighbourhood would eat the ritual 'hotpot', and another ancient tradition was the 'Dark Stranger', a tall, dark-haired man dressed in black who was invited to take the year's first step over the threshold, and who brought good luck with a lump of coal, a hunk of bread and a glass of whisky. 'When my father died the whole street contributed to the cost of the funeral,' says Walsh.

Because of its strong sense of community, the town survived the closure of the mines, the last of which shut in 1994, and the crisis of 2008. A number of big businesses absorbed the worst of the blows. The multinational Heinz has set up one of the largest food factories in the world near Wigan, where billions of cans of soup and baked beans roll off the production line every year.

The town also lies at the heart of a 'transition region'. In total, such regions in Britain received some €10 billion from European Structural Funds between 2007 and 2013, with another €11 billion allocated between 2014 and 2020, as well as €25 billion for rural development. 'Unemployment here, after everything that's happened, is still only around 5 per cent,' says Chris Ready, not without pride. 'People like living in Wigan, and they stay.'

Since 2010 the Conservative government has made cuts of more than £30 billion, or €33 billion, to unemployment benefits, rent subsidies and social welfare payments in the UK. In the summer of 2011 there were street protests, riots and mass looting in London, Manchester, Liverpool, Birmingham and elsewhere, yet the government pressed ahead with its austerity policies. Between 2010 and 2017 the ranks of the homeless doubled in size, and half a million people became dependent on food banks. The average British family's income fell by more than 6 per cent after 2010, while the pay gap, already far bigger than in the rest of Europe, steadily increased. The incomes of top managers rose four times as quickly as those of the average citizen.

Downright shocking was the impact on health. According to the Office for National Statistics, in 2018 average life expectancy in the poorest parts of Glasgow, Manchester and Blackpool was just seventy-four years, and the average resident lived no more than fifty-two years in good health, on a par with people in Somalia and Gambia. The difference between those neighbourhoods and the prosperous parts of Britain amounts to more than eighteen years of life.

In Wigan, they were well prepared for austerity in 2010. 'We had our strategy ready.' Although £160 million in spending cuts was imposed on the town, the damage was mitigated by a great deal of voluntary work in hospitals, libraries and night shelters. 'But we have far more homeless and beggars than before,' says Ready. 'At the churches there are baskets you can put food in and it's picked up immediately. Worse still, there are more and more working poor, people who have jobs but can't possibly manage on what they're earning. That's unacceptable. If you work you shouldn't need to be poor, but people are.'

Later I walk down a shop-lined street with Tom Walsh, past a war memorial with hundreds of names, to the Museum of Wigan Life. 'I was recently asked to talk to some schoolchildren about the history of Wigan. I had a lump of coal in my hand. One of the girls asked, "What's that, sir, coal?" The old Wigan, the old England, is just history now.'

'And Brexit?' I ask. He's silent for a moment. Then he says, 'I was shell-shocked. It's our biggest mistake since the First World War.'

The Brexit referendum that hijacked British politics from 2016 onwards and largely paralysed the British government – how necessary was it actually? If a year earlier, in 2015 or so, you had asked the British what they were most concerned about, they would have mentioned healthcare, income distribution, social security or education. Membership of the EU came somewhere near the bottom of the list, in eighth or tenth place. The theme of 'Europe' was irrelevant to the average Briton, let alone the idea that there should be a historic referendum on the subject. The origins of the decision to hold another referendum had nothing to do with Europe at all. The reason was purely and simply party political.

On 23 January 2013, David Cameron promised to hold a new referendum about the EU. As we have seen, he was against leaving, he mainly wanted to silence his internal opposition once and for all. He gambled that his coalition partners, the Liberal Democrats, would immediately quash any such proposal. If necessary he could force a few more concessions from the EU. Sarkozy warned him, saying it was a tragic and monumental mistake. Earlier still, in November 2012, Cameron laid out his strategy to Angela Merkel during a dinner at 10 Downing Street. Those present said that in response she looked at him for a long time in silence, clearly wondering whether she should take this seriously. Inviting such a historic decision, with such massive consequences for the future of the country, simply to solve an internal party problem – she could barely comprehend it.

Of course, the biggest political crisis in Britain for generations was caused by more than just a prime minister who consistently placed the interests of his Conservative Party above those of the country. He was merely playing with matches next to a barrel of gunpowder. Historians of the future will point to Nigel Farage, to the lying tabloids and to unprecedented manipulation of voters via the internet. Tony Blair will be named, the premier who, after the enlargement of the EU in 2004, immediately accepted an unlimited number of Eastern European labour migrants – most of the other European countries were far more cautious – and completely underestimated the social and political effects. It seriously undermined public confidence in the EU. His later successor, the socialist Labour leader Corbyn, also played his part; because of his ambivalent attitude, Labour remained divided. He allowed a political vacuum to emerge and his followers wavered, with many of his voters eventually opting for the Brexit camp.

One important factor was an apparent U-turn by the charismatic

London mayor Boris Johnson. It was only once he had joined that the Brexit campaign gained real momentum. Johnson was a theatre show in his own right. According to his biographer Andrew Gimson, with his carefully cultivated sloppiness he was the darling of 'Merry England', the jovial, rustic England of conservatives with a small 'c', rather than the aggressively nostalgic 'Little Englander' world of Nigel Farage. It was a common view at the time that Johnson's remarkable decision had only one motive: he believed it was a way to become a prime minister just like his great hero Winston Churchill. Shortly before making his move he wrote two columns for the *Daily Telegraph*, under the headings 'Out' and 'In'. The latter in particular was crystal clear yet it was the 'Out' column that was published, and on the morning of Sunday, 21 February 2016, he declared he was supporting the Leave campaign. Johnson had become a committed Brexiteer.

Johnson and Farage, with their well-organized band of Brexiteers, would have stood no chance had they not been able to draw upon the eternal doubt felt by millions of Brits as to whether they supported in or out, an issue reignited by a series of European crises.

The ambivalence began with geography. As an island off the rest of Europe, Britain had in many ways already chosen a path of its own – in a religious and legal sense but also regarding practical matters such as traffic rules, weights and measures, and its currency. When in 2014 Eurobarometer asked about the extent to which people felt European, affirmation of European identity came from 50 per cent of Italians, 60 per cent of French people and 70 per cent of Germans. The British figure was a mere 40 per cent, the lowest of all European countries.

Furthermore, since 1945 the British had regarded themselves as victors, despite the devastation wrought by the war. They felt they were typical representatives of the Atlantic world, faithful military allies of America – unlike demilitarized Germany and pig-headed France. Such feelings of triumph were virtually unknown in the rest of Europe, where the founding of the EU was seen as an important part of the process of peace and reconciliation. When Helmut Kohl and François Mitterrand stood hand in hand at Verdun in 1984, in the pouring rain, Margaret Thatcher found it simply ridiculous. Theresa May, her distant successor, was the only European government leader not to go to Compiègne when the others commemorated the armistice of 1918 there. Her notable absence was both symbolic and telling: Great Britain is not joining the European process of peace and recovery, its definitive liberation from the dark past. To the United Kingdom, the EU was a glorified trading block, and instinctively the British always stood with one foot outside it.

The British had taken a long time to become members. In the 1950s they remained outside by choice, and in the 1960s because French president Charles de Gaulle stood in the way. It was not until 1973 that the United Kingdom joined. The European Economic Community, as it then was, proved a great success, and the project had everything it needed to grow over time into a powerful political bloc. London believed Britain could not afford to stay out. But the hearts of the British weren't in it. A year later, in 1974, a new Labour government asked to renegotiate and in 1975 a referendum on EEC membership was held. Two-thirds of the British voted in favour but the ambivalence remained, along with some degree of anxiety.

In that sense too Britain was unique. There was never a period in which both major parties, Labour and Conservative, fully supported EU membership. Many Labour members were opposed because the Union might in future be able to obstruct a radical turn to the left. For Conservatives like Margaret Thatcher, the Second World War continued to influence thinking. During a famous speech in Bruges in 1988 she emphatically warned against a 'European super-state exercising a new dominance from Brussels'.

The latent split became a reality in 1992 over the Maastricht Treaty. Britain went along with the new European Union but rejected the line taken by the other members about 'ever closer union'. It did not join Schengen or the euro, and it negotiated more and more exemptions. The great enlargement of 2004 – of which the British were enthusiastic advocates, since it meant the power of France and Germany would be 'diluted' – increased their alienation. A huge number of Eastern European immigrants arrived, and on top of that the political centre of gravity of the EU shifted further eastwards, away from Britain.

The British started to withdraw from the centres of power in Brussels. 'Increasingly the conversation fizzled out because they didn't want to talk about Europe – the common story – but about themselves,' was the experience of Europe expert Caroline de Gruyter. 'Their own position in Europe became the issue, not Europe itself.' Former British ambassador to the EU

Ivan Rogers later declared in the House of Commons that almost all his instructions from London were negative: block this, torpedo that. The famous European training programme for British diplomats was discontinued; the quality of the British contribution, which had always been highly regarded, rapidly declined; and British diplomats, in contrast to those of the other non-eurozone member states, had hardly any part to play in the settlement of the euro crisis. Herman Van Rompuy, who chaired many crisis summits, said, 'They were not part of this story.'

Events gathered pace after that. The 2015 UK general election went far better for Cameron than he had expected. He won an absolute majority in the House of Commons, the Liberal Democrats were now out of the picture and his government was therefore stuck with its risky promise. As Donald Tusk said later, 'Paradoxically David Cameron became the real victim of his own victory.'

Cameron was still not particularly worried, since at that point the polls were showing a majority for Remain. To strengthen his position he went to Brussels to try to gain new exemptions for Britain, especially concerning immigration, but this time he returned virtually empty-handed. In reality he was asking the EU to renegotiate a whole series of European treaties, purely to help heal internal divisions in the Tory party. Daniel Korski, one of the British negotiators, later described how he and his colleagues barely gained a foothold. After all, there was no reason to make an exception for the British. 'To be honest, we failed to find any evidence of [British] communities under pressure that would satisfy the European Commission,' Korski said of the argument about immigration.

Threatening to leave actually weakened the British position. 'How do you convince a room full of people, when you keep your hand on the door handle?' said Herman Van Rompuy in a speech in London. 'How to encourage a friend to change, if your eyes are searching for your coat?' Furthermore, in February 2016 the European leaders had other things on their minds. The refugee crisis was at its political height; the end of Schengen was in the air. They failed to realize fully, however, being busy with too many other issues, that Cameron's opportunism might have disastrous consequences. Britain, contrary and difficult as it was, remained of immense political, economic and strategic importance to Europe. They sat on their hands and let Cameron stumble on.

A meagre deal was presented with great fanfare, but British voters were disappointed. 'It stinks,' wrote *The Sun*. The referendum was set for 23 June 2016.

5

The Battle for Britain began. The Brexiteers, despite all their demagoguery, faced a difficult task. They needed to unite 'the people' around Brexit, an abstract idea with a mainly negative charge. Yet they succeeded, with an extremely clever campaign, the support of rich financiers – of whom the most important, Arron Banks, had links with both Donald Trump and the Kremlin – and above all because of the fact that the old parties and their ideologies had completely lost their power of conviction and their capacity to unite.

After extensive market research, the Leave campaign entered the fray with the slogan 'Take Back Control'. According to campaign leader Dominic Cummings it was a killer argument that captured everything that had gone wrong over all those years – the influx of migrants, the financial crisis – as well as a dislike of the global elite and big money. After Brexit, British democracy would be triumphant again, sovereignty would be restored and everything that was unique and special about good old England would be cherished. It would be possible to say no to Germany's *Wir schaffen das* and to the bureaucratic power of a nevertheless shaky Brussels. 'There's nothing ignoble in being the first rat to leave a sinking ship,' wrote historian and Brexiteer Andrew Roberts in the *Sunday Times*.

Facts and the truth were no longer relevant. It was suggested that Turkey might become a member of the European Union as early as 2020 and that 5 million Turks were raring to leave for Britain. A video message sent out on social media claimed, 'Every week we send 350 million pounds to Brussels, money that's wasted. That's enough to build a new hospital every week.'

It set the tone. That £350 million could instead go to the ailing National Health Service. Double-decker buses drove all over the country with that promise written on their sides. The fact that most of the £350 million came back to Britain in the form of agricultural subsidies and by a thousand other

routes was conveniently ignored. In reality, the net payment to the EU fluctuated around £90 million, or about £60 per British citizen per year. The
Norwegians were paying more than double that, some €135 per head, just
to get access to the European single market.

The tabloids sang their own song. The British might lose control of their
coasts, it was claimed, if they remained in the EU. Their country would
eventually be forced to merge with France. *The Sun* 'revealed' the existence
of a guide for Polish immigrants describing how to live off state benefits, in
an article headlined 'How to be a Pole on the dole'.

In 1972 and 1994, comparable referendums had been held in Norway:
should we become members of the European Union, or are we better off
going our own way? On both occasions, a small majority (54 per cent and
52 per cent) rejected EU membership. Whatever you think of those referendum results, they were based on a comprehensive and unadulterated
democratic process, with local debates everywhere and a thorough weighing up of all the pros and cons.

How different was the course of events in the United Kingdom in 2016.
None of the Brexiteers ever pointed to possible problems. For them, Brexit
was simply a route to political power. It was never an ideal, not even a
dream. It was pure fantasy, and all the practical details were ignored. A new
trade agreement with the EU would be, in the words of Brexiteer Liam Fox,
'one of the easiest in human history'.

Meanwhile the Remainers were above all defending the status quo –
which many voters now wanted to change. To them, the risks of leaving
seemed enormous: British business would forfeit the largest market in the
world; the freedom to travel and settle in Europe would end; and the British
would find themselves a good deal poorer. Almost half of British trade was
with the EU, after all, and another 12 per cent with countries that had trade
agreements with the EU.

'It is a complete shambles,' declared an angry Terry Sargeant, British
CEO of one of the largest steel companies in the world, ThyssenKrupp, in
2018. He could not see how the German parent company could continue to
do business with the British after Brexit, since its supply lines all depended
on the EU's smooth customs regulations. 'It's not about me. I am 57 and
will retire in a few years. I can retire to Spain. But I am from a working-
class background and it is the working man who is going to be hit

hardest. This is about the future generations. I am passionate that we do what we can to stop the damage, that is why I am speaking out.'

Hardly anyone listened. Among voters, business had lost much of its authority and power of persuasion after the crisis of 2008. Brexiteers seemed unconcerned that nothing lay ready to replace all those EU agreements. The City of London, with a turnover roughly equal to that of the German car industry, might lose its position as the biggest financial centre in the world if there were a hard Brexit. Britain's own automotive industry, with a total of 856,000 jobs and an annual turnover of £82 billion, would be hit extremely hard. Whatever the outcome of the negotiations, farmers would lose their European subsidies, which represented 60 per cent of their income across the board. Economic growth, according to the Bank of England, would give way to recession.

Would the United Kingdom, that ancient federation of England, Scotland, Wales and Northern Ireland, survive? Brexit was primarily an English matter, a typical nationalist dream. There was a fair chance that the Scots would in the long run refuse to go along with it; the Irish too. The Irish Question might loom large again. All these warnings were brushed aside. 'Project Fear,' the Brexiteers scoffed.

In late April 2016 I was in London. There was a thunderstorm, and hail and rain hammered down over Whitehall and the rest of what was once the centre of an empire. I took part in a panel discussion about Brexit that evening. It was a shocking experience: a small room, a lacklustre debate, endless preaching to the converted. The audience was completely anti-Brexit but there was not so much as a spark. Although the polls were looking more and more worrying, it seemed as if the Remain campaign – slogan: 'Stronger In' – was fast asleep. Nobody could imagine that an earthquake was coming. My fellow journalist Misha Glenny was the only person present who let fly, mainly for the sake of the young, since 70 per cent of young people in Britain were in favour of Europe yet were not planning to go out and vote. Many elderly people supported Leave, and they always voted. Glenny announced that after thirty years of not being involved in British politics he intended to crawl from his hole 'full blazing out all my cannons'. 'The world is becoming a huge mess,' he said. 'Very, very dangerous.'

The class-ridden character of the campaign made it typically English.

Important Brexiteers, Boris Johnson first among them, were products of the English elite, man for man. Eton, Oxbridge: they seemed determined to comply with every single one of the preconceived notions about them. At Oxford, Boris Johnson – along with David Cameron and his later rival Jeremy Hunt – had been a member of the infamous Bullingdon Club, a student society founded more than two centuries ago. Born to rule, club members stressed their exclusivity – they once burned a fifty-pound note in front of a tramp – and their privilege. 'I don't think an evening would have ended without a restaurant being trashed and being paid for in full, very often in cash,' Andrew Gimson reported. Johnson and his friends knew they could do anything and smash everything, without ever having to suffer the consequences.

That attitude to life continued to shape their behaviour after their student years. As Brussels correspondent for the *Daily Telegraph* – having been sacked by *The Times* for making up a quote – Johnson was seen as the inventor of the 'Euromyth', a journalistic genre that we would now call 'trolling' or 'fake news'. Journalists who dutifully recorded the progress of the European project looked at Johnson's style with some envy. He turned Brussels into a drama, full of plots and traps set by the French for the solid and politely smiling British. 'Never let the facts get in the way of a good story,' colleagues said. He invented the 'banana police' who checked whether the fruit had the right curve and claimed that coffins would soon have to comply with European norms, that fishermen would henceforth have to wear hairnets and that condoms must be of a standard European format, 'one size fits all', clearly an unacceptable constraint for the better-endowed Brit. '[I] was sort of chucking these rocks over the garden wall,' Johnson explained, 'and I listened to this amazing crash from the greenhouse next door over in England.'

He reinvented Brussels and the EU as absurdist theatre, a hilarious spectacle in the style of Monty Python. His readers lapped it up, other papers began to mimic him and so the image arose in broad circles in England that everything from Brussels was madness, the product of overpaid EU despots who wanted nothing less than to found a European superstate. Irrespective of the truth, his bosses, and indeed Margaret Thatcher, thought it was all magnificent. At last Johnson was able to step from journalism into politics, as had always been his intention. To him, and to others, Brexit was not an ideal but a route to power.

*

From a historical point of view, Brexit resembles the start of the First World War: a political accident with catastrophic consequences. The way the Brexit campaign played out also brings to mind associations with those years, when an astonishing military confrontation developed that made everyone realize a new era had dawned, with a completely new means of fighting a war, involving machine guns, tanks and aircraft. A century later, in 2016, a political war was fought in a completely new way for the first time, making use of all the methods and techniques offered by the new era of information technology.

In 2016, campaigners on both sides of the Atlantic made grateful use of unprecedented data gold mines, with the Brexit campaign serving as an experimental arena for the Trump campaign. In the final days before the referendum, 7 million carefully selected British people were bombarded, mainly via Facebook, with no fewer than 1.5 billion messages. Truth and lies – about that threatening 'wave' of Turkish immigrants, for example – were artfully combined. All that mattered was the effect. Boris Johnson described with relish how 'Eurobureacrats' had now implemented a ban on much-loved prawn cocktail crisps. Everyone could see it was nonsense, since they were readily available in every shop, yet the story was lapped up. In the end, the Leave campaign managed to mobilize 3 million voters who would otherwise not have gone to the polling stations.

As the campaigning went on, the mood grew increasingly grim. A possible Brexit was no longer regarded as a political issue, a matter of opinion with arguments for and against, but as a test of a person's identity. You were either a Leaver or a Remainer, just as you were once either Labour or Tory, Catholic or Protestant. In fact, studies showed that the new dividing line was far more profound even than that between different religions, with a full 87 per cent of British people identifying as Remainers or Leavers. Families were split. Boris Johnson's father and sister, for example, were active Remainers. In the Brexit novel *Middle England* by Jonathan Coe, Brexit crops up as an important factor in the estrangement between a married couple. The wife thinks her 'Brexit' husband isn't open enough, while the husband reproaches his 'Remain' wife for naivety and 'an attitude of moral superiority'. Such marital disputes did indeed occur, as therapists will testify.

The Remain campaign grew stronger, but it was still on the defensive.

Mass demonstrations took place, but not until after the referendum. Particularly telling was an event on the Thames on Wednesday, 15 June 2016. Nigel Farage had mobilized dozens of fishing crews to protest against the EU from the water. Pop star Bob Geldoff organized a counter-protest from a pleasure cruiser, alongside a handful of dinghies and other vessels. Brendan Cox, one of the participants, raced across the Thames towards Farage's flotilla in a boat with his two children, with a big flag reading 'IN' attached to the stern. His wife, Jo Cox, waved to them from the riverside. She had appointments in her north of England constituency, having taken office just one year before as a promising Labour MP, but she was deeply worried: a Remain campaign supported by the government and the elite might not go down at all well with her voters.

The next morning, Brendan Cox received a telephone call. Jo had been shot and stabbed. On the train he heard she was dead. 'This is for Britain,' the killer had shouted. 'Britain first.'

On Friday, 24 June 2016, at 4.39 in the morning UK time, the BBC announced that Britain would be leaving the EU. Almost three-quarters of those eligible had cast their votes, 51.9 per cent were for Leave, 48.1 per cent for Remain. Scotland and Northern Ireland wanted to stay, while England and Wales had chosen to go. A majority of the young and those who lived in big cities were pro-EU. Loyal Tory voters, the elderly and people in the provinces had voted for Brexit, and on this occasion they had received unexpected support from large numbers of the working class who had moved to the right over the preceding decade.

Two television reporter friends of mine were present when the national result was announced in a packed Manchester Town Hall. 'In the UKIP corner a small group started cheering,' they told me later. 'In the rest of the room a deathly silence fell. The reporters, the presenters, the camera crews – everyone was literally struck dumb.' Based on the polls, they'd known Brexit was a real possibility, yet no one had imagined it might actually happen. That morning, in the cafés, the same bewilderment prevailed. Young people were in tears. 'They've stolen our future!'

The Brexiteers themselves were taken completely by surprise. Michael Gove, the secretary of state for justice and a former chief whip – and other than Johnson, the key figure in the Tory Brexit campaign – had gone to sleep calmly assuming that everything would continue as normal. At a quarter to five the phone rang. His wife, Sarah Vine, later described the scene. 'Michael, guess what? We've won!' said the caller. Gove put his glasses on and said, 'Gosh, I suppose I had better get up!' They had the unreal feeling, Vine wrote, that like Alice in *Alice in Wonderland* they had fallen 'through a rabbit hole'.

Nigel Farage was jubilant, although he too could barely believe what was happening. Boris Johnson, half awake, started writing a new speech – he had only a text for defeat. When his former university friend David Cameron appeared in the doorway of 10 Downing Street hand in hand with his wife Samantha, everyone knew what he was about to do: make a speech announcing his departure. Johnson sat in front of the television to watch. According to Brexit chronicler Tim Shipman he was thoroughly upset. 'Oh my God, oh my God, poor Dave. God, look at Samantha. This is terrible.'

The European regulatory machinery started up immediately. Brussels had prepared well. Less than an hour after the result, at six thirty in the morning continental time, Donald Tusk sent a Lines To Take to all EU governments laying out the legal aspects of Article 50, the position of the British in the transition period, and the strategic situation facing the EU in the negotiations. Behind the scenes there was both anger and relief: at last we're free of those eternally exasperating Brits.

Little if any attention was paid to the role in the drama of the European Union itself, or to the fact that so many voters in an important member state no longer saw any benefit in its stumbling project. Beneath all the populist rhetoric, real issues and dilemmas were all too often left slumbering, and that was certainly the case now.

The departure of the British, however sad and damaging, was a direct result of the undemocratic set-up of the European Union and especially the course of events surrounding the Treaty of Lisbon in 2007, as Anthony Barnett, writer and founder of openDemocracy, pointed out. 'Leaving is a mistake and should be reversed, preferably along with changes in the EU itself. But any European democrat, whether a citizen of the EU or not, needs to confront a bigger question: the fundamental legitimacy of the European Union.' Dutch commentator Martin Sommer responded by writing, 'From Brexit we can learn that a lack of space for national peculiarities inflames nationalist feelings. The British only really got into the anti-European mood when immigration increased enormously and Brussels refused to let them do anything about it.' Europe expert Timothy Garton Ash drove the point home: Brexit is a European problem as much as it's a British one. He described it as 'Europe's bad breath', which indicated that something was not right with the body.

In Brussels, however, hardly anyone saw any need for self-examination. The day after the referendum, at lunches on Luxembourg Square, the occasional champagne cork was popped.

The UK government was caught completely off guard. All the instigators of Brexit abruptly dropped off the radar; nobody knew where they were. David Cameron had explicitly forbidden his civil servants to work on a plan B for this eventuality. Only the Bank of England had a Brexit scenario ready – and it needed one. The London Stock Exchange reacted immediately, with share prices falling back that morning by more than 8 per cent, while the pound dropped in value. At a stroke, Britain lost its status as one of the world's five largest economies. The markets grew calmer only after the Bank of England announced it was prepared to inject £250 billion into the economy. By that time the stock market had lost more than £100 billion in value.

Out on the street it was a day of reckoning. The Institute of Race Relations recorded dozens of incidents, ranging from racist stabbings, neo-Nazi stickers and graffiti reading 'Kill a Muslim' or 'EU Rats Go Home Now', to a Swedish mother who was screamed at to 'Go back to Europe'. Many Poles were abused in the street and a few were severely beaten. 'Project Fear?' Remainers snarled. 'This is Project Reality.'

6

In Wigan, everyone watched in amazement. Their constituency had belonged to Labour since 1910. 'This town would vote for a cow if Labour put one up for election,' people used to say. Now no less than 64 per cent of residents had voted for Leave – far more than the national average – and only 36 per cent for Remain. The national exit polls showed that 49 per cent of Leave voters were concerned about the power to decide on all kinds of issues, which they wanted returned to the British. The aftermath of *Wir schaffen das* in 2015 certainly had its effects on British voters, but 'a better grip on immigration' was a decisive argument for only 33 per cent.

Wigan's Brexit voters had been driven above all by a deep, unarticulated sense of despair. Tom Walsh and Chris Ready had taken part in endless discussions in the pub and at family gatherings. They knew the arguments. 'We're voting "Out" to fix the country.' 'Without a Brexit it'll get even worse.' 'No more immigrants.' Many of their acquaintances were attracted by the Brexiteer promise of an additional £350 million a week for the NHS. 'They so badly wanted to believe all that.' Corbyn's half-hearted attitude had a part to play as well; many of his voters assumed that by voting Leave they were giving those Tory 'rich deadbeats' a kick up the arse. Nationwide, a full 40 per cent of Labour supporters voted for Brexit and, importantly, 'everyone thought that would be it, that not much else would change'.

Strikingly, although Paisley in Scotland was a former mining town like Wigan, with the same problems and the same kind of poverty, the figures there were precisely the reverse. A large majority, 64 per cent, voted for Remain like the rest of Scotland, and 36 per cent for Leave. It may have had something to do with the Scottish nationalists, who spoke unambiguously in favour of Europe, but perhaps the main reason was political distance. To voters in Paisley, the Scottish parliament in Edinburgh was their own, and close by, whereas for people in Wigan in north-west England, London and Westminster were far away. They'd had it with politics in general, and not without reason.

Like many comparable towns, Wigan had its own Coronation Street. I'd been to see it on a previous occasion. For many years the black smoke of the mills had hung over it, but now there were two rows of neat and austere houses, with the occasional car proudly parked outside. The programme *Who Wants to Be a Millionaire?* was hugely popular in such neighbourhoods, which made me think back to what a British acquaintance had told me. As in many such television quizzes, participants could choose at various points whether they wanted to carry on with more difficult questions or take their winnings. 'In recent years something remarkable happened,' I was told. 'More and more competitors chose not to gamble. They stopped as soon as they had two or three thousand pounds. To them that was an unthinkable amount of money, so they already felt like millionaires. Many people now are really very poor.'

Shortly after the referendum, the *New York Times* interviewed a resident of the neighbourhood – Colin Hewlett, a former refuse collector who earned a living at Heinz. He was a proud Labour voter, just like his father. Nevertheless he had voted for Brexit. 'I don't think a lot will change,' he said. 'But we have to give it a chance.' He was sixty-one. For the interview he sat next to his wife, who had Alzheimer's disease, in a room full of photos of their six children and fourteen grandchildren. His secure employment contract had morphed into a zero-hours contract, and in just three years his weekly wage had halved, from £590 to £300. 'Gone to the dogs' was how he described his life.

Was his decision to back Brexit prompted by his income alone? No, it was at least as much about his self-respect, his identity, the values that were even more important to him than those few pounds in his pocket – things all those number-crunchers had no idea about. This explains why some of the population groups that were most vulnerable to the consequences of Brexit voted 'Out'. The farmers, for example, who stood to lose large subsidies, and residents of Wales and areas like Yorkshire and the Humber, or those in the north-east of England, where more than half of everything the region produced was exported to the EU. Colin Hewlett too was motivated by those abstract values, despite the fact that Wigan's economy relied to a large extent on exports from the huge soup factory where he worked.

The connection between the public agenda and each individual's personal worries, which lies at the core of the democratic process, seemed all too often to have been broken. Sociologist Zygmunt Bauman wrote about mental worlds revolving independently of each other, utterly isolated, set in motion by all kinds of mutually unconnected mechanisms: 'It is a situation in which people who have been hit don't know what has hit them – and have little chance of ever finding out.'

Had I not come upon this all over Western Europe in the past twenty years? And a traditional politics that refused to confront the real issues? Just look at the YouTube clip of Beppe Grillo at the wheel of a car on the motorway, asking himself why the Italians are so quiet: 'Because there's something that has spoken instead of millions of Italians. That something is the markets. The financial markets. The Italians are quiet and they're sad because they realize that they no longer have any say. The markets speak for them.

And who are they, the markets? I'd like to get to know them. Hello market, my name is Beppe Grillo, and you? What's your name?'

Or read *Who Killed My Father*, a book by French sociologist and writer Édouard Louis about the fate of his father, a worker in Picardy who became disabled after an accident, lost his state benefits because of austerity and had to take the most menial jobs to get by. Sarkozy 'broke your back', Louis writes to his father, forced to become a refuse collector. François Hollande 'asphyxiated you' with reforms to the jobs market, and his liberal successor Emmanuel Macron took 'the bread out of your mouth' when he cut housing subsidies.

Or listen to Didier Eribon, who as early as 2009, in *Returning to Reims*, called attention to the same schism – to the high-spirited, cosmopolitan worldview of a large proportion of the mainly urban elite, which no longer chimes in any way with the life and economic reality of the majority of the population. In 2017 he went to take a fresh look at Reims. The ugly factory where his mother slogged away for fifteen years was still standing. He told an interviewer: 'When my mother worked there she had seventeen hundred fellow workers, five hundred of whom were members of the CGT, the communist union that regularly organized strikes. The factory was a bastion of the Reims working class.'

Now the factory building was empty and dilapidated, with posters of Marine Le Pen on every wall. That year Le Pen almost won the presidential election, garnering more than 10 million votes. And the children and grandchildren of all those workers, where were they now? Probably unemployed, said Eribon. 'Or they're at the checkouts of the big supermarkets, in call centres or delivering food for Deliveroo – poorly paid and insecure work.'

Or take the real story behind all those picturesque French villages. In 1955, a third of the French population still worked in agriculture; in 2017, only 3 per cent. The big grape growers and grain producers were doing just fine while the small farmers lived in poverty, a third of them earning less than €350 per month, a fifth making a loss, all having to manage by taking jobs on the side. These were lives that were largely 'out of control', and in such a situation the urge to 'take back control', by whatever means, was hard to resist.

The main reason for the mass protests by French *gilets jaunes* (yellow

vests), who in the winter of 2018–19 occupied traffic junctions and rounda-
bouts for months, is telling: a tax increase, to finance Macron's ambitious
climate promises, of 7.6 euro cents per litre on diesel and 3.8 euro cents
per litre on petrol. For many French people, who needed to drive to their
low-paid jobs, that was simply too much – a measure of how poor they
were.

Three-quarters of the *gilets jaunes* were older than thirty-five. They were
mostly self-employed or labourers, and now that new taxes had been
announced they felt everything shaking and shifting beneath them. Their
slogan was above all 'No'. No to Macron, no to Europe, no to everything.

That spiritual malaise was in evidence everywhere in the peripheral areas
of Western Europe in the second decade of the century, from Wigan and
Reims to the towns and villages of the former GDR. In Germany the term
Wutbürger (angry citizen) was heard more and more often. According to the
'trust barometer' of research company OpinionWay, nine out of ten French
people believed politicians weren't at all troubled by the concerns of ordinary folk; three-quarters regarded politicians in general as corrupt; and a
third no longer believed in elections, having written off all hope of improve-
ment. An old friend of mine wrote to me from the south of France, 'The *jeu
de boules* has turned into a political café. What fury behind those
moustaches!'

One afternoon in 2017, I had to wait for a while on a town square in
Wallonia, the French-speaking region of Belgium. I looked at how people
dressed, their postures, their rotting teeth: so much poverty. And that wasn't
all. There was deep despondency in the air, too many shop windows were
empty, the whole district was full of half-finished projects, of defunct
industry. The children had nineteenth-century faces.

In the 1970s, sociologist Kai Erikson described the phenomenon of 'collective trauma'. He was referring to events such as the closure of a mine, a
major reorganization, or the depopulation of a rural area, which meant a
complete break with all the human relationships and routines that have
shaped lives in that place for generations. People go into a state of 'social
shock', Erikson wrote. Not only their work but their entire social life is
abruptly swept away.

In Jonathan Coe's *Middle England*, the central character takes his father one last time to the car factory where he used to work. He is astonished and shaken. There's now a giant shopping centre, and where the old assembly line used to be is a huge Marks and Spencer, full of 'pre-packaged salads, cooked meats and imported wines'. The father becomes completely confused, saying, 'How can you replace a factory with shops? If there's no factory, how are people supposed to make the money to spend in the shops?' And: 'I mean, a building isn't just a place, is it? It's the people. The people who were inside it.'

Many peripheral areas of Western Europe have experienced a similar cultural trauma in recent decades, caused by the closure of mines and factories, the restructuring of businesses, the depopulation of rural areas, austerity and mass unemployment. Apart from all their economic and material consequences, such events represented a profound break with all the old relationships and traditions within which people felt safe. Work gave them status, while unions, political parties and the church brought them structure and conviviality; as a worker you had your own football club, brass band or drama society.

Who can still recall the songs of the workers' movement? 'You won't get me I'm part of the union.' 'We'll keep the red flag flying here.' '*Avanti popolo, alla riscossa. Bandiera rossa, bandiera rossa . . .*' All those intimate connections, all those social anchors: when they were gone it could be hard to give meaning to life and many people felt totally disorientated, cut adrift from everything.

It was one of the psychological effects of neoliberalism. Amid all those market forces, a human life was small and futile. The resulting feelings could often be summed up in a few words: 'Let's go home. Back to the good old days.' Any leader promising to take voters home was listened to. But that home no longer existed.

7

In London, after a brief power struggle at the top of the Conservative Party, the dutiful and obstinate home secretary Theresa May was appointed prime minister. Behind her stalwart exterior was a woman divorced from reality. 'She's so removed from the world her colleagues live in,' one of her aides said to Tim Shipman. Less than a year after she took office, Grenfell Tower, a cheaply built and poorly maintained tower block right next to one of the richest neighbourhoods in West London, burned down, a gruesome symbol of ever-increasing inequality. At least seventy-two people were killed. When May visited the scene, she could not bring herself to speak to the residents.

May was a Remainer at heart, but now she behaved like an overzealous convert. In the weeks after the referendum she could have concentrated on creating room for reconciliation and for a national debate about the meaning of the Brexiteers' narrow victory. She could have guided the country towards the Norwegian option, for example, by exploring the well-functioning collaboration between the EU and Norway, Iceland, Switzerland and Liechtenstein. Instead she stoked up further division by adopting the slogan 'Brexit means Brexit' and by drawing red lines: the free movement of people must be curbed, British participation in the customs union must end, and Britain must no longer fall under the jurisdiction of the European Court of Justice. What if the EU did not accept this? 'No deal is better than a bad deal.'

May's best diplomat in Brussels, Ivan Rogers, resigned. He had tried in vain to explain to her how the EU worked, and why for the EU one thing was even more important than good relations with Britain: its own internal cohesion. No exceptions could be made where that was concerned. But in May's view, Rogers was too pessimistic, a fatalist.

Brexiteers Boris Johnson and David Davis – neither of whom had any diplomatic experience – were now put in charge of the negotiations. Johnson set the tone immediately by likening the French president, who argued the EU must take a hard-line approach, to a German concentration camp guard. Davis allowed himself to be photographed in those early weeks relaxing on the empty side of the negotiating table, while the EU delegation, led by shrewd negotiator Michel Barnier, sat opposite him, behind stacks of files. The mornings on which negotiations took place never lasted long. Davis laughed off many of the problems and by lunchtime he was on the Eurostar heading back to London.

It became increasingly clear in the spring of 2017 that Brexit in 2019 would be a hard Brexit, perhaps even a crash-out Brexit. Everyone in Brussels knew what the appointment of Barnier meant. The former French foreign minister and European commissioner was known as an impassive and tough negotiator; extremely experienced, brilliant and relentless. The British were to be driven into a corner of the playground and beaten up so badly that no one would ever dare to damage the Union again – more or less as had happened to the Greeks in the case of the euro.

The British defence, on the other hand, was weak and chaotic. Frans Timmermans, first vice president of the Commission, later told the BBC that everyone in Brussels assumed the British ultimately had a firm plan at the ready: 'That in some vault somewhere in Westminster there will be a Harry Potter-like book with all the tricks and all the things in it to do.' But when he saw Davis not negotiating, just grandstanding, he realized, 'Oh my God, they haven't got a plan, they haven't got a plan.' He was astonished. After all, without a plan there was nothing left for British politicians and diplomats to do, as time went on, other than panic.

Most Britons still seemed unaware of the situation they were in. Boris Johnson and the other advocates of Brexit continued to insist they could retain access to the European single market, and Brexit would therefore bring only benefits: 'We can have the cake, and eat it!' President of the European Council Donald Tusk made a suggestion. 'To all who believe in it, I propose a simple experiment. Buy a cake, eat it, and see if it is still there on the plate.'

On the afternoon of Wednesday, 29 March 2017, the British ambassador handed to Donald Tusk, who wore a forced smile, the letter from 10 Downing Street that set the divorce proceedings in motion. 'We are leaving the European Union, but we are not leaving Europe.'

Thus the United Kingdom, bolstered by personal ambition, party politics and delusions of grandeur, marched undaunted towards chaos.

13. Alone

2017

IT HAD BEEN A SUNNY summer. Up to that point 2016 was the hottest year since records began. Of the warmest seventeen years, sixteen had been in the new century. The temperature in the city of Berlin was 1.5 degrees above normal across the year as a whole, in Amsterdam 1.8, in Rome 2.2 and in Istanbul a full 3 degrees. The trend was unmistakable.

In Europe, crises were now following each other at a feverish pace. The great refugee crisis of 2015 and early 2016 had only just started to ease and now the EU was convulsed by its historic break with Britain. No member state had ever left the Union before. Was it a portent?

France was tired. In 1999 I'd had the feeling that, in every respect, the country was twenty years ahead. In the Paris region a transport system was in place that was far more advanced than anything in London, Berlin or Amsterdam. Spectacular building work was going on, healthcare and the motorways were of unprecedented quality, and ever since the 1980s all French telephone connections had a primitive forerunner of the internet, called Minitel.

By 2016 that indomitable élan had gone. In Paris and other big French cities, soldiers and police officers stood on every street corner looking like RoboCops, decked out in all the armour and weaponry of the twenty-first century. Since January 2015, after the attacks on *Charlie Hebdo* and a kosher supermarket, a state of siege had weighed on public life everywhere. On the evening of 13 November 2015, Paris was again hit by a coordinated series of terror attacks, this time on popular cafés and restaurants. Forty people were killed. At the same time, visitors to a pop concert at the Bataclan theatre were fired upon, leaving 90 dead and more than 350 wounded.

Brussels too, from the spring of 2016 onwards, looked like a besieged fort. On the morning of 22 March three suicide terrorists attacked Zaventem airport and a metro station, killing 32 people and wounding another 340.

Less than four months later, in Nice, on the evening of Thursday 14 July, after the traditional Bastille Day fireworks display ended, a terrorist driving a hijacked truck ploughed through a crowd on the Promenade des Anglais. No fewer than 86 revellers were crushed to death and 434 were injured. A chain reaction of further attacks followed. On Friday 22 July, a man shot nine people dead in a shopping centre in Munich. A few days later, two men ran into the village church of Saint-Étienne-du-Rouvray and cut the throat of the eighty-five-year-old priest, who was celebrating mass. He died with the words *Vade retro, Satan* on his lips: 'Go back, Satan.'

That same month, on 13 July, the new British government of Theresa May took power. It staked everything on a hard Brexit. Some EU countries and large companies began cautiously developing emergency plans for a possible no-deal departure. Two days later, on 15 July, elements of the Turkish army staged an attempted coup. In Ankara, tanks drove through the streets and there was fierce fighting that night on the bridges of Istanbul. President Erdoğan narrowly escaped assassination. The coup failed; both the planning and the execution were amateurish, and after Erdoğan called for a mass popular uprising it was soon over. The next morning the counting of victims began: 173 civilians and more than 200 military personnel had been killed. The nation was traumatized.

According to Erdoğan the influential spiritual leader Fethullah Gülen, who had been living in the United States since 1999, was the brains behind it all. Gülen denied any involvement. There was brief national unity, with both left and right condemning the coup attempt, but then Erdoğan and his Justice and Development Party, the AKP, began widespread purges. Within a year, 150,000 alleged Gülenists lost their jobs, some 50,000 were arrested, more than 150 newspapers and radio and television stations were closed, and around 150 journalists were jailed. Relations with the EU reached an all-time low: it wanted nothing further to do with this police state, while Erdoğan reproached the EU for a lack of solidarity in dark times.

It was shock upon shock. Former EU president Herman Van Rompuy spoke in late summer of a 'polycrisis': 'So much happening in so short a time, it's very destabilizing.' He believed Europe was in an even worse state now than during the euro crisis and the migrant crisis. The effect on us, as observers, was rather different. We were beginning, inevitably, to find the abnormal normal.

2

On the other side of the Atlantic Ocean that summer, startling developments were taking place. In the presidential campaign there were now just two candidates, the Democrat Hillary Clinton, former secretary of state as well as wife of the former president Bill Clinton, and the real estate dealer and ringmaster Donald Trump, who had won the Republican nomination despite his total lack of experience at governing, or indeed interest in it.

That victory had caused a fair degree of surprise. Commentators predicted that if Trump lost, an acute crisis would break out within the Republican Party. The *New York Review of Books* published an essay in which the Republicans were advised to do some serious soul-searching after the election. How in heaven's name could a figure like Trump have got so close to the presidency?

Hillary Clinton, despite her immense capacities, was also a controversial choice. A strong working-class culture existed within what the Americans call the middle class, including a considerable trade union tradition. It was an attitude to life represented during the primaries by Bernie Sanders, Clinton's main rival for the nomination. The Democrat establishment in Washington, however, dismissed Sanders as a 'socialist' (for which read 'fool'). The Democrats had no time for the feelings of the middle class, their traditional voters, let alone for the fact that a rebellion had been brewing within it for years.

Yet the signs were abundantly clear. Since Barack Obama took office in 2009, election results had been worse for the Democrats than ever before. At state level they had lost more than 900 seats and 12 governorships; in the House of Representatives and in the Senate they had lost 69 and 13 seats respectively. Yet in 2016 the party put forward a candidate who was promising more of the same, who was generally regarded as a central figure within the Washington in-crowd and who opposed Trump's simple 'America First' slogan with the unspoken 'Now it's my turn!'

Even before her nomination, Hillary Clinton was at about the same level in all the polls as Donald Trump. According to the CBS News/New York Times poll of May 2016, 64 per cent of voters thought she was neither honest nor trustworthy. One telling incident was described by a member of Obama's staff. To support Clinton, the president had gone with her to a campaign meeting in a large barbecue tent somewhere in North Carolina. After barely five minutes she ran away, to Obama's great concern. In an interview in NRC Handelsblad, Ben Rhodes quoted Obama as saying, 'You need to be in a barbecue tent like that, where they hate you because they only know you from Fox News, because they think you're the antichrist. Those are exactly the people you need to talk to.' And Clinton didn't. In a major slip, she even called hostile voters a 'basket of deplorables'. With that, she sealed her fate.

Donald Trump capitalized adroitly. With his shows and his grubby insinuations about Clinton – he even commented on her toilet visits – he managed to build an uncommonly stable and faithful following. Later he would admit to Bill Clinton that he didn't mean to be so nasty to his wife, it was just that people were incredibly angry and he'd had to make sure that anger didn't get aimed at him. A compromising bit of video turned up in which he bragged about picking up women. 'Just grab them by the pussy.' Any other candidate would have been in big trouble with a remark like that, but for Trump's followers it was a recommendation: 'Look, he's one of us.' Flemish journalist Rudi Rotthier, travelling around America in 2016, found people everywhere 'who felt the simple desire come over them to be duped by someone else for a change'.

Trump was an extraordinary candidate in every respect. From May 2016 onwards Chris Christie, governor of New Jersey, led the transition team that would organize Trump's takeover of power, should he be elected president that November. In the final round both the remaining presidential candidates are obliged to get a team working on the transition, a huge operation with dozens of ministerial posts and hundreds of other vacancies to be filled, and thousands of people to screen. Continual consultation with the sitting president is needed to make the transition as smooth as possible, and given Trump's complete lack of experience such a team was more necessary than ever. Eventually Christie had more than a hundred people working for him. He consulted weekly with an 'executive committee', which mainly consisted of Trump's close family: two of his sons, his daughter Ivanka and his son-in-law.

Remarkably, Trump himself was not the least bit interested. In late August, Christie said later, the candidate could barely be prevented from dismissing the entire team because it was costing too much. 'Shut it down. Shut down the transition.' He didn't want to think about actually governing at all; for him it was all about the show and the Trump name.

Trump's campaign was a glaring manifestation of a radicalization that had been going on for quite some time in conservative circles. It marked the end of a Republican strategy deployed over the years, against the tide, for gaining and keeping power. The average American voter no longer lived in a rural area, was no longer white – in other words, no longer belonged to the traditional Republican electorate. That trend was accelerating. Yet the Republicans had managed to reinforce and retain their positions of power by continually fiddling with electoral boundary delimitation, by using judicial appointments and new forms of political financing, and by playing upon the same feelings of discomfort and dissatisfaction as were brewing in Europe. In the words of American historian Andrew Bacevich, 'Trump did not create the conditions in which the campaign of 2016 was to take place. Instead, to a far greater extent that any of his political rivals, he demonstrated a knack for translating those conditions into votes.'

Six years earlier, in 2010, I took a long trip through what's known as 'fly-over country', the unseen America of dirt-poor families. Not New York this time but Marshall, Minnesota. Not Yosemite but the potato fields of Maine. John Steinbeck did the same in 1960 and I followed his route. In the diners and McDonald's restaurants along the way I spoke to farmers, housewives, drivers, to all and sundry. Again and again I heard the same stories about how in the 1960s they lived frugally but had jobs, and security, and were full of hope that things would get better and better for them and their children. A half-century later all that had gone into reverse. These were years of despair, of confusion about an American dream that had promised so much and seemed to be delivering so little.

I recall arriving one November evening in the little town of Paducah in northern Texas, just south of the Panhandle. It was deathly quiet. Between the old brick houses were lawns and bare patches of ground – all that was left of the buildings that once stood there. The town square was dominated by a huge stone-faced courthouse, and around it was a variety of shops: a bookstore, a hardware store, a florist's, a pharmacy – a lively aggregate. But everything looked rusty and as if it could do with a fresh coat of paint, and most of the doors and windows were boarded shut. A light was on in just one of the buildings, on a corner. The local newspaper was somehow still going, the *Paducah Post*.

The owner, Jimmye Taylor, also acted as editor-in-chief and was the only member of staff. Circulation had fallen from 20,000 to 1,400. Jimmye was born in 1937 into a poor farming family. Her parents adored Roosevelt, she said, who had got them through the crisis. 'Now we know he was halfway to being a socialist.' Everyone in the little town voted Republican these days, she told me, but 'we don't trust anyone any more, not even our own members of Congress. We're all poor people, and poor people depend on really concrete things. If those fail to materialize, they become fearful and insecure.'

Jimmye Taylor was still proud of her paper, her town, her Texas and her country. But there was barely any connection left between her self-image as an American and the reality she saw around her.

The devastation of Wigan, Reims, Paducah: this too is globalization.

Once more I'm envious of my student of 2069. I often have a brief conversation with her and I notice that I want to know everything she knows, facts and connections that will probably be common knowledge in a couple of decades from now but of which at this point I only have a handful of jigsaw pieces. That's particularly true of the puzzling phenomenon that is Donald Trump.

Trump would later describe himself as 'the most transparent president' in American history. The opposite was the case. Anyone looking into Trump's past almost immediately came upon mystifications. There were large and inexplicable transactions, shady sources of money, and a great many instances of deception and trickery. His academic record, his health files, his relationships with various women, his family history, his financial situation: a fog of secrecy enveloped it all. He was eager to hide three dossiers in particular, at any cost: his tax returns, which in contravention of the

American tradition he refused to make public; his relationship with (yes, them again) Deutsche Bank; and his business and political links with Vladimir Putin's Russia. When in 2017 he heard that a special prosecutor was to be appointed to look into the Russia connection, he flopped back in his chair and said, according to a later report by Robert Mueller, the prosecutor appointed, 'Oh my God. This is terrible. This is the end of my presidency. I'm fucked.' That grim fear of disclosure was well founded. All three dossiers were dynamite under the carefully constructed palace of lies he'd been building all those years. They were also three keys to further research.

First, his tax returns. Out of his rise as a real estate mogul, Donald Trump, in his eternal narcissism, had constructed an image of himself as the most successful businessman in America. He bought shopping malls, hotels, a football team and the Mar-a-Lago resort in Florida. He opened Trump Tower in New York, *Forbes* magazine put him on its list of the 400 richest Americans, and later he would always claim that he made all his money himself, starting at the bottom.

In 1987 his guide to success in business was published, entitled *The Art of the Deal*. In reality the book was written by a hired writer, Tony Schwartz, but for his followers it became a political bible. The broad American audience came to regard him as a master wheeler-dealer, setting an example to others who have worldly ambition.

That effect was further reinforced by the television series he presented from 2004 onwards, *The Apprentice*, a reality show in which candidates competed for a job with business genius Donald Trump, and which for the losers always ended with the cry 'You're fired!' It was all a sham. The team knew perfectly well that the plutocrat Trump was a fake. 'We walked through the offices and saw chipped furniture,' one of the producers later told the *New Yorker*. 'We saw a crumbling empire at every turn. Our job was to make it seem otherwise.'

In reality, as was clear from the few tax returns the *New York Times* eventually hauled to the surface, Trump's success was based purely on loans and continual fresh injections of cash, to the tune of hundreds of millions, from his immensely rich father. Hardly ever did any of Trump's own 'golden deals' make a profit. In fact, between 1985 and 1995, the years in which he dazzled Americans with *The Art of the Deal*, his losses on real estate reached a total of $1.2 billion. Some years later, Trump suddenly had hundreds of millions to his name once more. Those millions were not made from real golden deals, however, but purely from Trump's fame as a 'dealmaker'. With *The Apprentice* he earned, according to his tax returns, $197 million, but with the fame and licensing deals the series brought him he made another $230 million. Having started out as a trader in real estate, Trump had become a brand. In the years that followed he successfully exploited that brand all over the world, but he continually needed to keep it alive with stunts and shows. When the Trump brand began to decline, a shot at the American presidency was an obvious next step.

Then the second dossier: Deutsche Bank. From the end of the 1990s onwards, Trump's empire was mainly based on an extremely risky symbiosis with that high-profile German institution. After a dark wartime past, Deutsche Bank restricted its activities to its home market for decades, but in the 1990s it decided to spread its wings. To make an international reputation for itself quickly, a bank has to do one thing: namely, take bigger risks than all other banks, with clients that provide the necessary dazzle and publicity.

That was how Donald Trump and Deutsche Bank found each other. By about 1998 Trump's reputation had reached rock bottom; no American bank would touch him. Deutsche Bank, just starting out in the American market, lent him hundreds of millions of dollars for his real estate projects, time and again – more than $2 billion in total. There are indications that those millions mostly came from Russia, and indeed Deutsche Bank was later involved in a huge Russian money-laundering scandal. Investigative journalists such as Craig Unger revealed connections between Trump and the shell companies set up abroad in the late 1980s by the KGB, and the tens of millions in Russian money that needed to be reinvested by that route. In 2008 Trump's son Eric referred to them: 'We see a lot of money pouring in from Russia.'

Which brings us to the third dossier: Russia. As early as August 2016, an open letter appeared in the American press from fifty senior Republican

Party national security officials, warning against Donald Trump as a security risk. 'Mr. Trump lacks the character, values, and experience to be President,' they wrote. If elected, he 'would put at risk our country's national security and well-being'. The signatories, who included top national security and foreign policy advisers to the George W. Bush administration, predicted that he 'would be the most reckless President in American history'.

During the election campaign, Trump's behaviour towards the Kremlin was remarkable. He openly called on Russia to make public the emails it had stolen from his Democrat rival Hillary Clinton, for example, an appeal to which the Russian hackers responded within hours. The former British MI6 expert Christopher Steele wrote, in the much-debated Steele dossier from 2016, that the KGB had been interested in Trump ever since the 1980s, and suggested that Trump was susceptible to blackmail as a result of a no-holds-barred visit by two prostitutes to the presidential suite at the Ritz-Carlton Hotel in Moscow, during the Miss Universe contest in 2013.

The Mueller report later described in detail how eight members of Trump's campaign staff worked closely with a handful of representatives of the Kremlin before and after the 2016 presidential election. They expected to 'benefit electorally from information stolen and released through Russian efforts'. The Senate intelligence committee also concluded – the report by both Democrats and Republicans fills almost a thousand pages – that Russian influence, reaching at least 125 million voters, was far more extensive than initially assumed. Trump's campaign created and maintained close links with Russian functionaries, the team provided the Russians with the data they needed to be able to help, and they precisely coordinated the release of damaging material from the Russians about Hillary Clinton. In short, there was probably a firm relationship of dependence between the future president of the United States and the Kremlin, although at the time of writing it is still too early to reach a comprehensive conclusion.

To be fair, when it comes to the manipulation and influencing of voters, the West had plenty of experience to draw upon. In 1996, for example, all available means were deployed to determine the outcome of the Russian election. On no account must the communists be allowed to get back into power. Under pressure from America, the IMF supported the Russian economy to the tune of $10.6 billion, while the Americans themselves forked out $24 billion. Whatever it took, Boris Yeltsin must not lose. Elsewhere too, Western intelligence agencies, especially the CIA, put up a fight – first mainly in South and Central America, and later in Serbia, Georgia and Ukraine.

The FSB, formerly the KGB, was an experienced opponent. In the Soviet years it had a special department for 'active measures'. Putin's Russia continued that tradition, but with all the technology of the twenty-first century. As we have seen, the Brexiteers in 2016, for example, had ties to Moscow through their financier Arron Banks, as did the Italian populist leaders. Up-and-coming Dutch populist Thierry Baudet increasingly attracted the attention of Western intelligence agencies for his eye-catching links with representatives of the Kremlin, his efforts to block the EU's Association Agreement with Ukraine and his consistent support for Russian standpoints. The same went for the party led by Marine Le Pen, which during the 2017 French presidential election campaign received a loan of €9.4 million from a Russian bank on extremely easy terms, while her opponent, Emmanuel Macron, had to fend off some 4,000 attacks almost certainly by Russian hackers.

Russia's influence was goal-oriented only to a limited degree. Its main purpose was to create chaos and sow doubt. The amateurishness of much of this Russian activity, often carried out by autonomous units hired for the purpose, was striking. According to political analyst Vladimir Frolov, the 'partisans' produced 'sloppy work that was laughed at by experts in Russia with knowledge of espionage'. In American intelligence circles too, there was surprise. One might be forgiven for thinking the Russians wanted to get caught. 'They were unusually loud in their intrusions,' said former FBI director James Comey later, in a congressional hearing. 'It was almost as if they didn't care if we knew.'

Perhaps that was indeed precisely the intention. Whether it was a matter of the EU, the United States or other Western countries, chaos made them weak. Cyberattacks would probably not change the results of elections, but they caused a general uncertainty and thereby damaged the legitimacy of a newly elected president or government – and with it, the stability and strength of Russia's opponents.

3

Early in the morning of Wednesday, 9 November 2016, we Europeans were again woken by a ballot-box result that hardly anyone had expected and that was to have historic consequences. Even 'safe' Democrat states turned out to have voted for Trump, and one by one they tumbled. It was still dark and we sat up in bed to watch. 'Goodness gracious,' we whispered to one another. On the screen, the American voting map had turned almost completely red, the colour of the Republicans. We held our breath. Trump hadn't won, Clinton had lost – that was the essence of what had happened. She was in a hotel, watching the results. 'It was as if the air had been sucked out of the room,' she wrote later.

Trump talked of a 'historic landslide'. In reality, after the count was over, his victory was extremely slim. If 79,000 voters in three states had made a different choice, Hillary Clinton would have been in the White House; she actually got 3 million more votes than Trump. But on that November morning we saw an astounded Donald Trump walk down the steps of the great hall of his New York palace, his wife Melania in his wake – white as a sheet; was this ever something she'd wanted? – along with his ten-year-old son Barron, drunk with sleep, and the rest of the family. He clearly hadn't prepared a victory speech and just improvised something.

Chris Christie, the man who had prepared the entire transition, was sitting next to Trump as the result gradually became clear. The atmosphere was oppressive. Trump sat in silence, staring obsessively at the television. Don Jr later told a friend that he looked 'as if he'd seen a ghost'. Whatever might have driven Trump – the kick of all those rallies, the international positioning of the Trump trademark, revenge against the New York elite that had always poked fun at him – this had surely never been the intention. Trump's close adviser Steve Bannon said, 'Hillary Clinton spent her entire adult life getting ready for this moment. Trump hasn't spent a second getting ready for this moment.'

Two days later, Christie reported to Trump Tower with the results of six months of hard and thorough work, a transition plan in thirty folders containing the design of an entire federal government, tailored to fit Trump and his Republican supporters. To his astonishment he came upon Michael

Flynn in the small circle of the executive committee. Flynn was a retired general with a bad reputation because of his close contacts with Russia – indeed the security people in the transition team had issued serious warnings about him – and now there he was, as the new national security adviser, one of the most important jobs in the vast American security apparatus. There were several striking appointments of this kind. ExxonMobil CEO Rex Tillerson, for example, leader of the lobby against the Paris Agreement on climate change, became the new secretary of state.

Steve Bannon took Christie aside. The way it had always gone on the set of The Apprentice was how it went now in the White House. He was sacked on the spot. 'You have no position of any kind in the transition, and we do not want you to be in the building anymore.' All thirty folders, the product of laborious work by him and his 140-strong staff, were dumped. Meanwhile, hundreds of public servants were waiting in the various departments, waiting to hand over to the new staff appointed by the Trump administration. No one showed up, not even in the weeks and sometimes months that followed. In the power centre of the Western world, no new government had taken office. Instead, there was a gigantic vacuum.

Nobody welcomes messages that turn an entire worldview upside down. The polls that had been so wide of the mark were sneered at. The national polls were correct, however, all those months: Trump at around 46 per cent, Clinton at around 48 per cent, reflecting a neck-and-neck race whose result was uncertain because of the complexity of the American voting system. But somehow or other, most observers, myself included, did not want to face up to that uncertainty. It was the same as with Brexit: despite all the calculations of probability, we simply could not imagine such an outcome. We knew that underneath that enchanting, bountiful, dynamic America lay an aggressive, racist and inward-looking America, but all too often we refused to face the fact. Now it was that America, in this world, that would predominate.

I had never before seen people burst into tears purely because of an election result. I did now. It happened everywhere around me, even behind the scenes of news broadcasts. When the outcome became clear, presenters turned pale. At Harvard, where climate research had been a priority for years, professors stood weeping in the lecture halls on the morning after the result.

Bikers for Trump offered to protect the new president during the inauguration. Trump embraced them in a grateful tweet. 'Hail Trump!' cried the American neo-Nazis. 'Hail the people!' The writer Philip Roth spoke of an innate American rage and the 'terror of the unforeseen'.

Obama set off on his farewell tour of Europe. According to security adviser Ben Rhodes, Angela Merkel had a tear in her eye when she took her leave of him on 17 November in Berlin. She told him she regarded it as her duty to stand for election for a fourth term, purely because of Trump. 'She's all alone,' Rhodes quotes Obama as saying at the time.

In those years, a television series about the American presidency was enjoying unprecedented popularity. President Frank Underwood and his wife made a diabolical couple, both of them literally stepping over dead bodies to achieve and secure top positions. Night after night we watched House of Cards breathless, engaging in long discussions about the veracity of the series. Wasn't this a bit over the top? Could a politician ever make it that far with so many lies and deceptions in his past? Wouldn't he have been brought down along the way by all the opposing forces that operate in an even partially functioning democracy? Underwood took viewers deliciously into his confidence now and again in an aside: 'Democracy is so overrated.'

What we saw in the final months of 2016 seemed like an impressive sequel to that series. The new central character was a brilliant invention, a complete outsider who saw himself as a divine genius and liked to spend the nocturnal hours in bed with candy bars and cheeseburgers, tweeting about anything that came into his head – in the company of television show Fox & Friends, of course. That alone was a splendid device. The president kept calling the presenters, so the programme worked like an echo chamber in which he continually saw himself and his supernatural talents confirmed.

Who can have forgotten the hilarious episode about Thanksgiving Day, when in his speech he thanked God for himself and for the difference his arrival had made to his country? Or how he dictated his own health certificate to his personal physician, a powerful statement about 'the healthiest individual ever elected to the presidency'? Or how, at least according to a sacked member of staff, he initially did not want to take his oath of office on the Bible but on his own book, The Art of the Deal, which he described as the 'best business book of all time'? Or how he announced in a tweet that his 'nuclear button' was far bigger than that of North Korean leader Kim Jong-un? And every evening a fairy tale before bedtime: after a hundred days of Trump, the fact-checking team at the *Washington Post* had counted 492 misleading presidential statements or downright lies – almost five per day.

The first episode of this real-life TV show, covering his inauguration, established the mood from the outset. First you saw the departing presidential couple, smiling and courteous, receiving the new president and his wife to hand the White House over to them formally. The new president, eager as a child, raced up the steps, forgetting his wife. After a bit of fumbling with an outsized gift, both couples went inside. Behind closed doors a confidential conversation ensued between the arriving and departing presidents, then the two couples appeared again at the door.

I watched that footage a second time. It was, after all, a historic moment. The new president stood there enjoying it all, his wife behind him, off to one side. Later he said something to her and you could see her tense up, a mask sliding over her face as if she'd just been given a hefty kick to the stomach. And look at the face of the departing first lady, now that she was outside again. It was taut and defeated. She got through the ceremonies with dignity, but she was clearly deeply shocked at what had taken place inside.

That same feeling soon spread to the viewers. The inaugural speech by the new American president was remarkably bitter. More than that, it was dark. Every historian with any knowledge of literature sat up. Here, again, a magical alliance was announced between a leader and 'the people' – whatever that hazy concept might mean – to the exclusion of all the other forces that make a democracy a democracy: the elected politicians, the judiciary, the press, the autonomy of states and cities. It was an address in which the new president laid the foundations for a totalitarian system. Not Republican, not conservative or right wing, but based on the alt-right philosophy of his sinister adviser Steve Bannon. 'We are at war,' Bannon had exclaimed time and again during his public appearances, and he spoke of an existential war, all over the world, against the radical jihadists and against China and, above all, although he did not say so, against the principles of open and free-thinking democracy.

So there we sat that evening, in Europe, watching. The television show with Trump at its centre had become reality, and reality was 'fake news'. We sat watching in the here and now. These were the words of the American president, and he was real.

In was dark and rainy in Washington on Friday, 20 January 2017. Hillary Clinton was confronted at the Capitol by a crowd yelling 'Lock her up! Lock her up!' Precisely at the moment when the new president began to speak, the skies opened. 'I felt the water run down my face,' wrote political journalist Mark Danner. 'Yet it took only a few hours to learn I'd been mistaken.' At one of the inauguration balls, Donald Trump said, 'You know, I looked at the rain – which just . . . *never came*!' He told the staff of the CIA that 'God looked down and he said, "We're not going to let it rain on your speech!"'

The next day, the new president reconfigured the facts even further to suit him. The inauguration had been an unimaginable event. 'This was the largest audience ever to witness an inauguration, period, both in person and around the globe,' his spokesman said. In reality, according to all the usual estimates, there were clearly fewer people present than at Obama's inauguration. Aerial photographs confirmed this. But according to Trump the reverse was true. 'Didn't I say so myself?'

The National Park Service, which had declared in all honesty that its estimates suggested there were fewer attendees than last time, was forced to close down its website immediately. The boss had received a furious phone call from the president in person, who spent a large part of his first working day on the issue. New photos must be shown – in the press too. His close adviser Kellyanne Conway introduced the term 'alternative facts' and the belief that science was just an opinion.

Only a few weeks earlier, the staff at Oxford Dictionaries had chosen 'post-truth' as its Word of the Year 2016. Post-truth: 'Relating to or denoting circumstances in which objective facts are less influential in shaping public opinion than appeals to emotion and personal belief.' This new Word of the Year signified a profound departure from the basic assumptions of the Western intellectual tradition, in which research and the verification of facts were central – the tradition that had shaped our part of the world for at least three centuries. 'Post-truth is pre-fascism,' wrote historian Timothy Snyder. 'To abandon facts is to abandon freedom. If nothing is true, then no one can criticize power, because there is no basis upon which to do so.'

*

In the weeks after the inauguration we saw the emergence of a presidency the likes of which had never been seen before in American history. In his very first introductory phone call, within half an hour Trump got into a blazing row with the prime minister of Australia, one of America's oldest and most faithful allies. In a couple of tweets he undermined the entire international security system. Three days after he entered the White House, the Trans-Pacific Partnership, the major trade agreement negotiated between America and Asia, was swept away in a single gesture. In Beijing, which had been kept out of the treaty, champagne corks must have popped, since in reality it meant the United States was withdrawing from that hard-won sphere of influence. In Asia, America was regarded from then on as a declining power.

Angela Merkel came to visit. Trump refused to shake her hand. He said that he wanted to negotiate a 'new trade deal' with Germany, since the existing one was bad for America. Merkel's team was astonished at the new American president's ignorance. The existing trade deal did not exist, since for many years America, like most countries, had a trade deal with the EU as a whole.

Critical news organizations such as the *New York Times*, CNN and the BBC were barred from presidential press conferences. One stunt followed another. This president didn't govern, he simply continued his television show to hold on to his audience of millions. You can sleep safely again, because from now on our president will look after us, was the message. The good old days with work and dignity are coming back. Watch Fox News to see how I'm creating tens of thousands of jobs at the stroke of a pen.

On 31 May 2017, Trump announced he was pulling out of the Paris climate agreement, the outcome of decades of meticulous scientific research and at least twenty years of patient diplomacy in which all the countries of the world had finally come together, with the exception of Syria and Nicaragua, which signed up later that year. 'I was elected to represent the citizens of Pittsburgh, not Paris,' the president said. The mayors of Pittsburgh and Paris responded with anger and, in a letter, pointed to all the sustainability projects in the two cities: 'Though separated by an ocean and a language, we share a desire to do what is best for our citizens and our planet.'

It was in every respect a baffling decision. Environmental activist Bill McKibben responded by writing that 'it amounts to a thorough repudiation of two of the civilizing forces on our planet: diplomacy and science. It undercuts our civilization's chances of surviving global warming, but it also undercuts our civilization itself, since that civilization rests in large measure on those two forces.'

'Will this president really last the full four years?' we asked ourselves in those early months. Would Trump not be impeached long before his term was up, or declared by Congress to be unfit to serve? In the streets, in bars and around kitchen tables, we speculated. At that point we still had some faith in the safety valves of Congress and the judiciary that the founding fathers had so carefully introduced into the American presidential system and the constitution. That the zeitgeist had changed to such an extent that a figure like Trump could set the tone all over the world as the Kennedys did in the 1960s was beyond our imagining. Only after some time had passed did they begin to dance more and more often through my head, those prophetic words of the legendary singer Leonard Cohen: 'Oh, and one more thing . . . You aren't going to like what comes after America.'

4

In a letter to his wife in May 1942, Evelyn Waugh mentioned a small military operation that had caused a bit of a stir among the higher social circles in Scotland. On his Kelburn Castle estate, Lord Glasgow was troubled by a huge old tree stump. A British commando unit was stationed nearby and the officers offered to blow the thing up with such accuracy that it 'falls on a sixpence'. After a well-lubricated lunch, the gathering walked out into the garden to watch the explosion. But instead of falling on a sixpence, the stump was blown into the air along with tens of cubic metres of soil and half the plantation of young trees next to it. When Glasgow walked back in silence to his castle and looked up, he saw that every single pane of glass in the building had been smashed. On going inside, he walked to his bathroom to cool off and recover himself. But when he pulled the plug out of the sink, Waugh wrote, 'the entire ceiling, loosened by the explosion, fell on his head'.

*

The Economist raked up the image of Lord Glasgow's castle in the summer of 2017, and it was indeed salient. At an international level, Britain had not cut such a sorry figure since the Suez Crisis of 1956, and in the months that followed it would only get worse.

At home, ceilings did indeed come down; reality could no longer be ignored. During the campaign the Brexiteers had expertly played upon the nation's emotions, without focusing any attention at all on how their vague ideal would be implemented, let alone on the sacrifices that would have to be made. 'There will be no downside to Brexit, only a considerable upside,' David Davis had promised, for instance. But what was to happen to the open border between the Republic of Ireland and Northern Ireland? Free passage was an essential part of the Good Friday Agreement of 1998 that had brought, after three decades, an end to the bloody Troubles. One in twenty citizens of Northern Ireland had been the victim of an attack or a shooting in those years; one in five had experienced a bomb explosion, and a similar number had seen someone close to them killed or seriously wounded.

During my journey in 1999 I found myself in Omagh, an ordinary small town where only a year earlier the biggest bomb attack of the entire civil war had taken place. The explosion happened on a Saturday afternoon, while families were out shopping, and it left two whole housing blocks in ruins and twenty-nine people dead, many of them children. 'There was blood everywhere – on the floor, on people's faces and bodies – you felt you were walking through blood,' one eyewitness said.

Just short of Belfast, at the foot of a motorway embankment, lay a hundred dead IRA heroes in a wilderness of long grass and crooked gravestones. I spoke to a woman there, who told me: 'Our men had already fallen behind when the civil war began, now it's much worse. That whole generation has to find a way back to a normal life.' If the border became a hard external border after Brexit, then an important element of the peace agreement of 1998 would be gone and all that misery might start up again.

Another issue was the new role of Britain in the twenty-first-century world order. Liam Fox, minister for international trade, had claimed that forty trade agreements would be ready for signing by the time Britain left the EU. Normally such complex negotiations take six to ten years. Could beneficial trade deals be made with America, Australia and, for instance,

India, without those countries making multiple demands of their own? In the form of military and political support in the case of America, for instance, or an end to restrictions on travel and immigration in the case of India?

Brexit had all the components required of a political infarct: a social crisis, along with growing distrust of politics in general and European politics in particular. Moreover, what was actually meant by 'Leave' or 'Remain'? How was Brexit supposed to happen? In what form? Donald Tusk rightly asked himself what the 'special place in hell' looked like for those who had promoted Brexit without 'even a sketch of a plan' for how to do it.

A balanced discussion was made particularly difficult by the British tradition of 'winner takes all', and by the habit of thinking purely in terms of winners and losers. It's a side effect of the constituency voting system in which, per constituency, there is only one winner and the losers and minorities don't count. Politics of that kind is always good for drama and sensation, as in a television series, but it leaves little room for the boring work of coalition, consultation and compromise. When the crisis surrounding Brexit escalated, opposition leader Jeremy Corbyn turned out not to have Theresa May's mobile phone number, nor to have any use for it. In many European countries, where informal contacts between party leaders are the norm, there was a sense of amazement. The British saw nothing odd about it.

Some Brexiteers were soon eagerly talking of a 'hard Brexit' and later even of a 'no-deal Brexit', although there was no indication that those who had voted Leave wanted such a radical outcome. Did the vote really have to result in an abrupt break with Europe, whereby their children could no longer go abroad to work and study, whereby their diplomas would not be valid anywhere else in the world, whereby chaos would arise around the delivery of medicines and a thousand other things, and their own jobs would be at risk? Was this really the intention? The House of Commons rejected such an outcome. A deadlock developed that would persist for years. Meanwhile, Brexit increasingly became a national obsession.

From Europe's perspective, all the windows were smashed. 'From the moment the British chose to leave the Union they were mentally absent, as far as the European Commission was concerned,' said Vincent Stuer. 'After all those crises, Europe was battle-weary and talking got us not one inch further. Moreover, the British did it to themselves.' Brexit was and remains an inexplicable step as far as European politics is concerned. 'As members of the EU they had absolutely the best of both worlds. They had a huge amount of power and influence and they threw it all away. The Germans held the "hard" power, the British all the rest – plus the language. If we in Brussels had any particular direction in our thinking, then it was usually Anglo-Saxon. Their leverage and clout were far greater than they realized.'

The Brexit negotiations were inevitably conducted in accordance with European rules. David Davis was not replaced for another two years, and by that time most of the British diplomats who knew how the EU works had long since been purged from Brussels. 'I don't negotiate,' a negotiator for the EU told Europe correspondent Caroline de Gruyter. 'I mainly sit there explaining our rules to the British. They keep asking for things we're unable to offer them.'

The sometimes aggressive attempts by May and her diplomats to play the twenty-seven remaining members off against each other failed miserably. The member states kept each other fully apprised and the British got nowhere. They seemed unaware, too, that up against the huge EU bloc they were the requesting party, so it was not a particularly clever tactical move, for example, to dismiss EU citizens in Britain as 'queue jumpers' or, as David Davis and Boris Johnson proposed, to threaten to scrap all financial arrangements with the EU if they didn't get their way. Relentless British goading kept the rest of the EU together. Noises in France and the Netherlands suggesting a possible Frexit or Nexit soon fell silent.

The breach between the EU and Britain was reminiscent of the course of events when a couple with many children leave their divorce settlement entirely up to the lawyers. For the EU, that was perhaps unavoidable. After all, the EU 27 already agreed on the rules, whereas creating a consensus on a relationship with a former member was far more difficult. The British must be made to feel the consequences, discipline must be maintained, it must not be made too easy to get up and leave the Union. The EU's approach was shaped by those limitations: stiff and formal, without any room for more flexible solutions – concerning the Irish border, for instance. First the divorce had to be finalized, and only then could talks begin on the future relationship – as if the way the divorce took place would not have a decisive impact on future relations. That same Irish border issue, which in a new kind of customs union with the British would have been fairly simple to resolve, now became an almost insuperable problem.

Nevertheless, Britain agreed to the process, and it also assented to the rapid triggering of the Article 50 procedure. That set the clock ticking. The definitive moment of departure would be 29 March 2019. It was one of Theresa May's greatest strategic mistakes, since it meant she would have to hurry, and in negotiations whoever is in a hurry is by definition the weaker party. In Brussels there was furtive laughter at the adulation with which the British prime minister was greeted by the Brexiteers for, as former ambassador Ivan Rogers put it, 'walking straight into the trap'.

'The European Commission doesn't negotiate, it systematically follows a procedure,' one commentator wrote. That rigidity was not the result of obstinacy, however, as many Britons suggested, but of weakness and impotence. The Union, an organization of twenty-seven countries interlinked by an endless series of agreements and compromises, had no other option. Negotiating pragmatically and politically, as would be natural for any mature and self-confident federation, was impossible for the EU.

In the short term the Union remained firmly united; in the long term it might perhaps pay a high price for the required tenacity. Many old economic and cultural ties, dating back to long before the EU, were now being disrupted or destroyed. Britain, however, along with France, remained Europe's most important military power. It was also an essential trading partner, home to a plenitude of top universities, the heart of the financial world along with New York and Frankfurt, and an inseparable part of Europe and of European history. Timothy Garton Ash rightly warned of a serious disturbance to the traditional balance of power in Europe, currently based on the triangle of France, Germany and Britain – and of a 'humiliated, divided, angry "Weimar Britain"', right on the edge of the European continent.

5

In the summer of 2018 I again set sail for this European island. Among the jetties and wharves of the port city of Newcastle there was silence and emptiness. The customs man sang 'Maria' from *West Side Story* when he saw my wife's forename. The country still seemed like a caricature of itself, strange and at the same time oddly dear to us. We passed seventeenth-century pubs, trees that had already been big and mighty under Queen Victoria, cricket pitches where people played as if nothing had changed since the 1930s. I saw all sorts of Brits walking along the Promenade: a lady wearing white spectacles and a wig; an older man in a yellow tracksuit; a father with his twins in a double pushchair; a proud Indian family; a girl of five in her prettiest purple dress, on a purple scooter, crying; a very elderly lady in a wheelchair, wrapped in a red blanket, pushed by her granddaughters, beaming. They all paraded through the chilly Saturday afternoon by the sea, and nobody had any idea where their country, their city, or they themselves were going.

Only six years earlier, at the opening ceremony of the 2012 Olympic Games, Britain had shown unforgettably what it was and what it could do: a country with a rich past, an old empire that had rediscovered itself and had stepped into the twenty-first century in high spirits and full of self-confidence. We watched its impressive history pass by once again, with an ode to the landscape, to poets like Shakespeare and Blake, but also to the great characters from British children's books: Peter Pan, Mary Poppins and Voldemort. The Industrial Revolution thundered past, the 'Tommies' and the 'Poppies' from the two world wars, and then Sergeant Pepper's Lonely Hearts Club Band. All of it with a wink. Even the elderly Queen Elizabeth joined in, with a film in which she flew over a jubilant London in a helicopter with James Bond, apparently jumped out and then appeared large as life in the stadium, happy and glorious.

Now nothing seemed glorious, the country and its government appeared paralysed and numb, and even the United Kingdom as such could no longer be taken for granted. My wife and I found ourselves in Hawick, in the green hills of the Scottish Borders. At the start of the High Street, where the town's drinkers were holding their morning session, stood a statue of a medieval knight being cheered by a grateful public. The Battle of Hornshole in 1514, when a handful of young Scots from Hawick beat off a group of English raiders and even seized their pennant, was still commemorated here. Little seemed to have happened in the town since then, except that in the rest of the High Street there were twenty-five abandoned shops, sucked dry by a massive shopping centre on the outskirts. Now 1514 was hugely topical once again, because of Brexit. Northern Ireland and Scotland, where a large majority had voted Remain, were after all being dragged out of the European Union by force, against their will. Might that not lead to renewed calls for independence?

In the spring of 2018 I'd been in London briefly, this time for a radio discussion with a few journalists and opinion-makers. In the reception hall of the BBC's old Broadcasting House, the air seemed stagnant. Around the ceiling the golden words DEO OMNIPOTENTI TEMPLUM HOC ARTIUM ET MUSARUM shone out: 'This temple of the Arts and Muses is dedicated to Almighty God'. This was not the vestibule of a broadcasting organization, this was the portal to a house of God; everything here was built and engraved for the eternal empire.

The programme was cut from the same cloth, fine and restrained. But as soon as we went off-air my fellow panellists let rip: 'Dear God, it's an incredible mess here, with a weak prime minister and a totally confused Labour Party.' 'Perhaps Labour will change tack and there'll be a second referendum.' 'But Boris Johnson has called his Brexiteers to arms, he's talking about a "historic victory" that they mustn't throw away.' 'Not a clue how this goes from here.'

Britain would now have to make fundamental choices. Which direction did it want to take over the coming decades? What role did it want to play in the world? What did it want to be? A neoliberal dream, a free-trade zone for the rest of the globe, an American outpost, liberated from all regulations and mollycoddling? Or, despite everything, a European country where workers and consumers were protected and not every chlorine-washed chicken would pass muster?

Membership of the EU was due to end in March 2019, so by October 2018 there needed to be a firm deal with the EU, yet nowhere could I detect any sense of urgency. Britain ought to have been buzzing with activity and debate. Nothing was happening.

The European Union, after the initial shock, had long since moved on to other matters. In the new German coalition agreement of February 2018, Europe and the EU were mentioned 312 times all told. There was just one reference to Brexit. In late June 2018, during a marathon meeting of European government leaders, mainly about the impossibility of reaching workable agreements on the influx of immigrants, less than sixty seconds was devoted to the subject. Theresa May was told to come up with a proposal for a 'realistic' Brexit quickly, or it would all end in a chaotic departure of the British. Tusk spoke of 'the last call to lay the cards on the table'.

If Britain had produced a reasonably workable plan for Brexit at that point, so people in Brussels believed, it would probably have been accepted quickly by the rest of the EU, since everyone was keen to move on. But there was nothing at all, and because May had drawn 'red lines' from the start that could not be crossed, she later experienced every necessary concession – concerning the Irish border, concerning the financial settlement with the EU, concerning the role of the European Court – as a defeat. According to the EU negotiators, a huge amount of time was wasted as a result. 'Every step forward was extremely painful.'

It was not until more than two years after the vote, in September 2018, that Britain produced a concrete proposal, at a special EU summit in Salzburg. When it was completely and unanimously rejected, the humiliation for May and her diplomats was immense. The EU 27 closed ranks. Eventually, after two months of tough negotiations, Britain and the EU reached a divorce settlement in Brussels on Sunday, 25 November 2018, including a transition period that would last until the end of 2020. Just how complex Brexit was in reality was clear from the size of the document: a volume of 600 pages. For the time being there could be no complete break. For the Irish border question, the EU had demanded – and got – an interim agreement known as the 'Irish backstop': even if no definitive accord was reached, the border must remain open.

That meant that as long as there were no agreements on a new trading relationship, Britain would remain within the customs union. The British reaped all the benefits of that arrangement, but it meant they would have to obey EU rules without having any say in the making of them. The Brexiteers were furious, claiming it made the country a vassal state of the EU. For the EU this was the final offer. May had overlooked one small detail: the deal with which she came home did not have the support of her cabinet, let alone her party and the British parliament.

*

The Brexit process gradually took on more and more of the characteristics of a slow and protracted vendetta between a handful of families, featuring affairs, intrigues and, above all, betrayal. We watched as each crisis followed the last. Between June 2018 and April 2019, thirty-six ministers and junior ministers resigned, purely because of Brexit. The damage to Britain's reputation was enormous, and repairing it would be difficult if not impossible.

The cause lay in part with the British system of government. Britain does not have a written constitution; instead, everything is held together by informal rules of precedent. Britishness – which is what Brexit was largely about – is closely bound up with the independent power of the Crown and parliament. The referendum cut right across that, and the question that seeped through all the discussions was what 'the will of the people' meant and which must prevail in the end – the referendum result or the majority in the House of Commons?

Theresa May was in a terrible bind. She was the messenger of international reality, the cold shower in a fantasy world, time and again. She was not thanked for it. Like Angela Merkel, she was a respectable clergyman's daughter, but her character was a major obstacle. She turned out to have none of the skills demanded by this complicated situation: she was blunt when she needed to be diplomatic, stubborn when flexibility was called for, conservative when creativity was required, blind when the country asked for vision, tight-lipped when she would have done better to approach her opponents with openness.

Her cliquish mentality led her to replace her top diplomats with third-rate figures. In her stubbornness she drew her famous red lines and set Article 50 in motion without any plan in place. In her blindness she organized a senseless election in which she lost her majority, then endlessly dragged out the negotiations and concocted a deal with the EU at the last possible moment, without asking herself whether she had sufficient support for it at home. By her final months in office she had no credibility left in the circle of European government leaders.

In the House of Commons she threw everything she had into forcing through her Brexit deal. After talks in Northern Ireland, she was convinced the continued existence of the United Kingdom itself was at stake, fearing that a no-deal exit might lead to it breaking apart, with Northern Ireland eventually deciding to join the Republic of Ireland. Three times over, her deal was swept away by a devastating majority. The EU granted a delay. Any other prime minister would have resigned long since, but May ploughed on, certain as she was that her deal was the only route to an orderly Brexit.

Everywhere in Europe the debates were followed keenly – in that sense, the continent was far more united than in 1999. But the scenes in the Commons gradually became impossible to watch. Time and again the British premier was chased around the arena like a wounded bull, to laughter and jeers, speared from all sides till she bled. Westminster had once been the mother of modern democracy. What we were watching now was a degenerate version, a game of words played by an elite that, according to the best traditions of the Bullingdon Club, would never personally suffer the consequences of its actions.

Labour leader Corbyn participated eagerly, in his own way. He raised not a finger to protect his followers from this torrent of misery; as an uncompromising socialist he seemed to embrace a kind of Marxist immiseration thesis. His absence from the huge London anti-Brexit demonstration in October 2017 – 700,000 people, one of the largest post-war street protests – spoke volumes. And the pretence that he could negotiate his own Brexit deal that would offer the same benefits as EU membership, with the exception of freedom of settlement, came from a similar la-la land as had produced the Brexiteers.

In England too, politics increasingly looked like a television series. As in all soaps, no one ever seemed to need to work, cook or clean; as far as British politics went, in those Brexit years normal work practically came to a standstill. Countless issues remained unaddressed, urgent problems – poor housing, faltering healthcare – remained untouched, and the government of the country stagnated. All time and energy was deployed in that mammoth political game, and in nothing else. French minister for European affairs Nathalie Loiseau joked that she had named her cat 'Brexit': 'He wakes me up every morning meowing to death because he wants to go out, and then when I open the door he stays put, undecided, and glares at me when I finally push him outside.'

In June 2019, Theresa May at last resigned. The new prime minister, Boris Johnson, came to power after a party leadership election in which only members of the Conservative Party were allowed to participate: largely provincial, white, older Britons with an average age of fifty-seven. Johnson thereby finally gained the position he had been after all his life. For him, Brexit had never been a goal, only a means. The about-turn was almost soundless: of the 65 million British people, precisely 92,153 voted: 0.14 per cent. Commentators spoke of a 'hard-Brexit coup' disguised as a normal course of events, and of an unparalleled seizure of power by the radical wing of the Conservative Party.

Whatever kind of Brexit might be in prospect, the effects of the referendum result were now tangible. The British economy was still doing well, but it was estimated to be between 1 and 2.5 per cent smaller in 2019 than it would have been had the referendum not taken place. The pound, having lost 15 per cent in value, was weaker in the summer of 2019 than during the depths of the crisis of 2008. Prices rose everywhere. Shortly after the referendum I spoke to a worried British couple: they supported their children, who had emigrated to Australia and were therefore receiving far less than before. And their pensions, now that inflation threatened, were no longer safe either.

Investment growth fell. Between 2013 and 2016, the year of the referendum, investment in British businesses grew by 16 per cent. Between 2016 and 2019 the rise was barely 1 per cent. The banks and insurance companies moved £900 billion worth of capital to the continent in the three years following the vote. A highly placed employee of the Ford Motor Company in the UK told me that people there still had little idea what was hanging over their heads. 'Brexit turns our whole company upside down. We have an engine factory in England, but the cars themselves, even though they still look so British, are made in Germany. The majority of what the factory produces is then sold in Britain. But nothing is certain any longer.'

Japanese car-maker Nissan was offered a secret deal by May, yet it nevertheless decided to cancel plans to set up an assembly plant for its sports cars in Britain. Honda closed its factory in Swindon at the cost of 3,500 jobs. Ford and Jaguar also announced closures, with the loss of another 6,200 jobs. The ferry and shipping freight operator P&O, almost two centuries old, had its entire fleet re-registered under the Cypriot flag. Thomas Cook, the world's oldest travel agency, went bankrupt. Sony moved some of its activities to Amsterdam. The costs increased. The Bank of America alone spent almost $400 million preparing for Brexit.

One comfort was that the British would get their coveted blue passports back – although they would be produced in Poland by a French-Dutch company, since that made the operation £140 million cheaper. The printing works was officially in Amsterdam. That European reality remained.

Meanwhile, British victimhood was deliberately cultivated by some. There were headlines, tweets and letters everywhere about 'the terrible way the EU has treated us'. Johnson presented himself as a modern Churchill, while Brexiteers spoke of heroism and the Dunkirk spirit. A no-deal exit would be a blessing in disguise for the country, television adventurer Anthony Middleton tweeted. 'It would force us into hardship and suffering which would unite & bring us together, bringing back British values of loyalty and a sense of community!'

But slowly the beginning of a different story could be heard, about a 'Remainer elite' that was deliberately sabotaging plans for a no-deal Brexit. It was the British version of the poisonous Dolchstoß (stab-in-the-back) myth, used by the German army leadership for years after the humiliation of Versailles to accuse social democrat politicians of treason. They had stabbed the glorious German army in the back. Treason, or at least accusations of it, now lurked everywhere.

6

Donald Trump had always been a great advocate of Brexit. A few days after his inauguration he took aim at the entire European unification project, central to the European policy of all American presidents since the Second World War. He described Brexit as 'smart', expected it to be a great success, and hoped that other European countries would follow the example of the United Kingdom. In his strategic vision, 'America First', the EU was not an ally but a potentially dangerous competitor that must be weakened as much as possible. Every instance of European division was encouraged. '[Trump] doesn't want negotiations with our allies and trading partners to succeed; he wants them to fail. And by the time everyone realizes this, the damage may be irreversible,' wrote commentator Paul Krugman.

There was much in the Brexiteers that Trump recognized. On both sides of the Atlantic, what had taken place was not merely a reaction to globalization and to existing politics, it was an act of resistance against the forms in which political power was exercised: the rules of democracy and the rule of law, the balance between the different state institutions, and undoubtedly also the international order the European Union was aiming to create. Like Trump and some European populists, the 'hard' Brexiteers rejected the notion that governing is a complicated, fact-based business that demands a lot of knowledge and expertise, requiring good special-ists and civil servants who concern themselves with it all their waking lives. That too was part of the Brexit drama: the collision between the magic of nationalism and the complexity of the modern world.

That same mentality caused Trump to call the American military pres-ence in and around Europe into question. In that he was not alone. Earlier American presidents had regularly contemplated withdrawing much of the American force currently stationed in Germany, some 50,000 troops in all. After so many years of American protection, Europe had become lazy and neglectful in the field of defence. The Americans had always been dominant in NATO, and after the fall of the Wall the Europeans had quietly shifted the responsibility for their defence and security further towards the Ameri-cans, who, whether on the left or the right, had gradually come to resent it. Urged on by their military-industrial complex, they were spending twice as much on defence as the Europeans, who had cut their budgets time and again.

In 2016 a retired British general, Richard Shirreff, published a thriller called *2017: War with Russia*, in which Russia almost effortlessly rolls into the Baltic states and annexes them. Meanwhile the British prime minister sits in his favourite pub, the Germans are paralysed with shock, and the Greeks and Hungarians secretly side with Russia. By the time Europe reacts, it's too late. Weak plot, bizarre central characters – clearly the anxieties of an old warhorse.

Except that Richard Shirreff was until 2014 the second-most important man in NATO. His playful thriller was primarily intended, as its subtitle states in so many words, as 'an urgent warning'. The first half of the book describes what all the critics and experts have confirmed to be a thoroughly realistic scenario, regarding both the possible Russian military initiative and the responses to it by NATO and the EU. The RAND Corporation, a think tank which analysed just such a Russian attack in detail in a war game, concluded in 2016 that Russia could complete a surprise invasion within sixty hours. 'The strategic goal of the invasion was to demonstrate NATO's inability to protect its most vulnerable members. ... The outcome was, bluntly, a disaster for NATO.'

In Germany, a pacifist philosophy had predominated for decades. For the Germans, war had lost all its heroism; after 1918 and 1945 they knew that their entire country could be destroyed by a belief in military heroics. According to former chancellor Willy Brandt, war was 'no longer the *ultima ratio* but the *ultima irratio*', and most Germans agreed with him. The defence budget for Europe's largest economy had hovered around 1.2 per cent of gross national product for years, far below NATO's agreed commitment of 2 per cent. According to an official report to the Bundestag in the autumn of 2018, of Germany's six submarines only half were fit for deployment, of its 128 Eurofighter jets only a third were battle-ready, and of its 244 tanks barely 95 were operational. According to German expert Claudia Major, her country 'would need at least fifteen years' to fill the holes left by the Americans, 'and a very, very great deal of money'.

Between 2010 and 2012 the Netherlands had made cuts to its armed forces worth a billion euros. Potential operational deployment had fallen by almost 20 per cent in those two years. In 2016 the Dutch Court of Auditors stated that the Dutch army no longer had the capacity to fulfil its first and most essential task: to defend its own territory. Lord Richards, former British chief of the defence staff, described the military position of his own country as 'Belgium with nukes'. The entire British Army would now fit into Wembley Stadium.

Nor was Europe sufficiently prepared for cyberattacks and hybrid forms of warfare such as blackmail, disinformation and hacking. In the words of a senior Dutch military officer, 'Nowadays you no longer have to fire artillery pieces to break the backbone of an army.' Not one European country could develop and produce new military technology on its own. Britain, Germany, Italy and Spain therefore jointly produced the Eurofighter Typhoon, the Dutch and Belgians integrated their naval activities, and France and Britain worked together closely on further developing their nuclear weapons.

These remained separate projects, however. The European NATO countries were spending a total of around €265 billion between them on defence, more than Russia (€65 billion) and China (€170 billion) combined. But that vast sum was fragmented, since it needed to finance all the traditional national configurations, with each country having its own army, navy and air force, its own policy on military development and acquisition, and hundreds of its own privileges for military personnel. According to information from 2018, the European armed forces – to the extent that there was such a thing – had 17 different types of tank, 20 types of aircraft, 26 types of artillery and 29 types of ship. It was not remotely possible to talk of an efficient and independent European military force.

Particularly hard for the Americans to understand was the laying of Nord Stream 2, a new pipeline to transport Russian gas to Germany via the Baltic Sea. It meant Germany was cutting its defence budget and at the same time supporting Russia with billions in gas profits, bypassing Poland and Ukraine, and making Germany more dependent on Russian gas. What kind of a strategy was this, for heaven's sake?

It was criticism that had been heard for years in Washington, but Donald Trump went further, calling the whole of NATO, which until then had more or less functioned as the armed wing of the EU, 'obsolete', claiming it was largely irrelevant to present-day security concerns.

Within four months of the accession of Donald Trump, on Sunday, 28 May 2017, Angela Merkel publicly drew her conclusion: the most successful military alliance in modern history was coming to its end. 'The time in which we could fully rely on others is over to some extent,' she said in a sweaty and crowded beer tent during the Truderinger Festwoche in Munich. 'We Europeans have to take our fate into our own hands.' She meant, in part, 'we Germans'.

After the transfer of power in the United States, the White House quickly descended into chaos. If Putin truly had been able to install a puppet there, it surely would have acted little differently from Donald Trump. The aims of the Russian president were clear: absolute power over Russia, restoration of the old pride, a tight hold on neighbouring countries, and a gradual weakening of the United States and the European Union, not so much by military means as by the sustained and systematic creation of confusion and unrest.

For Vladimir Putin, the arrival of this new US president was therefore a godsend. In no time at all he caused an infarct in the heart of the Western world. At the G7 summit in May 2017, the world leaders walked together through the streets of the beautiful little Sicilian town of Taormina, where the conference was held, with the new American leader following behind in a lurching golf cart. That image said it all.

We saw no political strategy unfolding in any form at all, only an endless series of stunts. Above all we saw a man who, in a normal business, would have been removed from any executive function as quickly as possible. Now he was in charge of the most powerful country on earth.

'Crazytown' was what Trump's former chief of staff General John Kelly called the White House. He stayed for less than eighteen months. 'He's an idiot. It's pointless to try to convince him of anything. He's gone off the rails.' For Kelly's predecessor, Reince Priebus, Trump's bedroom, where he watched television and ruled the world by Twitter from his bed, was 'the devil's workshop'. According to Trump's defence secretary, James Mattis, who stuck it out for almost two years, the president showed the under-standing and behaviour of 'a fifth or sixth grader', meaning a child of ten or eleven years old. 'The root of the problem is the president's amorality,' one senior official in the Trump administration wrote in September 2018, in an anonymous letter to the *New York Times*. 'Anyone who works with him knows he is not moored to any discernible first principles that guide his decision making.'

Trump's staff, as became clear from later memoirs and reconstructions, were meanwhile doing all they could to avoid calamities, sometimes by ignoring him, sometimes even by taking documents off his desk at the last moment to prevent him from signing them. Former White House staff secretary Rob Porter remarked, 'It felt like we were walking along the edge of the cliff perpetually.'

Week after week matters arose that would have got any normal president into serious trouble. Trump persistently refused to publish his tax returns. He sacked the director of the FBI for refusing to terminate an investigation into Russian interference in the American election. He became personally involved in the appointment of judges who needed to decide cases in which his businesses had interests. Gradually, his attacks on the press took effect. After more than a year of his presidency, 43 per cent of Republicans questioned said that Trump should indeed have the power to ban newspapers

and other media. We watched it happening almost every day, a brief com-
motion and then on we went. We grew numb.

Under Trump's slogan 'America First', the whole of post-war American
security policy was scrapped. The protective American umbrella over Europe abruptly shut; an end came to the – admittedly outdated – INF Treaty,
which had safeguarded Europe against the use of short-range and
intermediate-range nuclear missiles; and the EU was threatened with a
trade war. In May 2018, the Joint Comprehensive Plan of Action, an agreement on nuclear weapons between the United States, Iran, Russia, China
and the countries of Europe – the result of twelve years of negotiations –
disappeared down the rubbish chute at Trump Tower.

'The truth is that Trump represents a threat to the European Union at
almost every level,' warned former British diplomat and security adviser
Ian Kearns in 2018. The American sense of responsibility for Europe and
the rest of humanity (which had of course always involved a good deal of
self-interest, if covertly so) was over. 'Trump's world is a world of raw
power politics unconstrained by rules, and of transactional bilateral deals
wherever they can deliver narrow advantage,' wrote Kearns. 'From the economic sphere to efforts to avoid major power conflicts, Trump rejects the
ideas and institutions developed at the mid-point of the twentieth century
as an answer to protectionism and devastating war.'

The way in which the ambassadorship to the EU – in theory a central
post within transatlantic relationships – was filled by Trump was telling.
After leaving the position vacant for a year and a half, the president finally
presented his candidate to the Senate – one Gordon Sondland, a retail magnate in Portland, Oregon, whose only political experience consisted of the
fact that the previous year he had donated a million dollars to Trump's
inauguration celebrations.

During a warm July week in 2018, the president visited Europe. He
established the mood immediately during a working breakfast, plus press
briefing, at the start of the NATO summit in Brussels. NATO secretary general Jens Stoltenberg was publicly scolded about the paltry contribution of
other NATO countries to Western defence. Rich Germany, Trump said, was
a captive of Russia because of its total dependence on Russian gas. You could
see the look of bewilderment on the hard-bitten Norwegian's face; even he
had no response to that. Nor was he meant to. Trump had set up the whole

scene mainly as a television show for his following in Middle America. But at the same time, before the eyes of the world, he was taking aim at the foundations of the Atlantic alliance.

A few days later, on 16 July in Helsinki, the American president adopted a very different tone towards NATO's main opponent. Behind closed doors and in the presence of no one save the interpreters, he spoke for two hours with Vladimir Putin. He had not consulted any dossiers. Instead, he said later, he had relied on his own 'intuition'. The meeting was shrouded in the greatest possible secrecy. Trump refused to tell even his closest staff exactly what the two men had talked about, which made it impossible for them to outline further policy. In their despair, they later fell back on the help of the Special Collection Service, the intelligence agency that eavesdrops on all communications between the Russians. By that route the White House staff were able to gain, from Moscow, some idea of what had been discussed. The rest of the world knows nothing to this day.

Particularly striking was the servile attitude of the normally jaunty Trump at the press conference afterwards. He supported Putin in every respect, continued to insist that the Russians had not exercised any influence at all on the elections, and fiercely attacked his own FBI and CIA, calling their investigation 'a disaster for our country'. His statements were so much in conflict with the American political line, so opposed to the vision of his own government, so inexplicable, that practically everyone wondered what on earth was going on. It was so extreme that even Putin could sometimes seem barely able to contain his laughter.

We had gradually got used to a great deal from the president, but this beat everything. In America especially, reactions were of shock. 'It's hard to find words to describe,' said the presenter on ABC News. 'All of you who are watching today will be able to tell your friends, family, your children, your grandchildren, you were watching a moment of history.' Republican senator John McCain said, 'No prior president has ever abased himself more abjectly before a tyrant.' 'It was nothing short of treasonous,' said former CIA director John Brennan. 'Not only were Trump's comments imbecilic, he is wholly in the pocket of Putin.' The otherwise perpetually optimistic commentator Thomas Friedman responded by saying, 'My fellow Americans. We are in trouble.'

*

It was a historic transition that we Europeans, with some disbelief, saw taking place before our eyes in July 2018: the end of a *Pax Americana* that had been shaped and cherished, by Americans especially, after 1945. Germany above all was deeply disturbed. For the Germans it was not just a matter of their military protection but of their post-war value system, which was profoundly bound up with American ideals and traditions. Suddenly America's allies were no longer a support but a burden.

As so often in history, the process was at first slow and almost imperceptible. Now it became rapid and abrupt. The new American president's crude 'America First' marked the end of the 'American century', the period from America's intervention in the First World War in 1917 to Trump's break with Europe in 2017.

This dismantling was closely interwoven with an even deeper historical shift: the end of Western hegemony, which had held the rest of the world in its grip for at least five centuries, ever since Columbus.

The prestige and the soft power of our old Atlantic ally now rapidly melted away, perhaps for ever. There were no other natural allies. In this new world order, Europe stood alone.

Intermezzo

I

ON AN OCTOBER AFTERNOON IN 2017, on a café terrace in Barcelona, I drank coffee with my Spanish colleague José Martí Font. In 1999 he had seen in the new century surrounded by people flinging their glasses out of the windows. Now he had lost his steady job at *El País*, the streets of his city were full of Catalan flags, capes were being sold everywhere in Catalan colours, the Catalan language was a duty and a calling, and separatism hung in the air. 'I'm a mixture of everything,' José sighed. 'My father's family was Spanish, pro-Franco even. My mother's parents were Catalan nationalists. At home it was all openly spoken about, thank god, and the two identities lived at peace inside me. Now, from one day to the next, the nationalists want me to choose. You surely can't ask that of a person?'

The old nationalist tensions in Spain had flared up once more. In the late 1970s, after the Franco dictatorship, the country was divided into seventeen regions, giving it one of the most decentralized systems in the world. For basic matters such as education, policing, healthcare, language, culture, state broadcasting and public works, authority lay with the regional governments and the regional parliaments, but in some regions there were growing calls for independence. Until 1999 the Basques rebelled with much blood and violence, and now the Catalans were filling the streets and squares with vast peaceful crowds.

Within small groups there had always been a desire for independent nationhood. In 2012, however, they were joined by the large regional conservative party and by the Catalan government. The move was prompted by a universal sense of outrage when a new autonomy statute, approved by the

Spanish and Catalan parliaments, was thrown out by the deeply conservative supreme court in 2010. But the revival of nationalism among Catalan conservatives was reminiscent of the conversion of Slobodan Milošević in Yugoslavia in the 1990s. Almost overnight, grey and corrupt politicians were transformed into idealistic leaders, distracting attention from all the scandals in which they were embroiled. Blame for the economic crisis and subsequent spending cuts could then be heaped upon the central government in Madrid.

Aside from the Greeks, the Spanish were the hardest hit after 2008. Unemployment grew explosively, more than a quarter of Spaniards who were in work bounced about from one temporary job to the next like acrobats, and researchers discovered evidence of mass impoverishment everywhere. Half of all those aged between eighteen and sixty-five now found themselves, by their own account, in a lower social class. 'The call for protection against the major powers of this world is the driving force behind all forms of populism, and we are no exception,' said José. 'Elsewhere they blame "the South" or "Europe"; here most fingers are pointed at Madrid.'

In 2014, a non-binding referendum was held in Catalonia in which less than 40 per cent of voters took part. As predicted, 80 per cent of them voted for independence. In the propaganda put out by the nationalist parties, the regional elections of 2015 were recast as a referendum on separation: anyone voting for them was voting 'yes'. Even so, instead of achieving a majority of the vote, those parties found themselves with 48 per cent, although the electoral system meant it was enough for them to win a majority of seats in the Catalan parliament. In all the opinion polls, support for independence remained stuck at between 45 and 50 per cent. Half of all Catalans, in other words, had little or no appetite for secession.

That fact did not dissuade the president of the Catalan government, Carles Puigdemont – backed by his parliamentary supporters – from calling a fresh referendum on 1 October 2017. By doing so he was violating both the Spanish constitution, which speaks of 'the indissoluble unity of the Spanish nation', and the statute of Catalan autonomy, changes to which require a far more cumbersome procedure. The Spanish government, under the uncompromising leadership of the myopic Mariano Rajoy, immediately added fuel to the fire, sending troops to Catalonia to stop the referendum by force, thereby providing the Catalan nationalists, day after day, with the victim-hood they craved. Images of sometimes violent skirmishes were shown repeatedly on Catalan public television channels, which were entirely in the hands of the nationalists: 'Look how the Spanish state responds to a demo-cratic process.' It was impossible to imagine better propaganda.

The 2017 referendum was exceptionally chaotic. According to the inimit-able calculations of the Catalan authorities, 43 per cent of voters turned out and 92 per cent of them voted for separation. In the weeks that followed, tensions grew. Puigdemont made a few more vain attempts to strike a deal with Madrid. Would he have the audacity to declare independence unilater-ally? And would the EU accept it? The Catalan foreign minister claimed everything would turn out just fine; he was in touch with all the permanent representatives of the EU countries in Brussels. A Dutch journalist did some checking and found not a single representative who had been in con-tact with the Catalan government. They told him, incidentally, that they would avoid such contact 'at any price'.

At regular intervals large demonstrations were held in Barcelona and the energy of the enthusiastic crowds was overwhelming, but the repeatedly delayed independence started to get on everyone's nerves. In those months I frequently walked around the Plaça Sant Jaume, in front of the Palace of the Generalitat, seat of the Catalan government, and encountered there a warm bath of cheerful like-mindedness.

In 1937, in revolutionary Barcelona, George Orwell wrote, 'There was much in it that I did not understand, in some ways I did not even like it, but I recognized it immediately as a state of affairs worth fighting for.' After eighty years little had changed in that regard. Those standing and sitting on the square were mainly young people. African immigrants were selling plastic capes in the Catalan colours, and many of those present were wear-ing them. They looked like the kings, knights and jacks of Botifarra, the region's ancient card game. At least fifteen international camera crews kept the theatrics going. Now and then someone would give a speech, to cheers, or sing a song, to applause. 'There's only one thing I want,' a young man shouted. 'A Republic!' He was at the age when you secretly think you're immortal. Three older men started chanting all those forgotten red battle cries again: 'The people united will never be defeated . . .' I watched a pretty girl walk up to a Catalan flag and embrace it passionately. How joyfully straightforward a choice can be.

In the economics pages of the newspapers, meanwhile, this virtual Catalan nation state came up against international reality daily. More than a thousand Catalan businesses and almost all the major banks and insurance companies announced they were leaving Catalonia, since if it became independent it would no longer be in the eurozone. 'Barcelona was always a city of books,' said José Martí Font. 'At least 60 per cent of Spanish books used to be published here. That's all gone. Over the past few weeks almost all the publishing houses have moved to Madrid. Staying has become too risky.' Eventually, more than 4,000 companies left and the number of businesses located in Catalonia fell by 40 per cent.

We talked about the book José was writing, on the subject of cities. They are the points of light on the nocturnal map of Europe, and they strike a balance between 'space' and 'place' more effectively than nation states. 'If you bring the regional politicians together here, or in Europe the national leaders, then their discussions are mostly stiff, awkward and political,' José said. 'But a conference of mayors? They immediately start talking about concrete problems, about the solutions they've sought and found. They exchange ideas and generate a collective dynamism straight away, no matter where they come from. They all have their feet firmly planted in everyday life.'

As we sit talking, the bells suddenly start ringing, all over the city. What's going on? A religious festival? Surely it couldn't be . . . We turn straight to the news. José groans. On this very square, the Plaça Sant Jaume, in front of a euphoric crowd, Puigdemont has just declared independence.

When the bells fall silent, the streets are deathly quiet, as if the city's plug has been pulled. Forty-five minutes later the first armoured vehicles of the Spanish riot police race down La Rambla. In Madrid, the Spanish government has already declared a state of emergency. Catalonia has temporarily lost its autonomous status and is under direct rule from the capital until fresh elections can be held in two months' time. The half of Catalans who want to remain part of Spain now start to revolt and there are huge demonstrations, all over the country. Carles Puigdemont seems to have lost control of the situation and he flees to Belgium. Other separatist leaders are arrested, on charges of rebellion, sedition and misuse of public funds.

Less than three weeks after his triumphant declaration of independence on the Plaça Sant Jaume, Puigdemont tells Belgian newspaper *Le Soir* that 'a solution other than independence is possible'. The capitulation is a fact. The flags on all those Catalan houses start to fade and eyes turn dull again.

2

Nationalism must be blissful, I thought, walking around the Plaça Sant Jaume in its short-lived state of ecstasy. It must be something like a euphoric dream, about a life that in these hectic times at last becomes simple and orderly again. Every populist is a nationalist by definition, since a leader needs a people to cherish, to unite and protect against outsiders and other influences deemed harmful to it. All nationalism is a story of victimhood: a lost battle in the distant past, betrayal by other European countries, the repression of a language and identity. Catalonia is no exception. The generously subsidized Catalan broadcasters trumpeted all those myths abroad day after day, and so a make-believe world gradually emerged in which Catalonia was perpetually exploited and oppressed and in which all its problems would be solved when the country was finally 'liberated', as if by the waving of a magic wand. Nationalist politicians and commentators said that of course Catalonia would always remain in Europe. They never mentioned that the EU would not accept such a secession.

Nationalism is still young. Until the eighteenth century the 'fatherland' in which people felt at home was a city or a province, a shire or a duchy. The larger entity, a kingdom, an empire or, in the Dutch case, a republic, was generally too distant. Yet all nationalists speak as if nations have existed for ever and their talk of values is always bombastic, about blood and soil and traditions going back to prehistoric times. They fire barrages of timeless myths and illusions. In the Catalan independence movement, just as with Brexit, reality was almost an irrelevance. In Catalonia I passed colourful campaign posters that were translated for me. 'Yes means loving the earth; side with the ecological republic.' 'Yes means a right to health.' 'Yes means equal rights.' 'Yes means a roof over your head.' 'Yes means a proper job; support workers' rights.' But the referendum was not about any of those things and there was no plan to address such matters once independence was achieved.

During my frequent visits over the years I experienced delightful street parties in Catalonia, parades with giants and people on stilts, medieval-style processions featuring old men with falcons and owls on their shoulders, astonishing human pyramids – what strength, what unity! Compared to the knowable community of a small town or a village, a nation is a construct, an 'imagined community' as anthropologist Benedict Anderson called it. But at the same time it is an association that has gradually developed between countless shared experiences, large and small, across generations – a 'deep, horizontal comradeship' that is genuinely strong and sincere – and in some countries it has assumed almost religious proportions. In the twentieth century, those feelings became stronger, not weaker, as democratic welfare states were created under all the different national flags. With good reason, people are often prepared to fight for their country and to die for it. At the same time, those feelings are easy to manipulate.

I would have been able to muster rather more understanding for all this enthrallment – including that Catalan victimhood – had our Spanish grandchildren not lived in Catalonia. One was at university in Barcelona and the other two were at school in a small town nearby. From the moment the youngest two, fresh from the Netherlands and speaking perfect Spanish, started school, Catalan was obligatory. The teacher, who of course had a perfectly good command of Spanish, feigned blindness and deafness if any other language was spoken. It was the same at the homes of some of their school friends; Catalan seemed to be the only language on earth. Their first months at school were difficult. They were three and six. Language is a great way of shutting out a foreigner, even a child. Those who spoke only a little Catalan were given lower marks for diligence and behaviour. At secondary school, essays could be written in English, German or Catalan, but not Spanish.

Our eldest granddaughter was studying English literature, but her philosophy exam could be taken only in Catalan. A year went by before she found a teacher who was prepared to speak the occasional word of Spanish or English. To the nationalists, anyone who did not share their point of view was a fascist. 'Fascist!' 'Fascist!' Our grandchildren spoke Spanish: 'Fascists!' The youngest children were given notes to take home requesting that their parents allow them to demonstrate in favour of independence. If you didn't sign, then from that point on you had a reputation for being a 'fascist'. Graffiti had already appeared on some houses. In the school playground, children separated into two groups.

3

Can all these dreams and feelings of nationhood ever assume a European shape? Or rather, can a European identity ever arise on this continent, with its sixty languages and forty countries? The pioneers of Europe sincerely cherished that hope. We know better now, especially after the crises of the past two decades.

Some have compared the European project to the Habsburg Empire, described by Robert Musil as the state that no one understood, 'in many ways an exemplary state, though unappreciated'. It was an empire that stretched from western Ukraine and Bosnia to Switzerland, and for centuries it provided a stable basis for eleven nationalities, seventeen languages and ten religious groupings. This Danube monarchy had a number of cosmopolitan cities – Vienna, Prague, Trieste, Lviv, Kraków and Budapest – where all those Germans, Hungarians, Slavs and secular or religious Jews lived mixed together; cities that sparkled with innovation and creativity. Yet at root it was a medieval, feudal system that somehow, balancing and blundering, had managed to survive for six centuries.

Then came that June day in 1914. In his novel *The Radetzky March*, Joseph Roth describes a garrison on the border of the Austro-Hungarian Empire when the message arrives that the heir to the throne has been murdered in Sarajevo. A tumult erupts, the Hungarian officers immediately start talking among themselves in their own language, and laughing. A Hungarian officer eventually responds to a request for them to speak German. 'I will say it in German. We are in agreement, my countrymen and I: we can be glad the bastard is gone!'

And so it became clear how deep a gulf separated these nations, and how superficial imperial unity ultimately was, including all the pompous government offices, barracks, parades and rituals like the 'Radetzky March'. At that moment, Roth writes, the fatherland fell to pieces.

I often find myself thinking about the history of my own country, about the Republic of the Seven United Netherlands in the seventeenth and eighteenth centuries. It too was an unprecedented structure, holding together seven provinces and several cities in a political relationship. All those entities, like the EU member states, wanted to preserve their sovereignty and autonomy as far as possible. Decision-making was exceptionally tricky and time-consuming, a city like Amsterdam could sometimes operate as overbearingly as Germany does now in the EU, and it seemed the composite entity would never amount to much. Yet it worked. The Dutch Republic provided sufficient footing for a long series of cleverly improvising rulers to create something out of it, and slowly, in an apparent wilderness, all kinds of regulations and connections arose. Until, as in the Habsburg Empire, the impossible structure blocked almost all adjustments and innovations.

When the American founding fathers, seeking an inspiring example, garnered information about the United Provinces for their debates in 1787, they became aware of the 'collective indecision' of separate provincial powers. One of them, James Madison, found the Dutch to be in 'a most wretched situation – weak in all parts'. Eight years later, during the bitterly cold January of 1795, revolutionary French troops invaded by crossing the frozen rivers with ease, and the once so glorious Republic collapsed like a pudding from one moment to the next. After the French occupation ended, a new unitary state eventually arose, the Kingdom of the Netherlands.

Might the EU, that tottering construct, that anxious semi-federation, always dangling by a thread, which Jacques Delors called an 'unidentified political object' meet the same fate? In the first two decades of the twenty-first century the continued existence of the European project hung in the balance several times, especially around the time of the euro crisis. The system's fragility was obvious. The Greek euro crisis became a raging inferno partly because in the spring of 2010 the German government spent weeks waiting for election results in just one state, North Rhine-Westphalia. Negotiations between the EU (508 million inhabitants) and Ukraine were seriously hampered in 2016 by a referendum organized by a small Dutch pressure group, in which 2.5 million Dutch 'no' voters (the turnout was marginally above the threshold of 32 per cent) threatened to block the entire Association Agreement.

In that same year, the EU's CETA trade treaty with Canada was almost killed off by the regional parliament of one member state, Wallonia, home to just 3.5 million people. The Canadian trade minister Chrystia Freeland, after the initial failure, left Namur, the Wallonian capital, sobbing. Because of the treaty, certainly, but I suspect her tears after that experience were also shed for the future of the EU. In May 2018, French president Emmanuel Macron warned that we cannot permit ourselves 'the luxury of forgetting', especially when it concerns the suffering and fate of previous European generations. 'I don't want to belong to a generation of sleepwalkers that ignores its own past.'

The EU's democratic immaturity was particularly problematic in light of the rapid emergence of new powers and forces in the virtual world. Over the past twenty years we have seen their early manifestations: cyberattacks on Iran, Lithuania, Georgia and Ukraine, alleged manipulation of the Brexit referendum and the American presidential election, trolling wars over Ukraine, and spyware in foreign digital products. In 2007, Estonia became the first state to suffer a Russian cyberattack. Banks, media and government institutions were severely affected for more than three weeks. A year later, when armed conflict broke out between Georgia and Russia, hackers used a simple DDoS attack to pave the way for the Russian troops, paralysing command centres and the media. In 2015, during the Ukraine war, Russian hackers went all out, disabling the airport, railways and media organizations; and shortly before Christmas, for the first time in history, they treated western Ukraine to a total electricity blackout, including all its emergency systems. Heating, transport, monetary transactions: nothing worked.

In this new field of operations, which was utterly dominated by America and China, Europe was once again, for the time being at least, the weak party. Bringing up the rear, Russia played a role of its own, specializing in cyberwarfare and in repeatedly throwing highly developed societies off balance.

In the emerging 'imagined community' of the EU, however, all these threats and crises had the effect of binding nations together. In that sense the Union has clearly grown and strengthened since the start of the century. It emerged from the euro crisis stronger as a political construct, for example, even though agreement concerning immigration policy still seemed a long way off. As a geopolitical power, the EU needed to find a role for itself in important international developments, and in that sense too, things happened that would have been unthinkable twenty years earlier: joint sanctions against Russia, a common approach to the global technology giants, a shared climate policy, and unbroken unity during Brexit.

When I travelled around the continent in 1999, it was almost impossible to speak of a Europe-wide public debate. European news was marginal and European engagement minimal. Twenty years later, Europe was on the front pages every day; we followed the Greek, British, German and Italian elections as if they were being held in our own country; and whether I was in Zürich, Brussels, Stavanger, Vienna, Amsterdam or Berlin, people were discussing the same subjects, and the public had the same questions and the same worries. Something that in 1999 people talked of in theoretical terms was very slowly becoming a reality because of the internet: a European 'coffee house', featuring a permanent and open European debate.

Like nation states in the nineteenth century, Europe was now acquiring its own public space, with the inevitable accompanying ruckus. In 2006, 9 million Europeans were living in European countries other than their own; by 2018 the number had doubled to 17 million, or one in every twenty-five European citizens. According to Eurostat, after the worst of the recent crises abated, in the summer of 2018, 67 per cent of Europeans were convinced that their country benefited from the Union. Admittedly, 39 per cent had no faith in European leaders, but 46 per cent had more faith in them than before. And everywhere, as we have seen, trust in national governments was lower. Only 13 per cent of Greeks, for example, trusted their own government, whereas more than a quarter trusted the EU. In the Netherlands, Angela Merkel was for several years more popular than Dutch prime minister Mark Rutte.

The same effect could be seen in elections to the European Parliament. In May 2019, the turnout was higher by a quarter than in previous elections – at 51 per cent, up from 43 per cent. In Poland the turnout almost doubled.

That fact alone was spectacular. European citizens had woken up and wanted to join the conversation.

Research has revealed a striking contradiction. The percentage of voters who opted for Eurosceptic parties more than doubled across Europe as a whole over the first twenty years of the new century, from 15 to almost 35 per cent, yet at the same time support for the EU reached a record high. Brexit sent out shockwave after shockwave; now no one else was talking about leaving. The issues European voters were concerned about no longer fitted the frameworks of left and right, and political fragmentation, which had raised its head earlier at a national level, was clearly visible in European politics. It was a historic outcome: the European coffee house at last existed, and the public was showing its teeth.

So what happened in Spain, outside Catalonia? When I drove through the country in the turbulent autumn of 2017, fierce anti-nationalism could be felt everywhere. In Madrid, in the small towns of Aragon, Andalusia and elsewhere, Spanish flags hung from the houses. Everyone was furious with the rich and arrogant Catalans who were endangering the fragile peace of their shared country. In Madrid, people were demonstrating again with the old placards quoting Marx and Lenin. Everyone was in search of new banners under which to march. And, above all, new barricades to entrench themselves behind.

Bart

I'M FROM A 'BLACK' FAMILY — YES, that's what they call it here. A family of Flemish nationalists, some of whom were actually collaborators during the war. One of my uncles, Jan, was in Germany, with the Volkssturm, and died there. Another uncle fought on the Eastern Front; he was a prisoner of the Russians for five years after it ended. When Belgium was liberated the whole family fled to Germany, like thousands of other collaborators; they were so frightened of the consequences of their choice.

My father was still a boy then. It marked him for life. All those experiences turned him into a rebel, a man who stood firmly for freedom, a man who, like many war children, didn't care much for power and authority, and he certainly had an aversion to the Catholic Church. He remained a true Flemish nationalist, but with a deep dislike of uniforms and other manifestations of the extreme right.

For me that nationalist stuff was simply oppressive. I soon started looking for a political home and ended up with the liberal party led by Guy Verhofstadt. But I know the DNA of the nationalists better than they know it themselves; I grew up with it, with all the talk, the books, the magazines, the emotions, the drive. And that's precisely what worries me.

People who embrace nationalism often get stuck in a particular kind of logic, a groupthink that makes them drift away from the ideals of a free society. It's very difficult for nationalism to be open, it continually closes itself off, it's always a matter of assimilate and exclude, of 'us' and 'them'. It's very normative too. It always wants to decide what a 'good' Fleming is, or what a 'good' Dutch person is. That's at odds with real freedom.

You see it all over Europe. Bear in mind that many of these groups originally emerged out of emancipatory movements. Take my grandfather. He wasn't allowed to study in Dutch, since it was a second-rate language, so he never got anywhere. If you wanted to be part of the elite of Belgian society you had to betray the person you were. The Flemish Movement was eager to end all that. Over time, however, nationalism became so central to their thinking that they were prepared to throw in their lot with the devil himself. So yes, eventually you go so far astray that you find yourself working with forces that are downright pernicious. You end up on the wrong track altogether.

Just think, the Flemish Movement was originally a freedom movement, and pacifist, too, created in the trenches of the First World War. It's astonishing how such an open, progressive and innovating force could switch within four or five years to become an anti-democratic movement in which everybody fell into line, right arm raised.

My family has lived in Mechelen since 1520, so we're profoundly wedded to this city. In 2001, completely unexpectedly, I was elected mayor. I was born in 1964 and when I was growing up this was still a city inhabited almost exclusively by white Flemish families. By the time I took office a sixth of the population was of Moroccan origin, there was a prevailing sense of insecurity, local government was weak and ossified, and in league tables Mechelen stood out as one of the most miserable cities in Flanders. It was utterly polarized. You couldn't have an ordinary conversation with people any longer; everything they said was about how immigrants were making people feel unsafe, about squalor, about everything that was wrong.

Then came 9/11. I'd recently become mayor and I heard the news here, in that room next to this one. Panic all round. The dominant thought was that dozens of planes were in the air that could crash into vital buildings at any moment, even in Europe. In that mood my police chief came to see me. He had orders from Brussels to protect all American facilities and companies against possible attacks with aircraft. 'But how am I supposed to do that?' he asked. 'I'd have a hard job bringing down a plane with my service pistol.'

It was a lash of the whip, a further log on the fire of polarization. Like everywhere else, our Moroccan citizens got a new identity. No longer 'Moroccans' or 'immigrants'; from that point onwards they were 'Muslims'.

What's going on now all over Europe started far earlier here in Flanders, back in the 1990s: fear of the stranger, us-and-them thinking, nationalism. The nationalists talk all day about return and reverse migration, everyone living in their own country. The first child of Moroccan origin was born in the same year as me, 1964. In 2001 he was thirty-seven years old, with children of his own. How can you still talk about return? The only alternative in their mind was to make everyone become the archetypal Fleming: headscarf off, drink alcohol, eat pork – the ultimate proof of assimilation.

In response the left came up with an equally naive story: 'We have to tackle racism.' It often stopped there. Everyone was to have their own community, their own youth club – all identities were to be reinforced so that immigrants had a firmer footing in society. That was pretty much the left wing's only answer to the far right. It was well-meaning paternalism, which in essence came down to the creation of new ghettos. Because in practice the people in those youth clubs were concerned only about their own identity: what makes us Moroccans? So there was no alcohol, only Moroccan food, only Moroccan music.

I knew that atmosphere perfectly, it was exactly the same as the closed world of the Flemish nationalists. They held parties where all the music was from the 1930s, they had all sorts of rituals and stories that functioned as veiled norms, as signals that you're 'one of us'. I saw exactly the same cage as the one I'd struggled to escape. It was community thinking that focused on dividing lines, the kind of thinking that smothers all freedoms. Because if you didn't join in you were a collaborator.

That oppression was finally broken in the late 1990s by the young immigrants themselves, especially by the first generation to go to university. They realized that the way they were being treated was condescending, so they rebelled against it and started organizing themselves. It was comparable to the rise of the workers' movement a century earlier. Here again was an old question asked by every emancipation movement: do we seek strength from each other and among each other, or do we secure a place for ourselves in society? That was the tension that dominated in those days.

As mayor I never took part in any kind of groupthink. It was certainly tempting. All politicians have a tendency to prostitute themselves in election campaigns, to curry favour with the voters by telling racist, discriminatory or extenuating stories. In those early years I couldn't walk into a bar without people starting to talk like that. I kept my distance from it – my own upbringing had taught me how dangerous it was. I'd seen for myself the consequences of humiliation and exclusion. I told people that, too: we're not going to do to Muslims what was done to the Flemish militants, are we? I saw only a society of people, citizens of this city.

But I also knew we had to start with security. People quite understandably no longer felt safe on the streets. The rule of law needed to be restored. In that sense the city was traumatized. All it had left was a glorious past; the present was impoverished and there was no future. We combined those two issues. We put a lot of effort into policing and security and at the same time we were hard at work smartening up public space. A car park was built under the Grote Markt. There had been endless debate about it, claims it would bring chaos and misery, but I said, 'We're going to get things moving.'

With security as a priority, we tried to make connections. For example, we adopted the 'neighbourhood fathers' initiative from Amsterdam, with fathers walking through their own districts in the evenings. As social control it worked, in some very difficult neighbourhoods. The same went for the 'big brothers' project, which invited slightly older Moroccan boys to act as supervisors at children's play areas. They kept things in order to some extent, but that wasn't all: they grew into the job. I came upon one of those boys recently, he's now in his mid-thirties, and he said to me, 'I felt part of this city then, for the first time.' And for the kids in the playground 'the city' was no longer a white policeman but someone from their own world – a cousin, or literally a big brother. A change in perspective like that is spectacular.

Next we focused on standards and norms. If young people aren't reprimanded quickly and directly, things can easily go from bad to worse. We wanted to prevent that. If we picked up a young person, we billed them for the costs: a hundred euros. Then we had a talk, with the parents present. At that point we asked the parents for help: we're going to invest public funds and energy in you, are you prepared to work with us on this project? Or would you rather pay the hundred euros? And 98 per cent of parents worked with us. We got them to sign a six-month contract, and the terms might be quite banal. Such as: make sure your child joins a sports club. Or: for the next six months you pick up your child from school. Or: your child is no longer allowed in this or that neighbourhood, because he's got bad friends there.

That project alone had a huge impact. All the big Flemish cities have had to deal with radicalized Muslims who travelled to Syria to fight with Islamic State or some other group. A remarkably large number were Belgian. According to the Belgian security services, almost 100 came from Antwerp and some 200 from Brussels. From Mechelen: none.

For me personally that was a great emotional victory. My father talked on his deathbed about his older brother Jan, who was drafted into the Volkssturm by the Nazis, because his family had opted for radical Flemish nationalism, and then, barely fifteen years old, died in the wrong uniform. He was so young, it was just like the stories of Islamic State recruits. I thought: never another Jan Somers from Mechelen, never again. And the only way to stop it happening is by creating trust in society. We must recruit people for our community, so that Islamic State can't recruit them. If you feel you're part of society, you're not going to attack it. That's the most wonderful victory we achieved, that we managed to protect our children against the Pied Pipers of Hamelin.

In 2016, after the attacks in Brussels and Zaventem – the airport is just round the corner here – the whole city was in shock again. I went to a mosque. I hadn't done that before; I'd always wanted to keep my distance a bit as mayor. I found totally traumatized people there, people who'd been spat on and sworn at, people who really had only one question: 'When will the pogroms start here?' Those people were victims twice over, first as citizens, then as Muslims, because their identity had been hijacked by Islamic State. We tried to hold the city together. At the commemoration on the Grote Markt, around 40 per cent of those present were of non-European extraction.

In the end we got through the crisis years reasonably well. In the Flemish City Monitor, our city moved upwards each year in all categories. Child poverty fell, the middle classes came back, and every year we opened something new, lately a new library. As for trust in local government, in 2004 we were in thirteenth place, in 2018 at number one. Trust in fellow citizens with a different cultural background: from thirteenth place to number three. Pride in the city: from thirteenth place to number one. At the start of the century we were the sickly little brother among Flemish cities. Now we set an example.

You can see signs of the resurgence of the city and the region everywhere. In any number of European consultative bodies, cities and regions are plotting new courses, and they all understand one another. American political scientist Benjamin Barber says it plainly: the local and municipal level is far better equipped to address today's problems than the national level. In other words, the city is far stronger than the nation. I've seen that from close proximity, both as mayor and as minister-president of Flanders. In parliament you can spend months debating the difference between, say, sewage systems. In a city, if the sewers are broken you have to fix them as quickly as possible. That's a completely different starting point. Nationally you spend a lot of time on the question: where do our divisions lie? Locally it's: what unites us?

I'm convinced it's in the cities, along with the European level, that the future lies. The nation state is essentially a nineteenth-century concept. But it's tenacious, durable, tempting. A national identity all too often looks to the past: the Golden Age in the Netherlands, the Sun King in France. A city looks to the future. It's a connection project, whereas national identity is a demarcation project.

Muslim women's headscarves – that's a typical demarcation project. Opponents talk about women's emancipation and so on, whereas those same people, when I see what they're doing, hardly seem to be the driving force behind emancipation in other fields. I think: but guys, there are a billion people in this world who wear headscarves. Of course I'm all for equality between men and women, but have we truly emancipated a single woman by harping on about banning headscarves? Quite the opposite, we've turned it into a symbol of rebellion. Emancipatory movements come from the inside. So when will they emerge? When women and men no longer feel excluded but acknowledge that they're full members of this society.

Of course we have fundamental values: equality between men and women, the rule of law, democracy, the separation of church and state, the basic principles of the Enlightenment. But what do populists do? They broaden those principles to include everything from the past. Every tradition then becomes a fundamental value. That means you're doing exactly the same as the Salafists, fossilizing a society. The Salafists say that every change to Islam since the seventh century is blasphemy. Some populists essentially have the same attitude. That way you're going to kill our Western model, because it's based on freedom, on a society that's continually the subject of debate, continually changing. I once calculated that seven European countries have fewer Muslims than we have in this city. In other words, more Muslims live in our little city than in the whole of Hungary.

Here in Mechelen we have an ancient tradition. It's called the Giants Parade and it's held once every twenty-five years. There's a family of giants, with a father and a mother and a Janneke and a Mieke and a little Claeske, and a granddad too, called Goliath. In 2013 we expanded the family to include two new giants, Noa and Amir, one a black African, the other a North African.

When the influx of refugees arrived, our city immediately offered them refuge. It was our moral duty, and what's more, almost all families here have a history of being refugees from the First World War. My own grandfather was a refugee in the Netherlands for years. We accepted 250 refugees, which is no problem at all for a city of more than 80,000 people.

From the first week we made sure all the children could go to school. All the families were given a buddy, a guide to show them how things work here and keep in contact. You really can explain quite a lot that way, you know. That they were sincerely welcome here, for a start, but also that we have our own rules. About how men and women treat each other, all that sort of thing. We organized language courses straight away. Not like the nationalists, not because we're so proud of our language, but for purely practical reasons. After all, how can you function in a society if you can't communicate? We gave each newcomer a kind of uncle or aunt, someone from the city who had agreed to spend an hour every week or two taking a man or a woman out. I thought the people who signed up would mostly be progressive types. But no, almost half were very traditional people. And what happened? After a few weeks they'd invite the newcomer into their home; they'd sit at the kitchen table and ask the refugee about their parents, about what work they used to do. The immigrant turned into a person. The pairs became friends. It made at least as much difference for the guides as for the newcomers. Their worldview changed. And the newcomers, through this new friendship, started building networks outside their own group, so that they had a sound footing, and far more opportunities. I've seen it happen over and over again. Right in my own family too. In the intimacy of personal life – that's where it has to take place.

Recently I met a couple of mayors from Lebanon and told them what we were doing. 'Great,' they said. 'But what can we do? We have forty thousand refugees in a city of ten thousand. Even if we put our babies to work, it won't be enough.' That makes you feel really humble once more.

14. Great Expectations

2018–2021

I

A GERMAN DECEMBER DAY IN 2018. I'm on the train, Münsterland and the Ruhrgebiet are wet with fog and drizzle, and beyond the glass I can at first see only some hazy colours: the dark red of the tiled roofs, the brown of the barns and sheds, the grey of the station platforms, the flats and the factories. Here and there, behind the houses, a swing or a stray garden chair recalls happy summer evenings.

In 1999 I travelled on the *Marla*, a fully laden container ship, on the last high water of the year, the 'Advent water', along the Rhine on my way back to the Netherlands. That would be impossible now. After the extreme drought of the past summer the river is barely navigable. On that trip the German carriages still clattered and creaked across the country. Now the trains are silent, remarkably comfortable – can it get any better? – and full of electronic gadgets. Everything works and everything is on time. The *Berliner Morgenpost* reports that the U-Bahn isn't functioning properly. Why? Only 95.5 per cent of trains are on time. What a fortunate country, I think to myself. What un-European orderliness. Just 4.5 per cent of trains arrive late and the Senate is forced to intervene?

Over a quarter of a century ago I got to know the Winklers, a family from the far east of Germany, from the GDR town of Niesky in what was known as the Tal der Ahnungslosen (Valley of the Clueless), where you couldn't even pick up Western television. Eckart Winkler was a structural engineer, his wife Inge a paediatrician. They were active church members and independent thinkers who in the GDR years kept themselves going by working hard and then, in the evenings, shutting out the world beyond their flat with music and a good book. Nobody was rich, but rents were low, Eckart's company provided hot meals, and doctors, schools and universities were free of charge. The state guaranteed a secure existence. Just as long as you didn't get any wild ideas. If you did, you'd have a big problem.

The first time I was invited to stay with them, along with a fellow journalist, was in February 1990, shortly after the Wall fell. When it began to get dark the streets of the town looked blue from the fumes of the Wartburgs and Trabants – there were still hardly any other cars – not to mention the thousands of coal fires and stoves.

It was an intimate world, that world of great expectations that I'll never forget. The tiled stove in the corner of the living room gave out a gentle heat and daughter Gudrun sat leaning against it studying while the other daughter, Almund, made a doll from a handkerchief and an old tennis ball. Granddaughter Elisabeth played on the floor. Son-in-law Jens was in service with the Nationale Volksarmee. Yet those were months in which suddenly everything was possible. At last all the party bosses had been sent packing, everyone could travel freely – there were even trips to Paris on offer – and soon every home would have a shiny Opel or Mercedes parked outside. In three months, the price of a Trabant had halved.

'We were as happy as little rabbits let loose after all those years,' Gudrun told me later. 'But after we'd danced in the meadow for a bit, it occurred to us to wonder: what happens if a fox comes?' Eckhard was cursed with a good memory; all his bosses, who were now calling themselves 'entrepreneurs', were the same men as had worked for the Stasi for years. And all those new candidates standing for office – weren't they the very people who had always unquestioningly applauded the communist leader Erich Honecker?

In later years I went back a number of times. The free West had taken over the economy and the changes were astonishing. Everything that had taken your average West German city almost forty years to achieve came to pass here in just over twenty months: new roads, clean air, a hyper-modern mall where everyone shopped till they dropped for colour televisions and washing machines. The Winklers had got a new bathroom installed in their flat, a computer was humming away in the corner and outside was an almost-new Opel. Eckart now travelled around half of Europe with his technical director, the party bigwig he'd always quarrelled with in the past. He had a hundred men under him, he said, but by the end of that year there would be only around forty left.

The tiled stove carried on burning for years, but Gudrun had gone; she'd fallen in love with a *Wessi* and moved to a suburb of Dortmund. She wasn't the only one. Of her school class, almost half had moved to the West. The town's birth rate had dropped by a third since 1989. 'The women started to feel insecure,' Gudrun told me later. 'They were the first to lose their jobs, company meals became a thing of the past and they were sent back to the kitchen sink.' In her memory the GDR was an oasis of peace and orderliness, and even the repression – which the family encountered to no small degree – had something simple about it. 'We knew precisely who the enemy was. He was plump and dumb and unambiguous. Here in the West you run foul of all kinds of things too, but it's all vague and elusive.'

It's years since I last saw that studious girl next to the tiled stove, but now she's picking me up at the station. After two decades a great deal has changed, but we recognize each other immediately. She still lives close to Dortmund, she's a social worker and therapist, and with her husband Martin she has two sons and a daughter, Kathy, who still lives at home. Their house is full of artworks, books and music. In the middle of the living room is a grand piano, and in another room Kathy is painting.

After all these years Gudrun seems like a born *Wessi*, even if her old life sometimes raises its head when her eldest son comes home with horror stories about the privatized hospital where he works. 'The fact you can get so rich that way, that's just wrong, isn't it?' she says. 'With a clinic where the nurses are run off their feet for less and less money, and even the towels have been replaced with cheap paper crap? I'm too much of a child of the GDR to accept that.'

'What my mother learned in the GDR was "Keep quiet",' Kathy says. 'What she's learned here is "Speak up a bit more".'

'Angela Merkel has an ability to vanish into thin air in a trice,' says Gudrun. 'She's utterly impalpable. You learn that in a dictatorship. What I have more difficulty accepting is her engineer's mind. She thinks very mathematically, in terms of money and shortages – everything that's quantifiable and nothing else.'

Over dinner we talk about the past twenty years. 'Germany is still a class-based society. If you're poor you stay poor. Our children can go to a good university only because they put a lot of energy and money into it.' The culture of measuring and counting has taken root here as it has everywhere. Gudrun and Martin, who is also a therapist, now have to keep supplementing and correcting their patients' notes, and the pressure of work is increasing. 'Our actual work used to be taken seriously. No longer, it seems.'

Of the 2008 banking crisis she says, 'My husband had a lot of patients who lost all their money. I know a woman who used to talk proudly about her husband, a banker. Now she doesn't mention him. It's become an embarrassing occupation.' During the crisis their two sons used to read passages from *Das Kapital* by Karl Marx out loud, exclaiming, 'Dead right; he's dead right!'

Austerity has meant that retired women now take cleaning jobs, or move in with relatives. 'Here in the Ruhrgebiet you see many older people living with their children, or vice versa. Often the only jobs are far away, so elderly parents are left behind, lonely.' As for the Greek crisis, 'I heard nothing but sympathy around me, and nobody looked down on the Greeks, but no one knew what ought to be done. Everybody believed there was a big difference between the workers and the politicians. People could plainly see how ordinary Greeks were being crushed and as Germans they felt ashamed.'

In 2018, another 166,000 people applied for asylum in Germany, once again fewer than the year before. Yes, their little town of 8,000 residents has taken in immigrants, Gudrun tells me, almost 300 of them. At first that didn't create many difficulties; it was an old mining town, so people were used to workers coming from Turkey, Poland and Yugoslavia. In Kathy's class only seven of the pupils have German parents. 'In my generation, division is no longer relevant,' says Kathy. 'We really are united.'

Gudrun, Martin and Kathy were among those who took a Syrian refugee under their wing, but it wasn't always easy. He was a complicated young man. Even so, the family did its best to help him settle. 'I want to keep my country in order,' says Gudrun. 'He mustn't become a terrorist.'

Is there much more fear of immigrants now? 'Yes, especially since so many came all at once. Everyone lives and works together with the Turks just fine, the children play with each other all over the place. But in the evenings there's grumbling in many homes.'

Her cleaner said she intended to vote for the far right. Gudrun looked up a website designed to help voters discover which party best reflected their views and worked through the questions with her. 'And what was the result? The Greens.' Nevertheless, she voted AfD. Because of the foreigners. 'I'm not the only one to have volunteered,' says Gudrun. 'There are hundreds of thousands of us. But all the work that we do is buried under that cursing and grumbling.'

Martin comes in. They need to rehearse for a Christmas performance, so he goes to sit at the piano. Kathy has played the cello since the age of five and Gudrun plays the flute. The music fills the flat, familiar and safe. The local paper reports that a driver has saved a sleepwalker from the freezing cold, a wolf has been found dead on the road, and the local boy scouts have carried the peace light from Bethlehem into the cathedral. Tomorrow will see the first fall of snow.

In the days that follow I travel through a Germany full of Christmas decorations, candles, gnomes, broken slabs of chocolate, marzipan-filled loaves, woollen hats, lace, cuckoo clocks, angels, traditional woodcarvings, and slippers that cry out for the slow warmth of that old-fashioned tiled stove. Every self-respecting town has a Christmas market, each one an overwhelming avalanche of the cosiness many Germans can't get enough of, and again and again I wade through the smell of glühwein, hot doughnuts, sourdough loaves and bratwurst.

'Für ein Deutschland, in dem wir gut und gerne leben' was Angela Merkel's slogan in the last election campaign: 'For a Germany where we live well and enjoy living'. She won't be the figurehead of Germany and Europe much longer. She's talking about leaving office, our sober headmistress who in her pompous chancellery usually sits working at the corner of a conference table and goes back to her flat in the evening to make potato soup. At times like these December days, her ideal seems fulfilled. Satisfied couples stroll the streets, the wives beautifully dressed, the husbands with hands clasped at their backs. At eleven in the morning everyone starts drinking glühwein, and the supermarket has a whole frozen Polish goose on offer for €3.79.

At the Christmas market in Halle, students are meanwhile buying organic plum jam and postcards saying things like 'Islamization? Not here!' and 'Fortress Europe, close the borders!' and 'Defend yourself! This is our country!' They belong to the hippie branch of the Identitäre Bewegung, the youngest adherents of the great replacement theory – to get their own back, they write, 'on the '68 generation that is trying to eradicate our values, our traditions, our identity and our people'. They remind me of the students Joseph Roth ran into in Berlin almost a century ago, loudly singing their slurs: 'Down, down, down with the Jewish republic!', and of the ever-growing piles of *Volksdeutsche* pamphlets he came upon in kiosks on Potsdamer Platz.

In Dresden, some 20,000 AfD members are marching through the streets again. Since 2015 more than 4,000 attacks have been reported, big and small, on asylum centres and foreigners, some involving petrol bombs. The language on the streets is changing, and with it the language of the Bundestag. After almost three-quarters of a century, words like *Lügenpresse* (lying press) and *Volksverräter* (traitor of the people) are popping up again in German public debate.

'Grumbling and taking action, they go together here,' Gudrun told me, and she said she would continue to devote time and effort to 'her' refugees. Here in the Germany of 2018 that counter-movement is indeed strong and active, especially among generations younger than hers. In Berlin, anti-racism protests have attracted hundreds of thousands of people; in Chemnitz an anti-fascism concert was organized in response to a demonstration by 6,000 right-wing extremists, and 65,000 people attended. On German social media one prominent hashtag is *Wir sind mehr*: 'we are more'.

2

During my travels in 1999, Hotel Imperator, a time-worn Berlin townhouse with huge rooms, was my base of operations for Eastern Europe; I even had a couple of my own bookshelves there. Not long afterwards the big money swept away the stiff coffee, the crisp bread rolls, the neatly starched chambermaids, the creaking parquet floors and the corridors hung with contemporary art. It was all very sad. That street has nothing to offer now but swankiness.

The incomparable Hotel Savoy, with its mild smell of gentlemen and cigars at reception, is my new home. If the old Europe still comes together anywhere, it's here. I've heard so many stories told by elderly Berliners, bursting with history, and all from a single human lifetime. Bertolt Brecht, Joseph Roth, the Manns, Kurt Weill: you can still almost touch them in this hotel.

Over the past twenty years, the city has recovered much of its old dynamism, along with a peaceful modernity, an innate stylishness. All the projects that were underway in 1999 have long since become a natural part of the city. '*Der Westen ist besser, der Westen ist bunter, und schöner und schlauer, und reicher und frei,*' sang the East German singer-songwriter Wolf Biermann in the 1990s. 'The West is better, the West is brighter, and lovelier and smarter, and richer and free. The East is grimmer, the East is greyer, prospects are bleak and great is the need.'

Now there's a whole generation at work that did not experience the GDR, and there is little to be seen even of the border between the former East and West Berlin. The remains of the Wall are now the responsibility of museums and heritage preservation societies. An entire world, the really existing utopia of millions of communists, driven by an ideal that oppressed one and all, has been swept away. Only the dapper *Ampelmännchen*, that unique little man in a hat, is allowed to continue striding forth on pedestrian crossings. You see him all over the city now, one last relic of that utopia.

The old Berlin was bound together by rails. Every railway enthusiast knows the famous Gleisdreieck behind Kreuzberg, a wondrous node where all possible rail connections came together, a great confluence of noise, steel and hastening crowds. Now it's a big, quiet park; strange how all the energy has gone from it. Along what remains of that old steel, I spend a few days going back and forth with crowds of Berliners: out of the tram, onto the S-Bahn, and vice versa.

In 1999, beggars and indigents were still a rare element of the street scene. Now you find them everywhere, especially under viaducts, where it's crowded but dry. Many of the homeless have equipped their sleeping places professionally, their neat little beds firmly wrapped and made up – German thoroughness, even here. 'How the eye is sharpened by poverty!' wrote Roth, and it's still the case today. Here and there in the mornings you hear the rattle of the *Pfandsammler*, the men and women – mainly elderly or on welfare – who collect bottles and cans to earn a few cents from the deposit.

That sad army of litter pickers is broadly accepted these days, along with the dead-end poverty that drives Berliners to it.

Here the Christmas markets smell above all of roasted chestnuts and grilled goose. The market at the Gedächtniskirche has been strongly fortified ever since twelve people were crushed to death in a jihadist attack exactly two years ago. At this wounded church a new place of remembrance has been created, where hundreds of candles are flickering. It's scattered with flowers and wreaths. Inside, before the huge blue mosaic, a short evening service is being held. The organ plays and the brief sermon is about Christmas markets, the meaning of Christmas and heavenly peace. There are no more than thirty of us in the congregation, a few coats and knitted hats, a mother with her daughter. We say the 'Our Father' and receive the blessing: 'The Lord bless you and keep you.' Then we're outside again.

The next morning, from the train eastwards, I see white frozen fields, vegetable plots, flocks of black birds in the distance. In the local papers I read about wolves, which are having to be shot once again; about one of the Berlin nouveau riche who has turned his back on the city, wanting to live somewhere 'without hippies and ultra-feminism', a place 'where men still behave like men' and 'have normal jobs and careers'; about the climate, as 2018 will almost certainly go down as the warmest year since records began; and about a historic event – yesterday, the last German hard coal mine closed, the huge Prosper-Haniel colliery in Bottrop, dating back to 1871, where from the furthest coal-face it took an hour and a half to get back to the surface. The last lump was ceremonially presented to federal president Frank-Walter Steinmeier and European president Jean-Claude Juncker. Everyone sang 'Glück auf, der Steiger kommt' and that was the end of King Coal.

The once so tormented Dresden looks, after a little snow, like a perfect Christmas card once again. The station is a cathedral, the product of decades of order and industry, the ultimate Meccano set for grown-ups. The Frauenkirche, which was still a bare building site in 1999, looks glorious, as if no bombs ever fell. On the far side of the river the Saxon monarch Augustus I shines as if he's fallen, horse and all, into a trough of gold leaf. Beyond him the ordinary down-at-heel GDR begins again: the monotonous brick houses, the cobbles, the crumbling asphalt, the communist trees. Everything still has the flavour of Walter Ulbricht.

AlexA Senoirenresidenz is an old folks' home full of therapeutic nostalgia. The manager, Gunter Wolfram, receives me warmly and shows me around. 'For many elderly people, life here has become difficult now that pensions have been cut,' he says. They don't go hungry, but they can't play any part in things any longer, not even in the family, because they lack financial resources and the time to earn a little extra is behind them for good.' "*Jammerossi und Besserwessi*" – there's some truth in that,' he believes. 'In the West people learned to manage by themselves, whereas in the East they always relied on the community.' The community now serves mainly as a repository for complaints: about the weather, about money, and always about the insecure future. A few years ago the care home found itself increasingly confronted with depression, and of course with dementia. 'The atmosphere changed, the residents weren't having fun anymore, they grew dull and nodded off.'

Back then the home was unexpectedly given some extra space and a small subsidy. The manager decided to set up a cinema, by way of experiment, with proper cinema seats and films from the 1950s and 1960s. At the entrance he installed a Zschopau Motorroller, a GDR scooter from the 1960s, heavy as a piano. The old scooter, rather than the film, was the great success of the opening night. 'Four residents with dementia were impossible to part from it; they came up with stories they'd never told before, about friends, about trips to the Baltic coast. All of that from the mouths of people some of whom no longer knew the difference between a knife and a fork.'

I'm shown some of the rooms that were furnished after the new money came in, full of carefully collected and preserved relics of the GDR, including posters, radios and televisions, a few bits of furniture, a wallet full of those small East German banknotes, the TV guide FF *Dabei* – 'Some people suddenly recall the programmes' – the women's magazine *Guter Rat* and plastic bottles of a 'special detergent' called Reuwa. 'Everyone washed their front steps with this; it's the smell of my childhood.'

Carrying genuine GDR shopping bags, the residents now start their day in this part of the home. They go shopping in the past, light an old-fashioned stove as they always did, peel potatoes for soup – it keeps them busy all day. 'I see people doing all this who could no longer hold a knife or speak a word; they'd given up on themselves. Now they recite poetry, they dance, they have the feeling they can make something of their old age. Memories come to the surface that younger generations know nothing about. You see them become cheerful again, like the personalities they were, and are.'

Tea is served to four ancient ladies around a table. One of them jumps to her feet when she sees me, recognizing me as a foreigner. Her face starts to beam and glow. '*Kommst du bei mir, Charley? Bist du endlich, endlich zurück?*'

3

I travel on to Niesky in a diesel train. It's more like a bus on rails, cosy and simple. 'No talking to the driver while the train is moving.' The landscape grows quiet and hilly, with a dusting of snow, and here and there are some geese and cranes. We wait at a deserted station. Next door is a large brick factory with smashed windows, behind it something modern and office-like made of concrete, all implacably boarded up. 'FREEDOM' is written in black on a tumbledown house, even now.

In Niesky I stay in the Bürgerhaus, a former business hotel, still 100 per cent GDR even thirty years after the fall of the Wall – from the grey stair carpet to the bare ceiling in my room and the faded beach scene above my bed. The town has turned into a spruce old lady with a stunning facelift. Almost all the houses have been renovated, painted and insulated, and instead of communist grey, soft pastels dominate. The nearby brown coal mine has been transformed into a silent and infinitely deep lake. Waggon-bau Niesky, maker of train carriages, for a century the town's biggest employer, went bankrupt in 2018. The post office has been privatized. The cinema, where so many emotionally charged parties for young people were held, has gone. On that spot now is the car park for the Edeka supermarket, the monster that here too has swallowed up much of the town's retail trade. In nearby Görlitz the border with Poland was erased by the EU enlargement of 2004. On both banks of the Neisse a short distance away, a shared park has been laid out with a bridge, so that you can walk back and forth. Couples have photos taken there on their wedding day.

There's a new sports hall, the library is the pride of everyone here, but many schools have been demolished. Niesky has become a town of elderly people, where the young show their faces only at Christmas and Easter. Between 1990 and 2015 the former GDR lost 15 per cent of its population. Only the interior world of Eckart and Inge on Plittstrasse – now Wiesenweg – seems unchanged. They receive me like an old friend, dinner is ready, Inge inspects my coat and wants to resew one of the buttons immediately.

The tiled stove has gone, though, and that's not all. Granddaughter Elisabeth, along with her husband, now runs a farm in Ireland. Daughter Almund and son-in-law Jens currently live in Berlin – after all, that's where the jobs are. Eckart's technical bureau has projects everywhere, even in Africa and China. He no longer has to travel to China himself, since he can inspect every connection and every screw from Niesky, via the internet, and an assistant in China investigates all problematic nooks and crannies, camera in hand.

'Globalization has made my work a thousand times easier,' Eckart acknowledges. 'Just imagine, in the 1980s, in the GDR, if there was a technical problem that meant I needed to ring the West, I had to go through a "trustworthy" colleague. I wasn't allowed to make the call myself.'

'We've gradually grown into it, into Europe and the Western world,' they both say. 'In the 1990s that was all still a long way off. We had to get to know the West, learn to find our way in it, which was work enough in itself. Europe was far away. Very far.'

We catch up on events of the past twenty years. In the aftermath of the 1990s, in the former GDR as elsewhere, everything was enthusiastically plundered. Factories were sold for a pittance and dismantled, the machinery moved to the West. The jobs vanished. Treuhand, the organization set up to handle the privatization of state-owned enterprises, eventually posted a loss of more than 270 billion marks. Everything the GDR produced seemed contaminated, even though there were some excellent businesses. Eckart tells me about his own company, how they installed cooling systems with great expertise. That didn't count for anything. For them, the twenty-first century began with a prevailing sense of humiliation.

'In those years it was all about money,' says Inge. 'We knew nothing about that, because in the GDR everything was laid down. Even as a paediatrician you found yourself unable to do anything any longer because there wasn't any money for follow-up. In the first year after the Wende we talked more about money than in our whole lives up to that point.'

'It was the first time I'd come upon Western businesspeople who were proud of the fact that they'd never paid a cent in taxes,' Eckart tells me. 'I couldn't believe it, that you could think like that.'

The past also meant that, in 2001, 9/11 was experienced differently here compared to the rest of Europe. 'I thought: now you Americans finally know what war means,' says Eckart. As a boy in 1945 he'd seen signal flares above Dessau 'like lights on a Christmas tree'. He then watched the city burn. 'We were sitting in the air raid bunker and I thought: do those Americans actually know what happens to people here when the bombs fall? An Arab person I know said, "The Americans have only themselves to blame for this." I felt the same way. But I felt ashamed, too, for thinking like that.'

Eckart and Inge experienced more capitalism in recent years than they would have liked. They were horribly duped by a building project in which they invested their pensions, and their company was beset by lawyers who saw everything as a potential court case. They had some hard times. The humiliation has not gone away, either. Wages and salaries here are still 20 per cent lower than in the rest of Germany, almost all the big companies and institutions are still in the West, and former East Germans hold just 1.7 per cent of the top jobs in politics, government, academia, the economy and culture, despite making up 17 per cent of the population. Even the Tal der Ahnungslosen remains: there may well be more gaps in internet coverage here than in Albania.

However critical Eckart and Inge always were of the regime, you can't gloss over those long GDR years. As for so many other Eastern Europeans, their memories are indelible, an essential part of their identity. Berlin journalist Anja Maier has compared it to phantom pain after an amputation: 'What I still know for certain about East Germany is that I had a life there. A different life. And sometimes in a painful sense I long to have it back.' Inge says something similar: 'We're doing well, just fine in fact. But in my head things aren't right. The solidarity that was so natural then has gone completely. If a tree blew down in a storm, all the neighbours would come out to clear it away. That's over now. You just ring the housing corporation and it's taken care of.'

In Germany as a whole, memories of the GDR are fading fast. The younger generation knows nothing about it. Eckart and Inge often feel annoyed by all the dark stories about those times – because after all, those stories are about a part of themselves. Its reality was ambiguous, both oppressive and safe. 'We had unprecedented social security. We were never afraid. Yes, all right, of the state, we had to watch out for that, always.'

'You've lived and worked for more than half a century in this same quiet little town,' I say. 'In this same modest flat. And meanwhile your lives have been totally turned upside down.'

Eckart nods. 'At root, I think, it was all about money.'

4

Seventy-five years ago, on 16 June 1944, the legendary war correspondent Ernie Pyle published his first report from the beaches of Normandy. 'It was a lovely day for strolling along the seashore. Men were sleeping on the sand, some of them sleeping forever. Men were floating in the water, but they didn't know they were in the water, for they were dead.'

In the summer of 2019, D-Day was commemorated and all the leaders of the Allied nations of the time came together. For several days beforehand, the Trump family and their entourage more or less took possession of Buckingham Palace, flouting all the royal protocol, taking selfies on the balconies, acting like tourists in a newly conquered province. Trump saw the National Health Service as ripe for a takeover, said Nigel Farage ought to lead the negotiations with Brussels, and described the mayor of London as a 'stone cold loser'. Never in diplomatic history had a foreign leader interfered so openly and crudely in British domestic politics.

In 1964, on the twentieth anniversary of the Allied landings, former president Eisenhower stood in the American cemetery in Normandy among the remains of almost 10,000 of those sleeping and floating men. 'These people gave us a chance, and they bought time for us,' he said, 'so that we can do better than we have before.' Those now seem like words from a different world, from a generation that, for all its faults and short-comings, strove after a common goal: a state that provided for people, the dissemination of knowledge and prosperity, a robust public sector, the breaking down of borders and other national barriers, guaranteed human rights, the construction of European and other international institutions to safeguard those rights and to promote cooperation and preserve peace. It was a shared striving that united Western Europe and the United States, despite their many differences – and which united their armed forces too.

More than half a century after that anniversary, Franco crawled back out of his grave and the reactionary-nationalist Vox took almost 10 per cent of the votes in Spain. Benito Mussolini's great-grandson had found a place for himself in a neo-fascist party called Fratelli d'Italia, which attracted one in every twenty-five Italian voters. Marine Le Pen was hot on the heels of Macron in the polls.

The enemy on the Normandy beaches was by 2019 the dominant power on the continent, despite itself. After the first German empire, of Otto von Bismarck, founded in 1871, and the second, of Adolf Hitler, founded in 1933, it was the third time that Germany had emerged as an imperial power within Europe, if in disguise. This time it was an indirect and implicit power, based on consultation and collaboration, not military but economic, not national but cosmopolitan, a 'soft hegemony'. But it certainly could be a coercive power, as Europe saw in the euro crisis, for instance.

Guilt and history continued to prey on the minds of the Germans. The migrant crisis of 2015 was fuelled in part by Germany's fear of rapid ageing, but also to a great degree by its irrepressible need to 'make amends'. Germans were still terrified of leadership; Führung remains a loaded word to this day. 'I fear German power less than I am beginning to fear its inactivity,' said Polish foreign minister Radek Sikorski in 2011, in a speech in Berlin. 'You have become Europe's indispensable nation. You may not fail to lead.'

When I mentioned this later to a former German foreign minister, he laughed. 'Well, you should hear him and the other Eastern European leaders when we actually do that. It's totally unacceptable to them. You can take it from me!'

The heroic America of 1944 seems to have lost faith in its mission, and that won't change in a hurry. It no longer sees itself as an 'indispensable nation', a city on the hill, with a moral duty to defend Western freedom and democracy, although how it did so in practice is another story. After the Cold War ended, the balance of forces changed, military ties with Europe quickly loosened and competition with China took priority, a confrontation that Europe watches with sorrow. The most important imperial power of the twenty-first century turned inward. In 2019, at that same vast cemetery, the

American president mouthed a few platitudes and then resumed his familiar litany of accusations aimed at his domestic political opponents. He spent the rest of the day watching television.

The date on which he launched his 10,000th lie was Friday 26 April, five weeks before the Normandy commemoration. The frequency had increased markedly since he took office. At first the 'Fact Checker' run by the *Washington Post* had counted five a day; now the average was twenty-three.

The books on his list of favourites from 2018, despite this president's aversion to reading, had one characteristic in common: they were all about Donald Trump. At the top was *The Faith of Donald J. Trump: A Spiritual Biography*, in which the authors claim that God is using this man in a way that millions of mortals cannot comprehend. 'But God knows, and that's good enough.' If you saw it as a television series, it was all still hilarious.

In reality his administration was starting to look more and more like an absolute monarchy with a smattering of feeble democracy. History teaches that monarchs who have lost their bearings can cause irreparable damage in no time. More and more often there were moments at which the American president talked complete gibberish. In his speech on 4 July 2019, for instance, he cheerfully claimed that the American revolutionaries under George Washington in 1775 'took over the airports' from British forces. A few weeks later he tried to buy Greenland, ordered American companies to withdraw all their activities from China as if he were the Sun King, and declared openly that 'divine providence' had appointed him to fight a trade war with China: 'I am the chosen one.' What he thought about Europe became plain as day in a leaked video clip of a dinner with sponsors in 2018. 'The European Union is a group of countries that got together to screw the United States,' he told his guests. 'And, frankly, they're probably worse than China in a sense, just smaller.' When he put a foreign power, Ukraine, under severe pressure to collect damaging material on his likely Democrat rival at the next presidential election, Joe Biden, enough was enough. On 24 September 2019, the Democrats initiated an impeachment procedure. Despite convincing evidence, the process was blocked by the Republican majority in the Senate. After that, the president regarded himself as omnipotent.

In late 2019, Brexit, which sometimes looked rather like a polite coup d'état, was once again supported by British voters. In a general election called by Boris Johnson, the Conservative Party – using the simple slogan 'Get Brexit done!' – won such a comfortable majority in the House of Commons that his regime was guaranteed to keep its hold on power for years to come. Labour suffered its most crushing defeat since 1935. The party had refused to make a clear choice in the Brexit debate, and the figure of Jeremy Corbyn – who resigned as Labour leader in April 2020 – had repelled many voters. All the same, the results were distorted by the British constituency system, since in reality Johnson's support among voters had increased by only 1.2 per cent. Parties advocating for a second referendum had won more Britons to their side (16 million) than their opponents (14.5 million), but nowhere did that result manifest itself.

The actual Brexit negotiations, beneath the television screens of the dismal Albert Borschette Conference Centre in Brussels, dragged on. At the very last moment a Withdrawal Agreement came into being that settled the divorce, and on 31 January 2020 Britain officially left the EU. After that, a new trade agreement had to be put together under extreme time pressure, since the British refused to countenance further delay. In early September a profound breach of trust occurred. A bill was tabled in the House of Commons whose provisions directly contravened the protocol on Northern Ireland that was part of the Withdrawal Agreement. The Irish government in particular was furious. This crass move by London had a counterproductive effect, in that unity between EU member states became stronger than ever. Tensions rose to such a height that in mid-October Boris Johnson declared that the British must prepare themselves for a 'no-deal' scenario.

The powerful part played by populist sentiments was clear from the fact that the negotiations almost collapsed over fishing (0.1 per cent of the British economy), whereas the financial sector (7 per cent of the economy) was left out of the negotiations altogether. The consequences would be felt immediately. By January 2021 the centre of gravity of European stock exchange dealings had already moved from London, traditionally Europe's financial capital, to Amsterdam. The daily London trading volume had fallen to €8.6 billion; that of Amsterdam had quadrupled in the space of a month, to €9.2 billion.

Meanwhile, we were entertained by one British costume drama after another. The great television producers made a whole series of them, the onscreen castles and ballrooms dazzled us, the hundreds of crinolines and petticoats brought hours of overtime for the sewing workshops, and we wallowed day after day in that great British past that would never end. Then it was Christmas Eve and there, after all, was a trade agreement. It was 1,246 pages long.

The EU had been generous. The deal lacked the usual tariffs and export quotas. No other foreign trade partner was granted so much free access to the European single market. In return the British had to stay in line with EU rules on state aid, quality and safety, as well as the Union's social and environmental standards. But it was still a hard Brexit, an exceptionally painful break for both partners. On the staircase of possibilities once presented by negotiator Michel Barnier, with on the top step a position like Norway's, this was right at the bottom, only just above the chaos of a 'no deal'.

The EU lost one of its largest member states, an important economic and military power, a country with an uncommonly rich cultural and scholarly tradition, and a strong ally in the battle against the disruptive illiberalism of the Polish and Hungarian regimes. The British lost their vital position in one of the most important power blocs in the world, their central role in the financial sector, their opportunities to trade with the outside world problem-free and, especially important for young people, their right to study, work and live anywhere in Europe. That is to say nothing of the economic cost and the risk of far lower growth for years to come. 'Not one single person . . . has convinced me of the added value of Brexit,' Barnier said sombrely when it was over. 'It is a lose-lose game.'

British truck drivers who arrived at customs in Hook of Holland after New Year's Day 2021 were the first to be confronted with the reality. Even their favourite ham sandwiches had to be handed over, since the import of foodstuffs such as meat and fish was no longer permitted. 'Welcome to the Brexit, sir. I'm sorry.'

At this point, no one has any idea of the form in which the United Kingdom will rise again after so many years. What part will it play, severed from Europe? Will it be a bridge to America or a vassal state? Does it have sufficient weight to remain a permanent member of the UN Security Council and other international institutions? Will it even stay together? After all, Brexit is a specifically English nationalist project.

'What is happening now is not worthy of a serious country,' wrote Martin Wolf, an influential commentator at the *Financial Times*, when the Brexit chaos was at its height. 'The conclusion is that the UK is no longer such a country.' Great Britain as the world knew it – self-aware, pragmatic and respected – no longer exists, that much is clear.

At the end of the first two decades of the century, however, counter-movements were emerging that it would be foolish to underestimate. In the hot dry August of 2018, a shy fifteen-year-old Swedish schoolgirl began skipping school in a single-handed attempt to save the planet. In no time her climate protest grew into a dynamic global youth movement, with millions of school strikers in 135 countries.

Five times over, the Swiss citizens' movement Operation Libero successfully fought off attacks by the far right, winning referendums on constitutional rights and the rule of law. In Poland, an online resistance group uncovered a systematic defamation campaign by the government against the last remaining independent judges, and a secretary of state was forced to resign. In March 2019 in Slovakia, after months of demonstrations, liberal anti-corruption champion Zuzana Čaputová was elected president. In Malta, proceedings following the murder of journalist Daphne Caruana Galizia led to a popular revolt and the government stepped down. Everywhere in northern Europe the advance of the right-wing populists seemed to have been halted, and in Denmark, Sweden and Finland, as in Latvia and Lithuania, moderate pro-Europeans won elections.

The cities stirred themselves too. Istanbul and other large Turkish conurbations elected fierce opponents of Erdoğan as mayors, while Warsaw, Budapest, Prague and Bratislava joined a 'Pact of Free Cities' in late 2019. Their four mayors promised to act in concert to ensure their cities remained 'open, progressive, tolerant and above all European'.

In Italy, Matteo Salvini overplayed his hand by forcing a crisis purely because he was doing well in the polls. He now wanted 'full power', but 'his' purely populist government fell. In an impressive speech, Prime Minister Giuseppe Conte reproached him for having placed his own interests structurally and permanently above those of the state: 'When a political force concentrates on self-interest and party interest alone and assesses its options based only on the convenience of elections, it not only betrays the noblest calling of politics, it ultimately endangers the national interest.'

You no longer see Putin's portrait so often on young Russians' smartphones. By 2019, Russia seemed to be doing just fine. It was one of the top five countries in terms of natural resources, the national budget showed a surplus of 3 per cent and net national debt was zero. But because it was a kleptocracy, hardly any of that wealth reached the average Russian, whose spending power had been stagnant for years. Putin's cuts to pensions in particular created ill feeling. And sanctions were biting, trade between Russia and the rest of Europe having practically halved. The price of foodstuffs shot up. Before the Ukraine crisis in 2014, the average Russian had 10 per cent more to spend than they do now. In 2020 alone, sugar became 70 per cent more expensive, buckwheat 40 per cent, oil 24 per cent and flour 13 per cent, while average incomes haven't risen for five years. The 'reborn Russian world power' under Putin is largely for show. In reality the Russian economy is barely any bigger than Spain's and smaller than Italy's, and the defence budget is a third of the total amount spent by the EU on its own defence. The power of Russia is above all a power to disrupt, with an army of trollers and hackers. Among people aged between eighteen and twenty-four, Putin's popularity almost halved in a single year, from 36 to 20 per cent. However popular Putin might be, a poll by Russia's own Levada Center showed that more than 80 per cent of Russians were hoping for change, 42 per cent for 'fundamental change'. Only 11 per cent were content with the status quo.

Putin's answer lies in the past. Under the influence of twentieth-century thinker Ivan Ilyin, he has in recent years seen Russia mainly as the eternal victim: of the Ukrainian 'Nazis', of the 'traitors' on the home front and above all of the liberal West. It is an ideology full of resentment, the familiar toxic mixture of frustration and jealousy that we have seen raise its head before in the history of beaten and humiliated powers. Democracy and the rule of law merely stand in the way. When Belarussian tyrant Alexander Lukashenko lost the 2020 presidential election, he was able, with Putin's support, to resist a huge popular movement and calmly stay in office. In his last interview, Boris Nemtsov warned that Russia was quickly turning into 'a fascist state'. A few hours later he was murdered.

Opposition leader Alexei Navalny barely survived an attack in August 2020 that was claimed to have been staged by a team from the security service FSB. On board a domestic flight he fell seriously ill from one moment to the next, and the decision by the pilot to make an emergency landing in Omsk probably saved his life. After a fair amount of obstructionism by the local authorities, Navalny was transferred to a Berlin hospital, where international experts determined that he had been poisoned with a Novichok nerve agent. Once he had recovered he returned to Moscow in January 2021, where he was immediately arrested and sentenced to almost three years in a prison camp. His anti-corruption group had meanwhile published a video showing the megalomaniac country estate – 70 square kilometres – and the twenty-first-century Versailles – almost 18,000 square metres – that Putin had built between 2005 and 2010 on the coast of the Black Sea. Total cost, according to Navalny: $1.3 billion. The video has so far been watched by more than 100 million Russians. But for the time being, the opposition has been crushed completely.

5

What has become of my other main characters? And how was Europe doing at the end of those twenty years, in the late summer of 2019 and beyond?

In the Centrum Kafé in Kirkenes everyone was still extremely worried about Frode Berg. Against everyone's expectations, the friendly retired border guard had been sentenced by a Russian court to fourteen years in a prison camp. He'd admitted that he was indeed involved in spying. 'He's the victim of a botched operation by the Norwegian security service,' the men in the café say now. In November 2019 he was finally freed, in a prisoner swap. In Kirkenes they haven't recovered from the fright; enthusiasm for trips to Russia and for exchange programmes has declined markedly.

In 2016 Aydin Soei, who had come to Copenhagen as a refugee, published a book called Forsoning (reconciliation) that quickly became regarded as a classic of Danish literature. 'I'm thirty-five,' he says now. 'The generation of immigrant children ten years younger than me grew up in a very different reality. They're surrounded by various minorities that have done well. Ten years ago there was no ethnic-minority middle class, but there is now. They go out, they drink, they have boyfriends and girlfriends. But there's polarization too. Those who were excluded, like my brother, are leading a totally different life. They're among the young men that our society has lost along the way.'

Yet even Aydin's brother has abandoned radical Islam, including its dress codes and the belligerent language aimed at America. He is far more stable since becoming a father. 'He still has no work, he does a lot of sport, he walks along the street with a big sports bag, muscular, shaven-headed, but he wouldn't hurt a fly.' Aydin remains optimistic about his brother's future.

Umayya Abu-Hanna has set up a Finnish website called The Finnish Patriot. 'All Finns called themselves patriots, but in reality they were mostly racists. I was looking for true patriots, people with ideas about the future of Finland, who wanted to work hard on creating it. Out of nowhere I soon had ten thousand people signing up.' As for herself, she says: 'I'm a chameleon and always will be. I play with my identity: Finnish, Scandinavian, Palestinian, Amsterdammer, mother of a black child. It gives me great freedom, and my real energy comes from my work and from the city. No Nazareth for me but Amsterdam, New York, Beirut. For me, cities mean perennial learning.' She does admit that now she's getting older she tends to feel something is missing. 'Any animal can say: I come out of that cave or that nest. I don't have a home.'

Steven Seijmonsbergen, the assets and liabilities manager at Fortis, left the bank. He now works as a consultant and stresses that he and his colleagues need eternal vigilance. 'You think you're dealing with one bank, but behind it these days are ten or twenty separate service providers that are all links in the chain. That means your loan is subjected to more and more "transfer moments", each presenting new risks.' So although stricter banking regulations have provided more security, new uncertainties and complexities have arisen.

The financial machinery seems to be running as it always used to, but in reality everything is still largely reliant on emergency arrangements. A new recession is inevitable at some stage, the experts say, because the world economy always surges and then falls back. What measures can be taken when that happens is a big question, since the monetary means available have been deployed flat out over recent years in an attempt to stimulate growth.

Furthermore, the system is still extraordinarily opaque. The French banks alone have outstanding loans to Italy of €250 billion, but it's unclear exactly why or where. According to the latest annual report from the European

Banking Authority, the risks have risen sharply again. The banks have years of plenty behind them, yet they have not built effective buffers. Most of the profits, as before, have been spent on bonuses and dividends for the financiers. The *Financial Times* warns that if the eurozone does eventually fall apart, it will lead to 'probably the most violent shock in history, dwarfing the Lehman Brothers bankruptcy in 2008 and the 1929 Wall Street Crash'. Italy has already developed a parallel currency called the 'mini-BOT', featuring portraits of famous Italians who would be embraced by the public. The notes are held ready for distribution.

Iceland has long forgotten the financial crisis. Everyone is now far more worried about the melting of the glaciers. The Okjökull glacier was the first to disappear completely, transforming itself into a crater lake. More than 10 per cent of the country is still covered in glaciers, but all that ice will gradually disappear until 'Iceland' is merely a name.

In 2019, the Arctic had its warmest June ever. Canada, Siberia and Alaska experienced huge forest fires, as did Australia. In Germany, Belgium, France and the Netherlands, temperature records were broken yet again. According to the UN Environment Programme, the world needs to reduce CO_2 emissions by 7.6 per cent every year if the climate goals agreed in Paris are to be reached, with a maximum rise in temperature of 1.5 degrees. Not a single country, let alone the world as a whole, has ever succeeded in making such a reduction in one year, and it would need to be repeated year after year. At our granddaughter's birthday party on 25 July in Utrecht, the temperature reached 40 degrees. She was seven.

Greece appears to have survived all its financial perils. On 1 September 2019, the last of the restrictions on the movement of capital, introduced in 2015 to prevent a run on the banks, were lifted. The European Commission spoke of an 'important milestone' and the country was able to borrow everywhere again, at historically low rates of interest. The recently installed New Democracy government has already promised tax cuts. Unemployment is still the highest in the EU at 18.5 per cent, with 40 per cent of young people out of work. Wages are low, often half the level of the rest of the EU, and many jobs are temporary. The brain drain is continuing apace. Since 2010 some 400,000 young people have left the country, three-quarters of them university graduates. Almost a third of Greek households still have to make ends meet on an annual income of less than €10,000.

Manos Logothetis, the doctor who spent three years of his life in the 'oubliette' that was Samos, but who afterwards felt a need to ask awkward questions, returned to Athens after the change of government and is now junior minister for immigration. The asylum system for which he is responsible has seized up completely, and Greece, already poor, is having to accommodate more refugees and immigrants than Italy and Spain put together. Two journalist friends of mine who visited Samos in the summer of 2019 to report on conditions returned shocked: they had never seen anything like it on European soil before, and they'd seen a great deal. Despite millions in subsidy from Europe, there was still not a single toilet unit in the vast improvised camp, let alone washing and showering facilities. Meanwhile a handful of doctors and nurses at the local hospital have been arrested; for €500 they'd composed fake referral letters that enabled refugees to travel on to the mainland.

Nothing has come of a European asylum system. The consequences for Lesbos, too, were dramatic. As a result of deficient organization by the Greek immigration services, waiting times remained astoundingly long. Since quite a few migrants still managed to sneak in – 60,000 in 2019 alone – pressure on the islands increased even further. When in the spring of 2020 the coronavirus pandemic broke out, a total of 42,000 migrants were still stuck on the Greek islands, where there were facilities for only 6,200. The Moria camp on Lesbos was intended for a maximum of 3,000 people, yet in reality there were at least 12,000 camping there. That hopeless situation, in combination with all the restrictions of the Covid-19 crisis, led to an outburst of anger and despair. On a September night in 2020 the camp burned to the ground. Within two weeks a new camp had been built, with tents put up at an astonishing pace. But this time it was an internment camp; in theory at least, the refugees could no longer leave. The mud, the stench and the desperation remained.

Migration is once again a rich source of income for criminals, corrupt governments and the lucrative prisons industry. An estimated half a million illegal immigrants are currently wandering around Italy; its squares and stations are full of the homeless at night. As for the deal with Turkey, of the many tens of thousands of migrants since 2016, fewer than 2,000 have

ultimately been sent back to the supposed safety of Turkey. In Libya meanwhile, at least 20,000 migrants are being held by the Directorate for
Combating Illegal Immigration, paid for by EU subsidies. Conditions
there – mistreatment, extortion, sexual abuse – are appalling.

Within the European Council there is talk of setting up a common European border force and coastguard. The idea is to deploy a permanent
intervention force of some 10,000 border guards to deal with crisis situations. Around Greece a start has already been made by Frontex, with ships,
planes and 600 guards. But a collaborative effort by journalists, including
those of Bellingcat, *Der Spiegel* and ARD, revealed in the autumn of 2020 that
staff of this Operation Poseidon were involved on several occasions with the
random sending back by the Greek coastguard of rubber dinghies full of
refugees – a risky procedure that violates the most elementary principles of
international law. Rescues at sea, including those performed by the European rescue and anti-smuggling Operation Sophia, have been temporarily
suspended. The Libyan coastguard currently has the place virtually to itself.

The number of migrants reaching Europe by crossing the Mediterranean
has fallen significantly, according to the UNHCR. In 2018 there were 113,482,
as against 1,015,078 in 2015. The same organization states that the chances of
drowning have increased. With the eastern route more or less cut off by the
Turkey deal, more and more migrants hazarded the longer – and far more
dangerous – crossing to Lampedusa and Italy. According to figures from the
UN's International Organization for Migration (IOM), in 2016, 2.3 per cent
of the migrants on this central route died or disappeared; in 2019, the figure
was twice as high, at 4.8 per cent or almost one in twenty. Figures for the
westerly route were comparable: between the spring of 2016 and the summer of 2020 another 12,000 people died, and the IOM assumes this to be
an absolute minimum. I find reports like these hidden away in the pages of
my newspaper. The refugee drama is no longer news, merely a statistical fact.

Precious little has come of the 2016 Turkey deal. Most of the promises
made to Ankara, such as visa-free travel, relocation of the most vulnerable
refugees and a renewed prospect of EU membership, have not been kept.
The Erdoğan regime made use of the failed coup of that year to carry out a
coup of its own, by means of widespread purges. More than half a million
people were detained by the police and intelligence agencies, and some
77,000 were jailed, with or without trial. Seventeen generals – many but

not all of them suspected instigators of the coup – were condemned to a total of 171 'aggravated life terms', whatever that may involve. More than 140 journalists are still being held. Another 150,000 Turks, including 4,000 judges and prosecutors, have been sacked from their jobs.

In Ukraine, the war has become a ritual dance. Ukrainian troops and the separatists still face each other, sometimes only a few dozen metres apart. According to the most recent reports, people are still being killed, several each week. But neither side is able to mount an attack because of the cease-fire agreement known as the Minsk Protocol, and nor can they withdraw because there is still no political solution. When they fire their weapons, usually at night, it's to let off steam.

Sarajevo remains Sarajevo, eternally waiting for Prince Europe. China, Russia and even the Arab world are increasingly interested, since it provides access to the heart of Europe for a song. In the city there are jokes about the difference between optimists and pessimists: the optimists believe Turkey will join the EU during the Bosnian presidency, while the pessimists think Bosnia will join the EU during the Turkish presidency. In other words never, *nimmer, jamais*.

In Gdańsk the propaganda of hatred has led to murder. During a festive concert by the Great Orchestra of Christmas Charity in January 2019, free-thinking mayor Paweł Adamowicz was stabbed by a mentally disturbed man and died shortly afterwards. A fierce campaign had been waged against him in the state media. 'Polarization killed him,' said his widow. A week before his death, a puppetry film circulated on the internet in which he was given the central role. A puppet collects money for sick children during the concert, which he pockets before turning into a Jew with a Star of David. The animation was exuberantly liked and shared.

Meanwhile, the PiS regime has opted, like the Hungarian government, for direct confrontation with the EU. In late December 2019, a law was pushed through the Polish parliament under which judges can be punished if they insist on obeying the verdicts of the European Court of Justice. Polish human rights ombudsman Adam Bodnar responded by saying, 'If a judge has a case of any political importance on his desk, he needs to watch out.'

*

In Hungary, the 2018 election campaign was driven purely by fear: fear of immigrants, fear of Islam, fear of Brussels. Young television producer Eszter Hajdú recorded dozens of election meetings, so viewers could at last hear what was really being said in all those halls all over the country. A leader of Fidesz claimed that George Soros had earned his fortune with money from dead Jews; another Fidesz politician said that the Brussels elite was stimulating immigration to make Europe more left-wing and to weaken the European people. 'Just try walking with me through Paris; you won't see a single white person.' A shout from the audience: 'Shame it wasn't six million plus one.'

At present, 42 per cent of Hungarian families with children are living below the poverty line. In the countryside the figure is 54 per cent. Healthcare in Hungary is worse than anywhere else in Europe and the disabled have lost most of their state support. With his cocktail of hatred, Orbán has won more voters than ever and his majority in parliament is now overwhelming. Hungary, he explained on his re-election, is surrounded by a 'German Iron Chancellor in the west,' by 'Slavic military states in the east' and by 'Islamic robber masses from the south'. Six of the people who worked on Eszter Hajdú's documentary did not want their names included in the credits at the end, for fear of reprisals.

Around Carles Puigdemont, leader of the 2017 Catalan rebellion, silence has fallen. He is still living in exile, protected by kindred spirits in Flanders. In October 2019 the uncompromising high court in Madrid, which never misses an opportunity to add fuel to the fire, sentenced nine other Catalan members of parliament and political leaders to prison terms of between nine and thirteen years for violent insurrection. The extreme punishments led to new mass protest marches, with opponents of independence increasingly taking part alongside its advocates. In early 2020, however, for the first time since the 1930s, a progressive coalition government was formed in Spain with the declared aim of using a 'bilateral negotiating table' to find a way out of the impasse.

Bart Somers, mayor of Mechelen, was awarded the 'World Mayor Prize 2016' as the world's best mayor.

As an experienced member of the Bullingdon Club, Boris Johnson managed for years to escape every scandal and get away with every lie. Only after he was present at parties during the pandemic, when the whole country was in a strict lockdown, did the spell break; even the British refused to put up with that much inequity. Arriving at a service of thanksgiving for Queen Elizabeth II's platinum jubilee in June 2022, Johnson was booed by the crowd. The Conservatives found themselves in hot water, cabinet members resigned one after the other and in the end Johnson had no option but to go. On 7 July 2022 he announced he would resign as prime minister.

There followed a brief intermezzo under the leadership of the dogmatic Liz Truss – her ultraconservative 'Trussonomics' led to an unprecedented drop in the value of the pound – after which the moderate Rishi Sunak was put in place to pick up the pieces. In those same disastrous September weeks, Queen Elizabeth died. Her impressive funeral on 12 September signified, in every respect, the end of an era. And perhaps of a world power.

Angela Merkel has set out on her farewell tour. In December 2018 she stepped down as leader of the CDU and announced she would cease to serve as federal chancellor after the elections in 2021. When she was asked at a local meeting how she wanted school history books to describe her half a century from now, her answer was: 'She tried.'

6

Some historians have compared this point in history with the start of the sixteenth century, a period of what is known as 'paradigm change'. It was the time in which the Europeans 'discovered' the rest of the world. After the invention of printing, many people learned to read and write, so knowledge was no longer the privilege of a tiny elite. Martin Luther provoked the ecclesiastical leadership, revolts broke out here and there in Europe, and in the Low Countries cities and regions renounced their divinely appointed monarch, while established ideas and institutions everywhere began to shift and to crack. It was the start of developments that ultimately resulted in the revolutions of the eighteenth and nineteenth centuries.

After more than two centuries of freedom, equality and fraternity, are we now living through a comparable change in fundamental assumptions and priorities? Until the attacks of 9/11, immigration from Turkey and

North Africa was generally regarded as a social issue that, with sensible policies, might yet be steered in the right direction. From one moment to the next, as described by Aydin Soei and others, 'immigrants' became 'Muslims'. It was now a clash of religions, an almost insoluble conflict.

Dealings with reality started to acquire magical features in these years. Respectable scientific research, especially on climate, was regularly jeered off stage by populist politicians. In the Netherlands there were even proposals to withdraw the state subsidy to the renowned Royal Netherlands Meteorological Institute because the conclusions of all that research no longer left any room for climate scepticism. The 'alternative facts' of the American president were eagerly accepted by his followers, and the same went for those spouted by Salvini in Italy and Orbán in Hungary. It was the bombardment of lies on television and the internet in Poland that cost the life of Paweł Adamowicz. As for Britain, many of the Brexiteers' campaign promises were utterly detached from economic and political reality. British political author William Davies uses the term 'radical incompetence'. 'This is not simply a backlash after decades of globalization, but against the form of political power that facilitated it.' A power that, he adds, was 'increasingly divorced from local identities'.

With that abandonment of reason, the sober work of government was downgraded, along with the skill of diplomats and the extremely important but far from spectacular toil behind the scenes. All populists mislead, and in doing so ignore problems, complications and dilemmas. Throughout his long political career, Geert Wilders has stayed well away from the work of government. The Brexiteers had no plan at all when they began negotiations in Brussels. In Ukraine, the actor Volodymyr Zelenskiy got himself elected president while boasting of his total lack of experience in management and politics. Matteo Salvini was officially minister of internal affairs, but by halfway through 2019 he had spent precisely seventeen days in his department. The rest of the time, 'Selfini' was busy with his campaign performances.

This downgrading was linked to the dismantling of the public sector, which in these years, under the banner of austerity, gathered pace all over Europe. In Britain the social infrastructure – parks, pubs, libraries – was seriously affected, especially in poorer regions and neighbourhoods. Belgium – and this is merely one of many examples – witnessed the rapid rise of the private swimming pool while more and more public swimming facilities closed, almost 20 per cent of them between 2006 and 2017. In eastern Germany I regularly came upon fearful elderly people after the austerity programme known as Hartz IV. What other spending cuts might be hanging over their heads? They had nowhere left to go.

Inequality increased markedly in these years too, especially after the banking crisis of 2008. In the southern EU member states a new poverty-stricken class emerged, made up of young people with good educations who couldn't get jobs, who were dependent on temporary and poorly paid work from which it was impossible to earn a living, and who therefore had to rely on family, friends or charity. They were no longer able to build careers, something that for their parents' generation was still the most normal thing in the world. This was starkly illustrated when, during the political crisis in the summer of 2019, parliamentarians of the Five Star Movement, many of whom had been unemployed in the past, were prepared to join almost any coalition, so terrified were they of losing their well-paid parliamentary seats.

Swiss author Roger de Weck spoke of a 'revived aristocratization' of Western society. He was thinking of aristocracies in the worst sense of the word, as elites who are not prepared to answer to anyone, not willing to accept that in any society property brings responsibilities and duties with it, and who, certainly in the semi-public sector, often feel themselves to be above the rules of the market and capital. In these dying days of neoliberalism, we have seen robber barons of that sort turn up everywhere – locally, nationally and internationally – often displaying a stunning arrogance. In the financial world especially, and above all during the crisis of 2008, this new caste's unashamed greed and total lack of any sense of responsibility have been remarkable, undermining any form of civil society. Many people therefore turned against 'the system' itself, feeling that they had no further part to play in it, that no one was any longer paying attention to them. And they were right.

While these two decades that started the twenty-first century were a period of rapid and profound change, the reaction to it – nostalgia – was perhaps the strongest force in evidence. Nostalgia is a serious business, a form of homesickness, not in space but in time; a fundamental feeling of displacement. French political thinker Dominique Moïsi wrote in the early years of this century that the world was no longer confronting a clash of civilizations but instead a clash of emotions: a culture of hope in China and the rest of Asia, a culture of humiliation in the Arab and Muslim world, and a culture of anxiety in the West. Everywhere in the Western world, fear replaced trust – fear of the other, fear for the future, and a fundamental fear of a loss of identity in an increasingly complex world.

The European project proved particularly susceptible to the last of those fears, and it was a phenomenon visible everywhere. The great expectations of the start of the century were replaced by a melancholic longing for a home that, if we are honest, never existed in reality. The EU had acquired a boundless character, both literally and figuratively, an infinity, and that unpredictability turned European citizens into fearful fugitives, fleeing into the past and often into the illusion of the safe nineteenth-century nation state. Europe, which less than a century ago still shaped the world order of the day, turned in on itself, at a time in which the EU, at a global level, was facing a series of unprecedented and far-reaching choices. In his 2014 book *World Order*, Henry Kissinger wrote that Europe was 'drifting off into a geo-political vacuum' between a past it sought to overcome and a future it had not yet defined.

For many Europeans at the turn of the century, including those who thought in international terms, the EU and its continued existence seemed the only geopolitical goal they could imagine for Europe. Their dream became a reality: peace, for generations, and steadily increasing prosperity. But what the rest of the world would look like, what role Europe would have to play in it, how the special relationship with Russia in particular should be given new shape, how the continent should address the increasing pressure of immigration from a disintegrating Middle East and an overpopulated Africa – to all these geopolitical questions there was not even the beginning of an answer.

Are we now on the eve of an era in which the future will be shaped by forces that stand outside any form of order? The answer might well be 'yes'.

7

The interviewers of Eurobarometer regularly ask European citizens whether they expect the life of today's children to be better than their own. In 1999 the answer was an overwhelming 'yes'. Twenty years later it was an overwhelming 'no'.

That is the state of present-day Europe.

There are moments when politicians rise above themselves and their ingrained patterns of thought and behaviour. The founding of the European Coal and Steel Community in 1952 was one such moment, as the small club of pioneers of that time understood only too clearly. The deepening of the European Community, culminating in the Maastricht Treaty and the European Union, was another, guided and inspired by visionary and sometimes courageous diplomats and statespeople. But will anything like it be possible in the years to come?

The story goes that senior diplomat Robert Cooper, in the 1990s head of the policy planning section of the British Foreign Office, had a special rubber stamp made after the fall of the Berlin Wall that read 'OBE', for 'Overtaken By Events'. He got his diplomats to work through all the files with it, which cleared things up no end. I believe it's almost time to order another such stamp. In short, it's time for me to take my leave. From now on, you, dear reader, know more than I do.

I travelled to Budapest again. I wanted to visit the elderly György Konrád one more time. We sat together on his small balcony, the midday sun shining through the leaves of the avenue on which he lived, and drank a glass of cognac. His voice was soft, almost inaudible sometimes, but his sentences were clear and sharp – the way he still set them down on paper daily.

In today's Hungary he was boycotted once again. On the occasion of his eighty-fifth birthday the German president paid lavish tribute to him, but in his own Budapest a deafening media silence reigned. Konrád's response was laconic. 'It's an old problem, one I've always had, my whole life long. I was always a traitor to my country, first under the communists, now under the nationalists. It's my perennial title.' He showed me a comment: *It's a shame he's still alive, the rat*. 'No, they haven't learned much.'

We spoke at length about his country. 'When it comes down to it, Orbán isn't brave enough to go directly against the EU,' he told me. 'Putin is cleverer than the rest, calmer. Erdoğan is too hot-tempered. But Orbán is afraid.' He likened Orbán's followers to the old communist apparatchiks, who developed a similarly extreme flexibility in order to survive. 'They've even adopted Orbán's language. Mind you, if they don't they might as well write their letters of resignation. But Orbán knows perfectly well that his friends will betray him in an instant if the European money dries up. Don't forget, this country doesn't belong to Orbán, this country belongs to us.'

When we talked about Angela Merkel's *Wir schaffen das*, Konrád said, 'I have no wise answer. I understand German feelings about the Holocaust. But throwing the borders open out of a sense of guilt is not the best solution. You can't erase the Shoah by letting in a million immigrants.' Europe needs to treat its own culture with care, he added. 'Extreme exclusion should not now be followed by extreme inclusion. We must respect other cultures, certainly. And we should be glad that so many people want to live within European culture. It's wonderful that there's such a massive exchange going on – the dynamism of a city like Amsterdam, it's all magnificent. But we mustn't be blind to the differences.'

We discussed the populists who are now gaining ground in the West, the nationalists and romantics who want to go back to the nineteenth century. 'They wallow in the past, but I'm afraid that at the same time they are the future,' I said.

'I think so too,' said Konrád. 'People like that own the future, at this point at least. But all things pass; you'll learn that if you live a bit longer.'

We exchange a few more words and then fall silent. Eventually, rather awkwardly, we say our goodbyes. 'Will we see each other again in this life?' we both wonder.

Europe will continue on its course, yes, he's certain of that. 'Fall, get up, slowly learn something. We'll stay together – at least, unless external powers intervene.' The big cities, he says, that's where it will all happen. 'I'm not a nationalist, I'm an urbanist. Urbanism, that's the basis of twenty-first-century Europe.'

'How about one more cognac, after all?'

György Konrád died on 13 September 2019.

Epilogue

To my student of 2069

I

DEAR FRIEND,

Who could ever have imagined that our whirlwind existence would plunge into a vacuum. When I was writing this book in 2019, I thought we were done with this period, that you and I could shake hands and go our separate ways – I to my own time, you half a century ahead. I have to admit that in my sleepless moments, the alarming feeling sometimes crept over me that this entire book described what was merely a prelude, although I had no idea to what. We know a little more now. I therefore owe you this deferred account.

Like a bolt from the blue, our turn came. We, the sun-baked generations of these decades, were kicked out of our slumbers in the spring of 2020 and cautiously rolled the forgotten word 'fate' on our tongues. Weren't we immortal? Hadn't we all agreed, in this self-aware part of the world, that everybody was safe now, that everything could be taken care of?

A woman in Sarajevo once described to me how, as a young girl in 1992, she experienced the start of the Bosnian Civil War. 'Well,' she said, 'my parents, my grandparents, every generation had been through a war. We simply thought: okay, so it's our turn.'

And now we hang by a thread.

These days I'm one of my village's bell-ringers. When all this trouble started, I stood for fifteen minutes in the dark little space at the bottom of the tower pulling a bell rope, next to the bier and other old village stuff. I gave a few firm tugs and far above my head the peal of bells began, accompanied by hundreds of other bells, all over the country. The churches had got together and thought this up, to provide a moment of 'hope and comfort', although to me it was more suggestive of 'fire' and 'red alert'. Which it is too, of course. It's as if an angel from the Book of Revelation has come down to earth breathing death and disaster. A new virus has emerged, it's spreading invisibly, rapidly, and it can be fatal, especially for elderly and vulnerable people. The scientists have given it a fine-looking name, SARS-CoV-2, or severe acute respiratory syndrome coronavirus 2, the cause of a disease they have named Covid-19, but they still don't know it very well. It's capricious. It changes shape, too; new mutations keep turning up, some of which are more deadly still.

At first the doctors found themselves empty-handed. There were no proven treatments and a vaccine was a distant prospect. In the first wave the dead piled up in the churches and cold stores of Spain and Italy, and there was neither the space nor the time for so many burials. From Madrid to New York the hospitals looked like battlefield aid posts. At the same time, a great lonely dying was underway, especially in care homes.

For our generations this was new and unfamiliar territory. Everyone was worried and frightened. People we knew might die, perhaps even people we love, perhaps we ourselves. We followed the news. What we were going through seemed unreal. Almost all European countries were locked tight, supply lines were broken, a fifth of the world's population was isolated at home, schools were shut, meetings forbidden, theatres, cafés and restaurants closed, the streets empty of people.

Boccaccio wrote about all this long ago, describing the Florentine plague epidemic of 1348, writing that 'townsman avoided townsman' and 'kinsfolk seldom or never visited one another and held no converse together save from afar'. Now too, keeping at a distance became the new virtue. The handshake, a custom more than 2,000 years old in the West, abruptly disappeared.

In the centre of Amsterdam you walked through photographs of a silenced nineteenth century. In our village the card-game evenings and drama rehearsals had stopped. We watched advertisements on television featuring joyful gatherings, people embracing, and they were already images from a different era. Every night on its scoreboard the television news totted up the latest death toll.

All these months we have stood looking open-mouthed at our world's abrupt standstill, trapped and above all astonished. This crisis entails disruption to the economic and social order on a scale never seen before. The stock markets initially seemed bewitched. Everything collapsed at once in the early weeks: shares, bonds, gold – the value of all three went into freefall. Oil prices were at their lowest level this century, at one point even turning negative; buyers received forty dollars for every barrel they bought, since there was nowhere left to store all the unsold oil. But just as quickly and incomprehensibly, stocks rose, and by the end of the year records were being broken once again.

There were some who announced the end of an astonishing and dislocating period of globalization and neoliberalism. You, out there in 2069, are in a better position to judge the truth of that than I am. 'The future is impossible to predict,' my favourite columnist wrote. 'And as for the little we can predict, you don't want to know the half of it.' That's the position we were in during those months.

I am writing these lines on thin ice. There is no distance yet; the history is still too fresh. It's more than possible that you, in 2069, will describe this period, with a shake of the head, as a strange incident, a worldwide panic attack, an eruption of mortal dread that the West especially had repressed for too long. Yet in the early phase in particular, we had every reason to be extremely concerned. Along with all the fear, pain, death and grief, an economic storm of unknown magnitude was blowing towards us. There were concerns that it might be as great a crisis as the Great Depression of the 1930s. In the end the economy of the eurozone slumped by 6.8 per cent in 2020. For comparison: in the very depths of the 2008 banking crisis the contraction amounted to 4.5 per cent.

Banker Steven Seijmonsbergen, who as assets and liabilities manager at Fortis experienced that earlier crisis from the inside, had told me that in those September weeks of 2008 he regularly broke out in a sweat. The entire financial system might seize up at any moment. Money would cease to come out of the cash machines. He looked out of the window at life on the streets and thought: do you realize that all this could come to a halt from one day to the next?

What was narrowly avoided then became a reality in 2020, except that the cash machines kept on turning. All over the world, people stopped coming out of their houses. So this crisis, unlike those of 1929 and 2008, struck at the heart of the economy, immediately and directly, and at small and medium-sized businesses especially.

As ever, the catastrophe hit the poorest hardest: the slum dwellers in Asia and South America who had little in the way of medical services; the day labourers of India and Africa, representing half the working populations, who saw their chances of jobs and food evaporate; the millions of refugees and displaced persons; but also the countless people in Europe and the United States who were on below-average incomes. More than half the workers of the world saw their incomes fall after the outbreak of the pandemic, according to a Gallup poll in May 2021. Women were particularly hard hit. The major improvements in global living standards of the past thirty years were to some degree negated.

What were the initial reactions? To be honest, precisely what you would expect: every country immediately fell back on old traditions and patterns of behaviour. The smoothly organized welfare states of Norway and Denmark, for example, reacted with remarkable speed and discipline. For Sweden, a more individualistic society of trust, the responsibility of citizens themselves was central. Cafés, restaurants and schools remained open for a long time, with only sporting events and meetings of more than fifty people banned. It was not a success, incidentally. Sweden had many times the number of fatalities seen in other Scandinavian countries.

Centralized France, like Belgium and Spain, opted for overwhelming governmental intervention. Acting like an absolute monarch, President Macron boarded up the country completely. Nobody was allowed to leave home without a permit, the police controlled everyone and everything – even matters entirely unrelated to the virus – and punishments were severe, the grip of the authorities total. The country lay deserted; more than one in three employees was temporarily laid off as a result of the closures.

Italy, in immense confusion, came to a standstill. Some 100,000 to 150,000 businesses were in danger of bankruptcy, employing between them two to three million Italians. Southern Italy braced itself for the worst economic carnage since the Second World War. In poor districts of Naples the Camorra started handing out food parcels. After all, they provided the perfect cover for the distribution of drugs, as well as helping it to tighten its hold on the population.

Germany, with its carefully worked-out plans for a pandemic, succeeded in handling the outbreak reasonably well at first, although there was continual confusion about the powers and rules of all its different states.

In free-market Britain, however, so little protective clothing was available that in the early weeks hospital staff sometimes had to go around dressed in bin bags, wearing snorkels and welders' goggles. One British expert told the *Sunday Times*, 'If you were with senior NHS managers at all during the last two years, you were aware that their biggest fear, their sweatiest nightmare, was a pandemic, because they weren't prepared for it.'

2

It was a calamity foretold. 'A third of the world died,' wrote fourteenth-century chronicler Jean Froissart of the Black Death, the bubonic plague that depopulated entire regions of Europe in the middle of that century, especially in what is now Italy. He was probably right; contemporary historians arrive at similar estimates. In North and South America in the sixteenth century, the indigenous population was almost wiped out by the smallpox and measles brought by European colonists.

Pandemics, like wars, famines and natural disasters, have had a profound impact on human history time and again, over the centuries. They reinforce the position of monarchs and other rulers, and they justify the most drastic interventions by the state – from violations of domestic privacy to forced detention. American historian Frank Snowden, a specialist on epidemics, regards the campaign against the bubonic plague as a crucial moment in 'the emergence of absolutism'.

At the same time, epidemics were part of ordinary human life. It has been calculated that anyone born in Amsterdam in 1600 who lived to be seventy years old would have experienced six outbreaks of the plague. The smallpox that tormented Britain took the lives of at least a tenth of the population in the eighteenth century. Almost half of British people at the time bore the scars, and central characters in books by Charles Dickens often have to go through life with an appearance disfigured by the pox. Smallpox broke out time and again, well into the twentieth century. It was not until 1979 that the World Health Organization declared it the first disease ever banished from the earth.

When the plague ravaged London for the umpteenth time in the summer of 1665, senior naval administrator Samuel Pepys heard the groans of famished and dying seamen through the door of his office, and saw corpses lying in the streets. The city had emptied, and those few he came upon looked 'like people that have taken leave of the world'. Meanwhile he calmly chattered away in his diary about all his day-to-day worries: financial difficulties, too many letters, a pretty maidservant, a pleasant time spent with a friendly widow, an argument with his wife, problems at the office. He also mentions remarkable moments of contemplation that seem familiar to us today, about humanity and 'how little merit doth prevail in the world, but only favour'. Yet there is also intense enjoyment of life, as when at the height of the epidemic he gets himself rowed across the Thames to lodgings outside the city. An unknown man travels with him, who soon proves as fond of music as Pepys himself, 'and he and I sung together the way down with great pleasure'.

Pandemics are part of modern history too, a fact that we sometimes seem to forget. Take for example what became known as 'Russian flu', a disease that emerged in December 1889 in Saint Petersburg. It was the first pandemic able to spread rapidly across the globe by means of the railways and steamboat traffic. Some experts believe it was probably the first outbreak of a coronavirus; newspaper reports of the time mention symptoms, including the loss of taste and smell, that closely resemble those we are seeing now. An estimated 1 million people died.

The notorious Spanish flu of 1918 – my own father barely survived it as a young student – probably first emerged in Kansas. It was helped in its rapid spread by American troop transports to Europe. Then all those great festive gatherings to celebrate the end of the war formed further hotbeds of infection. Worldwide between 20 and 40 million people died; between 150,000 and 280,000 in Britain, 230,000 and 360,000 in France, 20,000 and 60,000 in the Netherlands, 30,000 and 80,000 in Belgium. In the 1980s a different epidemic arose, mainly among gay men but also drug users and haemophiliacs: AIDS, a fatal disorder of the immune system, caused by a virus named HIV. Effective drug treatments have now turned it into a chronic illness, in theory. Nevertheless, in 2019 it caused almost 700,000 deaths worldwide. In total, AIDS has so far killed close to 33 million people.

The virus that causes Covid-19 was described by pandemics specialist and science journalist David Quammen as neither anything new nor a fateful accident. 'It was – it is – part of a pattern of choices that we humans are making,' he wrote. Quammen points to the way we are turning the world upside down, disturbing ecosystems on a massive scale and continually shaking viruses loose, as it were, from their natural hosts. 'Virus leaps' have occurred increasingly over recent decades, initially from animals to humans, then from humans to humans, at which point a pandemic is never far away.

In the early 1990s, with rapidly increasing globalization and the rise of mass international air traffic, intelligence agencies such as the CIA began to regard a worldwide pandemic as one of the greatest security risks we face. There were plenty of examples: the Hong Kong flu that killed around a million people worldwide (1969–70), Ebola in Zaire and Sudan (1976), the Sin Nombre hantavirus in the US (1993), the Hendra virus in Australia (1994) and bird flu in Hong Kong (1997).

In tackling this pandemic, the WHO has played a central role on numerous occasions, but it has needed to fight with one hand tied behind its back. It could not introduce binding regulations and its budget was little larger than that of the average teaching hospital. It has always been forced to compromise and manoeuvre to maintain the cooperation of certain member states – China, but also some African countries – and nothing has changed in that regard. A great deal depends on the personality and authority of the director general leading the organization at the time of a crisis.

Gro Harlem Brundtland, former prime minister of Norway, was in charge of the WHO when in 2002 a farmer in the Chinese province of Guangdong became infected with a strange and fatal lung disease. It was the first case of SARS, a forerunner to the current virus. By March 2003 it had spread to Hong Kong, Vietnam and Canada. Rapid preventive action by Brundtland and her team, including testing, quarantine and negative travel advisories, limited the epidemic to fewer than a thousand fatalities.

When in March 2009 a new virus emerged in Mexico, quickly dubbed 'swine flu', the WHO's response was less convincing. By June, when the organization recognized that a pandemic was underway, more than 28,000 people had been infected, in seventy-four countries. The organization quite rightly raised the alarm. When the pandemic died out a year later, it had claimed fewer lives than expected. Most of the vaccine had to be discarded. Governments were already short of money after the financial crisis of 2008, so fierce criticism came from all sides, and the WHO bore the brunt of it. Its budget was reduced by at least $300 million, entire departments were abolished – including the research teams that were most important in combating pandemics – and its leadership became weak and hesitant.

In January 2014, Ebola once again brought death to West Africa, and this time the WHO lost control of the situation completely. This was a virus far less infectious than flu but far deadlier. As a result of all the previous criticism, it was not until August 2014 that the WHO dared to raise the alarm, seven months after the disease first broke out – to the despair of Doctors Without Borders, which had watched a local outbreak turn into a terrifying epidemic. When the virus threatened to spread to the Western world, America at last intervened. President Obama's White House created a special Ebola task force, Congress made more than $5 billion available, and a large medical-military mission was sent to West Africa, with 3,000 troops. The virus was brought under control at the eleventh hour. More than 11,000 people died in Africa, but without this effective intervention it might easily have been ten or a hundred times as many, right across the globe.

Some governments and intelligence agencies were now wide awake. Many security assessments pointed to the danger of pandemics and to the predicted shortage of equipment and intensive care beds during any major outbreak of disease. In America a special department of the National Security Council was set up, so that such disasters could in future be recognized at an early stage and contained. In January 2017, the possibility of a deadly flu epidemic was an important element of the transition talks between Obama's team and the new president.

All that information, like the transition files Chris Christie had so carefully compiled, was discarded under Trump. All the officials of the new government who had shown any interest left within the next two years, or were fired. In a new round of spending cuts, the special pandemic response team of the National Security Council was largely disbanded. Nevertheless, in 2019, under the code name 'Crimson Contagion', precisely such a new outbreak, including all its bureaucratic consequences, was acted out in twelve states. The scenario closely resembled what actually happened just a few months later: a virus that affects the respiratory organs spreads from China and turns up in Chicago, after which, the epidemiologists of Crimson Contagion estimated, around 110 million Americans are infected, some 7 million are hospitalized and 500,000 die.

'Nobody ever thought of numbers like this,' said President Trump. In reality they had. It was just that most political leaders failed to listen.

The pandemic currently horrifying the world probably began in the Chinese city of Wuhan, which has a population of at least 10 million. On 30 December 2019 Ai Fen, a doctor and director of the emergency department at Wuhan Central Hospital, spotted a lab report that set her thinking. It concerned a patient with severe pneumonia, and she already had six other patients with similar symptoms in quarantine. She took a photograph of the report and sent it to a couple of other doctors, with 'SARS-like corona virus' circled in red. Her colleague Li Wenliang, an ophthalmologist, passed the report on to a handful of old classmates from medical school. 'Scary,' was their response. 'Is SARS coming back?' A few hours later, in the middle of the night, he was taken to task by his bosses. How had he got hold of this information? On 3 January, he was ordered to report to the police station, for 'spreading rumours' and 'undermining the social order'. It all blew over, but not before he had been forced to sign a declaration stating that he would cease to engage in 'illegal activities'.

The origin of the virus remains unknown, but because its genetic pedigree can be traced back to the world of Asian mammals, practically all Western experts currently assume that it came from bats and was circulating in Wuhan by December 2019. One important focus of infection was probably the Huanan Seafood Market, where numerous wild animals were illegally sold. Such markets were already notorious as a source of new viruses. Six of the first seven patients in Wuhan had been there.

Although the number of victims in Wuhan increased rapidly from mid-December 2019 onwards, the local authorities spent weeks trying to silence whistle-blowers and keep the problem under wraps.

The city's health commission admitted on 31 December that there were indeed twenty-seven recorded cases of a previously unknown form of pneumonia, but claimed the disease was under control. The WHO's

representatives in Beijing were alerted that same day and the Huanan market was closed as a precaution. There was no attempt, however, to prevent
the exodus of 5 million potential carriers of the virus as various holidays
came round. To mark Chinese New Year a huge banquet was held in Wuhan,
with 40,000 families invited.

Meanwhile, first-aid posts were filling with patients who showed symptoms of the unknown lung disease. Although the public was still being kept
in the dark, scientists at the Wuhan Institute of Virology mapped the entire
genome of the new virus on 5 January. It was confirmed to be a relative of
the SARS virus, which had spilled over from bats. Their findings were com-
municated to the scientific world two days later and the reaction was rapid.
By 10 January, Berlin researcher Olfert Landt had developed a reasonably
reliable coronavirus test.

The Chinese authorities remained silent. The suspicion that the virus
could be passed from one person to the next was becoming stronger, as
more and more patients were emerging who had never set foot in the seafood market, yet on 14 January the WHO was still reporting that the
Chinese authorities believed there was no sign of human-to-human transmission. It was not until 18 January that a radical reversal took place. Beijing
sent top expert Zhong Nanshan to Wuhan, emergency assistance was flown
in from all sides, and from 23 January onwards the 10 million residents of
the metropolis were placed under strict quarantine. By that point the disease had spread to six countries. The Chinese 'people's war' against the
virus – an unprecedentedly tough but effective test-and-lockdown strategy –
was a success. According to official statistics at least, barely 5,000 people
died out of a population of 1.4 billion. Two months after the outbreak
began, Wuhan cautiously opened up again.

Whistle-blower Li Wenliang was allowed to resume his work. On 8 January he performed a cataract operation on an elderly patient. She did not
have a fever, so he treated her without wearing a surgical mask. It later
turned out that she ran a stall at the seafood market and had been experiencing strange symptoms. Two days later, Li started to cough. From that
moment on he began wearing masks and for safety's sake he sent his wife,
who was pregnant, and his young son out of the city. He was now becoming increasingly famous on the internet and via WeChat he gave interviews
all over the world: 'If the authorities had released information about the

epidemic sooner, we'd be in a better position now.' The truth needed to be told, even though from late January onwards he was dependent on supplementary oxygen. On 6 February he died, at the age of thirty-three.

Ai Fen, the other whistle-blower, was initially celebrated by state media, but when on 10 March she described her own experiences in the magazine *Renwu* (People), including all the obstructions she'd faced from the authorities, the article was removed from the website within three hours. After that, Ai Fen disappeared for several weeks.

When a pandemic threatens, the WHO calls together the world's most prominent experts in the basement of its head office in Geneva – the Strategic Health Operations Centre. This occurred on 22 January, three weeks after the first reports from China. Ought the organization to raise the alarm by declaring a public health emergency? Opinions within the group were divided. For reasons of prestige, China had little desire to see such an announcement and many other specialists had their doubts as well. A week or so later, however, on 30 January, the virus had proven itself so infectious that the declaration of an international state of emergency was unavoidable.

By now alarm bells were ringing everywhere. On 22 January, Richard Hatchett, who had served as the top epidemiologist in the Obama administration, warned the world leaders gathered in Davos of a catastrophe that was fast approaching. 'This is not China's problem,' he said. 'This is the world's problem.' Two days later Chinese doctors echoed that sense of urgency in medical journal *The Lancet*, writing that this new virus was as deadly as the Spanish flu.

The American intelligence agencies woke up immediately at that. On 18 January the White House and President Trump had been brought up to date, although the latter seemed uninterested and went off to play golf. The same cannot be said of his advisers, according to one senior official, but 'they just couldn't get him to do anything about it'. On 31 January the American government blocked the arrival of most travellers from China. Apart from that, Washington, once the world's leader whenever calamities arose, did practically nothing for five weeks.

France confirmed the first three coronavirus infections on the European continent on 24 January, all three of them connected with travel to China. Two days later the director of the prominent Johns Hopkins Center for

Health Security in Baltimore put out an urgent call to world leaders to increase their testing capacity on the double and stock up on protective equipment: 'Prepare for the worst'. The European Commission reacted with speed and agility, putting its internal crisis system into operation on 29 January. But the EU had few opportunities to intervene, since healthcare had always been regarded by member states as a national matter. The announcement of crisis measures took place in an almost empty press room, which says a great deal.

If you ask me how I responded to those first alarm signals, I have to say I was worried, yes, but it was all very hard to imagine. I remember seeing pictures in early February 2020 of the rapid construction of an emergency 1,000-bed hospital in Wuhan and regarding it mainly as a curiosity: the Chinese can pull off feats like that. The state of emergency seemed far away. In Taiwan, South Korea, Singapore, New Zealand and China, however, made wiser by earlier outbreaks, the authorities reacted effectively and rigorously, and there were remarkably few infections and deaths. In Europe and the United States, the opposite was generally the case.

'I cannot comment on why there was not much sense of an urgency,' an EU diplomat who had been present at many of the crisis meetings told Politico.eu. 'I think it was because everybody thought it would remain a local thing in certain areas of the world and they didn't want to spread panic.'

In 2005 Germany had put in place a Nationaler Pandemieplan für Deutschland, and based on that plan the medical industry immediately began laying in extra supplies. Most other European countries, however, were in no sense ready for a pandemic of such magnitude. Although the WHO had warned in early February of a 'global shortage of personal protective equipment', laboratories were not scaled up, the production of testing materials was not increased and additional PPE was not ordered or manufactured on a large scale.

In many other European countries too, there was a remarkable lack of urgency. In Britain the health minister insisted throughout February that the risk of an epidemic was 'low'. Yet he had already been given a shocking report by Neil Ferguson, the leading expert at Imperial College London, in which the infectiousness of the new virus was estimated to be higher than that of the Spanish flu.

Behind the scenes, senior British civil servants were preparing for something resembling a war situation. Britain has an established procedure for emergencies, with a national crisis committee, COBRA, chaired by the prime minister. It held crisis meetings in London almost weekly from 24 January onwards, although with little result. Boris Johnson himself was nowhere to be seen until early March. 'There's no way you're at war if your PM isn't there,' a senior government adviser told the *Sunday Times* later, on condition of anonymity. 'What you learn about Boris was he didn't chair any meetings. He liked his country breaks. He didn't work weekends. It was like working for an old-fashioned chief executive in a local authority 20 years ago. There was a real sense that he didn't do urgent crisis planning. It was exactly like people feared he would be.'

In Spain, a new and inexperienced government had just taken office. Even when in early March almost 600 cases and ten deaths were reported, the health minister claimed they all had their origins abroad. Alarm signals were ignored, including advice from the European Centre for Disease Prevention and Control to stop shaking hands, keep a distance from others and avoid crowds.

Practically unnoticed, in mid-February the first hotspots of the virus emerged in Europe. On Sunday 16 February, the French health minister stepped down from her job in tears. As a candidate for the post of mayor of Paris she was obliged to resign. 'I knew that a tidal wave was coming towards us,' she told *Le Monde* later. The following Monday an international week of contemplation began in Mulhouse, held by the Église Porte Ouverte Chrétienne, an evangelical megachurch, with five days of talks, prayer services and communal singing. At least 2,000 people took part, packed together in the huge church building, before fanning out again across the world. Just over a week later, one of them was discovered to have caught Covid-19. It then became clear that hundreds of members of the congregation had spread the disease across the globe, to places as far away as Burkina Faso and French Guyana. 'So we were in the same petri dish for a week,' the founder's son later told Reuters. From Mulhouse the virus was transferred to Strasbourg and the rest of France, while areas of Germany close to the French border were also infected.

In that same week, a thirty-eight-year-old man with symptoms typical of influenza reported to the hospital in Codogno, a small town in Lombardy. At first he refused to be admitted, but on Thursday 20 February he was taken into intensive care. He tested positive for the virus and since then he has been regarded in Italy as Patient Number One. The man turned out to be an unusually active type. He'd been out to dinner three times in the past week, he played football, he was in a running club, and of course he had twice walked into the hospital coughing and spluttering. In short, the man was a 'super spreader', in a highly populated part of the country. He'd had no contact with China, so he must have picked up the virus from other Italians who had not themselves shown any spectacular symptoms. That meant that in Lombardy – which does a great deal of trade with China – the virus had probably been active for weeks. 'The man we call Patient Number One was probably Patient Number 200,' one of the doctors said.

That weekend, all over Europe, skiing holidays and carnival gatherings began. It was the start of a stream of new infections, both at crowded ski resorts and among singing and dancing carnival-goers. The little town of Ischgl in the Tyrol, where everything is geared to winter sports and even more to the après ski, became a massive source of infection. For financial reasons, the hotels, party venues and cable cars were not closed until 13 March despite multiple warnings. Rich Russian skiers went home, as the mayor of Moscow put it, 'with suitcases full of virus'.

The evening of Friday 21 February saw Italy's first death from Covid-19. The second followed a day later. That Sunday, eleven towns in Lombardy were cordoned off by the police and the army. Schools and theatres were shut and the finale of the Venice Carnival was cancelled. On the morning of Monday 24 February, prices on the Italian stock market fell dramatically. There were now seven dead.

It was the start of a chaotic week, full of contradictory reports. On the Tuesday, after more than 300 cases had been confirmed and Lombardy was struggling to create more hospital beds and intensive care places, prime minister Giuseppe Conte announced that Italy was 'a safe country, probably safer than many other countries'. The health ministers of Italy, Austria, France, Germany, Slovenia and Croatia, meeting in Rome, declared that the closing of borders would be 'disproportionate and ineffective' and that large gatherings need not be cancelled. 'The problem is Italy, you know, not the virus,' was the mood at the meeting. The mayor of Milan even started an advertising campaign with the slogan 'Milan isn't stopping' and insisted that bars, restaurants and tourist attractions must remain open.

Behind the scenes, however, concern was rapidly growing. Hospitals in northern Italy could barely cope with the influx of patients, and there was a serious shortage of equipment. In late February the Netherlands finally started to set up a civil contingencies body to deal with the crisis, almost four weeks later than the Germans, the British and the EU. The Italian coronavirus crisis became noticeable on Wall Street as investors all over the world grew increasingly worried. That week, the New York Stock Exchange lost 10 per cent of its value, partly because American investors lacked faith in their president's nonchalant attitude. The rising panic was obvious from share values, with a run on safe investments like US government bonds.

On Friday 28 February, Italy activated the EU's Civil Protection Mechanism, with a request to all member states for face masks and other personal protective equipment. The move represented an acknowledgement by Rome that it really did have a problem. An embarrassing silence followed. It was clear that other member states now realized they had failed in their responsibility to stockpile sufficient equipment. 'The biggest alarm for us in the Commission came at the end of February when Italy requested assistance,' said Janez Lenarčič, European commissioner for crisis management. 'There was no response. All alarm bells started to ring. We then realized what nobody told us before, that there is a general shortage throughout Europe of personal protective equipment.'

At the end of carnival week, other European governments also began to realize that a major health crisis was rolling towards them. But another full week if not more went by before those worries were expressed publicly. The rest of Italy was finally shut down on Sunday 8 March. On the Saturday night, after news of the proposed lockdown leaked out, thousands of Milanese had stormed the trains to southern Italy, thereby ensuring that region too was infected. By then Italy had almost 10,000 cases, with 463 dead. The lockdown had come too late.

The death toll shot up. In the overwhelmed hospitals, dramatic scenes played out. Corridors filled with patients on ventilators. Everything was in short supply: intensive care beds, ventilators, personal protective equipment. Many doctors and nurses had to work without appropriate protection and became infected. In the Papa Giovanni XXIII hospital in Bergamo on 18 March, 500 of the 3,500 staff were infected. One of the doctors said, 'We carry on like soldiers going to war.' In Bergamo alone, fifty to sixty patients were dying each day. The priest in the nearby village of Zogno decided to ring the bells just once a day from then on, otherwise he'd be ringing them constantly for dead villagers. 'There's no room left for bodies,' said a paramedic. The San Giuseppe church, a temporary storage place, was full of coffins for weeks.

In late April 2020, the official number of Italian Covid-19 deaths was more than 25,000. In reality there were at least 10,000 more than that. Some thirty doctors had already died in and around Bergamo, more than 150 in Italy as a whole.

Italy's undersecretary at the ministry of health, Sandra Zampa, later admitted that her country had not looked at China as a practical warning but as 'a science fiction film that had nothing to do with us'. But when the virus broke out in Italy, Europe 'looked at us the same way we'd looked at China'.

The risk of infection within the EU was 'low to moderate', declared European Commission president Ursula von der Leyen on Wednesday 26 February. On the crucial weekend of 29 February, when almost all governments were jolted awake, the National Institute for Public Health and the Environment in the self-confident Netherlands announced that further measures were unnecessary. There seemed to be no evidence the virus was spreading; the two cases that had been found could both be traced back to Italy, so this was clearly an Italian problem.

On the evening of Friday 6 March, the Netherlands saw its first Covid-19 fatality. Barely a week later, only a handful of pigeons were walking the deserted streets of inner-city Amsterdam.

The European Union initially did what the member states had been demanding for years: little or nothing. Healthcare, as we have seen, had remained a national responsibility. Given the huge differences between European countries, this was only logical. The EU was allowed to fight a pandemic of mad cow disease with all means available, but human diseases were a matter for individual member states. Moreover, in early March the Union was still caught up with a ghost from the past. The European leaders had their hands full tackling a flare-up of the conflict with Turkey, which was again receieving large numbers of Syrian refugees. President Erdoğan was threatening to jettison all his agreements with Brussels if the EU continued to refuse to take more of them. For the umpteenth time there were harrowing scenes on the border between Greece and Turkey. The Turks had opened their side of the border, and thousands of refugees were gathering there in the hope that the Greeks would do the same. Fears arose of a repeat of the exodus of 2015.

Meanwhile nationalist sentiments were surfacing once more. The German government announced a ban on the export of personal protective equipment, including face masks and sanitizing gel, even to fellow members of the EU – putting its own people first. Fortunately the European Commission intervened quickly and successfully. The Turkish fires were extinguished too, at a meeting on 9 March between Erdoğan, Ursula von der Leyen and European Council president Charles Michel. The EU-Turkey deal of 2016 would be looked at again. Tensions on the border eased.

Of all European countries, Finland and Germany were the best prepared for a pandemic. By the middle of March, for example, Germany had a testing capacity of 700,000 a week, compared to 150,000 in France. It also had 25,000 ventilators ready for use and another 10,000 on the way, whereas France had no more than 5,000 in total. All the same, in a television address on 18 March, Angela Merkel did not mince words: 'The situation is serious. So take it seriously.' If nothing was done, an estimated 60 per cent of the German population might eventually become infected, and everyone could do the next calculation; even if the death rate was no more than 0.7 per cent, that meant 350,000 Germans might die of the virus. The country immediately implemented a policy of testing and quarantining, on a large scale, and it bore fruit.

In Spain, International Women's Day was celebrated on Sunday 8 March by tens of thousands of demonstrators, all over the country. Later they proved to have been a prodigious source of infection. The prime minister's wife and two female ministers were infected. Five days later a state of emergency was declared and at that point Spanish bureaucracy took over. Protective equipment entered the country in dribs and drabs. The virus spread unhindered in care homes, where staff, lacking any protection, were unable to cope. The army, entering the homes to disinfect them, found that some of the beds were occupied not by residents but by corpses.

The United Kingdom was the slowest to react of all European countries; not until eight days after the deaths of the first three Covid-19 patients were large public events banned, and only fifteen days later was a form of lockdown introduced. (In Greece, for instance, the delay was zero and eight days respectively.) It had thirteen coronavirus patients on 26 February.

On Monday 2 March, five weeks after the crisis committee's initial meeting, Boris Johnson chaired COBRA for the first time. He now started talking valiantly of a 'full battle plan'. The main advice to the public was to wash hands for at least twenty seconds, which Tory parliamentarian Jacob Rees-Mogg said was the time it took to sing 'God Save the Queen'. For the swelling number of coronavirus patients, special Nightingale hospitals were set up in great haste. Yet it was only on 11 March that the British government announced a lockdown, and pubs and restaurants were not ordered to shut until 20 March. 'I do accept that what we're doing is extraordinary,' Johnson said. 'We're taking away the ancient, inalienable right of free-born people of the United Kingdom to go to the pub.' In early April the perpetually flippant prime minister was taken into intensive care. He'd carried on shaking hands for too long. Again the country, without a premier, was rudderless for weeks. Meanwhile the virus was advancing at astonishing speed. One Dutch intensive care doctor, Dharmanand Ramnarain, described afterwards to *de Volkskrant* how on the night of 20–21 March the crisis swept into the Elisabeth-TweeSteden Hospital in Tilburg. 'At one thirty in the morning I thought: it has to get quieter now, otherwise I can't handle it.' But in his intensive care unit, patients who were struggling to breathe kept pouring in. 'It was so awful. In our department they saw more and more patients deteriorating. Nurses were crying; they'd lost control of the situation.'

3

The past two years have been a time of truth. All over the world the pandemic has both accelerated and intensified existing problems of all kinds, including those of my own country. Sometimes I've felt as if I were watching an Amsterdam canal being pumped dry. That happens sometimes during construction work, and it's always astonishing to see what, along with dozens of bicycles, gets pulled out of the blue mud.

I saw the steamroller of spending cuts, having crushed healthcare for years, emerge from the water in its full pitiless magnitude. In the Netherlands alone, cuts to healthcare amounted to €3 billion, and 70,000 jobs. The quality and dedication of all those men and women had for years been out of all proportion to their rewards, and now they were the heroes of the crisis, absolutely vital. A national pandemic plan, such as existed in Germany, had never been a priority.

This was closely related to another product of recent years, the wholesale commercialization of healthcare. It became clear that all over the world the pharmaceutical industry had moved away from developing vaccines and treatments for newly emerging viruses. It could rake in far more money with other activities, such as buying up and monopolizing patents on existing medicines.

Another mess that emerged from out of the mud: economies had been relying on debt to an extraordinary degree. Many businesses were unlikely to survive the current conditions for long, but it was astonishing how quickly large companies in particular started to fall apart. It seemed the normal buffers barely existed any longer. The reason was simple: with the extremely low interest rates of recent years, debt cost almost nothing, so all profits could go to the shareholders. Holding resources or cash in reserve was for idiots.

There was a danger that what we saw in the crisis of 2008 would be repeated; the primacy of the free market was fiercely defended year after year, insane profits were made, social inequality increased markedly everywhere, but when trouble came all the costs were loaded onto the public sector and the ordinary taxpayers. The international travel agency Booking.com was given massive support by the Dutch government, even though in 2019 it had recorded profits of $5 billion. That money had almost all gone on bonuses and dividend payments, and on the purchase, for $8 billion, of the company's own shares – a well-known trick for driving up profits for shareholders. That little speculation game had left it $3 billion in debt, so it would not take much to push the flourishing company over the edge.

Richard Branson, owner of airline Virgin Atlantic, tried something similar. Even though all his businesses were based in the tax-free Virgin Islands, he now demanded that the British come up with £500 million to save Virgin, and the Australians another £700 million. He was at least sent away with a flea in his ear.

Another moment of truth concerned the power of the nation state. During this pandemic it was entirely in the hands of governments almost everywhere, and they farmed it out to experts. As one Dutch insider said later, 'The politicians lay down on their backs like dogs, paws in the air.' One thing of vital importance in tackling the coronavirus was to discover who was infected, who had been in close proximity to them and who would therefore need to be put into quarantine. Each step entailed interference in a person's private life of a kind unacceptable in normal times. The pattern that Frank Snowden had detected from the Middle Ages onwards, with epidemics justifying radical government measures that reinforced the position of those in power, was repeating itself. The Economist spoke of 'a pandemic of power grabs'.

Russia and China, for example, developed high-tech systems for tracking the movements of every one of their citizens. In Hungary, Prime Minister Orbán initially used the temporary state of emergency as a pretext for ruling by decree, with severe penalties for journalists who displeased him. The Serbian president followed suit. In Poland, the government talked openly of 'martial law'. In France, President Macron introduced such strict quarantine measures, with a complete lockdown and police everywhere, that it looked more like an experiment in constructing a police state. Protests by the gilets jaunes and other tormenters of the president ended immediately.

Another phenomenon familiar from epidemics of the past was renewed aggression towards 'the other' and 'the foreigner'. In this new crisis it was once again unfamiliarity and uncertainty that increased the sense of impotence and made whipping up popular anger all the easier. A Welsh song of lamentation describes the plague as 'death coming into our midst like black smoke'. Bubonic plague spread so quickly that, in the words of an eyewitness, it was as if one sick person 'could infect the whole world'. The disease was the devil himself, and its demonic character was compounded by the fact that no one in those days had any idea of the cause, the bacterium

Yersinia pestis. That remained the case for another five centuries. During the plague epidemic of 1348–49, in Strasbourg, Basel and elsewhere, the blame was laid at the door of the Jews, who were said to have poisoned the wells as part of a plot to take over the towns from the Christians. In Strasbourg as many as a thousand Jews were herded into the Jewish graveyard and burned alive. In Basel practically the entire Jewish community was massacred by the same means.

In 2020 it was the Chinese, all over the world, who quickly became the target of discrimination and increasing racism. Nationalism thrived on the crisis. 'The Chinese virus,' the American president kept saying. 'The American virus,' the Chinese responded. 'The Madrid virus,' decided Catalan nationalists. And once again the preachers and flagellants went after the Jews. The UN rapporteur on freedom of religion or belief, Ahmed Shaheed, reported a 'horrifying increase' in anti-Semitic hate speech on the internet. The accusations were age-old: the Zionists were trying to use the virus to wipe out the non-Jewish population in order to get their hands on world power. Rich Jews, it was claimed, had been in possession of a vaccine for ages already; it was set to earn them a vast amount of money.

Sometimes the moment of truth concerned the truth itself. First, China put severe pressure on the rest of the world and an independent international inquiry into the origin of the virus was blocked for months; only China's version of the truth was the truth, and responsibility for the pandemic lay not with China but elsewhere, in an American laboratory. A critical draft report by the EU about the Chinese campaign of lies was softened at the insistence of Beijing.

During the London plague of 1665–66, the city authorities tried to prevent panic by keeping the official number of fatalities as low as possible. They preferred to note all kinds of invented illnesses as the cause of death. The Spanish flu was given the prefix 'Spanish' because in 1918 only the uncensored Spanish press wrote about it. Elsewhere in Europe the pandemic was covered up as far as possible.

In 2020 too, figures were initially fiddled all over the place. For weeks the regular medical specialist on Russian state television talked about a 'mild influenza', and the authorities reported infection percentages that seemed too good to be true, especially for a country with a long land border with

China and intensive trading relations with Italy. Doctors did, however, report a very high death rate among their colleagues. A friend of mine, a Russian doctor who has worked in the Netherlands for the past quarter-century, received innumerable calls from former colleagues asking her whether she knew what was really going on. In early 2021, the offices of statistical bureau Rosstat calculated that there had been 230,000 excess deaths in Russia in the first eleven months of 2020, an increase of more than 13 per cent. Only then did the Russian government admit that in reality not 55,000 but more than three times that number, 186,000, had succumbed to the virus. It was like a repeat of the unease and deathly silence after Chernobyl.

In the Netherlands, with its severe shortage of testing materials, daily reports at first gave only the 'official' death toll. In reality the number of victims may have been twice as high for weeks, to judge by population statistics. In other European countries too, thousands of deaths among people who had not been tested, especially in care homes, were more or less hidden in the early stages. In late April 2020 The Economist registered the differences: Spain reported only 71 per cent of the actual number of deaths, Belgium 87 per cent, while figures from Sweden, France and Germany were reasonably accurate, at 91, 93 and 97 per cent.

It was not just a matter of numbers, however. The clash between scientific and magical thinking, which increasingly set the tone in public and political debate, has gained extra sharpness and urgency in recent months. Online conspiracy theories have blossomed as never before, in thousands of varieties. In America the combination of internet, Fox News and President Trump proved a particularly poisonous mix – a powerful, self-reinforcing hotchpotch of prejudice, rumour, pseudoscience, racism and undisguised hatred.

For weeks the president, continually cheered on by Fox, dismissed all reports about the new coronavirus as a Democrat hoax. It was little more than ordinary flu, he said, which his government had 'completely under control'. When Covid-19 started killing thousands in America as elsewhere, it was all the fault of China; Trump claimed there was 'convincing evidence' that the virus had escaped from a lab at the Wuhan Institute of Virology. His own intelligence agencies and experts had firmly ruled out that possibility, having determined that the virus was of natural origin. Trump angrily sacked a senior official at the Department of Health and Human Services who had written a report about the desperate shortage of equipment in hospitals.

The election campaign was thrown into chaos. The mass rallies the president loved so much could not be held and instead he used the daily coronavirus briefings as an election platform. The result was an absurd spectacle, a series of improvised shows without any preparation beforehand, full of bizarre advice – 'People are really surprised I understand this stuff,' he was overheard saying. 'Every one of these doctors said, "How do you know so much about this?"' – and sneers aimed at critical reporters and Democrat governors. When Dr Anthony Fauci, the country's top epidemiologist and a senior adviser to a series of presidents, lowered his head despondently during one of the presidential bragging sessions, he immediately became the subject of a storm of criticism on Twitter for having undermined Trump's authority. Afterwards he received so many threats that he needed a permanent personal security detail.

In the White House, in other words, truth had become irrelevant. This president, with his misleading claims and outright lies, had gradually beaten everyone into submission. By the time he left office, the *Washington Post* had counted more than 30,000 presidential untruths. The reality was cruel and merciless. It was then that the American death toll passed 400,000, and still there was no end in sight.

'A nation's response to disaster speaks to its strengths – and to its dysfunctions,' wrote historian Anne Applebaum when the crisis broke out. That was certainly true of the United States in this pandemic. In the financial world, America, largely out of self-interest, soon resumed its traditional role: in the lead, all-powerful, stimulating and stabilizing. Everywhere politicians used terms like 'the enemy' and 'war', but it was not a useful image. In wartime there is great dynamism, with factories working at full throttle to support the war effort. Now we were dealing with the opposite, a profound stillness, with sports halls full of coffins and a global recession rolling our way.

The economic data made heads reel. In France, Spain and Italy alone, GDP dropped by between 6 and 10 per cent, the steepest fall since the Second World War. Tourism had virtually stopped. In Europe alone the tourism industry accounted for more than 11 per cent of employment, and the economies of Greece, Spain and Malta, for example, stood or fell by the number of tourists arriving.

The entire European economy slumped by 6.4 per cent in 2020, although a rapid recovery was expected to take place in 2021. The oil price recovered somewhat, although the price per barrel remained tens of dollars lower than the previous year. Governments all over the world showered their countries with money in a desperate attempt to salvage what they could. National debts were climbing to wartime heights. Across the world as a whole, more than €1 trillion was spent on measures to combat the coronavirus, and the average budget deficit in the eurozone rose from 0.6 per cent to 10.1 per cent.

In the United States, the Trump administration put together an aid package of over $2 trillion, more than double the size of the 'big bazooka' deployed by Obama after the crisis of 2008. It said all that needed to be said about the seriousness of the situation.

Furthermore, this was a dual economic crisis. Because of the threat emanating from the pandemic, demand for oil had markedly decreased. The new technique of fracking, by which means America had worked its way up over recent years to become the world's largest oil and gas producer, now proved far too expensive. The industry faced almost grinding to a halt; none of its investors wanted to chance their arm – exactly the outcome that another major oil producer, Russia, was hoping for.

In mid-March 2020, when most of the public was fully focused on the Covid-19 crisis, the global financial system became unstable again behind the scenes. On Monday 9 March, there was panic on the stock markets that lasted for several days. All confidence had evaporated, everything was being sold, everyone was rushing for the exits. Trading on Wall Street was paused several times. There was particular concern about Italy, with its extremely high government debt. How on earth would it be able to cover these insane levels of extra expenditure? Might all the uncertainty cause interest rates on government bonds to rise, with once again sums in the billions that the country could not find in time, triggering the terrifying doom loop that had been so narrowly avoided in the euro crisis?

On Thursday 12 March, Christine Lagarde, the new boss of the European Central Bank, made a feeble attempt to calm the mood. It backfired. She was not willing to guarantee that the ECB would come to Italy's aid, and immediately Italian interest rates rose by 0.65 per cent. Not much, on the face of it, but because of the volume of Italy's national debt it meant the country would have to find an additional €14 billion annually.

As in 2008, the American central bank, the Federal Reserve, took the lead, and its methods were even more rigorous this time. It printed dollars flat out. American government bonds were bought, to a value of $700 billion, and billions were funnelled to almost forty central banks and vital financial centres all over the world. But enormous financial firepower did not help this time; stocks and financial markets remained in chaos and the panic only grew. Whatever the Fed and the ECB did – and all they could do was offer financial buffers – it had no effect on the sources of the crisis: the virus and the lockdown.

On Wednesday 18 March, Lagarde rectified her mistake. She set up a Pandemic Emergency Purchase Programme, promising to pump €750 billion into the European economies by buying assets. She also announced that the ECB would review its 'self-imposed limits'. It was her way of saying what Mario Draghi had said on a momentous June day in 2012: 'Whatever it takes . . .'

Disquiet remained, now compounded by a profound political impasse in Washington. A huge rescue package was needed, and quickly, but in contrast to 2008 the Democrats and Republicans could not reach agreement. The American central bank was forced to take far-reaching measures. On the morning of Monday 23 March, before the stock market opened, the Fed gave the ultimate undertaking: not just government bonds but some of the better corporate bonds would become part of its programme of asset purchases. Two days later, on 25 March, the Republicans and the Democrats finally reached a deal. The markets calmed. Once again, the Americans had thrown their full financial and economic weight into the battle.

There was no sign of the 'shining city on the hill' in other fields, however. It was still 'America First'. At Shanghai Airport a shipment of surgical masks bound for severely hit eastern France was snatched away by a group of Americans who, with suitcases full of dollars, were prepared to pay three times the price agreed by the French. Within America too, decency and solidarity were strained to breaking point. While Europeans stood in line to buy face masks and sanitizing gel, many Americans were stocking up on weapons. In chaos and panic, states engaged in a bidding war, fighting over scarce medical equipment. The governor of New York, Andrew Cuomo, described in late March how the price of hospital ventilators was increasing: 'Because we bid $25,000, California says, "I'll give you $30,000" and Illinois says, "I'll give you $35,000" and Florida says, "I'll give you $40,000."'

The country faced an accumulation of problems: there had been no preparation; disease prevention centres had been slashed in half by spending cuts; healthcare was barely available in any form to large sectors of society; and the weak social safety net forced many people to carry on working when ill. Then there was the dominant presence of a foul-tempered president, who had appointed a son-in-law foolish and arrogant in equal measure as leader of the crisis team. The few remaining experts close to the president walked on eggshells for fear of upsetting him. In military circles, such a situation is known as a 'clusterfuck'.

The president's fabled ego occupied the main role, as in every other crisis. While residents of New York were dying in their thousands, he opined that he was at number one on Facebook – not true, incidentally. He insisted that the cheques for $1,200 going out to tens of millions of Americans must bear the name 'Trump', as if he were sharing out his own money. In the middle of the pandemic, he decided, to the astonishment of the rest of the world, to cancel America's subsidy to the WHO, since he believed the organization had listened too much to China and issued warnings too late. His voters would now surely forget his own procrastination, which had lasted for at least five weeks.

'The crisis demanded a response that was swift, rational, and collective,' wrote American essayist and historian George Packer. 'The United States reacted instead like Pakistan or Belarus – like a country with shoddy infrastructure and a dysfunctional government whose leaders were too corrupt or stupid to head off mass suffering.' Packer's conclusion: 'We are living in a failed state.'

For weeks, the leader of the Western world advocated taking hydroxychloroquine, a risky treatment for malaria, as the ultimate cure for Covid-19. In mid-April, although he later claimed he'd been asking a question sarcastically of reporters, Trump suggested that injecting patients with disinfectant might somehow help treat the virus, as 'almost a cleaning'.

*

'Post-truth is pre-fascism, and Trump had been our post-truth president,' wrote historian Timothy Snyder as Trump's term in office came to an end. Reporter Mark Danner – whom we encountered earlier at Trump's inauguration – heard how, during the campaign in Michigan, Trump worked a crowd of thousands of supporters into a state of thundering enthusiasm. 'We brought you a lot of car plants, Michigan! We brought you a lot of car plants. You know that, right?' The answer came instantly, from everywhere in the throng. 'Yes, Mr President, we know that!' In reality, not a single factory had been built in Michigan since Trump came to power; in fact the automotive industry had shed around 3,000 jobs. Many of Trump's listeners must have known that, but it didn't bother them. For them, the forty-fifth president was above earthly reality.

He convinced himself, too. Just as in 2016 he had been totally unprepared for victory – for him, entering the race had been mainly about name recognition – in 2020, despite extremely low approval ratings, he was not in any sense prepared for defeat. In the East Room of the White House, where the Trump clan gathered on the evening of election day, 3 November, after initial disbelief, fury erupted. As a first reaction, the president demanded the count be stopped immediately. Then he launched the big lie that would echo endlessly in the weeks that followed and would almost paralyse American democracy: 'This is a fraud on the American public. We were getting ready to win this election – frankly, we did win this election.'

In reality, Democrat Joe Biden, with an unprecedented turnout, had clearly won, with a majority of more than 7 million in the popular vote and 306 electoral college votes, as against 232 for Trump. If you looked more closely at the figures, however, as Pew Research did, you saw how strong and broad the support for Donald Trump still was. Almost half of American voters, 71 million, had voted for him. Furthermore, despite his many mistakes, he had strengthened his position among almost all demographic groups: from 39 per cent to 44 per cent of women voters, from 6 to 8 per cent of black voters, from 28 to 35 per cent of Hispanic voters, and from 8 to 35 per cent of Muslim voters. According to polling by YouGov, at least two-thirds of all those voters believed his story about an 'unprecedented landslide' and his 'stolen election'.

Seventy-seven days of chaos, lies, intimidation and abuse of power followed, right up to the inauguration of Joe Biden. The dozens of court cases brought by the Trump team, all the way to the supreme court, led nowhere. There was no evidence at all of large-scale fraud. On the contrary, the elections, as even Republican officials remarked, had been exceptionally well run. Local officials, the FBI and the Ministry of Justice were put under pressure by the White House to declare ballots and results invalid and to prosecute the perpetrators of this 'fraud'. Internally it was suggested that perhaps the army should be brought in to call 'fraudulent' states to order. The panic inside the White House even led to occasional fistfights among the presidential clique, according to a reconstruction by the *New York Times*.

The country was more deeply divided than ever. In 1960, less than 5 per cent of Americans felt it would be a problem if one of their children married a supporter of a different political party. According to a poll by *The Atlantic*, in late 2020 the figure was 35 per cent for Republicans and as high as 45 per cent for Democrats. Meanwhile, on the verge of leaving office, in violation of all the usual customs, Trump had one death sentence after another carried out, thirteen executions in total.

Most Republican representatives obediently went along with the lies Trump churned out, even if they knew perfectly well it was all downright nonsense. In some states with a Republican majority there was talk of replacing electors for Biden with supporters of Trump. The Republican secretary of state in Georgia was treated to a long telephone tirade by the president himself, who demanded he find another 11,780 votes, the precise number he needed to win the state. It all got him nowhere. On 14 December the electoral college confirmed the election result.

Meanwhile, tens of thousands of Trump supporters – ranging from respectable evangelicals to the violent Proud Boys and the conspiracy theorists of QAnon – took to the streets, egged on by Twitter salvos from the president: 'Stop the steal!' The movement reached a climax on 6 January 2021 in Washington, when Congress came together to count and confirm the votes of the electors – in normal times, a mere formality. Three-quarters of the Republican members of Congress tried to block the certification, while outside Trump called on his supporters to walk with him to the Capitol: 'We fight like hell, and if you don't fight like hell, you're not going to have a country anymore.'

Instead of walking with the crowd, he followed developments from the quiet of his home, in front of the television. Several thousand of his supporters stormed the Capitol, had little difficulty entering the building and caused the members of Congress inside several frightening hours. Five people died, but given the weapons available and the threatening tweets, it could easily have been more. Some Trump rebels were serious about getting their hands on 'treacherous' members. The gallows they set up outside was not purely symbolic and nor, perhaps, were their cries of 'Hang Mike Pence!'

It did not amount to a serious attempt at a coup. There was no systematic plan, the army was not involved: in that respect too, Trump and those around him were exceptionally incompetent. It was an impressive show, however, the start of a twenty-first-century stab-in-the-back legend that will haunt American politics for years to come.

Was this storming of the shrine of democracy 'un-American', as many people claimed? No, this kind of rebellion was once the foundation of American democracy. Moreover, the pro-Trump movement, also very American, was increasingly adopting the character of a religious sect: 'Jesus is my savior. Trump is my president.' On QAnon messageboards, images appeared of Trump who, standing on an advancing tank, would radically and definitively rescue the country from 'the bad people' in the Capitol and 'the paedophile Democrats'. This 'Great Awakening' – the term comes straight from the jargon of nineteenth-century religious sects – would take place on 20 January 2021, the day of the transfer of power to Joe Biden and vice president Kamala Harris. Nothing of the kind happened on that day. Yet Trump's supporters remained faithful; 40 per cent of Republican voters continue to believe in QAnon.

The spectacular Trump rebellion concealed the fact that on that same 6 January the Republicans suffered two phenomenal losses: the presidency and, after runoff elections in Georgia, their majority in the Senate. When Trump came to power in 2017, the party had both Congress and the White House in its grip. Now, after just one term, it had lost both. Such a complete loss had not been witnessed since 1892.

The rebellion rebounded on Trump. Because of his misleading and provocative posts, he lost his megaphones on the internet – Twitter, Facebook – for good. His brand and his business empire were now tainted, business associates wanted nothing to do with him, even Trump's faithful financial backer, Deutsche Bank, turned off the tap. The House of

Representatives decided for a second time to initiate impeachment proceedings against Trump: unique in American history.

America's loss of face in the rest of the world was now greater than ever. 'The US has lost its moral authority to preach democracy and human rights to other countries,' declared Malaysian parliamentarian and human rights activist Charles Santiago – and that was the general mood. 'It has become part of the problem.'

All the same, we felt liberated, even moved, as we watched the new president take the oath of office on 20 January 2021 in Washington. Suddenly normal people were walking about the place again, suddenly normal things were being said again, suddenly a reform and investment programme of Roosevelt-like proportions was on the table.

All those good intentions, however, could not conceal the fact that a fundamental change had taken place in Europe's most important ally. The core of every democracy, and certainly the American version, is the principle of the non-violent transfer of power: the winner of the election is allowed to govern, the loser accepts this, knowing that a new election will come round again, with a fresh opportunity for a change of power at the top. For the first time in American history, one of the two great parties, supported by more than a third of voters, was refusing to go along with that fundamental principle. In this most authoritative Western nation, it was a break with the basic principles of democracy. A break that could have far-reaching consequences, for Europe as well.

4

Yes, miracles still happen, in the form of breakthroughs that invariably occur around major shared experiences, such as wars and pandemics. A crisis removes the straitjacket of everyday life and makes space for new solidarity, a new sense of connection, new frameworks and ideas.

After the great 1348 epidemic of plague in Florence, Giovanni Boccaccio rose like a lark out of the rubble and created his *Decameron*, an outspoken masterpiece in which he celebrates freedom and lambasts the corruption and greed of the Catholic Church of his day, two centuries before the Reformation. The huge earthquake that flattened most of Lisbon in 1755, killing an estimated 40,000 people, a fifth of the population, had a major impact on Enlightenment philosophers, especially Rousseau, Voltaire and Kant, and therefore indirectly influenced the French Revolution. After that disaster, Kant rejected the very notion of a benign God; only reason could save the world.

One such miracle, of course, was the European project itself, after the horrors of the Second World War. For centuries, ever since the Peace of Westphalia in 1648, European politicians had assumed that international disputes, whether of trade or war, were essentially problems between states, which needed to be resolved between them. That model was no longer adequate for the complicated problems of the late twentieth century, let alone for those of our own. The financial collapse of 2008 was a global crisis, immigration was and remains a practical and moral dilemma for the whole of Europe and beyond, climate change and the question of how to generate enough energy is a global issue, and famines and epidemics can be tackled properly only on a planet-wide scale.

In this catastrophe too, miracles are happening. Once again we're facing a problem that is quintessentially international, with challenges that cry out for a coordinated international response. That is what we are seeing now. For example, after the Wuhan Institute of Virology detected the new virus in early January 2020, it was Olfert Landt in Berlin who was the first to develop a test. He immediately sent it to a Chinese colleague who was also a friend. 'Just try it. It works.' In the search for a vaccine, international collaboration – long live the internet! – assumed impressive forms.

The EU has learned a great deal from all those earlier crises. More than three years went by before ECB president Mario Draghi dared to say the magic words 'whatever it takes'. Christine Lagarde needed barely six days. European business life was given a dizzying cash injection, via the banks, of €3 trillion, at zero interest.

At the same time, we Europeans were stuck. The stations and airports were deserted for months, the intimidating peaked caps at the borders were back, while international air traffic largely collapsed. All those feverish dreams of globalization seemed over for good. The nation state was once more the obvious place of refuge, the centre of everything that moved; we seemed to seek comfort and safety again in that old home.

Within the European Union, both these forces were strongly in evidence. The practical need for internationalization and mutual assistance was accompanied by a tendency towards renationalization. Brussels certainly turned out to be capable of improvisation; in a huge combined effort, almost half a million stranded European travellers were brought back from all over the world. It was the EU that immediately seized the initiative by holding an international video summit to set in train joint efforts to develop a vaccine. The combined research and financial resources of all member states were deployed in order to acquire the best vaccines as quickly as possible. There was immense time pressure. Every day cost thousands of lives, every day brought fresh economic damage, every day counted.

In retrospect, we were lucky. In earlier times pandemics spent their fury only after tens of millions of deaths, whereas in 2020 scientists managed to put a series of excellent vaccines on the market within ten months. At first what became known as the Oxford vaccine from AstraZeneca was regarded as one of the best candidates – tried and tested technology, and cheap – but when in December 2020 it came onto the market, it turned out that there was no way the millions of doses that had been promised to the EU could be made available. The company and the EU had grossly underestimated the complexity of the production process. Britain and the United States, which had not only invested in the development of a vaccine but also in production capacity, were given priority and were able to begin vaccinating immediately.

The EU vaccination campaign therefore began slowly and laboriously. In late March 2021 only 10 per cent of all its citizens had received their first injection, compared to 25 per cent of Americans and 40 per cent of the British. Once the various teething troubles were overcome, however, lost ground was quickly made up. More vaccines arrived and in April Ursula von der Leyen managed to secure no fewer than 1.8 billion doses of the Pfizer vaccine on behalf of the EU. By mid-June more than half of Europeans had been vaccinated. Furthermore, that huge Pfizer contract – for far more than the EU itself needed – made it possible to give vaccines away or sell them on. Suddenly Europe had a powerful weapon in its hands in its vaccine diplomacy, an additional element of European soft power.

Not a single European country could have done all this on its own. All these successes were made possible by the unified action of all EU member states, and despite the many beginners' errors, joint procurement prevented competition between European countries that would have done immense harm to the Union. Such coordination was lacking in its lockdown strategy, especially at the start. Borders abruptly closed, regimes differed greatly from one country to another, Italian pleas for help were initially ignored, as they had been in the refugee crisis of 2015, and even the results of tests and other data were not exchanged. In the words of Von der Leyen, 'When Europe really needed to prove that this is not only a fairweather union, too many refused to share their umbrella.'

Moreover, around its two great fault lines, East–West and North–South, the European project began to grate and grind loudly once again. Viktor Orbán exacerbated the clash of values that had slumbered for years between East and West when he attempted to use the crisis to establish a wayward Hungarian police state. In Poland the independent press was meanwhile placed under extreme pressure. Most critical newspapers were bombarded with writs, more than sixty of which were thrown at *Gazeta Wyborcza*.

In the summer of 2021 new confrontations followed, this time concerning the fundamental rights of LGBTQ+ people and the principle of the rule of law. Poland's Constitutional Court, in a judgment concerning the politicized appointment of judges, even explicitly repudiated the jurisdiction of the European Court of Justice, saying that Polish law weighed more heavily than EU law and the European treaties. It was thereby in effect placing Poland outside the European legal order. After all, the European treaties state that the European Court always has the last word; that is the essence of the entire system. This was therefore a rebellion against the foundations of the Union, yet the EU found itself more or less empty-handed. A member state could opt to leave the EU, as had happened with Brexit, but it remained impossible to expel one. Another flaw from the years of dreams and great expectations had been revealed.

North and South clashed at least as fiercely over the approach to the new economic crisis. Countries like Germany and the Netherlands were able to draw upon considerable reserves to keep businesses going and give income support to millions of people who had lost their jobs. For Spain, Greece and Italy in particular, a vast debt problem lurked behind all those thousands of dead and all the upheaval. Spain would need an estimated €200 billion from European funds to keep itself going. In contrast to the €1.1 trillion or more that Germany was holding in reserve for its own economy, Italy could summon no more than €28 billion. There were predictions that without substantial support, some 65 per cent of Italian small and medium-sized businesses would not survive the crisis. Italy was barely credit-worthy, with a national debt twice that of Germany or the Netherlands before the crisis began. The trenches had therefore already been dug for a new euro crisis, this time centred on the EU's third-largest economy.

So a miracle was needed within the European family, an unambiguous sign of trust and solidarity, whatever the cost. The opposite happened. The ECB used all its monetary powers to the full, but it would be truly effective only if the European economies were boosted in other ways too. The main question was whether, after so many crises, there was in fact a sufficient sense of solidarity and trust among European citizens for radical measures to be implemented. The once so pro-European Italy felt abandoned by the rest of Europe during the refugee crisis, and now again, in the Covid-19 crisis. The Dutch and the Germans remembered all too clearly how its previous deputy prime minister, Matteo Salvini, had tried to violate all the budgetary rules of the eurozone only a year earlier, calling the imposition of sanctions a sign of the EU's lack of respect for Italy. Mutual trust was wearing thin.

Jacques Delors, former president of the European Commission, warned in a rare intervention that a lack of solidarity at such a crucial juncture represented a 'deadly danger for the European Union'. All the old ghosts, all those differences in economic culture that had been so expertly ignored at the introduction of the euro, were tumbling out of the closet once more. It all came down to that fundamental design fault of the common currency, the fact that it lacked a common financial system to counterbalance to some degree the disparities between its national economies, or at the very least buffers that could absorb some of the differences between them. After all, there were no exchange rates any longer to provide the necessary flexibility. A euro now cost more than a dollar, but if the eurozone had split in two in 2012, the northern euro would probably have been worth around $1.70 by 2020 and the southern euro perhaps fifty cents. This huge crisis was going to make the gap between them greater than ever.

Nine euro countries, including Belgium and France, therefore advocated issuing 'corona bonds', a variation on the eurobonds discussed earlier, meaning that the northern member states would implicitly underwrite deficits in the South. The economic differences between North and South would not become too extreme and the eurozone would avoid being thrown off balance completely. True solidarity was what was needed now, and as far as Spain, Portugal and Italy were concerned, this was no longer a request, it was a demand.

That starting point led to yet another fierce confrontation with the rich 'northern' countries. The Netherlands and Germany, along with Finland, Austria and Luxembourg, wanted to help but could not agree to finance deficits, especially Italy's, for ever and a day, without limit. Extending credit without conditions, they said, was not solidarity but irresponsibility; all democratic accountability, both national and European, would fall away. Moreover, it went against all the most basic agreements surrounding the euro, which stated that the currency was not to be held liable for the problems of individual member states. Such an outcome would be impossible to sell to northern voters. It was fine to allow a metro driver in Paris to retire at fifty-two, but would his colleague in Amsterdam, forced to slog away until he or she reached sixty-seven, be willing to pay for that? If yet another Italian government attempted to reduce the pension age, would it have to be paid for by an elderly German in Berlin who had already lost pension income under the punishing Hartz IV? So much for solidarity. Limited help, okay, but ultimately, the northerners believed, it was every country for itself.

An extremely delicate situation resulted. The negative dynamic that already existed in the eurozone was further boosted by the Dutch, who believed it was unnecessary even to deploy the existing emergency fund, the European Stability Mechanism. If the ESM were to be called upon, then there must be strict conditions, including severe cuts to public spending.

The Dutch finance minister, Wopke Hoekstra, caught up in a robust power struggle for the leadership of his Christian Democrat Appeal party, was eager for some extra ammunition, since his rival, the health minister, had inevitably been dominating the news for months. Moreover, his attitude was perfectly attuned to the self-satisfied tradition of Dutch Calvinism. 'Do we now have to throw open our granaries to countries like Italy, France and Belgium, who have spent seven years making merry?'

Hoekstra emerged, during a Eurogroup meeting on 9 April, as the Dutch version of Yanis Varoufakis; in many respects he was right, but with his patronizing and moralistic attitude he caused so much irritation that no one took him seriously any longer, to the great detriment of his own country. Despite the fact that this time the crisis was nobody's fault, he demanded once again that the South introduce 'macro-economic' reforms, including further cuts to pensions, along with savings on unemployment benefits and other welfare payments.

All the old pain of the euro crisis surfaced immediately. António Costa, the prime minister of Portugal, a country that in recent years had made great sacrifices to recover from the euro crisis and the cuts imposed by the North, was beside himself with fury. He called the insensitive attitude of the Dutch government 'repugnant'. This 'recurring meanness' was a threat to the future of the EU, he said. The Spanish foreign minister, Arancha González, wondered whether the Dutch realized that a first-class cabin was of little use if the whole ship sank. Even Germany, in the person of old budgetary hawk Wolfgang Schäuble, distanced itself from the Netherlands. German finance minister Olaf Scholz called Hoekstra's position 'unfocused and unbecoming'. Nout Wellink, the cautious former president of the Dutch central bank, said, 'We won't be the rich North any longer if the whole of the South goes under.' The Netherlands was forced to back down, the damage to its reputation immense.

With a great deal of effort, an emergency package worth €540 billion was finally put together, mainly intended for the poorest countries: €240 billion from the European Stability Mechanism, €200 billion from the European Investment Bank and €100 billion in the form of a new unemployment benefit. In the summer, a historic breakthrough took place when a coronavirus recovery fund of no less than €750 billion was created to help European countries save their economies from collapse. It is partly made up of loans, and partly – and this is new – of grants. For the necessary finance, the EU will now have to turn to the capital markets and borrow billions, and to pay them back it will impose a carbon tax: two further historic innovations. Another unprecedented aspect was that Germany, along with France, was taking the lead. In an emergency, the continued existence of the EU weighs more heavily there than any financial objections. This had everything to do with the identity of post-war Germany, closely interwoven as it is with the peace project that is the European Union.

The speed of decision-making was astonishing too. Whereas in the euro crisis years went by before some degree of agreement was reached, this time the European leaders concluded a settlement within a mere two months. Hidden beneath all the squabbling, and despite innumerable missed opportunities, huge steps had been taken. Yet again, the Union proved tougher than anyone expected.

Dear friend in the future,

Where are we headed? Will the Covid-19 crisis of 2020–21 be described in your history books, in 2069, as a 'disruptive' event or as 'transformative'? As a profound disturbance to order or, like 1945, as the start of massive change?

At this point the pandemic seems to be waning, in Europe and North America at least. We're slowly plodding back towards a kind of normality. According to the World Health Organization, within a period of two years, around fifteen million people worldwide died of causes related to the new coronavirus. Almost a quarter of a billion have fallen below the poverty line. The figure for the Netherlands is more than 22,000 dead, but there are huge differences between countries. Britain saw almost twice as many fatalities per hundred thousand inhabitants, while the death rate in efficient Norway and Denmark was a tenth and a third of the Dutch figure respectively. London's Imperial College School of Public Health has calculated that without all the lockdowns, the number of dead would have been several times larger; in the first wave alone the virus would have claimed more than three million lives in Europe as a whole.

The approach to the pandemic was the ultimate test of the quality – or lack of it – of the political systems and governments of all European countries. Quacks and false prophets seized their chance, in the public debate and beyond. In many European cities, demonstrations took place against curfews and other curtailments to freedom, and the Netherlands even saw riots and looting. This did not happen on a large scale, incidentally; the mood was rather one of resignation. But irritation was quick to mount, at home, in the streets, in politics, even at the Brussels negotiating tables. New terms came into being: 'virus fatigue', 'skin hunger'. The young generations, especially in southern Europe, were confronted once again with the prospect of chronic unemployment. After the crisis of 2008 many had already been plunged into depression and bitterness; now they were being denied access to a normal life for the second time.

All this inevitably had political consequences. In Spain and Italy the radical parties of both left and right were on the rise once more. In *NRC Handelsblad* journalist Hubert Smeets calculated that the Netherlands had climbed from seventh to third place 'in the European nationalist-populist competition'. In March 2021 almost a fifth of voters opted for parties that emphatically promised to put 'our own people first'.

After fifteen months of pandemic, the European Council on Foreign Relations (ECFR) observed a 'crisis of trust' all over Europe. It had a great deal to do with the initial Brussels bungling surrounding the acquisition and production of the AstraZeneca vaccine. Two-thirds of French people and more than half of Germans, Dutch, Italians, Spaniards and Austrians declared that their faith in the European project had declined. Discontent with national politics was a good deal greater, just as it had been according to earlier polls. In France and Portugal two-thirds of those asked said that their national politics was 'broken', in Italy and Spain as many as 80 per cent. A majority still recognized that the Union was 'a good thing' for their country and that the EU had a key role to play in recovery after the Covid crisis.

In those months of fear, anxiety and restrictions, commentary could be found everywhere that pointed to our 'unbounded consumption', our 'wild rampage across the globe'. Were these not the real causes behind the surging virus? Might it not be a foretaste of the coming climate crisis? Did we have any idea what was hanging over our heads?

I have a knot in the pit of my stomach as I write these final lines. On Thursday 24 February 2022, after months of menacing deployments, the Russian Army launched an assault on Ukraine. 'Everyone was waiting for the war, but nobody believed in it,' a Russian acquaintance writes – and that's how we all felt. 'For one reason or another, people can believe in God and in goodness, but they can't believe in war and in evil. That's illogical. After all, if evil doesn't exist, then neither does good.'

Ukraine immediately rose up. It resisted Putin's 'liberators' fiercely and competently, volunteers poured in, President Volodymyr Zelenskiy proved a strikingly courageous and charismatic leader – the show of solidarity was unprecedented. The West displayed an unexpected unanimity as well. There was a deluge of sanctions, NATO was on high alert, Finland and Sweden decided they wanted to become NATO members themselves now, while the Germans, confirmed pacifists ever since the Second World War, threw their *Ostpolitik* overboard in a single weekend and poured all their energies into building an effective fighting force. No less unprecedentedly, the EU decided to purchase weapons for Ukraine. The internal tensions between East and West and North and South seemed, for a moment, forgotten, and even the eternally neutral Switzerland took sides by introducing painful financial sanctions. What diplomats had failed to achieve in two decades, Putin managed to bring about inside two weeks: an exceptionally solid and united Europe.

This reversal does have its downside. 'Soft power', the principles of tolerance and cosmopolitanism, are the basic doctrines by means of which the European member states have managed to regulate their mutual relationships peacefully for more than three-quarters of a century, and indeed their relationships with the rest of the world. They form an essential part of the European identity. Now those foundations too were under threat.

It's a brutal and ruthless attack, the biggest European war since 1945, and it's already claimed tens of thousands of lives. The borders of Poland, the Baltic states, Hungary and Romania are being inundated by millions of desperate refugees and the end is nowhere in sight. The entire European security system has been thrown off balance. The old European order, the world of rules and agreements, the relaxed years after 1989 – all of that is now over. The risk of a nuclear war is present, for the first time since the 1980s. On the day of the invasion, President Putin threatened that everyone who stood in his way would feel 'consequences' the like of which 'you have never experienced in your history'.

As Russian author Vladimir Sorokin wrote, this is 'a war between past and future'. On one side is the past of Putin, who has now definitively broken with the perestroika project and revived a dictatorship where everything revolves around a single ideology: the restoration of the Holy Russian Empire, including the cruelty and abuses of power of the old tsarist regime.

On the other side is the future, the future of the Ukrainians and all those who want to be part of modern Europe, who are prepared to fight to their last breath to that end and in doing so make use of everything this new century has to offer them, from ultra-smart weapons to advanced cyber tactics and global information systems.

In Russia those who represent the future are leaving the country en masse: the young, the scientists, the innovative entrepreneurs. There's nothing left for them in their own country. In increasing isolation, Russia will sink back into the past, to its level of existence of decades ago. Because however fierce and cruel this war may become, ultimately it's a rearguard action by an empire in decline. Or rather, a nuclear power in decline – which is what makes this conflict so different and so dangerous.

At this point we are living in a painful balance between heart and mind. Everyone is afraid of further escalation, and equally terrified of a second Munich, that notorious moment just before the outbreak of the Second World War when the world believed a reliable agreement had been made with Hitler to preserve peace. In Europe a war fever has arisen that's distantly reminiscent of the mood of the summer months of 1914. After the isolation and division of the Covid years, both citizens and politicians seem to be embracing the warm feelings of solidarity that a common enemy induces. Perhaps shame is part of it too, after all those years of looking away, of constantly shrinking defence budgets, quiet collaboration and immensely lucrative gas contracts. That's certainly true in the case of Germany, which clung endlessly to the controversial Nordstream 2 pipeline and ignored all talk of the geopolitical downsides of the project. Until this spring, 40 per cent of the gas we use to heat our homes and power our industry came from Russia. According to calculations by the Brussels research institute Bruegel, this means Europe was pouring $850 million a day into Putin's war chest.

The West is now rushing headlong from targeted sanctions into all-out economic and financial warfare, but without explicit aims or clear conditions. Russia is hitting back. The blockade on the export of Ukrainian grain alone will inevitably lead to widespread food shortages all over the world. For Europe it marks the end of a long period of relative peace and stability. Our gas supply is being crimped, energy is becoming very expensive, major shortages of oil and grain threaten, the prices of bread and petrol are shooting up, inflation is surging – and this is only the start.

We knew our old world was shaky; I've described it that way in this book. But no one foresaw that it would come to an end so abruptly, with this 'perfect storm'. We stand at the beginning of a completely new phase in world politics. Over these past few weeks, this story has reached its definitive end.

> *We come from afar*
> *And have far to go*
> *Dear child.*

I don't have much more to say.

I walk to our village's church tower and pull the rope. The bell above my head starts ringing again. It dates from 1354, and having seen and experienced everything, it simply carries on tolling.

All the very best to you, there in 2069, dear friend.

September 2019 / May 2020 / July 2021 / October 2022

Acknowledgements

THIS IS TO A GREAT degree a historical essay, but without the patient, principled and resolute work of hundreds of journalists and others, the book could never have been written. In their courageous and persistent search for the complicated truth, they are the true chroniclers of our times.

My most important sources, ranging from the *Sächsische Zeitung* to the *Independent Barents Observer*, are listed in the bibliography. I could name names endlessly here: Luuk van Middelaar, who seized the chance to write in a short time an uncommonly intelligent and discerning account of his experiences as right hand to Herman Van Rompuy; Caroline de Gruyter, unmatched in her ability to provide, week after week, a clear insight into all the twists and turns of Brussels; the indomitable Ivan Krastev, with his consistently refreshing commentary from the eastern side of Europe; Hubert Smeets, whose insightful overview of the Putin years I fell back on time and again; Shaun Walker, who did fantastic work as a reporter in Ukraine; Adam Tooze, without whose exhaustive account I would probably have completely lost my way in the financial crises; Philipp Ther, one of the first to write the story of this neoliberal phase in European history; Manuel Castells and his fellow scholars, who charted the social and economic consequences of the euro crisis at an early stage; Tim Shipman, who reconstructed the Brexit process in detail in real time – I could go on and on.

The writing of this book was, in part, a collaborative project with VPRO Television. The television series that resulted went its own way, but we were able to share many discoveries and insights. Roel van Broekhoven, Stefanie de Brouwer, Mandy Duijn, Suzanne Hendriks, Frederique Melman, Maren Merckx, Mariska Schneider and colleagues: thanks for all the enjoyment and inspiration.

Friends and good people helped and supported me continually. In Vienna: Philipp Blom. In Kirkenes: Rune Rafaelsen and Thomas Nilsen. In Budapest: Péter Forgács, Gábor Demszky and György Konrád. In Vásárosbéc: Peter Flik and Edith van der Poel. In Novi Sad: Želimir Žilnik, Sarita Matijević and Sasa Matijević. In Copenhagen: Clause and Jusser Clausen and Aydin Soei. In Brussels: Bart Beirlant and Vincent Stuer. In London: Hieke Jippes and Misha Glenny. In Wigan: Tom Walsh and Chris Ready. In Amsterdam: Steven Seijmonsbergen and Umayya Abu-Hanna. In The Hague: Ko Colijn. In Lauwersoog: Ed Huisman and the men of the KNRM. In Warsaw: Anna Bikont and Jarosław Krawczyk. In Athens: Conny Keessen, and Efi and Kostas Karadimas. In Mechelen: Bart Somers. In Niesky: Eckart and Inge Winkler. In Dresden: Gunter Wolfram. In Bönen: Gudrun and Kathy Tucholski. In Barcelona: Stan Baggen, Mari Carmen Gaztañaga and José Martí Font.

Hubert Smeets and Harald Benink were critical and stimulating readers of the chapters on Russia and the financial crisis respectively. For their observations I am also deeply indebted to our friends Pieter Nijdeken and Saskia Dekkers, an outstanding journalistic duo that was continually out on the front lines for the television programme Nieuwsuur, all over Europe. René van Stipriaan was, as ever, a true friend and guide during the critical rereading and editing of the manuscript.

Writing is usually a lonely occupation, but not in this case. My wife Mietsie thought, read and lived intensely along with me. I felt constantly supported by her unconditional solidarity.

The same went for the people at the publishing house, especially my publisher and editor Emile Brugman and his wife Ellen Schalker. For more than a quarter of a century, with great calm and unparalleled professionalism, they have guided me through the jungle of the book trade. I have an untold amount to thank them for, and I know the same is true for dozens of other authors. I was always able to bask in the inspiring combination of work and friendship that only the best publishers can sustain.

After all these years, it is only natural that, with immense gratitude, I dedicate this book to the two of them.

Jorwert / Amsterdam, September 2019 / April 2020

Bibliography and Sources

General

Barnes, Julian, *A History of the World in* 10½ *Chapters*, London, Jonathan Cape, 1989.

Böll, Heinrich, 'Wir kommen weit her', written in his granddaughter's poetry album on 8 May 1985, two months before his death.

Castells, Manuel, et al., eds, *Europe's Crises*, Cambridge, Polity Press, 2018.

Garton Ash, Timothy, 'The New German Question', *New York Review of Books*, 15 August 2013.

Kearns, Ian, *Collapse: Europe after the European Union*, London, Biteback, 2018.

Kershaw, Ian, *Roller-Coaster: Europe, 1950 – 2017*, London, Allen Lane, 2018.

Krastev, Ivan, *After Europe*, Philadelphia, University of Pennsylvania Press, 2017.

Middelaar, Luuk van, *De passage naar Europa: Geschiedenis van een begin*, Groningen, Historische Uitgeverij, 2009.

————, *The Passage to Europe: How a Continent Became a Union*, trans. Liz Waters, London, Yale University Press, 2013.

————, *De nieuwe politiek van Europa*, Groningen, Historische Uitgeverij, 2017.

————, *Alarums and Excursions. Improvising Politics on the European Stage*, trans. Liz Waters, Newcastle upon Tyne, Agenda Publishing, 2019.

Mion, Giordano, and Dominic Ponattu, *Estimating the Economic Benefits of the Single Market for European Countries and Regions*, Gütersloh, Bertelsmann Stiftung, 2019.

Mishra, Pankaj, *Age of Anger: A History of the Present*, New York, Farrar, Straus and Giroux, 2017.

Percy, Norma, et al., *Inside Europe: Ten Years of Turmoil*, BBC documentary, London, 2019.

Sassen, Saskia, *Expulsions: Brutality and Complexity in the Global Economy*, London, Harvard University Press, 2014.

Saul, John Ralston, *The Collapse of Globalism: And the Reinvention of the World*, Toronto, Penguin Canada, 2005.

Ther, Philipp, *Die neue Ordnung auf dem alten Kontinent: Eine Geschichte des neoliberalen Europa*, Berlin, Suhrkamp Verlag, 2016.

Thomas, Casper, *De autoritaire verleiding: Over de opmars van de antiliberale wereldorde*, Amsterdam, Atlas Contact, 2018.

Tooze, Adam, 'The Secret History of the Banking Crisis', *Prospect*, August 2017.

————, *Crashed: How a Decade of Financial Crises Changed the World*, London, Allen Lane, 2018.

1. The Sky's the Limit — 1999

Engelen, Ewald, 'Koks erfenis', *De Groene Amsterdammer*, 25 October 2018.

Janssen, Roek, *De Euro: Twintig jaar na het Verdrag van Maastricht*, Amsterdam, De Bezige Bij, 2012.

Judt, Tony, *Postwar: A History of Europe since 1945*, London, Heinemann, 2005.

————, *Reappraisals: Reflections on the Forgotten Twentieth Century*, London, Heinemann, 2008.

Konrád, György, *Slingerbeweging*, Amsterdam, De Bezige Bij, 2011.

————, *A Guest in my Own Country. A Hungarian Life*, New York, Other Press, 2007.

Maier, Anja, 'Kanzlerin Angela Merkel: Verdammt lange da', *Tageszeitung*, 3 November 2018.

Michnik, Adam, 'On the Side of Geremek', *New York Review of Books*, 25 September 2008.

Montefiori, Stefano, 'Italians used to be fervently pro-EU. What went wrong?', *The Guardian*, 9 January 2019.

Mounk, Yasha, *The People vs. Democracy: Why Our Freedom Is in Danger and How to Save It*, Cambridge, MA, Harvard University Press, 2018.

Mudge, Stephanie L., *Leftism Reinvented: Western Parties from Socialism to Neoliberalism*, Cambridge MA, Harvard University Press, 2018.

Oudenampsen, Merijn, 'Een terugkeer naar rechts: De ideeënpolitiek van Frits Bolkestein', *De Groene Amsterdammer*, 18 October 2018.

Pessers, Dorien, interviewed by Marcel ten Hooven, 'Na mij geen zondvloed', *De Groene Amsterdammer*, 20 December 2018.

Piketty, Thomas, *Chronicles: On Our Troubled Times*, London, Viking, 2016.

Rifkin, Jeremy, *The European Dream: How Europe's Vision of the Future Is Quietly Eclipsing the American Dream*, New York, Penguin, 2004.

Roll, Evelyn, *Die Kanzlerin: Angela Merkels Weg zur Macht*, Berlin, Ullstein Verlag, 2009.

2. Peace – 2000

Alexievich, Svetlana, *Secondhand Time: The Last of the Soviets, an Oral History*, trans. Bela Shayevich, New York, Random House, 2017.

Drakulić, Slavenka, interviewed by Irene van der Linde, 'Wij kennen geen solidariteitsgevoel', *De Groene Amsterdammer*, 21 January 2016.

Judah, Ben, *Fragile Empire. How Russia Fell In and Out of Love with Vladimir Putin*, New Haven, CT, Yale University Press, 2013.

Pomerantsev, Peter, *Nothing Is True and Everything is Possible: Adventures in Modern Russia*, London, Faber, 2017.

Smeets, Hubert, *De wraak van Poetin: Rusland contra Europa*, Amsterdam, Prometheus/Bert Bakker, 2015.

3. Fear – 2001

Azab Powell, Bonnie, and Christiane Amanpour, 'UN Weapons inspector Hans Blix faults Bush administration for lack of "critical thinking" in Iraq', UC Berkeley NewsCenter, 18 March 2004.

Blix, Hans, *Disarming Iraq*, New York, Pantheon, 2004.

Böll, Heinrich, *Billard um halb zehn*, Cologne, Kiepenheuer & Witsch, 1959.

———, *Billiards at Half Past Nine*, trans. Patrick Bowles, New York, Melville House, 1962 / 2010.

Buruma, Ian, *Dood van een gezonde roker*, Amsterdam, Atlas, 2006.

————, Murder in Amsterdam: The Death of Theo van Gogh and the Limits of Tolerance, New York, Penguin Press, 2006.

Chorus, Jutta, and Ahmet Olgun, In godsnaam: Het jaar van Theo van Gogh, Amsterdam, Contact, 2005.

Chulov, Martin, 'My son, Osama: the al-Qaida leader's mother speaks for the first time', The Guardian, 3 August 2018.

Fens, Kees, Dat oude Europa, Amsterdam, Querido, 2004.

————, Het volmaakte kleine stukje, Amsterdam, Athenaeum-Polak & Van Gennep, 2009.

Gessen, Masha, The Future Is History: How Totalitarianism Reclaimed Russia, London, Granta, 2017, p. 130.

Hersh, Seymour M., 'War and Intelligence', New Yorker, 12 May 2003.

Kleijwegt, Margalith, Onzichtbare ouders: De buurt van Mohammed B., Zutphen, Plataan, 2005.

Klepel, Gilles, Die neuen Kreuzzüge: Die arabische Welt und die Zukunft des Westens, Paris / Zurich, Piper Taschenbuch, 2004 / 2005.

Leyers, Jan, Allah in Europa: Het reisverslag van een ongelovige, Amsterdam, Das Mag Uitgevers, 2018.

————, interviewed by Sheila Kamerman and Hendrik Spiering, 'Ik kreeg een boks van de haatimam', NRC Next, 21 April 2018.

Lubbers, Ruud, Persoonlijke herinneringen, Amsterdam, ONE Business BV, 2018.

Mak, Geert, De brug, Amsterdam, Stichting CPNB, 2007.

————, Gedoemd tot kwetsbaarheid, Amsterdam, Atlas, 2005.

Os, Pieter van, Nederland op scherp: Buitenlandse beschouwingen over een stuurloos land, Amsterdam, Bert Bakker, 2005.

Pamuk, Orhan, 'The Anger of the Damned', New York Review of Books, 15 November 2001.

Ruthven, Malise, 'The Big Muslim Problem!', New York Review of Books, 17 December 2019.

Sneifer, Andrei, and Daniel Treismann, 'A Normal Country: Russia After Communism', Journal of Economic Perspectives 19, no. 1, 2005, pp. 151 ff.

Whitlock, Craig, 'At War with the Truth, The Afghanistan papers', Washington Post, 9 December 2019.

4. Greatness – 2004

Batory, Agnes, 'Populists in Government? Hungary's "System of National Cooperation"', *Democratization*, 23, 2016, pp. 283 – 303.

Foreign Affairs, 73, no. 2, March / April 1994.

Marusic, Damir, 'The Dangers of Democratic Determinism', *American Interest* 13, no. 5, 5 February 2018.

Milanovic, Branko, 'Democracy of convenience, not of choice: why is Eastern Europe different', globalinequality [blog], 23 December 2017.

Roth, Joseph, 'Bei den Heimatlosen', *Neue Berliner Zeitung*, 23 September 1920.

————, *Joseph Roth in Berlin. Ein lesebuch für Spaziergänger*, Cologne / Amsterdam, Kiepenheuer & Witsch, 1993.

————, *What I Saw: Reports from Berlin 1920 – 33*, trans. Michael Hofmann, New York, W. W. Norton & Company, 2003.

Szabłowski, Witold, *Dansende beren. Heimwee naar het communisme*, Amsterdam, Nieuw Amsterdam, 2018.

————, *Tańczące niedźwiedzie*, Warsaw, Agora, 2014.

Zakaria, Fareed, 'The Rise of Illiberal Democracy', *Foreign Affairs*, November / December 1997.

5. Numbers – 2004

Andersson, Ruben, *Illegality, Inc.: Clandestine Migration and the Business of Bordering Europe*, Berkeley, CA, University of California Press, 2014.

Bromet, Frans, Sylvia and Ruben, *Muziek op de vlucht*, television documentary, Hilversum, 2016.

Cennetoğlu, Banu, and UNITED for Intercultural Action, 'The List', *Die Tagesspiegel / The Guardian*, 8 November 2017.

Es, Ana van, 'Zo kreeg de wetsuitman van Texel een naam', *de Volkskrant*, 15 June 2015.

Fjellberg, Anders, 'The Wetsuitman', *Dagbladet / De Groene Amsterdammer*, 20 April 2016.

Rosi, Gianfranco, *Fire at Sea / Fuocoammare*, television documentary, Rome, 2016.

6. No, Non – 2005

Cooper, Robert, *The Breaking of Nations. Order and Chaos in the Twenty-First Century*, London, Atlantic Books, 2004.

'Free Falling – What to Expect from a No-Deal Brexit: The Terrifying Consequences If Nothing Is Sorted', *The Economist*, 24 November 2018.

Higgins, Andrew, 'Volkswagen Scandal Highlights European Stalling on New Emissions Tests', *New York Times*, 28 September 2015.

Hobolt, Sara B., 'The Crisis of Legitimacy of European Institutions', in Castells et al., *Europe's Crises*, pp. 243ff.

Johnson, William M. *The Austrian Mind. An Intellectual and Social History 1848 – 1918*, Berkeley, CA, University of California Press, 1972.

Judt, Tony, *Ill Fares the Land*, London, Allen Lane, 2010.

Konrád, György, *Europa und die Nationalstaaten*, Berlin, Suhrkamp Verlag, 2013.

Menasse, Robert, *Die Hauptstadt*, Berlin, Suhrkamp Verlag, 2017.

————, *The Capital*, trans. Jamie Bulloch, New York, Liveright, 2019.

————, *Der Europäische Landbote: Die Wut der Bürger und der Friede Europas*, Vienna, Zsolnay Verlag, 2012.

————, *Enraged Citizens. European Peace and Democratic Deficits*, trans. Craig Decker, Chicago, University of Chicago Press, 2016.

————, interviewed by Kris Hendrickx, 'Brussel heeft me leren geduldig te zijn', *Podium Brussels*, 10 March 2018.

————, interviewed by Aris Shapiro, 'Robert Menasse Looks at the People Who Make the European Union Run in *The Capital*', NPR, 19 June 2019.

Michnik, Adam, 'On the Side of Geremek', *New York Review of Books*, 25 September 2008.

Middelaar, Luuk van, 'De Europese Unie en de gebeurtenissenpolitiek', oration, University of Leiden, 23 September 2016.

Musil, Robert, *Der Mann ohne Eigenschaften*, Berlin, Rowohlt Verlag, 1930 – 1943.

————, *The Man Without Qualities*, trans. Sophie Wilkins and Burton Pike, New York, Vintage, 1996.

Ornstein, Leonard, et al., eds, *Paleis Europa: Grote denkers over Europa*, Amsterdam, De Bezige Bij, 2007.

Pfaff, William, 'What's Left of the Union?', *New York Review of Books*, 14 July 2005.

Platteau, Pierre, *Rue Bonnevie*, Amsterdam / Brussels, Atlas, 2002.

Sadée, Tijn, 'Om 5 uur naar huis? Carrièrekiller. Kleine reisgids voor de beginnende eurocraat', NRC *Handelsblad*, 26 August 2017.

Schaake, Marietje, interviewed by Guus Valk and René Moerland, 'Ik had last van machtsmisbruik', NRC *Handelsblad*, 21 June 2019.

Siedentop, Larry, *Democracy in Europe*, London, Allen Lane, 2000.

Stendhal, *La Chartreuse de Parme*, Paris, Ambroise Dupont, 1839.

————, *The Charterhouse of Parma*, trans. Richard Howard, New York, Modern Library, 1999.

Stuer, Vincent, *Curb Your Idealism: The European Union as Seen from Within*, Brussels, VUB Press, 2018.

Verbeken, Pascal, *Brutopia: De dromen van Brussel*, Amsterdam, De Bezige Bij, 2019.

Verhofstadt, Guy, *De ziekte van Europa (en de herontdekking van het ideaal)*, Amsterdam / Antwerp, De Bezige Bij, 2015.

7. Brothers – 2008

Bos, Wouter, interviewed by Yan Ting Yuen and Robert Kosters, in *De achtste dag*, television documentary, Hilversum, 2018.

Cardoso, Gustavo, Guya Accornero, Tiago Lapa and Joana Azevedo, 'Social Movements, Participation and Crisis in Europe', in Castells et al., *Europe's Crises*, pp. 405ff.

Dijsselbloem, Jeroen, *De Eurocrisis. Het verhaal van binnenuit*, Amsterdam, Prometheus, 2018.

————, *The Euro Crisis: The Inside Story*, trans. David MacKay, Amsterdam, 2018.

French, Tana, 'The Psychology of an Irish Meltdown', *New York Times*, 27 July 2013.

Hessel, Stéphane, *Indignez-vous!*, Montpellier, Indigène éditions, 2010.

————, *Time for Outrage!*, trans. Marion Duvert, New York, Twelve Books, 2011.

Kuttner, Robert, 'The Crash That Failed', *New York Review of Books*, 22 November 2018.

Lewis, Michael, *Boomerang: The Meltdown Tour*, New York / London, Allen Lane, 2011.

Luyendijk, Joris, *Dit kan niet waar zijn: Onder bankiers*, Amsterdam, Atlas, 2015.

——, *Swimming with Sharks: My Journey into the World of the Bankers*, London, Guardian Faber, 2015 / *Among the Bankers : A Journey into the Heart of Finance*, New York, Melville House, 2016.

McKee, Martin, 'Austerity and Health: The Impact of Crisis in the UK and the Rest of Europe', in Castells et al., *Europe's Crises*, pp. 127ff.

Sen, Amartya, Charleston Festival speech, 23 May 2015, published as 'Amartya Sen: The Economic Consequences of Austerity', *New Statesman*, 4 June 2015.

Stiglitz, Joseph, *The Euro: And Its Threat to the Future of Europe*, London, Oxford University Press, 2017.

Teulings, Coen, *Over de dijken: Tien jaar na het uitbreken van de financiële crisis*, Amsterdam, Prometheus, 2018.

Trichet, Jean-Claude, interviewed by Yan Ting Yuen and Robert Kosters, *De achtste dag*.

Witteveen, Johan, interviewed by Marcel ten Hooven, 'Zuiniger dan Colijn', *De Groene Amsterdammer*, 21 February 2013.

Yan Ting Yuen and Robert Kosters, *De achtste dag*, television documentary, Hilversum, 2018.

8. Truth – 2010

Allenova, Olga, Jelena Geda and Vladimir Novikov, 'Blok NATO razosjoslja na blokpaketi', *Kommersant*, 7 April 2008.

Bikont, Anna, *The Crime and the Silence: Confronting the Massacre of Jews in Wartime Jedwabne*, trans. Alissa Valles, New York, Farrar, Straus and Giroux, 2015.

Garton Ash, Timothy, 'Jesus Rex Poloniae', *New York Review of Books*, 16 August 2018.

Gross, Jan T., *Neighbors: The Destruction of the Jewish Community in Jedwabne*, Princeton, NJ, Princeton University Press, 2001.

——, 'Poles Cry for "Pure Blood" again', *New York Times*, 16 November 2017.

Hoffman, Eva, 'Hearing Poland's Ghosts', *New York Review of Books*, 22 March 2018.

Santora, Marc, 'After a President's Shocking Death, a Suspicious Twin Reshapes a Nation', *New York Times*, 16 June 2018.

Shore, Marci, 'Poland Digs Itself a Memory Hole', *New York Times*, 4 February 2018.

Smeets, Hubert, 'Poolse en Hongaarse leiders trippen op het interbellum', NRC Handelsblad, 8 December 2017.

9. Solidarity – 2012

About, Edmond, La Grèce contemporaine, Paris, Hachette, 1854.

———, Greece and the Greeks of the Present Day, trans. by authority, Edinburgh, Thomas Constable and Co., and London, Hamilton, Adams and Co., 1855.

'Breaking Up the Euro Area – The Merkel Memorandum', The Economist, 11 August 2012.

Chryssópoulos, Chrístos, Une lampe entre les dents: Chronique athénienne, Arles, Actes Sud, 2013.

Dendrinou, Viktoria, and Eleni Varvitsioti, The Last Bluff: How Greece Came Face to Face with Financial Catastrophe and the Secret Plan for its Euro-exit, Athens, Papadopoulos Publishing, 2019.

Janssen, Roel, Afrekenen met Griekenland: hoe Syriza langs de euro-afgrond scheerde, Amsterdam, De Bezige Bij, 2015.

Kitsantonis, Niki, 'Greece, 10 Years into Economic Crisis, Counts the Cost to Mental Health', New York Times, 2 March 2019.

Konstandaras, Nikos, 'Greece's Great Hemorrhaging', New York Times, 10 January 2019.

———, 'Lessons of a German Tax Cheat', New York Times, 22 March 2014.

Mak, Geert, De hond van Tišma: Wat als Europa klapt?, Amsterdam / Antwerp, Atlas / Contact, 2012.

Markaris, Petros, Finstere Zeiten: Zur Krise in Griechenland, Zurich, Diogenes Verlag, 2012.

Mody, Ashoka, EuroTragedy: A Drama in Nine Acts, Oxford, Oxford University Press, 2018.

Offe, Claus, 'Narratives of Responsibility: German Politics in the Greek Debt Crisis', in: Castells et al., Europe's Crises, pp. 269ff.

Ovid, Metamorphoses, trans. A. D. Melville, Oxford, Oxford World's Classics, 2009.

Stiglitz, Joseph, The Euro: And Its Threat to the Future of Europe, London, Oxford University Press, 2017.

Trichet, Jean-Claude, interviewed by Egbert Kalse and Daan van Lent, 'Een Nexit of Frexit is voor mij altijd ondenkbaar geweest', NRC Handelsblad, 9 August 2017.

Varoufakis, Yanis, Adults in the Room: My Battle with Europe's Deep Establishment, London, The Bodley Head, 2017.

Wiessing, Eva, and Conny Keessen, Worstelen aan de rand van Europa:Verhalen achter de Griekse crisis, Amsterdam, Lebowski Publishers, 2016.

10. Old Ghosts – 2014

Applebaum, Anne, 'A New European Narrative?', New York Review of Books, 12 October 2017.

Barry, Ellen, and Sophia Kishkovsky, 'Putin Takes Helm as Police Punish Moscow Dissent', New York Times, 7 May 2012.

Dunlop, John B., The February 2015 Assassination of Boris Nemtsov and the Flawed Trial of His Alleged Killers: An Exploration of Russia's 'Crime of the 21st Century', Stuttgart, Ibidem Verlag, 2018.

Flaubert, Gustave, L'Éducation sentimental: Histoire d'un jeune homme, Paris, Michel Lévy Frères, 1869.

————, Sentimental Education, trans. Robert Baldick, rev. Geoffrey Wall, London, Penguin Classics, 1964/2004.

Galeotti, Mark, The Vory: Russia's Super Mafia, New Haven, Yale University Press, 2018.

————, We Need to Talk About Putin, London, Ebury Press, 2019.

Gessen, Masha, The Future is History: How Totalitarianism Reclaimed Russia, London, Granta, 2017.

Knip, Karel, and Steven Derix, 'Er vliegt een vogeltje in uw richting – reconstructie neerschieten MH17', NRC Handelsblad, 11 July 2015.

Kreling, Paul, and Huib Modderkolk, 'Gansch het raderwerk staat stil. Digitale oorlog in Oekraïne', NRC Handelsblad, 27 June 2018.

Kurkov, Andrey, Ukraine Diaries: Dispatches from Kiev, trans. Sam Taylor, London, Harvill Secker, 2014.

Mansky, Vitali, interviewed by Helen Saelman, 'Vitali Mansky: Poetin is slachtoffer van zijn eigen poetinisme', Raam op Rusland, 14 November 2018.

Müller, Jan-Werner, *What is Populism?*, Philadelphia, University of Pennsylvania Press, 2016.

Myers, Steven Lee, and Andrew E. Kramer, 'How Paul Manafort Wielded Power in Ukraine Before Advising Donald Trump', *New York Times*, 31 July 2016.

Noordaa, Robert van der, and Coen van de Ven, 'Het MH17-complot: De invloed van Russische trollen', *De Groene Amsterdammer*, 30 May 2019.

Quinn-Judge, Paul, 'The Revolution That Wasn't', *New York Review of Books*, 19 April 2018.

Smeets, Hubert, *De wraak van Poetin: Rusland contra Europa*, Amsterdam, Prometheus/Bert Bakker, 2015.

———, 'Rusland en de NAVO: woordbreuk of samenloop der omstandigheden?', *Raam op Rusland*, 10 January 2018.

Snyder, Timothy, 'Diaries and Memoirs of the Maidan', *Eurozine*, 27 June 2014.

———, *The Road to Unfreedom: Russia, Europe, America*, New York, Tim Duggan Books, 2018.

Starink, Laura, *De schaduw van de grote broer: Letten en Russen, Joden in Polen, Duits Kaliningrad, Oorlog om Oekraïne*, Amsterdam, Atlas, 2015.

Troitsky, Artemy, interviewed by Margreet Fogteloo, 'Het volk is passief, apathisch, cynisch', *De Groene Amsterdammer*, 22 June 2017.

Walker, Shaun, *The Long Hangover: Putin's New Russia and the Ghosts of the Past*, Oxford, Oxford University Press, 2018.

Intermezzo

McEwan, Ian, *Amsterdam*, London, Jonathan Cape, 1998.

McNeill, J.R., *The Great Acceleration: An Environmental History of the Anthropocene Since 1945*, Cambridge, MA, Harvard University Press, 2016.

11. The Promised Land – 2015

Alexander, Robin, *Die Getriebenen – Merkel und die Flüchtlingspolitik: Report aus dem Innern der Macht*, Munich, Siedler Verlag, 2017.

Algemene Rekenkamer, *Asielstroom 2014 – 2016: een cohort asielzoekers in beeld*, The Hague, 2018.

Anastasiadou, Marianthi, Athanasios Marvakis, Panagiota Mezidou and Marc Speer, *From Transit Hub to Dead End. A Chronicle of Idomeni*, www.border-monitoring.eu, 2017.

Andersson, Ruben, *Illegality, Inc. Clandestine Migration and the Business of Bordering Europe*, Oakland, University of California Press, 2014.

Blokker, Bas, and Jutta Chorus, 'Verhuizen naar Europa', *NRC Handelsblad*, 14 November 2015.

Colling Nielsen, Kaspar, *Den Danske Borgerkrig 2018 – 24*, Copenhagen, Gyldendal, 2013.

DeParle, Jason, 'The Sea Swallows People', *New York Review of Books*, 23 February 2017.

Eakin, Hugh, 'The Terrible Flight from the Killing', *New York Review of Books*, 22 October 2015.

————, 'Liberal, Harsh Denmark', *New York Review of Books*, 10 March 2016.

Joffe, Josef, *Der gute Deutsche: Die Karriere einer Moralischen Supermacht*, Munich, C. Bertelsmann Verlag, 2018.

Linde, Irene van der, 'Grenzen verleggen. Europa en Afrika houden samen migranten tegen', *De Groene Amsterdammer*, 21 September 2017.

Mardini, Yusra, *Butterfly: From Refugee to Olympian – My Story of Rescue, Hope, and Triumph*, New York, St. Martin's Press, 2018.

————, interviewed by Karolien Knols, 'Tegen de stroom in', *de Volkskrant*, 24 October 2018.

Polman, Linda, *Niemand wil ze hebben: Europa en zijn vluchtelingen*, Amsterdam, Uitgeverij Jurgen Maas, 2019.

Roth, Joseph, *The Wandering Jews. The Classic Portrait of a Vanished People*, trans. Michael Hofmann, Preface to the new edition (1937), New York, W. W. Norton and Company, 2001.

12. *Wigan* – 2016

Armstrong, Stephen, *The Road to Wigan Pier Revisited*, London, Little, Brown, 2012.

Barnett, Anthony, *The Lure of Greatness: Why 2016 Blew Away the World Order*, London, Unbound, 2017.

Boomkens, René, 'De cultuur van het neoliberalisme en het onbehagen in de politiek', in Martine Groen and Paul Kuypers, *Woorden breken*, Antwerp / Apeldoorn, Garant, 2018.

'Britain's Brexit Crisis', *Panorama*, BBC, 18 July 2019.

Coe, Jonathan, *Middle England*, London, Viking, 2018.

Corduwener, Pepijn, and Arthur Weststeijn, *Proeftuin Italië: Hoe het mooiste land ter wereld de moderne politiek uitvond*, Amsterdam, Prometheus, 2018.

Cox, Brendan, *Jo Cox: More in Common*, London, Two Roads, 2017.

Ehrenreich, Barbara, *Fear of Falling: The Inner Life of the Middle Class*, New York, Pantheon, 1990.

Eribon, Didier, interviewed by Jaap Tielbeke, 'Macron is hetzelfde liedje', *De Groene Amsterdammer*, 10 May 2018.

Eribon, Didier, *Retour à Reims*, Paris, Fayard, 2010.

Eribon, Didier, *Returning to Reims*, trans. Michael Lucey, Cambridge, MA, Harvard University Press, 2020.

Erikson, Kai, *Everything in Its Path: Destruction of Community in the Buffalo Creek Flood*, New York, Simon and Schuster, 1978.

Evans, Geoffrey, Noah Carl, and James Dennison, 'Brexit. The Causes and Consequences of the UK's Decision to Leave the EU', in Castells et al., *Europe's Crises*, pp. 380ff.

Frank, Thomas, 'Millions of Ordinary Americans Support Donald Trump. Here's Why', *The Guardian*, 8 March 2016.

Geysels, Jos, and Erik Vlaminck, *Uit woede en onbegrip: Een pamflet over de schande van de armoede*, Antwerp, Uitgeverij Vrijdag, 2019.

Gimson, Andrew, *Boris: The Rise of Boris Johnson*, London, Simon and Schuster, 2006.

Gross, Neil, 'Are Americans Experiencing Collective Trauma?', *New York Times*, 16 December 2016.

Gruyter, Caroline de, 'Misschien is het maar beter dat ze gaan', NRC *Handelsblad*, 9 March 2019.

Higgins, Andrew, 'Wigan's Road to "Brexit". Anger, Loss and Class Resentments', *New York Times*, 5 July 2016.

Istendael, Geert van, *De grote verkilling*, Amsterdam, Atlas / Contact, 2019.

Kadt, Jacques de, *De deftigheid in het gedrang*, Amsterdam, Van Oorschot, 1991.

Kearns, Ian, *Collapse: Europe after the European Union*, London, Biteback, 2018.

Korski, Daniel, 'Why we lost the Brexit vote', *Politico*, 20 October 2016.

Krugman, Paul, 'Austerity's Grim Legacy', *New York Times*, 6 November 2015.

Kruk, Marijn, interviewed by Marcel Gauchet, 'Een gevangenis zonder tralies', *De Groene Amsterdammer*, 27 July 2017.

Leparmentier, Arnaud, 'L'Europe est-elle mortelle?', *Le Monde*, 9 April 2016.

Louis, Édouard, *Who Killed My Father?*, trans. Lorin Stein, London, Harvill Secker, 2019.

Müller, Jan-Werner, *What is Populism?*, Philadelphia, University of Pennsylvania Press, 2016.

Orwell, George, *The Road to Wigan Pier*, London, Secker and Warburg, 1986.

O'Toole, Fintan, 'The Ham of Fate', *New York Review of Books*, 15 August 2019.

'Post-Brexit Racism', Institute of Race Relations, 7 July 2016.

Purnell, Sonia, 'Boris Johnson Is about to Inherit a Crisis His Euro-Bashing Helped Spawn', *The Guardian*, 15 July 2019.

Quatremer, Jean, 'Boris Johnson Is the Epitome of What's Worst about the English Ruling Class', *The Guardian*, 16 July 2019.

Radden Keefe, Patrick, 'How Mark Burnett Resurrected Donald Trump as an Icon of American Success', *New Yorker*, 7 January 2019.

Richards, Steve, *The Rise of the Outsiders: How Mainstream Politics Lost its Way*, London, Atlantic Books, 2018.

Rorty, Richard, *Achieving Our Country: Leftist Thought in Twentieth-Century America*, Cambridge, MA, Harvard University Press, 1998.

Sargeant, Terry, interviewed by Lisa O'Carroll, 'Brexit Plan "Complete Shambles", UK Boss of ThyssenKrupp Says', *The Guardian*, 12 November 2018.

Shipman, Tim, *All Out War: The Full Story of Brexit*, London, William Collins, 2017.

Sociaal en Cultureel Planbureau, *De sociale staat van Nederland 2017*, The Hague, 2017.

Tormey, Simon, *Populism*, London, Oneworld Publications, 2019.

Ven, Coen van de, 'Alles wat ons eigen is verdwijnt', *De Groene Amsterdammer*, 14 March 2019.

Zimmer, Undine, *Nicht von schlechten Eltern, Meine Hartz-IV-Familie*, Frankfurt am Main, S. Fischer Verlag, 2013.

13. *Alone* – 2017

Anonymous, 'I Am Part of the Resistance Inside the Trump Administration', *New York Times*, 5 September 2018.

Bacevich, Andrew, *The Age of Illusions: How America Squandered Its Cold War Victory*, New York, Macmillan, 2020.

Blom, Philipp, *Wat op het spel staat*, Amsterdam, De Bezige Bij, 2017.

Chait, Jonathan, 'Will Trump Be Meeting with His Counterpart – or His Handler?', *New York Magazine*, 9 July 2018.

Christie, Chris, *Let Me Finish: Trump, the Kushners, Bannon, New Jersey, and the Power of In-Your-Face Politics*, London, Hachette, 2019.

Clinton, Hillary Rodham, *What Happened*, New York, Simon and Schuster, 2017.

Danner, Mark, 'The Magic of Donald Trump', *New York Review of Books*, 26 May 2016.

Davies, William, 'Boris Johnson, Donald Trump and the Rise of Radical Incompetence', *New York Times*, 13 July 2018.

'Bagehot – Britain's Decline and Fall: The Country Has Not Cut Such a Pathetic Figure on the Global Stage since Suez', *The Economist*, 1 July 2017.

Enrich, David, 'A Mar-a-Lago Weekend and an Act of God. Trump's History with Deutsche Bank', *New York Times*, 18 March 2019.

Frank, Thomas, *Rendezvous with Oblivion*, London, Scribe UK, 2018.

———, *What's the Matter with Kansas?: How Conservatives Won the Heart of America*, New York, Metropolitan Books, 2004.

Friedman, Thomas, 'What if Trump Could Explain as Well as He Inflames? Building a Border Wall Won't Solve Our Immigration Problem', *New York Times*, 5 February 2019.

Frolov, Vladimir, 'Prutswerk van Prigozjins partizanen schaadt het Kremlin', *Raam op Rusland*, 20 February 2018.

Garton Ash, Timothy, 'A Humiliating Brexit Deal Risks a Descent into Weimar Britain', *The Guardian*, 27 July 2018.

Goodman, Peter, 'For Many British Businesses, Brexit Has Already Happened', *New York Times*, 2 April 2019.

Gruyter, Caroline de, 'Dit zijn helemaal geen onderhandelingen', NRC *Handelsblad*, 20 October 2018.

Hidalgo, Anne, and William Peduto, 'The Mayors of Pittsburgh and Paris: We Have Our Own Climate Deal', New York Times, 7 June 2017.

Hoeven, Rutger van der, 'Wereld in wachtstand. President Trump halverwege', De Groene Amsterdammer, 17 January 2019.

Hughes-Wilson, John, On Intelligence: The History of Espionage and the Secret World, London, Constable and Robinson, 2016.

Krugman, Paul, 'For Trump, Failure Is the Only Option', New York Times, 12 July 2018.

Lewis, Michael, '"This Guy Doesn't Know Anything": The Inside Story of Trump's Shambolic Transition Team', The Guardian, 27 September 2018.

Macintyre, Ben, interviewed by Sarah Lyall, 'Masters in Espionage', New York Times, 25 August 2017.

Mak, Geert, Reizen zonder John: Op zoek naar Amerika, Amsterdam, Atlas, 2012.

Mak, Geert, In America: Travels with Steinbeck, trans. Liz Waters, London, Harvill Secker, 2014

McKibben, Bill, 'Trump's Stupid and Reckless Climate Decision', New York Times, 1 June 2017.

McTague, Tom, 'How the UK Lost the Brexit Battle', Politico, 27 March 2019.

O'Toole, Fintan, Heroic Failure: Brexit and the Politics of Pain, London, Head of Zeus, 2018.

————, 'The King and I', New York Review of Books, 21 March 2019.

Rhodes, Ben, The World as It Is: A Memoir of the Obama White House, New York, Random House, 2018.

Rompuy, Herman Van, 'Less Europe, wat betekent dat dan?', de Volkskrant, 9 September 2016.

Rotthier, Rudi, De Verscheurde Staten van Amerika, Amsterdam, Atlas Contact, 2019.

Sanchez, Julian, 'Russia Wanted Trump to Win. And It Wanted to Get Caught', New York Times, 17 February 2018.

Shane, Scott, 'Russia Isn't the Only One Meddling in Elections. We Do It, Too', New York Times, 17 February 2018.

Shipman, Tim, Fall Out: A Year of Political Mayhem, London, William Collins, 2017.

Shirreff, Richard, 2017: War With Russia — An Urgent Warning from Senior Military Command, London, Coronet, 2016.

Shlapak, David, and Michael Johnson, Reinforcing Deterrence on NATO's Eastern Flank. Wargaming the Defense of the Baltics, Rand Corporation, 2016.

Snyder, Timothy, *The Road to Unfreedom: Russia, Europe, America*, New York, Tim Duggan Books, 2018.

———, *On Tyranny. Twenty Lessons from the Twentieth Century*, New York, Tim Duggan Books, 2017.

Sommer, Martin, 'Ieder land zijn eigen neurose', *de Volkskrant*, 19 January 2019.

Takken, Wilfred, 'Hillary verliet de barbecue na vijf minuten, Obama bleef', *NRC Handelsblad*, 19 July 2018.

Unger, Craig, *House of Trump, House of Putin: The Explosive Story of Donald Trump and the Russian Mafia*, New York, Dutton, 2018.

Wolff, Michael, *Fire and Fury: Inside the Trump White House*, New York, Henry Holt and Company, 2018.

Woodward, Bob, *Fear: Trump in the White House*, New York, Simon and Schuster, 2018.

Wylie, Christopher, interviewed by Wouter Woussen and Nikolas Vanhecke, 'Trump is verkozen dankzij een oorlogswapen', *De Standaard*, 17 July 2018.

Intermezzo

Barreiro, Belén, interviewed by Lex Rietman, 'La sociedad que seremos', *De Groene Amsterdammer*, 6 September 2018.

Bienert, Michael, *Joseph Roth in Berlin: Ein Lesebuch für Spaziergänger*, Cologne, Kiepenheuer and Witsch, 1996.

Minder, Raphael, *The Struggle for Catalonia: Rebel Politics in Spain*, London, Hurst and Company, 2017.

Puigdemont, Carles, *De Catalaanse crisis: Een kans voor Europa - Gesprekken met Olivier Mouton*, Tielt, 2018.

Roth, Joseph, *Radetzkymarsch*, Berlin, Kiepenheuer and Witsch, 1932.

———, *The Radetzky March*, trans. Joachim Neugroschel, New York, Overlook Press, 1995.

14. Great Expectations – 2018–2021

Andress, David, *Cultural Dementia: How the West Has Lost Its History and Risks Losing Everything Else*, London, Head of Zeus, 2018.

Barreiro, Belén, interviewed by Lex Rietman, 'La sociedad que seremos', *De Groene Amsterdammer*, 6 September 2018.

Baudet, Thierry, and Geert Mak, *Thuis in de tijd*, Amsterdam, Prometheus, 2014.

Bienert, Michael, *Joseph Roth in Berlin: Ein Lesebuch für Spaziergänger*, Cologne, Kiepenheuer and Witsch, 1996.

Castells, Manuel, 'Achilles' Heel: Europe's Ambivalent Identity', in Castells et al., *Europe's Crises*, pp. 178ff.

Chrislinger, David, 'The Man Who Told America the Truth About D-Day', *New York Times Magazine*, 5 June 2019,

Colijn, Ko, 'De nieuwe wereld volgens het boekje', in *De nieuwe wereld. Christendemocratische verkenningen*, Summer 2009.

————, 'Naar een integrale veiligheidsbenadering', *Internationale Spectator*, no. 3, 2015.

Eijck, Guido van, 'Statiegeld hoort naast de vuilnisbak. Armoede in Duitsland', *De Groene Amsterdammer*, 12 July 2018.

Europese variaties, Wetenschappelijke Raad voor het Regeringsbeleid, September 2018.

Garton Ash, Timothy, 'Dringend gezocht: bedreiging', *De Groene Amsterdammer*, 11 October 2012.

Garton Ash, Timothy, 'Is Europe Disintegrating?', *New York Review of Books*, 19 January 2017.

————, 'The New German Question', *New York Review of Books*, 15 August 2013.

————, 'Why We Must Not Let Europe Break Apart', *The Guardian*, 9 May 2019.

Gruyter, Caroline de, 'Habsburg Lessons for an Embattled EU', Carnegie Europe, 23 September 2016.

Henley, John, 'Why the EU Is Witnessing the Birth of Real European Politics', *The Guardian*, 14 May 2019.

Judson, Pieter M., *The Habsburg Empire: A New History*, London, Harvard University Press, 2016.

Kissinger, Henry, *World Order: Reflections on the Character of Nations and the Course of History*, London / New York, Routledge, 2014.

Krien, Daniela, *Die Liebe im Ernstfall*, Zurich, Diogenes Verlag, 2019.

Lukacs, John, *A Short History of the Twentieth Century*, Cambridge, MA, Harvard University Press, 2013.

Maier, Anja, 'Fantoompijn in het Oosten', *De Groene Amsterdammer*, 25 July 2019.

Middelaar, Luuk van, 'Het Europees Parlement heeft aan kracht gewonnen', *NRC Handelsblad*, 31 May 2019.

Moïsi, Dominique, 'The Clash of Emotions', *Foreign Affairs*, January / February 2007.

Münchau, Wolfgang, 'Italy May Be the Next Domino to Fall', *Financial Times*, 26 June 2016.

Rood, Jan, ed., *Een wankele wereldorde: Clingendael Strategische Monitor 2014*, Instituut Clingendael, 2014.

Roth, Joseph, *Joseph Roth in Berlijn*, ed. Michael Bienert, Amsterdam, 2009.

———, *Radetzkymarsch*, Berlin, Kiepenheuer and Witsch, 1932.

———, *The Radetzky March*, trans. Joachim Neugroschel, New York, Overlook Press, 1995.

Scheffer, Paul, *De vorm van vrijheid*, Amsterdam, De Bezige Bij, 2018.

———, *Freedom of the Border*, trans. Liz Waters, Cambridge, Polity Books, 2021.

Segers, Mathieu, *Reis naar het continent: Nederland en de Europese integratie 1950 tot heden*, Amsterdam, Prometheus, 2019.

Somers, Bart, *Samen Leven: Een hoopvolle strategie tegen IS*, Antwerp, Houtekiet, 2016.

Sopova, Alisa, 'How's Life in the War Zone? Not Great', *New York Times*, 26 May 2018.

Thunberg, Greta, Svante Thunberg, Malena Ernman and Beata Ernman, *Our House is On Fire: Scenes of a Family and a Planet in Crisis*, London, Penguin, 2020.

Tjeenk Willink, Herman, *Groter denken, kleiner doen*, Amsterdam, Prometheus, 2018.

Veld, Sophie in 't, *Een Europees ID*, Amsterdam, Prometheus, 2018.

Wolf, Martin, 'Brexit Means Goodbye to Britain as We Know It', *Financial Times*, 11 July 2019.

Epilogue

Applebaum, Anne, 'Epidemics Reveal the Truth about the Societies They Hit', *The Atlantic*, 2 March 2020.

Beirlant, Bart, 'Zuid-Europa heeft genoeg van Hollandse "kleinzieligheid" ', *De Standaard*, 28 March 2020.

Beunderman, Mark, and Maarten Schinkel, 'De ravage door het virus transformeert de hele economie', *NRC Handelsblad*, 10 April 2020.

Boccaccio, Giovanni, *The Decameron*, trans. John Payne, London, The Villon Society, 1886.

Boffey, Daniel, 'Bust-ups and Brinkmanship: Inside Story of How the Brexit Deal Was Done', *The Guardian*, 24 December 2020.

Buckley, Chris, and Steven Lee Myers, 'As New Coronavirus Spread, China's Old Habits Delayed Fight', *New York Times*, 7 February 2020.

Buranyi, Stephen, 'The WHO v Coronavirus: Why It Can't Handle the Pandemic', *The Guardian*, 10 April 2020.

Calvert, Jonathan, George Arbuthnott and Jonathan Leake, 'Coronavirus: 38 Days when Britain Sleepwalked into Disaster', *The Times*, 19 April 2020.

Danner, Mark, 'The Con He Rode In On', *New York Review of Books*, 19 November 2020.

Effting, Maud, 'Je ziet ze denken: daar is de ic-dokter, daar komt mijn vonnis', *de Volkskrant*, 1 April 2020.

Februari, Maxim, 'Van wat valt te voorspellen wil je de helft niet weten', *NRC Handelsblad*, 30 March 2020.

Garton Ash, Timothy, 'A Better World Can Emerge after Coronavirus. Or a Much Worse One', *The Guardian*, 6 May 2020.

Harari, Yuval Noah, 'The World after Coronavirus', *Financial Times*, 19 March 2020.

Hendrickx, Frank, and Huib Modderkolk, 'Februari, de verloren maand in de strijd tegen het coronavirus', *de Volkskrant*, 11 April 2020.

Herszenhorn, David, and Sarah Wheaton, 'How Europe Failed the Coronavirus Test', *Politico*, 7 April 2020.

Hoedeman, Jan, and Niels Klaassen, ' "Dat kutvirus," verzucht de premier. Reconstructie van een wanhopige strijd', *Het Parool*, 2 May 2020.

Krastev, Ivan, *Is It Tomorrow Yet?: Paradoxes of the Pandemic*, London, Allen Lane, 2020.

Landt, Olfert, in Sterre Lindhout, 'Hij maakte de eerste test voor corona', *de Volkskrant*, 14 April 2020.

Lievisse Adriaanse, Mark, and Derk Stokmans, 'Het virus kwam sneller dan de overheid reageerde', *nrc.next*, 22 March 2020.

'The Man Who Knew – Li Wenliang Died on February 7th', *The Economist*, 15 February 2020.

McNeill, William H., *Plagues and Peoples*, New York, Anchor, 1976.

Mishra, Pankaj, 'Grand Illusions', *New York Review of Books*, 19 November 2020.

Packer, George, 'We Are Living in a Failed State', *The Atlantic*, 15 June 2020.

Pepys, Samuel, *Everybody's Pepys, The Diary of Samuel Pepys, 1660 – 1669*, abridged by O.F. Morshead, London, G. Bell and Sons, 1967.

Pilkington, Ed, 'How Science Finally Caught Up with Trump's Playbook – with Millions of Lives at Stake', *The Guardian*, 4 April 2020.

Ploeg, Jarl van der, 'Zelfs de doden zijn eenzaam in Bergamo', *de Volkskrant*, 19 March 2020.

Quammen, David, *Spillover: Animal Infections and the Next Human Pandemic*, New York, W. W. Norton and Company, 2013.

Rice, Susan, 'The Government Has Failed on Coronavirus, but There Is Still Time', *New York Times*, 13 March 2020.

Rutenberg, Jim, et al., '77 Days: Trump's Campaign to Subvert the Election', *New York Times*, 31 January 2021.

Sanger, David, 'Before Virus Outbreak, a Cascade of Warnings Went Unheeded', *New York Times*, 19 March 2020.

Snowden, Frank, *Epidemics and Society: From the Black Death to the Present*, New Haven / London, Yale University Press, 2019.

Snyder, Timothy, 'The American Abyss', *New York Times Magazine*, 9 January 2020.

Tisdall, Simon, 'Power, Equality, Nationalism: How the Pandemic Will Reshape the World', *The Guardian*, 28 March 2020.

Tooze, Adam, and Moritz Schularick, 'The Shock of Coronavirus Could Split Europe – Unless Nations Share the Burden', *The Guardian*, 25 March 2020.

Tooze, Adam, 'How Coronavirus Almost Brought Down the Global Financial System', *The Guardian*, 14 April 2020.

Tuchman, Barbara, *A Distant Mirror: The Calamitous 14th Century*, New York, Knopf, 1978.

Walt, Stephen, 'The United States Is Getting Infected with Dictatorship', *Foreign Policy*, 13 April 2020.

Index

Page references in *italics* indicate images.

penguin.co.uk/vintage